WILLIAM MORRIS

Romantic to Revolutionary

ALSO BY E.P. THOMPSON

The Making of the English Working Class

Whigs and Hunters: The Origin of the Black Act

Albion's Fatal Tree: Crime and Society in Eighteenth-Century England
(with Douglas Hay, Peter Linebaugh, John G. Rule and Cal Winslow)

WILLIAM MORRIS

Romantic to Revolutionary

E. P. THOMPSON

PANTHEON BOOKS, NEW YORK

FIRST AMERICAN EDITION

 Published in the United States by Pantheon Books, a division of Random House, Inc., New York, and simultaneously in Canada by Random House of Canada Limited, Toronto. Originally published in Great Britain by The Merlin Press Ltd., London.

Library of Congress Cataloging in Publication Data

Thompson, Edward Palmer, 1924–
William Morris: Romantic to Revolutionary

Includes index.
1. Morris, William, 1834–1896. 2. Authors, English
–19th century–Biography. 3. Socialism in Great Britain.
PR5083.T6 1977 821'.8 [B] 76-62712
ISBN 0-394-41136-6

Manufactured in the United States of America

CONTENTS

LIST OF ABBREVIATIONS ix

Part One

CHAP. PAGE

WILLIAM MORRIS AND THE ROMANTIC REVOLT

I. Sir Launcelot and Mr. Gradgrind 1
i. The first revolt (1); ii. History and Romance (4); iii. Mr. Gradgrind (7); iv. John Keats (10)

II. Oxford—Carlyle and Ruskin 22
i. "Where is the battle?" (22); ii. Medievalism and Thomas Carlyle (27); iii. John Ruskin (32)

III. Rossetti and the Pre-Raphaelites 40
i. "My work is the embodiment of dreams. . ." (40); ii. The Pre-Raphaelites—and the "soonset floosh" (49)

IV. The First Joust with Victorianism 61
i. Janey (61); *The Defence of Guenevere* (76); iii. Conclusion (85)

Part Two

THE YEARS OF CONFLICT

I. William Morris and the Decorative Arts 88
i. Introduction (88); Red House and the Firm (90); iii. Morris as a designer and craftsman (98)

II. The Poetry of Despair 110
i. *Scenes from the Fall of Troy* (110); ii. *The Earthly Paradise* (114); iii. "A sense of something ill. . ." (119); iv. "The time lacks strength" (134)

III. "Love is Enough" 151

IV. Hope and Courage 171
i. Kelmscott (171); ii. Iceland (175)

V. Action 192
i. "There is no wealth but life" (192); ii. The Eastern Question (202)

VI. The 'Anti-Scrape' 226

VII. The River of Fire 243

Part Three

PRACTICAL SOCIALISM

I. The First Two Hundred 276
i. The refugees (276); ii. The "old guard" (279); iii. The intellectuals (287); iv. The "oddities" (297)

II. The First Propaganda 301
i. "All for the Cause" (301); ii. "So I began the business. . ." (305); iii. "Oh, it is monstrous" (316); iv. Letters and articles (322); v. An incident in Hyde Park (328)

III. The Split 331
i. Theory of socialism (331); ii. Socialist strategy (334); iii. Dissension begins (342); iv. The Executive and *Justice* (344); v. The Scottish Land and Labour League (350); vi. Resignation (357); vii. The aftermath (362)

IV. The Socialist League, 1885-6: "Making Socialists" ... 366
i. The Provisional Council (366); ii. The League's policy (378); iii. Fighting imperialism (382); iv. The membership—and *Commonweal* (390); v. The fight for free speech (393); vi. The S.D.F. and the unemployed riots (403); vii. The League in 1886 (412); viii. William Morris, agitator (423)

V. The Socialists make contact with the masses, 1887-8 ... 427
i. "Staying power is what we want" (427); ii. "Jonah's view of the whale" (430); iii. The Northumberland miners (435); iv. The Third Annual Conference (446); v. The policy of abstention (455); vi. John Lincoln Mahon (464); vii. The Jingo Jubilee (479); viii. "Bloody Sunday" (482); ix. Exit the Bloomsbury Branch (503)

VI. The Last Years of the Socialist League 512
i. "The League don't get on" (512); ii. The new unionism (523); iii. The Second International—and the Fabians (533); iv. Morris and the anarchists (549); v. Artistic and intellectual colleagues (552); vi. The "hobbledehoys" triumph (559); vii. "Where are we now?" (572)

VII. Towards a United Socialist Party, 1890-96 580
i. The Kelmscott Press (580); ii. Goodbye to the anarchists (585); iii. The rejection of purism (597); iv. An approach to unity (605); v. Mature theory (610); vi. Reconciliation with the S.D.F. (616); vii. The last year (624)

Part Four
NECESSITY AND DESIRE

Necessity and Desire 641
i. Architecture, machinery and socialism (641); ii. Theories of art (655); iii. *Chants for Socialism* and *The Pilgrims of Hope* (667); iv. The prose romances (673); v. The society of the future (682); vi. *News from Nowhere* (692); vii. Personality and influence (698); viii. Desire and necessity (717)

Appendices

I. The Manifesto of the Socialist League 732

II. William Morris, Bruce Glasier and Marxism 741

i. John Bruce Glasier (741); ii. William Morris and Marxism (751)

POSTSCRIPT: 1976 763

AUTHOR'S NOTE TO THE REVISED EDITION ... 817

INDEX 821

LIST OF ABBREVIATIONS

The following abbreviations have been used in the footnotes to the text:

Brit. Mus. Add. MSS.: British Museum Additional Manuscripts, comprising letters of Morris to his family, lectures, diaries, and other documents.

Glasier MSS.: Letters of Morris to J. Bruce Glasier in the Morris Museum, Water House, Walthamstow.

Hammersmith Minutes: Minutes of the Hammersmith Branch of the Democratic Federation and S.D.F. (until December, 1884), Hammersmith Branch, Socialist League (until December, 1890), and Hammersmith Socialist Society (until December, 1896). Preserved, with several gaps, among Brit. Mus. Add. MSS. 45891-4.

Int. Inst. Soc. Hist.: International Institute of Social History, Amsterdam. Documents collected by the historian of Anarchism, Dr. M. Nettlau, comprising correspondence of the Socialist League, 1885-8, and various letters of Joseph Lane, Frank Kitz, Ambrose Barker, and others. Correspondence of Morris and G.B. Shaw with Andreas Scheu.

Mattison MSS.: Correspondence and diaries of the late Mr. Alf Mattison in the Brotherton Library, Leeds University.

Works: *The Collected Works of William Morris* in 24 Volumes (Longmans, 1910-15).

Letters: *The Letters of William Morris to his Family and Friends,* Edited by Philip Henderson (Longmans, Green & Co. 1950).

Unpublished Letters: *Unpublished Letters of William Morris to the Rev. John Glasse* (Labour Monthly, 1951).

Glasier: J. Bruce Glasier, *William Morris and the Early Days of the Socialist Movement* (Longmans, 1921).

Mackail: J.W. Mackail, *The Life of William Morris,* 2 Volumes (Longmans, 1899).

Marx-Engels Sel. Cor.: *Selected Correspondence of Karl Marx and Frederick Engels,* translated and edited by Dona Torr (Lawrence & Wishart, 1936).

May Morris: May Morris, *William Morris, Artist, Writer, Socialist,* 2 Volumes, with an introduction to Vol. 2 by George Bernard Shaw (B. Blackwell, 1936).

Memorials: G.B[urne]-J[ones], *Memorials of Edward Burne-Jones,* 2 Volumes (Macmillan, 1904).

PART I

WILLIAM MORRIS AND THE ROMANTIC REVOLT

CHAPTER I

SIR LAUNCELOT AND MR. GRADGRIND

I. The First Revolt

WILLIAM MORRIS was born in March, 1834—ten years after the death of Byron, twelve years after Shelley's death, thirteen years after the death of Keats. As he grew to adolescence, the reputation of the last two poets was growing up beside him. He was caught up in the last great eddies of that disturbance of the human spirit which these poets had voiced—the Romantic Revolt. Romanticism was bred into his bones, and formed his early consciousness. And some of the last clear notes of this passionate revolt were sounded when, in 1858, the young William Morris published *The Defence of Guenevere:*

> "Poor merry Dinadan, that with jape and scoff
> Kept us all merry, in a little wood
>
> "Was found all hack'd and dead: Sir Lionel
> And Gauwaine have come back from the great quest,
> Just merely shamed; and Lauvaine, who loved well
> Your father Launcelot, at the King's behest
>
> "Went out to seek him, but was almost slain,
> Perhaps is dead now; everywhere
> The knights come foil'd from the great quest, in vain,
> In vain they struggle for the vision fair."[1]

Thereafter the impulse of revolt in English poetry was almost spent, and the current set—in the poetry of Morris himself, as well as of Tennyson and their contemporaries—away from the main channels of life, and towards ever-more-secluded creeks and backwaters. What had once been a passionate protest against an intolerable social reality was to become little more than a yearning nostalgia or a sweet complaint. But, throughout all the years of his despair,

[1] "Sir Galahad, A Christmas Mystery."

between 1858 and 1878, the fire of Morris's first revolt still burnt within him. The life of Victorian England was an intolerable life, and ought not to be borne by human beings. The values of industrial capitalism were vicious and beneath contempt, and made a mockery of the past history of mankind. It was this youthful protest, still burning within him, which brought him into contact, in 1882, with the first pioneers of Socialism in England. And when he found that these pioneers not only shared his hatred of modern civilization, but had an historical theory to explain its growth, and the will to change it to a new society, the old fire flared up afresh. Morris, the Romantic in revolt, became a realist and a revolutionary.

That is why a study of William Morris, the revolutionary, must start with some consideration of the Romantic revolt in poetry before his birth. But, first, let us summarize the main events of his first twenty-five years. Morris, in 1883 (the year in which he joined the Democratic Federation), described in a letter to the Austrian Socialist, Andreas Scheu, some of the events of his early life, as they appeared in importance from his new standpoint:

"I was born in Walthamstow... a surburban village on the edge of Epping Forest, and once a pleasant place enough, but now terribly cocknified and choked up by the jerry-builder.

"My Father was a business man in the city, and well-to-do; and we lived in the ordinary bourgeois style of comfort; and since we belonged to the evangelical section of the English Church I was brought up in what I should call rich establishmentarian puritanism; a religion which even as a boy I never took to.

"I went to school at Marlborough College, which was then a new and very rough school. As far as my school instruction went, I think I may fairly say I learned next to nothing there, for indeed next to nothing was taught; but the place is in very beautiful country, thickly scattered over with historical monuments, and I set myself eagerly to studying these and everything else that had any history in it, and so perhaps learned a good deal, especially as there was a good library at the school to which I sometimes had access. I should mention that ever since I could remember I was a great devourer of books. I don't remember being taught to read, and by the time I was 7 years old I had read a very great many books good, bad and indifferent.

"My Father died in 1847 a few months before I went to Marlborough; but as he had engaged in a fortunate mining speculation before his death, we were left very well off, rich in fact.

"I went to Oxford in 1853 as a member of Exeter College; I took very ill to the studies of the place; but fell to very vigorously on history and especially medieval history, all the more perhaps because at this time I fell under the influence of the High Church or Puseyite school; this latter phase however did not last me long, as it was corrected by the books of John Ruskin which were at the time a sort of revelation to me; I was also a good deal influenced by the works of Charles Kingsley, and got into my head therefrom some socio-political ideas which would have developed probably but for the attractions of art and poetry. While I was still an undergraduate, I discovered that I could write poetry, much to my own amazement; and about that time being very intimate with other young men of enthusiastic ideas, we got up a monthly paper which lasted (to my cost) for a year; it was called the *Oxford and Cambridge Magazine,* and was very *young* indeed. When I had gone through my school at Oxford, I who had been originally intended for the Church!!! made up my mind to take up art in some form, and so articled myself to G.E. Street. . . who was then practising in Oxford; I only stayed with him nine months however; when being . . . introduced by Burne-Jones, the painter, who was my great college friend, to Dante Gabriel Rossetti, the leader of the Pre-Raphaelite School, I made up my mind to turn painter, and studied the art but in a very desultory way for some time. . ."[1]

Here, in Morris's matter-of-fact narrative, the first great crisis of his life is described. The bill-broker's son, shielded in a prosperous middle-class home, sent to receive the stamp of the ruling class at a public school (which was still too disorganised and new to do its corrupting job effectively),[2] doomed to a clerical career—suddenly taking the decision to throw the respectabilities to the winds, to turn his back on the

[1] *Letters,* pp. 184-6.

[2] In an undated letter (1886 or 1887?) to the Reverend William Sharman, published in *Labour Leader,* April 18th, 1903, Morris again referred to his own education: ". . . my parents did as all right people do, shook off the responsibility of my education as soon as they could; handing me over first to nurses, then to grooms and gardeners, and then to a school—a boy farm, I should say. In one way or another I learned chiefly one thing from all these—rebellion."

recognized professions and careers, and to cast in his lot with Rossetti's circle of enthusiasts, Bohemians, and dedicated artists. It is true that the decision cost him no serious financial hardship. The toil, under appalling conditions, of the workers in the tin and copper mines of Devon and Cornwall shielded him from poverty, and gave him his freedom of choice—as he was later to understand only too well. But it was a real decision nonetheless. His whole life was to provide testimony that it was dictated by no mere whim or passing desire for amusement. Why did he take it? Why—when he had shown no particular aptitude in his youth—did he decide to dedicate his life to painting as an art?

II. History and Romance

It is easy enough to point to the leading passion of William Morris's life at Marlborough and at Oxford. He himself described it often enough in later life. At one time he recalled his journeys to France in these years:

> "Less than forty years ago I first saw the city of Rouen, then still in its outward aspect a piece of the Middle Ages: no words can tell you how its mingled beauty, history, and romance took hold on me; I can only say that, looking back on my past life, I find it was the greatest pleasure I have ever had. . ."[1]

Medievalism was not a new discovery in his adolescence. He had read Scott's novels before he was seven: had ridden the glades of Epping Forest in a toy suit of armour. From his childhood his eye and visual memory were sharp for the architecture and art of the Middle Ages: and his games were those of knights, barons and fairies. His father took him on occasion to see the old churches in their neighbourhood, and once they visited Canterbury and the Church of Minster in Thanet: fifty years later—having never returned in the interval

[1] "The Aims of Art", *Works,* Vol. XXIII, p. 85.

—he described the church from memory. In a lecture on *The Lesser Arts of Life* delivered in 1882, he recalled another early impression:

"How well I remember as a boy my first acquaintance with a room hung with faded greenery at Queen Elizabeth's Lodge, by Chingford Hatch, in Epping Forest... and the impression of romance that it made upon me: a feeling that always comes back on me when I read, as I often do, Sir Walter Scott's *Antiquary*, and come to the description of the green room at Monkbarns, amongst which the novelist has with such exquisite cunning of art imbedded the fresh and glittering verses of the summer poet Chaucer; yes, that was more than upholstery, believe me."

At Marlborough he was rather solitary, and thought to be eccentric, spending much of his time taking rubbings of brasses, visiting historical sites, and still in his teens storing in his imagination "endless stories of knights and chivalry."

But, for all this, he was not cut to the pattern of the romantic hero of late Victorian aestheticism—pale, nervous and sensitive, scorned and misunderstood by his fellows and the world. He was self-sufficient, it is true, and absorbed in a world of "romance": but the world of "romance" was not incompatible with the closest observation and study wherever his interest directed him:

"On Monday I went to Silbury Hill which I think I have told you before is an artificial hill made by the Britons but first I went to a place called Avebury where there is a Druidical circle and a Roman entrenchment... I think the biggest stone I could see was about 16 feet out of the ground in height and about 10 feet thick and 12 feet broad, the circle and entrenchment altogether is about half a mile",

he wrote in a letter from Marlborough to his sister. By the time he went up to Oxford he had assumed the forthright, assertive manner that springs to mind with the first mention of his name. His friend, Dixon (the same Canon Dixon with whom the poet, Gerard Manley Hopkins, was later to become intimate in correspondence) set down his memories of Morris at this time:

"At first Morris was regarded by the Pembroke men simply as a very pleasant boy... who was fond of talking, which he did in a husky shout, and fond of going down the river with Faulkner... He was also extremely fond of singlestick, and a good fencer. In no long time, however, the great characters of his nature began to impress us. His fire and impetuosity, great bodily strength, and high temper were soon manifested: and were sometimes astonishing. As... his habit of beating his own head, dealing himself vigorous blows, to take it out of himself ... But his mental qualities, his intellect, also began to be perceived and acknowledged. I remember Faulkner remarking to me, 'How Morris seems to know things, doesn't he?' And then it struck me that it was so. I observed how decisive he was: how accurate, without any effort or formality: what an extraordinary power of observation lay at the base of many of his casual or incidental remarks..."[1]

This accurate grasp of detail persisted in all his medieval studies, and not only in his chief interest, in architecture and the architectural arts. He fell enthusiastically upon the collection of illuminated manuscripts in the Bodleian Library, and founded the store of knowledge which so astonished H.M. Hyndman, the Socialist leader, when, in the days of the Democratic Federation, they visited Oxford together, and the Curator at the Bodleian asked Morris to help in the identification of some recent acquisitions:

"Morris... taking them up one by one, looked, very quickly but very closely and carefully at each in turn, pushing it aside after inspection with 'Monastery So and So, date Such and Such', 'Abbey this in such a year', until he had finished the whole number; his decision being written down as he gave it. There seemed not to be the slightest doubt in the librarian's mind that Morris's judgment was correct and final, and though Morris hesitated here and there... eventually his verdict was given with the utmost certainty."[2]

Amiens and Rouen: the grey, medieval streets of Oxford

[1] Mackail, I, p. 43.

[2] H.M. Hyndman, *The Record of an Adventurous Life* (1911), p. 335.

itself: illuminated manuscripts, brasses and carvings, already revealing their influence in the leaf patterns which he worked on the edges of his letters: the ballads, Chaucer, Froissart, Malory's *Morte d'Arthur,* and all that was written of the Arthurian cycle—these were the things which quickened his pulse and roused him to heights of enthusiasm in his youth. This enthusiasm for medievalism coloured all his contributions to the *Oxford and Cambridge Magazine,* and culminated in his first great achievement, *The Defence of Guenevere and Other Poems.* It imparted that special flavour of idealized chivalric romance blended with closely-wrought detail which is distinctive of his early *Story of the Unknown Church,* and which is marked in such a passage as this, from his adolescent romance, *A Dream:*

"She saw him walking down toward the gateway tower, clad in his mail coat, with a bright, crestless helmet on his head, and his trenchant sword newly grinded, girt to his side; and she watched him going between the yew-trees, which began to throw shadows from the shining of the harvest moon. She stood there in the porch, and round by the corners of the eaves of it looked down toward her and the inside of the porch two serpent-dragons, carved in stone; and on their scales, and about their leering eyes, grew the yellow lichen; she shuddered as she saw them stare at her, and drew closer toward the half-open door; she, standing there, clothed in white from her throat till over her feet, altogether ungirdled; and her long yellow hair, without plait or band, fell down behind and lay along her shoulders, quietly, because the night was without wind. . ."

III. Mr. Gradgrind

A Dream was written when Morris was twenty-one: the year, 1855. On every side industrial capitalism was advancing triumphantly. The challenge of Chartism had receded. Four years before, the Great Exhibition of 1851 had ushered in twenty-five years of British industrial supremacy. The most humane and intelligent men and women of the middle class were concerned with the practical problems involved in clearing up the worst squalor and muddles left by the speculators of the previous decades: sewerage and paving, municipal government, the regulation of industrial conditions and the elimination of its worst abuses—these were among the concerns of enlightened minds. What did Sir Launcelot and maidens in white ungirdled drapery have to do with such a time?

The answer (or a part of it) is implicit in the question. In 1854, when Morris had just gone up to Oxford, Dickens published in *Hard Times* one of his most angry attacks upon Victorian utilitarianism:

> "Now what I want is, Facts. Teach these boys and girls nothing but Facts. Facts alone are wanted in life. Plant nothing else, and root out everything else. You can only found the minds of reasoning animals upon Facts. . ."

So Mr. Gradgrind orders the schoolmaster at the opening of the book. The scene of the action, Coketown, is dedicated to Fact:

> "You saw nothing in Coketown but what was severely workful. If the members of a religious persuasion built a chapel there. . . they made it a pious warehouse of red brick with sometimes (but this only in highly ornamented examples) a bell in a bird-cage on the top of it. The solitary exception was the New Church; a stuccoed edifice with a square steeple over the door, terminating in four short pinnacles like florid wooden legs. All the public inscriptions in the town were painted alike, in severe characters of black and white. The jail might have been the infirmary, the infirmary might have been the jail, the town-hall might have been either, or both, or anything else, for anything that appeared to the contrary in the graces of their construction. Fact, fact, fact, everywhere in the material aspect of the town; fact, fact, fact, everywhere in the immaterial. The. . . school was all fact, and the school of design was all fact, and the relations between master and man were all fact, and everything was fact between the lying-in hospital and the cemetery, and what you couldn't state in figures, or show to be purchaseable in the cheapest market and saleable in the dearest, was not, and never should be, world without end, Amen."

Dickens's picture may be caricature: but it is of the best

order of caricature, which delineates the essential lines of truth. Mr. Bounderby, the coarse and avaricious mill-owner of *Hard Times,* the type of the earlier Industrial Revolution, was now giving way to his more sophisticated cousin, Mr. Gradgrind. Gradgrind not only has power and wealth: he also has a theory to justify and perpetuate exploitation. The Victorian bourgeoisie had constructed from bits of Adam Smith and Ricardo, Bentham and Malthus a cast-iron theoretical system, which they were now securing with the authority of the State and the Law, and sanctifying with the blessings of Religion. The laws of supply and demand were "God's laws," and in all the major affairs of society all other values must bend before commodity values. Capital and labour were bound together by indissoluble ties: and upon the prosperity of capital depended the prosperity of the working class. Even excessive charity might endanger the working of these "natural" laws, by subsidizing and encouraging poverty, and (Dickens maintained) "the *Westminster Review* considered Scrooge's presentation of the turkey to Bob Cratchit as grossly incompatible with political economy." State regulation of the hours and conditions of adult labour (unless extended to "defenceless" children, or, in exceptional cases, the "weaker" sex) was not only bad political economy but a monstrous interference with God's laws, which would bring down a terrible retribution. The market was the final determinant of value, and if there was insufficient demand to make fine architecture or beautifully planned towns *pay,* this was sufficient evidence that such commodities as these were insignificant in the realm of Fact.

Medievalism was one of the characteristic forms taken by the later flowering of the romantic movement in mid-nineteenth-century England. It was, in its essential impulse, a revolt against the world of the Railway Age, and the values of Gradgrind. It posed the existence, in the past, of a form of society whose values were finer and richer than those of profit and capitalist utility. Within this prevailing predisposition toward medieval themes and settings, some of the most significant conflicts of ideas of Morris's time found their expression. From this same soil, from this same yearning for the ideal, the heroic and the passionate, in a world of Cash and Fact, grew both the Jesuit Hopkins and the pagan and Communist, William Morris. And behind both poets there may be sensed a more specific influence, in the achievement of the moodiest of all our great poets, John Keats.

IV. John Keats

We must look more closely at Keats than at any other forerunner of Morris, for his shadow falls most markedly upon Morris's youth, and the evidence of his influence may be found in every page of *The Defence of Guenevere.* Within his work may be found the germ of the Pre-Raphaelite Brotherhood, the deepening influence of medievalism, the first assertion of the theory of "art for art's sake". There is no wonder that Morris later recalled that "our clique was much influenced by Keats."[1]

Keats was the contemporary and friend of Shelley. In Leigh Hunt's circle he mixed with advanced Radicals and free-thinkers. His private letters show that he was Radical himself in his sympathies, admired Orator Hunt, the chief speaker at Peterloo, and Richard Carlile, the courageous free-thinker, and shared Shelley's revulsion at the oppressive corruption of his times. And yet (if his late poem, "The Cap and Bells", be excepted) there is little evidence of direct political interest in his poetry. "Liberty, Equality, Fraternity"—none of these are made into themes for his great Odes.

Keats's poetry is highly self-conscious, highly wrought and finished. He is less concerned than Shelley with the communication of an all-important message, more concerned with the craftsmanship of his art. His vocabulary differs, significantly,

[1] *Works,* Vol. XXII, p. xxxi: "Our clique was much influenced by Keats, who was a poet who represented semblances, as opposed to Shelley who had no eyes, and whose admiration was not critical but conventional."

from that of his forerunners. Wordsworth's employment of the "language of conversation of the middle and lower classes" is abandoned: we rarely meet the abstractions so frequent in Shelley. In their place we find the conscious employment of a "poetic" vocabulary, of words coloured by their historical (in particular, medieval) associations, but no longer in the general currency of speech. These facts, on their own, would suggest, that the mood of dejection, which is to be found in Shelley, had become, in Keats, overpowering, and that he had found in his poetry a refuge from a social reality which he felt to be unbearably hostile.

But this is only a part of the truth. The greater part can be found in that sense of conflict which may be found in all Keats's poetry, from his early "Sleep and Poetry" to his final draft of "Hyperion". This conflict sometimes appears as one between the sensuous and the philosophic life ("O for a life of Sensations rather than of Thoughts!"), sometimes as between science and imagination ("Do not all charms fly/At the mere touch of cold philosophy?"): more often it is deeply embedded in the very structure of the poems themselves, in the acute tension between the richness of the life of the senses and imagination and the poverty of everyday experience, and in Keats's struggle to reconcile the two. It is his intense awareness of this conflict (which was of central significance to English culture), which gives greatness to his achievement. The "Ode to a Nightingale" makes this plain.

The poem opens with the invocation of the mood of unconsciousness—"drowsy numbness", "hemlock", "opiate", and "Lethe-wards"—and the nightingale's song is shown as the external cause of the poet's mood. The second verse intensifies the evocation of this mood, of the suspension of the active, conscious, suffering mind by the means of wine:

> "That I might drink, and leave the world unseen
> And with thee fade away into the forest dim. . ."

"Fade far away" is picked up in the third verse, and the world from which release is desired is defined. It is a world of "weariness", "fever" and "fret", "where men sit and hear each other groan", a world of mortality and sickness, where beauty and love are transient, and "but to think is to be full of sorrow". In the fourth verse, the list of those agents (hemlock, opiates, wine) which bring release from reality, is not only continued but is intensified by the invocation of "poesy" (and the choice of the archaic word is of significance):

"Away! away! for I will fly to thee,
Not charioted by Bacchus and his pards,
But on the viewless wing of Poesy,
Though the dull brain perplexes and retards. . ."

Poetry is now seen as the supreme means of escape to another world of art and imagination, where the active consciousness is numbed, and in the fifth verse Keats employs all his magnificent powers of sensual suggestion to evoke a blissful state on the very edge of the unconscious. The associations of "incense" and "embalmed" are realized in the next verse:

"Darkling I listen; and, for many a time
I have been half in love with easeful Death,
Call'd him soft names in many a mused rhyme,
To take into the air my quiet breath;
Now more than ever seems it rich to die,
To cease upon the midnight with no pain. . ."

Drugs, wine, "poesy"–all have led to Death, the ultimate escape from reality. Now, with the real world exorcised, the other world of art and beauty becomes (as in the "Ode on a Grecian Urn") *more* real than life itself: and, in the seventh verse, this world is left in sole possession, the nightingale becomes *all* nightingales, a symbol of ideal beauty persisting unchanged throughout history, a part of a magic world:

"The same that oft-times hath
Charm'd magic casements, opening on the foam
Of perilous seas, in faery lands forlorn."

But with "forlorn", the sense of the poet's alienation from the world of his everyday experience comes back to Keats—"the very word is like a bell/To toll me back from thee to my sole self!" The unreal world dissolves, the language becomes plain and everyday, the rhythm loses its drowsy incantation:

"Adieu! the fancy cannot cheat so well
As she is fam'd to do, deceiving elf.
Adieu! adieu! thy plaintive anthem fades
Past the near meadows, over the still stream
Up the hill-side; and now 'tis buried deep
In the next valley-glades;
Was it a vision, or a waking dream?
Fled is that music:—do I wake or sleep?"

The real world has re-entered: but the question hangs in the air—*which* world is the real one?

The conviction of feeling in the poem is undeniable. Why should Keats have felt this conflict to be of so deep and poignant a nature? Some critics read the poem as simply an attempt to dispel the consciousness of death and of change by invoking a dream-world of art. But this does not fully explain the profound attraction for Keats of the suspension of the active consciousness. Why is it that reality should appear so unbearable to Keats that "poesy" should be allied with opiates and drugs as a means of escape? Why is it that the idea of consciousness is inseparable, for Keats, from the idea of suffering? Why is it that growing maturity and insight "into the heart and nature of Man" convinced him that the "world is full of Misery and Heartbreak, Pain, Sickness, and oppression. . ."[1] No explanation taken from his personal life is sufficient to account for this extreme polarization between the pleasures of sensation and imagination, and the pain of consciousness; nor to explain why despite his own political convictions, the great part of his best poetry is marked by an

[1] Keats to Reynolds, May 3rd, 1818, *Letters of John Keats* (Ed. Buxton Forman, 4th Edition, 1952), pp. 142-3.

absence of warm or hopeful ambitions for mankind.

Now let us turn to one of Keats's letters, written to his friend Bailey in November, 1817. His friend had sustained some insult at the hands of the Bishop of Lincoln, and the spontaneous incoherence of Keats's rage reveals more of the very movement of his feelings than many of his more studied letters:

"It must be shocking to find in a sacred Profession such bare-faced oppression and impertinence—The Stations and Grandeurs of the World have taken it into their heads that they cannot commit themselves towards an inferior in rank. . . There is something so nauseous in self-willed yawning impudence in the shape of conscience—it sinks the Bishop of Lincoln into a smashed frog putrefying. . . Such is this World—and we live—you have surely in a continual struggle against the suffocation of accidents—we must bear (and my Spleen is mad at the thought thereof) the Proud Man's Contumely. O for a recourse somewhat human independent of the great Consolations of Religion and undepraved Sensations—of the Beautiful—the poetical in all things—O for a Remedy against such wrongs within the pale of the World."[1]

And so the invective continues, until it reaches a conclusion which takes us directly to the third verse of the "Ode to a Nightingale"—"The thought that we are mortal makes us groan".

"You have one advantage which the young men of my time lacked", William Morris wrote to the young Socialist, Fred Henderson, in 1885:

"We were borne into a dull time oppressed with bourgeoisdom and philistinism so sorely that we were forced to turn back on ourselves, and only in ourselves and the world of art and literature was there any hope. You on the contrary have found yourself confronted by the rising hope of the people. . ."[2]

These words might serve as a commentary on Keats's life. The warm aspirations for Liberty, "suffocated" by his times and

[1] *Letters of John Keats*, p. 59. [2] See first edition of this book, p. 878.

denied hope of realization, turned back upon their source. The imagination, he suggested in one letter, must either "deaden its delicacy in vulgarity and in things attainable", or "go mad after things that are not". Faced by the "Proud Man's Contumely", Keats exalted the pride of his own creative genius. "Undepraved sensations. . . the Beautiful. . . the poetical in all things"—these at least were beyond the contamination of the "Stations and Grandeurs of the World". The timeless world of art and literature provided a democracy of its own, open not to place-seekers and pensioners but to those with the inborn right of their own talent. "The Beautiful" is posed as a "Remedy" for the oppressions of the world: but, in the heat of Keats's rage, it seemed to him an inadequate remedy, as he cried out for a recourse "somewhat human", a remedy "within the pale of the World". Almost without intending it, his letter reveals that the "world" of culture and imagination, and the "world" of his daily experience in society has become opposed to each other and distinct.

Keats was one of the first poets to feel in his own everyday experience the full shock of "bourgeoisdom and philistinism." In his "Epistle to Reynolds" there is a passage where the "world" of dream and poesy breaks down sharply, and he writes:

> ". . . I saw
> Too far into the sea, where every maw
> The greater on the less feed evermore.—
> But I saw too distinct into the core
> Of an eternal fierce destruction. . .
> The Shark at savage prey,—the Hawk at pounce. . ."

"Big fish eat little fishes"—the image of the ethic at the heart of capitalism, of ruthless competition, self-interest, and struggle for survival, the same as used by Shakespeare in *Timon.* Keats was not screened by birth or wealth (as were Byron and Shelley) from the full impact of this competitive struggle. In the publication of his poetry, he found himself exposed on two fronts. On the one hand, much of the influence in the world of letters still rested with men who sought to continue the servile tradition of dependence upon aristocratic patronage, even after the substance had gone. When Keats and his friends (drawn mostly from the poorer professional classes) sought to claim a share in the cultural life of the nation, they were ridiculed as "Cockneys". The very idea of a medical student or a schoolmaster writing poetry, independent of the patronizing encouragement of the Great, was laughable: and when the circle was found to be grouped around Leigh Hunt, a convicted Radical, it was dangerous! *Blackwood's,* reviewing some of Keats's poems, declared:

> "The egotism of the Cockneys is. . . an inexplicable affair. None of them are men of genius. . . they are lecturers of the Surrey Institution, and editors of Sunday papers and so forth. They have all abundance of admirers in the same low order of society to which they themselves originally belong, and to which alone they have all their lives addressed themselves."[1]

On the other hand, Keats, no less than Shelley, found that the middle classes who were pressing forward the industrial revolution and who were soon to gain the day with the Reform Bill of 1832, had little time for poetry—a commodity which could not easily be measured by Mr. Gradgrind's measuring-rod, and which "you couldn't state in figures, or show to be purchaseable in the cheapest market and saleable in the dearest", unless it was concerned with hymning the virtues of those marketable assets, prudence, enterprise and thrift.

Already in Keats's time the way was being prepared for the triumph in the mid-century of Victorian utilitarianism. Such perspectives filled Keats with no more enthusiasm than he felt for the decadent "Stations and Grandeurs of the World". Under this strain, he revealed in his letters a morbid sensitivity to money relations and transactions. He found his

[1] *Blackwood's Magazine,* April, 1819.

poems on sale in the capitalist market, subject to the same laws of supply and demand as any commodity. The equation of human and artistic values to money values aroused his disgust, and revealed itself in a feeling of estrangement from his audience:

> "A Preface is written to the Public; a thing I cannot help looking upon as an Enemy, and which I cannot address without feelings of Hostility."[1]

In reaction he turned his attention from the business of communication to the art product itself. If art-values were irrelevant to the market, they could only be realized through the integrity, the "self-concentration", of the artist himself. He became the prototype of the "pure" artist, producing art for its own sake:

> "I should say I value more the privilege of seeing things in loneliness than the fame of a prophet. . . I never expect to get anything by my Books: and moreover I wish to avoid publishing—I admire Human Nature but I do not like *Men.* I should like to compose things honourable to Man—but not fingerable over by *Men.*"[2]

This should not be seen as a desire on the part of Keats to escape from all social responsibilities. As he saw it, he was defending art itself in a world which had no place for it. "His nonsense. . . is quite gratuitous", declaimed one supercilious reviewer: "He writes it for its own sake."[3] And the implication of this violent philistine attack was that poetry *ought* to be written to the greater glory of a society which Keats

[1] Keats to Reynolds, April 9th, 1818, *Letters of John Keats, op. cit.,* p. 129. "I have not the slightest feel of humility towards the public—or to anything in existence—but the eternal Being, the Principle of Beauty, and the Memory of great Men. When I am writing for myself for the mere sake of the moment's enjoyment, perhaps nature has its course with me—but a Preface," etc.

[2] Keats to Haydon, December 22nd, 1818, *Ibid.,* p. 271.

[3] *Quarterly Review,* April, 1818.

despised. At every turn Keats was racked by the conflict between the ideal and the real. Rather than hand over poetry to the utilitarians he was *proud* to write it for "its own sake", and to nourish his aspirations for beauty and a nobler humanity in the loneliness" of his own heart. Even in his tormented personal relations with Fanny Brawne he sought to attach ideal attributes to her sadly at variance with the vapid society within which the real girl had her being. The same conflict was posed in "Lamia" in the opposition of the imaginative, sensuous, intuitive life, to the power of an analytical science which in his lifetime was carrying all before it. Even the "Eve of St. Agnes" is a supreme essay in illusion: an interval between storms, where the cold light of the moon is transformed by the coloured glass of windows against which the sharp sleet beats—the same image which Morris was to use with such effect in the final verses of his Apology to *The Earthly Paradise.*

This inward-turning of the great romantic impulse brought to Keats a heightened sensitivity to every shade of subjective experience, and in expressing the complexities of a vividly self-centred consciousness he anticipated new generations of writers (and of people) to come. But we are concerned here, not with an assessment of Keats but with the sources of that conflict which was to prove of such importance to Morris. For this conflict was not personal to Keats alone: it was central to the position of the artist in capitalist society. The terrible prophetic vision of Blake was becoming realized. All values were becoming, in Keats's day, tainted with the property-values of the market, all life being bought and sold. The great aspirations at the source of the Romantic Revolt—for the freeing of mankind from a corrupt oppression, for the liberation of man's senses, affections, and reason, for equality between men and between the sexes—were being destroyed by each new advance of industrial capitalism. But, with these aspirations (or the *hope* of their realization "within the pale of the World") denied, this seemed to Keats to be an ugly, non-human, objectless world of oppression and pain, redeemed only by the pleasures of sensual experience, which themselves were evanescent and subject to mortality and change. On the other hand, the culture of the past, "the realms of gold", in which finer values than those of Cash and Fact were enshrined, seemed saturated with a richness not to be found in life.

So it was that the words "Beauty" and "work of art" acquired a new meaning, which first crystallized in the writings of Keats, and which was accepted almost unreflectingly by the young Morris and Rossetti. "Beauty", for Keats, was something "abstract", not to be found in reality. It belonged especially to the world of artifice, art, imagination. Its source was in those aspirations within the artist's heart, denied adequate expression in the realms of social existence and human action:

> "I am certain of nothing but of the holiness of the Heart's affections and the truth of Imagination. What the Imagination seizes as Beauty must be truth—whether it existed before or not—for I have the same idea of all our passions as of Love: they are all, in their sublime, creative of essential Beauty."[1]

It is not the objective world (we should note) but the "passions" of the artist which are the source of "Beauty". These passions (unfulfilled in action) in the heart of the artist seemed to Keats to be the source, the inspiration, for the finished "work of art". The work of art embodied these feelings in its unchanging, intrinsic beauty, and it could, in its turn, evoke these feelings, this sense of beauty, in the heart of the beholder. And so, between the heart of the artist and the work of art, the work of art and the audience, a self-enclosed aesthetic was fashioned, excluding the world of action and social reality. Art was no longer conceived, as by Shelley, as an agent in man's struggle to master nature and discover himself. Art (if we set aside a lingering faith in its

[1] Keats to Bailey, November 22nd, 1817, *Letters of John Keats, op. cit.,* p. 67.

refining moral influence) was conceived as a compensation for the poverty of life.

Again and again, in the life of young Morris and Burne-Jones, in the Pre-Raphaelite circle and their friends, we shall meet with echoes of Keats's life. Like Keats, they were (in the main) unorthodox and advanced in their opinions—free-thinkers, or Republicans, or simply "Bohemians"; and, like Keats, their opinions found little expression in their art or their actions, they were without "hope" of their effective realization, they were "suffocated" and oppressed on all sides by "bourgeoisdom and philistinism". When Morris became an active Socialist, it was this re-birth of "hope" to which he recurred, again and again, in lectures and poems. The heroes of his long Socialist poem he called "The Pilgrims of Hope". Their "hope" was the vision of 1789, with a new brightness and certainty—"Liberty, Equality, Fraternity"—reborn "within the pale of the world".

But in Morris's youth, the world of art and imagination was both a palace of refuge and a castle in revolt against the philistines. He turned to a dream-world more strange and fantastic than that of Keats. The continual conflict in Keats's life, between rich aspiration and drab reality, could no longer be sustained with such intensity. Rather, the poetry of the mid-nineteenth century appears to oscillate between the two poles contained within Keats's sensibility. On the one hand, the poetry of "realism" (at its worst, the poetry of Tupper) was soiled by the drab or brutal reality of life within industrial capitalism. It was impoverished and infected by philistine attitudes. Where it was not moralizing or sentimental, but was most sincere (as in some poems by Clough and Arnold) it was rarely far from disillusion or irony. And, alongside this, there was the poetry of "romance"—of medievalism, trance, and escape, filled with nostalgia and a yearning for values which capitalism had crushed, and which were projected into archaic or dream-like settings. The two kinds of poetry were not mutually exclusive. Tennyson, Arnold and Browning moved between them both. But neither kind of poetry rose to the sustained greatness of the earlier Romantics. The poetry of "romance"—as is emphasized by its special "poetic" attitudes and vocabulary—was always a little detached from the essential human conflicts of the time. But notwithstanding this, the love of art, the cherishing of aspirations threatened by philistinism, gave rise to poems of great poignancy and beauty. And it was to this poetry of "romance" that William Morris's youthful contribution was made.

CHAPTER II

OXFORD–CARLYLE AND RUSKIN

I. *"Where is the Battle?"*

WILLIAM MORRIS's father, a partner in a Quaker firm of bill and discount brokers, made his wealth from mines. His holding of 272 £1 shares in the Devon Great Consols (controlling copper and tin mines in the South-West) suddenly boomed: and they did not stop booming until they had realized a sum approaching £200,000. When he died, in Morris's boyhood, his death made no difference to the prosperity of his family. Regularly the handsome dividends came in to the rural village of Walthamstow, on the edge of Epping Forest, bringing with them nothing to indicate the miseries at the bottom of the cramped and ill-ventilated shafts from which they had their source. At the age of twenty-one William Morris came into his own share—at the rate of £900 a year.

Morris's father was exceptionally lucky, his rise to affluence was hardly arduous. He did not provide those texts for industry and prudent enterprise to qualify him for inclusion in Samuel Smiles's gallery of exponents of "Self-help". But his son's upbringing, far from factory, mine or mill, was much the same as that of tens of thousands of others who were to become pillars of the Victorian middle class during Britain's age of industrial supremacy. For some reason, William Morris did not run true to type. Perhaps his upbringing was *too* comfortable for a child with a most active imagination and practical, inquisitive temper—his head filled with stories of heroic actions, great conflicts against overmastering odds, hard adventures and sacrifices. J.W. Mackail in his biography of Morris mentions a story of a schoolboy rebellion at Marlborough, of which Morris was one of the leaders, and which resulted in his withdrawal from the school to study under a private tutor.

By the time he reached Oxford, he was certainly inclined towards rebellion.[1] A good account of these early years is preserved in the recollection of Canon Dixon and of his close friend, Edward Burne-Jones. He and his small circle of friends lived a strenuous, imaginative and intellectual life, isolated from the general run of university activities. Oxford was still preoccupied by the discussions which had been aroused, twenty years before, by the "Oxford Movement", and had been more recently inflamed by Newman's "return" to the Catholic Church. Morris and Burne-Jones were swept into the same current. Canon Dixon recalled:

> "At this time, Morris was an aristocrat, and a High Churchman. His manners and tastes and sympathies were all aristocratic. His countenance was beautiful in features and expression, particularly in the expression of purity. Occasionally it had a melancholy look. He had a finely cut mouth, the short upper lip adding greatly to the purity of expression. I have a vivid recollection of the splendid beauty of his presence at this time."[2]

Burne-Jones, writing to a friend in 1854, drew a similar picture—but with a significant qualification: he could not quite fit him to the perfect model of the young romantic genius:

> "He is full of enthusiasm for things holy and beautiful and true, and, what is rarest, of the most exquisite perception and judgement in them. For myself, he has tinged my whole inner being with the beauty of his own, and I know not a single gift for which I owe such gratitude to Heaven as his friendship. If it were not for his boisterous mad outbursts and freaks, which break the romance he sheds around him—at least to me—he would be a perfect hero."[3]

That was the trouble. If it were not for this damned cheerfulness, he would have seemed set fair to become a Canon, Judge, or minor romantic poet.

[1] Jack Lindsay, *William Morris, His Life and Work* (1975), pp. 33-5, finds new evidence on the Marlborough "rebellion", but no evidence that Morris was a leader.
[2] Mackail, I, p. 46.
[3] *Memorials,* I, p. 96.

The attraction of medievalism and Catholicism were in no sense an impulse originating with Morris and his circle. The tide had long been set in that direction: or rather, this may be seen as part of the reaction to the tide of utilitarianism. Revolutionary and reactionary alike were caught in the same current. Disraeli and Lord John Manners, the Tory Young Englanders, dreamt of feudal ideals taking shape in the form of an alliance between the aristocracy and the proletariat (the inheritors of the peasantry) in opposition to the manufacturers and speculators. Staunch "Tory" Radicals, like Richard Oastler, cherished the same illusions in their horror at the naked exploitation and self-interest of industrial capitalism. At Oxford Morris and Burne-Jones admired *The Heir of Redclyffe,* whose hero was an embodiment of saintly, chivalric honour in a sordid and commercial world, and Kenelm Digby's romanticized pictures of noble and knightly virtue.[1] Malory, Froissart, legends, ballads and chronicles of medieval Europe—all heightened the sense of contrast between the world of the imagination and the world of Fact. Catholicism, and its near cousin, the Oxford Movement, fed the same emotions. On the one hand was the complacent evangelicalism of Morris's childhood memories: on the other, the saintly renunciation of the world practised by Pusey—and the attractions of ritual and plainsong, with their historical associations. In a world which had no use for the human spirit, Catholicism appeared to offer a spiritual refuge free from the taint of commerce.

It was during this early period of revulsion against utilitarianism that Morris and Burne-Jones first formed the idea of founding a sacred order or Brotherhood on medieval lines —a small group of friends, celibate, dedicated to the purity of art and religion and to the service of the things of the spirit in a world given over to Mammon. The idea was first

[1] Especially *The Broad Stone of Honour.* An interesting discussion of the sources of Morris's medievalism can be found in the first two chapters of Margaret R. Grennan, *William Morris, Medievalist and Revolutionary* (1945). See also R. Furneaux Jordan, *The Medieval Vision of William Morris* (1960).

mooted even before they had any acquaintance with the more famous "Brotherhood", the Pre-Raphaelites. Edward Burne-Jones, a pale witty, self-effacing youth, at this time (unlike Morris) inclined to dramatize his own emotions, mentioned the project in a half-flippant way in May, 1853, to his friend Cormell Price at Birmingham:

> "I have set my heart on our founding a Brotherhood. Learn Sir Galahad by heart. He is to be the patron of our Order. I have enlisted *one* in the project up here, heart and soul."[1]

The enlisted *"one"* was soon the moving spirit. In mid-1854 Burne-Jones was writing to the same friend that he longed to be back at Oxford "with Morris and his glorious little company of martyrs".[2] Morris was debating seriously the idea of devoting his fortune to the foundation of a monastery. The aim of the Brotherhood was summed up in Burne-Jones's words, as a "Crusade and Holy Warfare against the age".[3]

But how was this "Holy Warfare" to be fought? Indeed, where was the battleground? Many young men of the middle classes whose aspirations for a life with finer ends than the amassing of wealth and social position had not been utterly crushed, felt at this time a desire to do battle with the forces around them: but their aspirations drained away into the sands of hopelessness as they faced the immovable facade of Victorian society. "Yet is my feeling rather to ask, where *is* the battle?", wrote Arthur Hugh Clough in a long poem published several years before: and, finding no answer, the feeling recedes into disillusion:

> "O that the armies indeed were arrayed! O joy of the onset!
> Sound, thou Trumpet of God, come forth, Great Cause, to array us,
> King and leader appear, thy soldiers sorrowing seek thee.
> Would that the armies indeed were arrayed, O where is the battle?
> Neither battle I see, nor arraying, nor King in Israel,
> Only infinite jumble and mess and dislocation,
> Backed by a solemn appeal, 'For God's sake, do not stir, there!'
> Yet you are right, I suppose; if you don't attack my conclusion.

[1] *Memorials,* I, p. 77. [2] *Ibid.,* I, p. 103. [3] Mackail, I, p. 63.

Let us get on as well as we can, and do the thing we are fit for;
Every one for himself, and the common success for us all, and
Thankful, if not for our own, why then for the triumph of others,
Get along, each as we can, and do the things we are meant for."

Here, faced by:

"... the whole great wicked artificial civilised fabric—
All its unfinished houses, lots for sale, and railway out-works—"[1]

where was the chosen battlefield?

For Morris, it did not long seem to be in a return to purer religion. Religion of all varieties was deeply compromised by the same evils. Gradually, aided partly by the Christian Socialism of Kingsley and Maurice and the hostility to Rome of John Ruskin, but mostly by his own warm and concrete response to the world about him which prevented him from becoming, like nearly all his contemporaries—Christian and atheist alike—enmeshed in the abstract "doubts, disputes, distractions, fears", and ceaseless searching of conscience of his time, the emotional lure of High Anglicanism began to fade. In May, 1855, Cormell Price noted solemnly:

"Our Monastery will come to nought, I'm afraid... Morris has become questionable in doctrinal points, and Ted [Burne-Jones] is too Catholic to be ordained. He and Morris diverge more and more in views though not in friendship."[2]

And from this time onwards the divergence was to increase.

But, when Cormell Price was writing this note, a decision of vital importance was already being formed in the minds of both friends. In the summer of 1855 they were in France together, visiting the cathedrals of Amiens, Beauvais, and Chartres. From Chartres, Burne-Jones recalls, they—

"made northwards from Rouen, travelling gently and stopping at every Church we could find. Rouen was still a beautiful medieval city, and we stayed awhile and had our hearts filled. From there we walked to Caudebec, then by diligence to Havre, on our way to the churches of the Calvados: and it was while on the quay at Havre at night that we

[1] "The Bothie of Tober-na-Vuolich." [2] *Memorials*, I, p. 109.

resolved definitely that we would begin a life of art, and put off our decision no longer—he should be an architect and I a painter. It was a resolve only needing final conclusion; we were bent on the road for the whole past year, and after that night's talk we never hesitated more. That was the most memorable night of my life."[1]

The battlefield had been found.

II. Medievalism and Thomas Carlyle

The banner of the Romantic Revolt was passing from the literary to the visual and architectural arts. Indeed, by the late 1860s, when Morris was writing *The Earthly Paradise* it seemed to him that literature was no more than a skirmish on the edge of the main battlefield. Poetry could withdraw into a world of its own: and the poets could shut out the philistines by refusing to read their work. But architecture it was impossible to ignore. Everywhere, at every turning, Morris and his friends were confronted with the degradation of the human spirit at the hands of industrial capitalism—in the railway stations, slum quarters and bogo-Gothic buildings of Victorian prosperity and in those hybrid monstrosities of architecture, Egyptian, classical and utilitarian by turns, against which the Catholic architect, Pugin, had for some years been writing in protest.

The young architects of the 1850s were already deeply involved in the medieval revival, and this was indeed a congenial climate to Morris, who had felt the lure of the Middle Ages since his boyhood. In 1850, the cult of the medieval had already revealed itself in various forms. Appearing, both in literature and architecture, in the latter half of the eighteenth century, the fascination with the "Gothic" was rarely more than a freak of aristocratic decadence—the attraction of the bizarre, the "barbarous", and the grotesque, in reaction against the sophistications of eighteenth-century society. Later, Keats enriched his poetry

[1] *Memorials,* I, pp. 114-15.

with medieval associations, not so much from any close interest in the thought or society of the Middle Ages, as from the desire to heighten the illusion of his art, and to give his fantasy-world a strange and colourful habitation. We have seen that Morris spent his adolescence surrounded, as if by a palpable atmosphere, by the sense of the mystery and interest of the life of past times. This powerful historical imagination which never died in him, which—rather—became disciplined and deepened during a lifetime of study, was perhaps his greatest single intellectual strength. In his youth, this faculty was quickened to intensity by his growing hatred of his own civilization, and, in common with other great romantics, the contemplation of the past brought with it a sense of nostalgia and loss:

> ". . . the plaintive numbers flow
> For old, unhappy, far-off things,
> And battles long ago."

Heroism, beauty, high endeavour, love—all overthrown, and all contrasting with the tawdry present—these were the reflections aroused by the contemplation of the past.

But, as the nineteenth century advanced, a new content was being infused into the cult of medievalism. Increased scholarship added daily to the knowledge of medieval times. For Morris, the most important result of the new scholarship was in the reconstruction of a picture of the Middle Ages, neither as a grotesque nor as a faery world, but as a real *community* of human beings—an organic pre-capitalist community with values and an art of its own, sharply contrasted with those of Victorian England. However much this reconstruction may have been modified by twentieth-century scholars, it was an influence of the very first importance in liberating Morris's mind from the categories of bourgeois thought. In this reconstructed world, Morris found a place, not to which he could retreat, but in which he could stand and look upon his own age with the eyes of a stranger or visitor, judging his own time by standards other than its own.

And the two men who most influenced him in effecting this liberation were Thomas Carlyle and John Ruskin.

Carlyle's *Past and Present* was published in 1843, and read by Morris and Burne-Jones during their years at Oxford. The whole book is a blistering Old Testament attack on the morality of industrial capitalism, contrasted with an idealized picture of life in the monastery of St. Edmunsbury in the twelfth century. Carlyle's books, with their perverse, ejaculatory, repetitive and arrogant style, find few readers to-day. Consistency is not among his merits: pretentious mysticism, white-hot moral indignation, pious mumbo-jumbo, lie side by side. But his writings are among the greatest quarries of ideas in the first half of the nineteenth century, shot through with occasional gleams of the profoundest revolutionary insight.

Carlyle was essentially a negative critic. In his political conclusions he was not only reactionary, but actively malignant—jeering at the Chartist leader, Ernest Jones, in prison—letting fall his denunciations on the heads of Owenites, Chartists and industrialists alike:

> "All this dire misery, therefore: all this of our poor Workhouse Workmen, of our Chartisms, Trades-strikes, Corn-Laws, Toryisms, and the general breakdown of Laissez-faire in these days,—may we not regard it as a voice from the dumb bosom of Nature, saying to us: 'Behold! Supply-and-demand is not the one Law of Nature; Cash-payment is not the sole nexus of man with man,—how far from it! Deep, far deeper than Supply-and-demand, are Laws, Obligations sacred as Man's Life itself: these also, if you will continue to do work, you shall now learn and obey.' "[1]

His position was closely akin to that brilliantly characterized by Marx and Engels in the *Communist Manifesto* as "Feudal Socialism":

> "Half lamentation, half lampoon; half echo of the past, half menace, of the future; at times, by its bitter, witty and incisive criticism, striking the bourgeoisie to the very heart's core, but always ludicrous in its effect,

[1] *Past and Present,* Book III, Ch. 9.

through total incapacity to comprehend the march of modern history . . . What they upbraid the bourgeoisie with is not so much that it creates a proletariat, as that it creates a *revolutionary* proletariat."

But it was within the social dialectic of this time that progressive human feelings might keep company in the same man with reactionary thought. The same current is found to run not only in Thomas Carlyle, but in such men as Richard Oastler. The Manchester School of political economists was now in almost sole possession of the field: under the shiboleths of *laissez-faire,* Free Trade, freedom from all restraint, the Railway Age was being pressed forward. If it brought misery in its wake—that was unfortunate. But if this advance were necessary for commercial prosperity, it was argued, then it must in the end bring prosperity for the "nation":

" 'I am almost ashamed,' said Sissy, with reluctance, 'But to-day, for instance, Mr. M'Choakumchild was explaining to us about Natural Prosperity.'

" 'National, I think it must have been,' observed Louisa. . .

" 'National Prosperity.' And he said, 'Now, this school-room is a nation. And in this nation, there are fifty millions of money. Isn't this a prosperous nation? Girl number twenty, isn't this a prosperous nation, and ain't you in a thriving state?'

" 'What did you say?' asked Louisa.

' 'Miss Louisa, I said I didn't know. I thought I couldn't know whether it was a prosperous nation or not, and whether I was in a thriving state or not, unless I knew who had got the money, and whether any of it was mine. But that had nothing to do with it. It was not in the figures at all. . ."

" 'That was a great mistake of yours,' observed Louisa."

—*Hard Times* once again. If reason and economics taught this philosophy, then men like Carlyle and Oastler, were tempted to cast reason and economics aside, to appeal to the heart, to "Obligations sacred as Man's Life itself". But when these Obligations came to be described, they often took on the colour of feudal obligations and relationships: relationships which, however severe and binding, at least appeared as human relationships, relations between men, and not between man and an impersonal labour-market.

It is in Carlyle's disgust at the reduction by capitalism of all human values to cash values that his greatness lies: it is this which exercised most influence over Morris, and—while it ran underground awhile—found full and constant expression in his later years. It is the perpetual refrain of *Past and Present:*

> "Cash-payment never was, or could expect for a few years be, the union-bond of man to man. Cash never yet paid one man fully his deserts to another; nor could it, nor can it, now or henceforth to the end of the world."[1]

Work and Wages—these Carlyle put forward as the "largest of questions" in his time, and while his positive proposals are either feudal nonsense or too paltry to do more than scratch the surface of the problem, his denunciation of the "cash-nexus" won a response from Marx, and remained indelibly printed upon William Morris's consciousness. Years afterwards, in his Socialist lectures, he refers again and again to capitalism as this "so-called society", and reiterates that a "society" based upon cash and self-interest is not a society at all, but a state of war. This all-important idea he learnt, in his Oxford days, directly from Carlyle:

> "We call it a Society; and go about professing openly the totallest separation, isolation. Our life is not a mutual helpfulness; but rather, cloaked under due laws-of-war, named 'fair competition' and so forth, it is a mutual hostility. We have profoundly forgotten everywhere that *Cash-payment* is not the sole relation of human beings. . ."[2]

And, all the while, Carlyle stressed the contrast between capitalist society and the feudal obligations and relations of the monks of St. Edmundsbury to point his moral—a contrast from which Morris was only too ready to learn.

[1] *Past and Present,* Book III, Ch. 10. [2] *Ibid.,* Book III, Ch. 2.

One other doctrine of Carlyle was profoundly important to Morris—his constant emphasis on the value of work—that labour is the root of life. "All work, even cotton-spinning is noble; work is alone noble".[1] "All true Work is sacred; in all true Work, were it but true hand-labour, there is something of divineness."[2]

> "A man perfects himself by working. Foul jungles are cleared away, fair seed-fields rise instead, and stately cities; and withal the man himself first ceases to be a jungle, and foul unwholesome desert thereby... The man is now a man."[3]

This teaching, of the dignity of all labour, Morris learnt to practise in his own life. It formed one of his first bonds of sympathy and understanding with the working class. But Carlyle saw labour as a religious sacrament; he was not concerned with art. And it was from John Ruskin that Morris gained a new outlook on the role of creative satisfaction in labour.

III. John Ruskin

To the end of his life, Morris looked back to Ruskin with gratitude. Ruskin was the "Master": and though Morris, the pupil, in the end left him far behind, he was always quick to acknowledge his great debt. In his article of 1894, *How I Became a Socialist,* Morris recalled:

> "Before the uprising of *modern* Socialism almost all intelligent people either were, or professed themselves to be, quite contented with the civilisation of this century... This was the *Whig* frame of mind, natural to the modern prosperous middle-class men...

[1] *Past and Present,* Book III, Ch. 4. [2] *Ibid.,* Book III, Ch. 12.
[3] *Ibid.,* Book III, Ch. 11.

"But besides these contented ones there were others who were not really contented, but had a vague sentiment of repulsion to the triumph of civilisation, but were coerced into silence by the measureless power of Whiggery. Lastly, there were a few who were in open rebellion against the said Whiggery—a few, say two, Carlyle and Ruskin. The latter, before my days of practical Socialism, was my master towards the ideal aforesaid, and, looking backward, I cannot help saying, how deadly dull the world would have been twenty years ago but for Ruskin! It was through him that I learnt to give form to my discontent, which I must say was not by any means vague. Apart from the desire to produce beautiful things, the leading passion of my life has been and is hatred of modern civilisation."

On another occasion in his later years, when a speaker at an Art Congress in Edinburgh referred slightingly to Ruskin, Morris declared: "That's all nonsense. Why, man, Ruskin has made Art possible for us!"[1]

When Morris went up to Oxford, Ruskin's *Modern Painters* and *The Seven Lamps of Architecture* had already been published. Canon Dixon recalled:

"It was when... Burne-Jones and he got at Ruskin, that strong direction was given to a true vocation... Morris would often read Ruskin aloud. He had a mighty singing voice, and chanted rather than read those weltering oceans of eloquence as they have never been given before or since, it is most certain. The description of the Slave Ship, or of Turner's skies, with the burden, 'Has Claude given this?' were declaimed by him in a manner that made them seem as if they had been written for no end but that he should hurl them in thunder on the head of the base criminal who had never seen what Turner saw in the sky."[2]

But it was Ruskin's *The Stones of Venice,* the second and third volumes of which were published in the year after Morris went up to Oxford, that gave Morris a theory of art and society which was to influence all his later thought.

Ruskin's interest in art was essentially moral: and in the

[1] A. Compton-Rickett, *William Morris* (1913), p. 54.
[2] Mackail, I, pp. 46-7.

moral inter-relation between art and society. He was not, of course, the first nineteenth-century critic to assert that the arts had a moral function although he was the first to give the visual arts this special prominence. It was generally held that the arts had some didactic, or even utilitarian, task to perform. But between the generally held view and Ruskin's view there was the difference that lies between the words "moralizing" and "moral". The Victorian critics were content that art should moral*ize,* should point *a* moral congenial to established society: and, in his weaker moments, Ruskin fell as deeply into this error as any other. But, at his best, Ruskin sought to treat the arts as the expression of the whole *moral being* of the artist, and—through him—of the quality of life of the society in which the artist lived.

Great art, said Ruskin, "compasses and calls forth the entire human spirit", and should the art of a period be poor, it was an unfailing indication of the poverty of life of the people; while, in their turn, the poverty or health of the arts effect the quality of life. His criticism is made up of a continual passage from life to art, and from art to life. He was, like Carlyle, a man of deep but fitful insight ("Of Ruskin Morris said that he would write the most profound truths and forget them five minutes later"),[1] and while the moments of insight lasted he had the courage to follow his thought to a conclusion. Such a moment was reached in the sixth chapter of the second volume of *The Stones of Venice,* when the mists of Victorian sentimentality parted and he saw directly the Great Lie at the heart of capitalist society:

> "The great cry that rises from all our manufacturing cities, louder than the furnace blast, is all in very deed for this,—that we manufacture everything there except men; we blanch cotton, and strengthen steel, and refine sugar, and shape pottery; but to brighten, to strengthen, to refine, or to form a single living spirit, never enters into our estimate of advantages."[2]

[1] May Morris, II, p. xxxii.
[2] *The Stones of Venice,* "The Nature of Gothic", para. 12.

"We manufacture everything... except men." "From the time at which he wrote this chapter... those ethical and political considerations have never been absent from his criticism of art; and, in my opinion, it is just this part of his work, fairly begun in 'The Nature of Gothic'... which has had the most enduring and beneficial effect on his contemporaries, and will have through them on succeeding generations". So wrote Morris in 1892, when he printed this chapter, "The Nature of Gothic", separately at the Kelmscott Press. And he added: "To my mind... in future days it will be considered as one of the very few necessary and inevitable utterances of the century."

In "The Nature of Gothic" Ruskin set himself the task of analysing the main characteristics–and, more than this, the essential character–of Gothic architecture. The first characteristic he singled out as "Savageness or Rudeness", and the sections dealing with this are the ones which impressed themselves upon Morris's mind. The rough, irregular character of the stonework of late medieval buildings, Ruskin declared, can only be understood by considering the nature of the craftsmen who built them. Every man, Ruskin asserted, has creative powers slumbering within him. Moreover, the act of self-realization in labour was, for Ruskin, no mere luxury. Like Carlyle, he believed that through labour man achieved his own humanity: but with Ruskin there was this difference –the labour must be *creative* labour, summoning up the intellectual and moral–and not only physical and mechanical –powers of the labourer. This led him to a direct contrast between medieval and nineteenth-century society:

"Observe, you are put to a stern choice in this matter. You must either make a tool of the creature, or a man of him. You cannot make both. Men were not intended to work with the accuracy of tools, to be precise and perfect in all their actions. If you will have that precision out of them, and make their fingers measure degrees like cog-wheels, and their arms strike curves like compasses, you must inhumanize them. All the energy of their spirits must be given to make cogs and compasses of themselves... On the other hand, if you will make a man of the working creature, you cannot make a tool. Let him but begin to imagine, to think, to try to do anything worth doing; and the engine-turned precision is lost at once. Out come all his roughness, all his dulness, all his incapability; shame upon shame, failure upon failure, pause after pause: but out comes the whole majesty of him also. . ."[1]

The very precision of the products of the modern engineering industry were—Ruskin asserted—the visible indications of the slavery of the modern worker; "all those accurate mouldings, and perfect polishings, and unerring adjustments of the seasoned wood and tempered steel" upon which Victorian society so prided itself were the marks of the murder of the human soul by the exclusion of the worker's moral and intellectual faculties. By contrast, in medieval times,

"There might be more freedom in England, though her feudal Lord's lightest words were worth men's lives, and though the blood of the vexed husbandman dropped in the furrows of her fields, than there is while the animation of her multitudes is sent like fuel to feed the factory smoke, and the strength of them is given daily to be wasted into the fineness of a web, or racked into the exactness of a line.

"And, on the other hand, go forth again to gaze upon the old cathedral front, where you have smiled so often at the fantastic ignorance of the old sculptors; examine once more those ugly goblins, and formless monsters, and stern statues, anatomiless and rigid; but do not mock at them, for they are signs of the life and liberty of every workman who struck the stone; a freedom of thought, and rank in scale of being, such as no laws, no charters, no charities can secure; but which it must be the first aim of all Europe at this day to regain for her children."[2]

Ruskin was not the first to notice or to protest against "this degradation of the operative into a machine": but he was the first to declare that men's "pleasure in the work by which they make their bread"[3] lay at the very foundations of society, and to relate this to his whole criticism of the arts. Moreover, he went on to declare, in a passage that may have

[1] *The Stones of Venice,* "The Nature of Gothic", para. 12.
[2] *Ibid.,* para. 13. [3] *Ibid.,* para. 15.

had an incalculable influence on Morris's future career, that the separation of manual and intellectual labour was equally destructive of both:

"We are always in these days endeavouring to separate the two; we want one man to be always thinking, and another to be always working, and we call one a gentleman and the other an operative; whereas the workman ought often to be thinking, and the thinker often to be working, and both should be gentlemen, in the best sense. As it is, we make both ungentle, the one envying, the other despising, his brother; and the mass of society is made up of morbid thinkers, and miserable workers... It would be well if all of us were good handicraftsmen in some kind, and the dishonour of manual labour done away with altogether... In each several profession, no master should be too proud to do its hardest work. The painter should grind his own colours; the architect work in the mason's yard with his men; the master-manufacturer be himself a more skilled operative than any man in his mills; and the distinction between one man and another be only in experience and skill, and the authority and wealth which these must naturally and justly obtain."[1]

In this passage may, perhaps, be found the germ of the Morris Firm.

In the next decade–as we shall see–Ruskin turned his attention more and more to political economy and questions of social morality, and took several further impetuous zig-zag steps in the direction of a revolutionary understanding of capitalist society. For all his moral courage and indignation, his eyes were fixed longingly upon the craftsmanship of pre-capitalist modes of production. In his negative criticisms, however, he was in his time without rival–

"We have much studied, and much perfected, of late, the great civilized invention of the division of labour; only we give it a false name. It is not, truly speaking, the labour that is divided; but the men: –Divided into mere segments of men–broken into small fragments and

[1] *Ibid.*, para. 21.

crumbs of life; so that all the piece of intelligence that is left in a man is not enough to make a pin, or a nail, but exhausts itself in making the point or the head of a nail."[1]

William Morris read this and discussed it excitedly with Edward Burne-Jones in 1853. In 1883 he was reading excitedly once again, and wrote at the top of a sheet of notes:

"It is not only the labour that is divided, subdivided, and portioned out betwixt divers men: it is the man himself who is cut up, and metamorphosised into the automatic spring of an exclusive operation "Karl Marx."[2]

And the sheet continues with notes from Chapter XIV of the First Volume of Marx's *Capital,* "Division of Labour and Manufacture". Repeatedly, when reading this chapter, Morris must have felt the hand of Ruskin on his shoulder:

"The knowledge, the judgement, and the will, which, though in ever so small a degree, are practised by the independent peasant or handicraftsman... these faculties are now required only for the workshop as a whole. Intelligence in production expands in one direction, because it vanishes in many others. What is lost by the detail labourers, is concentrated in the capital that employs them."[3]

And, in another part:

"Within the capitalist system all methods for raising the social productiveness of labour are brought about at the cost of the individual labourer; all means for the development of production transform themselves into means of domination over, and exploitation of, the producers; they mutilate the labourer into a fragment of a man, degrade him to the level of an appendage of a machine, destroy every remnant of charm in his work, and turn it into a hated toil; they estrange from him the intellectual potentialities of the labour-process in the same proportion as science is incorporated in it as an independent power;

[1] *Ibid.,* para. 16.

[2] Walthamstow MSS. The notes comprise passages of free translation (for his own use) from the French. They refer especially to Volume One of *Capital,* Chapter XIV, section 5.

[3] *Capital,* (1938), p. 355.

they distort the conditions under which he works, subject him during the labour-process to a despotism the more hateful for its meanness; they transform his life-time into working-time, and drag his wife and child beneath the wheels of the Juggernaut of capital. But all methods for the production of surplus-value are at the same time methods of accumulation. . . of capital. Accumulation of wealth at one pole is, therefore, at the same time accumulation of misery, agony of toil, slavery, ignorance, brutality, mental degradation, at the opposite. . ."[1]

"It is not the place, here", Marx wrote, "to go on to show how division of labour siezes upon, not only the economical, but every other sphere of society, and everywhere lays the foundation of that all engrossing system of specialising and sorting men, that development in a man of one single faculty at the expense of all other faculties, which caused A. Ferguson, the master of Adam Smith, to exclaim: 'We make a nation of Helots, and have no free citizens.' "[2]

What Marx did not have place nor time to develop at this point was subsequently to be a central preoccupation of Morris's thought.

[1] *Ibid.*, pp. 600-1. Mr. R. Page Arnot first called attention to the relation between this passage of Marx and Morris's thought in his *William Morris: a Vindication* (1934).
[2] *Ibid.*, p. 347.

CHAPTER III

ROSSETTI AND THE PRE-RAPHAELITES

I. "My work is the embodiment of dreams. . ."

AT the time when he was reading Carlyle and Ruskin, Morris had very little first-hand experience of working people, of their conditions of life and labour. Of the life of the workers he had a vague but continual guilty apprehension. But his knowledge (and hatred) of capitalism in the 1850s was derived not from contact with the sources of exploitation, but from the squalor and anarchy which he passed through in London and the great towns: from the degradation of its architecture: and from the sham and hypocrisy prevading its manners and thought. In their influence upon Morris in the fifties, Ruskin's writings were perhaps of greatest importance in helping towards his choice of art as the central battleground in the "Holy Warfare against the age."

For "politics"—the intrigues and shadow-boxing of the two great political parties—he was already forming a contemptuous indifference, which was nourished by Carlyle's scorn of democratic fetishes, and Dickens's ridicule of Parliament. He was attracted by (and learnt something from) the "Christian Socialism" of Charles Kingsley and F.D. Maurice. But when, early in 1856, he came under the influence of the engaging and arresting personality of Dante Gabriel Rossetti, these ideas were left to mature in the back of his mind. In July, 1856, he was writing to his friend, Cormell Price:

> "I can't enter into politico-social subjects with any interest, for on the whole I see that things are in a muddle, and I have no power or vocation to set them right in ever so little a degree. My work is the embodiment of dreams in one form or another. . ."

In one sense, this letter reveals that Morris was aware of the severity of the disease from which society was suffering: he put forward no petty quack remedies: the immensity of the problem left him helpless. In another it reveals the weak point in his vision at this time. "Things are in a muddle"—can it be an accident that almost the identical phrase—"It's aw a muddle", "Fro' first to last, a muddle!"—is the refrain of the sentimentalized workingman, Stephen Blackpool, whose central position in the structure of Dickens's *Hard Times* destroys the artistic integrity of the novel, and blunts the edge of its attack? *Hard Times* appeared in 1854, and Morris —already an admirer of Dickens—was certain not to have passed it by. And Blackpool—and, above all, this very phrase, "a muddle"—serves in the novel to obscure the one fact which Dickens could never bring himself to look in the face—the fact of the class struggle, the irreconcilable interests of the employers and the employed.

In the 1850s, however, Morris abandoned the effort to analyse the cause for his "hatred of civilisation", and surrendered to the over-mastering attractions of "romance". For it was just at this time that he came under the influence of Dante Gabriel Rossetti, and—through him—met the members and associates of the Pre-Raphaelite Brotherhood. This "Brotherhood" was a high-sounding name adopted by a small circle of young artists (and would-be artists) determined to raise the banner of revolt against the academic art of their time, but incoherent in their ideas, and ill-assorted in their talents. The name itself was derived from the banter of fellow art-students, who thought that the reverence paid by John Everett Millais and William Holman Hunt to the religious art of the early Italian Renaissance was exaggerated and ludicrous. The "Brotherhood" had been founded in 1848, to give a sense of mystery, dedication, formality, to the group, when they met in each others' rooms and studios for earnest discussion. Of its seven original members, three were of especial prominence—the two very young professional painters, with marked abilities, Hunt and Millais: and Rossetti himself, the brilliant London-born son of an Italian refugee. Rossetti's younger brother, William Michael, was another member (critic and recorder of the Brotherhood, since he had no talent as a painter), and his sister, Christina Rossetti the poet, was a close associate. Ford Madox Brown, the painter—a few years older than the others—was welcomed as an unofficial associate, while John Ruskin came to the aid of the Brotherhood when they were hard-pressed by outraged critics, and adopted a position of qualified patronage. In 1849 and 1850 Millais, Hunt and Rossetti exhibited paintings adorned with the mystic initials, "P.R.B.", which aroused both attention and rage in academic circles: and in 1850 a paper named *The Germ* was published, which lasted for only four numbers, and whose contents were written almost entirely by members of the Brotherhood or their associates.

The fame of the Brotherhood had reached Morris and Burne-Jones at Oxford, through the storm of critical controversy, and through Ruskin's defence of their work. The rumour of revolt within the visual arts excited their interest: when they found a copy of *The Germ* they read it with enthusiasm, and they made it their business to view any paintings by the group which they could find. In January, 1856 (when the original Brotherhood was already breaking up), Burne-Jones contacted Rossetti at the Great Ormond Street Working Men's College which the Christian Socialist, F.D. Maurice, had helped to found, and at which both Rossetti and Ruskin gave lectures and tuition. He fell completely under Rossetti's spell: and was flattered to find at a subsequent meeting that Rossetti was taking a close interest in the *Oxford and Cambridge Magazine*. Burne-Jones recalled:

"He received me very courteously, and asked much about Morris, one or two of whose poems he knew already, and I think that was our principal subject of talk, for he seemed much interested about him. He showed me many designs for pictures; they tossed about everywhere in the room: the floor at the end was covered with them and with books... I stayed long and watched him at work, not knowing till many a day afterwards that this was a thing he greatly hated, and when, for shame, I could stay no longer, I went away, having carefully concealed from him the desire I had to be a painter."[1]

Even after the passage of years, Burne-Jones could still recall with excitement the spell which Rossetti's studio cast upon him. Here—after all the youthful conversations at Oxford, the awed discussions with Morris of this new, revolutionary, movement in art of which they had read in the pages of their master, Ruskin, and the visits they had made to see the pictures of members of the Brotherhood—here at last he seemed to have stepped directly into the presence of Art itself, and—what is more—Art treated him familiarly and courteously, and had even noticed the work of his best friend.

Rossetti, on his side, was flattered by the attention he received, for the "great" man was himself still in his late twenties: and, no doubt, he was not so disturbed to be watched at his work as Burne-Jones later came to fear. Indeed only a few days later he was writing to his friend, Allingham:

"That notice in the Oxford and Cambridge Magazine was the most gratifying thing by far that ever happened to me—being unmistakeably genuine... It turns out to be by a certain youthful Jones, who was in London the other day, and whom... I have now met. One of the nicest young fellows in—Dreamland. For there most of the writers in that miraculous piece of literature seem to be. Surely this cometh in some wise of the *Germ*..."[2]

Morris, by now articled to G.E. Street, the architect (where he met his life-long friend, Philip Webb), but still with one foot in the university, was the next to be introduced to the shrine of Art. Burne-Jones, indeed, was now worshipping at it almost daily, having thrown over his Oxford degree and

[1] *Memorials,* I, pp. 129-30.

[2] *Ibid.,* I, p. 130. "That notice" was a reference to Rossetti's work in an article by Burne-Jones on Thackeray, published in *The Germ.*

moved to London to dedicate his life to painting. Here Morris joined him on many weekends in the early summer, and they basked together in Rossetti's patronage:

> "Our Sundays were very peaceful days... often spent by Morris reading aloud the Morte d'Arthur while I worked, and often Rossetti would join us in the afternoon, and it became clear that he cared to be with us."[1]

"We fell under the influence of Rossetti", Morris recalled in 1892,[2] "perhaps I even more than Burne-Jones,[3] and he did us a great deal of good." It was the only time in his life that Morris was completely—and almost uncritically—swept off his feet by another personality. Rossetti was most decisive: Keats was the climax of romantic poetry: the course of poetry was now nearly run, and the next Keats must be a painter. In fact, *every* man ought to be a painter. Within a matter of weeks, architecture was abandoned. In July, 1856, Morris was writing to a friend (in the same letter in which he declared that "my work is the embodiment of dreams"):

> "I have seen Rossetti twice since I saw the last of you; spent almost a whole day with him the last time, last Monday... Rossetti says I ought to paint, he says I shall be able; now as he is a very great man, and speaks with authority and not as the scribes, I *must* try...

[1] *Memorials,* I, p. 133. [2] *Works,* Vol. XXII, p. xxxi.

[3] It is difficult to believe this, in view of the tone of adulation in some of Burne-Jones's private letters and recollections, e.g. "One autumn evening Gabriel and I were alone, and... we were chatting together—and he to me was as Pope or Emperor—it was so nice, for when he loved man or woman they knew it and it was happy; and it was just then that a note came from —— to say that he would come in a few minutes to fetch us to dine to meet this and that... Gabriel ... rang the bell and asked the man when the next train for Euston started for London, and a cab was got and we were in the train for Euston when —— came. It was ten o'clock when we got to Euston Hotel, and we... were back in Oxford by nine [the next morning]... I thought, 'this man could lead armies and destroy empires if he liked; how good it is to be with him' " (*Memorials,* I, p. 167).

"I shall have enough to do, if I actually master this art of painting: I dare scarcely think failure possible at times, and yet I know in my mind that my chances are slender; I am glad that I am compelled to try anyhow: I was slipping off into a kind of small (very small) Palace of Art. . ."[1]

By August he was sharing a studio in London with Burne-Jones, who wrote:

"Topsy and I live together in the quaintest room in all London, hung with brasses of old knights and drawings of Albert Durer. We know Rossetti now as a daily friend, and we know Browning too, who is the greatest poet alive, and we know Arthur Hughes, and Woolner, and Madox Brown. . . Topsy will be a painter, he works hard, is prepared to wait twenty years, loves art more and more every day. He has written several poems, exceedingly dramatic—the Brownings, I hear, have spoken very highly of one that was read to them; Rossetti thinks one called 'Rapunzel' is equal to Tennyson. . . The 'Mag.' is going to smash—let it go! the world is not converted and never will be."[2]

Rossetti continued to drum into the two lads his gospel:

"If any man has any poetry in him, he should paint, for it has all been said and written, and they have scarcely begun to paint."[3]

And—while Morris was learning to do it—he could be useful in other ways: for Rossetti had not overlooked the fact that his protégé had money, and this enabled him to extend the range of his good-natured patronage. "Yesterday", Ford Madox Brown noted in his diary for August 24th, 1856, "Rossetti brought his ardent admirer Morris of Oxford, who bought my little Hayfield for £40."[4]

In the next two years, if the Palace of Art was evacuated, Morris set up in real style in a Gothic castle in Bohemia. The studio at Red Lion Square was furnished with enormous

[1] *Letters,* pp. 17-18.

[2] Mackail, I, pp. 107-8.

[3] *Ibid.,* I, p. 110.

[4] *Ibid.,* I, p. 112.

"intensely medieval furniture", including a huge settle surmounted with three great cupboards, on the panels of which Rossetti painted scenes from Dante and Malory. Morris, working to master the art of painting, became noticeably more variable in mood—at some times hilarious, at others taciturn and morose, at others flying into uncontrollable rages. In 1857 the famous descent of the artists and amateurs on Oxford was made, in order to paint murals on the walls of the Oxford Union. Rossetti took with him a mixed bag of friends and protégés, and they set to work to paint with distemper on a ground of whitewash on damp mortar scenes out of Malory. Morris's picture was entitled "How Sir Palomydes loved La Belle Iseult, with exceeding great love out of measure, and how she loved not him again but rather Sir Tristram". The remaining members of the Oxford "Brotherhood" were enlisted to help in the execution of the work. Dixon, the fledgling Canon, took a hand, while C.J. Faulkner—now an Oxford Fellow and Mathematics Tutor—"comes out tremendously strong on the roof with all kinds of quaint beasts and birds".[1] They sat for each other as models, and Cormell Price noted in his diary for October 18th, 1857, "Stood for Top for two hours in a dalmatic".[2] Morris's head was "always fit for Lancelot or Tristram",[3] while his (now portly) figure, with legs straddled like Henry VIII, served to decorate angles in the roof. "For the purposes of our drawing we often needed armour", recalled Burne-Jones:

"Therefore Morris, whose knowledge of all these things seemed to have been born in him. . . set to work to make designs for an ancient kind of helmet called a basinet, and for a great surcoat of ringed mail with a hood of mail and a skirt coming below the knees. These were made for him by a stout little smith who had a forge near the castle. Morris's visits to the forge were daily, but what scenes happened there we shall never know; the encounters between these two workmen were always stubborn and angry as far as I could see. One afternoon when

[1] Mackail, I, p. 120.
[2] *Ibid.*, I, p. 126. "Dalmatic"—a long-sleeved clerical vestment.
[3] *Ibid.*, I, p. 120.

I was working high up at my picture, I heard a strange bellowing in the building, and turning round. . . saw an unwonted sight. The basinet was being tried on, but the visor, for some reason would not lift, and I saw Morris embedded in iron, dancing with rage and roaring inside. The mail coat came in due time, and was so satisfactory to its designer that the first day it came he chose to dine in it. It became him well; he looked very splendid."[1]

The story of the armour is one among many humorous anecdotes of Morris at Oxford. He was now known by his friends as "Topsy", partly in honour of his mop of matted hair, partly after the character in *Uncle Tom's Cabin.* One of his associates recalled him as being, at this time,

"a short, very square-built, spectacled man with a head that appeared too big from the length and thickness of his dark, matted locks. His movements were jerky and full of humour, for Morris was an excellent mimic. . . He was very shy, and had a way of shifting his legs and twiddling with his watch-chain which gave him somewhat of a grotesque appearance. He was the essence of good-nature, and stood chaff with extra-ordinary tolerance."

In the circle of enthusiasts, he was the butt of their laughter. His painting was amateurish—the figures fourteen feet high, their legs hidden by sun-flowers, above which great heads and shoulders appeared. Rossetti told him his Iseult was ugly, and sent him back to "nature" to make sketches of a local *b lle.* The wary mother refused to allow Morris to draw her daughter, and on his return, disconsolate, he was confronted by some rhymes:

"Poor Topsy has gone to make a sketch of Miss Lipscombe.
But he can't draw the head, and don't know where the hips come."

When painting the roof, he was covered from head to foot—hair, beard, and clothes—in paint. "My good man, can you tell me the subject of these pictures?" enquired one officious

[1] Mackail, I, pp. 120-1.

don, examining the work in progress:

"Morris turned suddenly on the don, glaring at him through his tempera-splashed spectacles. *Morte d'Arthur* he shouted, and mounting a ladder, he vanished into the chaos of the roof scaffolding."[1]

The next day Rossetti received from the don a complaint as to the rudeness of his workmen. The stories of Morris's hatred of any formal or fashionable social intercourse are many. Day and night, he lived with the stain of paint on his hands, the dreams of Malory in his head. "Morris went to Jones's on Sunday night", noted the sister of Cormell Price in her diary, "and his hair was so long and he looked so wild that the servants who opened the door would not let him in, thinking he was a burglar."

This Oxford adventure was the culminating period of Morris's youthful revolt. In these dizzy weeks, surrounded by other young enthusiasts, he came nearest to bringing to life his dream-world in the heart of Victorian England. During these weeks several of his best early poems were written, in a medieval volume with a large clasp. A hilarious and eccentric undergraduate, with scarlet hair, who flaunted revolutionary, atheist and republican convictions, became one of the circle: his name was Swinburne. Rossetti discovered the beautiful Jane Burden, with her deep mystic eyes, shapely neck, and plenitude of dark hair, who was to become William Morris's wife. The co-operative work at the Union, under the inspiration of the master-artist, Rossetti, seemed to give a new reality to the idea of "Brotherhood": in such a manner (it seemed) the frescoes on some stately church might have been painted in Italy during the early Renaissance. Nineteen-year-old Val Prinsep, aspiring to become a painter, who was one of the circle, could still recall fifty years later the "singular charm" of the adventure. The medieval dream was built into their everyday life. Like other such cliques a special slang, private jokes

[1] Val. C. Prinsep in *The Magazine of Art,* 1904.

and allusions, were cultivated. Every lodging was a "crib", all beautiful women were "stunners". "For a man not to know the difference between a basinet and a salade was shameful". They asserted the same artistic doctrines: "in all art there was to be an abundance of pattern". Above all, underlying their high spirits and affectations, there was a tremendous sense of dedication to art, an earnest passion to achieve something worthy of the beauty of past times, despite the commercialism and philistinism of their age. "I can still picture to myself the little dining-room at that 'delightful crib' "; recalled Val Prinsep:

"I can recall the animated discussions on Art subjects that we held there. I can hear Rossetti from his sofa interrupting us, and saying:

" 'It's all very well talking, but if I could paint like ——', mentioning a painter, who was then the most popular artist of the day, 'why, by Jove, I should do it.'

"I can see Morris stop aghast in his stumping backwards and forwards, as was his wont, and Ned look up from his drawing, and crying a pained, 'Oh, Gabriel', and then bursting forth in a roar of laughter at the idea of 'our Gabriel' being anything but what he was. Then Morris recovers himself and chuckles, 'What a lark!' "[1]

II. The Pre-Raphaelites—and the "Soonset Floosh"

That these years of discipleship to Rossetti were ones of high-spirited revolt—Bohemian, enthusiastic, iconoclastic—is clear enough. Analysis of the nature of this revolt is more difficult. If we consider the aims of the original Pre-Raphaelite Brotherhood (which was already dissolving when Morris and Burne-Jones met Rossetti) we meet with a good deal of confusion. Hunt and William Michael Rossetti attempted to write the history of the movement in later life, and they by no means agreed on the original objectives of the Brotherhood, nor even on the course of events. Certainly, all who took part in its early stages believed that they were in revolt

[1] Val C. Prinsep in *The Magazine of Art*, 1904.

against the academic art of the time. Several of the group came from impoverished professional or lower middle-class backgrounds: like Keats, they found the need to fight to gain entry and recognition in artistic circles, and, like Keats, they resented the tradition of deference to aristocratic taste which had by no means been ousted by the mid-century. The Royal Academy (to their minds) represented the bastion of reaction in the visual arts, and William Morris, in 1891, still regarded the Pre-Raphaelite movement as "a really audacious attempt: a definite revolt against the Academical Art which brooded over all the Schools of civilized Europe at the time. . ."

"One must look upon it as a portion of the general revolt against Academicism in Literature as well as in Art", continued Morris. "In Literature the revolt had taken place much earlier. . ."[1] And, in truth, the movement started with a strong literary influence. The painters influenced by the great romantic poets, sought to discard the cold conventions of a mechanical "grand manner", and to return to the direct observation of nature. F.G. Stephens, one of the original Brotherhood, wrote in *The Germ:*

> "The Public are taught to look with delight upon murky old masters, with dismally demonaic trees, and dull waters of lead, colourless and like ice, upon rocks that make geologists wonder, their angles are so impossible, their fractures are so new. . . so it is that the world is taught to think of nature, as seen through other men's eyes, without any reference to its original powers of perception. . ."[2]

Holman Hunt, more than fifty years later, reconstructed a conversation with Millais in the early days, when the two young painters decided to challenge the stylized manners of the Schools:

> "Let us go on a bold track. . . It is simply fuller Nature that we want. . . Why should the several parts of the composition be always

[1] Lecture on "The English Pre-Raphaelites", May Morris, I, p. 297
[2] *The Germ*, No. 4.

opposed in pyramids? Why should the highest light be always on the principal figure? Why make one corner of the picture always in shade? For what reason is the sky in a daylight picture as black as night?"[1]

So far, so good—but overshadowing the "return to Nature" of the romantic literary tradition there was the particular influence of the poems of John Keats. The discovery of Keats's poems had nourished the adolescent revolt of both Hunt and Rossetti. Hunt's first picture exhibited at the Academy was *The Eve of St. Agnes:* the first avowedly Pre-Raphaelite painting of Millais was taken from *Isabella,* and Rossetti's first important poem, *The Blessed Damozel,* was written as a heavenly complement to the same poem. The desire to make their painting the medium for the expression of more intimate and personal feelings than were capable of expression in the conventional "grand manner" was thus, in its early stages, coloured by the attractions of Keats's imaginative "realms of gold". Many years later William Michael Rossetti sought to find a formula which reconciled both the "return to Nature" and the lure of "romance"—

"the predominant conception of the Pre-Raphaelite Brotherhood," he wrote, was "that an artist, whether painter or writer, ought to be bent upon defining and expressing his own personal thoughts, and that these ought to be based upon a direct study of Nature."[2]

But John Ruskin, in the letter to *The Times* in 1851 in which he came to the defence of the Brotherhood (placing, admittedly, his own interpretation on their aims, rather than that of Hunt or Rossetti) emphasized quite different points:

"They intend to return to early days in one point only—that. . . they will draw either what they see, or what they suppose might have been the actual facts of the scene they desire to represent, irrespective of any

[1] W. Holman Hunt, *Pre-Raphaelitism and the P.R.B.,* Vol. I, p. 59.
[2] W.M. Rossetti's Preface to a facsimile edition of *The Germ* (1905).

conventional rules of picture-making: and they have chosen their unfortunate though not inaccurate name because all artists did this before Raphael's time and after Raphael's time did *not* do this, but sought to paint fair pictures rather than represent stern facts. . ."

The representation of "stern facts" and the expression of the artist's "own personal thoughts" need not necessarily be opposed. But the two phrases indicate the contradictory nature of Pre-Raphaelite aims. "Truth to Nature" proved to be one of the most deceptive slogans of any artistic movement in history. The Pre-Raphaelite painters devoted exceptional pains to copying the external appearances of reality. They took each other (and each other's friends) for models, and posed in strange costumes and in stranger attitudes. William Morris, raging inside a basinet, is only one piece of vociferous testimony among many to the literal enthusiasm with which the group of painters adopted their fallacy—painting each vein and mottle on a leaf, painting the coat of a sheep hair by hair, or tethering a calf in the studio—in the belief that by so doing they were approaching closer to the portrayal of reality.

But the very last impression that is given by the majority of Pre-Raphaelite paintings is that they are engaged in any serious way with the exploration of contemporary experience. The painters understood perfectly well that "Truth to Nature" pushed to its extreme would become mere copywork naturalism. In fact, they took themes for their painting which varied like the two extremes of Victorian poetry. At both extremes they were subject to a strong literary inspiration. In the first stage of the movement, Keats, Dante and the Bible, provided most of the texts. In the second stage—of Morris, Burne-Jones and Rossetti—Malory supplanted these, and Morris's first full-scale picture (commissioned for Thomas Plint, a Leeds stockbroker) was entitled "Sir Tristram after his illness, in the garden of King Mark's Palace, recognized by the dog he had given to Iseult". One of Burne-Jones's earliest paintings (also commissioned for Plint) was taken from Rossetti's poem, *The Blessed Damozel:*

> "I have chosen The Blessed Damozel for my year's work. In the first picture I shall make a man walking in the street of a great city, full of all kinds of happy life; children, such as he will never have, and lovers walking, and ladies leaning from windows all down great lengths of street leading to the city walls; and there the gates are wide open, letting in a space of green field and cornfield in harvest; and all round his head a great rain of swirling Autumn leaves blowing from a little walled graveyard.
>
> "And in the other picture I shall make lovely Heaven, where the lady stands at the edge of the garden and leans over, trying to count a thick flight of little souls in bright flames, and the garden of Heaven full of flowers on every side of her and of lovers who have met again. Oh dear, I dare say it will turn out something awful."[1]

And at the other extreme, something equally awful, if not even more grisly, was perpetrated by members of the movement—their attempt to fit into their laborious backgrounds dramatic scenes from contemporary life. Just as remote idealized beauty—La Belle Iseult and Guenevere and the Blessed Damozel—provided the first source, so Vice provided the second. Hunt hit rock-bottom with *The Awakened Conscience,* whose scene is "one of those *maison damnées* which the wealth of a seducer has furnished for the luxury of a woman who has sold herself and her soul to him". The Seducer is portrayed with one hand striking the keys of the piano, and with the other arm embracing the Victim of his Passions, who stands "her wide eyes straining on vacancy as if seeing Hell open, the trinkets on her hands driven into the flesh and the fingers intertwined with a spasmodic power".[2] But, while Rossetti also tried his hand at Vice, the original intention of the Brotherhood had been to treat contemporary reality in other aspects as well. An article in *The Germ* entitled "Modern Giants" declared that we miss "the poetry of the things about us":

[1] *Memorials,* I, p. 153.

[2] See William Gaunt, *The Pre-Raphaelite Tragedy* (1942), p. 54.

"our railways, factories, mines, roaring cities, steam vessels and the endless novelties and wonders produced every day; which if they were found only in the One Thousand and One Nights, or in any poem classical or romantic, would be gloried over without end; for as the majority of us know not a bit more about them, but merely their names, we keep up the same mystery, the main thing required for the surprise of the imagination."[1]

"Truth to Nature." "Stern facts." "Flight of little souls in bright flames." "*Maisons damnées.*" "Mystery—the main thing required for the surprise of the imagination." Perhaps the last phrase provides the best clue in this Babel. Once again, we are forced to return to the conflict voiced in the poems and letters of John Keats. But, in the minds of these young artists, the sense of opposition between the world of "romance" and that of everyday experience has reached a further stage. Reality, the world where "men sit and hear each other groan", is presented as Vice: an attempt to represent the truth of suffering, which is tarnished by the sentimental moralizing from which even Dickens did not escape. This impoverished sentimentalizing was based, in the last analysis, upon a refusal (or inability) really to look the facts of capitalist exploitation and class conflict in the face. Ruskin himself admitted, he had "naturally a great dread of subjects altogether painful". As for railways, factories, mines—these remained subjects for Art only so long as they remained to the artist a "mystery", miraculous magic powers summoned into being by genii. Once the "mystery" was penetrated, they revealed themselves to the artist only as squalid scenes of suffering, exploitation and money-making, drained of all the aspirations transfigured in the world of "romance".

Rossetti, indeed, tried his hand at Vice (in his long uncompleted painting, *Found*) but, finding it uncongenial, he had dedicated himself to the other extreme of "romance" when Morris and Burne-Jones came under his influence. The

[1] F.G. Stephens in *The Germ*, No. 4.

Pre-Raphaelite doctrine of "Truth to Nature" finds a marked parallel in the concrete, richly ornamental language of Keats's *Eve of St. Agnes* (a poem bound to exert a special attraction on a painter, with its splendid colour-imagery), and in the matter-of-fact realistic details which Tennyson embroidered into *Mariana:*

> "The rusted nails fell from the knots
> That held the pear to the gable-wall. . ."

or the colourful visual detail of the *Lady of Shallott:*

> "All in the blue unclouded weather
> Thick-jewell'd shone the saddle-leather,
> The helmet and the helmet feather
> Burn'd like one burning flame together,
> As he rode down to Camelot. . ."

Browning, and, later, Morris, employed similar realistic devices in their poems on medieval themes in order to evoke their romantic dream in concrete terms and with the semblance of life. In Burne-Jones's paintings from Malory, in Rossetti's early paintings from Dante, and in Morris's own painting of Guenevere, minutely naturalistic detail—of costume, rich ornament, and hangings—was used to like effect. But the impression left by the pictures is not one of realism. Rather, Keats's world of "poesy" and "romance" appears to have lost its last root-holds in the soil of contemporary experience, and to be becoming emaciated, sapless, and drooping. We are no longer conscious (as we are in Keats's greatest work) of the real sense of conflict between rich aspiration and drab reality, and of the struggle to reconcile the two. Rather, the extreme of "romance" (like that of Vice) seems always tainted by the evasion of life. At their worst, Pre-Raphaelite versions of Keats or the Bible or Malory were (like the worst of Tennyson's *Idylls*) little more than the projection of the impoverished sensibility of the Victorians into a medieval setting, with conventional Victorian gentlemen and ladies dressed up in fancy costume. At their best, they were remote and ethereal, saturated with a yearning for values lost to the world, and whose impossibility of realization was accentuated rather than relieved by the naturalistic detail of the painting.

This version of contemporary experience was directly related to the concept of "Beauty" which Rossetti and his friends had taken over, perhaps unconsciously, from Keats: or which, it may be, they had reached independently from the pressure of a similar hatred of their times. Victorian society (they held) was inimical to all "Beauty", and to the end of his life Morris maintained that the true artist at work within capitalist society must always be forced to "Look back!" In 1891 he delivered a lecture on "The English Pre-Raphaelites" in which he came to the defence of Burne-Jones and Rossetti on this very point, in terms which throw some light back upon his views as a young man:

> "I must just say one word about the fact that both Rossetti and Burne-Jones have very little to do with representing the scenes of ordinary modern life as they go on before your eyes. One has often heard that brought against the 'Romantic' artists, as a shortcoming. Now, quite plainly, I must say that I think it *is* a shortcoming. But is the shortcoming due to the individual artist, or is it due to the public at large? for my part I think the latter. When an artist has really a very keen sense of beauty, I venture to think that he can not literally represent an event that takes place in modern life. He must add something or other to qualify or soften the ugliness and sordidness of the surroundings of life in our generation. That is not only the case with pictures ... it is the case also in literature... The difficulty is even greater, perhaps, for the painter. In painting, you cannot get so far away from the facts as you can in literature... By all means, if anyone is really moved by the spirit to treat modern subjects, let him do so... but ... I don't think he has a right, under the circumstances and considering the evasions he is absolutely bound to make, to lay any blame on his brother artist who turns back again to the life of past times; or, who, shall we rather sav. since his imagination must have some garb or another, naturally takes the raiment of some period in which the surroundings of life were not ugly but beautiful."[1]

[1] May Morris, I, pp. 304-5.

"My work is the embodiment of dreams. . ." The tone of the remark is almost aggressive—damn Gradgrind's age, with all its "practical" men, its cant of progress, its hypocrisies and its ugliness! Morris, in the years of Rossetti's greatest influence upon him, placed himself firmly in the etherialized extreme of Pre-Raphaelite "romance". It was, perhaps, here that the most positive aspect of the movement was to be found. "Why is it", asked Thomas Dixon, a working-man from Sunderland, writing to William Michael Rossetti about *The Germ,*

> "these pictures and essays being so realistic, yet produce on the mind such a vague and dreamy sensation, approaching as it were the Mystic Land of a Bygone Age?. . . There is in them the life which I long for, and which to me never seems realizable in this life."

So it seemed to many other men and women, dissatisfied with the poverty of their lives, and finding their sense of loss reflected in these canvasses, their yearning for something finer, more "ideal". It was as if the human spirit was being driven to more and more remote regions, but was still struggling to keep alive. As Burne-Jones once declared: "The more materialistic Science becomes, the more angels shall I paint."

But angels frightened no one—least of all Mr. Gradgrind. Of all the contradictory vicissitudes of the Pre-Raphaelite movement, none was more curious or unexpected to the artists than the assortment of patrons which they collected around them. In their early days, none of the dwindling stream of aristocratic patronage was diverted towards them: indeed, when Millais (before he turned renegade, and entered the portals of the Academy) had dared to intrude democratic sentiments and realistic detail into his *Christ in the House of His Parents,* the critics met him with an outburst of fury. *The Times,* calling the picture "plainly revolting", continued: "To attempt to associate the Holy Family with the meanest details of a carpenter's shop, with no conceivable omission of misery, of dirt and even disease, all finished with the same loathesome minuteness, is disgusting." But the dissenting middle class had less fastidious sensibilities, and in the later years of Victoria's reign, Millais's picture was to become a favourite in the Sunday school and the Bible class. Something similar can be found in the adoption of Rossetti and his friends by such patrons as Marshall, a Leeds millionaire: MacCracken, a Liverpool shipping-magnate: and Thomas Plint, the Leeds stock-broker. Although several patrons of this kind were said to have a weather-eye open towards successful financial speculation, this certainly was not the main motivation of Plint.

We are indebted (once again) to Val Prinsep for a glimpse of Plint, visiting Rossetti in his studio:

> "On the easel was a charming water colour of an 'Annunciation', the angel appearing to the Virgin in the grey dawn as she wanders by the side of a stream. The charm of the picture was the pearly grey tones of the figures and landscape. Plint sat down before the picture. He was a Yorkshire man, and talked with a strong accent.
>
> " 'Nobutt, Mr. Rossetti,' he said, 'that's a fine thing.' Then, after a pause, he added: 'Couldn't you put a soonset floosh over the whole thing?' "[1]

Rossetti was stung to fury, and despite the abject penitence of the Dissenting stock-broker, refused to sell him the painting. Plint was able to impose more easily on the impoverished Ford Madox Brown, buying his *Work* on the condition that he introduced into it both Carlyle and Kingsley, and changed "one of the four *fashionable* young ladies into a *quiet, earnest, holy*-looking one, with a book or two and tracts".[2] Plint, dying at thirty-nine, left pictures which fetched the sum of £18,000 at a Leeds sale in 1862. His obituaries commended his high reputation on the stock exchange, his life spent in the service of religion and benevolence, and his selection of *Hymns and Sacred Poetry.*[3] Whatever qualities Thomas

[1] *The Magazine of Art,* 1904.

[2] See Oswald Doughty, *A Victorian Romantic, Dante Gabriel Rossetti* (1949).

[3] Rev. R.V. Taylor, *Biographia Leodensis,* pp. 497-8.

Plint may have had (and no doubt he was both well-intentioned and enlightened) he can hardly have seemed to the young Morris and Burne-Jones—when he came forward as their first patron—to have been fitted to take a seat at the Round Table or to shake a lance in the jousts at Camelot.

But Plint (and his like) were important and neglected characters in what one critic has termed "The Pre-Raphaelite Tragedy". First, he helps us to understand the gathering cynicism of Rossetti, who despised his patrons while at the same time he was forced to meet their tastes. Later, Plint's successors were to lead Morris, also, to an understanding of the inadequacy of the Firm in the "Holy Warfare" with the age—although with altogether different results. Second, Plint points to the nature of the "tragedy" itself. Romanticism, when "hope" had perished, when revolt no longer grappled with the enemy but evaded it in a world of "romance", when aspiration no longer summoned forward the future but yearned for the past, was no longer a source of fear to the enemy. It might be ignored, or jeered at as "effeminate". More dangerous, it could be courted as an ally. It could provide a "soonset floosh".

This was the tragedy of Pre-Raphaelitism, beside which the differences and defections of the Brotherhood sink into unimportance. At the end of his life, Rossetti dismissed the early mysteries of the Brotherhood as "the mere affectations of a parcel of boys", and so showed himself wiser than both Holman Hunt and his own brother who were to treat the origins of the affair with such solemnity. But Rossetti did not deny the earnestness of the revolt itself. "What you call the movement was serious enough," he told Hall Caine,

> "but the banding together under the title was all a joke. We had at that time a phenomenal antipathy to the Academy, and in sheer love of being outlawed signed our pictures with the well-known initials."[1]

[1] See Hall Caine, *Recollections of Rossetti* (1928).

The element of tragedy in the movement comes from the very devotion and ambition of this original revolt, which yet never succeeded in moving into serious engagement with the enemy. In their lives and, often, in their occasional sketches, Rossetti, Madox Brown, and Burne-Jones showed abilities, humour, and a quality of self-criticism which was rarely present in their more studied canvasses. The reason (in the case of Burne-Jones in particular) must partly be found in the conditions of work which they imposed upon themselves. The fire of their original conceptions became lost in the desert of interminable copywork from which their paintings were assembled. But the greater reason lies in the extravagance of their ambition. In their youth, they looked upon success in the esteem of fashionable circles with contempt. They refused all compromise with the Academy, and Millais was damned when he capitulated. Rossetti, indeed, showed a dislike of exhibiting before the public which recalls the letters of Keats. They thought of themselves as revolutionaries, who intended to bring back a world of feeling and meaning to the visual arts—irony or critical restraint were targets set far too low. They sought to create great Art with their backs turned on the world. "Dream" is not an affectation: it is a precise description of the character of the movement. They desired to paint Visions: but the result was "dream", a world of compensation, in which the frustrations and repressions, both personal and social, of their lives found release. Great art is not made of such stuff: and, while many minor works of permanent value were painted in the process, the major "masterpieces" of the Pre-Raphaelites remain as testimony to this truth.

CHAPTER IV

THE FIRST JOUST WITH VICTORIANISM

I. "Janey"

WHAT lasting impression did these five years of excitement, painting and studying in the studio at Red Lion Square, decorating the Oxford Union, defying the conventions of the Respectable and the Good, leave upon William Morris?

First, one reservation must be made. Morris has been treated by some critics as though the original impulse of his life came from his contact with the Pre-Raphaelite Brotherhood. This is not the case. Although Morris came under Rossetti's influence when he was (in his own words) a "mere boy" of twenty-three, his revolt reached back into his teens, and many of his guiding ideas were formed in earlier years. The decision to devote his life to Art had been made on the quay at Le Havre, before Burne-Jones stood awestruck in Rossetti's studio. However literally Morris adopted the idea of discipleship to the master-artist,[1] he was no creature blown into life by Rossetti's breath.

Next, we should guard against the danger of interpreting these years of the late 1850s in terms of later developments, when the Pre-Raphaelite movement drifted towards its insipid close. We should recall, not the failures, defections and despondencies, but the clear note of excitement of the young men in revolt against the orthodoxies on every side. Political revolt was present in the movement, though it was not uppermost in young Morris's or Burne-Jones's mind. Hunt and Millais had been touched by the spirit of 1848: they had even joined the Chartist procession on April 10th; Woolner, the sculptor, an original member of the Brotherhood, with

[1] See Mackail, I, p. 111: "Once, when Burne-Jones complained that the design he made in Rossetti's manner seemed better than his own original work, Morris answered with some vehemence; 'I have got beyond that: I want to imitate Gabriel as much as I can.' "

whom Morris and Burne-Jones were acquainted, held fervently democratic convictions. Rossetti was too extreme an individualist to take interest in political matters: but he had behind him the Republican background of his home, and his brother (whom Morris thought to be a bore) earnestly maintained his ex-patriate father's principles. It was natural for Burne-Jones and Morris in the sixties to regard themselves as "People's Men", although the absence of any powerful popular movement in the late fifties meant that this was less a matter of conviction than of private sentiment.

Moreover, the circle of artists and intellectuals felt themselves to be, in other ways, an island of unorthodoxy amidst the encroaching seas of Victorian conventions. Both Rossettis were free-thinkers. Madox Brown's home in London in the sixties (which Morris frequently visited) was noted for its easy Bohemian atmosphere where eccentric artists, atheists, foreign refugees (even "communists") would foregather. Among some of the circle, unconventional personal relations and behaviour—the flouting of respectable "manners"—were not only tolerated: they were necessary as a true hall-mark of genius.

But all these various forms of "revolt" stemmed from the same source—hatred of Victorianism, the attempt to fight back the insidious pressure of respectability. Among all the members of this circle, Rossetti was perhaps the most earnest both in his hatred and in his devotion to art. His unhappy relations with "Lizzie" Siddal (who became his wife) were redeemed throughout by his respect for her personality, his desire that she should develop her independent abilities as a painter and poet. The misery of Rossetti's last years, when he became the victin of laudanum, insomnia, and of a morbidity only occasionally uppermost in his youth, have hidden from view the man whom Morris and Burne-Jones first met and loved. But, despite all the clouds which later came between them, Morris never denied his debt to Rossetti in the early years of their friendship. "He was not a happy man", he wrote in 1892, "being too self-centred, though very kind, and fair in his judgement of other people."[1] His main reflection remained. "He did us a great deal of good". And this was no more than the truth. Rossetti, in the late fifties, was aroused by the enthusiasm of his two young friends to a renewal of his own excitement, when plotting the "P.R.B." revolt with Hunt and Millais. "He was very kind and sincere . . . Art was his religion", recalled one of the students whom he had taught at the Working Men's College in 1855. "He could inspire and thrill us, we loved him so, and were happy to render him the smallest service. . . He did not want our worship."[2] The tribute reveals Rossetti's real interest and quick sympathy for people, irrespective of considerations of class or social convention, in all matters of art or ideas. The startling influence which he exerted over so many of his contemporaries was not based (as is sometimes supposed) upon a bizarre, "magnetic", egocentric personality, but, far more, upon this quality of sympathy, his ability to give them confidence in their own powers.[3] Good-natured, accomplished, assured, a brilliant conversationalist continually throwing out new whims and theories as if they were infallible doctrine, yet still ready to enter into the enthusiasm of his friends and make them his own, saturated from childhood in the poetry of Dante and the atmosphere of the arts, he seemed to embody in himself the life for which the young men were searching. Through his influence Morris was weaned from the last bourgeois fetishes which held him back. The pressure of "respectability", the desire to acquire a sound professional status—these were set behind him. Rossetti was the first man to recognize the evidence of genius in the two friends: he nourished it, encouraged it with friendship rather than patronage, and paid it a succession of most generous

[1] *Works,* Vol. XXII, p. xxxi.

[2] Quoted Doughty, *op. cit.,* pp. 167-8.

[3] See T. Watts Dunton, "A Glimpse of Rossetti and Morris at Kelmscott", in *The English Review,* January, 1909: "I am never tired of iterating, and reiterating, that Rossetti could, and did, take as deep an interest in another man's work as in his own. It was this that made all his friends love him."

tributes. In 1869, when he and Morris were drifting apart, he was still writing of him in a private letter as "the greatest literary identity of our time", and praising his "width of relation to the mass of mankind"—a quality in which Rossetti well knew that he was himself lacking. "He has done things in decorative art which take as high and exclusive a place in that field", the letter continued.[1] Here is no sign of that self-absorption and jealousy which is sometimes attributed as a constant trait to Rossetti's character. "Rossetti always urged Morris to follow his artistic tendencies", wrote one mutual friend, criticizing the "unjust" treatment of Rossetti in Mackail's biography of Morris.[2] And, for Burne-Jones, the liberating influence of Rossetti's friendship was one which he never ceased to cherish: "He gave me courage to commit myself to imagination without shame."[3]

But these years were to bring their lasting influence in yet another form—in Morris's choice of the beautiful Jane Burden as his wife. As we have seen, the pursuit of "romance" was not confined to the painting and poetry of the Pre-Raphaelites: it also intruded into their lives. Rossetti, Burne-Jones, and Morris sought to create a romantic world of their own, in despite of their society—and even to flaunt it in the faces of the philistines. The studio at Red Lion Square, the fraternity of artists painting at Oxford, the building by Morris of Red House at Bexley Heath—these were acts of defiance, or refuges from the world of Gradgrind. So long as money could command it (even if the money came from the same world which they denounced) it was possible to live their lives of make-belief. But no amount of money could bring back an idealized Guenevere or Beatrice for a lover. In their first conception, the Pre-Raphaelite and the Oxford Brotherhood were to have celibacy as a binding condition upon the artists of the "Order". Such a condition was bound to break

[1] Sir J. Skelton, *Table Talk of Shirley* (1895), p. 85.

[2] W.J. Stillman, *Autobiography of a Journalist* (1901), p. 91.

[3] Quoted by Lethaby, *William Morris as Work-Master* (1901).

down. Moreover, in pursuit of "Truth to Nature", models for Beatrice and Guenevere had to be found. And so an attitude to women, shared in different degrees by Rossetti, Burne-Jones, Morris, and others of their circle, was formed.

This attitude (once again) was foreshadowed in the personal relationships of Shelley and of Keats. On the one hand, there was a persistent underlying element of respect for the personality of women, and a yearning for a fully-equal relationship of love and companionship between the sexes. On the other, there was an extreme idealisation of Love itself, which (it has been suggested) could sometimes degenerate into narcissism—the woman was the "soul" of the man, to be isolated and sheltered from the cares and realities of life. For Rossetti, nourished on the *Vita Nuova* of Dante, this yearning for ideal Love, both in his life and his art, was to become an over-mastering obsession.

Certain physical characteristics recur frequently in the models preferred by the Pre-Raphaelites—wide masses of hair, often red; large eyes which, for Morris, must always be grey; pale colouring; a long, finely-defined neck. Here, she is presented (in an unpublished novel of 1870) by Morris:

> "She was slim and thin... a little above the middle height of women, well-knit and with a certain massiveness about her figure... Her face, like her figure, had something strong and massive amidst its delicacy... dark brown abundant silky hair, a firm clear cut somewhat square jaw, and round well-developed lips... a straight nose with wide nostrils and perfectly made... high cheeks... and to light all this up, large grey eyes set wide apart."[1]

And while there cannot be said to have been a rigid "type" of Pre-Raphaelite womanhood, nevertheless the idealization of Love in the early paintings of Rossetti, the early poems of Morris, and the paintings of Burne-Jones, has something in common.

These attitudes find one of their most remarkable expres-

[1] Brit. Mus. Add. MSS. 45328.

sions in Morris's poem, "Praise of My Lady," addressed to Jane Burden, his future wife:

"My lady seems of ivory
Forehead, straight nose, and cheeks that be
Hollow'd a little mournfully.
Beata mea Domina!"

"Mournful"—that is a key word. Languorous melancholy—not a Platonic idealization to the abstract extreme of Dante's love for Beatrice, but a physical beauty which is nevertheless remote, unattainable, and sad. It is as if the idealized Lady had been created in an idealized Heaven, only to languish, as in Rossetti's early poem, *The Blessed Damozel,* for a mortal and a physical love in the real world:

"Her great eyes, standing far apart,
Draw up some memory from her heart,
And gaze out very mournfully;
—*Beata mea Domina!*

"So beautiful and kind they are,
But most times looking out afar,
Waiting for something, not for me.
Beata mea Domina!

"I wonder if the lashes long
Are those that do her bright eyes wrong,
For always half tears seem to be
—*Beata mea Domina!*

"Lurking below the underlid,
Darkening the place where they lie hid—
If they should rise and flow for me!
Beata mea Domina!"

But directly contradicting the melancholy, soulful eyes are the frankly sensuous lips:

"Her full lips being made to kiss,
Curl'd up and pensive each one is;
This makes me faint to stand and see,
Beata mea Domina!

"Her lips are not contented now,
Because the hours pass so slow
Towards a sweet time: (pray for me),
—Beata mea Domina!—

"Nay, hold thy peace, for who can tell;
But this at least I know full well,
Her lips are parted longingly,
—Beata mea Domina!—

"So passionate and swift to move,
To pluck at any flying love,
That I grow faint to stand and see.
Beata mea Domina!"

And so the idealized image was projected on to the canvas or on to the page; a love perpetually yearning for fulfilment, but bringing with it the fear that with the fulfilment of love the ideal would be shattered. It is as if the figures on Keats's "Grecian Urn" had become part of the pattern of their lives:

"Bold Lover, never, never canst thou kiss,
Though winning near the goal—yet, do not grieve;
She cannot fade, though thou hast not thy bliss,
For ever wilt thou love, and she be fair!"

So it was that the legend of Launcelot and Guenevere came to exercise so powerful an influence over Morris and Rossetti—the story of a love in idealized chivalric colours which remained for ever poised on the brink of physical satisfaction: —a satisfaction which, in the world of Victorian morality, seemed to imply either the squalid scenes of Vice, or the respectable bourgeois property contract:

"In that garden fair

"Came Launcelot walking; this is true, the kiss
Wherewith we kissed in meeting that spring day,
I scarce dare talk of the remember'd bliss,

"When both our mouths went wandering in one way,
And aching sorely, met among the leaves;
Our hands being left behind strained far away. . .

"Nevertheless you, O Sir Gauwaine, lie,
Whatever happened on through all those years,
God knows I speak truth, saying that you lie.

"Being such a lady could I weep these tears
If this were true? A great queen such as I
Having sinn'd this way, straight her conscience sears;

"And afterwards she liveth hatefully
Slaying and poisoning, certes never weeps. . ."

This is from the title poem of Morris's first volume of poems, *The Defence of Guenevere*—a poem whose intensity springs not only from the defence of a love which trembles at the point of adultery, but from the dramatic situation of the poem itself—the passionate defence of that love against a hostile inquisition:

"This Mellyagraunce saw blood upon my bed—
Whose blood then pray you? is there any law
To make a queen say why some spots of red

"Lie on her coverlet?. . . so must I defend
The honour of the Lady Guenevere?
Not so, fair lords, even if the world should end

"This very day, and you were judges here
Instead of God."

So powerfully is the beautiful, defiant, figure of Guenevere evoked, that it seems as if Beauty and Love themselves are defying the world:

". . . There was one less than three

In my quiet room that night, and we were gay;
Till sudden I rose up, weak, pale and sick,
Because a bawling broke our dream up, yea

"I looked at Launcelot's face and could not speak,
For he looked helpless too, for a little while,
Then I remember how I tried to shriek,

"And could not, but fell down; from tile to tile
The stones they threw up rattled o'er my head,
And made me dizzier; till within a while

"My maids were all about me, and my head
On Launcelot's breast was being soothed away
From its white chattering, until Launcelot said—

"By God! I will not tell you more to-day,
Judge any way you will—what matters it?"

But in the poem's sequel, "King Arthur's Tomb", the dream-world of love, once again so powerfully evoked in the body of the poem (this time in Launcelot's words):

". . . She held scarlet lilies, such
As Maiden Margaret bears upon the light

"Of the great church walls, natheless did I walk
Through the fresh wet woods, and the wheat that morn,
Touching her hair, and hand and mouth, and talk
Of love we held, nigh hid among the corn.

"Back to the palace, ere the sun grew high,
We went, and in a cool green room all day
I gazed upon the arras giddily,
Where the wind set the silken kings a-sway."

is shattered by the death of Arthur. The very poignancy of their love was in its offence against the moral sanctions of society:

"We went, my maids and I, to say prayers when
They sang mass in the chapel on the lawn.

"And every morn I scarce could pray at all,
For Launcelot's red-golden hair would play,
Instead of sunlight, on the painted wall,
Mingled with dreams of what the priest did say;

"Grim curses out of Peter and of Paul;
Judging of strange sins in Leviticus:
Another sort of writing on the wall,
Scored deep across the painted heads of us."

Here—on the one word "painted"—the worlds of illusion and reality are reversed. The "dreams" of the moral sanctions voiced by the priest become suddenly more real than the "painted" illusion of their love. And so Arthur's death, which at last permits Guenevere and Launcelot to consummate their love in marriage with the moral approval of society, by destroying this tension between their passion and the sanctions of society at the same time destroys their desire, leaving the lovers in a grey world of everyday reality:

"Still night, the lone
Grey horse's head before him vex'd him much,

"In steady nodding over the grey road—
Still night, and night, and night, and emptied heart
Of any stories; what a dismal load
Time grew at last, yea, when the night did part,

"And let the sun flame over all, still there
The horse's grey ears turn'd this way and that. . ."

All the rich colours of the illusory world, the "scarlet lilies", the "fresh wet woods", the "arras", and the "silken kings", are drained away, and

"suddenly the thing grew drear,
In morning twilight, when the grey downs bare
Grew into lumps of sin to Guenevere."

But the sense of "sin" is, for Guenevere, less a feeling of remorse for Arthur, then the realization that the moral sanctions of society (expressed as an implacable Heaven and Hell), once broken, will in the end have their revenge. "Banner, and sword, and shield," Guenevere addresses Launcelot at the end of the poem:

"you dare not pray to die,
Lest you meet Arthur in the other world,
And, knowing who you are, he pass you by,
Taking short turns that he may watch you curl'd

"Body and face and limbs in agony,
Lest he weep presently and go away,
Saying, 'I loved him once,' with a sad sigh—"

These poems are so much more violent and intense than (for example) Tennyson's domestic bourgeois moralities in medieval dress, the *Idylls of the King,* that it has been suggested that they represent a complete escape into the Middle Ages, a true imaginative realization of the life of medieval times. But this is only a part of the truth. The intensity of the feelings in these poems comes, not from the Middle Ages, but from William Morris, the young nineteenth-century poet: it is a measure of the intensity of his own revolt against the impoverished relationships of his own society.

This impoverishment can be illustrated by referring once again to Arthur Hugh Clough's long poem *(The Bothie of Tober-Na-Vuolich),* published a few years before *The Defence of Guenevere.* In this poem, Clough, sensitive, intelligent, and sincere, tried to handle a contemporary theme, of the moral, intellectual and emotional conflicts of a young undergraduate, Philip Hewson, of radical (even "Chartist") views. Clough's manner is at times the mock-heroic (in itself a confession of the poverty of the subject), but more often of serious intent. Hewson oscillates in love between a lovely peasant girl and a sleek and beautiful daughter of the aristocracy, before coming to rest at Elspie, an unspoiled Highland lass who nevertheless has gentility and cultural attainments. The confession of love is a climax to the poem:

"So he retained her hand, and, his tears down-dropping on it,
Trembling a long time, kissed it at last. And she ended.
And as she ended, uprose he: saying, What have I heard? Oh,
What have I done, that such words should be said to me? Oh, I see it,
See the great key-stone coming down from the heaven of heavens;
And fell at her feet, and buried his face in her apron.
But as under the moon and the stars they went to the cottage,
Elspie sighed and said, Be patient, dear Mr. Philip,
Do not do anything hasty. It is all so soon, so sudden.
Do not say anything yet to any one.
Elspie, he answered,
Does not my friend go on Friday? I then shall see nothing of you,
Do not I go myself on Monday?
But oh, he said, Elspie!
Do as I bid you, my child: do not go on calling me Mr.;
Might I not just as well be calling you Miss Elspie?
Call me, this heavenly night for once, for the first time, Philip.
Philip, she said, and laughed, and she said she could not say it;
Philip, she said; he turned, and kissed the sweet lips as they said it."

At their next encounter, the foregoing scene of passion is chewed over:

"As we went home, you kissed me for saying your name. It was dreadful.
I have been kissed before, she added, blushing slightly,
I have been kissed more than once by Donald my cousin, and others;
It is the way of the lads, and I make up my mind not to mind it;
But, Mr. Philip, last night, and from you, it was different, quite, Sir.
When I think of all that, I am shocked and terrified at it.
Yes, it is dreadful to me."

Yes—it is laughable. And yet Clough succeeded (and the poem as a whole shows both sincerity and sensitive understanding of his times) in portraying only too faithfully contemporary middle-class sensibility, the extinction of a straining passion in gentility, fears, and repressions. The young poets lived in a time when every relationship, no matter how intimate, was becoming tainted by the tribe of Tuppers—the pressure of respectability and the acute sense of property values of the

Victorian middle class. Here is a sample of Martin Tupper's *Proverbial Philosophy* (from the section "Of Marriage"):

"Mark the converse of one thou lovest, that it be simple and sincere;
For an artful or false woman shall set thy pillow with thorns.
Observe her deportment with others, when she thinketh not that thou art nigh,
For with thee will the blushes of love conceal the true colour of her mind.
Hath she learning? it is good, so that modesty go with it:
Hath she wisdom? it is precious, but beware that thou exceed;
For women must be subject, and the true mastery is of the mind.
Be joined to thine equal in rank, or the foot of pride will kick at thee;
And look not only for riches, lest thou be mated with misery:
Marry not without means; for so shouldst thou tempt Providence;
But wait not for more than enough; for Marriage is the DUTY of most men. . ."

Samuel Butler and Thomas Hardy, at the end of the century, were to expose (in *The Way of All Flesh* and *Jude the Obscure*) the terrible inhumanity of the bourgeois marriage-relationship—an "iron contract", a title deed to property, a "license to be loved on the premises". All the rich colours of the bourgeois dawn, of *Romeo and Juliet* and *Hero and Leander,* were draining into these grey "lumps of sin", Grundyism, and guilt.

This, then, was William Morris's youthful world. At one extreme was Vice, gaudy, blatant, and miserable: at the other Mrs. Grundy and Theobald Pontifex, giving moral names to the tyranny of possession. And, in between, as the constant background to his revolt, there was the muted gentility of the Philips and Elspies, whose mild aspirations were soon huffed out by the winds of hypocrisy, respectability, and philistinism (those winds which always circle the brutal storm-centre of class oppression and imperialist aggression), unless they shelter them carefully in a Highland cottage or candle-lit cabin of Art or (like the original Philip and Elspie) seek to step back an hundred years to the more heroic climate of New Zealand. Here is one source of the elusive, yearning passion of these poems: the aspiration for a richer love could only be a dream: embodied in morning coats, or Victorian manners, it became a farce: embodied in armour, and the atmosphere of chivalry, it had an illusory reality, but of a beauty that was always unattainable, a love that was haunted by the fear of loss:

> "Over those bones I sat and pored for hours,
> And thought, and dream'd, and still I scarce could see
> The small white bones that lay upon the flowers,
> But evermore I saw the lady; she
>
> "With her dear gentle walking leading in,
> By a chain of silver twined about her wrists,
> Her loving knight, mounted and arm'd to win
> Great honour for her, fighting in the lists.
>
> "O most pale face, that brings such joy and sorrow
> Into men's hearts—yea, too, so piercing sharp
> That joy is, that it marcheth nigh to sorrow
> For ever—like an overwinded harp."[1]

Poignant in art, but disastrous in life:

> "Life's eyes are gleaming from her forehead fair,
> And from her breasts the ravishing eyes of Death."[2]

So wrote Rossetti, torn all his life, and in much of his poetry, by the conflict between the yearning melancholy ideal and the grey reality, between the deathly-pale and passive "Lizzie" Siddal and the sensuous Fanny Cornforth. How far the most famous Pre-Raphaelite models—and in particular "Lizzie" Siddal and Jane Burden—were cast by temperament and nature for their role, and how far they were created anew in the image of the ideal it is impossible to judge. Both were discovered early by Rossetti. Jane Burden was only seventeen when she was thrown (in the days of the Oxford Union) into the constant company of this group of artists in their deepest

[1] "Concerning Geffray Teste Noir."

[2] D.G. Rossetti's fragment, "The Orchard Pit".

medieval phase. Her melancholy, large-eyed beauty struck all who knew her. Perhaps the young girl was swept into the role of Guenevere and Iseult before she herself had found out who she was. In 1869, ten years after her marriage to Morris, she seemed to Henry James the very type of "Pre-Raphaelite womanhood":

> "Oh, *ma chère,* such a wife! *Je n'en reviens pas*—she haunts me still. A figure cut out of a missal—out of one of Rossetti's or Hunt's pictures: to say this gives but a faint idea of her, because when such an image puts on flesh and blood, it is an apparition of fearful and wonderful intensity. It's hard to say whether she's a grand synthesis of all the Pre-Raphaelite pictures ever made—or they a 'keen analysis' of her—whether she's an original or a copy. In either case she is a wonder. Imagine a tall lean woman in a long dress of some dead purple stuff, guiltless of hoops (or of anything else, I should say), with a mass of crisp black hair heaped into great wavy projections on each side of her temples, a thin pale face, a pair of strange, sad, deep, dark Swinburnian eyes, with great thick black oblique brows, joined in the middle and tucking themselves away under her hair. . . a long neck, without any collar, and in lieu thereof some dozen strings of outlandish beads—in fine complete."[1]

But of her character all accounts are reticent: she is silent, languorous, frequently unwell or supposedly unwell, occasionally high-spirited and good-humoured in more intimate company. Few accounts go beyond such appearances, and all dwell upon her remarkable melancholy beauty. The truth is more difficult to penetrate: but one thing at least seems to be clear. William Morris had married not her, but a picture, an ideal from his Pre-Raphaelite dream-world. The dream-world was so all-embracing in these years that it unfitted him for an equal human relationship. It was no fault of hers that, when the dream passed away and he came to know her as a real person, she was not suited to the fuller relationship he then desired. It certainly was no fault of hers: indeed, when this time came she was already so moulded to his dream that she

[1] *Letters of Henry James* (1920), Vol. I, pp. 16-18.

could not change the poses and affectations he had helped to create. But none-the-less it must be acknowledged that this marriage was to provide an element of tragedy in his life, and perhaps in the lives of them both.

II. The Defence of Guenevere

William Morris and Jane Burden were married in April, 1859. He was then twenty-five, and she was more than five years younger. The ceremony was the occasion for one of the last gatherings of the "Oxford Brotherhood". Dixon officiated, joining them by mistake by the names of "William and Mary".

His marriage, and the building of Red House, mark the climax of the first phase of Morris's revolt—the attempt to build a world within a world, whose values and relationships, architecture and manners, were distinct from those of the modern civilization which he hated. But the building of Red House opens, at the same time, the second phase—the attempt to reform the outer world, in some measure, by means of Art, and especially by means of the decorative arts.

The real achievement of the first phase of Morris's life was in his first volume, published in 1858, *The Defence of Guenevere and Other Poems.* It was at Oxford that Morris had discovered (or, rather, reopened) in himself his vein of poetry. His friend, Canon Dixon, later recalled:

> "One night Crom Price and I went to Exeter, and found him with Burne-Jones. As soon as we entered the room, Burne-Jones exclaimed wildly, 'He's a big poet.' 'Who is?' asked we. 'Why, Topsy. . .'
>
> "We sat down, and heard Morris read his first poem. . . As he read it, I felt that it was something the like of which had never been heard before. It was a thing entirely new: founded on nothing previous: perfectly original, whatever its value, and sounding truly striking and beautiful, extremely decisive and powerful in execution. . . I expressed my admiration in some way, as we all did: and I remember his remark, 'Well, if this is poetry, it is very easy to write.' From that time onward for a term or two, he came to my rooms almost every day with a new poem."[1]

[1] Mackail, I, pp. 51-2.

He continued to write fluently. Two years later, when Val Prinsep joined the artists painting the Oxford Union, he took dinner with Rossetti, Morris and Burne-Jones at their lodgings:

"When dinner was over, Rossetti humming to himself as was his wont, rose from the table and proceeded to curl himself up on the sofa. 'Top,' he said, 'read us one of your grinds.' 'No, Gabriel,' answered Morris, 'you have heard them all.' 'Never mind,' said Rossetti; 'here's Prinsep who has never heard them, and beside they are devilish good.' 'Very well, old chap,' growled Morris, and having got his book began to read in a sing-song chant some of the poems afterwards published in his first volume. All the time he was jigging nervously about with his watch-chain. . . Forty years after, I can still recall the scene: Rossetti on the sofa with large melancholy eyes fixed on Morris, the poet at the table reading and ever fidgetting with his watch-chain, and Burne-Jones working at a pen-and-ink drawing:

" 'Gold on her head, and gold on her feet,
And gold where the hems of her kirtle meet,
And a golden girdle round my sweet,
Ah qu'elle est belle, La Marguerite,'

"still seems to haunt me, and this other stanza:

" 'Swerve to the left, son Roger, he said,
When you catch his eyes through the helmet slit,
Swerve to the left, then out at his head,
And the Lord God give you joy of it.' "[1]

Val Prinsep was a man of perception, and the two verses he recalled well represent the two elements—ideal decorative beauty and brutal realism—which are so striking in Morris's first (and best) volume of poetry. If the master influence is that of Keats, two more immediate influences can be felt in the poems—the sensuous lyricism of Tennyson, the rough vigour of early Browning. But, while many poems in the volume are directly derivative from these two poets, and others are little more than bizarre "medieval" experiments, the best among them are entirely original, in the sense that

[1] *Memorials,* I, pp. 161-2.

Morris has thoroughly absorbed the influence of his forerunners, and achieved a synthesis of his own. These poems—among which are the title poem, "Sir Peter Harpdon's End", "Concerning Geffray Teste Noire", "The Haystack in the Floods", "The Judgement of God", and "King Arthur's Tomb"—are the great achievement of Morris's youth, an achievement which has only rarely received due recognition. They are, indeed, among the last true and uncorrupted works of the Romantic Revolt.

When Morris was at Oxford, this Revolt was already in its autumn, and was beginning to enter its long decline. We have already seen something of the causes of this in the parallel movement of Pre-Raphaelitism in art. The aspirations of the great romantic poets, denied by the advances of industrial capitalism and the triumph of a philistine middle class, were being driven into a dream-world of imagination. "Only in ourselves and the world of art and literature was there any hope" (see p. 14). The romantic movement was escapint to a world of "romance", in compensation for the poverty of life, where beauty, the energies of youth, love, and heroism, were conjured up in ancient heroic or medieval chivalric settings, or by frequent allusions to the culture of the past, or by hypnotic and sensuous incantation. But always in this dream-world these values are evoked with a savour of nostalgia, of loss, of the unattainable. It was in Tennyson's early poetry that this savour of nostalgia first found overwhelming lyrical expression.

According to Canon Dixon, Tennyson at this time carried everything before him among the young men at Oxford:

"Poetry was the thing: and it was felt with justice that this was due to Tennyson. Tennyson had invented a new poetry, a new poetic English; his use of words was new, and every piece that he wrote was a conquest of a new region. . . There was the general conviction that Tennyson was the greatest poet of the century; some held him the greatest of all poets, or at least of modern poets."[1]

[1] Mackail, I, p. 44.

Tennyson's "Palace of Art" had not yet, in the 1850s, capitulated before the siege of Victorianism. Still feelings of guilt, "uncertain shapes" lurked in the corners, inspiring the remarkable opening verses of *Maud,* which appeared in 1855 when Morris was at Oxford, and which disappointed Tennyson's more respectable admirers. But the charm which Tennyson cast upon the young men was derived less from the persistence, in muted form, of the romantic protest, than from his new expression of the colours of the romantic twilight.

A reference in a letter of twenty-year-old Burne-Jones gives insight into the nature of their enthusiasm. Writing of the lyric, "Tears, idle tears, I know not what they mean", in *The Princess,* he said: "In some hot dreamy afternoons I have thought upon it for hours, until I have been exquisitely miserable."[1] So the young men pined in the luxurious misery of languishing after "the days that are no more". The sweet autumnal tints of departed heroism were present in his verse, the nostalgia of the death of King Arthur, and the last years of Ulysses among a hostile, spiritless people. But—despite his effort to shake free in "Ulysses"—Tennyson was falling in love with the disease itself, becoming becalmed in the land of "The Lotus-Eaters".

Morris shared in the admiration for Tennyson. But there was a difference, one of the greatest significance. "The attitude of Morris I should describe as defiant admiration", recalled Dixon:

> "This was apparent from the first. He perceived Tennyson's limitations. . . in a remarkable manner for a man of twenty or so. He said once, 'Tennyson's Sir Galahad is rather a mild youth.' "[2]

He responded to the feelings of loss, the musical languor of Tennyson, yet still his feelings rose in protest at the acceptance of defeat. He refused to relax passively in the currents of nostalgia, however much he felt their attractions. This

[1] *Memorials,* I, p. 77. [2] Mackail, I, p. 45.

resistance must have prepared the way for his ready response to Browning's *Men and Women,* which appeared in 1855. Moreover, he found in Browning a realism in the treatment of medieval themes, which served as an antidote to the tendency already becoming apparent in Tennyson to intrude into his world of "romance" Victorian middle-class values in medieval fancy dress. Tennyson's Sir Galahad is indeed a "mild youth", a pious genteel prig, a "maiden knight" on a "goodly charger":

"How sweet are looks that ladies bend
  On whom their favours fall!
For them I battle till the end,
  To save from shame and thrall:
But all my heart is drawn above,
  My knees are bow'd in crypt and shrine:
I never felt the kiss of love,
  Nor maiden's hand in mine.
More bounteous aspects on me beam,
  Me mightier transports move and thrill;
So keep I fair thro' faith and prayer
  A virgin heart in work and will."

Contrast the Galahad of Morris—by no means one of the best of his early poems:

"I thought: O! Galahad, the days go by,
Stop and cast up now that which you have found,
  So sorely you have wrought and painfully.

"Night after night your horse treads down alone
  The sere damp fern, night after night you sit
Holding the bridle like a man of stone,
  Dismal, unfriended, what thing comes of it.

"And what if Palomydes also ride,
  And over many a mountain and bare heath
Follow the questing beast with none beside?
  Is he not able still to hold his breath

"With thoughts of Iseult?"

The enervated hymnal rhythm, the featureless vocabulary,

the smug spiritual complacency of the first: the sinuous, irregular, meaningful rhythm, the evocation of a concrete environment ("your horse treads down... the sere damp fern"), the sense of real conflict in the oath of chastity, in the second. It is as if Morris's poem is a declaration of war against Tennyson's Galahad and all he symbolizes.

The autumnal tints of late romanticism are all to be found in this first volume of Morris. But with these, there is still a rough vigour to be found only in occasional passages of Browning–nowhere else. The sense of loss and failure is there:

> "... everywhere
> The knights come foil'd from the great quest, in vain;
> In vain they struggle for the vision fair."

Sir Peter Harpdon, defeated, laments the end of an heroic age:

> "Day after day I see the French draw on;
> Hold after hold falls as this one will fall.
> Knight after knight hangs gibbeted like me,
> Pennon on pennon do they drain us out..."[1]

But the poems are not therefore exquisite luxuries of misery:

> "sometimes like an idle dream
> That hinders true life overmuch,
> Sometimes like a lost heaven, these seem–"[2]

Certainly, the idle dream, the use of poetry as a refuge from life, is present in some of the poems. But in others (and these, the best) it is not nostalgia but protest, protest at the "lost heaven", which is dominant. Sir Peter Harpdon, holding on to a rotten outpost in France, the great days of chivalry long past, doomed as he knows to certain over-throw, still keeps his courage up:

[1] Omitted fragment of "Sir Peter Harpdon's End", *Works*, Vol. I, p. xxviii.
[2] "Old Love".

"Men will talk, you know,
(We talk of Hector, dead so long agone),
When I am dead, of how this Peter clung
To what he thought the right; of how he died,
Perchance, at last doing some desperate deed
Few men would care to do now, and this is gain
To me, as ease and money is to you,
Moreover, too, I like the straining game
Of striving well to hold up things that fall;
So one becomes great; see you! in good times
All men live well together, and you, too,
Live dull and happy—happy? not so quick,
Suppose sharp thoughts begin to burn you up,
Why then, but just to fight as I do now,
A halter round my neck, would be great bliss."

And so it is not only "the great dim broken walls he strove to keep", but also the old heroic values, even after the conditions for their existence had disappeared. The very choice of themes is a declaration against the ageing Ulysses, the dying Arthur. Sir Peter Harpdon and Alice, Robert and Jehane in "The Haystack in the Floods", even Launcelot and Guenevere, are full of the colours of youth, instinct with hope and eagerness, cut short by the hostile external world. "Lord Jesus!" cries out Jehane:

". . . pity your poor maid!
For in such wise they hem me in,
I cannot choose but sin and sin,
Whatever happens. . ."

And the soldier who recounts Sir Peter's death to Alice declares:

"Few words he spoke; not so much what he said
Moved us, I think, as, saying it, there played
Strange tenderness from that big soldier there
About his pleading; eagerness to live
Because folk loved him, and he loved them back,
And many gallant plans unfinished now
For ever."

Few poems are so pervaded by this poignancy of eager life struggling against overmastering odds as "The Haystack in the Floods". Here all the ingredients are apparently those of the most heavy-handed Victorian melodrama—the wicked baron and the defenceless maiden watching her knightly lover slain. And yet the incident—the extinction of life and beauty in a brutal act of revenge and lust in the drenching rain—is evoked with the pain of reality:

> ". . . she,
> Being waked at last, sigh'd quietly,
> And strangely childlike came, and said:
> 'I will not.' Straightway Godmar's head,
> As though it hung on strong wires, turn'd
> Most sharply round, and his face burn'd. . .
>
> "From Robert's throat he loosed the bands
> Of silk and mail; with empty hands
> Held out, she stood and gazed, and saw
> The long bright blade without a flaw
> Glide out from Godmar's sheath, his hand
> In Robert's hair; she saw him bend
> Back Robert's head; she saw him send
> The thin steel down; the blow told well,
> Right backward the knight Robert fell,
> And moan'd as dogs do, being half dead,
> Unwitting, as I deem: so then
> Godmar turn'd grinning to his men,
> Who ran, some five or six, and beat
> His head to pieces at their feet."

Morris was not the first to counterpose violence and the idealization of love. Browning had already done this, notably in "Count Gismond". Both poets used the device to give flesh and blood and the semblance of realism to their romances—to prevent the idealization of love from declining into the pious sentimentalities of Tennyson's Sir Galahad. This idealized love was not to be reached through a respectable Victorian courtship but only through trial and hardship, brutality and cunning, and acts of heroism: while the straining of these opposites towards union gave poignancy to the love:

"I see her pale,
Her mouth half open, looking on in fear
As the great tilt-yard fills. . ."[1]

Perhaps it is in the poem "Concerning Geffray Teste Noire" that the distinctive qualities of the volume find their most perfect expression. The poem is narrated (in the manner of Browning) by an old man, in whose memory the intensity of past experience struggles with the present mood of dispassionate reflection. The perspective of the poem is deepened by the inter-mingling, within the narrative itself, of memory and of action. Strand by strand, the bright primary colours of opposed emotions are laid side by side—the colour of heroic chivalry:

"The dancing trumpet sound, and we went forth;
And my red lion on the spear-head flapped
As faster than the cool wind we rode North,
Towards the wood of Verville. . ."

—the sharp eye for matter-of-fact detail:

". . . fold

"Lying on fold of ancient rusted mail;
No plate at all, gold rowels to the spurs,
And see the quiet gleam of turquoise pale
Along the ceinture. . ."

—the sudden memory of the Jacquerie, and the burnt skeletons of women hanging in the church at Beauvais—the passage of reflective passion—

"I saw you kissing once, like a curved sword
That bites with all its edge, did your lips lie,
Curled gently, slowly, long time could afford
For caught-up breathings. . ."

[1] *Works,* Vol. I, p. xxviii.

broken abruptly by the intrusion, once again, of the main action of the poem, and the whole rounded by the return to the autumn-mood of age. This poetry has little in common with the dream-world of Burne-Jones's paintings. Although seen through the veils of medievalism and memory, the passions and vigour of youth are evoked with more realism than by any Victorian poet who treated contemporary themes.

Indeed, Morris in the best poems of this group is the true inheritor of the mantle of Keats. His best poems are both more limited than those of Keats, and more poignant. After this volume, no English romantic poet, within the main tradition, succeed in achieving so successful an illusion of the very appearance and movement of life. The closely-imagined detail: the flat restraint of the continuously-moving rhythms, broken with an apparently casual roughness: the constant mingling of memory and present narrative, reflection and action: the deliberate muddling of time in the perception of the moment: all these devices heighten the illusion of reality, and maintain the dramatic tension.[1] It is not difficult to find in the Morris of these poems the master of W.B. Yeats.

III. Conclusion

The distinction of Morris's contribution was recognized only by a small circle of friends. Fewer than 300 copies of the book were sold, and a number of these were bought by Morris himself, as gifts for his acquaintances. The press generally ignored the book, although one reviewer (in the *Athanaeum*) found it "a curiosity which shows how far affectation may mislead an earnest man towards the fog-land of Art". The Editor of *Fraser's* "could make nothing of them":

[1] See Jack Lindsay, *William Morris, Writer* (William Morris Society, 1961) and *William Morris* (1975), pp. 89-100.

"Nor could a very able man who looked at the MS. for me. Surely nineteen-twentieths of them are of the most obscure, watery, mystical, affected stuff possible?. . . I am sick of Rossetti and his whole school. I think them essentially unmanly, effeminate, mystical, affected, and obscure. . ."[1]

It may be that the poem's reception served to harden Morris's "hatred of civilization". At any rate, he now had no difficulty in finding the great issues on which to do battle. He saw them to lie on every hand. But to find the enduring courage–to nourish his hatred with "hope", and to select some skirmish where the odds were not too unequal–that was a different matter. Nearly every one of Morris's early circle of friends either gave up in despair, or came to terms with the enemy.

But underneath the shy, gruff, Bohemian exterior of the young William Morris were qualities these others lacked–the qualities of a fighter: a capacity for endless devotion to detail, of practical application, foreshadowed in his own delineation of a character in a story, "Frank's Sealed Letter", which appeared in the *Oxford and Cambridge Magazine:*

"I could soon find out whether a thing were possible or not to me; then, if it were not, I threw it away for ever, never thought of it again, no regret, no longing for that, it was past and over for me; but if it were possible, and I made up my mind to do it, then and there I began it, and in due time finished it, turning neither to the right hand nor to the left hand till it was done. So I did with all things that I set my hand to."

These qualities of character, his wealth (which enabled him to chose his own profession and to be his own master), and, above all, his direct, poetic response to life–the source of his glorious wrath and ever-burning indignation at cant, injustice, misery and ugliness–these were among the things which saved him from either compromise or total despair.

[1] Sir J. Skelton, *Table Talk of Shirley,* pp. 78-9.

PART II

THE YEARS OF CONFLICT

"He who desires but acts not, breeds pestilence."

WILLIAM BLAKE: *Proverbs of Hell*

CHAPTER I

WILLIAM MORRIS AND THE DECORATIVE ARTS

I. Introduction

IN the next twenty years William Morris established his reputation as a poet, and as a craftsman in the decorative arts. His activities during these years have been described in close on an hundred different books—among the best of which are the first two which were written: J.W. Mackail's biography and a study by Aymer Vallance. These years are usually regarded as those of his most fruitful achievement. The building of Red House; the establishment and growth of the Firm of Morris & Co.; the writing of *The Earthly Paradise* and *Sigurd the Volsung;* the formation of the Society for the Protection of Ancient Buildings; and the famous series of public lectures on art and society—all these took place during those twenty years.

It was during these years, also, that Morris's personality appeared to take confident shape. In place of the shy, self-conscious youth, with his outbreaks of rage or boyish humour, Morris presented a face to the world made up of bluff self-assertive decision, vigorous application to detail, matter-of-fact workmanship. He was damned if he would let anyone take *him* for an ineffectual aesthete! "I sits with my feet in a brook", he used to recite,

> "And if anyone asks me for why,
> I hits him a crock with my crook,
> For it's sentiment kills me, says I."[1]

In artistic circles he became familiar, with his rough beard, his disordered hair, his fierce intolerance of fools and fashions —a character resembling the King of Thrace in *The Knight's Tale* of his favourite poet, Chaucer:

[1] Edward Carpenter, *My Days and Dreams* (1916), p. 216.

"Blak was his berd, and manly was his face. . .
And lyk a griffoun lokèd he aboute,
With kempe heres on his browes stoute."

His robust bearing, and a slight roll in his walk, led him to be mistaken more than once for a sailor. He was delighted when he was stopped by a fireman in Kensington High Street, and asked: "Beg pardon, sir, but were you ever Captain of the *Sea Swallow*?" Acquaintances were amazed at the gusto with which Morris could enter into all the pleasures of life. Madox Brown recalled a period when he sat down regularly to a dinner of roast beef and plum pudding. Visiting him one day at the house of the Firm in Red Lion Square, he saw Morris come on to the landing and roar downstairs: "Mary, those six eggs were bad. I've eaten them, but don't let it happen again."[1] Others were surprised to meet a poet with so straightforward and business-like a manner. Henry James, visiting him in 1869 was impressed "most agreeably":

"He is short, burly, corpulent, very careless and unfinished in his dress. . . He has a very loud voice and a nervous restless manner and a perfectly unaffected and businesslike address. His talk indeed is wonderfully to the point and remarkable for clear good sense. He said no one thing that I remember, but I was struck with the very good judgement shown in everything he uttered. He's an extraordinary example, in short, of a delicate sensitive genius and taste, saved by a perfectly healthy body and temper."[2]

Later anecdotes show Morris in one or other of his occupations with the Firm, designing, weaving, wood-engraving or dyeing, as when—

"in the cellars of his old house in Bloomsbury Square. . . on heavy sabots of French make, aproned from the armpits, with tucked-up shirt-sleeves, his fore-arms dyed up to the elbow, the great man lectured

[1] Ford Madox Hueffer, *Ancient Lights* (1911), pp. 3-4.

[2] *Letters of Henry James,* Vol. I, pp. 16-18.

most brilliantly in the high art of dyeing, illustrating his lecture with experiments in the various dyes he wanted for his silks and wools."[1]

Finally, he is seen—as he became familiar to the Socialists in the 1880s—greying early, but as brisk and vigorous as in his youth—

"with gray beard like the foam of the sea, with gray hair through which he continually ran his hands erect and curly on his forehead, with a hooked nose, a florid complexion, and clean, clear eyes, dressed in a blue serge coat, and carrying as a rule, a satchel."[2]

Such recollections as these do not give us the whole picture of the man. It is not easy to reconcile them (as we shall see) with the pervasive melancholy of Morris's poetry in the 1860s and early 1870s, nor with the note of despair in some of his more intimate letters. The true picture of Morris during these years must be made up of far more conflict and of more private unhappiness than was revealed in the sturdy public character which he turned towards the world. Nevertheless, throughout the vicissitudes and disappointments of these years, he drew sustaining strength and kept a practical and sane grip on life by means of the constant activities in which he was engaged connected with the famous Firm.

II. Red House and the Firm

After his marriage, Morris turned his attention to building a house which might embody the Palace of Art upon earth. He wished to reject the age of Gradgrind, not only in his opinions and actions, but in his daily surroundings. The architects of the time (he later recalled)—

"could do nothing but produce on the one hand pedantic imitations of classical architecture of the most revolting ugliness, and ridiculous

[1] E. Magnusson, "William Morris", *Cambridge Review,* November 26th, 1896.

[2] Hueffer, *op. cit.,* p. 18.

travesties of Gothic buildings, not quite so ugly, but meaner and sillier; and, on the other hand, the utilitarian brick box with a slate lid which the Anglo-Saxon generally in modern times considers as a good sensible house with no nonsense about it."

Morris and his friends refused to accept such buildings as the inevitable expression of their age. If the romantic revolt had broken through in the fields of literature, could it not also transform their architecture? they asked:

"Were the rows of square brown brick boxes which Keats and Shelley had to look on, or the stuccoed villa which enshrined Tennyson's genius, to be the perpetual concomitants of such masters of verbal beauty?... was the intelligence of the age to be for ever so preposterously lop-sided? We could see no reason for it, and accordingly our hope was strong; for though we had learned something of the art and history of the Middle Ages, we had not learned enough. It became the fashion among the hopeful artists of the time... to say that in order to have beautiful surroundings there was no need to alter any of the conditions and manners of our epoch; that an easy chair, a piano, a steam-engine, a billiard-table, or a hall fit for a meeting of the House of Commons, had nothing essential in them which compelled us to make them ugly, and that if they had existed in the Middle Ages the people of the time would have made them beautiful."[1]

Accordingly, Morris and his friend Philip Webb, the architect, set to build Red House at Bexley Heath in Kent. The house was built, not—as in previous Gothic revivals—in an attempt to combine a number of superficial medieval characteristics which pleased the taste of the architect, but in a definite attempt to adapt late Gothic methods of building to the needs of the nineteenth century. To-day Red House may no longer excite wonder: but in its time it was revolutionary in its unashamed use of red brick, its solid, undisguised construction, and absence of fussy facades and unfunctional ornamentation. A visitor in 1863 described his first reaction

[1] "The Revival of Architecture", *Works,* Vol. XXII, pp. 321-3.

on seeing the house as one of "astonished pleasure":

> "The deep red colour, the great sloping, tiled roofs; the small-paned windows; the low, wide porch and massive door; the surrounding garden divided into many squares, hedged by sweetbriar or wild rose, each enclosure with its own particular show of flowers; on this side a green alley with a bowling green, on that orchard walks amid gnarled old fruit-trees; all struck me as vividly picturesque and uniquely original."[1]

On entering the porch, the same visitor found that the hall "appeared to one accustomed to the narrow ugliness of the usual middle-class dwelling of those days as being grand and severely simple". A solid oak table stood upon a red tiled floor. Opposite the door a wide oak staircase was placed, with no skirting or cupboard beneath it, so that its construction was unconcealed. The keynote of simplicity and straightforward construction recurred in many rooms: the open roofs: the tall bricked open hearth, without any mantlepiece: the pale distemper on the walls: the black, rush-seated chairs. Side by side with the essential simplicity of the whole, there were to be found examples of rich decoration; painted panels on the solid cabinets: embroidered serge on the walls of the principal bedroom: experiments in ceiling decoration and in stained glass. Burne-Jones declared that Morris was making Red House "the beautifullest place on earth". There is no cause for surprise that contemporaries saw it as the prototype of a daring new revival.[2]

It was the need to furnish Red House which led to the formation of the famous Firm. At first it was merely a matter of decorating Morris's Palace. Morris and Burne-Jones had already tried their hand when furnishing their studio in Red Lion Square. At Red House, Rossetti, Philip Webb, Madox

[1] See Aymer Vallance, *William Morris, His Art, His Writings, and His Public Life* (1897), p. 49.

[2] See Nicolaus Pevsner, *Pioneer of the Modern Movement from William Morris to Walter Gropius* (1936), pp. 65-6.

Brown and others were all brought in to help. Burne-Jones, who had already undertaken one or two commissions for stained glass, now set to work on painted tiles for the fire-places. Morris designed flower patterns in wool for the walls. Webb designed table-glass, metal candlesticks, and furniture. The successes of the small group made them think of more ambitious projects. In Rossetti's recollection, the actual origin of the Firm was in a casual discussion:

> "One evening a lot of us were together, and we got talking about the way in which artists did all kinds of things in olden times, designed every kind of decoration and most kinds of furniture, and some one suggested—as a joke more than anything else—that we should each put down five pounds and form a company. Fivers were blossoms of a rare growth among us in those days, and I won't swear that the table bristled with fivers. Anyhow the firm was formed, but of course there was no deed or anything of that kind. In fact, it was a mere playing at business, and Morris was elected manager, not because we ever dreamed he would turn out a man of business, but because he was the only one among us who had both time and money to spare. We had no idea whatever of commercial success, but it succeeded almost in our own despite."[1]

Burne-Jones recalled rather more of conscious decision on Morris's part. His income from the copper mines was diminishing fast: his apprenticeship as a painter had not been an unmixed success: he was forced to consider some practical means of earning a living without compromising with the age. On every side it was apparent that the minor arts were "in a state of complete degradation" (he recalled in 1883), and accordingly "with the conceited courage of a young man I set myself to reform all that".[2]

In its origin, then, the Firm had both a private and a public significance. In its private significance, it was the last and most ambitious attempt to project the old "Brotherhood" into life, to build a world of art in the face of the nineteenth

[1] Theodore Watts-Dunton in the *Athanaeum,* October 10th, 1896.

[2] *Letters,* p. 186. See also *Memorials,* I, p. 213.

century. This attitude persisted in Morris's mind for several years, and found expression in 1865 when it was planned to extend Red House into a great quadrangle, in which the workshops of the Firm would be housed, and Burne-Jones (now married to "Georgie" MacDonald) should live. When this plan fell through, Morris, who was recovering at this time from an attack of rheumatic fever, was plunged into dejection and wrote to his friend:

> "As to our palace of art, I confess your letter was a blow to me at first. . . in short, I cried, but I have got over it now; of course, I see it from your point of view but I like the idea of not giving it up for good even if it is delusive."[1]

Shortly afterwards Morris and the Firm moved into a convenient house in Queen Square, and left Red House, never to return.

From this time onwards the public significance of the Firm became all-important for Morris—the attempt to "reform all that", to reform a philistine age by means of the decorative arts; and, as a first step, to reform the arts themselves. The first circular of the Firm (drafted, most probably, by Rossetti) proposed self-confidently to undertake work in "any species of decoration, mural or otherwise, from pictures, properly so called, down to the consideration of the smallest work of art beauty".[2] Branches of work offered included Mural Decoration, Carving, Stained Glass, Metal Work, as well as Jewellery, Furniture and Embroidery.

In an article published shortly after Morris's death Walter Crane[3] characterized this movement as—

> "in the main a revival of the medieval spirit (not the letter) in design; a return to simplicity, to sincerity; to good materials and sound work-

[1] *Letters,* p. 22.

[2] See Mackail, I, pp. 150-2, for the full circular.

[3] Walter Crane was not an early associate of the Firm. At the time when it was founded he was apprenticed as an engraver to W.J. Linton, the old Chartist and Republican. See Walter Crane, *An Artist's Reminiscences* (1907), p. 46.

manship; to rich and suggestive surface decoration, and simple constructive forms."[1]

Since the Great Exhibition of 1851, domestic decoration and furniture had fallen under the Second Empire taste in upholstery, the "antithesis of the new English movement". The impulse towards Greek and Roman forms (Walter Crane wrote)—

"which had held sway with designers since the French Revolution, appeared to be dead. The elegant lines and limbs of quasi-classical couches and chairs. . . had grown gouty and clumsy, in the hands of Victorian upholsterers. . . An illustrated catalogue of the exhibition of 1851 will sufficiently indicate the monstrosities in furniture and decoration which were supposed to be artistic. The last stage of decomposition had been reached, and a period of, perhaps, unexampled hideousness in furniture, dress and decoration set in which lasted the life of the second empire, and fitly perished with it. Relics of the period I believe are still to be discovered in the cold shade of remote drawing-rooms, and 'apartments to let', which take the form of big looking-glasses, and machine-lace curtains, and where the furniture is afflicted with curvature of the spine, and dreary lumps of bronze and ormulu repose on marble slabs at every opportunity, where monstrosities of every kind are encouraged under glass shades, while every species of design-debauchery is indulged in upon carpets, curtains, chintzes and wallpapers, and where the antimacassar is made to cover a multitude of sins. When such ideas of decoration prevailed, having their origin or prototypes, in the vapid splendours of imperial saloons, and had to be reduced to the scale of the ordinary citizen's house and pocket, the thing became absurd as well as hideous. Besides, the cheap curly legs of the uneasy chairs and couches came off, and the stuffed seats, with a specious show of padded comfort, were delusions and snares. Long ago the old English house-place with its big chimney-corner had given way to the bourgeois arrangement of dining and drawing-room. . . The parlour had become a kind of sanctuary veiled in machine-lace, where the lightness of the curtains was compensated for by the massiveness of their poles, and where Berlin wool-work and bead mats flourished."[2]

[1] *Scribner's Magazine,* July, 1897.

[2] Walter Crane, *William Morris to Whistler* (1911), pp. 51-3.

The building of Red House, and the unorthodox methods by which it was decorated and furnished—this was all well so long as it remained a rich man's private hobby. But when the Firm challenged the established trade in the public market, it was bound to provoke the fierce opposition of philistine taste and vested interests. The amount of prejudice which the Firm aroused, wrote Aymer Vallance, "would scarcely be believed at the present time."

"The announcement came with the provocation and force of a challenge, and dumbfounded those who read it at the audacity of the venture. . . Professionals felt themselves aggrieved at the intrusion, as they regarded it, of a body of men whose training had not been strictly commercial into the close premises of their own particular domain; and, had it been possible to form a ring and exclude Messrs. Morris, Marshall, Faulkner and Co. from the market, the thing would infallibly have been done."[1]

As it was, the early expansion of the business was hindered not only by philistinism amongst the only public wealthy enough to buy the Firm's products, but by the active hostility of the trade. This was one of the factors which caused the Firm to specialize in its first years in particular in ecclesiastical work, where little rivalry existed. At the 1862 Exhibition, where the Firm presented some of its first work, opponents went so far as to start a petition to get the exhibits disqualified, maintaining amongst other things that the stained glass was a fraud, and was old glass re-touched. It was not until 1867 that the Firm obtained an important commission to decorate a non-ecclesiastical building—the Green Dining Room at the South Kensington Museum.

As the Firm expanded, it became the spear-head of a movement which challenged the fussy and pretentious in one field after another of decorative art. Walter Crane (looking back on the half-century) described some of the points of conflict:

[1] Vallance, *op. cit.,* p. 58.

"The simple, black-framed, old English Buckinghamshire elbow-chair, with its rush-bottomed seat, was substituted for the wavy-backed and curly-legged stuffed chair of the period, with its French polish and concealed, and often very unreliable, construction. Bordered Eastern rugs and fringed Axminster carpets, on plain or stained boards, or India matting, took the place of the stuffy planned carpet; rich, or simple, flat patterns acknowledged the wall, and expressed the proportion of the room, instead of trying to hide both under bunches of sketchy roses and vertical stripes; while, instead of the big plate-glass mirror, with ormulu frame, which had long reigned over the cold white marble mantlepiece, small bevelled glasses were inserted in the panelling of the high wood mantleshelf, or hung over it in convex circular form. Slender black wood or light brass curtain-rods, and curtains to match the coverings, or carry out the colour of the room, displaced the heavy mahogany and ormulu battering-rams, with their fringed and festooned upholstery, which had hitherto overshadowed the window of the so-called comfortable classes. Plain white or green paint for interior wood-work drove graining and marbleing to the public-house; blue and white Nankin, Delft, or Gres de Flandres routed Dresden and Sevres from the cabinet; plain oaken boards and trestles were prefered before the heavy mahogany telescopic British dining table of the mid-nineteenth century, and the deep, high backed, canopied settle with loose cushions ousted the castored and padded couch from the fireside."[1]

By the 1870s the Firm was not only well established: it was beginning to set the pace among wealthy circles where any claim was made to cultivation. Even the fiercest opponents were forced to alter their designs, and to adapt some of the minor superficial characteristics of the Firm's work to their own.[2] In short, Morris and Co. (for the original partnership was broken up with some acrimony in 1874, and Morris—still with the assistance of Burne-Jones and Philip Webb—took sole command) had become fashionable: and, moreover, the revolt had begun to bring rich returns in the form of commercial success.[3]

[1] *Scribner's Magazine,* July, 1897.

[2] See Crane, *op. cit.,* p. 55. For Peter Floud's opinion that "Morris must be regarded not as a revolutionary pioneer and innovator, but rather as the great classical designer of his age", see *Listener,* October 7th, 1954 and Postscript below.

[3] But for Morris's "financial crisis" in the late 1860s, see J. Le Bourgeois, *Durham Univ. Journal,* LXVI, 1974.

If Morris had been concerned only with the effecting of some reform within the decorative arts, it would seem that at the end of the 1870s he might have rested satisfied. In fact, it was exactly at this time that his bitter discontent found its expression in his famous lectures on art and society. For the reform for which he looked went beyond his own practice of the arts; these arts were the forum which his early revolt had chosen, in which to conduct the "holy warfare against the age". But on every side the age remained undismayed. His work had opened many new vistas in the decorative arts; but at the end of each one he was faced by the soiled, utilitarian chimneys, and the facts of mass production of shoddy goods for profit. By means of his own private income, and with the assistance of a clientele made up variously of enterprising men of wealth, nostalgic parsons, and persons of genuine sensitivity and taste, he might widen for a moment the charmed circle of his art. But, outside that circle, the age remained indifferent or hostile as before, so that he was impelled to write to Andreas Scheu in 1883:

> "In spite of all the success I have had, I have not failed to be conscious that the art I have been helping to produce would fall with the death of a few of us who really care about it, that a reform in art which is founded on individualism must perish with the individuals who have set it going. Both my historical studies and my practical conflict with the philistinism of modern society have *forced* on me the conviction that art cannot have a real life and growth under the present system of commercialism and profit-mongering."[1]

It was his success, rather than any failure, which brought him into conflict with his age.

III. Morris as a Designer and Craftsman

During the early stages of the Firm Morris was too busy to concern himself with this kind of problem. He and his friends

[1] *Letters,* p. 187.

had engaged upon a considerable venture—the establishment of a company of artists and craftsmen who intended to revive the minor arts of England, on a sound financial basis and in the face of an age of shoddy. Morris took upon himself the major responsibility. He was one of the Firm's principal designers, the main link between the other designers and the craftsmen who executed their designs and the man responsible for much of the day-to-day business management.[1]

From the very outset, Morris showed that he had taken to heart John Ruskin's works:

> "It would be well if all of us were good handicraftsmen in some kind, and the dishonour of manual labour done away with altogether . . In each several profession, no master should be too proud to do its hardest work."

Disturbing as such a doctrine was to the servant-supported middle-class, it was inescapable in the work Morris had on hand. In the view of W.R. Lethaby, one of the "Morris group", there were two quite different currents of "Gothic revival" among the architects and designers of the nineteenth century. The fashionable one, represented by men like Sir Gilbert Scott—

> "for the most part. . . followed the movement—backward—of attempting to 'revive the Gothic style of design' rather than settling down to perfect a science of modern building."

[1] For example, in the Firm's work in stained glass, the designs of Burne-Jones and Madox Brown came normally to Morris in the form of plain, uncoloured cartoons. It was his task to mark the lead-lines, to select the colours, sometimes to design the background, etc. This could not be done without the most thorough understanding of the processes of painting and firing the glass, which he gained by working at the small kiln constructed in the Firm's basement at Red Lion Square. To gain an idea of his complete mastery of the techniques of glass-firing and staining, see his letter to John Ruskin, *Letters,* pp. 168-9. See also *Life and Letters of Frederick Shields,* p. 98.

The letters of Warington Taylor (business manager of the firm between 1865 and 1869) to Philip Webb (printed in *Philip Webb and his Work* by W.R. Lethaby) provide an amusing commentary on Morris's qualities (or lack of them) in the financial affairs of the Firm. See also Philip Henderson, *William Morris* (1973 edn.), pp. 105-112.

To Ruskin and the group around Morris and Philip Webb, the architecture "to which we gave the modern name 'Gothic' was the customary way in which masons and carpenters did their work". In their view, an "Architecture of Aristocracy",[1] originating at the time of the Renaissance and coming to dominance in the eighteenth century, had destroyed these natural manners of work. "The national arts were flattened out and destroyed in the name of gentility, learning, and 'taste'." The two schools of nineteenth-century medievalists, can therefore be sharply distinguished. The fashionable architects attempted to impose a superficial Gothic style upon their work, copying interesting Gothic features, often disregarding both structure and modern requirements. Philip Webb and Morris and their group, on the other hand, were concerned with the *manner* of work in the Middle Ages, with the handling of materials by the medieval builder and craftsman, with substance and structure rather than with "style".

This distinction can be clearly seen in all Morris's work as a designer. While he may have occasionally fallen into the faults of the first attitude, the essence of his approach was in the second. Looking back upon his work, he told a *Clarion* interviewer in 1892:

> "I have tried to produce goods which should be genuine so far as their mere substances are concerned, and should have on that account the primary beauty in them which belongs to naturally treated natural substances; have tried for instance to make woollen substances as woollen as possible, cotton as cotton as possible, and so on; have used only the dyes which are natural and simple, because they produce beauty almost without the intervention of art; all this quite apart from the design in the stuffs or what not."[2]

Since many of the arts in which the Firm commenced to work were—to all intents—extinct in England, Morris had no alternative but to concern himself with the substance of the arts

[1] W.R. Lethaby, *Philip Webb and his Work* (1935). See esp. Ch. V.
[2] *Clarion*, November 19th, 1892.

and the practical details of the craftsman's work first of all.

From the foundation of the Firm until the end of his life, Morris was continually busy with close study, experiments, and practical engagements with the materials of his craft. Glass-firing, the glazing of tiles, embroidery, woodcutting and engraving, pottery and book-binding, weaving and tapestry-work, illuminating—all these were among the skills he mastered to a greater or lesser degree. Characteristic of his thorough application was his determination in the mid-1870s to revive the use of vegetable dyes. For months the problem absorbed his mind, and he studied the question in old books and in the London museums. He experimented at his own dye-vat, and his mind was running on it even during his favourite relaxation:

> "I was at Kelmscott the other day, and betwixt fishing, I cut a handful of poplar twigs and boiled them, and dyed a lock of wool a very good yellow. . ."[1]

Next, he paid visits to Leek, in Staffordshire, where at a large dye-works he could experiment on a larger scale, and gain the advice of workmen who remembered using the old dyes in their youth. From here he wrote to Georgie Burne-Jones:

> "I shall be glad to get back to the dye-house at Leek to-morrow. I dare say you will notice how bad my writing is; my hand is so shaky with doing journey-man's work the last few days: delightful work, hard for the body and easy for the mind. For a great heap of skein-wool has come for me and more is coming: and yesterday evening we set our blue-vat the last thing before coming here. I should have liked you to see the charm work on it: we dyed a lock of wool bright blue in it, and left the liquor a clear primrose colour, so all will be ready for dyeing to-morrow. . ."[2]

"His way was to tackle the thing with his own hands", recalled Walter Crane—

[1] Mackail, I, p. 315. [2] *Letters,* pp. 65-6.

"and so he worked at the vat, like the practical man he was in these matters. An old friend tells the story of his calling at the works one day and, on inquiring for the master, hearing a strong cheery voice call out from some inner den, 'I'm dyeing, I'm dyeing, I'm dyeing,' and the well-known, robust figure of the craftsman presently appeared in his shirt-sleeves, his hands stained blue from the vat."[1]

The problem had at last been solved to his satisfaction.

Morris was also a first-rate scholar in the history of the decorative arts. Study and practice he regarded as inseparable. This union was expressed in his own experiments in tapestry weaving. Here he found no living craftsmen to learn from. Gobelins, the old French centre, he declared had degenerated into a "hatching-nest of stupidity". After close study, he set up a handloom in the bedroom of his Hammersmith house. There he worked from one of his own embroidery patterns, and wove—

"a piece of ornament with my own hands, the chief merit of which, I take it, lies in the fact that I learned the art of doing it with no other help than what I could get from a very little eighteenth century book."[2]

This constant interplay of study and practice gave him his great authority in all the decorative arts. "They talk of building museums for the public", he once said:

"but South Kensington Museum was really got together for about six people—I am one, and another is a comrade [Philip Webb] in the room."[3]

When called before the Royal Commission for Technical Instruction in 1882 he remarked of the same museum,

[1] *Scribner's Magazine,* July, 1897.

[2] Letter of Morris in the *Journal of the Derbyshire Archaeological Society,* April 5th, 1893, quoted in the *History of the Merton Tapestry Works* by H.C. Marrillier, p. 16.

[3] Lethaby, *op. cit.,* pp. 39-40.

"perhaps I have used it as much as any man living". Testimony to the regard in which his knowledge was held can be seen in the fact that he was consulted by the Museum as a professional referee when important purchases in tapestries and textiles were to be made.[1] "Went to S.K.M. yesterday", he noted in his diary of a visit to the Museum in January, 1887—

"to look at the Tray tapestry again since they have bought it for £1250: I chuckled to think that properly speaking it was bought for me, since scarcely anybody will care a damn for it."[2]

In his lectures and papers on the decorative arts delivered in the 1880s—in such a lecture as "The History of Pattern Designing"—he reveals the astonishing body of knowledge which he had acquired during these years of his most active practice within the minor arts: knowledge derived from close study of Ancient, Egyptian, Byzantine, Persian, Indian, and Northern European and English traditions in particular.

This study of the traditions of the past he held to be essential for any designer. "My view is", he declared before the Royal Commission for Technical Instruction—

"that it is not desirable to divide the labour between the artist and what is technically called the designer, and I think it desirable on the whole that the artist and designer should practically be one. . . There are two chief things that would have to be thought of, in providing facilities for study for the art of design. However original a man may be, he cannot afford to disregard the works of art that have been produced in times past when design was flourishing; he is bound to study old examples, but he is also bound to supplement that by a careful study of nature, because if he does not he will certainly fall into a sort of cut and dried, conventional method of designing. . . It takes a man of considerable originality to deal with the old examples and to get

[1] I am indebted to the Keeper of the Library of the Victoria and Albert Museum for the information that a number of Morris's professional reports are still in his files.

[2] *Socialist Diary,* 1887, Brit. Mus. Add. MSS. 45335.

what is good out of them, without making a design which lays itself open distinctly to the charge of plagiarism."[1]

But Morris's interest did not stop short with the mastery of the designer's work:

"What I want to see really is, and that is the bottom of the whole thing, an education all round of the workmen, from the lowest to the highest, in technical matters as in others. . ."

While Morris was interested in the quality of the art products themselves, he was equally interested in the manner in which these products were made, and in the people who made them. On the one hand, he deprecated the separation between the artist in his studio and the technical designer to whom nothing was left but the "grinding work" of adapting the design to the lathe or the loom. In textiles:

"I think it would be better. . . that the man who actually goes through the technical work of counting the threads, and settling how the thing is to be woven, through and through, should do the greater part of the drawing."

On the other hand, he desired that the man who executed the work should be given opportunity to exercise his own creative abilities. Of all the principles which Morris shared with Ruskin, this was the most difficult to put into operation. Certainly, many attempts were made, and as the Firm expanded and the Merton Abbey works were established, a method of work was built up distinct from normal commercial practice. In several branches of work experienced craftsmen were engaged from the beginning, who taught Morris their business, and worked side by side with him in all experiments. When apprentices were taken on, a point was

[1] Morris's evidence before the Royal Commission (1882) is reprinted in full in May Morris, I, pp. 205-25.

made of not seeking out the exceptionally gifted and outstanding lad; it was taken for granted that any intelligent lad had the makings of an artist and craftsman in him. This was especially justified in the case of the tapestry work at Merton Abbey, where on Morris's death—not twenty years after he had revived the art with an old book and a handloom—a body of skill had been trained up adequate to ensure the art's continuance. Morris was gratified to be able to say of one piece which was exhibited at the Arts and Crafts Exhibition in 1893:

> "The people who made it—and this is by far the most interesting thing about it—are boys, at least they are grown up by this time—entirely trained in our own shop. It is really freehand work, remember, not slavishly copying a pattern. . . and they came to us with no knowledge of drawing whatever, and have learnt every single thing under our training. And most beautifully they have done it!"[1]

Carpet-making, weaving, jewellery and metal-work, glass-making—all provided some opportunity for the exercise of the craftsman's creative initiative; while the atmosphere in every branch of the Firm was one which tended to draw out the workman's initiative and intellectual powers. But, looking back upon his results in 1892, it was here that Morris felt that his achievements had most fallen short:

> "Except with a small part of the more artistic side of the work," he told a *Clarion* reporter, "I could not do anything (or at least but little) to give this pleasure to the workman, because I should have had to change their methods of work so utterly that I should have disqualified them from earning their living elsewhere. You see I have got to understand thoroughly the manner of work under which the art of the Middle Ages was done, and that that is the *only* manner of work which can turn out popular art, only to discover that it is impossible to work in that manner in this profit-grinding society."[2]

[1] Quoted by Vallance, *op. cit.*, p. 121.
[2] *Clarion*, November 19th, 1892.

This practical work—directing, experimenting, above all designing—must be remembered as the constant background to all other activities of Morris from the formation of the Firm until the end of his life. "It is very characteristic of Morris", wrote Edward Carpenter on his death, "that his chief recreation was only another kind of work."[1] The volume of this work was prodigious. In 1881, when he was giving up much time to the Society for the Protection of Ancient Buildings and to the National Liberal League, such an entry as this in his diary is by no means exceptional: "Up at 6.15. 2½ hours tapestry. Then pointing carpet: to S.P.A.B. in afternoon: then to N.L.L. meeting."[2] Most of his tapestry work was done in this way, before the main business of his day had started. During his most active period as a Socialist propagandist, the work had sometimes to be laid aside for weeks at a time; but nevertheless it was still fermenting in his mind. On the back and at the bottom of his lecture notes there are often found the leaf designs and experiments in lettering, which indicate that the Kelmscott Press was already occupying a part of his thoughts.

Morris set down the principles which guided him in his pattern designing in two essays in his later life, and in these several precepts frequently recur:

> "The aim should be to combine clearness of form and firmness of structure with the mystery which comes of abundance and richness of detail... Do not introduce any lines or objects which cannot be explained by the structure of the pattern; it is just this logical sequence of form, this growth which looks as if... it would not have been otherwise, which prevents the eye wearying of the repetition of the pattern... Do not be afraid of large patterns.
>
> "The geometrical structure of the pattern, which is a necessity in all recurring patterns, should be boldly insisted upon, so as to draw the eye from accidental figures...
>
> "Above all things, avoid vagueness; run any risk of failure rather than involve yourselves in a tangle of poor weak lines that people can't make out. Definite form bounded by firm outline is a necessity for all

[1] *Freedom*, November, 1896. [2] Brit. Mus. Add. MSS. 45407.

ornament... Rational growth is necessary to all patterns... Take heed in this growth that each member of it be strong and crisp, that the lines do not get thready or flabby or too far from their stock to sprout firmly and vigorously; even where a line ends it should look as if it had plenty of capacity for more growth if so it would... Outlandishness is a snare... Those natural forms which are at once most familiar and most delightful to us, as well from association as from beauty, are the best for our purpose. The rose, the lily, the tulip, the oak, the vine, and all the herbs and trees that even we cockneys know about, they will serve our turn..."

In the same essays he emphasized his preference for pictorial suggestion or direct expression, which was pushed to its extreme in his late tapestry-work with Burne-Jones:

"You may be sure that any decoration is futile, and has fallen into at least the first stage of degradation, when it does not remind you of something beyond itself, of something of which it is but a visible symbol.

"I am bound to say that... I, as a Western man and a picture-lover, must still insist on plenty of meaning in your patterns; I must have unmistakable suggestions of gardens and fields, and strange trees, boughs, and tendrils, or I can't do with your pattern, but must take the first piece of nonsense-work a Kurdish shepherd has woven from tradition and memory; all the more, as even in that there will be some hint of past history."[1]

These passages reveal clearly the leading characteristics of Morris's designs. In the opinion of his colleague, W.R. Lethaby the architect:

"They stand supreme in modern pattern work, and will necessarily remain supreme until as great a man as Morris again deals with that manner of expression with his *full force* as he did... Even the most formal of his work recalls to us the strong growth of healthy vegatation ... Others, more directly, speak in ordered pattern-language, of a flower-

[1] See "Textiles" (1888), May Morris, I, pp. 244-51; "Some Hints on Pattern-Designing" (1881), *Works,* Vol. XXII, pp. 175-205; "Textile Fabrics" (1884), *Works,* Vol. XXII, pp. 270-94.

embroidered field; of willow boughs seen against the sky; of intertwined jessamine and whitethorn, of roses climbing against a background of yew; of branching pomegranate, lemon and peach, of a rose trellised arbour in a garden. . ."

Nearly all his designs show the same vigour and boldness, both in the strong recurring lines, and heavy curling leaves, and in their unashamed use of bright colour ("If you want mud, you can find that in the street", he told an important customer who thought his colours were not sufficiently "subdued"): copious in their luxuriant growth and foliage: suggestive in their pictorial detail. His years of research into the problems of dyeing brought their reward. In Lethaby's opinion:

"Even in the choice of single colours, reds, greens, yellows, Morris's mastery appears; if it be kermes and indigo in dyes, or red lead and yellow ochre in pigments, he looked on these colours when *pure* as in themselves beautiful natural products, the individuality and flavour of which would be destroyed by too much mixing."[1]

Everything which left his hand, or which had been produced at the Firm under his eye, reveals the excellence of materials and of workmanship.

Shoddy—that was his enemy. "It is a shoddy age", he once shouted in his last years. "Shoddy is king. From the statesman to the shoemaker, all is shoddy."[2] The Firm fought shoddy from start to finish, and nothing it turned out could come under this accusation. In his work as a designer Morris desired to combine two things: sound workmanship on good materials, and richness of decorative detail. In his first objective, simplicity and good quality, he was the main pioneer of that trend which is continued in the best design of our own day. If he is taken to task to-day by some critics for over-

[1] W.R. Lethaby, *William Morris as Work-Master* (1901).
[2] *Clarion*, November 19th, 1892.

elaboration and sweetness in some of his work—for the heavy and intricate ornamental lines of some of his later wallpapers and chintzes—yet it is still Morris himself who first laid down both the text and the practice on which his critics stand. Moreover, it should be remembered that Morris's second objective (that of richness of decoration) could only be reached by finding customers among the wealthiest class. Here he was subject to a constant sense of impatience and irritation which was one of the forces impelling him forwards to Socialist conclusions. His brusqueness of manner with his customers, and his steadfast refusal to compromise the standards of his art, became famous and even made his Firm a centre of fashionable curiosity. As Rossetti once remarked: "Top's very eccentricities and independent attitude towards his patrons seem to have drawn patrons round him."[1] But it was only to be expected that younger designers who followed him would turn away from such difficult customers as these, with their freakish fashions and desire for ostentation, and in consequence, would turn aside from the extravagance of some of Morris's work, which—while not compromising in any way with the philistinism of his patrons—nevertheless was planned in a grand and costly manner, and was suited to large rooms and long perspectives. Towards the end of his life, Morris remarked to Edward Carpenter (moved for a moment by the simplicity of the life he found in Carpenter's cottage at Millthorpe):

> "I have spent, I know, a vast amount of time designing furniture and wall-papers, carpets and curtains; but after all I am inclined to think that sort of thing is mostly rubbish, and I would prefer for my part to live with the plainest whitewashed walls and wooden chairs and tables."[2]

[1] T. Watts-Dunton's recollections in *The English Review*, January, 1909.
[2] Carpenter, *op. cit.*, p. 217.

CHAPTER II

THE POETRY OF DESPAIR

I. Scenes from the Fall of Troy

WHEN Morris joined the Democratic Federation in 1883, he signed his membership card, "William Morris, Designer". But his comrades in the Federation and the Socialist League, when advertising his lectures or pamphlets, preferred to identify him as "The Author of *The Earthly Paradise*". In doing this, they echoed the opinion of Morris's importance which was held by the Victorian middle-class public. With the publication of *The Earthly Paradise* in 1868-70, and of its forerunner, *The Life and Death of Jason,* in 1867, Morris's reputation as a major poet and notable personality of the age first became established.

To-day it is rare to find readers who have read all, or most, of the twenty-four poetic narratives which make up *The Earthly Paradise.* Few of the works of the Victorian Age have been brushed aside in this century so conclusively as the poem which was once acclaimed as Morris's masterpiece. Only one line (from the "Apology" at the opening of the poem) remains in common currency—"the idle singer of an empty day"—and around this line there have gathered vague associations of sweetness and languorous melody. And from these associations there has been built, in turn, the common picture of Morris: of a bluff, straightforward extrovert, part designer, part sweet singer, with wide interests but with a shallow response to life, who in some miraculous way is supposed to have by-passed the acute mental conflicts and emotional stresses which racked and wasted even the greatest of his contemporaries. This supposed absence of arduous intellectual or spiritual struggle in Morris's life has given rise to an air of condescension in the treatment of him by contemporary scholars.

But a careful reading of *The Earthly Paradise* must lead us to quite different conclusions. Alongside our picture of "William Morris, Designer", with his great capacity for application and his constructive confrontation of life, we must set another picture—of Morris, the late romantic poet, over whom flowed those waves of objectless yearning, nostalgia for the past and dissatisfaction with the present, which dragged him backwards towards despair. The middle years of Morris's life were years of conflict: and only when "hope" was reborn within him in the 1880s do the "poet" and the "designer" become one, with integrated aim and outlook. Only when Morris became a Communist did he become (as W.B. Yeats was to describe him) the "Happiest of the Poets".

The evidence of this conflict may be found in Morris's poetry, and some of the causes of it in the climate of his times and in his personal life. First, let us turn to the poems.

Nine years of silence passed between the publication of *The Defence of Guenevere* and *Jason.* During a part of this time, at least, Morris continued writing. In the months after he returned from his honeymoon and had moved into Red House he was working on a poem in dramatic form, *Scenes from the Fall of Troy,*[1] which he left unfinished, and whose parts were not published in his lifetime. The manner of writing, the stress of feeling, in these fragments is closely related to the earlier poems, especially to "Sir Peter Harpdon's End". The pervasive sense of inevitable failure in the face of overwhelming odds, already present in the earlier poem, is deepened. Continually the note recurs of the passing of the old heroic values—Helen's beauty, Hector's courage, the heroic story of the siege itself becoming, in its later stages in the description of Paris, a tale of brutality, cunning and fraud:

[1] *Works,* Vol. XXIV.

"... here we are, glaring across the walls
Across the tents, with such hate in our eyes
As only damned souls have, and uselessly
We make a vain pretence to carry on
This fight about the siege which will not change
However many ages we stay here.

But now—alas! my honour is all gone
And all the joy to fight that I had once
Gone mouldy like the bravery of arms
That lie six feet under the Trojan turf.
Ah when I think of that same windy morn
When the Greeks landed with the push of spears:
The strange new look of those our enemies,
The joyous clatter, hurry to and fro,
And if a man fell it was scarce so sad—
'God pity him' we said and 'God bless him,
He died well fighting in the open day'—
Yea such an one was happy I may think,
Now all has come to stabbing in the dark."

Contrast with these passages the final stanza of "The Death of Paris", one of the tales of *The Earthly Paradise,* and something of the very marked change between these two phases of Morris's poetry will become evident. In this verse the narrator is made to reflect, in conventional late romantic manner, upon the oblivion of time:

"I cannot tell what crop may clothe the hills,
The merry hills Troy whitened long ago—
Belike the sheaves, wherewith the reaper fills
His yellow wain, no whit the weaker grow
For that past harvest-tide of wrong and woe;
Belike the tale, wept over otherwhere,
Of those old days, is clean forgotten there."

We pass, in this contrast, from poetry which (for all its unfinished effect and occasional clichés) lays a constant claim upon the reader's intellect and perception, to poetry of imprecise dreamlike moods, soothing and relaxing to the mind. In the *Scenes from the Fall of Troy,* the great legend is used, not—as in Morris's later manner—as an antique picture-land with decorative figures but as the setting within which the heroic values lost to the nineteenth century can be evoked with freshness and conviction. It is true that the sense of failure is ever-present. But the forces, human and natural, making for failure are evoked with a sense of active conflict, rather than recorded with passive nostalgia. Courage, beauty, endurance, wisdom—all are overthrown but their value is never denied. Rather, the dramatic method of narration, the occasional sharp realistic details, the meaningful irregularities of rhythm—all work together to evoke the feeling of real struggle and life. As in the earlier poems, Morris lays brutality side by side with beauty and melancholy: the scenes of battle are treated with realism and care, as in Aeneas' account of the encounter between Troilus and Diomed:

> "Into the press came Diomed softly
> And like a cunning fighter, on each side
> He put the strokes that met him: traversing
> With little labour till his turn might chance.
> Then came my lord King Priam's youngest son,
> With no hair on his face, Sirs, as you see,
> Who all day long had struck the greatest strokes
> And bent his knees and stiffened up his back;
> But when his eye caught Diomedes' eye
> He cried and leapt—crur, how the handles jarred!"

There is no slackness here in rhythmic control. We are made to share in the aspirations of the heroes and when Hector is trapped by Achilles, his death, like that of Sir Peter Harpdon, strikes a note of affimation rather than defeat, and the concluding line of the whole poem evokes not disaster alone, but a boundless vista of further endeavour and experience:

> "To the ships!
> Aeneas and Antenor—to the ships!—"

There are failures and immaturities enough in the *Scenes from the Fall of Troy* to account for Morris's abandoning the work uncompleted. But even so, many problems remain. At some time between leaving off work on the *Scenes* and the full adoption of his plans for *The Earthly Paradise,* Morris took a conscious decision to alter the whole manner of his writing. Moreover, in this alteration he turned his back upon much of what is strong and moving in his earlier work, while maintaining—in a more sophisticated and self-conscious form—the weakness and immaturities. This decision is an important one. An understanding of it provides a key to the poetry of his middle period. It reveals much of the change of attitude from revolt to disillusion in his personal outlook during these years. And it marks a stage in the degeneration of the English Romantic movement.

II. The Earthly Paradise

The Earthly Paradise is a collection of twenty-four poetic narratives, of greatly varying lengths, and from many sources, classical, Eastern, medieval, and Norse. They are grouped in pairs for each month of the year, prefaced by verses for the months. As in *The Canterbury Tales,* the poems are bound together by a slender narrative. In the long Prologue, "The Wanderers", a group of Northern warriors in the Middle Ages set sail in quest for a land of eternal life and youth, and after many adventures and much disillusionment, they reach in their old age a friendly and fertile land where Greek traditions still linger. They are welcomed, entertained, and the stories are those with which the Wanderers and their hosts entertain each other. The resemblance to the method and plan of *The Canterbury Tales,* however—despite Morris's invocation of his "master", Geoffrey Chaucer—is only superficial, and the comparison much to Morris's disadvantage. While Chaucer's plan is dynamic the framework of *The Earthly Paradise* is entirely static. It is the pretext, not the occasion for the stories. Neither among the Wanderers nor the hosts is there any differentiation of character: the stories whether intended as tragic or felicitous, express similar attitudes to life throughout which are always felt to be those adopted by Morris the poet, rather than those held by the narrators he has shadowed forth. In this way, the framework, so far from giving added vigour and interest to the narrations, acts to dull the immediacy of their impact, to remove them even further from the region of everyday belief. We are reading not stories, but a story about people telling stories; and these stories were told very long ago about events which took place in an even further distant and fabulous past.

Moreover, Morris adopts, as the prime narrator, the character of the careless folk-bard, beguiling, saddening, or sweetening the lives of his listeners by his tales, but always avoiding any full treatment of their implications. Since he speaks not in his real voice but in a self-consciously assumed character, this is a further means by which the impact of life is distanced in the poem.

The method of narration throughout is leisurely—"a smooth song sweet enow"—and full of archaisms. That this style was adopted after deliberation is clear from some of the earliest rejected drafts of the poems.[1] A comparison between two passages of the Prologue, "The Wanderers" (one of the first to which Morris turned his hand), will reveal the change in manner. The first Prologue was written in quatrains, both more diffuse and more regular than his early poems, but still preserving some roughness and overrunning from verse to verse when demanded by the action. In these two passages, the Wanderers are the victims of a night-attack in a strange land. In the rejected version Morris wrote:

"But in the dead of night I woke,
And heard a sharp and bitter cry,
And there saw, struck with a great stroke,
Lie dead, Sir John of Hederby.

"We armed us with what speed we might,
And thick and fast the arrows came,
Nor did we any more lack light,
For all the woods were red with flame.

[1] See *Works,* Vol. XXIV, and May Morris, I, pp. 397 ff.

"Straight we set forward valiantly
While all about the blacks lay hid,
Who never spared to yell and cry—
A woeful night to us befell.

"For some within the fire fell,
And some with shafts were smitten dead,
Neither could any see right well
Which side to guard, nor by my head

"Did we strike stroke at all that night,
For ever onward as we drew
So drew they back from out our sight. . ."

This is thin verse, with several careless and flat lines thrown in, as it seems, to marry off a rhyme. But it is still verse which can carry action: the sudden awakening is vividly shown: the sequence of events is clear: the confusion and impotence of the warriors at night presented with movement and conviction. The published version is in the usual rhyming couplets:

"But therewithall I woke, and through the night
Heard shrieks and shouts of clamour of the fight,
And snatching up my axe, unarmed beside
Nor scarce awaked, my rallying cry I cried,
And with good haste unto the hubbub went;
But even in the entry of the tent
Some dark mass hid the star-besprinkled sky,
And whistling past my head a spear did fly,
And striking out I saw a naked man
Fall 'neath my blow, nor heeded him, but ran
Unto the captain's tent, for there indeed
I saw my fellows stand at desperate need,
Beset with foes, nor yet more armed than I,
Though on the way I rallied hastily
Some better armed, with whom I straightway fell
Upon the foe, who with a hideous yell
Turned round upon us. . ."

On the surface this passage reveals that technical accomplishment so often claimed by nineteenth-century critics for *The Earthly Paradise.* The verse seems to scan all right, there are no grammatical howlers, a few "felicities" of poetic diction.

But—as too often in these poems—it is a "technical mastery" at odds with real poetic achievement. The passage describes action: it does not begin to evoke it—what line could with less conviction convey speed and confusion than the sedate, "And with good haste unto the hubbub went"? The archaisms underline the static, decorative effect—"therewithall", "beside", "at desperate need", "beset with foes". Even more characteristic, in the press of imminent death the narrator can find time to note the conventional poetic beauties, "the star-besprinkled sky". The confusion at the end of the passage, in which by an afterthought the narrator reaches the captain's tent with some better-armed comrades, conveys not the confusion of battle but an imprecision in the poet's imaginative realization of the scene. The rhythms are ugly and clogged: the action muddled.

Not all of Morris's scenes of action in *The Earthly Paradise* can come under all these criticisms. But the general sense of the criticism is true throughout. These leisurely narratives never falter: but at the same time they never mend their pace. They are old tales re-told, and this is constantly emphasized by the liberal use of archaic, or "poetic" diction. The poem marks an important stage in the tendency, so often commented upon, for the later romantics to confine both their themes and their vocabulary to certain limited fields of experience. Even in the first version of the Prologue, Morris described the ship of the Wanderers, when they first set out, as supplied with "stockfish and salt-meat": in the published version, it is a "fair long-ship", "well victualled". Consistently the vocabulary is limited so as to prevent the intrusion of the humdrum, the sharp realistic detail, the unpleasant or shocking fact. If scenes of labour are presented, they are seen by the observer as picturesque—the sickle, the barefooted damsels, the mellowing grapes. If scenes of battle, they are decorative, as seen through a dim heroic mist. If scenes of love, they are sensuous but featureless, presented as a mood of luxury rather than a human relationship. The characters are the simplest shadows of folk types, the fabulous king, the hero, the lovelorn maiden, the scholar, the traveller, the misanthrope. They are brought into relationship, not through the pressures of character, but through the incidents of the story. From the very opening of the poem, the "Apology" and the first lines of the Prologue:

> "Forget six counties overhung with smoke,
> Forget the snorting steam and piston stroke,
> Forget the spreading of the hideous town;
> Think rather of the pack-horse on the down,
> And dream of London, small, and white, and clean. . ."

we are transported to a "shadowy isle of bliss", in which we are not invited to judge either the events or the characters according to our own experience. In the *Defence of Guenevere* volume we are made to feel that the characters—Sir Peter Harpdon, the narrator of "Geffray Teste Noire", Guenevere herself—are motivated by passions whose nobility or intensity may exceed our own, but which we still recognize in ourselves. The conditions within which they act may be strange to us, but the consequences of their actions follow with the same logic that we experience in our own lives. With *The Earthly Paradise* we enter through Keats's "magic casements" into "the realm of gold":

> "A nameless city in a distant sea,
> White as the changing walls of faerie,
> Thronged with much people clad in ancient guise
> I am now fain to set before your eyes."

The realism which was the very salt of Morris's youthful poetry is deliberately abandoned; and the tension between the closely-imagined detail and the atmosphere of dream is broken. The laws of everyday experience no longer hold good, and we enter a land of the marvellous and strange, in which the poet may make and break his own laws—a land filled with dragons, magic of several kinds, fabulous kingdoms and hoards of wealth, Gods on earth and pagan sacrifices. The land is a land of dream.

So much is generally recognized, although the distinction between the romantic realism of *The Defence of Guenevere,* and the dream-like "romance" of *The Earthly Paradise* is not always understood. But romance, however far-fetched and dream-like, cannot escape from some indirect relevance to living experience. Morris himself, indeed, claimed this relevance for one of the most miraculous of his tales, "The Land East of the Sun and West of the Moon":

> "A dream it is, friends, and no history
> Of men who ever lived; so blame me nought
> If wonderous things together there are brought,
> Strange to our waking world—yet as in dreams
> Of known things still we dream, whatever gleams
> Of unknown light may make them strange, so here
> Our dreamland story holdeth such things dear
> And such things loathed, as we do; else, indeed,
> Were all such marvels nought to help our need."

Morris did not think that he was writing fairy stories for children, but adult poetry. Moreover, he had shown himself in his first volume to have one of the most original poetic talents of the century, and he showed throughout his life a deep reflective seriousness inconsistent with the character of a casual entertainer. What impelled him to chose the form of romance for his most sustained poetic work? Why did his tales of magic and dragons establish for him so high a reputation among his contemporaries? What relevance did these stories have to his own experience? These are among the problems which demand some answer.

III. "A sense of something ill. . ."

Romance is often seen as a sympton of decadence within a culture. In its sophisticated literary forms it has flourished among the idle class, divorced from the labour of production. But in the nineteenth century it found an even wider and growing audience, among the exploited as well as among the exploiters. This audience found in it a refuge from the drabness of their own lives: a compensation for the extinction of the heroic and beautiful in their everyday existence. And the manifesto of this new romance was in the often-quoted "Apology" which prefaces *The Earthly Paradise:*

> "The heavy trouble, the bewildering care
> That weighs us down who live and earn our bread,
> These idle verses have no power to bear;
> So let me sing of names remembered,
> Because they, living not, can ne'er be dead. . ."

Here there is evidence enough that Morris's turn to romance was deliberately and consciously taken:

> "Dreamer of dreams, born out of my due time,
> Why should I strive to set the crooked straight?
> Let it suffice me that my murmuring rhyme
> Beats with light wing against the ivory gate,
> Telling a tale not too importunate
> To those who in the sleepy region stay,
> Lulled by the singer of an empty day.
>
> "Folk say, a wizard to a northern king
> At Christmas-tide such wondrous things did show,
> That through one window men beheld the spring,
> And through another saw the summer glow,
> And through a third the fruited vines a-row,
> While still unheard, but in its wonted way,
> Piped the drear wind of that December day.
>
> "So with this Earthly Paradise it is,
> If ye will read aright, and pardon me,
> Who strive to build a shadowy isle of bliss
> Midmost the beating of the steely sea,
> Where tossed about all hearts of men must be;
> Whose ravening monsters mighty men must slay,
> Not the poor singer of an empty day."

Because this "Apology" is concerned with a real and personal experience—the poet's own creative problems—and because it claims the attention of the reader with its constant sense of contrast between the rich illusions of art and the hostile realities of life, it is finer poetry than all but a few passages of the poems for which it serves as a Preface. It carries still the flickering spirit of revolt—"Of Heaven and Hell I have no power to sing"—where Morris turns his back upon the impoverished moralizing of contemporary schools, rejecting the age of "improvement". But in its sum it is a confession of defeat: considered within the traditions of the romantic movement, it is a rejection of Shelley's claims for the poet, a refusal to sustain the struggle of Keats for full poetic consciousness and responsibility. The tension between the ideal and the real, between the rich aspirations of life and art and the ignoble and brutal fact, which underlies the best of Keats's poetry and (in a more complex way) Morris's own early poems, is no longer present. It is restated in the "Apology": but when the main poem is entered the open conflict has been abandoned.

But the conflict cannot be exorcised as easily as that. While the conscious effort to reconcile, or merely to bring into poetic opposition, man's desire and the reality of his life, is abandoned, the same conflict persists in a muted form upon nearly every page of *The Earthly Paradise.* A close reading of every poem in the sequence reveals that Morris is not really interested in either the characters or in the action —in the sense that the action is in itself either significant or purposeful. The poetry is a poetry of *mood:* the climaxes are climaxes of mood: the real action lies in variations of mood. The narratives are little more than the machinery for this variation, the basic movement of which is an almost mechanical oscillation between sensuous luxury and horror, melancholy or despair. "The Lady of the Land" is discovered by a voyager among fabulous cloisters stored high with precious gems and gold:

> "Naked she was, the kisses of her feet
> Upon the floor a dying path had made

From the full bath unto her ivory seat;
In her right hand, upon her bosom laid,
She held a golden comb, a mirror weighed
Her left hand down, aback her fair head lay
Dreaming awake of some long vanished day."

At the end of the tale she is transformed into a vile dragon:

"A fearful thing stood at the cloister's end,
And eyed him for a while. . .

And as it came on towards him, with its teeth
The body of a slain goat did it tear,
The blood whereof in its hot jaws did seeth,
And on its tongue he saw the smoking hair. . ."

This movement is repeated in poem after poem. It is stated early in the Prologue, where the narrator tells of a dream that he was a king,

"Set on the throne whose awe and majesty
Gold lions guard; before whose moveless feet
A damsel knelt, praying in words so sweet
For what I know not now, that both mine eyes
Grew full of tears, and I must bid her rise
And sit beside me; step by step she came
Up the gold stair, setting my heart a-flame
With all her beauty, till she reached the throne
And there sat down, but as with her alone
In that vast hall, my hand her hand did seek,
And on my face I felt her balmy cheek,
Throughout my heart there shot a dreadful pang,
And down below us, with a sudden clang
The golden lions rose, and roared aloud,
And in at every door did armed men crowd,
Shouting out death and curses. . ."

Repeated once again, purely in terms of mood, in "The Hill of Venus":

"Time and again, he, listening to such word,
Felt his heart kindle; time and again did seem
As though a cold and hopeless tune he heard,
Sung by grey mouths amidst a dull-eyed dream;
Time and again across his heart would stream
The pain of fierce desire whose aim was gone,
Of baffled yearning, loveless and alone."

It is found in a significant image which recurs several times in the poems, of the living struck dead in the postures of life: the human sacrifice met by the Wanderers: the figures in the tomb in "The Writing on the Image": the dead-alive people at the end of "The Land East of the Sun and West of the Moon": the land peopled with the dead images—

"Of knights and ladies sitting round,
A set smile upon every face;
Their gold gowns trailing on the ground,
The light of gold through all the place."

in the first version of the "Wanderers".

In fact Morris has made this oscillation of mood the prevailing movement in many whole poems. It is a mechanical oscillation: the sense of real conflict and struggle is absent. In "King Arthur's Tomb" (one of the *Defence of Guenevere* volume) Morris speaks of "that half-sleep, half-strife/(Strange sleep, strange strife) that men call living". It is a significant phrase. In this early volume, life—while strange and idealized—is made up equally of action and of desire. Men are not content with moods alone: they fight, work, enter into relations with each other, in the effort to make their desires into realities. A symbolical incident takes place at the opening of *The Earthly Paradise.* The Wanderers, setting out on their quest for the land of eternal life (a desire which Morris would never have put into the head of Sir Peter Harpdon or even Launcelot) encounter King Edward III in the Channel. He is perhaps the only real character in the poem:

"Broad-browed he was, hook-nosed, with wide grey eyes
No longer eager for the coming prize,
But keen and steadfast, many an ageing line,
Half-hidden by his sweeping beard and fine,
Ploughed his thin cheeks. . ."

He, after hearing of their quest, gives them licence to proceed:

". . . the world is wide
For you, I say,—for me a narrow space
Betwixt the four walls of a fighting place."

Then he is left in the world of strife and action: the Wanderers go on into the world of sleep and of dream, leaving the "fighting place" behind. It is true that they meet adventures enough: but these adventures happen to them: they are not willed, and their significance is only in their shattering of the subjective illusions of the Wanderers. The ambitions, strife and achievements of men and women have little more significance than they have to "The Man Who Never Laughed Again":

"But all the folk he saw were strange to him,
And, for all heed that unto them he gave,
Might have been nought; the reaper's bare brown limb,
The rich man's train with litter and armed slave,
The girl bare-footed in the stream's white wave—
Like empty shadows by his eyes they passed,
The world was narrowed to his heart at last."

We are left with the question asked in the verses for November:

"Art thou so weary that no world there seems
Beyond these four walls, hung with pain and dreams?"

The four walls of the "fighting-place" have contracted to the four walls of the solitary individual's heart.

It is impossible not to judge *The Earthly Paradise* within

the context of romanticism in decline. To Morris, oppressed by "bourgeoisdom and philistinism", the real world of "the piston stroke" and "hideous town" (and also of his unhappy personal life) had become unbearable. We do not need to reconstruct his state of mind from hints and suggestions, for he did this himself in a remarkable passage in his article, "How I became a Socialist" (1894):

> "Apart from the desire to produce beautiful things, the leading passion of my life has been and is hatred of modern civilization... What shall I say concerning its mastery of and its waste of mechanical power, its commonwealth so poor, its enemies of the commonwealth so rich, its stupendous organisation—for the misery of life! Its contempt of simple pleasures which everyone could enjoy but for its folly? Its eyeless vulgarity which has destroyed art, the one certain solace of labour? All this I felt then as now, but I did not know why it was so. The hope of the past times was gone, the struggles of mankind for many ages had produced nothing but this sordid, aimless, ugly confusion; the immediate future seemed to me likely to intensify all the present evils by sweeping away the last survivals of the days before the dull squalor of civilization had settled down on the world. This was a bad look-out indeed, and, if I may mention myself as a personality and not as a mere type, especially so to a man of my disposition, careless of metaphysics and religion, as well as of scientific analysis, but with a deep love of the earth and the life on it, and a passion for the history of the past of mankind. Think of it! Was it all to end in a counting-house on the top of a cinder-heap, with Podsnap's drawing-room in the offing, and a Whig committee dealing out champagne to the rich and margarine to the poor in such convenient proportions as would make all men content together, though the pleasure of the eyes was gone from the world, and the place of Homer was to be taken by Huxley? Yet, believe me, in my heart, when I really forced myself to look toward the future, that is what I saw in it, and, as far as I could tell, scarce anyone seemed to think it worth while to struggle against such a consummation of civilization."

This passage was written at the end of Morris's life, when his new convictions enabled him to express his earlier attitudes with greater logic than they were felt by him at the time. But what is important is that Morris was not imagining emotions which he *might* have felt when he was in his thirties, but striving to re-create his earlier state of mind with precision. It is rubbish to suppose that Morris, in his middle years, was a bluff craftsman, insensitive to the life around him; or that *The Earthly Paradise* is a sweet song of pleasure written carelessly by a man advancing by easy steps to the effortless acceptance of Socialist convictions. Such an interpretation lessens the splendour of the struggle for the human spirit enacted in Morris's life. In truth, the underlying note of *The Earthly Paradise* is neither sweet nor careless: it is a note of despair. If we set some of Swinburne's poems aside, the poem closest in mood to much of *The Earthly Paradise* is that of James Thomson, the unhappy alcoholic and insomniac—*The City of Dreadful Night.*

"The hope of the past ages was gone..." As we have seen "hope" was a key-word in Morris's vocabulary. By "hope" he meant all that gives worth and continuity to human endeavour, all that makes man's finest aspirations seem possible of achievement in the real world. Of his later conversion to Socialism Morris wrote (in the same article): "I did not measure my hope, nor the joy it brought me." But without hope the romantic movement lost its forward impetus: it was no longer a movement of revolt, but one of compensation or escape: "only in ourselves and the world of literature and art was there any hope". Aspiration, denied the hope of fulfilment, could only be nourished and brooded upon in the solitary individual's heart. But, as William Blake had warned, "He who desires but acts not, breeds pestilence". The romantic is caught in the mood of "The Man Who Never Laughed Again":

> "If, thinking of the pleasure and the pain,
> Men find in struggling life, he turned to gain
> The godlike joy he hoped to find therein,
> All turned to cloud, and nought seemed left to win.
>
> "Love moved him not, yea, something in his heart
> There was that made him shudder at its name;
> He could not rouse himself to take his part

> In ruling worlds and winning praise and blame;
> And if vague hope of glory o'er him came,
> Why should he cast himself against the spears
> To make vain stories for the unpitying years?"

The world is "empty" because it is an entirely subjective world. No matter how rich the illusion of happiness it is always transient and poisoned by the knowledge of mortality. The Wanderers, in the Epilogue of the poem, recall

> ". . . That day of their vanished youth, when first
> They saw Death clear, and deemed all life accurst
> By that cold overshadowing threat—the End."

The "isle of bliss" is amid the "beating of the steely sea": the wizard to the northern king transforms the room by his miraculous windows, but the continuous reality outside is the piping of the December wind: always we are on the verge of—

> ". . . the waking from delight
> Unto the real day void and white."

of "The Land East of the Sun and West of the Moon".[1] Never are we permitted to escape into illusion for long: rather, we are trying in anxious wakefulness to recall a dream. Nor are the illusions themselves free from the same taint: more often, like "The Golden Apples",

> ". . . the tale did seem
> Like to the middle of some pleasant dream,
> Which, waked from, leaves upon the troubled mind
> A sense of something ill that lurked behind."

Mortality is a theme common to all poetry. But the attitude

[1] Cf. *The City of Dreadful Night,* Section XII, with its refrain "I wake from daydreams to this real night."

of poets to the fact of death has changed no less than attitudes to other aspects of man's experience. Death has been faced with resignation or with fear of the unknown: it has been seen as a leveller or as a welcome release. Mortality has given value to heroism and poignancy to love. Rarely, before the nineteenth century, was death felt as the poisoner of all value in life. Darwin's evidence of evolution published in the mid-century had made men view themselves in a diminished perspective. Even Tennyson was impelled to question, in *In Memoriam,* not only whether individual men were doomed to extinction, but the human race itself,

> "Who loved, who suffer'd countless ills,
> Who battled for the True, the Just,
> Be blown about the desert dust,
> Or seal'd within the iron hills?"

Tennyson quickly put the question back behind a veil of wishful religious sentiment. But for James Thomson—who must have been at work on *The City of Dreadful Night* at the same time as Morris was finishing *The Earthly Paradise* —the question had become an accepted fact:

> "The world rolls round for ever like a mill;
> It grinds out death and life and good and ill;
> It has no purpose, heart or mind or will."

And, to the horror of the fact of mortality in an indifferent universe, James Thomson could only oppose the refrain. "No hope could have no fear".

It is the total absence of hope which is new—hope not for a future life, but for human fulfilment upon earth. Moreover, this absence of hope fell within the context of a society whose basic ethic was that of naked individualism, where every pressure tended to isolate man from his neighbour, and to deny the objective values of men acting together in society, striving for goods both wider and more permanent than those of the individual's satisfaction. "The place of Homer was to be taken by Huxley. . ."–it is no accident that Morris singled out as the enemy not the great scientist Darwin, but the notable publicist of evolutionary theory and polemical rationalist, T.H. Huxley. For it was Huxley, far more than Darwin, who was responsible for that caricature of science commonly mistaken for "the theory of evolution" by the Victorian public: a caricature in which nature was seen as "red in tooth and claw", engaged in a merciless and meaningless struggle for survival on the pattern of the competitive ethics of industrial capitalist society, in which the predatory instincts formed the motive power of "progress". Indeed, Huxley repeatedly crossed the border into political theory, and declared in a phrase which lodged in the popular memory: "For his successful progress man has been largely indebted to those qualities he shares with the ape and the tiger." Moreover, he came forward as the champion of a mechanical materialism which–while it helped to liberate scientific enquiry from the trammels of superstition–was closely akin in spirit to Mr. Gradgrind's utilitarianism, the deadly foe of Morris's youth. Where Morris's master, Keats, had written, "Truth is Beauty, Beauty Truth", T.H. Huxley declared that he had no faith "in any source of truth save that reached by the patient application of scientific methods". Morris had (perhaps unfairly) taken Huxley as the Prophet of a society utterly careless of beauty, of art, and the finer human virtues, which looked upon both nature and the past of mankind as an "ugly confusion", a jungle of accidents within which predatory passions and lusts fought for survival, and in which self-interest and the values of possession contaminated every relationship, from the labour market to the marriage bed.

These are among the reasons why the recognition of mortality fell with such horror upon Morris's mind, and those of many of his more sensitive contemporaries. On every side he was faced by the "sordid, ugly, aimless confusion". Death appeared as doubly bitter: as closing with terrible finality a life whose potentialities had never been even partially fulfilled, whose aspirations, denied by a hostile society, must always remain unsatisfied: and as sealing a life whose focus was becoming ever more subjective, without the compensation of that sense of continuity which the active participation in the struggle for wider social ends must always bring. But, paradoxically, this horror bred its opposite. Since the romantic mind, once "hope" was abandoned, could not contemplate life without turning to the fact of death, so a desire for death was generated as a means of escape from the "unpitying" reality of life. So marked in Swinburne, it is also one of those undertones in *The Earthly Paradise* which bring the "sense of something ill that lurked behind".

Morris, in *The Earthly Paradise,* rarely turned to look his fear in the face—perhaps only in the finest of the verses for the months, as at the close of "November":

> "Yea, I have looked, and seen November there;
> The changeless seal of change it seemed to be,
> Fair death of things that, living once, were fair;
> Bright sign of loneliness too great for me,
> Strange image of the dread eternity,
> In whose void patience how can these have part,
> These outstretched feverish hands, this restless heart?"

In these lines, because Morris dared to look steadily at his enemy, we are left with the sense, not of death, but of life. But whenever he took refuge from his fear in the world of romance, we meet, not life, but the constant undertow back towards death. The dream, so much desired, is always breaking down:

> "Ah, these, with life so done with now, might deem
> That better is it resting in a dream,
> Yea, e'en a dull dream, than with outstretched hand,
> And wild eyes, face to face with life to stand...
> Than waking in a hard taskmaster's grasp
> Because we strove the unsullied joy to clasp—
> Than just to find our hearts the world, as we
> Still thought we were and ever longed to be,

To find nought real except ourselves, and find
All care for all things scattered to the wind,
Scarce in our hearts the very pain alive.
Compelled to breathe indeed, compelled to strive,
Compelled to fear, yet not allowed to hope—"

he concludes "The Man Who Never Laughed Again". Indeed, it may be suggested that one of the pressures which impelled him to write *Jason* and *The Earthly Paradise* was the desire to shake off that morbidity of preoccupation which contributed in making James Thomson into an alcoholic. The speed with which he wrote—on occasion upwards of 700 lines in a night—not only accounts for much of the technical slackness (the easy, often repeated rhymes, the clumsy archaisms—"therewithal", "gan", "uswards", etc.—thrown in to enable the rhythm to muddle through) but is also evidence that neither his mind nor his feelings were seriously engaged in much of the work. It is as if his feverish activity, both in the crafts and in poetry in these years, is like the labour of the craftsman in "Pygmalion and the Image", which "soothes his heart, and dulls thought's poisonous sting".

The reason for the constant oscillation of mood in the poem now becomes more clear. It is caused by the constant undertow of death. The movement reminds us of Keats once again, and of the "Ode to Melancholy":

"She dwells with Beauty—Beauty that must die;
  And Joy, whose hand is ever at his lips
Bidding adieu; and aching Pleasure nigh,
  Turning to poison while the bee-mouth sips:
Ay, in the very temple of Delight
  Veil'd Melancholy has her sovran shring. . ."

"Veil'd melancholy", the consciousness of the passing of life and of beauty, may only be seen by him "whose strenuous tongue/Can burst Joy's grape against his palate fine". This melancholy is met and accepted as the price of consciousness in the revised *Hyperion.* What may be called a "muted *Hyperion* theme" persists in *The Earthly Paradise.* It is the theme of the hero, dissatisfied with humdrum life, aspiring to some goal, which, once achieved, brings a moment of bliss, and then disaster or despair. Among whole poems where this theme predominates are "The Watching of the Falcon", "The Man Who Never Laughed Again", "The Writing on the Image", "The Hill of Venus", while it appears with slight variations in "The Wanderers" and "The Lady of the Land", and, in an inverted form, in "Pygmalion and the Image" and "The Land East of the Sun and West of the Moon", which, while ending happily, do so with many suggestions of the evanescence of mortal happiness. But, because Morris never treats with full awareness the conflict which this theme symbolizes, it has gone tawdry and picturesque. The aspirations of the heroes have diminished to the lust for wealth or sensuous pleasure or mere romantic restlessness and curiosity: the struggle is replaced by the miraculous, the satisfaction suited to the aspiration, the disaster mechanical, and having little more moral implication than that "curiosity killed the cat". The conflict is never openly stated or posed in terms of human choice or agency: certainly it is never resolved. Its recurrence represents little more than a profound dissatisfaction with life, and a fear of death under whose shadow all human values seem to fall apart.

Here, then, is some answer to our questions. *The Earthly Paradise* is the poetry of despair. The extinction of hope in the world around him drove Morris to abandon Keats's struggle, and the struggle of his own youth, to reconcile his ideals and his everyday experience, and he turned his back on the world by telling old tales of romance. But, as Keats had warned in his revision of *Hyperion*, this road must lead to the death of the poetic genius, by excluding from poetry the active, suffering consciousness, and limiting its themes to certain "poetic" regions of experience. Since one of his main impulses towards writing poetry was in the desire to shake free from despair, the poetry itself reveals this feeling of despair as a constant undertow: but since he rarely met his despair openly, he rarely evoked it with any depth of feeling or dignity. For these reasons, *The Earthly Paradise* must be seen as romantic poetry which has entered the phase of decadence. Much of it is exceedingly competent narrative verse: "The Man Born to Be King"; "The Writing on the Image"; "The Man Who Never Laughed Again"; these and others are well-told tales. Morris has a persuasive manner of telling a story, an unfaltering self-possessed passage from event to event. But the essential qualities of great art are absent.

Is this all that can be said of the poem? Fortunately, no. If it were, then we would be hard put to it to explain that capacity for change, for the re-birth of life and hope, evident in Morris's life. As another constant underswell to the poem, never dominant except in the verses for the months, and rarely found without a note of melancholy, there is a suggestion of that "deep love of the earth and the life on it" recalled in his essay. It is found, again and again, in the sensitive evocation of natural beauty and of the seasons. It is found in touches of description of ordinary human life, which, while still picturesque, carry a feeling of a world outside the circle of despair in which men and women carry on the business of life, perhaps without conscious aim, but at least with faith in life and confidence in the future. This sense of normality comes with freshness in the return of "The Man Who Never Laughed Again" from his sojourn of horror to human habitation, passing—

> "The slender damsel coming from the well,
> Smiling beneath the flashing brazen jar,
> Her fellows left behind thereat, to tell
> How weary of her smiles her lovers are. . .
>
> "The trooper drinking at the homestead gate,
> Telling wild lies about the sword and spear,
> Unto the farmer striving to abate
> The pedler's price; the village drawing near,
> The smoke, that scenting the fresh eve, and clear,
> Tells of the feast; the stithy's dying spark,
> The barn's wealth showing dimly through the dark,
>
> "How sweet was all! how easy it should be
> Amid such life one's self-made woes to bear!"

Above all, it is found in the struggle to throw off the mood of death-longing at the end of the verses for "October":

> "—O hearken, hearken! through the afternoon,
> The grey tower sings a strange old tinkling tune!
> Sweet, sweet, and sad, the toiling year's last breath,
> Too satiate of life to strive with death.
>
> "And we too—will it not be soft and kind,
> That rest from life, from patience and from pain;
> That rest from bliss we know not when we find;
> That rest from Love which ne'er the end can gain?—
> —Hark, how the tune swells, that erewhile did wane!
> Look up, love!—ah, cling close and never move!
> How can I have enough of life and love?"

IV. "The time lacks strength"

"This sordid, aimless, ugly confusion", "a counting-house on the top of a cinder-heap, with Podsnap's drawing-room in the offing"—so Morris was later to describe England in the years when *The Earthly Paradise* was first published. And yet, despite the "hatred of modern civilisation" which underlay the poem, it was immediately received with acclaim among a very wide section of the middle-class reading public. Morris (declared the reviewer in *St. James's Magazine*) was "one of those men this age particularly wants". The "world"—"all that roar of machinery and that bustle about wealth—is too much with us":

> "It is not necessary that Mr. William Morris, or indeed, any single man whatsoever, should supply a full and adequate antidote to prevalent feverishness; but he does a distinct and notable service when he provides one possible means of escape."[1]

[1] *St. James's Magazine,* January, 1878. See Oscar Maurer, in *Nineteenth-century Studies,* edited Davis, De Vane, and Bald (Cornell U.P., 1940). See also Karl Litzenburg "William Morris and the Reviews", *The Review of English Studies,* October, 1936; P. Faulkner, *William Morris: The Critical Heritage* (1973).

The reviewer of the *Pall Mall Gazette* also found himself "glad to retire from the stress and the cares of his ugly workaday English life and be entertained. . . with that succession of gracious pictures. . . of a remote romantic world".[1] The *Saturday Review,* attacking Browning for his obscurity found it refreshing to meet "with a modern poem of the Chaucerian type":

> "There is a fairer chance for poetry to be read and appreciated and taken back into favour by a busy material age, if its scope is distinct and direct, its style clear and pellucid, and its manner something like that of the old rhapsodists, minnesingers, and tale-tellers who in divers climes and ages have won such deserved popularity. So seems Mr. Morris to have thought."

So seem also to have thought a class of readers who bring to mind Mr. Plint, the Leeds stockbroker, and the industrialists who patronized Burne-Jones, Rossetti, and the Morris firm:

> "Mr. Morris's popularity has. . . something remarkable about it. He is, we have noticed, appreciated by those who as a rule do not care to read any poetry. To our personal knowledge, political economists and scientific men to whom Shelley is a mystery and Tennyson a vexation of spirit, read the 'Earthly Paradise' with admiration."[2]

If the poem had been intended to voice a revolt against the age, then it would seem to have been a signal failure. Rather, it seemed to strike a chord in the very age which Morris despised. How can this startling reception of the poem be explained?

Morris's readers were largely drawn from the great middle class into which he himself had been born, which had been enriched by the Industrial Revolution, and which was reaching the climax of its power and prosperity during Morris's youth and middle age—in the twenty years which followed the Great Exhibition of 1851, when Britain was indeed the workshop of the world. In the census of 1851, 272,000 were

[1] *Pall Mall Budget,* December 11th, 1869.

[2] *The Saturday Review,* May 30th, 1868.

numbered in the professions: in 1871, 684,000. In the same years the numbers classed as domestic servants swelled from 900,000 to 1½ millions. Between 1854 and 1880 British capital invested overseas (largely in foreign loans and railways) jumped from about £210 millions to £1,300 millions. By this latter date there were close on 50,000 shareholders in Indian railway stock alone, most of whom lived in Great Britain. At the climax of these years, shortly after the passing of the Reform Bill of 1867, John Bright, champion of Free Trade, uttered one of his many paeons of triumph. "The aristocracy of England which so lately governed the country has abdicated", he declared:

> "There is no longer a contest between us and the House of Lords; we need no longer bring charges against a selfish oligarchy; we no longer dread the power of the territorial magnates; we no longer feel ourselves domineered over by a class; we feel that denunciation and invective now would be out of place; the power which hitherto has ruled over us is shifted."[1]

This vast middle class, part actively engaged in commerce and industry, part *rentier,* part professional, which felt itself to be the real ruler not only of England but of the greater part of the world, was the soil in which the characteristic attitudes which we now name "Victorianism" flourished.

"Victorianism" did not arise suddenly in 1851. Wilberforce the prototype of so many "Victorian" public men, was dead before Queen Victoria came to the throne. Ernest Jones had pilloried the Victorian middle-class Liberal when Chartism was still a living force:

> "Against the slave trade he had voted,
> 'Rights of Man', resounding still;
> Now, basely turning, brazen-throated,
> Yelled against the Ten Hours Bill."[2]

[1] Address to the working men of Edinburgh, November 5th, 1868, *Public Addresses by John Bright, M.P.* (1879), pp. 122-3.

[2] "A Christmas Story", *The Labourer,* Vol. I (1847).

and when Samuel Fielden denounced the "cotton conscience" in 1849, he was commenting on a theme which had been familiar to Lancashire and Yorkshire working-men for twenty years:

> "These masters about Stalybridge, he heard, were principally dissenters, and many of them unitarians, his [Mr. Fielden's] own set-[*Laughter*]—and he believed he was among a very bad lot; for true it was, that unitarians and quakers were the worst politicians in existence. They had agitated, defended, and passed more measures tending to enslave and oppress the poor man than any set of men in the country. Their cry of civil and religious liberty all the world over was now pretty well understood. It meant liberty for them to help themselves, and put down all who were in the way of their doing so. These were the men who made all the hubbub about black slavery, but who thought nothing of working their own people to death. . ."[1]

What was new in the years after 1851 was the widespread power exercised by the breed of Wilberforce and the Stalybridge masters in every field of public life; the permeation of the arts, the sciences, of all intellectual life by many of their attitudes; the increasing complacency of a triumphant class, surfeited with wealth and self-importance; and the great extension in the *rentier* class which drew its dividends but took no direct part in the exploitation of labour.

For Morris, it was always Dickens' inspired chapter, "Podsnappery", in *Our Mutual Friend* (1864-5) which described (for his mingled delight and fury) the characteristic attitudes of this class. Mr. Podsnap was "well to do, and stood very high in Mr. Podsnap's opinion":

> "Beginning with a good inheritance, he had married a good inheritance, and had thriven exceedingly in the Marine Insurance way, and was quite satisfied. He never could make out why everybody was not quite satisfied, and he felt conscious that he set a brilliant social example in being particularly well satisfied with most things, and, above all other things, with himself."

[1] Speech at Stalybridge, August 10th, 1849.

Other countries he considered "a mistake", and would dismiss their customs and culture with the devastating observation, "Not English!" Mr. Podsnap's world was entirely well-regulated and respectable:

"The world got up at eight, shaved close at a quarter past, breakfasted at nine, went to the City at ten, came home at half-past five, and dined at seven. Mr. Podsnap's notions of the Arts in their integrity might have been stated thus. Literature; large print, respectfully descriptive of getting up at eight, shaving close at a quarter past, breakfasting at nine, going to the City at ten, coming home at half-past five, and dining at seven. Painting and Sculpture; models and portraits representing Professors of getting up at eight... Music; a respectable performance (without variations)... sedately expressive of getting up at eight..."

But Mr. Podsnap's greatest faculty lay in his ability to evade and dismiss all unpleasant realities "calculated to call a blush into a young person's cheek":

"There was a dignified conclusiveness—not to add a grand convenience—in this way of getting rid of disagreeables... 'I don't want to know about it; I don't choose to discuss it; I don't admit it!' Mr. Podsnap had even acquired a peculiar flourish of his right arm in often clearing the world of its most difficult problems, by sweeping them behind him..."

Should anyone stray into Podsnap's company and commit such a breach of etiquette as to refer to the death by starvation of paupers in the London streets, he was soon brushed aside:

"I must decline to pursue this painful discussion. It is not pleasant to my feelings... I... do not admit these things... If they do occur (not that I admit it), the fault lies with the sufferers themselves. It is not for *me*... to impugn the workings of Providence... The subject is a very disagreeable one... It is not one to be introduced among our wives and young persons..."[1]

Was Podsnap a conscious hypocrite? Possibly: but the

[1] Morris was later to publish extracts from this chapter in *Commonweal*.

working of man's conscience is a complex matter, and certainly many typical "Victorians" did not *feel* themselves to be hypocrites. Even the Podsnaps like to appear to themselves, as well as to others, as enlightened, humane, in the forefront of progress. To Matthew Arnold (whose *Culture and Anarchy* was published in 1869, the same year as a part of *The Earthly Paradise*) the middle classes were not so much hypocrites as the "Philistines", "mechanically worshipping their fetish of the production of wealth and of the increase of manufactures and population, and looking neither to the right nor left so long as this increase goes on". The Philistines, he said "have developed one side of their humanity at the expense of all others, and have become incomplete and mutilated men in consequence". The word "mutilated" gives a clue perhaps as important as any other in Matthew Arnold's book. The characteristic "Victorian" middle-class sensibility was made up of a veritable complex of involuntary inhibitions and evasions, the sum of which made up that shallow culture in which both sentimentality and hypocrisy flourished. The greatest evasion of all was to be found in the hallowing of the "laws of supply and demand", as "God's laws" or "Nature's simplest laws", to hide the fact of the exploitation of man by man. Around this central evasion a thousand others grew unchecked. The *rentier* class in the London suburbs, in the cathedral and university cities, might cultivate a love of nature or an interest in foreign missions and charities, while remaining in ignorance of the source of their own incomes. The sons of the self-made millowners were given an expensive education, which equipped them with an earnest sense of their own moral mission of leadership, for no better reason than that their fathers had been able to pay their fees. In every field of life and of art these evasions and this confusion of wealth with righteousness re-appear. In complex ways (which Butler was to lay bare in *The Way of All Flesh*) the reduction of human values to property values, the pressure of "respectability" and of orthodoxy, made the "Victorians" ashamed of all the vitalities of life which could not be harnessed to the chariot of "Self-Help". The middle classes eased their own consciences by accusing the poor of being guilty of indigence, intemperance, and sensual and sexual excess. Mrs. Grundy covered her bare skin down to her ankles, gathered her children close to her, and tightened her lips in hostility to life.

Of course, such a limitation of intellect and sensibility was not imposed suddenly and uniformly upon a whole class. Rather, it resembled a poison seeping through the veins of society, and yet continually resisted by the forces of life. These years are also years of great advances in scientific theory: of the battle between Darwinism and obscurantism: of the movement among women of the middle classes for educational, legal and professional rights: of the militant secularist and birth-control agitations in the face of Mrs. Grundy. But even these courageous opponents of "Victorian" attitudes revealed in one part or another of their outlook the same impoverished sensibility. Even the finest and most sensitive minds did not entirely escape the taint of this poison (not Dickens nor George Eliot nor Matthew Arnold) although the fight they put up was strenuous, and their victories many times more noble than their defeats.

Examine for a moment a judgement upon a painting from a critic who should not be called a "typical Victorian":

> "Go into the Dulwich Gallery, and meditate for a little over that much celebrated picture of the two beggar boys, one eating, lying on the ground, the other standing beside him. We have among our own painters one who. . . as a painter of beggar or peasant boys, may be set beside Murillo, or any one else,—W. Hunt. He loves peasant boys, because he finds them more roughly and picturesquely dressed, and more healthily coloured, than others. And he paints all that he sees in them fearlessly; all the health and humour, and freshness and vitality, together with such awkwardness and stupidity, and what else of negative or positive harm there may be in the creature; but yet so that on the whole we love it, and find it perhaps even beautiful, or if not, at least we see that there is capability of good in it, rather than of evil; and all is lighted up by a sunshine and sweet colour that makes the smock frock as precious as cloth of gold. But look at those two ragged

and vicious vagrants that Murillo has gathered out of the street. You smile at first, because they are eating so naturally, and their roguery is so complete. But is there anything else than roguery there, or was it well for the painter to give his time to the painting of those repulsive and wicked children? Do you feel moved with any charity towards children as you look at them? Are we the least bit more likely to take any interest in ragged schools, or to help the next pauper child that comes in our way, because the painter has shown us a cunning beggar feeding greedily? Mark the choice of the act. He might have shown hunger in other ways, and given interest to even this act of eating, by making the face wasted, or the eye wistful. But he did not care to do this. He delighted merely in the disgusting manner of eating, the food filling the cheek; the boy is not hungry, else he would not turn round to talk and grin as he eats.

"But observe another point in the lower figure. It lies so that the sole of the foot is turned towards the spectator; not because it would have lain less easily in another attitude, but that the painter may draw, and exhibit the grey dust engrained in the foot. The lesson, if there be any, in the picture, is not one whit the stronger. Do not call this the painting of nature; it is mere delight in foulness. We all know that a beggar's bare foot cannot be clean; there is no need to thrust its degradation into the light, as if no human imagination were vigorous enough for its conception."[1]

Here, side by side with those magnificent passages in *The Stones of Venice* which set young Morris's mind aflame, John Ruskin himself falls to the depths of "Victorian" sentiment. Even the "fearless" painting of "nature", it seems, must be done in such a way as to make poverty seem "picturesque", and to light up all "by a sunshine and sweet colour". Two children bear the full weight of the Prophet's indignation: the stops of Ruskin's rich moral organ are all opened: the boys are "ragged and vicious", "cunning", "repulsive and wicked", "gathered out of the street"—and all because they have committed the sin of being born poor. But this is not the only source of Ruskin's indignation. The poor are all very well, providing that they show signs of a sense of their own sin, and excite feelings of benevolence and charity which

[1] John Ruskin, *The Stones of Venice,* Vol. II, Ch. 6, sections 60-1.

flatter a middle-class beholder. Murillo's crime is to depict, not a "wasted" and "wistful" "pauper child", but the vitality of childhood (and even, perhaps, of the working class itself?) shattering the middle-class concepts of shamefaced suppliance on the one hand and righteous philanthropy on the other. The children are evil because they do not plead for charity and they do not care what the middle-class beholder thinks of them: they are guilty of open sensual indulgence ("the food filling the cheek"), and (the tone implies) they robbed the parson's orchard to get their apples without the least sense of guilt; and, final horror of all, they are not even ashamed of their own dirty feet. In short, they have committed the crime of being happy without the help of a philanthropist.

John Ruskin was to set aside some (but not all) of this rubbish in his middle and later years. But the fact that so fine a mind could be guilty of such lapses serves to emphasize Arnold's phrase, "mutilated men". The conscience and sensibility of men could not be cheapened without doing them injury. Where public professions and the facts of experience were at variance, where the culture of the past criticized the commonplace sentimentalities of the present, conflicts and tensions were bound to be set up in the individual's mind.

Despite the public applause of "progress", the daily experience of tens of thousands even among the professional workers in the great cities was far different:

> "The facts of life for most of us are a dark street, crowds, hurry, commonplaceness, loneliness, and worse than all a terrible doubt, which can hardly be named, as to the meaning and purpose of life",

wrote Mark Rutherford. Gerard Manley Hopkins, one of the few men who escaped the shallowness of his time, and who (whenever he dared to look) registered in the depths of his being the impact of the truths of his society, wrote in 1881 to Morris's old friend, Canon Dixon:

> "My Liverpool and Glasgow experience laid upon my mind a con-

viction, a truly crushing conviction, of the misery of town life to the poor and more than to the poor, of the misery of the poor in general, of the degradation even of our race, of the hollowness of this country's civilisation: it made even life a burden to me to have daily thrust upon me the things I saw."[1]

Both Mark Rutherford and Hopkins were exceptional men: but what they could feel and express was present as an incommunicable dissatisfaction among even their Philistine contemporaries. Personal experience and public utterances were at odds: the energies of life, however repressed, still sought an outlet. The more that is known of the lives of the great Victorians, the more the acute conflict in their minds becomes apparent. And these conflicts were present not only in the leaders of thought and of art. They are found in an hundred forms in the life of the Victorian middle class, revealing a vast accumulation of half-conscious anxieties and guilt.

This may help us to understand why almost no literature of permanent value was written during these years which voices the dominant faith in "progress" and "Self-Help": why, on the contrary (in the words of Mark Rutherford):

"The characteristic of so much that is said and written now is melancholy, and it is melancholy, not because of any deeper acquaintance with the secrets of man than that which was possessed by our forefathers, but because it is easy to be melancholy, and the time lacks strength."

"The time lacks strength"—a curious comment on the age of England's industrial supremacy, but one which, in its turn, may help us to understand the almost universal welcome given to *The Earthly Paradise* when it first appeared.

This welcome came from two apparently incompatible schools of thought. On one hand stood the utilitarians. Frederick Harrison, the positivist, had already aroused

[1] *Correspondence of G.M. Hopkins and R.W. Dixon* (1935), p. 97.

Matthew Arnold's wrath by setting forward the doctrine of the separation of the arts and public life. "The man of culture is in politics one of the poorest mortals alive. . . No assumption is too unreal, no end too unpractical for him."[1] Poetry was no *use* in public life, and might be actively dangerous by reason of its encouragement of unpractical idealism. On the other hand, *in its proper place,* it might be given the active encouragement of enlightened men. It was Morris's distinction (in the view of this school of critics) to have found this proper place in *The Earthly Paradise.* This was the opinion of the *Saturday Review,* which thought that a "busy material age" could find room for Morris's "clear and pellucid style", also, it seems, of the "political economists and scientific men" to whom most poetry was a "vexation of spirit".

It was Harrison's positivist colleague, John Morley, who applied the doctrine of the immunization of art with most sympathy to Morris. First, he welcomed Morris's liberation of poetry from theology, and "the turgid perplexities of a day of spiritual transition". While (he pointed out) Morris was careless not only of religion, but also of "the conventional aims and phrases of politics and philanthropy", Morley was prepared to accept this:

> "Morality is not the aim and goal of fine art. . . Art has for its end the Beautiful only. Morality, so far from being the essence of it, has nothing to do with it at all."[2]

This was a fairly comforting conclusion, since it meant that man's aspirations towards Beauty might be fed in quiet,

[1] Quoted by Matthew Arnold in the Introduction to *Culture and Anarchy:* "Culture is a desirable quality in a critic of new books, and sits well on a professor of *belles lettres:* but as applied to politics, it means simply a turn for small fault-finding, love of selfish ease, and indecision in action. The man of culture is in politics, &c."

[1] *The Fortnightly Review,* January 1st, 1867. This review does not refer directly to Morris, but indicates the standard by which Morley welcomed *The Earthly Paradise.*

without being to the detriment "of energetic social action in the country". Moreover, this relegation of poetry to a world of private satisfaction and escape, might in the end bring social fruits:

"Only on condition of this spacious and manifold energizing in diverse directions, can we hope in our time for that directly effective social action which some of us think calculated to give higher quality to the moments as they pass than art and song."[1]

This school welcomed *The Earthly Paradise,* then, quite simply because it was poetry of escape. For one thing—although this was stated only by implication—it was "safe". By retreating to a world of "Beauty" it did not ask that kind of question about the capitalist ethic which was so pronounced in the writings of Carlyle and Ruskin, and which appeared through the fitful mists of yearning of Tennyson's youthful poetry. Since it was safe, it had clearly found the proper place for poetry in the scheme of social advance. It could be read—and read publicly—by men of action and men of business as a mark of culture. But this line of argument was little more than a rationalization of more subterranean emotional currents—those same currents which were at work in Morris's own creative impulses. And so there was to be found another school of criticism, which also praised the escapism of the poem, but which started from different premises.

This was the school of Romanticism in its decline. Flaubert, watching the ravages upon the human spirit of the bourgeois victory in France, commented in *Madame Bovary:*

"Every bourgeois in the flush of his youth, were it but for a day, a moment, has believed himself capable of immense passions, of lofty enterprises. The most paltry libertine has dreamed of sultanas; every notary bears within him the debris of a poet."

[1] *The Fortnightly Review,* 1873, p. 476.

Writing in a not dissimilar vein, Morris commented in a letter to his wife, presumably about some middle-class acquaintance:

> "People like you speak about don't know either what life or death means, except for one or two supreme moments of their lives, when something pierces through the crust of dullness and ignorance, and they act for the time as if they were sensitive people."[1]

Both passages strike the authentic note of a time that "lacks strength" when melancholy is "easy". The flames of the Romantic Revolt could not be dowsed in a couple of decades. The Victorians may have been "mutilated men", but mutilation cannot be accomplished without pain. The embers of romanticism persisted, and they lacked only the wind of hope to fan them into flame. But desire without hope, as we have seen, turns into nostalgia, luxurious melancholy, individualist gestures of protest, self-pity, and all that complex of emotions springing from a self-absorbed dissatisfaction with life which has no outlet in action. Those who, like Edward Burne-Jones, had felt "exquisite misery" in brooding upon "Tears, Idle Tears" during the hot summer afternoons of their adolescence, found in *The Earthly Paradise* more food for indulging their melancholy. The *Academy* declared:

> "The main current of intellectual energy runs now to science and politics and history and prose-fiction. . . Poets themselves are a 'survival'; and it is the law of survivals to dwindle and become extinct; while there are any left they might be allowed to feed in peace upon their natural food, the transformed emotions which arise from a vanished, decaying past."[2]

The concluding image is extraordinarily apposite.

So, to the approval of a section of the utilitarians, there was added a chorus of praise from the reviewers who—while taking no objective action to revolt against the humdrum routines of their existence—still enjoyed the luxury of feeling

[1] *Letters*, p. 36. [2] *The Academy*, August 1st, 1873.

that they too, like Morris, were misfits "born out of due time", capable of "immense passions" and "lofty enterprises" in any other age. They looked to poetry to fulfil the task defined in France by Lesconte de Lisle—to "give an ideal life to those who no longer have a real one."[1] So we find that the reviewer of the *Pall Mall Gazette* (like the reviewer of *St. James's Magazine*) was a confirmed escapist, "glad to retire from the stress and the cares of his ugly workaday English life and be entertained... with that succession of gracious pictures... of a remote romantic world."[2] And so, indeed, was the reviewer in the popular *John Bull,* glad to be free from the "turmoil of the restless driving life" and the "fierce intellectual struggles" of his age, while Morris "tells us in strains most musical his quaint old-world stories."[3]

Just as Morley lifted the platitudes of the utilitarian critics to a more serious level of discussion, so among the escapists Walter Pater was to be found. In Pater we find full-blown the theories of Art for Art's Sake already implicit in Keats. To prevent the soiling of art by utilitarianism, to defend it from a "tarnished actual present", Morris was right, Pater thought, to project—

> "above the realities of its time a world in which the forms of things are transfigured. Of that world this new poetry takes possession, and sublimates beyond it another still fainter and more spectral, which is literally an artificial or 'earthly paradise'. It is a finer ideal, extracted from what in relation to any actual world is already an ideal... The secret of the enjoyment of it is that inversion of homesickness, that incurable thirst for the sense of escape, which no actual form of life satisfies..."[4]

Man's aspirations can never break through and be realized in life: they can only find relief in the creation of the Beautiful

[1] Quoted in G.V. Plekhanov, *Art and Social Life* (1953), p. 178.
[2] *Pall Mall Budget,* December 11th, 1869.
[3] *John Bull,* December 31st, 1870.
[4] *Westminster Review,* October, 1868: reprinted in the 1st edition of Pater's *Appreciations.*

in art; and, since Pater believed this to be true, it followed that artistic beauty of form became an end in itself.

The reception of *The Earthly Paradise,* then, gives an insight of extraordinary interest into the emotional cross-currents of the age, against which Morris was to be in such uncompromising revolt barely ten years later. It provoked throughout the reviews a discussion of "escapism" in art, in which the most incompatible schools of thought joined in Morris's praise. This discussion served to give rise to that theory of art, which Oscar Wilde—taking Morris as a leading example of the "English Renaissance of Art"—was later to defend:

> "Art never harms itself by keeping aloof from the social problems of the day: rather, by so doing, it more completely realizes that which we desire... Into the secure and sacred house of Beauty the true artist will admit nothing that is harsh or disturbing, nothing that gives pain, nothing that is debatable, nothing about which men argue."[1]

Moreover, this reception "placed" Morris in the mind of the Victorian reading public once and for all. He was the sweet unpractical singer, the poet of escape, of the Beautiful and the antique. When Morris began to reveal quite different capacities and attitudes, the public was either disappointed or refused to notice the change. When Morris shocked his public by appearing in the Thames Police Court on the charge of assaulting a policeman, he was sadly admonished by H.D. Traill in the *Saturday Review* to return to his "Earthly Paradise":

> "Were it not better that ye bore him hence,
> Muses, to that fair land where once he dwelt,
> And with those waters at whose brink he knelt
> (Ere faction's poison drugged the poet-sense)
> Bathed the unhappy eyes too prone to melt
> And see, through tears, men's woes as man's offence?"[2]

[1] Lecture, "The English Renaissance of Art", delivered in New York, January, 1882. See Davis, De Vane, and Bald, *op. cit.,* pp. 266-7.

[2] *Saturday Review,* September 26th, 1885.

In all this profusion of comment, the underlying note of the poem, the note of despair, received very little attention. A few reviewers commented upon it in passing, as proof that even Morris could not shake free entirely from the doubts of his age. Only one—Alfred Austin, writing in *Temple Bar*—faced the issue clearly, and drew some conclusions:

"The realities of the latter half of the nineteenth century suggest nothing to him save the averting of his gaze. They are crooked; who shall set them straight? For his part, he will not even try. . . He sings only for those who, like himself, have given up the age, its boasted spirit, its vaunted progress, its infinite vulgar nothings, and have taken refuge in the sleepy region."

In Austin's view, Morris was wise to "give the go-by" to an age which will be known to posterity as "the age of Railways, the age of Destructive Criticism, or the age of Penny Papers". On the other hand—

"in doing so not only has he not produced great poetry—he has evaded the very conditions on which alone the production of great poetry is possible. Even in co-operation with an age—as the present one, for instance—it may be impossible to develop it; but without that co-operation all hope of such is bootless and vain. . . [Morris] is not a great poet—at most and at best the wisely unresisting victim of a rude irreversible current; the serene martyr of a mean and melancholy time."[1]

What was the reaction of the poet himself to the critical controversy which he had stirred up? His letters reveal very little. The favourable reception of the poem gave him pleasure. When his publisher sent him Austin's unfavourable review his reply was untroubled:

"from the critical point of view I think there is so much truth as this in his article, as that we poets of to-day have been a good deal made by those of the Byron and Shelley time—however, in another sixty years

[1] *Temple Bar,* May and August, 1869. Later this bitter young critic was to accept the Poet Laureateship which Morris contemptuously rejected on Tennyson's death, and so provided an ironic commentary on the need to "co-operate with the age."

or so, when it won't matter three skips of a louse to us (as it don't matter much more now), I suppose we shall quietly fall into our places."[1]

When the whole poem was completed in 1870, he felt that the time hung on his hands:

"I confess I am dull now my book is done; one doesn't know sometimes how much service a thing has done us till it is gone: however one has time yet; and perhaps something else of importance will turn up soon."[2]

It was well enough for the critics to discuss the pros and cons of the poetry of escape: but for William Morris the despair he felt was no affectation but compulsive and real. When, in his last years, his despair had been overcome by his new hope for humanity, it is related that he "pooh-poohed the ideal beauty of *The Earthly Paradise,* and said that there was 'more real ideal' in *News from Nowhere*". "The best thing about it", he is reported to have said of *The Earthly Paradise,* "is its name". "Some day or other that will inspire others when every line of the blessed thing is forgotten. *That is* what we're all working for."[3]

[1] *Letters,* p. 28. [2] *Ibid.,* p. 37.
[3] Recollections of William Sharp in the *Atlantic Monthly,* December, 1896.

CHAPTER III

"LOVE IS ENOUGH"

IN 1871 Morris was already at work on his next poem, *Love is Enough.* "He makes a poem these days", wrote Edward Burne-Jones—

"in dismal Queen Square in black old filthy London in dull end of October he makes a pretty poem that is to be wondrously happy; and it has four sets of lovers in it and THEY ARE ALL HAPPY; and it ends well and will come out some time next summer and I shall make little ornaments to it—such is Top in these days."[1]

The poem—despite Rossetti's praise—has very few virtues. At times it captures a mellow note of melancholy:

"Rather caught up at hazard is the pipe
That mixed with scent of roses over-ripe,
And murmer of the summer afternoon,
May charm you somewhat with its wavering tune
'Twixt joy and sadness. . ."

But even this is submerged in the after-traces of that "maze of re-writing and despondency" in which—in Morris's own words—it was written. The technical intricacies of the poem's structure, which have sometimes been praised, are largely mechanical. The characters (except perhaps the sentimentalized rustics with whom the poem opens and concludes) are mere shadows of the shadows in *The Earthly Paradise.* The long lines with their facile rhythm in which the "dramatic" portions of the poem are written seem to have such a deadly langour of feeling and emptiness of thought that they must pause at each line-ending for breath, and only with an effort of will can either poet or reader gather his energies for the

[1] *Memorials,* II, p. 23.

next. The narrative itself is a sort of shadow, reminiscent in parts of "The Land East of the Moon and West of the Sun", and the poetry of mood, divorced from any particularities of events, situations or relationships, relapses again and again into either rhetoric or cliché. It is a poem which might as well be forgotten—the lowest ebb of Morris's creative life.

Only in the "music"—the lyrics which intersperse the scenes of the narrative—does any genuine impulse behind the poem find expression:

"Love is enough: draw near and behold me
Ye who pass by the way to your rest and your laughter,
And are full of the hope of the dawn coming after;
For the strong of the world have bought me and sold me
And my house is all wasted from threshold to rafter,
—Pass by me, and hearken, and think of me not!

* * * * *

"Ye know not how void is your hope and your living:
Depart with your helping lest yet ye undo me!
Ye know not that at nightfall she draweth near to me,
There is soft speech between us and words of forgiving
Till in dead of the midnight her kisses thrill through me.
—Pass by me and hearken, and waken me not!

"Wherewith will ye buy it, ye rich who behold me?
Draw out from your coffers your rest and your laughter,
And the fair gilded hope of the dawn coming after!
Nay this I sell not,—though ye bought me and sold me,—
For your house stored with such things from threshold to rafter.
—Pass by me, I hearken, and think of you not!"

This verse is less like music than embroidery, with its repeated decorative motifs, its leisurely movement, its moody imprecise vocabulary. Just for a moment the languorous movement of the rhythm is broken—"Nay this I sell not"—and real feeling struggles to enter. Here is the impulse of the poem: it is a logical continuation of the feeling expressed in the "Apology" to *The Earthly Paradise.* If the world is crooked, if everything is soiled by the ethic of buying and selling, then at least the value of life may be found in those personal relationships which can be defended from the crooked world. "Love is Enough" because it is a human and not a cash relationship.

This is straightforward enough. But in Morris's handling it is found not as a prevailing attitude but as an assertion, and the assertion is never felt to carry conviction. In fact, "Love" is not presented in the poem as a human relationship, but as a languorous yearning, a saturation of the senses, a weakening of the will, in short, as the attraction of the unconscious. Indeed, towards the end of the narrative the longing for death and the yearning for "Love" become almost indistinguishable. The muddy movement of the poem suggests that Morris was so possessed by the desire to escape from some important fact in his conscious thoughts that he was incapable of fashioning his experience into convincing art. The superficial subject may be "Love", but the underlying theme is the desire for unconsciousness and death.

The poem itself is unworthy of Morris, and may be dismissed. But the bearing which it may have upon Morris's personal life is important. J.W. Mackail, the first serious biographer of Morris, was the son-in-law of Georgie Burne-Jones, and he had access not only to her memories but also to intimate letters which were later destroyed. He confessed in a private letter of 1899 that his account of "all those stormy years of *The Earthly Paradise* time and the time following it must be excessively flat", owing to the amount of tact ("a quality unpleasantly near untruthfulness often") that "had to be exercised right and left".[1] In his biography he permitted himself only the comment that in the verses for the Months in *The Earthly Paradise* "there is an autobiography so delicate and so outspoken that it must needs be left to speak for itself". Recurrent in several of these poems is the theme of failure in love—the failure to establish a relationship of true confidence and intimacy, the longing of

[1] Philip Henderson, *William Morris* (1973 edition), p. 120.

an intense love not fully reciprocated. It finds its finest expression in the beautiful verses for January:

"From this dull rainy undersky and low,
This murky ending of a leaden day,
That never knew the sun, this half-thawed snow,
These tossing black boughs faint against the grey
Of gathering night, thou turnest, dear, away
Silent, but with thy scarce-seen kindly smile
Sent through the dusk my longing to beguile."

Then the lamps in the house are lit:

"There, the lights gleam, and all is dark without!
And in the sudden change our eyes meet dazed—
O look, love, look again! the veil of doubt
Just for one flash, past counting, then was raised!
O eyes of heaven, as clear thy sweet soul blazed
On mine a moment! O come back again
Strange rest and dear amid the dull long pain!"

It is a simple and moving image—the sudden darkening of the windows suggesting both the fear of mortality and the hostility and emptiness of the outside world, and emphasizing the dependence of the lovers upon each other. But the flash of confidence is momentary:

"Nay, nay, gone by! though there she sitteth still,
With wide grey eyes so frank and fathomless—
Be patient, heart, thy days they yet shall fill
With utter rest—Yea, now thy pain they bless
And feed thy last hope of the world's redress—
O unseen hurrying rack! O wailing wind!
What rest and where go ye this night to find?"

The struggle to establish the relationship is neither won nor admitted as lost: and yet in its outcome Morris rests his "last hope of the world's redress", his touchstone of value. And meanwhile, without, those symbols of hurrying mortality, the dark clouds and the wind, can be sensed. There is no poem or sequence in *Love is Enough* which is so strangely moving, or whose imagery carries the same conviction.

When so much of the poetry which Morris wrote at this time bears the mark of carelessness and shallow feeling, one is justified in taking those poems where a deep and personal feeling is expressed as bearing some direct relation to his personal life. This is confirmed by a group of poems, written during this period which Morris suppressed during his own lifetime, and which were later published by his daughter, May.[1] Since Morris was rarely reluctant to publish his own work, it is clear that these poems were written without publication in mind, in an effort to express and master his own perplexities and despair. One of the most striking of these poems is "The Doomed Ship":

> "The doomed ship drives on helpless through the sea,
> All that the mariners may do is done
> And death is left for men to gaze upon,
> While side by side two friends sit silently;
> Friends once, foes once, and now by death made free
> Of Love and Hate, of all things lost or won;
> Yet still the wonder of that strife bygone
> Clouds all the hope or horror that may be.
>
> "Thus, Sorrow, are we sitting side by side
> Amid this welter of the grey despair,
> Nor have we images of foul or fair
> To vex, save of thy kissed face of a bride,
> Thy scornful face of tears when I was tried,
> And failed neath pain I was not made to bear."

The astringency of this poem, the unified imagery, and the absence of heroic or romantic posturing, is in marked contrast to the published poetry of this period.

Another unfinished poem of this time demands a biographical interpretation. The poem, after the first verse and a half, is put into the mouth of the beloved:

[1] *Works*, Vol. XXIV, pp. 347-66, and May Morris, I, pp. 538-9.

"Why doest thou struggle, strive for victory
Over my heart that loveth thine so well?
When Death shall one day have its will of thee
And to deaf ears thy triumph thou must tell.

"Unto deaf ears or unto such as know
The hearts of dead and living wilt thou say:
A childish heart there loved me once, and lo
I took his love and cast his love away.

"A childish greedy heart! yet still he clung
So close to me that much he pleased my pride
And soothed a sorrow that about me hung
With glimpses of his love unsatisfied—

"And soothed my sorrow—but time soothed it too
Though ever did its aching fill my heart
To which the foolish child still closer drew
Thinking in all I was to have a part.

"But now my heart grown silent of its grief
Saw more than kindness in his hungry eyes:
But I must wear a mask of false belief
And feign that nought I knew his miseries.

"I wore a mask, because though certainly
I loved him not, yet there was something soft
And sweet to have him ever loving me:
Belike it is I well-nigh loved him oft—

"Nigh loved him oft, and needs must grant to him
Some kindness out of all he asked of me
And hoped his love would still hang vague and dim
About my life like half-heard melody.

"He knew my heart and over-well knew this
And strove, poor soul, to pleasure me herein;
But yet what might he do some doubtful kiss
Some word, some look might give him hope to win.

"Poor hope, poor soul, for he again would come
Thinking to gain yet one more golden step
Towards Love's shrine, and lo the kind speech dumb
The kind look gone, no love upon my lip—

"Yea gone, yet not my fault, I knew of love
But my love and not his; how could I tell
That such blind passion in him I should move?
Behold I have loved faithfully and well;

"Love of my love so deep and measureless
O lords of the new world this too ye know. . ."

At this point the poem breaks off. It would be of the greatest interest if the date could be established. In its flexibility of psychological insight, in following through the paradoxical logic of human feeling, and in the manner in which the rhythm probes, hesitates, returns and moves forward with renewed confidence, only to hesitate again—in all this it is strongly reminiscent of the Morris who wrote *The Defence of Guenevere:* and yet throughout there is a note of disillusion which sets it apart.

These two poems most probably belong to the years between 1867 and 1870, and the lament over unreciprocated love is persistent in other poems of the same period. Quite clearly, Morris felt that his marriage with Jane Burden had failed: and this failure was the source of profound unhappiness. The Pre-Raphaelite courtship of Jane Burden, leading to their marriage in 1859, has already been discussed. "Calf love, mistaken for a heroism that shall be life-long, yet early waning into disappointment. . .": "the unhappiness that comes of man and woman confusing the relations between natural passion, and sentiment, and the friendship which, when things go well, softens the awakening from passing illusions"—perhaps these two phrases of old Hammond in *News from Nowhere* carry a part of Morris's judgment upon his own marriage. The earliest years of their marriage, in the days of Red House and the birth of their two daughters—Jenny (born in 1861) and May (in 1862)—seem to have been happy enough. But it was in the nature of things that Morris, confronted in marriage not with the high romantic ideal of *The Defence of Guenevere,* but with a real person, should have striven to create a new and truer relationship—one of mutual confidence, companionship and intellectual equality. And it was in this attempt, in the passing from romantic enchantment to intimacy, that he met with failure.

And yet, was it human intimacy he sought, or was there still a restless yearning in his romantic impulses for some intense idealized experience, seeking in Love, as in art, a refuge from life, "midmost the beating of the steely sea"?

Certainly, the idealization of Love, the "last hope of the world's redress", both in *The Earthly Paradise* and *Love is Enough,* suggests that this was also present in his mood. Whichever impulse was dominant—that towards closer human intimacy, or that towards some idealized "union of souls"—both foundered on the rock of Janey's passivity. Throughout she remains the enigma in the relationship. Perhaps unresponsive by nature or through the inhibitions of her upbringing, perhaps spoilt by the attention of poets and painters, it seems that she had allowed herself to fall into a character of inaccessible beauty, and to wear not only the Pre-Raphaelite draperies designed by Morris, but also the airs of a Guenevere. All accounts agree upon her strange, moody beauty, her poise and majestic presence—and also on her silence. For many years she was the victim of unexplained ailments, which seem to have had some nervous origin. Her letters (the few which are published, or are open to inspection) reveal no more than an ordinary concern for the details of life, with an undertone of dissatisfaction, occasionally of self-pity.[1] "I fancy that her mystic beauty must sometimes have weighed rather heavily upon her", wrote Graham Robertson in half-serious reminiscence:

> "Her mind was not formed upon the same tragic lines as her face; she was very simple and could have enjoyed simple pleasures with simple people, but such delights were not for her. . . She was a Ladye in a Bower, an ensorcelled Princess, a Blessed Damozel, while I feel sure she would have preferred to be a 'bright, chatty little woman' in request for small theatre parties and afternoons up the river. . ."[2]

And in this banter there may be a truth which more solemn observers overlooked. Certainly, Morris's letters to her

[1] See Helen Rossetti Angeli, *Dante Gabriel Rossetti* (1949), p. 210. A few noncommittal letters on family matters, with the same mournful undertone, are in Brit. Mus. Add. MSS. 45341.

[2] W.G. Robertson, *Time Was* (1931), p. 94.

especially in the middle and later years of their marriage, while always affectionate—even dutiful—are in marked contrast to his letters to Georgie Burne-Jones or Aglaia Coronio. Largely concerned with domestic affairs, they sheer away from any topic requiring intellectual or imaginative effort: and in one of the last letters (at the end of 1870) when he touches on such a topic, he breaks off with a confession of failure:

> "For me I don't think people really want to die because of mental pain, that is if they are imaginative people; they want to live to see the play played out fairly—they have hopes they are not conscious of—Hillao! here's cheerful talk for you. I beg your pardon, dear, with all my heart."[1]

In this context, the poem "Why doest thou struggle?" may be seen as a sensitive chart of their relationship:

> "I wore a mask, because though certainly
> I loved him not, yet there was something soft
> And sweet to have him loving me:
> Belike it is I well-nigh loved him oft—"

Every approach (as it seemed to Morris) was met by Janey's passivity, her melancholy self-absorption—perhaps by the conventionality and inhibitions suggested by the "rags of pride and shame" of another poem in this group.[2] In moments of passion he felt they had attained to an intimacy which eluded him in its aftermath: surely this is one of the sources of that constant oscillation between sensuous desire and emptiness or horror to be found throughout *The Earthly Paradise?* On Janey's side he surmised not an unwillingness, but an inability to respond:

> "I knew of love
> But my love and not his; how could I tell
> That such blind passion in him I should move?"

[1] *Letters,* p. 36. [2] See *Works,* Vol. XXIV, p. 360, "Song".

Perhaps he felt at times bitterness at her lack of response to his efforts to make their relationship anew. But gradually an acceptance of failure prevailed—the mood of the "Doomed Ship"—and with this (in fact implicit in the recognition of failure rather than the imputation against her of blame) a continued but diminished love. After all, it was he who, in the days of Launcelot and Guenevere, had helped to create the image which could not now respond.

Janey, it seems, was not the kind of person to take much blame upon herself for this failure, although she may well have been wounded by Morris's evident disillusion. As she grew older, her personality seems to have grown less, rather than more, sympathetic, and her air of aloof discontent to have become more marked. At what stage Rossetti became the centre of her interest it is impossible to say: but there seems to be no reason to give much credit to Hall Caine's story that they had loved each other since the days of the painting of the Oxford Union. Whatever sympathy existed between the beautiful model and the romantic young painter in earlier days, Janey and Rossetti were drawn together in the late 1860s after an emotional separation had already begun to take place between her and Morris.

From 1867 onwards Janey and Rossetti were often in each other's company. She was the model who dominated Rossetti's artistic imagination, and, as Professor Doughty has established, Rossetti's "regenerate rapture" in his love for Janey inspired much of *The House of Life* and many other poems of this period.[1] In 1870 and 1871 they were customarily to be seen together at social occasions in artistic circles: at Ford Madox Brown's receptions in Fitzroy Square, where Janey, "in her ripest beauty, and dressed in a long, unfashionable gown of ivory velvet, occupied the painting-throne, and Dante Gabriel Rossetti. . . too stout for elegance, squatted . . . on a hassock at her feet"; or (again at Brown's) among "anarchists, poets, musicians, all kinds and sorts", "Rossetti

[1] See Doughty, *op. cit.*, pp. 378f.

and Mrs. Morris sitting side by side in state, being worshipped"; or, at the receptions of Marston, the dramatist, Rossetti would be seen "sitting beside Mrs. Morris, who looked as if she had stepped out of any one of his pictures, both wrapped in motionless silence as of a world where souls have no need of words", or (more prosaically) he was "seated in a corner feeding Mrs. William Morris with strawberries", and carefully scraping off the cream, which was bad for her, before presenting them to her in a spoon.[1] Even in her Bohemianism the same impression of Janey's silence and passivity prevails.

It was in 1871 that Kelmscott Manor was taken on a joint tenancy by Morris and Rossetti, and there is no doubt that Morris hoped it would provide a home where Janey and the children could share Rossetti's company during his own absence. For similar motives, he paid his first visit to Iceland in this year. The theme of an uncompleted novel of this period (and the theme of several poems, written both now and later) concerned the love of two brothers (or friends) for the same woman: in the 1880s he returned to the theme in *The Pilgrims of Hope,* where both the sorrow and the magnanimity of the husband whose wife has fallen in love with his friend finds expression. Both in *News from Nowhere* and in a letter written in later years he stated clearly his belief that husband and wife in married life must remain "free people": "artificial bolstering up of natural human relations is what I object to". The enforcement of a property-contract when sentiment no longer went with it was immoral and odious to him; equally he rejected any jealous sense of property-rights in love. While the withdrawal of Janey's love from him caused him grief and pain, her attachment to Rossetti did not seem to him necessarily to exclude a continuing friendship between all three. Had the situation been reversed, and Janey been, in conventional terms, the "injured party", the orthodox Victorian moralists would probably have advised her to

[1] See Doughty, *op. cit.,* pp. 452f.

"suffer in silence". But for a *man* to do the same ran counter to every clause in the code of Mrs. Grundy. For Morris was prepared not only to talk about equality and respect for the rights of women, he was prepared to recognize this equality in his own actions.

Towards Rossetti, Morris's old feelings of admiration and friendship were changing, it is true. "I have been backwards and forwards to Kelmscott a good deal this summer & autumn", he wrote to Aglaia Coronio in October, 1872, "but shall not go there so often now as Gabriel is come there, and talks of staying permanently."[1] Two weeks later, he wrote to her of a visit to Kelmscott: "the *days* went well enough: but Lord how dull the evenings were: with William Rossetti also to help us. Janey was looking and feeling much better."[2] His acquaintance, C.F. Murray, related to A.C. Benson that Morris "grew almost to hate Rossetti down at Kelmscott: he had the natural dislike of the perfectly healthy man for the unhealthy man".[3] Rossetti was a changed man from the days of the painting fraternity at Oxford: and in the early 'seventies he could be seen to be degenerating year by year. His short-lived marriage with Lizzie Siddal had ended in tragedy. He was becoming now the victim of laudanum, obsessed by morbid fears and a sense of persecution, arrogant to the neighbours at Kelmscott, increasingly losing his old ebullience in self-absorption. There are reasons enough to explain the estrangement between the two friends, even without this greater complication.

Moreover, it must have become clear to Morris that his friend's attachment to Janey was becoming obsessional. Perhaps Morris had hoped that the summer of 1871, when Janey and Rossetti were at Kelmscott and he was in Iceland, would be only a passing interlude: and that the two would outgrow their attachment. Perhaps Rossetti also, on the eve

[1] *Letters*, p. 47. [2] *Ibid.*, p. 49.
[3] A.C. Benson, *Memories and Friends*, p. 214.

of his departure from Kelmscott that summer, intended to break free from Janey:

> "And now the mustering rooks innumerable
> Together sail and soar,
> While for the day's death, like a tolling knell,
> Unto the heart they seem to cry, Farewell,
> No more, Farewell, no more!"

But no decision was taken. At the end of August, shortly before Morris's return, Rossetti was speaking of "keeping the house on".[1] Next year, separated from Janey and suffering from Buchanan's attack on the "Fleshly School of Poetry", he attempted suicide. On his recovery, he returned to Janey at Kelmscott, writing to Madox Brown: "Had I not renewed correspondence and resolved to come here, I should never have got a bit better or been able to take up work. . ."[2] For the next two or three years Rossetti and Janey were much in each other's company, and thereafter Janey visited him (although less frequently) until his last years.[3]

The clearest insight into Morris's own feelings comes only at this period, in letters addressed to his friend, Aglaia Coronio. On November 25th, 1872, he was writing:

> "When I said there was no cause for my feeling low, I meant that my friends had not changed at all towards me in any way and that there had been no quarrelling: and indeed I am afraid it comes from some cowardice and unmanliness in me. One thing wanting ought not to go for so much: nor indeed does it spoil my enjoyment of life always, as I have often told you: to have real friends and some sort of an aim in life is so much, that I ought still to think myself lucky: and often in my

[1] W.M. Rossetti, *Letters and Memoir of Dante Gabriel Rossetti*, Vol. II, p. 244.

[2] Angeli, *op. cit.*, p. 215.

[3] Hall Caine, *Recollections of Rossetti* (1928), p. 141, speaks of the "rare and valued visits" from Janey in Rossetti's last years, when Caine was living with him. In 1874 Morris offered to surrender his half-share of the tenancy of Kelmscott since Rossetti had "fairly taken to living [there] which I suppose neither of us thought the other would do when we first began the joint possession": Henderson, *op. cit.*, p. 179.

better moods I wonder what it is in me that throws me into such rage and despair at other times. I suspect, do you know, that some such moods would have come upon me at times even without this failure of mine."

"One thing wanting", "this failure of mine"—these phrases remind us directly of the poems, and suggest that Morris was far from any mood of recrimination. The letter continues:

"I am so glad to have Janey back again: her company is always pleasant and she is very kind & good to me—furthermore, my intercourse with G. [Georgie Burne-Jones] has been a good deal interrupted; not from any coldness of hers, or violence of mine; but from so many untoward nothings; then you have been away so that I have had nobody to talk to about things that bothered me... Another quite selfish business is that Rossetti has set himself down at Kelmscott as if he never meant to go away; and not only does that keep me from that harbour of refuge (because it is really a farce our meeting when we can help it) but also he has all sorts of ways so unsympathetic with the sweet simple old place, that I feel his presence there as a kind of slur on it: this is very unreasonable when one thinks why one took the place, and how this year it has really answered that purpose: nor do I think I should feel this about it if he had not been so unromantically discontented with it & the whole thing which made me very angry and disappointed... O how I long to keep the world from narrowing on me, and to look at things bigly and kindly!

"I am going to try to get to Iceland next year, hard as it will be to drag myself away from two or three people in England: but I know there will be a kind of rest in it, let alone the help it will bring me from physical reasons. I know clearer now perhaps than then what a blessing & help last year's journey was to me; what horrors it saved me from."[1]

On January 23rd, 1873, he wrote to the same friend:

"Don't be alarmed for any domestic tragedy; nothing has happened to tell of and my dullness comes all out of my own heart; and—in short I am ashamed of it and don't like talking of it."

[1] *Letters*, pp. 50-1.

The letter continues with details of domestic changes. They have moved into a small house in Hammersmith, keeping the house in Queen Square for the work of the Firm. "I keep my study and little bedroom here, and I dare say as time goes on shall live here a good deal." The new house "will suit Janey and the children".

> "It is some ½ hour's walk from the Grange [the Burne-Jones's new house in Fulham] which makes it quite a little way for me; on the other hand I can always see anyone I want at Queen Sq.: quite safe from interruption: so in all ways it seems an advantage—does it not?"

The letter concludes with a further reference to Iceland: the voyage "will be a necessity to me this year: sometimes I like the idea of it, and sometimes it fills me with dismay".[1]

Throughout these years Morris was the victim of successive waves of the deepest depression. The sympathy which he had lost in his relations with Janey, he sought increasingly in his friendship with Georgie Burne-Jones. At about this time, it became one of the only constant habits of his life to visit the "Grange" every Sunday morning for breakfast, and spend the morning with Burne-Jones and his wife. His letters to her carry a warmth that is quite lacking from his letters to Janey. Certainly their friendship was close and without reserve.[2]

As it was, Morris's friendship with Georgie never replaced that feeling of loss, that sense of "one thing wanting", that accompanied him to the end of his life. For the moment he took refuge in work, applying himself to his translations from the Icelandic and his work with the Firm. Occasionally he referred in his letters to his moods of depression:

[1] *Ibid.*, p. 52.

[2] At about this time Edward Burne-Jones was also having a love affair (with Marie Zambaco), and, as Henderson and Lindsay have noted, this may have thrown Georgie and Morris even more closely together: P. Henderson, *William Morris* (1973 edition), p. 124-5; J. Lindsay, *William Morris* (1975), pp. 151-168; O. Doughty and R. Wahl (eds.), *Letters of Dante Gabriel Rossetti* (1965), II, p. 685.

"I am ashamed of myself for these strange waves of unreasonable passion: it seems so unmanly: yet indeed I have a good deal to bear considering how hopeful my earlier youth was, & what overweening ideas I had of the joys of life,"

he wrote to Aglaia Coronio in March, 1875. And, a few days later:

"I am in the second half of my life now; which is like to be a busy time with me, I hope till the very end: a time not lacking content too, I fancy, I must needs call myself a happy man on the whole: and I do verily think I have gone over every possible misfortune that may happen to me in my own mind, and concluded that I can bear it if it should come."[1]

Occasionally he expressed the fear that he might be losing creative inspiration:

"My translations go on apace, but I am doing nothing original: it can't be helped, though sometimes I begin to fear that I am losing my invention. You know I very much wish not to fall off in imagination and enthusiasm as I grow older. . ."[2]

Once or twice he cast a regretful glance back to the days of his youthful ideals, those "well-remembered days when all adventure was ahead!"

"Manly", "unmanly"—these are words as important in Morris's vocabulary as "hope". They reveal a quality in him which was absent in the characteristic make-up of the Victorian romantic. Man ought to be the master of his emotions, not their victim: if there was sorrow and disappointment in his life, he must not indulge in the luxuries of self-pity, but master them and fit himself to the work of the world in its despite. As the influence of Iceland and of the old sagas grew upon him, so this mood in him drew nourishment:

[1] Morris to Mrs. Alfred Baldwin, *Letters*, p. 67. [2] *Ibid.*, p. 53.

"Ah! shall Winter mend your case?
Set your teeth the wind to face.
Beat the snow, tread down the frost!
All is gained when all is lost."[1]

Moreover, as he became in later years more possessed by new and wider "hope", so all references to his private despondency and failure cease. The matter, perhaps, was never mentioned in his last years, except with his closest friend, Georgie Burne-Jones. Wilfred Scawen Blunt, a friend of his later years (although not a close friend) with that intuitive sense which seems always a shade too clever for the genuine insight of sympathy, detected something of it: "One thing only, I think, he did not know, much as he had written about it, the love of women, and that he never cared to discuss."[2] In general there was a surprising absence of comment among his contemporaries. If there were secrets, they were well kept. Morris's family and friends long outlived him, and no doubt it was delicacy towards their feelings which prevented comment.[3]

Perhaps (since the matter went for many years undiscussed) it were better passed over in silence now. And yet, without this knowledge, much would remain unexplained in Morris's life and in his writing. A relationship can rarely stand without alteration throughout changing years: the relations between Morris and Janey may well have degenerated in the last years of his life. Jane Morris, in her spoiled and indifferent way, was hostile to Morris's Socialist views, activities and friends. At the suppers on Sunday evenings in Kelmscott House, when the comrades gathered, she was usually absent. "Will you

[1] *The Academy*, March, 1871.

[2] Wilfred Scawen Blunt, *My Diaries* (1919), Part One, pp. 30-1.

[3] Jane Morris lived until 1914, Lady Burne-Jones until 1920, while May Morris, who kept a careful supervision over all manuscripts in her possession died in 1938. Certain letters between Rossetti and Jane Morris not available to me in the first edition are discussed by R.C.H. Briggs, "Letters to Janey", *Journal of the William Morris Society*, Vol. I, No. 4, Summer 1964. See also Philip Henderson's perceptive discussion of the relationship in his *William Morris* (1973 edition), pp. 128-140, which draw upon Rossetti's letters to Janey.

. . . come over tomorrow?" we find him writing at the end of his life to Andreas Scheu, one of his closest friends among the Socialists: "There will be no one to object to you as I am alone with the girls at present."[1] When Morris died, many of the comrades—in defence to Janey's known feelings—were absent from the funeral. Even Shaw, the irrepressible, felt embarrassment in her company:

"I always felt apologetic with Mrs. Morris. I knew that the sudden eruption into her temple of beauty, with its pre-Raphaelite priests, of the proletarian comrades who began to infest the premises as Morris's fellow-Socialists, must be horribly disagreeable to her. . . Fortunately she did not take much notice of me. She was not a talker: in fact she was the silentest woman I have ever met. She did not take much notice of anybody, and none whatever of Morris, who talked all the time."

The times when she broke silence were therefore memorable. Shaw, as a vegetarian, was forced—when dining with them—to reject the main dish:

"Mrs. Morris did not conceal her contempt for my folly. At last pudding time came; and as the pudding was a particularly nice one, my abstinence vanished and I showed signs of a healthy appetite. Mrs. Morris pressed a second helping on me, which I consumed to her entire satisfaction. Then she said, 'That will do you good: there is suet in it.' And that is the only remark, as far as I can remember, that was ever addressed to me by this beautiful stately and silent woman, whom the Brotherhood and Rossetti had succeeded in consecrating."[2]

But where Shaw could find humour, Morris may have found wasteful conflict and misery. In the manuscript of an unfinished prose romance of his last years, *The Story of Desiderius,* there is a character who seems closely modelled upon Rossetti in his decline, and a woman is drawn who is the very image of the woman who recurs so often in his earlier writing. This time she is above forty years of age:

[1] Morris to Scheu, March 11th, 1895, *Socialist Review,* May, 1928.

[2] May Morris, II, pp. xxiv-xxv.

"Her face was like the marble image of a good imaginer, so right and true were all the lines therein, and so shapely was the compass of it. Dark smooth and fine was her hair, her lips full and red, her skin smooth and clear of hue, her limbs and all her body excellently fashioned, her eyes great and grey... and seeming as if they were the very windows of a true and simple soul."

One is reminded at once of a poem of *The Earthly Paradise* period, "Near But Far Away":

> "She wavered, stopped and turned, methought her eyes,
> The deep grey windows of her heart, were wet,
> Methought they softened with a near regret..."[1]

But in this later picture there is a significant and terrible change. All this was "only seeming". In truth, she was "a friend in the morning, a stranger at mid-day, a foe in the evening". Beneath her beautiful presence she was indifferent and cruel: "she cared for no soul of man or beast what grief might happen to them". "Lovers had she had in her time, and yet had: yet had their love lasted but a little while: for presently they found that there was nought to be loved in her save her fair body."[2] Can this be the last portrait which the most famous of the Pre-Raphaelite models sat to—and would it be only charity to suppose it to be as unfairly distorted as the previous ones were idealized?

However this may be—and however Morris may have felt in his moods of depression—he maintained some affection and loyalty towards her to the last. But it is in *News from Nowhere* that the depths of his sense of loss, of "one thing wanting", are made plain. Into his portrait of Ellen, the girl who guided him up the Thames to Kelmscott Manor, are projected all those qualities he desired to find: and in the suggestion of the emergent relationship between Ellen and the narrator there will be found that tenderness, frank intimacy, comradeship and equal intellectual exchange, which he could envisage

[1] May Morris, I, p. 538. [2] Brit. Mus. Add. MSS. 45328.

between the lovers of the future and yet which he knew he could never achieve in his own life.

Ellen is far different from the remote and languorous type of the Pre-Raphaelite ideal. Even in repose "She was far from languid; her idleness being the idleness of a person, strong and well-knit both in body and mind, deliberately resting". She is suffused with an "indefinable interest and pleasure of life", her beauty "interfused with energy". She is without affectation or false reserve. Their love grows until the moment when they sit down to the feast in Kelmscott Manor, and the narrator suddenly realizes that he has become unnoticed by all the company:

> "I turned to Ellen. . . but her bright face turned sad directly, and she shook her head with a mournful look, and the next moment all consciousness of my presence had faded from her face.
>
> "I felt lonely and sick at heart past the power of words to describe."

The loss is final and without retrieve:

> "Ellen's last mournful look seemed to say, 'No, it will not do; you cannot be of us; you belong so entirely to the unhappiness of the past that our happiness even would weary you.' "

But the loss does not bring the emptiness of his middle years. Now there is hope within it—not for himself, it is true—but still the compensation of having seen his aspirations fulfilled in the lives of others in a future time:

> "She had arisen and was standing on the edge of the bent, the light wind stirring her dainty raiment, one hand laid on her bosom, the other arm stretched downward and clenched in her earnestness.
>
> " 'It is true', she said, 'it is true! We have proved it true!' "

CHAPTER IV

HOPE AND COURAGE

I. Kelmscott

WE have come a long way from the conventional picture of William Morris—the bluff, uncomplicated extrovert. But it would be a mistake to draw the other picture—the picture of conflict and of restless despair—in too uncompromising lines. During these years between 1866 and 1876, Morris found a hundred sources of interest and enjoyment. The work of the Firm went ahead at an amazing rate. His two daughters, Jenny and May, were growing up. His frequent visits to Kelmscott Manor, on the Gloucestershire-Oxfordshire border, brought relaxation and refreshment to his senses.

It might almost have seemed that he was in danger of forgetting, like so many of his circle, the fervour of his early revolt, and of withdrawing altogether to the consolations of his poetry and the work of the Firm. He was coming to react against the more extreme affectations of romanticism:

> "Just because I string a few rhymes together, they call me dreamy and unpractical, I can't help writing verses, I must do it, but I'm just as much a business man as any of them",

he once said. In the war scare of 1859-60, just after his marriage, he had joined the Volunteers. If his dress and his manners, in the early 1870s, were still considered by the orthodox to be eccentric, this was simply because he consulted his own convenience and was indifferent to conventional canons: he had little desire to enrage the Respectable and the Good. His private misery he concealed behind a self-sufficient manner which observers (from this time until his death) often confused with self-centredness, or lack of "warmth and responsiveness".[1] To Rossetti he appeared (not

[1] Angeli, *op. cit.*, pp. 110 f., 210.

surprisingly) "insolently solid": while the Hon. Mrs. George Howard (later Lady Carlisle), for whom Philip Webb had built and Morris had decorated a house in Kensington in 1868, recorded her impressions of him in 1870, when he visited her country home:

"Morris arrived early this morning... He was rather shy—so was I —I felt that he was taking an experimental plunge among 'barbarians' [*Culture and Anarchy*, with its characterization of the aristocracy as 'barbarians', had appeared in the previous year]... However, he has grown more urbane—and even three hours has worked off much of our mutual shyness—A walk in the glen made me know him better and like him more than I fancied I should. He talks so clearly and seems to think so clearly that what seems paradox in Webb's mouth in his seems convincing sense. He lacks sympathy and humanity though—and this is a fearful lack to me—only his character is so fine and massive that one must admire—He is agreeable also—and does not snub me..."[1]

Clearly, the lady was flustered to know *what* to make of her unconventional visitor. In 1871 (the year of *Love is Enough*) Morris made a more surprising intrusion, this time into the world of the "Philistines". He accepted a directorship on the board of the company controlling the copper-mines from which a part of his income was still derived, and he attended the meetings of the board in the full regalia of top hat and formal dress.

His personal unrest seemed only to strengthen his capacity for complete absorption in whatever work he had on hand. "Whatever chanced to be Morris's goal of the moment", wrote his acquaintance, Theodore Watts-Dunton, "was pursued by him with as much intensity as though the universe contained no other possible goal." Even his favourite relaxations, rowing on the Thames and fishing, were pursued in this whole-hearted manner. Watts-Dunton gives an amusing picture of his first meeting with Morris during these years. Watts-Dunton was staying as Rossetti's guest at Kelmscott, when Morris

[1] E.V. Lucas, *The Colvins and their Friends*, (1928), p. 35.

arrived for a day's fishing:

"When Rossetti introduced me, the manager [of the Firm] greeted him with a 'H'm! I thought you were alone.' This did not seem promising. Morris at that time was as proverbial for his exclusiveness as he afterwards became for his expansiveness.

"Rossetti, however, was irresistible to everybody, and especially to Morris, who saw that he was expected to be agreeable to me, and most agreeable he was, though for at least an hour I could still see the shy look in the corner of his eyes. He invited me to join the fishing, which I did. Finding every faculty of Morris's mind and every nerve in his body occupied with one subject, fishing, I (coached by Rossetti, who warned me not to talk about *The Defence of Guenevere*) talked about nothing but the bream, roach, dace, and gudgeon I used to catch as a boy in the Ouse... Not one word passed Morris's lips, as far as I remember... which had not some relation to fish and baits. He had come from London for a few hours' fishing, and all the other interests which as soon as he got back to Queen's Square would be absorbing him were forgotten. Instead of watching my float, I could not help watching his face with an amused interest at its absorbed expression, which after a while he began to notice, and then the following little dialogue ensued...

" 'How old were you when you used to fish in the Ouse?'

" 'Oh, all sorts of ages; it was at all sorts of times, you know.'

" 'Well, how young, then?'

" 'Say ten or twelve.'

" 'When you got a bite at ten or twelve, did you get as interested as excited, as I get when I see my float bob?'

" 'No.'

"The way in which he said, 'I thought not,' conveyed a world of disparagement..."[1]

Kelmscott—a large farm-manor dating, probably, from Charles the First's time—and its surroundings, brought a continual renewal of his "deep love of the earth and the life on it", which he so often expressed. At first, it seems, the house was taken not for Morris himself, but for Jane and Rossetti. "We have taken a little place deep down in the country", he wrote to a friend after his first visit to Iceland in 1871,

[1] *Athenaeum*, October 10th, 1896.

"where my wife and the children are to spend some months every year, as they did this—a beautiful and strangely naif house, Elizabethan in appearance though much later in date, as in that out of the way corner people built Gothic till the beginning or middle of last century. It is on the S.W. extremity of Oxfordshire, within a stone's throw of the baby Thames, in the most beautiful grey little hamlet called Kelmscott."[1]

At the end of 1872 he wrote to Aglaia Coronio:

"I went down to Kelmscott on Saturday last till Tuesday, and spent most of my time on the river. . . It was such a beautiful morning when I came away, with a faint blue sky and thin far away white clouds about it: the robins hopping and singing all about the garden. The fieldfares, which are a winter bird and come from Norway are chattering all about the berry trees now, and the starlings, as they have done for two months past, collect in great flocks about sunset, and make such a noise before they go off to roost. The place looks as beautiful as ever though somewhat melancholy in its flowerless autumn gardens. I shall not be there much now, I suppose."[2]

The "faint" sky, the "far-away" clouds, the winter birds from Norway, the starlings at sunset, the "flowerless" gardens—the selection suggests a melancholy as much within him as in the objects themselves. But as he came to know the place more intimately, it seemed to chime in with all his moods. Kelmscott Manor aroused in him a sense of history, of mingled labour and repose, and a mellow mood of content. In his last years he described the house in an article,[3] which concluded:

"A house that I love with a reasonable love I think: for though my words may give you no idea of any special charm about it, yet I assure you that the charm is there; so much has the old house grown up out of the soil and the lives of those that lived on it: some thin thread of tradition, a half-anxious sense of the delight of meadow and acre and

[1] *Letters,* p. 45. [2] *Ibid.,* p. 49.

[3] Quoted in Mr. Henderson's introduction to *Letters,* pp. xiii-xviii, and Mackail, I, pp. 228-32.

wood and river; a certain amount (not too much let us hope) of common sense, a liking for making materials serve one's turn, and perhaps at bottom some little grain of sentiment: this I think was what went to the making of the old house."

It is at the end of *News from Nowhere* that the most famous description of the place—and of all that it came to mean to Morris in his later years—can be found. Now, at the end of his life, full of hope in the future, Morris's haunting melancholy is all but extinguished in the sense of fruition and harvest—the "ripened seeding grasses", the sheep-pastures in the distance, the rich beauty of the garden:

"Ellen echoed my thoughts as she said: 'Yes, friend... this many-gabled old house built by the simple country-folk of the long past times, regardless of all the turmoil that was going on in cities and courts, is lovely still amidst all the beauty which these latter days have created... It seems to me as if it had waited for these happy days, and held in it the gathered crumbs of happiness of the confused and troubled past.'

"She led me up close to the house, and laid her shapely sun browned hand and arm on the lichened wall as if to embrace it, and cried out, 'O me! O me! How I love the earth, and the seasons, and weather, and all things that deal with it, and all that grows out of it,—as this has done'...

"She led me on to the door, murmuring a little above her breath as she did so, 'The earth and the growth of it and the life of it! If I could but say or show how I love it!' "

II. Iceland

Morris's greatness is to be found not so much in his rejection of the ideals and practice of an "age of shoddy"; in this he was accompanied by Carlyle and by Ruskin, as well as by other contemporaries. It is to be found, rather, in his discovery that there existed within the corrupt society of the present the forces which could revolutionize the future. "So there I was in for a fine pessimistic end of life", he wrote in 1894 (see p. 125), "if it had not somehow dawned on me that amidst all this filth of civilization the seeds of a great change . . . were beginning to germinate":

> "The study of history and the love and practice of art forced me into a hatred of the civilization which, if things were to stop as they are, would turn history into inconsequent nonsense, and make art a collection of the curiosities of the past, which would have no serious relation to the life of the present.
>
> "But the consciousness of revolution stirring amidst our hateful modern society prevented me, luckier than many others of artistic perceptions, from crystallising into a mere railer against 'progress' on the one hand, and on the other from wasting time and energy in any of the numerous schemes by which the quasi-artistic of the middle classes hope to make art grow when it has no longer any root, and thus I became a practical Socialist."[1]

The insight which enabled him to become conscious of "revolution stirring", and the moral courage which enabled him to meet that discovery, not with fear, but with joy and hope—these qualities in Morris were quite exceptional. Fitfully stirring in his earlier life and writing, it was in the early 1870s, the years of his despair, that they suddenly found nourishment and grew to stature. This new strength came to him, in the first place, not from his work, nor from Kelmscott, nor from new friendships, nor from contact with the industrial proletariat, nor from any experience in his everyday life. He drew this strength, as it seemed, from the energies and aspirations of a poor people in a barren northern island in the twelfth century. There can be few more striking examples of the regenerative resources of culture than this renewal of courage and of faith in humanity which was blown from Iceland to William Morris, across eight hundred years of time.

Already in the 1860s Morris had made some acquaintance with Northern sagas in translation, but while he felt something of their attraction he did not feel the full impact of their

[1] "How I Became a Socialist", *Justice*, June 16th, 1894.

heroic qualities, and unconsciously translated them in his mind into the language of medieval romance. In 1868 he was introduced to Eirikr Magnusson, by Warington Taylor, the Firm's business manager, who felt sure that Morris "would like to make the acquaintance of a real Icelander". Taylor was right: Morris took to Magnusson at once, and proposed that they should read Icelandic together three times a week.[1] His lessons from Magnusson were unsystematic:

> "Morris decided from the beginning to leave alone the irksome task of taking regular grammatical exercises. 'You be my grammar as we go along,' was the rule laid down. . . and acted upon throughout."[2]

For this reason Morris's acquaintance with Icelandic was never entirely at first-hand. Very soon the two men were at work on translations, which Morris worked up from a literal version prepared by Magnusson.[3] *The Saga of Gunnlaug Worm-tongue* and *The Story of Grettir the Strong* were published in 1869. Prefaced to the latter was a sonnet, in which Morris wrote of the new interest brought by the sagas "to fill life's void". In the prose foreword, he strove to define the values he found within the story–attitudes very different to those expressed in his own *Earthly Paradise:*

> "To us moderns the real interest in these records of a past state of life lies principally in seeing events true in the main treated vividly and dramatically by people who completely understood the manners, life and, above all, the turn of mind of the actors in them. . . The sagaman never relaxes his grasp of Grettir's character, and he is the same man from beginning to end; thrust this way and that by circumstances, but little altered by them; unlucky in all things, yet made strong to bear all ill-luck; scornful of the world, yet capable of enjoyment, and determined to make the most of it; not deceived by men's specious ways, but disdaining to cry out because he needs must bear with them. . ."

[1] *Works,* Vol. VII, pp. xvi, xxxii-xxxiii.
[2] *Ibid.,* p. xvii. [3] *Ibid.,* p. xliii.

Endurance and courage in the face of a hostile material and social environment—these are the qualities which he seemed to find in the first sagas which he came to know closely.

In the summer of 1869 he was introduced for the first time to the Volsunga Saga. Magnusson had made a translation, and had sent it to him:

"He was not so impressed with it as I had expected he would be; but added that as yet he had had time to look only at the first part of it . . . Some time afterwards—I forget how long—when I came for the appointed lesson, I found him in a state of great excitement, pacing his study. He told me he had now finished reading my translation of the 'grandest tale that ever was told.' "[1]

He set to work on a prose translation directly, and in December, 1869, was writing of the saga to Professor Norton:

"It seems as though the author-collector felt the subject too much to trouble himself about the niceties of art, and the result is something which is above all art; the scene of the last interview between Sigurd and the despairing and terrible Brynhild touches me more than anything I have ever met with in literature; there is nothing wanting in it, nothing forgotten, nothing repeated, nothing overstrained; all tenderness is shown without the use of a tender word, all misery and despair without a word of raving, complete beauty without an ornament, and all this in two pages. . . It is to the full meaning of the word inspired; touching too though hardly wonderful to think of the probable author; some 12 century Icelander, living the hardest and rudest of lives, seeing few people and pretty much the same day after day, with his old religion taken from him and his new one hardly gained—It doesn't look promising for the future of art I fear. . . I am not getting on well with my work, for in fact I believe the Volsunga has rather swallowed me up for some time past, I mean thinking about it. . . I had it in my head to write an epic of it, but though I still hanker after it, I see clearly it would be foolish, for no verse could render the best parts of it, and it would only be a flatter and tamer version of a thing already existing."[2]

[1] *Works,* Vol. VII, p. xviii. [2] *Letters,* p. 32.

The translation was published in 1870. At the conclusion to the Preface he set down his noblest praise:

"This is the Great Story of the North, which should be to all our race what the Tale of Troy was to the Greeks—to all our race first, and afterwards, when the change of the world has made our race nothing more than a name of what has been—a story too—then should it be to those that come after us no less than the Tale of Troy has been to us."[1]

Clearly, nothing had moved him so much or influenced him so deeply, since the days when he and Burne-Jones had broken with the conventions and thrown in their lot with Rossetti. His impressions were reinforced by his visits to Iceland in 1871 and 1873.[2] On the first voyage out, as the ship skirted the northern islands and turned towards the home of Grettir and Sigurd, Morris wrote to Janey:

"I have seen nothing out of a dream so strange as our coming out of the last narrow sound into the Atlantic, and leaving the huge wall of rocks astern in the shadowless midnight twilight: nothing I have ever seen has impressed me so much."[3]

The *Journals* he kept of the voyages are full of interest. The account of the first trip—which he took in the company of Magnusson and his old friend Charles Faulkner—is over-full of detail, but the detail is often amusing or revealing—the long journeys on ponies, the camping and the pride Morris took in his own cooking, evenings spent with the local people discussing the old sagas which lingered as verbal traditions, quarrels and accidents. "I find sleeping in a tent very comfortable even when the weather is very cold", he wrote to his wife:

"Last Thursday week we had a very bad day riding over the wilderness in the teeth of a tremendous storm of snow, rain, and wind. You've no idea what a good stew I can make, or how well I can fry bacon

[1] *Works,* Vol. VII, p. 286.
[2] See J. Purkis, *The Icelandic Jaunt* (William Morris Society, 1962).
[3] *Letters,* p. 42.

under difficulties. I have seen many marvels and some terrible pieces of country; slept in the home-field of Njal's house, and Gunnar's, and at Herdholt: I have seen Bjarg, and Bathstead, and the place where Bolli was killed, and am now a half-hour's ride from where Gudrun died. I was there yesterday, and from its door you see a great sea of terrible inky mountains tossing about. . ."[1]

On August 6th he permitted himself some reflections in his *Journal:*

"Just think, though, what a mournful place this is—Iceland I mean—setting aside the pleasure of one's animal life there: the fresh air, the riding and rough life, and feeling of adventure—how every place and name marks the death of its short-lived eagerness and glory; and withal so little is the life changed in some ways.. But Lord! what littleness and helplessness has taken the place of the old passion and violence that had place here once—and all is unforgotten; so that one has no power to pass it by unnoticed: yet that must be something of a reward for the old life of the land, and I don't think their life now is more unworthy than most people's elsewhere, and they are happy enough by seeming. Yet it is an awful place: set aside the hope that the unseen sea gives you here, and the strange threatening change of the blue spiky mountains beyond the firth, and the rest seems emptiness and nothing else: a piece of turf under your feet, and the sky overhead, that's all; whatever solace your life is to have here must come out of yourself or these old stories, not over hopeful themselves."

The *Journal* of his second visit in 1873 is more condensed, with occasional descriptions of the bare scenery which—by means of their free use of strong active verbs—"break", "cleave", "strike", "sweep"—give the sense of challenge:

"It was terrible-looking enough", runs his entry for August 12th, "all in great flakes at this latter end, otherwise with great waves tossed up sometimes, or broken all into rough fragments, or the familiar regular flowing stream. . . A few rods further on and we are among the black sand, and huge clinker rocks of lava at the foot of the sulphur hills, an

[1] *Letters*, p. 44.

ugly place: a valley sloping up into a narrow pass among steep sand-heaps of hills burned red and buff and yellow by the sulphur, grassless of course; and every here and there the reek of a sulphur kettle with the earth about it stained bright yellow and white. So up the pass, going past a cloven sand peak with a kettle at the foot of it, and winding along the path till on the hill's brow we can look across a wide open country, lava-covered, grey and dismal, walled by a sweep of ink-black peaks and saw ridges. . . the whole view dismays one beyond measure for its emptiness and dolefulness."

It was a long way from here to Kelmscott Manor; and the sense of contrast was ever present to him. "The journey was very successful, & has deepened the impression I had of Iceland, & increased my love for it", he wrote on his return to Aglaia Coronio:

"Nevertheless I was very full of longing to be back, and to say the truth was more unhappy on the voyage out and before I got into the saddle than I liked to confess. . . but the glorious simplicity of the terrible & tragic, but beautiful land with its well remembered stories of brave men, killed all querulous feeling in me, and have made all the dear faces of wife and children, and love, & friends dearer than ever to me. . .

"You wrote a very kind letter to me at Reykjavik: you won't want to be thanked for it I know, but you will like to hear that it answered its kind purpose & made me happier—What a terrible thing it is to bear that moment before one gets one's letters after those weeks of absence & longing.

"Do you know I feel as if a definite space of my life had passed away now I have seen Iceland for the last time: as I looked up at Charles' Wain tonight all my travel there seemed to come back to me, made solemn and elevated, in one moment, till my heart swelled with the wonder of it: surely I have gained a great deal and it was no idle whim that drew me there, but a true instinct for what I needed."[1]

"A true instinct for what I needed"—what was it that he found in the cold volcanic island and its fierce mythologies which was strong enough to carry him out of his despair to

[1] *Letters*, pp. 58-9.

the greatness of his last years? He asked the question himself in his poem, "Iceland First Seen":

"Ah, what came we forth for to see that our hearts are so hot with desire?
Is it enough for our rest, the sight of this desolate strand,
And the mountain-waste voiceless as death but for winds that may sleep not nor tire?
Why do we long to wend forth through the length and the breadth of a land,
Dreadful with grinding of ice, and record of scarce hidden fire. . .?"

Courage—this quality he mentioned again and again. "What a glorious outcome of the worship of Courage these stories are", he exclaimed at the end of one letter.[1] Recalling the impact upon him of his first acquaintance with the sagas, he wrote to Andreas Scheu in 1883:

"The delightful freshness and independence of thought of them, the air of freedom which breathes through them, their worship of courage (the great virtue of the human race), their utter unconventionality took my heart by storm."[2]

Courage, not in the presence of hope and success, but in the face of failure and defeat and hostile fate—this quality so opposed to the self-indulgent melancholy of romanticism in its decline, was surely one of which he felt the need, not only to face the world, but in his personal life as well?

"Self-restraint was a virtue sure to be thought much of among a people whose religion was practically courage: in all the stories of the North failure is never reckoned as a disgrace, but it *is* reckoned a disgrace not to bear it with equanimity, and to wear one's heart on one's sleeve is not well thought of",

he said in one of his Socialist lectures.[3] In a manuscript poem of 1871 he addresses the author of one of the sagas, and

[1] Mackail, I, p. 335. [2] *Letters*, p. 186. [3] May Morris, I, p. 450.

refers directly to that "mist of fear", the enervating sense of the presence of mortality so often encountered in his writing at this time:

> "Tale-teller, who 'twixt fire and snow
> Had heart to turn about and show
> With faint half-smile things great and small
> That in thy fearful land did fall,
> Thou and thy brethren sure did gain
> That thing for which I long in vain,
> The spell, whereby the mist of fear
> Was melted, and your ears might hear
> Earth's voices as they are indeed.
> Well, ye have helped me at my need."[1]

"Earth's voices as they are indeed"—here was another quality he valued in the sagas which was in marked contrast with the trend of feeling within and without himself at this time. In them he found heroic actions set forth, not in terms of motive or mood, but simply as deeds judged by the society in which the actors moved. "The hero is made manifest by his deeds", he recalled in his Socialist lecture. " 'Many a man lies hid within himself', says their proverb." This gave him a quite new focus on the world, a quite new value to human action—viewing it no longer in terms of the subjective moods of the actors. "The Man Who Never Laughed Again" had asked:

> "Why should he cast himself against the spears
> To make vain stories for the unpitying years?"

The world had "narrowed to his heart at last". In the sagas the world grew as wide as mankind again, the focus was taken from the individual's heart:

"Their morality is simple enough: strive to win fame is one percept. Says Havamal:

[1] Mackail, I, p. 264.

> "Waneth wealth and fadeth friend,
> And we ourselves shall die;
> But fair fame fadeth nevermore,
> If well ye come thereby.
>
> Be it understood that this was not the worship of success; on the contrary, success that came without valour was somewhat dispised. . . Perhaps the serious consciousness of the final defeat of death made that mere success seem but poor to those men, whereas the deeds done could no longer be touched by death."[1]

But such attitudes could only be valid in a society whose aims had something of the noble and the heroic about them. They could not be applied within a society whose dominant ethic was self-interest. So it was that there ran through Morris's response to the sagas and to Iceland a continual sense of the contrast between the ideals of the Northern past and those of his own society. Even in the Iceland of the nineteenth century he found a manliness and independence among the crofters and fishermen lacking in capitalist Britain. As he wrote to Andreas Scheu, in 1883; "I learned one lesson there, thoroughly I hope, that the most grinding poverty is a trifling evil compared with the inequality of classes."[2]

The literature of the North provided him with a quite new measure of value to set beside his own age. Just as Carlyle, Ruskin, and Morris himself, had been enabled to criticize their own time by standing in the pre-capitalist ground of the Middle Ages, so now Morris could view his society from a new position. Some of the things he found in the old Icelandic society he expressed—once again with more logic than he may have held at the time—in his lecture to the Socialists:

> "As to the manners of these early settlers they were naturally exceedingly simple, yet not lacking in dignity: contrary to the absurd feeling of the feudal or hierarchal period manual labour was far from being

[1] May Morris, I, p. 453. [2] *Letters,* p. 187.

considered a disgrace: the mythical heroes have often nearly as much fame given them for their skill as weapon-smiths as for their fighting qualities; it was necessary of course for a Northman to understand sailing a ship, and the sweeps on board their long-ships or fighting-craft were not manned by slaves but by the fighting-men themselves . . . In addition the greatest men lent a hand in ordinary field- and house-work, pretty much as they do in the Homeric poems: one chief is working in his hay-field at a crisis of his fortune; another is mending a gate, a third sowing his corn, his cloak and sword laid by in a corner of the field: another is a great house-builder, another a ship-builder: one chief says to his brother one eventful evening: 'There's the calf to be killed and the viking to be fought. Which of us shall kill the calf, and which shall fight the viking?'

"The position of women was good in this society, the married couple being pretty much on an equality: there are many stories told of women divorcing themselves for some insult or offence, a blow being considered enough excuse."[1]

Moreover, while the qualities which attracted him in the Middle Ages only served to heighten the meanness of the present, the Northern message of endurance and courage seemed to give him the strength and the hope to struggle in his own time. In some manuscript notes on the northern mythologies which he made in the 1870s,[2] he touches upon the destruction of the Gods, and seems to be brooding more upon his own time than on the myth itself:

"It may be that the world shall worsen, that men shall grow afraid to 'change their life,' that the world shall be weary itself, and sicken, and none but faint-hearts be left—who knows? So at any rate comes the end at last, and the Evil, bound for a while, is loose, and all nameless merciless horrors that on earth we figure by fire and earthquake and venom and ravine. . . till at last the great destruction breaks out over all things, and the old earth and heavens are gone, and then, a new heavens and earth. What goes on there? Who shall say, of us who know only of rest and peace by toil and strife? And what shall be our share in it? Well, sometimes we must needs think that we shall live again:

[1] May Morris, I, pp. 449-50.
[2] Mackail, I, p. 333 (MS. at Walthamstow).

yet if that were not, would it not be enough that we helped to make this unnameable glory, and lived not altogether deedless? Think of the joy we have in praising great men, and how we turn their stories over and over, and fashion their lives for our joy: and this also we ourselves may give to the world.

"This seems to me pretty much the religion of the Northmen. I think one would be a happy man if one could hold it, in spite of the wild dreams and dreadful imaginings that hung about it here and there."

Dismal as the contrast between that nobility and this self-interest might be, yet the sagas seemed to carry the message that men must not repine hopelessly under their misfortunes, but must meet their destiny halfway, and strive to master their conditions. The myth of the destruction of the Northern gods prepared his mind, also, for the idea of a revolution in his own society: and it was perhaps the influence of these myths which coloured his view of "the Revolution" as one sharp swift, climactic encounter, sombre and dramatic,

"When at the last tide gathered wrong and hate
Shall meet blind yearning on the Fields of Fate."

From Iceland, then, Morris gained a draught of courage and hope, which was the prelude for his entry into active political life in the later 1870s. But critics with a knowledge of Icelandic literature are agreed that he was not wholly successful in his translations and free renderings of saga material. He shared with his contemporaries certain misconceptions as to the nature of the material with which he was dealing. Moreover, in his prose translations he sought for a style (labelled by critics "Wardour Street English") in which (in the words of Magnusson) he could bring about "such harmony between the Teutonic element in England and the language of the Icelandic saga as the not very abundant means at his command would allow."[1]

[1] *Works,* Vol. VII, p. xvii ff., Introduction by Magnusson.

But it was inevitable that the "new tongue" which Morris felt bound to make for the purposes of translation should emphasize not the vivid simplicity of the original but its strangeness and antiquity. This criticism of Morris's style was voiced in his own lifetime. More recently, one scholar of Icelandic, Dr. Dorothy Hoare, has added further strictures. "His faults in manner", she writes in relation to the prose translations,

> "of reducing the speed, economy, plainness and vividness of the original to diffuseness, false rhetoric, obscurity, unfamiliarity, by making too literal a translation where the idiom needs to be translated by a *corresponding* English idiom, or by using phrases and syntax not in modern usage, and thus giving a kind of remote, medieval flavour to what is fresh and modern in spirit—may ultimately be reduced to the same first cause, the idea that the life dealt with was heroic in the ideal sense, a kind of earthly paradise where men were simple and free and noble, and untroubled by the misfortunes and oppressions of the modern world."[1]

There is more than one stile to cross between comprehension and artistic communication, and these Morris seemed unable to surmount. It is noticeable that in those passages of his letters, journals, prefaces and lectures, where Morris is describing his own response to the sagas, he evokes their spirit with enthusiasm and conviction. But the creative problems which he faced in his own renderings of the saga material were enormous. And the matter is important, not only for a consideration of his work in this field, but also because he was faced with very similar problems in his later Socialist writings. Morris, as a poet, was a child of the romantic movement: the vocabulary, the associations of words, the very movements of thought and feeling of romanticism were part of his youthful being. Whenever he took pen in hand, these were the words, the attitudes, the conventional

[1] Dorothy M. Hoare, *The Works of Morris and Yeats in Relation to Early Saga Literature* (1937), p. 55. See also J.N. Swannell, *William Morris and Old Norse Literature* (William Morris Society, 1961).

attributes of literature which arose unprompted in his mind. No literature could be more opposed, in its essential nature and outlook, to nineteenth-century romanticism than saga. "Realism is the one rule of the Saga-man", wrote Morris himself:

"no detail is spared in impressing the reader with a sense of the reality of the event; but no word is wasted in the process of giving the detail. There is nothing didactic and nothing rhetorical in these stories; the reader is left to make his own commentary on the events, and to divine the motives and feelings of the actors in them without any help from the story-teller. . ."[1]

If Morris were to have re-created the sagas in nineteenth-century English, he would have had to have broken decisively with romanticism—not only with its conscious themes and moods, but also with those associations of words, turns of phrases, facilities and languors of rhythm, at which he had first put himself to school, and which he had himself helped to mature.

Such a revolutionary transformation of his art could only have been achieved by the greatest creative concentration. But, in the 1870s, Morris was coming to regard his writing as (in the words of Henry James), a "sub-trade"—a form of pleasurable recreation and relaxation from other work—rather than as his central place of encounter with his age. He was coming to adopt an attitude towards his writing (derived in part from his own version of Ruskin's doctrine of pleasurable labour) which was incompatible with the fullest concentration of his intellectual and moral energies. "I did manage to screw out my tale of verses, to the tune of some 250 I think", he wrote to his wife in 1876 while working on *Sigurd the Volsung*. "That talk of inspiration is sheer nonsense", he is quoted as saying in later years. "I may tell you that flat. There is no such thing: it is a mere matter of craftsmanship." And again: "If a chap can't compose an epic poem while he's

[1] Morris to Magnusson, *The Saga Library* (1891), Vol. I, pp. x-xi.

weaving tapestry he had better shut up; he'll never do any good at all."[1] Morris adopted this attitude partly in antagonism to the excessive airs of the romantically "inspired": and in part he was influenced by his pictures of the folk-poet, the scald, the bard who could in earlier societies entertain the company in the hall or round the open fire almost impromptu with an epic tale. But these poets, with every incident, every image and turn of phrase, every description of hero or heroine, were drawing upon the collected traditions of past singers, were evoking the memories, associations and accepted judgements of a people. To write in the same unconcentrating manner in the nineteenth century could only mean that Morris must draw upon the only similar body of images and associations which existed—the romantic tradition.

If Morris did not succeed in conveying the true spirit of saga into English, and if his romantic equipment tended to soften and distort his material, his services as a pioneer must not be under-estimated. "Old Northern Literature in England owes an incalculable debt" to William Morris, in the opinion of one modern scholar of Icelandic.[2] It was, unexpectedly, in his most ambitious and freest rendering of saga material—in his epic poem *Sigurd the Volsung*—that he succeeded best in impressing his own age with the power of Icelandic literature. Despite the hesitation expressed in his letter to Professor Norton in 1869, he embarked on the work in 1875 and completed it in November, 1876. In one sense, such a free re-creation of the literature of another society was an impossibility from the outset. Morris, on occasion, consciously used the old story as a vehicle for contemporary themes. In the result, the poem is a medley of different elements. It is possible to feel the pressure of Morris's feelings about his own society, the imminence of his own participation in political life, straining the fabric of the epic, as in the words put into Brynhild's mouth in her last encounter with Sigurd (in Morris's first version):

[1] Mackail, I, p. 186. But for Morris's careful drafts and revisions of *Sigurd* see J.R. Wahl, *No Idle Singer* (Cape Town, 1964).

[2] Bertha S. Phillpotts, D.B.E., *Edda and Saga* (1931), p. 214.

"O where are the days and the hours and the deeds they brought to birth!
Are they dead, are they dreams forgotten, are they solacing dreams of the earth,
Are they stones in the House of Heaven, are they craven work of the shrine
Where the days and the deeds earth failed of in heaven's fulfilment shine?
Ah once was I far-foreseeing, but the vision fades and fails;
They have set down a sword beside me, they have cumbered the even with tales
And I grow weary of waking, for gone is the splendour of day;
In my hand are the gifts of Sigurd, but Sigurd is vanished away.
But the windy East shall brighten and the empty house of night
And the Gods shall arise in the dawning and the world shall long for the light."[1]

As Dr. Hoare reveals,[2] the original passionate motivations of the characters have been softened, and in their place greed and the lust for gold have been raised to be the main motivating force of the tragedy: and, while this is yet another indication of Morris's preoccupation with the problems of his own society, it is at the expense of the tragic situation of the original.

But *Sigurd the Volsung* cannot be judged in the same light as a close translation. It is a new poem, inspired by the saga, but translated into the language of romantic poetry. Morris was no longer striving to create a special language adequate to carry the spirit of the saga. He was content to employ his romantic technique (modified to some degree to suit the material) in order to convey, less the spirit of the original, than the feelings aroused in him by the old legends. In the significance given to action rather than to mood, in its suggestion of heroic values, the poem marks a complete break with *The Earthly Paradise.* The poem never reaches epic stature in its own right. The self-conscious alliteration, the long set speeches, the lack of hardness and muscle in the long lines—all these

[1] *Works,* Vol. XII, p. xxix. [2] Hoare, *op. cit.,* pp. 67-76.

tend to keep Morris, the poet, in between the reader and the action of the poem. And yet the poem *does* succeed, time after time, in suggesting heroic values, as it were at second remove—in calling to mind the qualities of other epic literature of other times. It does not so much generate heroic feeling as "fix" heroic associations, generated in other ages and by other poets. This was enough to arouse in some of his contemporaries an excitement akin to his own when first he encountered the saga. "That is the stuff for me", said young George Bernard Shaw, after Morris had recited some passages: "there is nothing like it."[1]

[1] May Morris, II, p. xxxvii.

CHAPTER V

ACTION

I. "There is no Wealth but Life"

IN January, 1876, William Morris returned from resigning his directorship of the Devon Great Consols Company, put his top-hat on a chair, and sat down on it. He never bought another. During the months of spring and summer he was at work on *Sigurd the Volsung,* renewing in the work his youthful impulse to wage a "holy warfare" against the age. In the summer, with the work nearly complete, he felt his "rebellious inclinations" turning towards Iceland again.[1] One wonders if it was while he was at work on *Sigurd* that he glanced up from the page to ponder the newspaper headlines, with their gathering warnings of a major European war.

On October 24th, 1876, the readers of the Liberal *Daily News* read at their breakfast table a long letter from "William Morris. Author of 'The Earthly Paradise' ", headed "England and the Turks".

> "Sir
>
> I cannot help noting that a rumour is about in the air that England is going to war: and from the depths of my astonishment I ask, On behalf of whom? Against whom? And for what end?"

Later in the letter, he wrote:

> "I who am writing this am one of a large class of men—quiet men who usually go about their own business, heeding public matters less than they ought, and afraid to speak in such a huge concourse as the English nation, however much they may feel, but who are now stung into bitterness by thinking how helpless they are in a public matter that touches them so closely."[2]

Early next year he was writing to *The Athenaeum:*

[1] *Letters,* p. 78. [2] *Ibid.,* pp. 81-4.

"Sir

My eye just now caught the word 'restoration' in the morning paper, and, on looking closer, I saw that this time it is nothing less than the minster of Tewkesbury that is to be destroyed by Sir Gilbert Scott. Is it altogether too late to do something to save it—it and what ever else of beautiful or historical is still left us on the sites of the ancient buildings we were once so famous for? Would it not be of some use once for all, and with the least delay possible, to set on foot an association for the purpose of watching over and protecting these relics. . ."[1]

In May, 1877, now Treasurer of the Eastern Question Association, he wrote his famous Manifesto "To the Working-men of England". Towards the end of it he struck a note that seems to reveal a change, almost overnight, in the quality of his insight and understanding:

"Working-men of England, one word of warning yet: I doubt if you know the bitterness of hatred against freedom and progress that lies at the hearts of a certain part of the richer classes in this country: their newspapers veil it in a kind of decent language: but do but hear them talking among themselves, as I have often, and I know not whether scorn or anger would prevail in you at their folly and insolence:—these men cannot speak of your order, of its aims, of its leaders without a sneer or an insult: these men, if they had the power (may England perish rather) would thwart your just aspirations, would silence you, would deliver you bound hand and foot for ever to irresponsible capital —and these men, I say it deliberately, are the heart and soul of the party that is driving us to an unjust war."[2]

A dramatic alteration had taken place in the direction of William Morris's activities and interests. And a new force had entered English public life.

Of course, this peal of thunder did not come entirely unannounced out of a clear sky. Morris was thoroughly conversant with advanced democratic and republican opinion in his time, and his interest in the "social question", while it had lain dormant since his Oxford days, had certainly not been

[1] *Letters,* p. 85. [2] For the full Manifesto, see *Letters,* Appendix II.

extinguished. Foreign refugees of advanced opinions were often to be seen at Madox Brown's receptions, and at other social occasions of his immediate circle: acquaintances such as W.B. Scott, Woolner and William Rossetti, took an active interest in Radical issues or in the progress of free thought: Mme. Bodichon (Barbara Leigh Smith), the notable advocate of women's rights, was another member of his circle. His closest friends, Edward Burne-Jones and Charles Faulkner, had taken an interest in the agitation of the Reform League which preceded the 1867 Reform Bill, and Allingham described "Ned" in 1866 as "a People's Man".[1] William Rossetti, who was the first to introduce Walt Whitman to the English public, noted with surprise in his diary for March, 1868, that Morris took an "interest in politics", holding views "quite in harmony with the democratic sympathies of Jones, Swinburne", and himself.[2]

Whatever his private sympathies may have been, he seems to have set political questions aside with the feeling of hopelessness which had come over him in the late 1850s. However, in the early 1870s, there are suggestions that these questions were once again beginning to thrust themselves forward in his thoughts. In March, 1874, he was writing to Mrs. Alfred Baldwin, from London:

> "Monday was a day here to set one longing to get away: as warm as June... though town looks rather shocking on such days, and then instead of the sweet scents one gets an extra smell of dirt. Surely if people lived five hundred years instead of threescore and ten they would find some better way of living than in such a sordid loathsome place, but now it seems to be nobody's business to try to better things —isn't mine you see in spite of all my grumbling—but look, suppose people lived in little communities among gardens and green fields so that you could be in the country in five minutes' walk, and had few wants, almost no furniture for instance, and no servants, and studied the (difficult) arts of enjoying life, and finding out what they really wanted: then I think one might hope that civilization had really begun. But as it is, the best thing one can wish for this country at least is, meseems, some great and tragical circumstances, so that if they cannot

[1] William Allingham, *A Diary,* p. 139. [2] Angeli, *op. cit.,* p. 117.

have pleasant life, which is what one means of civilization, they may at least have a history and something to think of—all of which won't happen in our time. Sad grumbling. . ."[1]

In August of the same year, when he wrote to the Hon. Mrs. George Howard, the presence in his mind of the Norse mythology is even more evident:

"I hope you will let me come again some time: and that then you will think me less arrogant on the—what shall I say?—Wesleyan-tradesman-unsympathetic-with-art subjects than you seemed to think me the other day. . . but I think to shut one's eyes to ugliness and vulgarity is wrong, even when they show themselves in people not un-human. Do you know, when I see a poor devil drunk and brutal I always feel, quite apart from my aesthetical perceptions, a sort of shame, as if I myself had some hand in it."

Mrs. Howard had evidently been taking him to task for contrasting the "Pax Brittanica" unfavourably with the past of the Northern legends, since the letter continues:

"Neither do I grudge the triumph that the modern mind finds in having made the world (or a small corner of it) quieter and less violent, but I think that this blindness to beauty will draw down a kind of revenge one day: who knows? Years ago men's minds were full of art and the dignified shows of life, and they had but little time for justice and peace; and the vengence on them was not increase of the violence they did not heed, but destruction of the art they heeded. So perhaps the gods are preparing troubles and terrors for the world (or our small corner of it) again, that it may once again become beautiful and dramatic withal: for I do not believe they will have it dull and ugly for ever. Meantime, what is good enough for them must content us: though sometimes I should like to know why the story of the earth gets so unworthy. . ."[2]

The thunder-clouds are there—but in both cases, while threatening, they pass on overhead: "nobody's business. . . isn't mine you see in spite of all my grumbling", "meantime, what is good enough for them must content us".

[1] *Letters*, p. 62. [2] *Ibid.*, p. 64.

Apart from these few letters, there are few forewarnings of the outburst into public affairs. It is necessary to take notice, not only of the few anticipations that exist, but also of the omissions. Two are particularly surprising. In all Morris's published correspondence and surviving papers there seem to be no contemporary references either to the Paris Commune of 1871, or to Ruskin's later writings on political economy and morality, *Unto this Last, Munera Pulveris,* and the series of letters entitled *Fors Clavigera,* which were addressed "To the Workmen and Labourers of Great Britain" between 1871 and 1877. In his later years, the story of the Commune so gripped Morris's imagination that it provided the climax for his long poem, *The Pilgrims of Hope:* while his references to Ruskin show that he was quite well aware of his later writing. But, in the 1870s, he seems to have suppressed, half-consciously, the effect of these events and writings upon his mind. Still, despite the contrary urge of the Icelandic influence, he felt himself to be the "dreamer of dreams, born out of my due time. . ."

Nevertheless, he cannot have been unaware of these things. About the true course of events in the Commune he was unlikely to have had any clear understanding, in the chorus of fear and vilification of the bourgeois Press: but if (as was likely) he read the *Fortnightly Review* he would not have missed Frederick Harrison's courageous defence of the Communards:

> "For the first time in Modern Europe, the workmen of the chief city of the Continent have organized a regular government in the name of a new Social order."[1]

nor his exposure of the hysteria on platform and Press, which (in Harrison's words) "was as if the horses had made an insurrection against men. . . the frenzy which seizes a white population when their black slaves grow insubordinate."[2]

It is likely that Morris's reactions to the news of the

[1] *Fortnightly Review,* May, 1871. [2] *Ibid.,* August, 1871.

Commune were influenced by those of his "master", Ruskin. Two of the most remarkable letters in *Fors Clavigera* were numbers VI and VII, the former "written under the excitement of continual news of the revolution in Paris", the latter "upon the ruin of Paris". Ruskin broke from the chorus of fear and hatred of his class by attributing the cause of the revolution to "the idleness, disobedience, and covetousness of the richer and middle classes" themselves.[1] He declared in Letter VI:

> "This cruelty has been done by the kindest of us, and the most honourable; by the delicate women, by the nobly-nurtured men . . . This robbery has been taught to the hands,—this blasphemy to the lips, —of the lost poor, by the False Prophets who have taken the name of Christ in vain, and leagued themselves with His chief enemy, 'Covetousness, which is idolatry'.
>
> "Covetousness, lady of Competition and of deadly Care; idol above the altars of Ignoble Victory; builder of streets, in cities of Ignoble Peace."

In Letter VII he was even more specific:

> "Occult Theft—Theft which hides itself even from itself, and is legal, respectable, and cowardly—corrupts the body and soul of man, to the last fibre of them. And the guilty Thieves of Europe, the real sources of all deadly war in it, are the Capitalists—that is to say, people who live by percentages on the labour of others; instead of by fair wages for their own. The *Real* war in Europe, of which this fighting in Paris is the Inauguration, is between these and the workmen, such as these have made him. They have kept him poor, ignorant, and sinful, that they might, without his knowledge, gather for themselves the produce of his toil. At last a dim insight into the fact of this dawns on him; and such as they have made him he meets them, and *will* meet."

This was the farthest point of understanding which Ruskin ever reached. His sympathies with the workers were sharply repressed by an event which must have fallen as a heavy blow upon Morris as well—the burning of the Louvre. "I am myself a Communist", he wrote in Letter VII.

[1] *Fors Clavigera,* Letter XLIII.

"I am myself a Communist of the old school—reddest also of the red; and was on the very point of saying so at the end of my last letter; only the telegram about the Louvre's being on fire stopped me. . ."

And the "Communism" which he went on to elaborate is a ridiculous eclectic dream-picture, made up of patches of Sir Thomas More, of patriachal reaction, and medieval nostalgia.

In truth, John Ruskin had advanced with strong (if uneven) strides since the writing of *The Stones of Venice.* In the late 1850s and early 1860s, he had become a declared disciple of Thomas Carlyle and had turned his main energies to developing the social criticism implicit in *Past and Present* and in his own "The Nature of Gothic". In all his writings he returned again and again to the assault upon industrial capitalism. A passage from the *Crown of Wild Olive* strikes the recurrent note:

"Our cities are a wilderness of spinning wheels instead of palaces; yet the people have not clothes. We have blackened every leaf of English greenwood with ashes, and the people die of cold; our harbours are a forest of merchant ships, and the people die of hunger."

In a series of articles in the *Cornhill Magazine* in 1860, later published as *Unto this Last,* he entered the field of "Political Economy", developing his ideas in 1862-3 in some essays in *Fraser's Magazine,* reprinted as *Munera Pulveris.* In one sense, these essays are no more than an elaboration of Carlyle's warning: "We have profoundly forgotten everywhere that *cash-payment* is not the sole relation of human beings." But in their negative application of this warning these essays are devastating. *Unto this Last* is in many respects the most logical of all Ruskin's writings: it reveals an effort of mental discipline for which he rarely had the patience. By striking at the root assumptions of orthodox capitalist economics, again and again he succeeds in making the "Prophets" of the Manchester School look silly, contradictory, and shallow. The orthodox economists, he writes in *Unto this Last,* say that "the social affections are accidental and disturbing elements in human nature; but avarice and the desire for progress are constant elements. Let us eliminate the inconstants, and considering the human being merely as a covetous machine, examine by what laws of labour, purchase, and sale, the greatest accumulative result in wealth is obtainable." His analysis of these assumptions was so disturbing, his indictment of capitalist ethics so unpardonable, that in both cases the outcry of the readers of the periodicals forced their editors to ask Ruskin to bring his contributions to an end.

On the positive side, too, Ruskin added much to Carlyle's early precepts. True value, he declared, could not be expressed by the capitalist laws of supply and demand: "to be 'valuable'... is to 'avail towards life'. A truly valuable ... thing is that which leads to life with its whole strength." "The real science of political economy... is that which teaches nations to desire and labour for the things that lead to life: and which teaches them to scorn and destroy the things that lead to destruction." His definition of "labour", again, must have puzzled the orthodox: "Labour is the contest of the life of man with an opposite—the term 'life' including his intellect, soul, and physical power, contending with question, difficulty, trial, or material force." "The prosperity of any nation", he continued, "is in exact proportion to the quantity of labour which it spends in obtaining and employing means of life. Observe—I say, obtaining and employing; that is to say, not merely wisely producing, but wisely distributing and consuming... Wise consumption is a far more difficult art than wise production... The vital question, for individual and for nation, is, never 'how much do they make?' but 'to what purpose do they spend?' " And —with the notice to conclude the series already issued by the editor—Ruskin could do no more than throw down his last challenge in a phrase which seems to have haunted Morris's imagination throughout his last years: "I desire, in closing the series of introductory papers, to leave this one great fact clearly stated. THERE IS NO WEALTH BUT LIFE."

The value which Morris set on this work was clearly

expressed in his Preface to "The Nature of Gothic" when it was issued from the Kelmscott Press in 1892.[1] But the Ruskin of *Fors Clavigera* was in some respects a poorer man than the Ruskin of *Unto this Last.* The bourgeois periodicals had been barred to him, and the middle classes turned a deaf ear towards him. Although in his new Letters he addressed directly the working men, it was not with any sense of identity of interest, but in the hope that among them might be found a few individuals who had escaped a little of the contamination of a contaminated age. The first Proposition with which he started his new series was one of bitter despair:

> "The English nation is beginning another group of ten years, empty in purse, empty in stomach, and in a state of terrified hostility, to every other nation under the sun."

The series had hardly begun before the blow of the Commune fell upon him: it was as if the last leg of hope had been knocked from under him. Henceforward an element of fear entered into his feelings towards the working-people, which provoked in him a tone of moral hectoring. The burning of the Louvre made him see the workers as a brutalized, destructive force, bearing the stamp of the masters who had oppressed them. The Commune he seemed to regard at times almost as a divine warning, the revenge upon the capitalists brought about by their neglect of human responsibilities, the Doom that overshadowed society if it did not heed the teachings of the "Master" of St. George's Guild—Ruskin himself. The revolutionary forces he identified with the bourgeois caricatures of the blood-stained *ouvrier* and the *petroleuse.*

Moreover, like many people who speak without being listened to, he was beginning to turn deaf himself. No doubt he was perfectly sincere when he wrote, in Letter XVII:

> "St. George's war! Here, since last May. . . have I been asking whether any one would volunteer for such battle? Not one human

[1] See May Morris, I, p. 295.

creature, except a personal friend or two, for mere love of me, has answered.

"Now, it is true, that my writing may be obscure, or seem only half in earnest. But it is the best I can do: it expresses the thoughts that come to me as they come. . . And, whether you believe them or not, they are entirely faithful words; I have no interest at all to serve by writing, but yours.

"And literally, no one answers. . ."

"I have given you the tenth of all I have, as I promised." Yes, certainly, Ruskin's sincerity is one of the incontrovertible and redeeming facts of the mid-nineteenth century. But he had ceased to listen to the world. Isolation had made him indifferent to the thought of his contemporaries: had strained the egotism already apparent in his earliest writings: had made his style eccentric, arrogant, and self-absorbed. Ruskin was still entrapped in the "feudal Socialism" of *Past and Present,* and it was almost impossible to recognize the world of the 1870s in this queer amalgam of wicked Tory squires (who must still be protected), monarchs, crusades and religious ejaculations which made up his Letters. While it is possible that Morris may have been one of those unnamed personal friends who—out of "mere love"—gave donations to Ruskin's fund for St. George's Guild, there is no doubt at all that he saw the pitiful impracticability of Ruskin's latter-day Crusade. He agreed with Ruskin well enough about the dragon: but he saw that it needed more than an art-critic or a "literary man" with a medieval spear to kill it.

Thus, whatever insight into capitalist society Morris gained in the early 1870s from the Commune and Ruskin's writings, on one point both may have combined to hold him back. The burning of the Louvre—and all that it seemed to symbolize—and the pitiful tilting of Ruskin—neither gave him any *hope.* Both served, rather, to estrange him from the source of hope, the working-class movement. Morris had reached a point where—if he was to progress at all and not decline into being a cynic and "railer against progress"—it was of vital importance that he should learn the truth about society by active participation and engagement within it. Three occasions all combined at the same time to force this active participation in social life upon him—the "Eastern Question", the destruction or "restoration" of ancient buildings, and a seeming deadlock in his creative ambitions with the Firm.

II. The "Eastern Question"

Morris could scarcely have chosen a more complex issue for his initiation into public life than the "Eastern Question" agitation. On the surface the moral issues appeared clean-cut: beneath the surface were the intricacies of secret diplomacy and rival imperialist interests. During the course of the agitation, all the elements of nineteenth-century political melodrama were present: impassioned public professions, and private intrigue: widely publicized splits in both the Conservative and Liberal Parties: the disclosure of secret agreements by a temporary Foreign Office clerk, paid at the rate of *8d.* an hour: rumours of the impending abdication of the Queen: Conferences and Congresses of the major European powers. Morris—whose social contacts had up to this time extended little further than to his literary and artistic associates and to his business clients[1]—was thrown into the company of prominent politicians and business-men, and leaders of the London trade unions and radical associations. Whereas up to this moment his political experience was limited to voting for Liberal candidates, and rare attendance at public meetings,[2] he was now a frequent attender at demonstrations, rallies and conferences, at some of which he was called upon to speak. At the age of forty-three he had suddenly started upon a new course of education.

[1] Morris avoided the usual social round, and very rarely attended any social function. When he did, he was miserable for days in advance. See his letter to Mrs. Alfred Baldwin, March 26th, 1874: "I have got to go to a wedding next Tuesday: and it enrages me to think that I lack the courage to say, I don't care for either of you, and neither of you care for me, and I won't waste a day of my precious life in grinning a company grin at you two" (*Letters,* p. 62).

[2] See Mackail, I, p. 338.

The immediate cause for the formation of the "Eastern Question Association" was to promote resistance to Disraeli's alliance with the Turks, following the revelations of atrocities committed by Turkish mercenaries upon the Christian population of Bulgaria. The Conservative administration had come to power in 1874, and Disraeli had embarked on his grandiose policies of Oriental imperialism. "You have", he declared,

> "a new world, new influences at work, new and unknown objects and dangers with which to cope... The relations of England to Europe are not the same as they were in the days of Lord Chatham or Frederick the Great. The Queen of England has become the Sovereign of the most powerful of Oriental States. On the other side of the globe there are now establishments belonging to her, teeming with wealth and population... What our duty is at this critical moment is to maintain the Empire of England."

In November, 1875, the British Government purchased 176,000 shares in the Suez Canal. The Prince of Wales was sent on a mission to receive the loyalty of his mother's Indian subjects, and early in 1876 it was announced that Queen Victoria would soon be blessed with the title of "Empress of India". Meanwhile, in the preceding year, outbreaks of revolt had occurred within the corrupt Turkish Empire—an empire which, since the time of the Crimean War, had increasingly been regarded as a British satellite, and in which the British Ambassador, Sir Henry Elliot, wielded extraordinary influence. The nationalist and "Christian" outbreaks extended from Bosnia and Herzogovina, Montenegro and Serbia, to (1876) the most subjugated province of all, Bulgaria, and they were not only watched with interest, but prompted and aided by the great power of Russia to the north. Intent upon distracting attention from misery and the cry for reform at home, the Tsar nourished the sentiments of Pan-Slavism among Russian intellectuals by threatening Turkey with the seizure and liberation of the Christian provinces. Within the councils of British imperialism itself, two extreme policies were debated: the partition of the Turkish Empire in Europe and North Africa between Russia and the other major European powers—Britain looking for Egypt, Cyprus and a foothold in Syria as her share: or uncompromising opposition to the Russian claims, and the preservation of the Turkish Empire intact and within the sphere of British influence.

Disraeli inclined towards the second policy (while hoping by threats, secret diplomacy, and force, to make the best of both worlds), and, in the summer of 1876, when the news of the nationalist uprising was disturbing the British public, he contented himself with admonishing the Turks to carry through reforms within their European provinces. On June 23rd, however, the Liberal *Daily News* published the first full accounts of the appalling savagery of the mercenary Bashi-Bazouks against the Christian population of Bulgaria which came to be known as the "Bulgarian atrocities". Disraeli, partly because he was misinformed by Sir Henry Elliot, partly because he did not have the same sharp eye of the "nonconformist conscience" as Gladstone, dismissed the revelations as "to a large extent inventions"; the accounts of the torture of victims he thought unlikely, since the Turks usually adopted "more expeditious methods". He was soon to regret the phrase. A storm of protest broke out in the country, coming in the first place, not from any leading Liberal politicians, but from the organizations of the people. Meanwhile, the extent of the atrocities was daily confirmed, and was finally substantiated at the beginning of September by an official Government investigator. Spontaneous meetings of protest were held throughout the country during August and the first week of September. The storm of feeling rose to such heights that Lord Derby, Disraeli's Foreign Minister, was forced to inform the Turks that the outrages had "aroused an universal feeling of indignation in all classes of English society, and to such a pitch has this risen, that, in the extreme case of Russia declaring war on Turkey Her Majesty's Government would find it practically impossible to interfere in defence of the Ottoman Empire".

Until this time the agitation in the country had been without a central leadership, springing from the initiative of local Liberal Associations, radical and nonconformist groups, and working-class organizations. But now a new figure emerged on the scene. Gladstone, who had retired in a disgruntled mood from the leadership of the Liberal Party after his defeat in 1874, saw in the popular agitation a matchless opportunity for rehabilitating the Party and strengthening his own hand against the aristocratic Whigs, Lords Hartington and Granville, who had resumed its leadership. When the summer parliamentary session came to an end, he later recalled, he thought the Eastern Question was "all up" for the time being:

> "I knew it would revive, and I thought it would revive in the next Session; but I gave it up for the moment until I saw in the newspapers by accident that the working men of England were going to meet on the subject of it. I said to myself that moment, 'Then it is alive'. Seeing that it was alive, I did what I could, and we all did what we could: and we stirred the country. . ."[1]

This hardly reveals the character of the impassioned crusader in which he publicly emerged. On September 6th he published his famous pamphlet, *The Bulgarian Horrors and the Question of the East,* in which—to the consternation of his more cautious colleagues in the parliamentary leadership of the Liberal Party—he demanded the evacuation by the Turks of Bulgaria:

> "Let the Turks now carry away their abuses in the only possible manner, namely by carrying off themselves. Their Zaptiehs and their Mudirs, their Bimbashis and their Yuzbashis, their Kaimakams and their Pashas, one and all, bag and baggage, shall, I hope, clear out of the province they have desolated and profaned."

Three days later he addressed an enormous meeting on Blackheath. As feeling rose even higher, politicians on the Radical wing of the Liberal Party—motivated equally, it

[1] *Life of W.E. Gladstone,* Ed. Wemyss-Reid (1899), p. 619.

would seem, by an interest in the cause itself and by the magnificent opportunity provided for strengthening their own position and organization within the country—considered means of giving the agitation a central leadership. Chief among these was A.J. Mundella, Radical M.P. for Sheffield, whose whole career was devoted to strengthening the alliance between the Liberal Party and organized labour, and to promoting policies of enlightened capitalist administration, arbitration in trades disputes, and "class peace". Early in October he and his Sheffield friend, Robert Leader, were discussing the calling of a national Conference on the Eastern Question. The politicians were to keep in the background. "I think the 'Great Guns' should *hardly be Parliamentary*", he wrote to Leader. "Get clergy, ministers, representatives of great bodies, Mayors of towns, etc."[1] The Liberal leader, Lord Hartington, with the Whig dislike of any popular movement, opposed the Conference for fear "it would get into the hands of men of extreme opinions". Gladstone continued speaking on the Question, but havered at the idea of giving the agitation a more pronounced organizational form. While the politicians manoeuvred, the Labour Representation League was rallying the London workers, resolving on October 20th that:

> "Should Russia make war upon Turkey, it will be the duty of the English people to oppose any action of the Government which has for its object any defence of the Ottoman Empire, or which shall prevent the establishment of such an independent Government for the Turkish provinces of Eastern Europe as shall be in accordance with the wishes of the people of these provinces. . ."[2]

The agitation, at its height in September, had begun to fall away at the end of October when William Morris published his first letter in the *Daily News.* He was in no way breaking with the opinions of his friends or associates in declaring his

[1] W.H.G. Armytage, *A.J. Mundella* (1951), p. 170.
[2] Minutes of the Labour Representation League (British Library of Political and Economic Science).

mind on the question even if his turn of phrase might have seemed a little extreme. In a letter to Mundella on November 15th 1876, he sent a list of friends, all of them "feeling strongly and rightly about the matter. . . their letters to me all express the desire that something should be done, and done as speedily as possible". The names included (with Morris's comments) William Allingham, Literary man, Editor of *Fraser's*; William De Morgan, Artist; F.S. Ellis, "my publisher"; "Not a parson"; W.B. Scott, Artist, Writer on Art; Henry C.J. Faulkner, Fellow and Tutor of University College, Oxford Wallis, Artist; Philip Webb, Architect; and W.T. Stead, Editor of the *Northern Echo* (later to become Assistant Editor of the *Pall Mall Gazette*).[1] In addition to his own friends, a score of other prominent cultural personalities were associated with the agitation during its early stages—among them Professor Thorold Rogers, Professor Fawcett, Robert Browning, the Reverend Stopford Brooke, D.G. Rossetti, and Thomas Carlyle (author of the phrase, "the unspeakable Turk"). Edward Burne-Jones was at Morris's side throughout, and in the early stages of the movement, when he wrote to Ruskin for support, he received the reply:

> "I hope neither Morris nor you will retire wholly again out of such spheres of effort. It seems to me especially a time when the quietest men should be disquieted, and the meekest self-asserting."[2]

Morris, indeed, for once in his life seemed only to be following the fashion.

Neither is it in any way surprising to find that in Morris's first letter there are many confusions and naiveties of thought —his faith in the complete integrity of Gladstone, in the honour of British intentions "except in trade", and his apparent lack of suspicion of Russian aims. On the other hand for the first public utterance of a poet and artist, there is a quite surprising understanding of the power of popular organization. From the very outset Morris saw the working

[1] Mundella Correspondence (Sheffield University Library).
[2] *Memorials,* II, p. 73.

class as the real force behind the agitation: "the nation is dumb, if it were not for the 2,000 working men who met last Sunday at Clerkenwell": and expressed his faith in the power of organized and determined opinion:

> "In matters of peace and war, no Government durst go against the expressed will of the English people, when it has a will and can find time to express it. . . I say it would be impossible even for that clever trickster [Disraeli] to do this, not only if united England were in earnest to gainsay him, but even if a large minority were but half in earnest and spoke and said 'No'."

The distinguished new recruit to the agitation did not deflect Disraeli from his course. At the Lord Mayor's Banquet on November 9th he made the provocative statement:

> "If England were to go to war in a righteous cause. . . a cause that concerned her liberty, her independence, or her Empire, her resources would prove inexhaustible. She is not a country that, when she enters into a campaign, has to ask herself whether she can support a second or third campaign. If she enters a campaign she will not terminate it until right is done."

These lofty sentiments were soon put into rhyme, and became the popular song of the war party:

> "We don't want to fight, but by jingo if we do,
> We've got the ships, we've got the men, we've got the money too!"

They also provoked, on November 10th, an angry reply from the Tsar, and a distinct heightening of the danger of war. The issues now became increasingly complex. For half a century Russia had been regarded by British radical opinion as the greatest bastion of reaction in Europe. A small group of the extreme left, together with a few Radicals—men as diverse as Karl Marx, Frederick Harrison, the Positivist leader, H.M. Hyndman and Joseph Cowan, the Radical M.P. for Newcastle —were inflexibly opposed to any compromise with Russia, believing that every diplomatic or military defeat suffered by the Tsar would hasten the cause of the progressive movement throughout the world. Objectively, they had constantly to ward off the danger of becoming aligned with the imperialist party, headed by Disraeli and the Queen herself, whose support for the Turks was motivated by grandiose plans of British influence in the Near East, and the even more dubious anti-Russian propaganda on Press and platform promoted by financial speculators who had bought up enormous numbers of depreciated Turkish bonds, £165,000,000 of which had come on to the market at this time. On the other hand, the Liberal Associations, the Labour Representation League, and the rank-and-file Radicals and trade unionists who were conducting in the country the anti-Turkish agitation in favour of the oppressed European nations were in equal danger of becoming the tools of interested Liberal politicians and of Russian imperialism. A letter of Morris's of November 15th, 1876, receiving his old friend Charles Faulkner, the Oxford mathematician, into the agitation, shows him floundering in an attempt to rebut the latter charge:

> "I know that the Russians have committed many crimes, but I cannot accuse them of behaving ill in this Turkish business at present, and I must say I think it very unfair of us, who freed our black men, to give them no credit for freeing their serfs: both deeds seem to me to be great landmarks in history... My cry and that of all that I consider *really* on our side is: 'The Turkish Government to the Devil, and something rational and progressive in its place.' "[1]

"Something rational and progressive"—this is the note of the old Benthamite radicalism. Another passage in the same letter shows Morris condemning the commercial imperialism of the "age of shoddy", but still with the suggested reservation that this is a degeneration from an enlightened liberal imperialism of the past. Supposing, he asks Faulkner, Britain were to be victorious in a war against Russia as Turkey's ally,

[1] *Letters,* p. 99, and transcript in Mackail's notebook. Morris Museum, Walthamstow.

"what should we do with Turkey, if we didn't wish to be damned? 'Take it ourselves', says the bold man, 'and rule it as we rule India.' But the bold man don't live in England at present I think; and I know what the Tory trading stock-jobbing scoundrel that one calls an Englishman to-day would do with it: he would shut his eyes hard over it, get his widows and orphans to lend it money, and sell it vast quantities of bad cotton."

It is also clear from this letter that Morris was from the outset impatient with the tactics of the parliamentary supporters of the agitation. "I do not feel very sanguine about it all", he wrote, describing the plans for the Conference, "but it is the only thing that offers at present, and I do not wish to be anarchical: I must do the best I can with it." Mundella, after bombarding Gladstone with letters, requesting him to address the Conference in which he forecast that "we shall have such a demonstration as England has not seen since the Anti-Corn Law days", and of "associations and committees organizing all over the country",[1] finally got a grudging and hedging reply in the affirmative: "Many thanks for your various communications. . . If, upon full consideration, it is thought that my appearance at one of your meetings. . . is desirable . . . I am ready to say that as at present advised I will come."[2]

The Conference was fixed for St. James's Hall on December 8th, and on the evening before Mundella was able to relax and look back on his good political management of the previous few weeks which had brought the "Eastern Question Association" into being:

"What a work it has been. . . as hard as a general election. I found that my first business was to extinguish the irrepressibles. . . I don't intend that any Radicals shall speak *if I can help it.* I want to fire off the Bishops, the Parsons, the Peers, the Literati, etc., not those who have been the actors heretofore but *a new set.* I have been twice with Gladstone giving him his role. It is like a moth going to the candle to go near him; he is all light and flame."[3]

The salvo on the next day was an enormous success. The

[1] Armytage, *op. cit.*, p. 172. [2] *Ibid.*, p. 173. [3] *Ibid.*, p. 173.

heavy artillery of Gladstone was saved for the evening. In the afternoon the howitzers and light field guns were arrayed—Anthony Trollope and the Duke of Westminster, the Pacifist Henry Richard and Samuel Morley, the wealthy Radical M.P., while George Howell and Henry Broadhurst brought supporting fire on behalf of the working men. Indeed, the bombardment aroused the fury of Queen Victoria herself, who wished to set the Attorney-General on to the speakers: "It can't be constitutional."[1]

As a result of the Conference, the Eastern Question Association was officially established. Its figure-heads included the Duke of Westminster and Lord Shaftesbury, but Mundella emerged from his unpublicized wire-pulling to become Chairman of the Executive Committee, while Morris became Treasurer. No doubt Mundella was pleased with himself at having hooked this particular member of the "Literati", although later in the agitation he must have asked himself what it *was* he had got on the other end of the line. The first job of the E.Q.A. was the issuing of tracts, one of which—*Lessons in Massacre*—was from Gladstone's pen. The agitation was no longer so urgent, owing to the lull of the Constantinople Conference. It was in the excitement immediately before and after the declaration of war by Russia upon Turkey on April 24th, 1877, that the danger of war became once again acute. In their efforts to prevent Disraeli's bringing Britain into the conflict on the Turkish side, Morris and Mundella were in constant contact with Henry Broadhurst, George Howell, and others of the Labour Representation League. Since this was Morris's first close contact with any working-class organization, it is necessary to explain something of its make-up and aims.

For ten years the L.R.L.—an alliance of the survivors of the old trade union leaders of the "Junta", of the London trade

[1] G.E. Buckle, *Life of Disraeli* (1920), Vol. VI., p. 107. *See also* p. 130 for the Queen's statement: "This mawkish sentimentality for people who hardly deserve the name of real Christians... forgetting the interests of this great country—is really incomprehensible."

unionists who had served on the General Council of the "First International", and of a few middle-class Radicals—had been promoting the candidatures of working men to Parliament. Despite occasional moments of independence, it had been falling increasingly under the wing of the Liberal Party. Influential and far-seeing Liberal M.Ps.—among them Samuel Morley and A.J. Mundella—had been attempting to secure the support of the working-class vote for the Liberal Party by setting aside a handful of seats in the mining and industrial areas for working-men Liberal M.Ps. Their efforts were continually frustrated by the die-hard attitude of the mill-owners and industrialists in the leadership of the Liberal machine in the localities, who—while perhaps giving lip-service to the general principle of working-class representation—were not prepared to permit a working man to sit in their own constituencies. Despite this opposition, in 1874 Thomas Burt, the Northumberland miners' leader, was returned without a Liberal opponent for Morpeth, and Alexander Macdonald was returned for the two-seat constituency of Stafford. In 1875 the L.R.L. issued a "Manifesto" which finally marked the end of any pretence of independence from the Liberal Party:

> "We have ever sought to be allied to the great Liberal Party, to which we, by conviction, belong. If they have not reciprocated this feeling, the fault is theirs, and the cause of disruption is to be found in them, and not in the League... But, happily, this exclusive feeling is fast dying out, as evidenced by the fact that men of the highest standing in the Liberal ranks have both written and spoken in favour of the objects of the League..."[1]

In home affairs, the next four or five years of the L.R.L.'s existence (with its most popular leaders, Broadhurst and Howell, themselves eager to secure places in Parliament) make up a record of the abasement of working-class interests to those of the Liberal Party, so that early in 1878 Marx was

[1] Reprinted in *Labour's Formative Years,* Ed. J.B. Jeffreys, p. 155.

writing to Liebknecht in disgust of "the corrupt trade union leaders and professional agitators", who had reduced the working-class movement to being "nothing more than the tail of the great Liberal Party".[1]

However, notwithstanding the degeneration at home from independent working-class politics to "Lib-Lab-ism", the Eastern Question agitation revived in the movement the old traditions of radical internationalism. Among the leaders of the League were several, including John Hales, of the Elastic Web Weavers, and Thomas Mottershead of the Silk Weavers, who had signed the Address of the General Council of the International welcoming the Paris Commune in 1871. On this issue at least, the L.R.L. acted not as the "tail" but as the head of the popular movement. Among even the most typical exponents of "Lib-Lab-ism" during this period—men like Henry Broadhurst of the Stonemasons, and Thomas Burt—the ideals of democratic internationalism were the last to be jettisoned.

At what time William Morris first met the leaders of the Labour Representation League it is difficult to say. Probably he was introduced to Broadhurst, Daniel Guile, and George Howell, at the Conference on December 8th 1876. Russia's declaration of war threw the E.Q.A. and the L.R.L. into joint action. Henry Broadhurst called a meeting of "Workmen's Political Associations and Trade Societies of the Metropolis" to meet at the Cannon Street Hotel on May 2nd, 1877, to support five anti-Turkish resolutions which Gladstone had tabled in the house. Thomas Burt, M.P., and Thomas Hughes, Q.C., presided over a meeting of 150 delegates of trade unions and Radical associations, and "a larger number of middle-class men".[2] Morris was in the front of the activity[3] and wrote of the meeting two days later:

"I was at the working-men's meeting... on Wednesday, it was quite a success; they seem to have advanced since last autumn. Some

[1] *Marx-Engels Sel. Cor.*, p. 356. [2] Minutes of Labour Representation League.
[3] See *Letters*, p. 90.

of them spoke very well, nor would the meeting so much as listen to George Potter on the other side. Burt (M.P. for Morpeth and who is, or was, a working man) was chairman, and spoke excellently though shortly, with a strong Northumbrian tongue: he seemed a capital fellow. Meantime the Liberal party is blown to pieces, and everything is in confusion."[1]

On the following Monday, May 7th, a further great Conference was held in St. James's Hall under the auspices of the E.Q.A. Meanwhile—as Morris had written—the Liberal Party was "blown to pieces". Incessant manoeuvres were going on among the parliamentarians to tone down Gladstone's five anti-Turkish resolutions, one of which only—in a modified form—was taken to a division on May 14th. The agitation had achieved a part of its aim in so far as on May 6th the Foreign Minister, Lord Derby, had been forced to declare that Britain was concerned in the war only to protect her own interests, which were defined as centring on the Suez Canal, the overland route to the Persian Gulf, and the use of the Dardanelles. It was within this context, irritated at the vacillation of the Parliamentary Liberals and admiring by contrast the stand of the L.R.L., that Morris issued his Manifesto "To the Working-men of England" on May 11th, over the signature of "A Lover of Justice". It reveals the enormous educational effect upon him of his recent participation in the agitation, the great stride forward in understanding of class issues which he had taken since his original letter of the previous October:

"Who are they that are leading us into war? Let us look at these saviours of England's honour, these champions of Poland, these scourges of Russia's iniquities! Do you know them?—Greedy gamblers on the Stock Exchange, idle officers of the army and navy (poor fellows!) worn-out mockers of the Clubs, desperate purveyors of exciting war-news for the comfortable breakfast tables of those who have nothing to lose by war, and lastly, in the place of honour, the Tory Rump, that we fools, weary of peace, reason, and justice, chose at the last election to 'represent' us: and over all their captain [Disraeli, recently made Earl of Beaconsfield] the ancient place-hunter, who,

[1] Mackail, I, p. 350.

having at last climbed into an Earl's chair, grins down thence into the anxious face of England while his empty heart and shifty head is compassing the stroke that will bring on our destruction perhaps, our confusion certainly:—O shame and double shame, if we march under such a leadership as this in an unjust war against a people who are *not* our enemies, against Europe, against freedom, against nature, against the hope of the world."[1]

Throughout it is to the working class that Morris appeals as the true force of internationalism and the backbone of the agitation:

"If you have any wrongs to be redressed, if you cherish your most worthy hope of raising your whole order peacefully and solidly, if you thirst for leisure and knowledge, if you long to lessen those inequalities which have been our stumbling-block since the beginning of the world, then cast aside sloth and cry out against an UNJUST WAR, and urge us of the Middle Classes to do no less. . ."

The success of the agitation contributed to ensure an ambiguous kind of neutrality during the next few months. Until November the stubborn resistance of the Turks at Plevna made it seem possible that the Russians would fail to break their defences. Meanwhile the "patriotic" newspapers used every event to arouse sympathy for the "gallant Turk", whether victorious or in defeat: and when on December 19th the fall of Plevna signalized the collapse of the main Turkish armies, a war temper was skilfully engineered in the country. On December 19th it was announced that Parliament would be recalled three weeks early, on January 18th 1878. The next day Morris was writing to his wife:

"Great things have happened since your letter. . . the marshal [Osman Pasha] has given way; Plevna has fallen; Servia is on the frontier—and things seem most like the Jew wretch & that old Vic forcing us into the war. You will see how the sprightly widow went to Hughenden & then said she would stay at Windsor Christmas over: & now Parliament is to meet for business on Jan. 17. So we are all alive at the E.Q.A. . . . I am so bothered by it all that I can do little else.I

[1] See *Letters*, Appendix II, pp. 388-9.

even tried to flit a few words at a small meeting we had at Lambeth yesterday: I can't say I got on very well but I did manage to get a few words out & get to the end. . ."[1]

This seems to have been Morris's first impromptu public speech. Five days later he was writing to his daughters:

"I have been much agitated for the past week by the goings on of an august personage and my Lord Beaconsfield; but we hope to agitate others in our turn next. I do not think it will really end in war: but the party of stupidity will do their best to bring it about: neither is there any doubt that the A.P. aforesaid is helping them and that this fact, strange as it may seem to us, makes many people, especially professional politicians, feeble in resistance. On the whole our side has got weaker, and many people are sluggish and hard to move who thoroughly agree with us. . ."[2]

On January 4th he was writing that "we are *all* of opinion that we must go on agitating". He had unwillingly agreed to address a Liberal Association at Chichester, and had spent the whole morning with Henry Broadhurst arranging a joint meeting between the E.Q.A. and L.R.L.—the "Workmen's Neutrality Demonstration" held in Exeter Hall on January 16th, 1878. The Trafalgar Square meeting, though disgracefully reported in the Liberal *Daily News*, was "a glorious victory for us: though I believe some blood was shed (from noses): the enemy spent huge time & trouble & plenty of money all to be spoilt in the end". Once again he returned to the attack on the Queen:

"You may be sure the Empress Brown has a great deal to do with it all: what a rage she will be in! For I really cannot think that the country will go to war when all is said: it would be too monstrous: the London Working men have got their backs well upon our side. . ."[3]

[1] *Letters*, p. 103. [2] *Letters*, pp. 103-4.
[3] *Ibid.*, p. 106. William De Morgan, the potter, first christened Queen Victoria the "Empress Brown", and Morris eagerly adopted the title. In 1878 Queen Victoria was intending to set up a tapestry and stained-glass manufactory, and Morris wrote to his daughter, Jenny (March 6th, 1878): "The Empress Brown is hard at work at her rival establishment: I am sure she expects to get the whole of the ornamental upholstery of the kingdom in to her hands: let her tremble! I will under-sell her in all branches" (Brit. Mus. Add. MSS. 45339).

In fact, the situation was very different from the widespread and spontaneous agitation at the time of the "Bulgarian atrocities". The war party within the Cabinet was being goaded on by Queen Victoria who went so far as to threaten to lay down her "thorny crown" if a war policy were not pursued. On January 10th she wrote to Disraeli: "The Queen is really distressed at the low tone which this Country is inclined to hold... Oh, if the Queen were a man, she would like to go and give those Russians . . . such a beating! We shall never be friends again till we have it out."[1] In the country, the propaganda of the "patriotic" Press, playing upon traditional hostility to Tsarism, had begun to show its effect. Successful anti-Russian demonstrations were held in the provinces, with some working-class support: and in London gangs of roughs broke up or threatened anti-war meetings. The parliamentarians, always with one eye to the constituencies, were more unreliable than ever, and the E.Q.A. and L.R.L. had their biggest job yet upon its hands. Jingoism was appearing on all sides, and in the critical last week of December and first fortnight of January Morris and his friends only just held their own.

The most important meeting was held in January 6th, on the eve of the opening of Parliament. It is significant of the change in political temperature that the meeting was called by the "Workmen's Neutrality Committee"—the joint committee co-ordinating the L.R.L. and E.Q.A.—rather than by the E.Q.A. itself. At the afternoon session in Willis's rooms the main speakers included the courageous Radical, Professor Thorold Rogers, and the leader of the agricultural workers, Joseph Arch, rather than the Dukes of Westminster and Anthony Trollopes of a year before. Even in this less respectable gathering it was left to Morris to commit the unforgivable breach of tact, and unmask the biggest war-monger of the lot. According to *The Times:* "Mr. W. Morris spoke in strong terms against the action of the 'war-at-any-price-party'." After praising Gladstone, he went on:

[1] Buckle, *op. cit.,* Vol. VI., p. 217.

"He must also face the fact that the Court was using all the influence which it possessed—(Cries of 'No, no,' and 'Three cheers for the Queen'). The speaker, having been reminded by the chairman that it was not desirable to introduce the name of the Sovereign into political discussion, concluded by expressing his regret that fortune had placed at the head of affairs in England a man who was unfitted to be a statesman, a man without genius. . . to whose shiftiness the nation. . . must oppose a steady resistance."[1]

After the meeting Morris wrote to his wife:

"As to the agitation I must confess I have been agitated as well as agitating: you will have got the newspapers by this time with a sort of report of our proceedings including the speech of me, & it's—may I call it amiable indiscretion: of course I said more, and more connected words than that: the little meeting was very noisy, but I call it a success . . . at least it quite refused to cheer the Empress Brown: you see I had to speak at the end by wh: time the peace-party desired to fight for peace, and the war party was blue with rage."

This afternoon meeting was only preparatory to a great demonstration in Exeter Hall in the evening, at which Mundella took the chair. Morris wrote, in the same letter, that it had been—

"magnificent: orderly and enthusiastic: though mind you it took some heavy work to keep the enemy's roughs out; the noise of them outside was like the sea roaring against a lighthouse."[2]

Admission was by tickets which had been distributed among London trade unions and Radical and Liberal clubs. Henry Broadhurst was in charge of a party of stewards at the doors,

[1] *The Times*, January 17th, 1878. It was probably of this meeting that George Wardle recalled: "Morris tried to speak, but was so hoarse from excitement that he could scarce utter a word. I stood near but could only catch 'He is a trickster—a trickster', meaning Dizzy. This was screamed or hissed with a voice so weakened by his emotions that it was scarce audible. Sir Robert Peel, who stood by, his hat cocked on the side of his head, was highly amused" (May Morris, II, p. 604).

[2] *Letters*, p. 107.

"all acquainted with the features of the leaders of the Jingo mob", and personally threw one suspect on the floor.[1] A good many penetrated into the Hall, but they were in too small a minority to cause disturbance. Broadhurst had persuaded a fellow stonemason, organist at a London chapel, to bring a choir "composed entirely of working men and women". While the audience filled the Hall, the organist and choir prepared them for singing the song which either Broadhurst or F.W. Chesson had persuaded Morris to write for the occasion. It went to the tune of 'The Hardy Norseman's Home of Yore':

> "Wake, London Lads, wake, bold and free!
> Arise and fall to work,
> Lest England's glory come to be
> Bond servant to the Turk!

There were five verses to the song, and a copy was at every place. A nonconformist minister read it through, verse by verse, and then the choir went through it twice. When the great assembly rose to their feet and thundered it out together, people as different in their backgrounds as Henry Broadhurst and Georgie Burne-Jones were deeply moved.

> "It went down very well", Morris wrote, "& they sang it well together: they struck up while we were just ready to come onto the platform & you may imagine that I felt rather excited when I heard them begin to tune up: they stopped at the end of each verse and cheered lustily: we came onto the platform just about the middle of it."

Next day, when the Queen's Speech was less bellicose than had been feared, Morris was able to write with confidence:

> "There is no doubt that the last fortnight's agitation has stopped Dizzy from asking for money & proposing a Gallipoli expedition: that is to say from proposing immediate war: this is encouraging: but the danger will not be over until peace is signed."[2]

1 Henry Broadhurst, *From a Stonemason's Bench to a Cabinet Bench,* pp. 81-4.
2 *Letters,* p. 107.

In fact the next two and a half months were ones of ceaseless activity and war rumours. On January 23rd, 1878, the news was given that the fleet had been ordered to sail to the Dardanelles. The war spirit in the country was unscrupulously fanned by professional Jingoists: a Trafalgar Square meeting on January 31st was broken up with the aid of a large party of workmen brought down from Woolwich Arsenal and paid a gratuity for their day's work: "people on our side had to hide away in cellars & places & get out anyhow".[1] "I was at a very noisy meeting last night down at Stepney, where we had a bare majority", Morris wrote the next day. "I feel very low & muddled about it all: but we have one shot in the locker yet, to whit a big, real big demonstration in Hyde Park." In the first week of February officially-sponsored rumours suggested that the Russians were on the point of occupying Constantinople, even that the Indian Empire was in danger. Successful pro-war demonstrations were held in several towns. The Parliamentary Liberal Party, which was screwing up its courage to oppose a Vote of Credit, collapsed on the receipt of a bogus telegram about the imminent Russian occupation of the city. Even before this debacle, on February 7th, Morris was writing to Faulkner:

> "I am full of shame and anger at the cowardice of the so-called Liberal Party. A very few righteous men refuse to sit down at the bidding of these yelling scoundrels and pretend to agree with what they hate: these few are determined with the help of our working-men allies (who all along have been both staunch and sagacious) to get up a great demonstration in London as soon as may be. . . There will certainly be a fight, so of course you will come up if you can."[2]

The day before this "there was a meeting of the E.Q.A. & it was obvious that our party in Parliament were getting out of heart: so some of us conscious of how dangerous things were

[1] *Ibid.*, p. 108. See also the account in Maccoby, *English Radicalism 1853-1886*, p. 229, and Armytage, *op. cit.*, pp. 181-4.
[2] *Letters*, p. 109.

getting met at Mr. Broadhurst's & talked about holding a great demonstration in Hyde Park to keep up their spirits". Together with Auberon Herbert he had visited Samuel Morley for money, and then spent a part of that day and the next lobbying the Liberal M.Ps. He was decidedly unimpressed by the experience. "The worst part of it all is that the war fever is raging in England, & people go about in a Rule Britannia style that turns one's stomach."[1]

The final stage in the Eastern Question "education"—as far as Morris was concerned—came in the following fortnight. The fleet was now anchored off the Dardanelles in earnest, waiting for Turkish permission to make the passage. The idea of a grand Hyde Park demonstration was abandoned because of the uncertain winter weather and the exposure to the thuggery of the Jingoists. Instead, Morris pushed through the ambitious plan of a meeting in the Agricultural Hall, the largest building in London. Several members of the E.Q.A., including Morris and Burne-Jones, contributed £50 each to guarantee the expenses.[2] The story—or Morris's version of it—is told by him in a letter of February 15th:

"As to my political career, I think it is at an end for the present: & has ended sufficiently disgustingly, after beating about the bush and trying to organize some rags of resistance to the war-party for a fortnight, after spending all one's time in committees & the like: I went to Gladstone with some of the workmen & Chesson, to talk about getting him to a meeting at the Agricultural Hall: he agreed and was quite hot about it, and as brisk as a bee . . . to work we fell & everything got into trim: but—on Monday our parliamentaries began to quake, and tease Gladstone, and they have quaked the meeting out now: the E.Q.A. was foremost in the flight, & really I must needs say they behaved ill in the matter: Gladstone was quite ready to come up to the scratch & has behaved well throughout: but I am that ashamed that I can scarcely look people in the face though I did my best to keep the thing up: the working-men are in a great rage about it, as they well may be: for I do verily believe that we should have made it a success . . . There was a stormy meeting of the E.Q.A. yesterday . . . I am out of it now, I mean as to bothering my head about it: I shall give up reading the

[1] *Letters,* pp. 110-11. [2] *Memorials,* II, p. 84.

Papers, and shall stick to my work . . . After this fiasco it will be impossible to hold another meeting in London on the subject: we have been terrorized by the Medical Students & the Civil Servants, and are now slaves of the Tories for life."[1]

There seems to be little doubt that Morris's account is substantially accurate. On one point, perhaps, Morris was misled—Gladstone's simulated enthusiasm for the meeting. On January 3rd, 1878, he had turned down Mundella's request to him to speak with his characteristic tone of moral ambiguity:

"You cannot, I think, doubt from the moment I take a more active part the whole parliamentary forces of the Tories will be set to work against us.

"But pray continue to write as you see occasion and be assured that every word will be weighed."[2]

By the end of January it was becoming difficult to hold any meeting in London without danger of rioting and Jingoist attack. From Sheffield on January 29th came the news that 20,000 inhabitants had passed a resolution in favour of the Government. This being Mundella's own constituency, there was some cause, it seemed for "quaking". Mundella's letters assumed a note of tragic self-sacrifice:

"It is utterly discouraging to our side, and damaging to my influence on the Eastern Question. Personally, I can bear it. . . but I grieve for the sake of the cause and party, and the country."[3]

"I have had a sleepless night", he wrote the next day, "and feel a weaker man in *every way* this morning, but I shall put a good face on it, and go into the fight following my own convictions regardless of all consequences." Such professions —as is usual with politicians—were a prelude to his backing out altogether. Horror upon horrors, Gladstone's windows were broken by the Jingoists. The "Bishops, Parsons, Peers,

[1] *Letters,* p. 112. [2] Armytage, *op. cit.,* p. 183. [3] *Ibid.,* p. 184.

Literati, etc.", who had been so keen on the expulsion of the Turks from Europe just over a year before, were thoroughly cowed, in London at least. Morris found himself left out on a limb, with only Chesson and the L.R.L. standing firm. The day after they had lobbied Gladstone and found him "brisk as a bee", the great man was writing anxiously to Mundella:

> "I told the gentlemen last night that I could only attend a meeting
> "1. seated all through the Hall.
> "2. without any admission of the public, i.e. promiscuous persons.
> "3. with an ample allocation of stewards to each position to keep order.
> "They were sanguine as to the feeling—and they seemed to think the operation required to fulfil these conditions could be effected in the time. . ."[1]

No doubt the quaking was not quite so one-sided as Morris imagined. As soon as Gladstone discovered that Mundella himself had cold feet, he seems to have dropped the matter with relief. But Morris refused to lay any responsibility upon him and still regarded him as "the most illustrious statesman of England, the most single-hearted statesman in the world."[2]

The pass had been sold to the war party, so far as any resistance from the parliamentarians was concerned. Had Disraeli been determined upon war, there seemed to be little to restrain him. But, while the Queen was thirsting for another Crimean adventure, Disraeli was alternating the threat of force with tortuous diplomacy, and was more concerned with securing new footholds in the Mediterranean than with entering upon a major military operation. On March 3rd Peace Preliminaries were signed between Russia and a Turkey thoroughly disgruntled with the British "alliance". On March 8th the Cabinet resolved (in private) that in the event of the Peace Treaty compromising British maritime interests, "a new station in the east of the Mediterranean must be obtained

[1] Mundella Correspondence.
[2] "Address to English Liberals", delivered to the Chichester Liberal Association (1878), May Morris, II, p. 379.

and if necessary by force". On March 27th Disraeli announced the immediate calling-up of the Reserves and privately proposed the seizure—with Indian troops—of ports in the Levant and of Cyprus. As a result of the modified acceptance of these proposals, Lord Derby, who had for some time exerted a restraining influence within the Cabinet, resigned as Foreign Minister. "Yesterday morning", Morris commented on this news, "I suppose there were few people in England who did not think war as good as declared: but it is strange how a feeling of backing out on both sides seems growing this morning so that I should not wonder if the Jingoes were disappointed after all. E.Q.A. as good as dead."[1] The Labour Representation League, on the other hand, was by no means dead, and noted in its minutes for April 4th that it had issued a powerful manifesto against the machinations of the Turkish bondholders, and also that a petition for neutrality had received the signatures of about 15,000 "leading men" of various trade unions, "the whole transaction occupying less than a week", having been launched upon the news of the call-up of the Reserves.[2] In the end, Disraeli achieved one of his main aims, not by force of arms but through the Congress of Berlin, from which he returned with "peace with honour"—and Cyprus![3]

[1] *Letters,* p. 119.

[2] Minutes of Labour Representation League. The Manifesto is reprinted in full in *Labour's Formative Years,* pp. 193-4. See also Broadhurst, *op. cit.,* p. 84, for an account of the petition.

[3] Marx and Morris were diametrically opposed on the Eastern Question. Marx's view—set forward in a letter to Liebknecht on February 4th, 1878—was that "a *Russian defeat* would have greatly *hastened the social revolution in Russia,* for which the elements exist on a mass scale, and with it *the revolution throughout Europe*" (*Marx Engels Sel. Cor.,* p. 357). He was appalled by the hypocrisy of those Liberal politicians who were exploiting the "Bulgarian atrocities" propaganda for their own tactical interests, and he condemned the "corrupt trade union leaders" who tagged on behind them: "These fellows shouted and howled behind Gladstone, Bright, Mundella, Morley and the whole gang of factory owners, etc., *in majorem gloriam* of the Tsar as emancipator of nations, while they never raised a finger for their own brothers in South Wales, condemned to die of starvation by the mineowners" (Marx to Liebknecht, February 11th, 1878, *Marx-Engels Sel. Cor.,* p. 356). The letter to Liebknecht concludes with the suggestion that the growing opposition of the workers to Russia early in 1878 was prompted, not by Jingoism, but by the British people's traditional and healthy opposition to Tsarism. It is interesting to note that H.M. Hyndman was also in the opposite camp to Morris during the Eastern Question agitation.

This, then, was Morris's first introduction to the political world. It was an experience which was likely either to teach him many lessons or to drive him off in disgust. The latter seemed the more likely result. In the last two months of the agitation he took little part.[1] He seems to have been taking in earnest his own threat; "I shall give up reading the Papers, and shall stick to my work." On the other hand, he may well have been meditating upon his lessons: the depth of cynicism and unscrupulousness of the Tory Party: the opportunism and moral cowardice of professional politicians: the power of the working class, even when only a mere fringe are organized.

Two years later, when he had occasion to write to Mundella now elevated to Vice-President of the Council in Gladstone's Government, he recalled the days of the Jingo terror:

> "I wonder sometimes as I walk through the streets and look at the people if they are the same flesh and blood as made things so pleasant for us in the spring of 1878; and I feel enclined to say., what the deuce then *was* it all about?"[2]

When eight more years had passed, he understood the answer well enough. "Gladstone-worship" was now a thing of the past although he felt now an admiration of a different nature. "What will be left of Liberalism", he asked,

> "when this old man has gone; with his astonishing physical vigour, his belief in himself, his capacity of shutting his eyes to everything that his momentary political position forbids him to see, and his keen delight in playing the political game?"

True, his "soft fighting was discouraging enough" in the days of the Eastern Question—

> "but after all it was perhaps good enough for the occasion, for the Jingoes and Dizzy at their head never intended to go to war; they only meant bragging—I admit that we didn't know it at the time."[3]

[1] He was preparing, at this time, to join his family in Italy, and was also suffering from one of those rheumatic attacks which came upon him more than once at the end of a period of severe nervous tension.

[2] Mundella Correspondence.

[3] *Commonweal*, January 7th, 1888.

CHAPTER VI

THE "ANTI-SCRAPE"

WHILE the Eastern Question agitation was giving William Morris his first education in the workings of the political world, he was gaining insight from another direction into the depth of philistinism of his century. Even since his early days in Street's office in Oxford, when he had planned to enter the profession of an architect, Morris had fulminated in private against the excesses of "restoration". In his first lecture, *The Lesser Arts,* Morris referred to the "restoration" of ancient monuments:

> "Thus the matter stands: these old buildings have been altered and added to century after century, often beautifully, always historically; their very value, a great part of it, lay in that. . .
>
> "But of late years a great uprising of ecclesiastical zeal, coinciding with a great increase of study, and consequently of knowledge of mediaeval architecture, has driven people into spending their money on these buildings, not merely with the purpose of repairing them, of keeping them safe, clean, and wind and water-tight, but also of 'restoring' them to some ideal state of perfection; sweeping away if possible all signs of what had befallen them at least since the Reformation, and often since dates much earlier: this has sometimes been done with much disregard of art and entirely from ecclesiastical zeal, but oftener it has been well enough meant as regards art: yet. . . this restoration must be as impossible to bring about, as the attempt at it is destructive. . . I scarcely like to think what a great part of them have been made nearly useless to students of art and history. . ."[1]

This is a moderate statement of the case—as moderate as ever came from Morris's pen. In fact, as Morris well knew, "restoration" was an extremely profitable business for a few fashionable architects. Chief among these was Sir Gilbert Scott, the perpetrator of the Albert Memorial, who died in 1878. An enormous amount of work passed through his

[1] "The Lesser Arts", *Works,* Vol. XXII, p. 19.

office, over which he could hardly have exercised even the most superficial supervision. It is related of him that once on a journey he noticed a church that was being built, and enquired the name of the architect. "Sir Gilbert Scott," was the reply. "The cathedral-restoring business was very thoroughly organized by him," relates W.R. Lethaby, one of Morris's colleagues in the Society for the Protection of Ancient Buildings.[1] Describing the work done by Scott and his fellows, Lethaby writes:

> "It is impossible to give any notion of the violence and stupidities which were done in the name of 'restoration'. The crude idea seems to have been born of the root absurdity that art was shape and not substance; our ancient buildings were appearances of what was called 'style'. When the architect had learned what his text-books taught of the styles he could then provide thirteenth- or fourteenth-century 'features' at pleasure, and even correct the authentic old ones. Professional reports would run: 'The Tudor roof is incongruous with the Early English chancel arch, and it should be replaced by a thirteenth-century roof of steep pitch.' At Canterbury a wonderful twelfth-century tower was destroyed to put in its place a nineteenth-century 'fifteenth-century' erection. At St. Albans eleventh-century and fifteenth-century work were both destroyed to satisfy the whims of a lawyer-lord. It never struck any one that antiquity is being old. . . A practice of producing professional office-made versions of the art of any century which passed as the art itself was at full blast when the much-hated, much-revered Society for the Protection of Ancient Buildings was founded by Morris, Webb and Faulkner."[2]

The idea first occurred to Morris in the summer of 1876. "The sight of Burford Church being pulled about set my father to making notes for a letter of appeal for some united action", May Morris relates.[3] It is significant that he did no more about the matter until March of the next year, by which time his experience of the first successful months of the Eastern Question agitation may have given him confidence

[1] Lethaby, *op. cit.*, p. 67. [2] *Ibid.*, pp. 145-6.
[3] *Works*, Vol. XII, p. xiii.

in the effectiveness of public action. His first blast was provoked by the proposed "destruction" by Sir Gilbert Scott of Tewkesbury Minster, and was printed in March, 1877, in *The Athenaeum,* a periodical which had long been raising the issue in its columns. Although the tone of his letter was scarcely diplomatic—"the architects are, with a very few exceptions, hopeless, because interest, habit, and ignorance bind them, and... the clergy are hopeless, because their order, habit, and an ignorance yet grosser, bind them"—it aroused an immediate response. Morris had appealed for—

> "an association... to keep a watch on old monuments, to protest against all 'restoration' that means more than keeping out wind and weather, and... to awaken a feeling that our ancient buildings are not mere ecclesiastical toys, but sacred monuments of the nation's growth and hope."[1]

The Society, which Morris dubbed "Anti-Scrape", was formed in the next month, and Morris became its Honorary Secretary. Morris's enthusiasm was supplemented by the tact and persistence of Philip Webb. At the first annual meeting in June the adhesion of an imposing list of notabilities was announced, including—after some persuasion—Thomas Carlyle, as well as John Ruskin, James Bryce, Sir John Lubbock, Leslie Stephen, Coventry Patmore, Burne-Jones, Holman Hunt, Lord Houghton, and A.J. Mundella. A Manifesto, drafted by Morris, together with some passages reprinted from Ruskin's *Seven Lamps of Architecture,* were issued by the Society.

From this time until the end of his life, the Anti-Scrape never ceased to occupy a part of Morris's time. For more than a year he acted as Secretary, and afterwards he continued as one of the most active members of the Committee. His work included the undertaking of correspondence in the Press, and from time to time the visiting and making of reports upon buildings due for destruction or restoration.

[1] *Letters,* p. 86.

In the first year alone, some of the major issues which came before the Society included Tewkesbury Minster, the restoration of the choir at Canterbury Cathedral, the destruction of Wren's city churches, and the rebuilding of the roof at St. Albans. In 1879, an even bigger issue came up—the threatened replacement of the mosaics and rebuilding of the west front at St. Mark's, Venice. The campaign to arouse European opinion on this included the presentation of a Memorial which was signed, among others, by Disraeli and Gladstone, to the Italian Ambassador.[1] The work at St. Mark's was stopped: but whether as a result of the pressure of the Committee, or as the result of an independent decision of the Italian Government, became a matter of some heated dispute.

Tact was never Morris's strong point, whether in international or parochial affairs. Perhaps that was one of the main reasons for the success the Society achieved. If his thundering letters sometimes only made his opponents stand on their dignity and refuse to alter their plans, they at least had the effect of making the next lot of restorers a great deal more wary for fear that the same outspoken public wrath would fall upon them. The guardians of old property began to consult the Anti-Scrape rather than the fashionable architects before forming their plans, especially when it became known that a group of highly skilled architects would give their free advice on behalf of the Society. On several occasions, the Anti-Scrape helped to raise funds for essential repairs to parish churches and other buildings in danger of decay. On other occasions, they gladly issued publicity with the aim of finding some use for buildings in danger of destruction.

On the Committee itself Morris was a tower of strength. As a visitor for the Society, he was not such a success: and perhaps it was the restraining influence of Webb and his other colleagues which accounts for the fact that he did little

[1] This campaign was actually organized by an independent Committee, with G.E. Street as Vice-Chairman and H. Wallis as Hon. Sec. The correspondence of the Committee is preserved in Brit. Mus. Add. MSS. 38831, and Morris's letter soliciting Gladstone's signature is preserved in Brit. Mus. Add. MSS. 44461. f.123.

visiting after the first two or three years. After visiting one church which was being thoroughly "restored", he "rushed to the window of the inn shaking his fist as the parson passed by".[1] On being shown a piece of nineteenth century Gothic carving in another cathedral, he burst out: "Why, I could carve them better with my teeth." Another anecdote does not concern an official visit for the Society, but a chance moment during the Socialist propaganda in Glasgow in the late 1880s. In the company of Bruce Glasier, Morris was on his way to a meeting when they stopped to look at the Cathedral:

> "We were within a few yards of the doorway when he stopped abruptly, as if struck by a rifle ball, his eyes fixed furiously on some object in front of him. As he glared he seemed to crouch like a lion for a leap at its prey, his whiskers bristling out. 'What the hell is that? Who the hell has done that?' he shouted, to the amaze, alarm, and indignation of the people near by.
>
> "I looked. . . and saw at once what was the offending object. There it was. . . a sculptured memorial or sarcophagus in shining white marble jammed into the old grey stone-work of the aisle. . completely cutting off a portion of the window above. . . 'What infernal idiot has done *that*?' Morris again demanded, and heedless of the consternation around him poured forth a torrent of invective against the unknown perpetrators of the crime. For the moment I thought he might actually spring upon the excrescence and tear out the hateful thing with his bare fists."[2]

But his visits did not only bring him rage. There is a pleasant description by Philip Webb of Morris's love for a certain barn in Berkshire, which illustrates the richness of the pleasure he gained from old buildings—and which, indeed, helps us to understand his rage at their destruction. Great Coxwell Barn, "had great hold on William Morris's imagination".

> "Before I had seen it", recounts Webb, "I laughingly scorned his determination that it was the most wonderfully beautiful example in

[1] Lethaby, *op. cit.*, pp. 149-50. [2] Glasier, *op. cit.*, pp. 103-4.

England. When at last he exultingly carried me to it (almost tremblingly for fear of my judgement) I was obliged to agree with him that it was unapproachable in its dignity. I clearly understood in this case as in others that his insight and judgement were unfailingly right . . . One turned up a narrow lane. . . when the ridge of the mighty roof. . . rose foot by foot over the grassy bank till one got over the top of the knoll, when its whole impressiveness was clearly seen, so large in its lines as to make one draw breath sharply with wonder. There it was, dominating the farmhouse adjoining, and with nothing but the simple fields of Berkshire about them. Its magnitude, nice precision of building and dainty parts of pure architecture, all done in handsome freestone, made it as beautiful as a cathedral, but with no ostentation of building whatever: a perfectly suitable barn and nothing else. The workmen who set it up did well once and for all time. . . If I saw what it all meant in the quiet Berkshire landscape and its clear history of the builders and their craft, how much more must he have seen into and round it? This building and all of its like, were infinite delight to him."[1]

It may seem an unlikely road to Communism by way of Great Coxwell Barn. Nevertheless it is true that Morris's work for the Anti-Scrape contributed as much to bring him on the final stages of his journey as any other influence. In giving leadership to the Anti-Scrape he was forced again and again to examine and set into words his deepest preoccupation—the relation of the arts to society. In the controversies which sprang up around the work he was continually forced to define (and to revise) the basic assumptions which had guided his life from his Oxford days.

In the first place, Morris was brought directly into conflict with the property sanctions of capitalist society. In the negative sense, he had to fight against both commercial rapacity and views of ecclesiastical propriety. When he remonstrated with the Vicar of Burford, the Vicar replied that it was his own Church and he could stand on his head in it if he wanted to. The Dean of Canterbury, in a controversy in *The Times* in 1877, struck a rather more lofty note:

[1] Lethaby, *op. cit.,* p. 154.

"Mr. Morris's Society probably looks on our Cathedral as a place for antiquarian research or for budding architects to learn their art in. We need it for the daily worship of God."

When Wren's city churches were being threatened with destruction, Morris was able (in *The Times* of April, 1878) to call upon those same religious sentiments which had been outraged by his earlier interference:

"Surely an opulent city, the capital of the commercial world, can afford some small sacrifice to spare these beautiful buildings the little plots of ground upon which they stand. Is it absolutely necessary that every scrap of space in the City should be devoted to money-making, and are religion, sacred memorials, recollections of the great dead, memorials of the past, works of England's greatest architect, to be banished from this wealthy City?"[1]

But this—strong as it is—is the expression of Morris's more diplomatic self—the loyal servant of his own Society. While he might score valid points in this way, with every case that came forward he was given further and more horrifying insight into the insensibility of commercial philistinism, the absolute lack of any public conscience where questions of individual profit or loss were concerned. "Even now mere cynically brutal destruction, not veiling itself under any artistic pretence, is only too common", he reported to the First Annual General Meeting of the Anti-Scrape in June, 1878: "It is still only too commonly assumed that any consideration of Art must yield if they stand in the way of money interests."[2] The next few years gave him more than enough examples to prove this statement. He was forced to contrast the attitude of feudal society in this respect with that of industrial capitalism. This contrast—while a frequent theme of his lectures and addresses in the late 1870s—found its fullest expression in his address to the Twelfth Annual

[1] *Letters*, p. 122.
[2] Address to 1st Annual Meeting, S.P.A.B., May Morris, I, pp. 116-17.

Meeting of the Anti-Scrape in 1889:

> "Consider London of the fourteenth century: a smallish town, beautiful from one end to the other; streets of low whitewashed houses with a big Gothic church standing in the middle of it; a town surrounded by walls, with a forest of church towers and spires, besides the cathedral and the abbeys and priories; every one of the houses in it, nay, every shed, bearing in it a certain amount of absolute, definite, distinct, conscientious art. Think of the difference between that and the London of to-day. . ."

The mind is thrown back directly to the "London, small and white and clean" of the opening of *The Earthly Paradise*. But this time it is evoked, not with a sense of nostalgia, but as an aggressive and fully-realised comparison, exposing the indifference of his own time:

> "Just consider what England was in the fourteenth century. The population. . . at about four millions. Think then of the amount of beautiful and dignified buildings which those four millions built . . . Not only those churches and houses which we see, but also those which have been destroyed. . . Those buildings. . . contained much art: pictures, metal-work, carvings, tapestry, and the like, altogether forming a prodigious mass of art, produced by a scanty population. Try to imagine that. Why, if we were asked (supposing we had the capacity) to reproduce the whole of those buildings with their contents, we should have to reply, 'The country is not rich enough; every capitalist in the country would be ruined before it could be done.' Is not that strange?"[1]

Thus the work of the Anti-Scrape quickened and deepened his insight into the destructive philistinism of capitalist society. His friends, like Edward Burne-Jones, followed him this far, but then were content to leave it at that. If clergymen or landowners wished to destroy old works of art, they were prepared to fight them tooth and nail, to fulminate against the age, to point out that people in earlier times had viewed the matter differently. But Morris's mind worked in a different

[1] May Morris, I, pp. 153-4.

way. He was not a systematic thinker, although he forced himself on occasion to discipline his intuitions with very great logic: but, whenever he was aware of the existence of a problem, he had a quite remarkable persistence in worrying at it until he was satisfied that he had reached a solution. One of the aims of the Society (proposed in his first letter to *The Athenaeum*) was "to awaken a feeling that our ancient buildings are not mere ecclesiastical toys, but sacred monuments of the nation's growth and hope". Faced with the jealous property-rights of capitalism, he wished to argue, first, that—irrespective of their position at law—"our ancient historical monuments are national property and ought no longer to be left at the mercy of the many and variable ideas of ecclesiastical propriety that may at any time be prevalent among us":[1] and, second, to convince the public in general that they had both responsibilities and rights in relation to these buildings. Since the law denied that this was true, he was forced to ground his case upon canons of social morality unacknowledged in capitalist society.

This view of men's responsibilities towards the art of past ages was not, in the first place, his own, but had come to him through Carlyle and Ruskin. It was suggested in those passages which he reprinted for the Anti-Scrape propaganda from the *Seven Lamps of Architecture:*

> "It is. . . no question of expediency or feeling whether we shall preserve the buildings of past times or not. *We have no right whatever to touch them.* They are not ours. They belong, partly to those who built them, and partly to all the generations of mankind who are to follow us. The dead have still their right to them: that which they laboured for. . . we have no right to obliterate. What we have ourselves built we are at liberty to throw down; but what other men gave their strength, and wealth and life to accomplish, their right over does not pass away with their death; still less is the right to the use of what they have left vested in us only. It belongs to all their successors."

[1] *Letters,* p. 92.

These words, Morris wrote to Ruskin, "are so good, and so completely settle the whole matter, that I feel ashamed at having to say anything else about it."[1]

"A Society like ours is nothing if it is not aggressive", he said in 1889; "therefore we have to try to convince even the most ignorant; and to do that properly, we ought to be able to get in the habit of putting ourselves in their position." In doing this, he found himself from the outset forced to rebut the charge that he wished only to preserve, in order to feed the sentiments of a handful of artists, the ruinous and the "picturesque". The interest in ancient buildings, he agreed, was "romantic"—"but what romance means is that capacity for a true conception of history, a power of making the past part of the present".[2] The romantic building "recalls to the mind the interest of the life of times past". Each attempt which he made to define in social terms the meaning of this beauty, the value of this interest in the past, brought him closer to Marxist conclusions. The beauty of the masterpieces of the past, he declared in a hundred different ways, lay in their embodiment of the aspirations of past generations of men, of their "hopes and fears", the vicissitudes of their affairs and the quality of their lives.

This conclusion forced upon him yet another series of questions. Why should men care to preserve the record of history at all? What could be learnt from the monuments of past aspirations beyond the sense of mortality, and the bitterness and degradation of the present? The answer lay in that astonishing rebirth of hope which permeated all Morris's writing and activity in these years. The masterpieces of the past were not dead relics, but a living inspiration and warning to the present, a proof of qualities in man which—however suppressed and slumbering—could not be extinguished for ever. "I love art, and I love history", he declared in a Lecture delivered in 1882 in support of the Anti-Scrape—

[1] *Letters*, p. 93. [2] May Morris, I, p. 148.

"but it is living art and living history that I love. If we have no hope for the future, I do not see how we can look back on the past with pleasure. If we are to be less than men in time to come, let us forget that we have ever been men. It is in the interest of living art and living history that I oppose so-called restoration. What history can there be in a building bedaubed with ornament, which cannot at the best be anything but a hopeless and lifeless imitation of the hope and vigour of the earlier world?. . . Let us leave the dead alone, and, ourselves living, build for the living and those that shall live."[1]

This theme recurs in all his early addresses to the Society. But it was in a most remarkable paper read to the Society in 1884, after he had become an active Socialist, that he achieved his finest expression of his views. Our ancient architecture, he commenced—

"bears witness to the development of man's ideas, to the continuity of history, and, so doing, affords never-ceasing instruction, nay education, to the passing generations, not only telling us what were the aspirations of men passed away, but also what he may hope for in the time to come."

After discussing the distortions of past historians, presenting history without pattern or development, he referred to the modern understanding of the past, which, now that the "mists of pedantry" were beginning to lift, revealed a different picture—

"inchoate order in the remotest times, varying indeed among different races and countries, but swayed always by the same laws, moving forward ever towards something that seems the very opposite of that which it started from, and yet the earlier order never dead but living in the new, and slowly moulding it to a recreation of its former self. How different a spirit such a view of history must create it is not difficult to see. No longer shallow mockery at the failures and follies of the past, from a standpoint of so-called civilization, but deep sympathy with its half-conscious aims, from amidst the difficulties and shortcomings that

[1] "The History of Pattern-Designing", *Works,* Vol. XXII, p. 233.

we are only too sadly conscious of to-day; that is the new spirit of history; knowledge... has brought us humility, and humility hope of... perfection..."

The two instruments of this new knowledge of history Morris declared to be the study of language and the study of archaeology ("the record of man's creative deeds"); the preservation of this latter record was the special aim of the Society.

Morris then turned to examine the second great argument which had been brought against the Anti-Scrape. The whole case of the restorers rested upon it. Granted the beauty of the medieval buildings, they said, why could not nineteenth-century architects and craftsmen, by patient research and practice, make copies of thirteenth-century work to replace the old stone where it had decayed? Once again, Ruskin had been the first to give an answer:

"Do not let us deceive ourselves in this important matter; it is *impossible,* as impossible as to raise the dead, to restore anything that has ever been great or beautiful in architecture. That which I have... insisted upon as the life of the whole, that spirit which is given only by the hand and eye of the workman, can never be recalled. Another spirit may be given by another time, and it is then a new building; but the spirit of the dead workman cannot be summoned up, and commanded to direct other hands and other thoughts."

Morris, starting from the arguments of "The Nature of Gothic", examined in detail the conditions and organization of labour in ancient, feudal, and in capitalist society. "Every architectural work is a work of co-operation", he commenced. "The very designer, be he never so original... [is] under the influence of *tradition;* dead men guide his hand even when he forgets that they ever existed." The closely-reasoned arguments with which Morris followed through the various changes in the skill and organization of the craftsmen cannot be summarized here. But this address is one of Morris's most important contributions to the theory of architecture. The inspired insights of Ruskin have been embodied within a coherent analysis of the techniques and productive relations of the societies within which the crafts were practised. Finally, Morris reached the point of change between the domestic industries and crafts of the eighteenth century, and modern industrial capitalism:

> "This strange and most momentous revolution was brought about by the machinery which the chances and changes of the world. . . *forced* on our population. You must think of this great machine industry as though on the one hand merely the full development of the effects of producing for profit instead of for livelihood, which began in Sir Thomas More's time, yet on the other as a revolutionary change from that of the mere division of labour. The exigencies of my own work have driven me to dig pretty deeply into the strata of the eighteenth century workshop system, and I could clearly see how very different it is from the factory system of to-day. . . therefore it was with a ready sympathy that I read the full explanation of the change and its tendencies in the writings of a man, I will say a great man, whom, I suppose, I ought not to name in this company, and who cleared my mind on several points (also unmentionable here) relating to this subject of labour and its products. . ."[1]

We can see here a clear example of the converging paths by which Morris was advancing towards Socialism. In the years between 1879 and 1884 he had been very active in practical work with tapestry and textiles, setting up his new workshops at Merton Abbey:[2] this work had brought him increasing insight into the contrast between the domestic and factory systems. At the same time his propaganda for the Anti-Scrape had brought him down a different path towards an understanding of the relations of the artist to his society. A few paces separated the paths, and the reading of *Capital* joined the two. Here is the explanation for the extraordinary clarity of this address.

Thus he had solved the problem, to his own satisfaction, of why restoration was impossible. The solution brought him back once again to his constant pre-occupation of the time

[1] May Morris, I, p. 139.

[2] See P. Henderson, *William Morris* (1973 edition), pp. 273-82.

—the change and movement of history:

"Surely it is a curious thing that while we are ready to laugh at the idea of... the Greek workman turning out a Gothic building, or a Gothic workman turning out a Greek one, we see nothing preposterous in the Victorian workman producing a Gothic one... I may be told, perhaps, that... historical knowledge... has enabled us to perform that miracle of raising the dead centuries to life. But to my mind it is a strange view to take of historical knowledge and insight, that it should set us on the adventure of trying to retrace our steps towards the past, rather than give us some glimmer of insight into the future; a strange view of the continuity of history, that it should make us ignore the very changes which are the essence of that continuity...

"Surely such a state of things is a token of change—of change, speedy perhaps, complete certainly: of the visible end of one cycle and the beginning of another."

It is important to make these views of Morris clear, since they scatter the charges of nostalgic medievalism or sentimental pedantry still sometimes levelled ignorantly at his name. In fact, it was his work for the Anti-Scrape which urged him forward from a passive to an active view of history. Persons with a false idea of the continuity of history, he told the Society in a notable passage of his address in 1889,

"are loth to admit the fatal words, 'It cannot be, it has gone'. They believe that we can do the same sort of work in the same spirit as our forefathers, whereas for good and for evil we are completely changed, and we cannot do the work they did. All continuity of history means is after all perpetual change, and it is not hard to see that we have changed with a vengeance, and thereby established our claim to be the continuers of history."[1]

At times Morris was despondent, saying: "It seems as if they will see what we mean just as the last old building is destroyed."[2] He was faced by that general apathy and defeatism which he himself was only shaking off, when he wrote to Georgie Burne-Jones in July, 1881:

[1] May Morris, I, p. 152. [2] Lethaby, *op. cit.*, p. 159.

"As to Anti-Scrape, I have little comfort there. . . As to the buildings. . . the destruction is not far from being complete already. What people really say to themselves is this: I don't like the thing being done, but I can bear it maybe—or certainly, when I come to think of it—and to stir in it is such obvious suffering; so I won't stir. Certainly to take that trouble in any degree it is needful that a man should be touched with a real love of the earth, a worship of it, no less; and I think that as things go, that is seldom felt except by very simple people, and by them. . . dimly enough. You know the most refined and cultured people, both those of the old religions and those of the vague new ones, have a sort of Manichean hatred of the world (I use the word in its proper sense, the home of man). Such people must be both the enemies of beauty and the slaves of necessity, and true it is that they lead the world at present, and I believe will so till all that is old is gone, and history has become a book from which the pictures have been torn."

But the conclusion to the letter is equally revealing:

"If you ask me why I kick against the pricks in this matter, all I can say is, first because I cannot help it, and secondly because I am encouraged by a sort of faith, that something will come of it, some kind of culture of which we know nothing at present."[1]

The work of the Anti-Scrape both arose from and contributed to Morris's rebirth of hope. How can we ever analyse the sources of such a change in a man's outlook? Which contributed most—the contact with Iceland, the practice of his crafts, the study of history, the concrete response to life of the poet (the "real love of the earth"), the public activity and contact with the working class? Certainly all had their part in his rising tide of confidence in the future. From the outset of his work with the Society he pleaded not for a complete halting of restoration, but for a "truce" lasting perhaps for a century, the preservation of the buildings intact until then, for the future to decide. Naturally, when he became a Socialist in 1883, he argued this with ever stronger conviction. In his address of 1884 he said plainly that capitalism was dying, and

[1] *Letters*, p. 150.

a new society coming to birth:

> "On the genuineness and reality of that hope the existence, the reason for existence of our Society depends. Believe me, it will not be possible for a small knot of cultivated people to keep alive an interest in the art and records of the past amidst the present conditions of a sordid and heart-breaking struggle for existence for the many, and a languid sauntering through life for the few. But when society is so reconstituted that all citizens will have a chance made up of due leisure and reasonable work, then will all society, and not our 'Society' only, resolve to protect ancient buildings. . . for then at last they will begin to understand that they are part of their present lives, and part of themselves."[1]

"Although I am engaged with other societies, who might consider themselves more useful", he said in his address in 1889, "I think the work of this Society is thoroughly worth doing. . . . Let us do what seems to us our duty in this matter, and let those that come after us do theirs; that will suffice; but my belief is that our descendants will thank us for our share of the work."[2]

Perhaps his most remarkable expression of confidence was in his address of ten years earlier—before he had any acquaintance with Socialism, and before he had even heard of Marx's name. "The workman of to-day is no artist", he said:

> "It is the hope of my life that this may one day be changed; that popular art may grow again in our midst; that we may have an architectural style, the growth of its own times, but connected with all history."

After making his appeal for a "truce" which would leave the decision to the future, he continued:

> "As for that decision of the future times of perfect and living art, I am not afraid of it. . . I believe that then the little grey weather-

[1] May Morris, I, p. 145. [2] *Ibid.*, p. 157.

beaten building, built by ignorant men, torn by violent ones, patched by blunderers, that has outlived so many hopes and fears of mankind, and yet looks friendly and familiar to them—I believe that this relic of past times will be no offence to the beauty and majesty of their streets. . . Rather I believe they will honour it the more for the many minds and hands of men that have dealt with it, and they will religiously guard it as a holy symbol of all the triumphs and tribulations of art: of art, the constant companion and expression of the life and aspirations of the world."[1]

[1] May Morris, I, p. 124.

CHAPTER VII

THE RIVER OF FIRE

SPEAKING at a Socialist meeting in Oldham on July 11th, 1885, a notorious agitator declared:

> "I have lived through and noted the most degrading epoch of public opinion that ever happened in England, and have seen the triumphant rule of the swindler in private and public life, the rule of hypocrisy and so-called respectability, begin to shake and totter."[1]

This agitator, normally reported in the Press as "Mr. W. Morris" should be distinguished from "William Morris, Author of 'The Earthly Paradise' ", who was still acknowledged in polite society. The transformation of the eccentric artist and romantic literary man into the Socialist agitator may be counted among the great conversions of the world. Morris was not only taking a step of far-reaching significance in his own life; nor was he only bringing the struggling Socialist pioneers their most notable recruit. He was also—if he is viewed (as he once viewed himself) as "the type of a certain group of mind" rather than as an isolated individual—taking a step which broke through the narrowing charmed circle of defeatism of bourgeois culture.

The years when this transformation took place were those between the end of the Eastern Question agitation in 1878 and the early months of 1883. Morris was by no means alone in his time in analysing the disease of capitalist society: from their different standpoints Carlyle, Ruskin, Matthew Arnold —even Dante Gabriel Rossetti and John Stuart Mill—either revolted in disgust against the ethic of capitalism or questioned its immutable economic basis. Yet all these men, the "railers against 'progress' ", were somehow held back from a final

[1] Unpublished Lecture, "The Depression of Trade", Brit. Mus. Add. MSS. 45333.

positive and revolutionary understanding. Discussing the death of the old art in a lecture of 1881, Morris declared:

> "We of the English middle classes are the most powerful body of men that the world has yet seen. . . And yet when we come to look the matter in the face, we cannot fail to see that even for us with all our strength it will be a hard matter to bring about that birth of the new art: for between us and that which is to be, if art is not to perish utterly, there is something alive and devouring; something as it were a river of fire that will put all that tries to swim across to a hard proof indeed, and scare from the plunge every soul that is not made fearless by desire of truth and insight of the happy days to come beyond."[1]

What a remarkable insight this is! At the time Morris could do little to define the nature of this "river of fire", and yet he could see around him his most gifted contemporaries—men who had helped to lead him to this point—hesitating upon its brink. Rossetti, the inspiration of his youth, died in April, 1882, and Morris reflected upon his lack of interest in politics:

> "The truth is he cared for nothing but individual and personal matters. . . He would take abundant trouble to help one person who was in distress of mind or body; but the evils of any mass of people he couldn't bring his mind to bear upon. I suppose in short it needs a person of hopeful mind to take disinterested notice of politics, and Rossetti was certainly not hopeful."[2]

If Rossetti was without hope, Arnold (in Morris's view) fell short in another direction—determination and courage. It is true that Arnold, in his last years, was carried by his hatred of the philistines to the point of declaring "Our middle classes know neither man nor the world; they have no light, and can give none", and of appealing directly to the working class to take the remedy into their own hands. But in his lecture upon

[1] "The Prospects of Architecture", *Works,* Vol. XXII, p. 131.

[2] Mackail, II, p. 93.

"Equality", which Morris read in the *Fortnightly Review* in 1878, he proposed as a practical programme little more than some reform in the law of bequest—"Self-Help" starting afresh with each generation, the Transport House distant ideal. Morris was impressed by Arnold's sincerity:[1] but not with his conclusions:

"With the main part. . . I heartily agree: the only thing is that if he has any idea of a remedy he dursn't mention it. I think myself that no rose-water will cure us: disaster and misfortune of all kinds, I think, will be the only things that will breed a remedy: in short, nothing can be done till all rich men are made poor by common consent. I suppose he dimly sees this, but is afraid to say it, being, though naturally a courageous man, somewhat infected with the great vice of that cultivated class he was praising so much—cowardice, to wit."[2]

As we have seen, even John Ruskin, whom Morris called "the first comer, the inventer",[3] drew back at this "devouring" barrier. In truth, Carlyle, Ruskin, Arnold—all were too ready to appeal to the working class to lead the nation forth in battles for objectives which they themselves had at heart, which were derived from their own special discontent, but which had little relevance to the immediate grievances under which working people were suffering. They were too inclined to see the workers as the rank and file of an Army of Light, struggling valiantly for culture or for a new morality, under the generalship of themselves and a few enlightened leaders who had broken free from the philistine middle class.

Morris also fell into this error in the years between 1878 and 1880. At the same time as he was beginning to write and lecture for "Anti-Scrape", he started on a new series of lectures in which he sought to take the cause of art to the workers. Discussing "The Lesser Arts" in his first lecture in December, 1877, he put the case at its simplest. The flood of "cheap and nasty" products on the market was the fault of all classes of society, he declared, producers and consumers

[1] May Morris, II, p. 69. [2] *Letters*, p. 113. [3] May Morris, II, p. 584.

alike. In particular—

"manufacturers (so called) are so set on carrying out competition to its utmost, competition of cheapness, not of excellence, that they meet the bargain-hunters half way, and cheerfully furnish them with nasty wares at the cheap rate. . ."

The remedy must therefore lie with the producers,

"the handicraftsmen, who are not ignorant of these things like the public, and who have no call to be greedy and isolated like the manufacturers or middlemen; the duty and honour of educating the public lies with them, and they have in them the seeds of order and organization which make that duty easier."[1]

Moreover, all his researches into Gothic architecture and into the decorative arts reinforced his conviction that the true roots of these arts were in the traditional skills of the people. "History", he said in one of his most striking phrases, "has remembered the kings and warriors, because they destroyed; Art has remembered the people, because they created."[2] What was more natural then that he should turn to the people for the rebirth of art? The only hope for the arts lay in a future when the working class,

"the 'residuum' of modern civilization, the terror of radical politicians, and the tool of reactionists, will become the great mass of orderly thinking people, sweet and fair in its manners, and noble in its aspirations, and that. . . is the sole hope of worthy, living, enduring art: nothing else, I say, will help. . ."[3]

His first lecture was delivered for a body called the "Trades Guild of Learning", promoted by Professor Warr, a Positivist

[1] "The Lesser Arts", *Works,* Vol. XXII, p. 22.

[2] *Ibid.,* p. 32.

[3] From a pre-Socialist Lecture (1880), reprinted in part in May Morris, II, p. 68.

colleague of Marx's old Radical friend, Professor Beesly, and for some years Secretary of the Cobden Club. George Wardle, the Manager of the Firm, recalled (in a letter to Sir Sydney Cockerell) that Warr established the Guild with Morris's aid because he "had visions of moralizing the Capitalist" by means of educating the young carpenters, stonemasons, and apprentices. In the beginning, for Morris as well,

> "it was rather a question of educating the workman, more especially the artizan or worker in some of the fine arts... I need hardly say there were very few workmen of any kind there [at the first lectures], except the men from Queen Square [the Firm] and that the bulk of the audience was formed by Morris's *clients*."[1]

Here, then, was Morris, in 1879 and 1880, even as late as 1881, standing on the brink of the "river of fire", hesitating before the plunge. Of the real lives of the workers he knew very little. He knew and respected the craftsmen who worked for the Firm, and the villagers of Kelmscott: but he saw the sordid scenes of the metropolis as an outsider glimpsing a garish interior of vice:

> "Look you", he said in 1881, "as I sit at work at home, which is at Hammersmith,[2] close to the river, I often hear go past the window some of that ruffianism of which a good deal has been said in the papers of late... As I hear the yells and shrieks and all the degradation cast on the glorious tongue of Shakespeare and Milton, as I see the brutal reckless faces and figures go past me, it rouses recklessness and brutality in me also, and fierce wrath takes possession of me, till I remember, as I hope I mostly do, that it was my good luck only of being born respectable and rich that has put me on this side of the window among delightful books and lovely works of art, and not on the other side, in the empty street, the drink-steeped liquor-shops, the foul and degraded lodgings. What words can say what all that means?"[3]

[1] May Morris, II, p. 605.

[2] Morris moved to Kelmscott House, Hammersmith (not to be confused with Kelmscott Manor in Lechlade) in 1878. It was Kelmscott House which became famous as a Socialist meeting-place.

[3] "Art and the Beauty of the Earth", *Works,* Vol. XXII, p. 171.

"Then indeed I fall a-wondering at the strange and slender thread of circumstances which has armed me for doing and forebearing with that refinement which I didn't make myself, but was born into. That, I say, I wonder at. . ."[1]

By the early 1880s it is clear that Morris was disappointed in the great ambitions with which he had started the Firm. In order to understand this, it must be remembered that in its origin the Firm had appeared to him not as a commercial venture and scarcely even as a strictly artistic one. It was the form taken by his "holy crusade against the age": it was intended to fight the flood of philistinism in one field of Victorian life, to inject into the very sources of production pleasurable and creative labour, to re-create conditions of artistic production found in medieval times. But the age had not flinched in the face of this form of attack. The slums grew, and the respectable suburban jerry-building thrived:

"I think you will understand me. . . but too well when I ask you to remember the pang of dismay that comes on us when we revisit some spot of country which has been specially sympathetic to us in times past. . . but where now as we turn the corner of the road or crown the hill's brow we can see first the inevitable blue slate roof, and then the blotched mud-coloured stucco, or ill-built wall of ill-made bricks of the new buildings; then as we come nearer and see the arid and pretentious little gardens, and cast-iron horrors of railings, and miseries of squalid out-houses breaking through the sweet meadows and abundant hedgerows. . ."[2]

It might have been something if the age had ignored the Firm altogether, or fought it tooth and nail. But, instead, it had been absorbed by fashionable and wealthy circles.[3] Lady Tranmore's

[1] Address to Nottingham Kyrle Society, 1881, May Morris, I, pp. 201-2.
[2] "The Prospects of Architecture", *Works,* Vol. XXII, p. 125.
[3] See "The Lesser Arts" (1877): "People say to me often enough: If you want to make your art succeed and flourish, you must make it the fashion: a phrase which I confess annoys me; for they mean by it that I should spend one day over my work to two days trying to convince rich, and supposed influential people, that they care very much for what they really do not care in the least, so that it may happen according to the proverb: *Bell-wether took the leap, and we all went over*" (*Works,* Vol. XXII, p. 13).

house, in Mrs. Humphrey Ward's novel, *The Marriage of William Ashe,* is described as reflecting "the rising worship of Morris and Burne-Jones":

> "Her walls were covered with the well-known pomegranate or jessamine or sunflower patterns; her hangings were of a mystic greenish blue, her pictures were drawn either from the Italian primitives or their modern followers."[1]

Moreover, Morris was enraged to find commercial manufacturers turning out cheap imitation-Morris products, including one wall-paper which he described as "a mangy gherkin on a horsedung ground".[2] "Morris" was becoming the code-word for a kind of ostentatious cultivation among a fringe of the upper and middle classes, and the designer himself was beginning to regard his own customers with increasing distaste.

From its early days the Firm had held fast to certain principles in its work: its first Manager, Warington Taylor, had (unbeknown to Morris) once lost a good contract for decorating a church because he had written on the estimate, under the item: "To providing a silk and gold altar cloth":

> "*Note.*—In consideration of the fact that the above item is a wholly unnecessary and inexcusable extravagance at a time when thousands of poor people in this so-called Christian country are in want of food—additional charge to that set forth above, ten pounds."[3]

When Morris started the Anti-Scrape he turned down all orders for decorations or stained glass in old churches, in order not to appear to be profiting from restoration himself. In the decoration of private houses he felt even more constrained. Philip Webb had built one of his most ambitious houses for Sir Lowthian Bell, the ironmaster, and Morris,

[1] See also Mary Howitt, *An Autobiography* (1889), Vol. II, p. 170.

[2] Mackail, II, p. 97.

[3] Glasier, *op. cit.,* p. 56.

called in to do the decoration, was so well pleased with his friend's building that he decided to attend to the work in person. One day, Sir Lowthian Bell related,

"he heard Morris talking and walking about in an excited way, and went to inquire if anything was wrong. 'He turned on me like a wild animal—"It is only that I spend my life in ministering to the swinish luxury of the rich." ' "[1]

In January, 1882, he was writing to Georgie Burne-Jones:

"I have perhaps rather more than enough of work to do, and . . . am dwelling somewhat low down in the valley of humiliation. . . It sometimes seems to me as if my lot was a strange one: you see, I work pretty hard, and on the whole very cheerfully, not altogether I hope for mere pudding, still less for praise; and while I work I have the cause always in mind, and yet I know that the cause for which I specially work is doomed to fail, at least in seeming; I mean that art must go under, where or how ever it may come up again. . . It does sometimes seem to me a strange thing indeed that a man should be driven to work with energy and even with pleasure and enthusiasm at work which he knows will serve no end but amusing himself; am I doing nothing but make-believe then, something like Louis XVI's lock-making?"[2]

In his designing, he was, in general, coming to favour simplicity rather than richness of finish: and when he came to lecture upon the lesser arts—in such a lecture as "Making the Best of It"—he was continually striving to translate his principles into terms of a working-class income. Fine carving, costly carpets and hangings, rich painting—all these might be desirable: but they were not the most important thing. Shoddy must be driven out first. "Simplicity of life, begetting simplicity of taste. . . is of all matters most necessary for the birth of the new and better art", he said in his first lecture. It was a constant theme of those that followed. "Simplicity of life", he said in 1881,

[1] Lethaby, *op. cit.,* p. 94. [2] *Letters,* p. 157.

"is not a misery, but the very foundation of refinement: a sanded floor and white-washed walls, and the green trees and flowery meads and living waters outside; or a grimy place amid the smoke with a regiment of housemaids always working to smear the dirt together so that it may be unnoticed; which, think you, is the most refined?. . ."[1]

Even the richness of the future seemed to him to be more one of quality than abundance:

"In looking forward towards any utopia of the arts. I do not conceive to myself of there being a very great quantity of art of any kind, certainly not of ornament, apart from the purely intellectual arts; and even those must not swallow up too much of life. . . Looking forward from out of the farrago of rubbish with which we are now surrounded, [I can] chiefly see possible negative virtues in the externals of our household goods; can see them never shabby, pretentious, or ungenerous, natural and reasonable always; beautiful also, but more because they are natural and reasonable, than because we have set about to make them beautiful."[2]

"I decorate modern houses for people", he told the young Yeats,

"but the house that would please me would be some great room where one talked to one's friends in one corner, and ate in another, and slept in another, and worked in another."[3]

And to his Socialist friend, Scheu, who must often have exchanged with him anecdotes of the trade, he said:

"I would like to be able to make a good fitting boot or a good suit of clothes; not always only those things that are the toys of rich folk. As things stand at the moment, I hang along with my creative work on to the apron-strings of the idle privileged classes."[4]

[1] "The Prospects of Architecture", *Works,* Vol. XXII, p. 150.

[2] "Textile Fabrics", *Ibid.,* p. 294.

[3] *Fortnightly Review,* March, 1903.

[4] Andreas Scheu, *Umsturzkeime* [Seeds of Revolution] (?1920), Part III, Ch. VI.

"Morris's writings about Socialism", Shaw wrote, "really called up all his mental reserves for the first time."[1] This is profoundly true: and among these writings the pre-Socialist lectures on art must be included. In preparing these lectures —writing them out in a beautiful hand with only an occasional abbreviation or correction—Morris was exercising and disciplining his mind in a way he had never done before. Nothing would be more mistaken than to suppose that the lectures were casually undertaken or easily prepared. Apart from those delivered to a general audience in support of the funds of the Anti-Scrape, Morris carefully selected his audience, going to the men practically engaged in artistic production, design or craftsmanship. In the lectures it is possible to see his thought advancing step by step—the discovery of one conclusion, the forced-march forward to the next. In 1880 he referred to the preparation of a lecture for the "Trades Guild of Learning" as his "autumn work". Of another lecture promised to the London Institute for the following March he wrote in the same letter:

> "I will be as serious as I can over them... the subject... still seems to me the most serious one that a man can think of; for 'tis no less than the chances of a calm, dignified, and therefore happy life for the mass of mankind."[2]

"I know what I want to say, but the cursed words go to water between my fingers", he wrote of another lecture. A lecture delivered early in 1881 took him the whole month of February to prepare, including—his journal suggests—eight complete days, while of another lecture he wrote: " 'tis to be a short one, but will give me a fortnight's work, I know."[3] And even after a lecture's delivery his mind was flooded with fresh problems, or he was left puzzled and bewildered:

[1] May Morris, II, p. xxxvi. [2] *Letters,* p. 134.
[3] Brit. Mus. Add. MSS. 45407, 45330.

"My audience. . . was polite & attentive; but I fear they were sorely puzzled at what I said; as might well be, since if they acted on it Nottingham trade would come to an end."[1]

In all his lectures he was moved—as in his addresses to the Anti-Scrape—by his increasing understanding of the movement of history, of the fact of class division and the class struggle. If simplicity was the aim, its attainment would liberate rich and poor alike:

"A state of things that produces vices among low people, will produce, not opposing virtues among high people, but corresponding vices; if you weave a pattern on a piece of cloth, and then turn it over and look at the back of it, you will see the back of the pattern, and not another pattern: material riches bred by material poverty and slavery produce scorn, cynicism and despair."[2]

And again:

"Luxury cannot exist without slavery of some kind or other, and its abolition will be blessed. . . by the freeing both of the slaves and of their masters."[3]

Or the uncompromising declaration of his first lecture of all:

"Sirs, I believe that art has such sympathy with cheerful freedom, open-heartedness and reality, so much she sickens under selfishness and luxury, that she will not live thus isolated and exclusive. I will go further than this and say that on such terms I do not wish her to live. . . I do not want art for a few, any more than education for a few, or freedom for a few.

"No, rather than art should live this poor thin life among a few exceptional men, despising those beneath them for an ignorance for which they themselves are responsible, for a brutality that they will not struggle with,—rather than this, I would that the world should indeed sweep away all art for awhile. . . rather than the wheat should rot in the

[1] *Letters*, p. 148. [2] May Morris, II, p. 66.
[3] "The Art of the People", *Works*, Vol. XXII, p. 48.

miser's granary, I would that the earth had it, that it might yet have a chance to quicken in the dark."[1]

In truth, these lectures are less concerned with a close criticism of the arts than with a criticism of civilization itself, as measured in the perspective of history, and as revealed by the evidence of contemporary public art. The danger, he said in one lecture, is that—

"the present course of civilisation will destroy the beauty of life—these are hard words, and I wish I could mend them, but I cannot, while I speak what I believe to be the truth."[2]

And in another:

"Civilization... has let one wrong and tyranny grow and swell into this, that a few have no work to do, and are therefore unhappy, the many have degrading work to do, and are therefore unhappy... Of all countries ours is... the most masterful, the most remorseless, in pushing forward this blind civilization... For our parts, we think that the remedy is to be found in the simplification of life, and the curbing of luxury and the desires for tyranny and mastery that it gives birth to..."

If this cannot be done, the alternative must be—

"the rending asunder for a time of all society by the forces of greediness and self-seeking, by the strife of man against man, nation against nation, class against class."[3]

This strife of class against class he felt still to be something only destructive—and yet still to be preferred to the gradual extinction of all art and noble aspirations in bourgeois vulgarity. If "civilization" meant no more than the attainment

[1] "The Lesser Arts", *Ibid.*, p. 25.

[2] "The Beauty of Life", *Ibid.*, p. 53.

[3] Brit. Mus. Add. MSS. 45331.

of comforts for the middle class, he said in 1880, then "farewell my hope!":

"I had thought that civilization meant the attainment of peace and order and freedom, of goodwill between man and man, of the love of truth and the hatred of injustice... a life free from craven fear, but full of incident: that was what I thought it meant, not more stuffed chairs and more cushions, and more carpets and gas, and more dainty meat and drink—and therewithal more and sharper differences between class and class."[1]

If this was all that was meant by "a civilization that is too apt to boast in after-dinner speeches; too apt to thrust her blessings on far-off peoples at the cannon's mouth",[2] then—

"I for one wish we had never gone so far... rather than we should never be other than we are, I would we had all together been shepherds ... among the hills and valleys; men with little knowledge, but desiring much; rough men if you please but not brutal; with some sort of art among them, genuine at least and spontaneous; men who could be moved by poetry and story, working hard yet not without leisure... neither malicious nor over soft-hearted, well pleased to live and ready to die—in short, men, free and equal.

"No, it cannot be: it has long passed over, and civilization goes forward, swiftly, if unsteadily..."[3]

And he declared in a passage from another lecture of 1880 which anticipates his full Socialist criticism of society:

"If civilization is to go no further than this, it had better not have gone so far: if it does not aim at getting rid of this misery and giving some share in the happiness and dignity of life to *all* the people that it has created... it is simply an organized injustice, a mere instrument for oppression, so much the worse than that which has gone before it, as its pretensions are higher, its slavery subtler, its mastery harder to

[1] "The Beauty of Life", *Works,* Vol. XXII, p. 76.

[2] "Art and the Beauty of the Earth", *Ibid.,* p. 170.

[3] May Morris, II, p. 70.

overthrow, because supported by such a dense mass of commonplace well-being and comfort."[1]

"It is strange indeed", he said in 1881,

"it is woeful, it is scarcely comprehensible, if we come to think of it as men, and not as machines, that, after all the progress of civilization, it should be so easy for a little official talk, a few lines on a sheet of paper, to set a terrible engine to work, which without any trouble on our part will slay ten thousand men... and it lies light enough on the conscience of *all* of us; while, if it is a question of striking a blow at grievous and crushing evils which lie at our own doors.. not only is there no national machinery for dealing with them... but any hint that such a thing may be possible is received with laughter or with terror, or with severe and heavy blame. The rights of property, the necessities of morality, the interests of religion—these are the sacramental words of cowardice that silence us!"[2]

"If we... think of it as *men*"—it is here, in his steadfast refusal to admit that men were mere victims of circumstances of their own creating, that the influence of the Norse sagas, and their "worship of courage" can be most strongly felt. "You may think", he said at the end of 1881, that we are "mere straws" in the "resistless flood": "But don't let us strain a metaphor; for we are no straws, but men, with each one of us a will and aspirations, and with duties to fulfil..." *Action*—this is the constant theme of his lectures. In 1880 he was writing to Georgie Burne-Jones:

"I do most earnestly desire that something more startling could be done than mere constant private grumbling and occasional public speaking to lift the standard of revolt against the sordidness which people are so stupid as to think necessary."[3]

1 "The Beauty of Life", *Works,* Vol. XXII, p. 65.
2 "The Prospects of Architecture", *Ibid.,* p. 137.
3 *Letters,* p. 139.

Educational ventures, campaigns for the enforcement of the Smoke Act, societies like the Commons Preservation and Kyrle Societies which were doing something to prevent the worst desecrations of town and countryside, to all these he was ready to give his public support. But his analysis of society was far too profound to suppose that these efforts would do more than scratch the surface. In August, 1881, he wrote again to Georgie, who seems to have suggested that he should be satisfied with such limited forms of action:

"I don't agree with you in condemning grumbling against follies and ills that oppress the world, even among friends, for you see it is but now and then that one has a chance of speaking about the thing in public, and meantime one's heart is hot with it, and some expression of it is like to quicken the flame even in those one loves and respects most, and it is good to feel the air laden with the coming storm even as we go about our daily work or while away time in light matters. To do nothing but grumble and not to act—that is throwing away one's life: but I don't think that words on our cause that we have at heart do nothing but wound the air, even when spoken among friends: 'tis at worst like the music to which men go to battle."[1]

Here, in his lectures, then, Morris was continually reconnoitering the banks of the "river of fire". "When he spoke offhand", one of his contemporaries recalled,

"he had a knack at times of hammering away at his point until he had said exactly what he wanted to say in exactly the words he wished to use, rocking to and fro the while from one foot to the other."[2]

The lectures were the anvil on which he beat out his thoughts. His mood varied often between hope and depression. On the one hand, he felt the gathering of the storm, that he was no longer isolated and that people were beginning to move in the same way: "it is a real joy to find the game afoot, that the thing is stirring in other people's minds besides mine",

[1] *Letters*, p. 151. [2] Mackail, II, p. 7.

he wrote in 1881.[1] In one of the most penetrating passages of his very first lecture, he had sensed that the movement of ideas and their influence in history was more than a mere accident of individual discontent:

> "I suppose that if some half-dozen men at any time earnestly set their hearts on something coming about which is not discordant with nature, it will come to pass one day or other; because it is not by accident that an idea comes into the heads of a few; rather they are pushed on, and forced to speak or act by something stirring in the heart of the world. . ."[2]

On the other hand, he felt often enough powerless in the face of the unbroken capitalist facade. In the summer of 1882, with trouble at home, colonial wars abroad, a famine in Ireland, he wrote to Georgie Burne-Jones:

> "Indeed I am older, and the year is evil; the summerless season, and famine and war, and the folly of peoples come back again, as it were, and the more and more obvious death of art before it rises again, are heavy matters to a small creature like me, who cannot choose but think about them, and can mend them scarce a whit."[3]

Here, indeed, he might have remained, had his work for Anti-Scrape, his lectures and practice of the arts, been his only line of advance. However revolutionary his theoretical insight into the problems that most concerned him, he was likely to fall into hopelessness or nostalgia if he did not have practical confidence in the possibility of overthrowing capitalism, practical contact with the working class. This was the point at which Morris broke so decisively with both Ruskin and Arnold. "To do nothing but grumble and not to act—that is throwing away one's life." Once his mind was decided,

[1] Mackail, II, p. 24.
[2] "The Lesser Arts", *Works,* Vol. XXII, p. 13.
[3] *Letters,* pp. 160-1.

he always looked for the most likely form of action that was at hand to realize his desires. From the time that the Eastern Question agitation had come to its sorry end, Morris had maintained his links with the radical movement of the London workers. It is true that the break-up of the E.Q.A. did not leave him in a hopeful frame of mind. Jingoism, it appeared to him, had swept the country:

> "The peace-party are in a very small minority... *there is no doubt of it...* For some years to come, until perhaps great disasters teach us better, we shall be a reactionary and Tory nation. I believe myself that the best way would be for all worthy men to abstain from politics for a while; so that these fools might be the sooner filled with the fruit of their own devices."[1]

But this "leave-them-to-stew-in-their-own-juice" attitude was little more than a new enthusiast making faces when he meets with his first check; and Morris was quickly shocked out of it by the events of the next year.

Imperialism was continuing its brutal advance, from the Fiji Islands to Burma, from South Africa to the Mediterranean. At the end of 1878 Disraeli and his military advisers took advantage of the Jingo spirit and the anti-Russian phobia to set to work to "rectify" the North-West Frontier of India, which (Disraeli explained) was a "haphazard and not a scientific one". The campaign thus launched in Afghanistan dragged on for several years, through disastrous setbacks and inglorious "victories". The miners' M.P., Thomas Burt, made one of his best speeches in the house at its outset.[2] The Government over-reached itself in 1879, with this war, the annexation of the Transvaal, wars against the Kaffirs and —least popular of all—against the Zulus. Had these wars been

[1] *Letters*, p. 120.

[2] See *Thomas Burt: an Autobiography* (1924), p. 52. Frederick Harrison and other Positivists organized a Committee to oppose the Afghan War, and Morris attended one of its meetings.

successful, no doubt the wave of Jingoism might have carried Disraeli back to power in the General Election which took place in the first months of 1880. But all were indeterminate, brutal, and expensive: and the rising disgust of the British people, which Gladstone enlisted in the rolling phrases of his "Mid-Lothian" campaigns, helped to bring a Liberal administration into power.

Imperialism, Morris saw, was the inevitable and most vicious outcome of the "Century of Commerce". He denounced it both in artistic and political terms. "While we are met here in Birmingham", he said at the beginning of 1879,

> "to further the spread of education in art, Englishmen in India are . . . actively destroying the very sources of that education—jewellery, metal-work, pottery, calico-printing, brocade-weaving, carpet-making—all the famous and historical arts of the great peninsula have been. . . thrust aside for the advantage of any paltry scrap of so-called commerce."[1]

At the end of January, 1880, in a lecture which was probably designed for some working-class Radical Club in connection with the election campaign, and which was devoted to combating "the tribe of Jingoes", and the slogan "Our country Right or Wrong" blazoned upon their banners, he declared:

> "England's place—what is England's place? To carry civilization through the world? Yes, indeed, the world must be civilized, and I doubt not that England will have a large share in bringing about that civilization.
>
> "And yet, since I have heard of wine with no grape-juice in it, and cotton-cloth that is mostly barytes, and silk that is two-thirds somach, and knives whose edges break or turn up if you try to cut anything harder than butter with them, and many another triumph of Commerce in these days, I begin to doubt if civilization itself may not be sometimes so much adulterated as scarcely to be worth the carrying—anyhow it cannot be worth much, when it is necessary to kill a man in order to make him accept it. . ."[2]

[1] "The Art of the People", *Works,* Vol. XXII, p. 36.
[2] Brit. Mus. Add. MSS. 45334. Some extracts from the lecture are in May Morris, II, pp. 53-62.

At the time when he delivered this lecture Morris was in that transitional period which he came later to describe as "a brief period of political radicalism during which I saw my ideal clear enough, but had no hope of any realization of it."[1] In the autumn of 1879 he became Treasurer of the National Liberal League, a small and largely ineffective organization which strove to keep together what influence the Labour Representation League still held when the latter petered out towards the end of 1878. Its first Secretary was Henry Broadhurst, Morris's old colleague of the "Workmen's Neutrality Committee" and also Secretary of the Parliamentary Committee of the T.U.C. To the Parliamentary Committee now fell the main responsibility for the promotion of working-men candidatures within the patronage of the Liberal Party: and the N.L.L. seems to have been mainly designed by its promoters, Broadhurst and its Chairman, George Howell (ex-Secretary of the L.R.L.), as a means of uniting the London Radical Clubs and trade unions, together with some middle-class men, behind certain specific and short-term democratic reforms. Its first important campaign came in the election of 1880, when it helped to rouse the London working class behind Gladstone's platform of "Peace, Retrenchment, Reform". Morris, still under the spell of Gladstone's oratory, worked as a loyal electioneer in the campaign.[2] It is true that he could not refrain from suggesting objectives more far-reaching:

> "I think of a country where every man has work enough to do, and no one has too much: where no man has to work himself stupid in order to be just able to live: where on the contrary it will be easy for a man to live if he will but work, impossible if he will not. . . where every man's work would be pleasant to himself and helpful to his neighbour; and then his leisure. . . (of which he ought to have plenty) would be thoughtful and rational. . ."[3]

[1] "How I Became a Socialist", *Justice*, June 16th, 1894.
[2] Morris campaigned enthusiastically for Sir Charles Dilke, with the help of Burne-Jones and William De Morgan. See A.M.W. Stirling, *William De Morgan and his Wife* (1922), p. 144.
[3] May Morris, II, p. 60.

But these views, he said, were only personal "crochetts":

> "I understand clearly that my crochett has no chance of being heard till Peace, Retrenchment, and Reform are abroad. . . I intend at the coming election to vote for any good man and true who will help me to those, and to let my crochett bide its time; and others of you who are like me, crochetteers, I give the advice to do the same."[1]

The formation of Gladstone's ministry put the promoters of the League in a quandary. "We have now to consider the possibility of making the League a force: if that be not possible, better dissolve at once", Howell wrote to Broadhurst in April 26th, 1880.[2] Broadhurst had little reason to continue his interest in the League. The honest stonemason had suffered the disaster of being elected to Parliament himself, and, exposed to the patronizing flattery of the bourgeoisie for the representative of the "British working man", his feet were set on the road which led to his total surrender at Sandringham in 1884, where the Prince of Wales even went so far as to accompany him to the village pub on the royal estate:

> "The Prince invited me to partake of the refreshment of the house, and I was quite ready to comply. We had, I think, a glass of ale each and sat down in the club-room, where we found several farm labourers enjoying their half-pints and their pipes. No excitement, no distubance, no uncomfortable feeling, was envinced by those present . . . The beer was very good and of a homely and acceptable flavour. . . I left Sandringham with a feeling of one who had spent a week-end with an old chum of his own rank in society rather than one who had been entertained by the Heir-Apparent and his Princess."[3]

No wonder Morris was to write in a letter of this year (when lamenting the lack of real working-class leaders to make con-

[1] Brit. Mus. Add. MSS. 45334.

[2] Howell Collection, Bishopsgate Institute.

[3] Broadhurst, *op. cit.*, pp. 151-3.

scious the "vague discontent and spirit of revenge" of the workers):

> "But you see when a man has gifts for that kind of thing he finds himself tending to rise out of his class before he has begun to think of class politics as a matter of principle, and too often he is just simply 'got at' by the governing classes, not formally but by circumstances. . ."[1]

However, John Hales took Broadhurst's place as Secretary and it was agreed that it was desirable "in the interests of the Liberal party generally and of the principles of Liberalism specially" that the League should continue and extend its work. Morris wrote to Broadhurst congratulating him on his election, and adding: "How to broaden and deepen the stream of radical principles, keeping meanwhile the government both alive and steady, without harrassing or frightening it,—that is the question, I fancy."[2] A programme of reforms was drawn up, including demands for detailed electoral reform and shorter parliaments, the abolition of paid canvassing, the codification of electoral law, a (vague) demand for reform of the Land Laws, the long-standing demand for municipal government for London, and—added in April, 1881, as a result of the hostility of the Tory Lords to certain of Gladstone's policies—the replacement of the House of Lords by an Elective Chamber.[3] "Unsatisfactory", Morris noted in his journal for March 26th, 1881, after attending a meeting of the League.[4] Reluctantly he was coming to admit his own disillusion in the Liberal Government and in any movement which attached itself to its tail. The momentum of imperialism was not checked in the least by the new administration: the only apparent result was the introduction of a certain indecisiveness into colonial policy, which led to further set-

[1] May Morris, II, p. 72.

[2] Morris to Broadhurst, April 4th, 1880, Brit. Lib. Polit. Science.

[3] Handbill in Howell Collection.

[4] Brit. Mus. Add. MSS. 45407.

backs and inglorious defeats. Gladstone, his former idol, was still not overthrown: he pictured him as sincere and progressive but enchained by his more reactionary colleagues. "Politics: Not pleasant", he wrote in February, 1881:

> "I don't trust the present government... to show as radical,—Whig it is and will remain... I doubt the Liberal Majority in the house, and the Government may get timid... In that case Gladstone's influence will be so shaken that the Liberal Party will fall to pieces, and good men and true must set to work to build up a Radical Party out of them and make themselves leaders out of the stones of the streets for all I can see. But... Gladstone is much stronger in the country than I thought for, and if he could only stop these damned little wars he might stop in till he has carried the regular liberal programme, and we should make a good step forward. But little wars with defeats and inglorious victories... shake a Government terribly..."[1]

A few days later he was even more anxious. The war was dragging on in Afghanistan: "I do think our side ought to start putting a little pressure on Government to make them do what they doubtless want to do... what a pity it is that there is not a proper radical club properly organized for political purposes, who could act speedily in such junctures."[2] Less than a month later affairs in the Transvaal shook Morris's confidence in Gladstone himself. During his second Midlothian campaign Gladstone had treated Disraeli's annexation with his intensest moral indignation:

> "If Cyprus and the Transvaal were as valuable as they are valueless, I would repudiate them because they are obtained by means dishonourable to the character of the country."

Reminded of these words now that he was in power, he explained that he had used the word "repudiate" in the sense of "dislike". Grievous as his moral revulsion might be, he could not see his way to letting them regain their indepen-

[1] May Morris, II, p. 581. [2] *Letters,* p. 144.

dence—although the defeat inflicted by the Boers on the British troops at Majuba Hill brought morality and practice a little closer together. "I am in hopes the matter will be taken up somewhat by people outside parliament for inside it all or nearly all people seem to be behaving ill enough" wrote Morris.[1]

Perhaps it was owing to Morris's persistence that among the objects of the National Liberal League there was added, at the end of 1881, the demand for the application to foreign policy of the "same moral principles" as in private relations. Otherwise, the programme of the League[2] showed little advance on the previous year, except in its emphasis on the need for extensive reform in the laws regarding land tenure—a question very much in the air in Radical circles. But shortly after this Morris resigned as Treasurer of the League, declaring: "I do so hate—this in spite of my accounts—everything vague in politics as well as in art."[3] Shortly after his resignation the League disappeared from public view.

Much of Morris's work for the E.Q.A. and the N.L.L., then, brought him education only in a negative sense. The work of the former, Wardle recalled, introduced him "to some politicians he had not known personally before, but acquaintance did not increase any respect he may have had for them."[4] His relations with the "Lib-Lab." working-class leaders were even more important in the development of his political views. George Howell, the patient wire-puller, can never have commanded much of his respect. Henry Broadhurst was a man of more sincerity, but a typical product of a skilled craft union in a time of industrial peace. Morris had ample opportunity to observe the stages by which Howell and Broadhurst became pawns of Mundella and of his colleagues, and it is not difficult to see—behind such passages as this in a lecture of 1883—not doctrinaire opinion but the weight of Morris's own personal experience: "The Trade Unions, founded for the

[1] *Letters*, p. 146. [2] Handbill in Howell Collection.
[3] Mackail, II, p. 8. [4] May Morris, II, p. 604.

advancement of the working class as a class, have already become conservative and obstructive bodies, wielded by the middle-class politicians for party purposes."[1]

By 1882 his disillusion in the Liberal Party was almost complete. He wrote, of a by-election, to the Hon. George Howard (Earl of Carlisle to be), amateur artist, Liberal M.P., and colleague of his on the E.Q.A.:

"I suppose your election is the North Riding... I make... the unpolitical remarks that I hope you have a good candidate: 'tis better to be beaten with a good one than be successful with a bad one. I guess there will be a fine procession of rats before this parliament is over: that will teach us, I hope, not to run the worst man possible on all occasions. Excuse the spleen of a kind of Radical cobbler."[2]

What finally opened Morris's eyes to the impossibility of advance within the shadow of the Liberal Party was the policy of the Government in Ireland and Egypt. The introduction of the infamous Coercion Bill in 1881 had aroused Morris's anxiety, but he had softened his fears with the reflection that they "don't *intend* to use it tyranically."[3] In fact, the Minister responsible for its operation, Foster—who had spoken so nobly on the platform of the E.Q.A. five years before—employed his powers so tyranically that even a section of the Conservatives thought his actions injudicious. In Egypt the Liberal measures of "pacification" in the summer of 1882 included the shelling of Alexandria by British warships. This made the lesson complete. The Coercion Bill, the worship of Liberal "leaders" who " 'led' the party into mere Jingoism", the "Stockjobber's Egyptian War, quite destroyed any hope I might have had of any good being done by alliance with the Radical party".[4] "Radicalism", he wrote in June of the next year, "will never develop into anything more than Radicalism... It is made for and by the

[1] "Art Under Plutocracy", *Works,* Vol. XXIII, p. 188.
[2] *Letters,* p. 156. [3] *Ibid.,* p. 144. [4] *Ibid.,* pp. 176, 188.

middle classes, and will always be under the control of rich capitalists: they will have no objection to its political development, if they think they can stop it there: but as to real social changes, they will not allow them. . ."[1]

The last of his illusions had perished under the criticism of practical experience. No barrier remained in his mind to prevent his acceptance of Socialist conclusions. But changes as great as this cannot be accomplished without the severest tensions. As early as the end of 1879 he was lamenting the seeming drying-up of the sources of his creative writing:

"As to poetry, I don't know, and I don't know. The verse would come easy enough if I had only a subject which would fill my heart and mind: but to write verse for the sake of writing is a crime in a man of my years and experience. . ."[2]

The great intellectual effort of his lectures must have exposed to him the facility of much of his verse. At the same period there are unexplained passages in his letters to Georgie Burne-Jones which suggest the breaking apart of old and intimate ties. In October, 1879, he wrote from Kelmscott:

"I am sitting. . . in the tapestry-room, the moon rising red through the east-wind haze, and a cow lowing over the fields. I have been feeling chastened by many thoughts, and the beauty and quietness of the surroundings, which latter, as I hinted, I am, as it were, beginning to take leave of. That leave-taking will, I confess. . . seem a long step towards saying good-night to the world."[3]

His estrangement from his wife seems to have become more pronounced. Indeed, the sense of his personal isolation during these critical years is extreme. He was turning his back upon his own class, and this meant that he was facing the separation from many old friends and colleagues. It was only the

[1] *Letters*, p. 173. [2] *Ibid.*, p. 132.

growing sense of "the Cause" which sustained his courage. "Little by little it must come, I know", he said in 1879:

"Patience and prudence must not be lacking to us, but courage still less. Let us be a Gideon's band. 'Whosoever is fearful and afraid, let him return, and depart early from Mount Gilead.' And among that band let there be no delusions; let the last encouraging lie have been told, the last after-dinner humbug spoken. . ."[1]

"Every man who has a cause at heart", he said in 1881, "is bound to act as if it depended on him alone, however well he may know his own unworthiness; and thus is action brought to birth from mere opinion."[2]

In the summer of 1882, then, he was ready "to join any body who distinctly called themselves Socialists",[3] although for a few months his action was delayed by the breakdown of his daughter, Jenny's, health,[4] his practical endeavours to relieve a famine in Ireland, and also his distrust of the ex-Tory leader of the Democratic Federation, H.M. Hyndman.[5] He had almost no acquaintance with individual Socialists, no knowledge of the theory of Socialism. In the summer of 1881 he had been enraged by the Liberal Government's prosecution of Johann Most, the German anarchist editor of the paper *Freiheit,* published from London, which had printed an article extolling the assassins of Tsar Alexander II:

"I suppose you have seen the sentence on Herr Most. . . just think of the mixture of tyranny and hypocrisy with which the world is governed! These are the sort of things that make thinking people so sick at heart that they are driven from all interest in politics save revolutionary politics: which I must say seems like to be my case. Indeed I have long known, or felt, say, that society in spite of its

[1] "Making the Best of It", *Works,* Vol. XXII, p. 117. [2] *Ibid.,* p. 174.

[3] "How I Became a Socialist", *Justice,* June 16th, 1894.

[4] Jenny's breakdown shattered Morris for several months: see Mackail, II, p. 73.

[5] The Federation's Radical character in 1882 is discussed by M.S. Wilkins, "The Non-Socialist Origins of England's First Socialist Organization", *Int. Rev. Social Hist.* IV, (1959), pp. 199-207.

modern smoothness was founded on injustice and kept together by cowardice and tyranny; but the hope in me has been that matters would mend gradually, till the last struggle, which must needs be mingled with violence and madness, would be so short as scarcely to count."[1]

As for theoretical knowledge, when he took the step of joining the Democratic Federation, he later wrote: 'I was blankly ignorant of economics; I had never so much as opened Adam Smith, or heard of Ricardo, or of Karl Marx."[2] In 1882 he read Henry George's *Progress and Poverty* and Wallace's *Land Nationalisation*[3] and something of Robert Owen and the French Utopian Socialists and also—it is evident from the many references—he was reading a good deal of William Cobbett, who seems to have had a pronounced influence upon the forthright polemical style of his later Socialist writings. In the winter of 1882-3 he attended a series of meetings at the Westminster Palace Chambers, organized by the Democratic Federation, on the subject of "Stepping-stones" to Socialism. The Austrian refugee Andreas Scheu, a furniture designer by trade, recalled Morris's first attendance:

"One evening, the meeting had scarcely started when Robert Banner, the book-binder, who sat behind me, passed me a note. . . 'The third man on your right is William Morris.' I had never seen Morris before and looked at once in his direction. The fine, highly intelligent face of the man, his earnestness, the half-searching, half-dreamy look of his eyes, his plain unfashionable dress, made a deep sympathetic impression on me."[4]

On January 13th, 1883, he joined the Federation. In the same week he was made an Honorary Fellow of Exeter College, Oxford. His membership card for the Federation, counter-

[1] *Letters,* p. 149.

[2] "How I Became a Socialist", *Justice,* June 16th, 1894.

[3] Morris to his daughter Jenny, November 13th, 1883, refers to Wallace's *Land Nationalisation:* "not nearly such a good book as George's but there are some nice things to remember in it", Brit. Mus. Add. MSS. 45339.

[4] Scheu, *op. cit.,* Scheu gave a similar account to Mackail, II, pp. 95-6.

signed by H.H. Champion, was simply inscribed, "William Morris, Designer".

The next few months were the true months of conversion In one of his earliest Socialist lectures he spoke of that feeling of joy,

"when at last, after many a struggle with incongruous hindrances, our own chosen work has lain before us disentangled from all encumbrances and unrealities, and we have felt that nothing could withhold us, not even ourselves, from doing the work we were born to do, and that we were men and worthy of life."[1]

He plunged at once into the day-by-day round of activities:

"When I joined the Communist folk, I did what in me lay
To learn the grounds of their faith. I read day after day
Whatever books I could handle, and heard about and about
What talk was going amongst them; and I burned up doubt after doubt,
Until it befel at last that to others I needs must speak. . ."[2]

On February 22nd, a friend noted in his diary: "He was bubbling over with Karl Marx, whom he had just begun to read in French. He praised Robert Owen immensely."[3] In March he delivered a lecture in Manchester so trenchant as to bring down the wrath of the leader-writers upon him. But nothing was more appropriate in his whole life than that one of his first public announcements that he was "one of the people called Socialists" was made with the "first comer", Professor Ruskin, in the chair. At the close of his address, in the Hall of University College, Oxford, Morris turned his appeal to the middle class:

"I have a last word or two to say in begging them to renounce their class pretensions and cast in their lot with the working men. . . It may

[1] "The Lesser Arts of Life", *Works,* Vol. XXII, p. 269.

[2] *The Pilgrims of Hope,* Section VI.

[3] Mackail, II, p. 97.

be that some of them are kept from actively furthering the cause which they believe in by that dread of organization. . . which is very common in England. . . more common among highly cultivated people, and. . . most common in our ancient universities. Since I am a member of a Socialist propaganda I earnestly beg those of you who agree with me to help us actively, with your time and your talents if you can, but if not, at least with your money, as you can. Do not hold aloof from us, since you agree with us, because we have not attained that delicacy of manners. . . which the long oppression of competitive commerce has crushed out of us."[1]

The reactions of the academic Podsnaps was immediate. "At the close of his address", *The Times* reported the next day,

"Mr. Morris announced himself a member of a socialist society and appealed for funds for the objects of the society. The Master of University then said to the effect that if he had announced this beforehand it was probable that the loan of the College-hall would have been refused."

Morris had crossed the "river of fire". And the campaign to silence him had begun.

What was the "river of fire", the something "alive and devouring", but the class division within society? Morris's conversion was a true conversion. It was not sudden, unannounced, a bolt out of the blue. It was in every sense a qualitative change in understanding and in action, for which all his life had prepared the way. In a certain sense he had already in his lectures advanced the theory of Socialism in relation to the decorative arts beyond any point which any other theorist had yet reached. But the final understanding was lacking. The understanding of the class struggle, submerged in many of his lectures, was only made apparent on his reading of *Capital,* in his discussions with Scheu and Bax and Hyndman, and his first Socialist activities. Once made apparent, all his previous thought came into unity, his action acquired new purpose and direction. One of his earliest

[1] "Art Under Plutocracy", *Works,* Vol. XXIII, p. 191.

Socialist lectures, in which he makes acknowledgement to Marx, shows clearly how all his old pre-occupations—his resistance to imperialism, his work for the National Liberal League—fell suddenly into place:

> "Once again I tell you that our present system is not so much a confusion. . . as a tyranny: one and all of us in some way or other we are drilled to the service of Commercial War; if our individual aspirations or capacities do not fit in with it, so much the worse for them: the iron service of the capitalist will not bear the loss, the individual must; everything must give way to this; nothing can be done if a profit cannot be made of it: it is for this that we are overworked, are made to fear starvation, live in hovels, are herded. . . into foul places called towns . . . it is for this that we let half Scotland be depopulated. . . and turn its stout peasants and herdsmen into mere flunkies of idle fools: it is for this that we let our money, our name, our power, be used to drag off poor wretches from our pinched fields and our dreadful slums, to kill and be killed in a cause they know nothing of."

Imperialism he saw no longer as the outcome of ambitious statesmen and generals: "It is simply the agony of capitalism driven by a force it cannot resist to seek for new and ever new markets at any price and any risk." England is losing her favoured position in the world:

> "What is to be done?. . . Conquer new markets from day to day; flatter and cajole the men of our colonies to consider themselves what they are not, Englishmen responsible for every quarrel England may lead them into: conquer valiant barbarians all over the world: rifle them rum them missionary them into subjection, then train them into soldiers for civilization. . ."

And so to the most uncompromising paragraph of all:

> "Here are two classes, face to face with each other. . . No man can exist in society and be neutral, no-body can be a mere looker on: one camp or another you have got to join: you must either be a reactionary and be crushed by the progress of the race, and help it that way: or you must join in the march of progress, trample down all opposition, and help it that way."[1]

[1] Unpublished lecture, "Commercial War", Brit. Mus. Add. MSS. 45333.

Here was Morris's greatest discovery—the discovery which his friends, for all their genius, could not make. Marx helped him to make it, but once it was made he accepted it as the inevitable conclusion of all his past thought. In its discovery he found his way forward both as an artist and as a man. His old dream of healing the division between artist and the people now became a vision to look forward to with certainty: that time when—

"the man of the most refined occupation, student, artist, physician . . . shall be able to speak to him who does the roughest labour in a tongue that they both know, and to find no intricacy of his mind misunderstood."[1]

The finest aspirations of the romantic revolt, which aroused his own desires for "Liberty, Equality, Fraternity" in his youth, now seemed possible of fulfilment:

"Not in Utopia, subterranean fields,
Or some secreted island, Heaven knows where!
But in the very world, which is the world
Of all of us. . ."

Blake's Jerusalem might yet be built in earnest, and Shelley's Phantoms and Sages be given flesh and blood. The long romantic breach between aspiration and action was healed.

So it was that William Morris crossed the "river of fire". "How can we of the middle classes, we the capitalists, and our hangers-on", help the workers? he asked in January, 1884. His answer was decisive:

"By renouncing our class, and on all occasions when antagonism rises up between the classes casting in our lot with the victims. . . There is no other way: and this way, I tell you plainly, will in the long run give us plenty of occasion for self-sacrifice. . ."[2]

[1] Speech to the Kyrle Society, May Morris, I, p. 195.
[2] "Art and Socialism", *Works,* Vol. XXIII, p. 213.

Of his old friends, only Philip Webb and Charlie Faulkner, both of whom fully knew his greatness, went with him. It was "the only time when I failed Morris", said Edward—soon to be Sir Edward—Burne-Jones many years later.[1] Swinburne, when Morris tried to enlist his aid, gave only his "sympathy":

"I do trust you will not. . . regard me as a dilettante democrat if I say that I would rather not join any Federation. What good I can do to the cause. . . will I think be done as well or better from an independent point of action and of view. . ."[2]

His years of revolt had ended in breakdown, and he was now the "prisoner of Putney", beginning his thirty years of genteel retirement with the solicitor, Theodore Watts-Dunton. Ruskin watched with encouragement from the further bank. He had had one mental crisis already, and he knew his powers to be failing:

"It is better that you should be in a cleft stick than make one out of me—especially as my timbers are enough shivered already. In old British battles the ships that had no shot in their rigging didn't ask the disabled ones to help them."[3]

But Morris was finding new friends and comrades on every side. He was in his fiftieth year, but he looked to the future with the excitement of youth. In an allegorical poem, "The Three Seekers", he exorcised for the first time the old despair, the fear of death, the restless fret of his middle years: and, in its singing refrain, we hear the joy of his "new birth":

" 'There is no pain on earth', she said,
'Since I have drawn thee from the dead.'

"Laughing, 'The world's my home,' she said,
'Now I have drawn thee from the dead.'

"Now life is little, and death is nought,
Since all is found that erst I sought."[4]

[1] *Memorials*, II, p. 97.
[2] Brit. Mus. Add. MSS. 45345.
[3] *Ibid.*
[4] *To-Day*, January, 1884.

PART III

PRACTICAL SOCIALISM

CHAPTER I

THE FIRST TWO HUNDRED

I. The Refugees

WHEN William Morris joined the Democratic Federation in January, 1883, the propaganda of Socialism in England had been under way for less than two years. "Those who set out 'to make the revolution' ", he recalled some years later:

> "were a few working men, less successful even in the wretched life of labour than their fellows; a sprinkling of the intellectual proletariat. . . one or two outsiders in the game political; a few refugees from the bureaucratic tyranny of foreign governments; and here and there an unpractical, half-cracked artist or author."[1]

In the years between 1870 and 1880 (and even for ten years before 1870) no consistent Socialist propaganda—not even of a dozen or twenty members—had existed in Britain.

Small bodies of Owenite "Socialists", it is true, could still be found up and down the country. They were mostly aged survivors, with little influence. In fact, "Socialism" no longer meant Owenism to the British public in 1880. Most frequently it was used as a bogy-word to cover the "outrages" of the Commune, the terrorist methods of the Russian nihilists—bomb-plots, assassination, dynamite. "Socialism! Then blow us up! There's nothing left for it but that", cried Dr. Warre, Headmaster of Eton, when informed by one of his masters, Henry Salt, of his conversion in 1880.[2] Useful bogy as this was, it was in part a recognition of the fact that modern Socialism now meant European Socialism, and it was from European sources that the Socialism of the 1880s drew both its theory and its initial impetus. Not only were Marx and

[1] "Where are We Now?", *Commonweal*, November 15th, 1890.

[2] H.S. Salt, *Seventy Years Among Savages* (1921), p. 65.

Engels living in London, and in contact with working-class and Radical circles, but also there passed through London and were scattered in all the major cities of Britain refugees from the terror in Russia, from the Commune, from the persecutions of the Austrian police, and—after 1878—from Bismarck's Anti-Socialist laws in Germany. It is the veteran of 1848 who is described as the first Socialist influence upon the hero of *The Pilgrims of Hope:*

> "At last it befel on a day
> That I came across our Frenchman at the edge of the new-mown hay,
> A-fishing as he was wont, alone as he always was. . ."

It is the refugee who first describes "the tale that never ends":

> "The battle of grief and hope with riches and folly and wrong.
> He told how the weak conspire, he told of the fear of the strong;
> He told of dreams grown deeds, deeds done ere time was ripe,
> Of hope that melted in air like the smoke of his evening pipe;
> Of the fight long after hope in the teeth of all despair;
> Of battle and prison and death, of life stripped naked and bare. . ."

Such men as this influenced the conversion of a number of the pioneers—Adam Weiler, the journeyman joiner and friend of Marx, who raised the standard of the eight-hour day in the T.U.C. in the 1870s, and who first introduced James MacDonald, the tailor, to Engels' articles in *The Labour Standard* in 1881:[1] Hermann Jung, the Vaudois watchmaker of Clerkenwell, an opponent of Marx after the break-up of the First International, who assisted Belfort Bax on his way: Frederick Lessner, "white of hair and beard, dignified of aspect", a refugee of 1848, close friend of Marx and Engels, and member of the General Council of the First International, who was later to become a pillar of the Hammersmith Branch of the Socialist League.[2]

[1] James MacDonald, "How I Became a Socialist", *Justice*, July 11th, 1896.
[2] See May Morris, II, p. 186.

Of all groups refugees are notoriously subject to bickering and schisms, which can only be healed when some opportunity arises of sinking their differences in common action. On escaping from Vienna to London in 1874, Andreas Scheu found two clubs of exiles in existence in 1874.[1] The largest group were followers of Lassalle, and met in a public house in Rupert Street: they could muster nearly 200 members. The smaller group of Marxists numbered perhaps forty, and met in the first story of "The Blue Post" in Newman Street. Presiding over them was Leo Frankel, the "beloved comrade", Hungarian goldsmith and Minister of Labour in the Commune, who "brought the last word" of Marx and Engels to the meetings. "They were mostly men past middle age, and already long-standing members of some English trade union or other."[2]

In the next two or three years, after a good deal of internecine warfare, the "Rupert-Streeters" and "Internationalists" at length merged into the General Communist Workers' Union, with headquarters at the Rose Street Club. Membership was open to all nationalities, and a few slender contacts were made with English workers. In 1878 a new disruptive influence entered the Club in the person of Johann Most, who was—like Scheu—a refugee from the "Left" Socialists of Vienna. After his arrival in Britain Most moved rapidly towards anarchism. He and Victor Dave succeeded in gaining control of the Club, and the Marxists retired to form a new Club at Tottenham Street.[3] "The Workers Assoc. is splitting up into all sorts of parties. . . and we have trouble enough in preventing our-

[1] Andreas Scheu, *Umsturzkeime* [Seeds of Revolution] (?1920), Part III, Ch. I. Scheu wrote his reminiscences when he was a very old man, and, since he was extremely partisan and rather vain, they should be treated with some care. They are, however, at least as accurate as Hyndman's various reminiscences. See also the reminiscences of Frank Kitz, *Freedom*, February-April, 1912; H.W. Lee, *Social-Democracy in Britain* (1935), Ch. III, Section I; F. Lessner, *Sixty Years in the Social-Democratic Movement* (1907), pp. 41-2.

[2] Scheu, *op. cit.*, Part III, Ch. 3.

[3] Cf. *Freedom*, February-April, 1912; Lee, *op. cit.*, Ch. III. Section I.

selves from being dragged into the whirl", Engels wrote to Becker on April 1st, 1880:

> "It is all a storm in a teacup, which may in some ways have a very good influence on those who take part in it. . . but so far as the course of the world is concerned it is more or less indifferent whether a hundred German workers here declare themselves for one side or the other. If they could exercise *any influence on the English*—but there is *absolutely no question* of that."[1]

Andreas Scheu, at about the same time, was feeling the same frustration at the internal bickering of the exiles: younger than many of his comrades, and with a better mastery of the English language, he turned to give his aid to the workers of his country of refuge:

> "The political activity of my fellow-countrymen became more and more limited to either playing billiards or cards. . . in the rooms at Tottenham St. or to passing bloodthirsty resolutions at the Anarchist Club under the leadership of tried *agents provocateurs;* so I turned my gaze upon the purely English working-class movement which promised to move into a new phase of activity. I began to visit their meetings."

II. The "Old Guard"

With the death of Chartism, and the absorption of the Chartists into the radical wing of the Liberal Party and into the Co-operative movement, a few individuals here and there remained loyal to the republican and socialist ideas of O'Brien, Harney and Ernest Jones, and provide in their lives a link between the old Chartism and the new Socialism.

John Sketchley was born in 1822, and appointed at the age of seventeen to be Secretary of the South Leicestershire Chartist Society, a post he held for ten years. In 1870 he settled in Birmingham, which was soon to become the headquarters of Joseph Chamberlain's and Dilke's short-lived

[1] *Marx-Engels Sel. Cor.*, p. 380.

republican agitation. He was outstanding among the old Chartists for his attention to international events, and his patient compilation of facts and statistics. In 1872-3 he was one of the chief contributors to the *International Herald,* edited by W.H. Riley, who later published a few numbers of a paper called *The Socialist* in Sheffield. Sketchley founded in 1875 a "Birmingham Republican Association", which three years later changed its name to the "Midland Social Democratic Association". This body can almost certainly claim to have been the first English society of the modern Socialist movement: but it has yet to be shown that it was more than a paper organization. In 1879, certainly, Sketchley himself was very active: he was contributing to German Socialist papers: and published *The Principles of Social Democracy: an Exposition and a Vindication*—a book full of statistical information on profits and working-class incomes, and in which were published the Principles of the Social Democratic Party of Germany and of the Social Democrats of America (1877). "Our comrade never remained stationary", Morris wrote in a Preface to Sketchley's later *Review of European Society*: "He was always advancing, always searching for truth, always working for the realization of justice." He was the first Secretary of the Birmingham Branch of the Democratic Federation, an active member of the Socialist League and one of the most regular contributors to *Commonweal,* and (after he removed to Hull) a member of the S.D.F. into the present century.[1]

Sketchley's *Principles of Social Democracy* introduced a few of the first of the Socialist pioneers to the ideas of European Socialism,[2] and his activities may have stirred a few minds in the Midlands. The brothers James and Charles

[1] See *Proposed Testimonial to Mr. John Sketchley* (August, 1900) signed by E. Copeland and H. Percy Ward of Birmingham; John Sketchley, *A Review of European Society* (1884), with Preface by William Morris; John Sketchley, "Personal Experiences in the Chartist Movement", *To-Day,* July, 1884.

[2] Frank Kitz recalled in *Freedom,* March, 1912, that "many thousands" of Sketchley's book were sold in London in 1880-2.

Murray played a small part in setting the London propaganda afoot. The Murrays had been active members of the Chartist locality in Soho, and they had worked with Bronterre O'Brien, who lodged with Charles Murray during some of his last years of obscurity. After his death, the Murrays and their friends maintained contact, and held political discussions, in the "Three Doves", in Berwick Street, Soho.[1]

Here they were joined by a young recruit, Frank Kitz, who left recollections of their meetings. Kitz, who was to play a prominent part in the Socialist League, was the son of a German exile, and was born in Kentish Town in 1848 or 1849. His lonely childhood, in conditions of extreme poverty turned him into a rebel: "I decorated the walls of my lonely room with pictures of the French Revolution. . . Brought up in the neighbourhood of the West End. . . I needed no lectures upon surplus value. . . to cause me to challenge the justice of a system which confers wealth upon the parasites of society and clouds the lives of thousands. . . with care and poverty." After tramping the country in search of work, he settled in Soho in the early 1870s, where he was introduced to the discussions of a society styled "the Democratic and Trades Alliance Association", composed in the main of Soho tailors and shoemakers. Among the circle he recalled the two Murrays, G. Eccarius, J. Bedford Leno (the Buckinghamshire poet, active in both the Chartist movement and the agitation before the Reform Bill of 1867), W. Townshend ("a tall, gaunt, kindly old shoemaker, the possessor of a vast accumulation of books and knowledge pertaining to the cause"), John Rogers (a friend of Marx) and Maltman Barry, Dr. Henry Travis, Dr. Gammage (the historian of Chartism–an "associate"), and others. Frank Kitz's entrance into this circle was in the immediate aftermath of the Paris Commune, when the British section of the First International was falling apart. The survivors formed themselves into the "Manhood Suffrage

[1] Charles Murray, *A Letter to Mr. George Jacob Holyoake* (1854); recollections of the late Mr. Ambrose Barker.

League" (which persisted, in name at least, into the late 1880s): but when the Rose Street Club was founded (1877), Kitz (who spoke fluent German) took part in its formation and quickly came under the influence of Johann Most and Victor Dave.[1]

James Murray was Chairman of a demonstration called in Hyde Park, on April 16th, 1871, in support of the Paris Commune.[2] The meeting was called by the "International Democratic Association", but in truth in the 1870s it is difficult to keep track of the high-sounding titles which the old guard employed in the hope of attracting public interest. At one time Kitz formed an "English Revolutionary Society": at another, the English Section of the Rose Street Club went under the *alias* of the "Local Rights Association for Rental and Sanitary Reform".[3] "I am prepared to be called an opportunist, an intriguer", wrote Joseph Lane, the founder of the Labour Emancipation League, in later years,

> "but little do any of those in the movement to-day know the trials and troubles of the early days, the dodges and subterfuges we had to resort to to get a hearing at all, in the streets, in halls, anywhere except in the Press."

If the pioneers were reported when they held their annual meeting to commemorate the Commune, it was, "I suppose, because we were a strange species of animal."[4] Joseph Lane himself, who was to play a leading part in the Socialist League, was one of the most remarkable of these "strange animals". Born in 1850, at the age of fifteen he was attending political

[1] *Freedom*, January-May, 1912: *Commonweal*, September 11th, 1886. An important forerunner of these little London organizations of the late 1870s is the "Land and Labour League", described by R. Harrison, *Bulletin of the International Institute of Social History Amsterdam*, 1953, No. 3.

[2] Handbill among Nettlau MSS., Int. Inst. Soc. Hist.

[3] *Freedom*, April, 1912.

[4] Nettlau MSS., Int. Inst. Soc. Hist. (in a letter to Ambrose G. Barker, March 22nd, 1912).

meetings in his home village of Wallingford. Coming to London in 1867, he joined, in 1871, the remnant of the English section of the First International, and became a member of the "Manhood Suffrage League". In the early 1870s he took an active part in the republican agitation, accompanying Dilke on one of his tours, and earning the nick-name of "Dilke's boy". He was a carter by trade, widely read in political theory, and "a born organizer and intensely earnest propagandist".[1] From 1878 onwards he was associated with every move to set an organized Socialist propaganda afoot.

However, it is perhaps misleading to describe as "Socialist" the activities of Lane, Kitz and the Murrays in the 1870s. They, and other ultra-Radical groups, were pressing demands on a medley of issues, among which the "Land Question", the realization of advanced democratic rights and opposition to coercion in Ireland were pre-eminent. The landed aristocracy and the mine-owners were still in the 1870s the main targets for Radical attack. At the end of the decade, the severe agricultural depression revived the agitation on "the Land Question", which contributed to the birth of modern Socialism. But, at the same time, the demand for land nationalization was in no way a specifically Socialist demand, and could, indeed, set earnest Radicals off on a false scent, since it directed attention only to the robbery of the people accomplished by means of the private ownership of the land and raw materials, and distracted attention from the far greater robbery accomplished by means of the private ownership of the means of production and exchange. This one-sidedness was to persist among some members of Morris's Socialist League: to Frank Kitz, land nationalization was always the "Question of Questions" until the end of his life.[2] But Joseph Lane took a step forward from the advanced radical position when, in the late 1870s, he took part in a land agitation in the East End of London. His propaganda directed

[1] Reminiscence of Ambrose G. Barker in *Freedom*, May, 1931.

[2] Letter of Kitz to Nettlau, 1912, Nettlau MSS., Int. Inst. Soc. Hist.

the eyes of the workers, not to the Highlands or the rural fastnesses of the feudal brigandage, but to their own conditions:

> "30,000,000 of our People own no Land, while Seven London Landholders draw £14,640,000 per annum from the People of London alone as Ground Rents for Land which was originally pasture lands.—What are these 30,000,000 of people with no Land or means of living, but the hired slaves of those who hold the Land or of the capitalist class who hold the Means of Production and Exchange?"[1]

From this point it was only a short step to the adoption of a thoroughgoing Socialist outlook.

In the late 1870s, then, there was a small but active group, in contact with the working-class Radical Clubs of East London, which advocated universal manhood suffrage and the fullest democratic rights: republicanism: the nationalization of the land: solidarity with democratic movements abroad: and which had hazy ideas of Socialist theory, drawn both from Owenite and from European sources. Lane, in 1878, was working actively in the Marylebone Radical Association, and this group induced several influential Radical Clubs to sign an "Address to the Heroes and Martyrs of the Commune", in May, 1879.[2] Events in 1880 and 1881 served to bring a few of these pioneers—refugees, class-conscious old Chartists, rebels like Frank Kitz and Jack Williams[3] who had formed the English Section of the Rose Street Club—into contact with the younger militant Radicals.

[1] Handbill, *An Open Letter to Baron De Forest, M.P. of West Ham, or any other Public Spirited Member of Parliament who will take up THE LAND QUESTION on behalf of the people,* by Joseph Lane.

[2] Organizations signing this Address "from the Social Democrats of London" included the Westminster Democratic Club, Tower Hamlets Radical Association, Patriotic Club, Lambeth Reform Union, Federal Workmen's League, Manhood Suffrage League, and Sketchley's Midland Social Democratic Association.

[3] John Edward Williams escaped from a workhouse at the age of ten, and was in the thick of every fight he could find from that time onwards. See *John E. Williams and the Early History of the S.D.F.* (1886), and H.W. Lee, *op. cit.*, (1935), pp. 86-7.

In 1881 James MacDonald, the tailor, coming to London from Edinburgh, found that a small propaganda was already under way. Attending a meeting of a Scottish Club in a public house in Tottenham Street he was told one evening by the landlord that "some of the most red-hot Fenians and dynamiters in England" were meeting in another room:

> "Some of us were curious. . . and eventually got introduced to them. There were Frank Kitz, James and Charles Murray, Garcia, Townsend, Butler, and others. They were vehemently denouncing the Coercion Bill. . . I was an enthusiastic admirer of Mr. Gladstone and his party, and at once took up the cudgels on behalf of my heroes. We followed up the meetings of these men and formed a sort of opposition. . . But gradually we found we were losing ground, and then we threw in our lot with the others and formed the Central Marylebone Democratic Association. . ."[1]

Thus, many of the radical working men who (like William Morris in the days of the National Liberal League) had for six years been dreaming great things of Gladstone's return to power, were month by month sinking into bitter disappointment at the imperialist policies of the Liberal Government in Ireland and overseas, and at its failure to relieve the misery intensified by the "Great Depression" at home. By the end of 1881 Joseph Lane and a few ultra-Radicals formed the first Socialist organization in London with any influence—the Labour Emancipation League.[2]

The Labour Emancipation League, which drew into a common organization many of the individuals already active in London, was a halfway house, in which the theories of the old guard and of the new pioneers both found expression. Its object was declared to be "the establishment of a Free Social Condition of Society, based on the principle of Political

[1] *Justice*, July 11th, 1896.

[2] For the part played by the prosecution of Most, and the *Freiheit* Defence Committee, in bringing Socialists together, see first edition, pp. 320, 329-31.

Equality, with Equal Social Advantages for All". The first six points in its programme were based on the advanced democratic demands of the Chartist and Radical traditions.[1] The seventh demanded the nationalization of land, mines, and means of transit. The final two served as a bridge to modern Socialism:

"(8) As Labour is the foundation of all Wealth. . . the Regulation of Production must belong to Society, and the Wealth produced be equitably shared by All.

"(9) As at present the Instruments of Labour and the Means of Employment are monopolised by the Capitalist Classes, which Monopoly is the cause of the misery and servitude of the Working People; the Emancipation of Labour requires the transformation of the said Instruments of Production and the Means of Employment into Collective or Public Property, for the benefit of All Members of Society."

Soon the L.E.L. claimed branches at Mile End, Canning Town, Hoxton, Bethnal Green, Millwall, Stamford Hill and Hackney. Joseph Lane became Secretary (after the defection of the first Secretary, Moseley Aaron) and he urged forward open-air propaganda, occasionally in Hyde Park and Regent's Park, but consistently on Mile End Waste, Clerkenwell Green, at Stratford and Millwall. Without financial backing or middle-class support, Lane and his comrades printed amateurish leaflets on an antiquated hand-press. They denounced Gladstone's Irish policies. In the poverty-stricken and crowded streets of the East End they distributed Manifestos calling for a Rent Strike. In co-operation with the English Section of the Rose Street Club they held a large demonstration on Mile End Waste to expose the policy of State-aided emigration for the unemployed, demanding a programme of public works, and declaring:

[1] (1) Equal Direct Adult Suffrage and Ballot, (2) Direct Legislation by the People, (3) Abolition of a Standing Army—the People to decide on Peace or War, (4) Free Secular Education, (5) Liberty of Speech, Press, and Magazine, (6) Free Administration of Justice. Points (3) and (4) had also been part of the Programme of the Land and Labour League; see R. Harrison, *op. cit.*

"1. . . . instead of assisting Canadian Speculators to get cheap labour by Public Charity, the people should demand the restitution of their common birthright, the Land. . .

"2. The only emigration at all necessary or desirable is that of the idle, aristocratic, and capitalist classes."[1]

The agitation soon won attention, not only from the police, but also from a few of the younger Radicals who, disillusioned with the actions of Gladstone's Ministry, were seeking for a profounder analysis of the causes of social misery than that of Charles Bradlaugh or of Joseph Chamberlain. Among them were members of yet another organization which had been formed in 1881—the Democratic Federation.

III. The Intellectuals

While Joseph Lane and his colleagues were beginning to start a Socialist agitation among the London workers, Socialism was also beginning to attract the curiosity of some young middle-class intellectuals. "I have a pile of half a dozen German pamphlets on Socialism which I must read to-day", George Gissing, serving his apprenticeship on Grub Street, was writing to his admiring younger brother in August, 1880.[2] In April of the next year Marx was complaining half-humorously to his daughter Jenny, of "an invasion from Hyndman and spouse, who both have too much staying power".

"I don't dislike the wife, for she has a brusque, unconventional and decided way of thinking and speaking, but it is funny to see how admiringly her eyes fasten upon the lips of her self-satisfied, garrulous husband."[3]

In December, 1881, he was writing to Sorge: "The English have recently begun to occupy themselves more with

1 L.E.L. Handbill, *State Emigration.*

2 See A. and E. Gissing, *Letters of George Gissing to His Family* (1927).

3 *Marx-Engels Sel. Cor.*, p. 389.

Capital." The *Contemporary Review* had published a "very inadequate" and inaccurate article on Socialism: Hyndman had published (in the previous June) *England for All*: and *Modern Thought* had just published an article by Ernest Belfort Bax on Marx himself, "the first English publication of the kind which is pervaded by a real enthusiasm for the new ideas themselves and boldly stands up against British Philistinism."[1]

Bax was to be one of Morris's closest socialist colleagues. As a boy of sixteen he was moved to tears by the news of the bloody repression of the Communards in 1871, "this martyrdom of all that was noblest (as I conceived it) in the life of the time."[2] Some time after this, he attached himself to the Positivists, since they were "the only organized body of persons at that time in the country who had the courage systematically to defend. . . the Commune".[3] Following his talent for musical composition, he went to study in Stuttgart in 1875, and on the Continent made closer contact with European thought and political movements. He became a student of German philosophy, and his studies and political sympathies both led him in 1881 to *Capital.* As a result of his monograph on Marx in *Modern Thought,* Marx sent him "many appreciative messages", but was too ill to make his acquaintance. It was not until 1883, after Marx's death, that Bax was introduced to Engels and entered more deeply into Marxist studies.

In any school of thought at war with Victorian orthodoxies there were bound to be minds receptive to Socialist influences. Both Positivists and Secularists contributed recruits to the early Socialist movement. The revolt against Victorian prudery, the influence of the old watchwords "Equality" and "Fraternity" which were now returning to a few young intellectuals by way of the literature of America and Europe, stirred other minds:

[1] *Marx-Engels Sel. Cor.,* pp. 397-8.

[2] E. Belfort Bax, *Reminiscences and Reflexions of a Mid and Late Victorian* (1918), p. 29.

"The long advances of history, the lives of men and women—the men that scratched the reindeer and mammoth on bits of bone, the Bushmen painting their rude rock-paintings, the mud-hovels clustering round mediaeval castles, the wise and kindly Arab with his loving boy-attendants, the Swiss mountain-herdsmen, the Russian patriot, the English mechanic.

"Know ME. I am Happiness in them, in all—underlying. . ."

No, not Walt Whitman, but his most famous English disciple, Edward Carpenter, in his *Towards Democracy,* written between 1881 and 1882. During the years of his adolescence, Shelley had been Carpenter's ideal: at Cambridge in 1869 (at the age of twenty-five) he first read William Michael Rossetti's edition of Whitman's poems, and felt "a great leap of joy".[1] A few years later he visited Whitman and renewed his inspiration. In Whitman's *Democratic Vistas* he found shadowed forth an ideal of brotherhood beside which the conventions of Victorian society seemed vicious and tawdry. Working as an extension lecturer at Sheffield, he tried, somewhat self-consciously, to win terms of friendship with the industrial proletariat:

"Railway men, porters, clerks, signalmen, ironworkers, coach-builders, Sheffield cutlers. . . from the first I got on excellently and felt fully at home with them—and I believe, in most cases, they with me. I felt I had come into, or at least in sight of the world to which I belonged."[2]

Class divisions were so rigorous that it seemed eccentric for a middle-class man to visit the public bar of the "local": an adventure to travel steerage to America and back: and—despite all the preachings of Carlyle and Ruskin—a strange affront to his class for Carpenter to help with the harvesting at the local farms, to try his hand at manual jobs, and to relax of an evening in the cottage of one of the labourers. Because

[1] Edward Carpenter, *My Days and Dreams* (1916), p. 64.

[2] *Ibid.,* p. 102.

Carpenter's revolt was individualistic, undisciplined, and (backed by a legacy of £6,000) not especially arduous, it is easily underestimated to-day. Established at his small-holding at Millthorpe, near Sheffield, with Thoreau's *Walden* on the shelves, receiving the visits of working-class admirers in the North, it all seems too easy.

But Carpenter can no more be held responsible for the vapidity of his followers than Morris can be held responsible for rustic garden furniture. His revolt against the Victorian orthodoxies was whole-hearted enough, even if it was expressed in an individualistic form. The two ex-Eton masters, Henry Salt and J.L. Joynes—and especially the former—were moved by somewhat similar currents of feeling. Joynes was intellectually tougher than either Carpenter or Salt, and his contribution to the early movement correspondingly greater. At King's College, Cambridge, Joynes and Salt had kicked against the pricks of authority, their major exploit being to release a mole to desecrate the sanctity of the Senior Fellow's lawn.[1] As masters at Eton both were under suspicion as Radicals, free-thinkers and possessors of tricycles. Meanwhile Joynes was reading the German revolutionary poetry of 1848, especially of Freiligrath, translations of which he later published as *Songs of a Revolutionary Epoch.* He entered the Socialist movement at its outset, and won some notoriety in 1882 by being arrested, in the company of Henry George, the author of *Progress and Poverty,* by the Irish Constabulary while on a speaking tour. This incident forced his resignation from Eton, and his total immersion for two years in the Socialist movement. A "quiet, gentle, unobtrusive man, tall and fair, with rather stooping shoulders and ruddy, almost boyish, face",[2] he gave the impression rather of a scholar than a fighter. But there were few Socialist activities in 1883 or 1884 in which he was not a leading spirit.

[1] Henry Salt, "James Leigh Joynes: Some Reminiscences", *The Social-Democrat,* Vol. I, No. 8, August, 1897. See also Salt, *Seventy Years Among Savages.*

[2] *Ibid.,* (a note by Harry Quelch).

George's *Progress and Poverty,* in which he set forward the demand, "We must make land common property", and proposed a means of effecting this by a drastic Single Tax, was being very widely read among advanced intellectuals and Radicals in 1881, and when he visited England and Ireland on a lecturing tour in 1882 he met with a ready welcome. The book's mixture of libertarian and Christian rhetoric with chapters of closely-argued political economy struck an answering chord among those who had already been interested in Mill's advocacy of land nationalization, and in the active campaign of Michael Davitt and the Irish Land League. The "sensation" of George's book, Marx wrote to Sorge in June, 1881, "is significant because it is a first, if unsuccessful attempt at emancipation from the orthodox political economy".[1] Many of George's converts, like Joynes, remained Single-Taxers for a short period only before moving forward to Socialism. A speech of George's, Shaw recalled, "sent me to political economy, with which I had never concerned myself, as fundamental in any social criticism."[2]

Trefusis, the hero of Shaw's early novel, *An Unsocial Socialist,* first published in serial form in *To-day* (where Morris read it) in 1884, but written a couple of years before, pokes fun at Erskine, a rhetorical poet of republicanism of the Swinburne breed:

" 'Erskine's next drama may be about liberty, but its Patriot Martyrs will have something better to do than spout balderdash against figurehead kings who in all their lives never secretly plotted as much dastardly meanness, greed, cruelty, and tyranny as is openly voted for in London by every half-yearly meeting of dividend-consuming vermin whose miserable wage-slaves drudge sixteen hours out of the twenty-four.'

" 'What is going to be the end of it all?' said Sir Charles, a little dazed.

" 'Socialism or Smash. Socialism if the race has at last evolved the

[1] *Marx-Engels Sel. Cor.,* pp. 395-6. 100,000 copies of *Progress and Poverty* were sold in England, 1881-3.

[2] May Morris, II, p. xii.

faculty of co-ordinating the functions of a society too crowded and complex to be worked any longer on the old haphazard private-property system. Unless we re-organize our society socialistically. . . Free Trade by itself will ruin England. . .' "[1]

But this sense of a system in crisis did not necessarily imply any pleasure at the prospect, any rebirth of the "hope" felt by Morris. Even to some of those middle-class men who supported the Socialist Movement, the proletariat appeared as primarily a destructive force. Morris's son-in-law, H. Halliday Sparling, wrote in a pamphlet on unemployment some years later:

"A million of starving people, with another million on the verge of starvation, represent a potential of destructive force to measure which no dynamometer has yet been made, but which will, if suddenly liberated, assuredly and absolutely destroy every vestige of nineteenth century civilization so-called; will destroy it more completely than time has destroyed the traces of the society of Nineveh, of Babylon, Greece and Rome, or even Mexico."[2]

Crazed faces, incendiary torches, dynamiters and assassins— there were men within the Socialist movement as well as without who could not shake off the bourgeois caricature of the proletarian revolution.

Even H.M. Hyndman, the "Father of English Socialism", and the man primarily responsible for bringing together in a single organization the various elements, proletarian and middle-class, moving towards Socialism in 1881, was not free from this attitude. A wealthy middle-class man, just over forty years of age, with enormous self-confidence and a taste for adventure, Hyndman had tried his hand at county cricket, globe-trotting and journalism before he read *Capital* in 1880 and became acquainted with Marx. His conversion to

[1] G.B. Shaw, *An Unsocial Socialist,* Ch. XV.

[2] H. Halliday Sparling, *Men versus Machinery* (1888).

Socialism was rapid—suspiciously rapid in the view of Joseph Lane and his friends.[1] At the beginning of 1880 he was dabbling in politics, with some idea of a "Tory-Radical" revival in which he tried to interest the aged Disraeli. In March of that year he offered himself as an Independent candidate at Marylebone, with a programme of "wide, steady, progressive Liberalism" at home and imperialism abroad: "The war in Afghanistan was the unavoidable consequence of the breach of Muscovite engagements. . . I am altogether opposed to Home Rule in Ireland. . ." The Colonies he declared to be "the special heritage of our working-class", and he demanded an increase in the size of the Navy: "In short, I am earnestly bent upon reform at home and resolute to maintain the power and dignity of England abroad."[2] Before the year was out, he was attempting to promote under his own leadership a union of the Radical Clubs in London—efforts which were brought to success in June, 1881, with the formation of the Democratic Federation. At its first Conference, Hyndman distributed copies of his own *England for All,* in two chapters of which he borrowed liberally (and without acknowledgement) from Marx. But, despite the Socialist content of these chapters, the Jingoism present in the previous year's programme was still apparent. The demand for a strong Navy (persistent throughout Hyndman's later career), and the presentation of the Colonies as the special heritage of the English working-class—these ideas were set forward in rolling passages of rhetoric:

> "In the Atlantic and Pacific, in European waters and the China Seas, from the Cape of Good Hope to Cape Horn, and from the British islands to Australia and India, we hold a chain of posts which will enable us to exercise at the fitting moment an almost overwhelming pressure. . . Halifax and Vancouver's Island, Bermuda and the Falkland

[1] See the letter of Lane to Ambrose Barker, deriding Hyndman's claims to be *The "Father and Founder" of the Modern English Socialist Movement,* published as a leaflet in 1912.

[2] The full Programme is printed in Lee, *op. cit.,* Appendix I.

Islands, Gibraltar, Malta, and Aden, Sydney, Melbourne, King George's Sound, and Auckland, to say nothing of the Indian ports, and scarcely less valuable possessions elsewhere, such as Hong-Kong, Fiji, and the Mauritius, constitute an array of maritime citadels which, maintained in proper defence by ourselves and our colonies, must, in conjunction with a fleet proportioned to our maritime interests, render future naval war against us almost impossible."

From this time forwards, Hyndman was to appear as a puzzling contradiction to Morris and to many another Socialist. The difference in temperament between Morris and Hyndman is aptly illustrated in their respective attitudes to the ceremonial headgear of their class, the top hat. Morris, resigning from his Directorship, had sat on his, and he never bought another. The top hat figures in nearly every reminiscence of Hyndman during the early years: in this dress he sold *Justice* in the streets, addressed open-air meetings, and earned his livelihood on the Stock Exchange. It symbolized a quite consciously adopted attitude in his propagandist work:

"At almost every meeting he addressed, Hyndman would cynically thank the audience for so 'generously supporting my class'. Indeed, he brought in 'my class' to an objectionable degree. It seemed to some of us that it would have been better if he could have dropped this reference, but none of us doubted his whole-souled advocacy of Socialism as he conceived it."[1]

Hyndman's reading of *Capital,* and his discussions with Marx, had convinced him that a proletarian revolution was inevitable, "whether we like it or not".[2] Marx he described as "the Aristotle of the Nineteenth Century",[3] and he asserted for himself the role of interpreter and chief apostle of a mechanical "Marxist" dogma. The working class he tended to regard as the raw material of the revolution, the motive-force which he could harness for his political strategy,

[1] Tom Mann, *Memoirs,* p. 40.
[2] See Hyndman, *The Social Reconstruction of England* (1884).
[3] *To-Day,* April, 1889.

rather than as made up of fellow-comrades actively and consciously participating in the struggle. Always the note of Jingoism ran underneath the surface:

> "There is still not wanting evidence that the English people, under better arrangements, would soon rise to the level of the most glorious periods of our past history. Those very lads who now fall into the dangerous classes from sheer ignorance and bad management—there are, according to the police, at least 300,000 such people in London alone—form, if taken early and thoroughly fed and trained, the flower of our navy. The race is really as capable as ever. In America, in Australia, all the world over, the Anglo-Saxon blood is still second to none. . ."[1]

To Edward Carpenter it seemed that Hyndman lived in imminent expectation of revolutionary events, when in a sudden crisis impelled by the spontaneous revolt of suffering and hunger, "the S.D.F. would resolve itself into a Committee of Public Safety, and. . . it would be for him as Chairman of that body to guide the ship of State into the calm haven of Socialism."[2] Although he was to win the loyal support of a few notable working-class comrades, among them Harry Quelch and Jack Williams, he alienated many hundreds more by his dictatorial manner and sectarian indifference to the wider organizations of the trade union and labour movement. While his books on political theory, and especially his *Historical Basis of Socialism in England* (1883), were arsenals of fact and argument for the pioneers, when he came to express the wider objectives of Socialism, he fell back upon the commonplaces of any middle-class gentleman.

To the inexperienced members of the Democratic Federation in 1882, however, Hyndman's supreme self-confidence, his fluent pen and imposing platform presence, his political contacts and even his ambition appeared as sources of strength.

[1] *The Coming Revolution in England* (reprinted from the *North American Review*, October, 1882).

[2] Carpenter, *op. cit.*, pp. 246-9.

Moreover, his political writings and his expositions of Marxist theory—faulty as both were—were in advance of any other English work of the time. While some of the prominent Radicals originally associated with the Federation were driven off by the socialist flavour of *England for All*, and by the vigour of the Federation's agitation against the Irish Coercion Bill, Hyndman gathered around him a group of enthusiasts—among them J.L. Joynes, Jack Williams, Herbert Burrows (who had for some time been active in the London Radical Clubs), Andreas Scheu, and the veterans, Charles and James Murray—who (in Scheu's view) were pushing Hyndman forward rather faster than he wished to go.[1] On May 31st, 1882, a Conference was held at which, for the first time, the Federation passed a distinctively Socialist resolution:[2] and the organization began to lose the taint, which the presence of Hyndman had at first given it, of being "a sort of Tory drag to take the scent off the fox".[3] By the end of 1882 the Federation was considered, at least by outsiders, to be a Socialist organization, although it had not as yet adopted any Socialist programme. Hyndman was now thoroughly convinced, not only of the soundness of Marxist theories, but also that the revolution was due to take place in England before all other countries.[4] It was not until 1883 that the Federation issued its first Socialist pamphlet, *Socialism Made Plain*: but in the winter of 1882-3, several Conferences were organized to discuss a series of immediate demands, which would serve as "stepping-stones" to Socialism. These included: "the compulsory construction by Public Bodies of healthy dwellings for the people": "free, secular and technical education": the legislative enactment of an eight-hour day: cumulative taxation of incomes over £300: public work for the

[1] See Scheu, *op. cit.*, Part III, Ch. V.

[2] See Lee, *op. cit.*, p. 48.

[3] William Morris to C.E. Maurice, June 22nd, 1883, *Letters*, p. 174.

[4] See his table of eight reasons why the Revolution must take place first in England, in *The Coming Revolution in England* and *The Historical Basis of Socialism in England*, (1883), pp. 374-5.

unemployed: the repudiation of the National Debt: State Appropriation of the railways, and municipal ownership of gas, electricity and water supplies: and the nationalization of the land. Thus, when William Morris joined the Democratic Federation in January, 1883, modern Socialism was on its point of emergence from the advanced radicalism of the previous decade, and the teething troubles of the new organization were scarcely begun.

IV. The "Oddities"

William Morris was one of perhaps 200 men and women who took the same step in 1882 and 1883. They represented a small eddy of ideas, part old, part new, rather than a movement of the masses: and this fact goes far to explain the doctrinaire and sectarian outlook of several of the pioneers. Until the new unionism of the later 1880s, the loyalty of the majority of the skilled trade unionists to Gladstonian Liberalism was still unbroken, and the apathy of the masses of the unskilled had scarcely been stirred. It is in the 1880s, rather than in the 1870s, that the full fruition of "Lib.Lab.-ism" can be seen. It was in the 1880s that the first working man (Henry Broadhurst) was given a Government post: that the first working men were appointed as magistrates: that local Liberal Parties admitted working men as candidates to School Boards and local Councils. "The great body of working men", Morris wrote, recalling the years of pioneering,

> "and especially those belonging to the most organized industries were hostile to Socialism: they did not really look upon themselves as a class, they identified their interests with those of their trade-union, their craft, their workshop or factory even: the capitalist system seemed to them, if not heaven-born, yet at least necessary and undoubtedly indefeasible."[1]

[1] "What We Have to Look For" (March 30th, 1895), Brit. Mus. Add. MSS., 45334.

But, while the pioneers of 1883 could only be counted in tens and twenties, there were among them names which were to figure prominently in the hard propaganda battle of the next few years. While, in Engels' words, the movement was largely proceeding "among 'educated' elements sprung from the bourgeoisie",[1] a small number of exceptionally gifted working men—among them John Burns and Tom Mann, Harry Quelch, a London meat-porter, John Lincoln Mahon, a young Scottish engineer, Robert Banner, a bookbinder, Tom Maguire of Leeds, and Tom Barclay of Leicester—were beginning to take a leading part in the propaganda of ideas. From this time forward, Socialist ideas were to become of increasing influence within the broader working-class movement, so that it is possible to date the effective birth of modern Socialism in Britain from 1883. The working men attracted to the movement in its first years, Morris recalled,

> "were there by dint of their special intelligence, or of their eccentricity; not as working-men simply. . . As a friend. . . once said to me, We are too much a collection of oddities. . ."[2]

And yet their conversion to the Socialist cause was a sympton of those deep upheavals in the economic and political life of Britain which were, in the next few years, to prepare many thousands more for their message.

It was the ending of English monopoly in the world market which, in Engels' judgement, was the "secret of the sudden—though it has been slowly preparing for three years—but the present sudden emergence of a Socialist movement" in England at the beginning of 1884.[3] And the repercussions of this event in political and social life were instrumental in bringing the "collection of oddities" together. Some were impelled forward by the bankruptcy of the Gladstonian

[1] *Marx-Engels Sel. Cor.*, p. 419, August 30th, 1883.

[2] "What We Have to Look For", Brit. Mus. Add. MSS. 45334.

[3] See *Marx-Engels Sel. Cor.*, p. 422.

administration in dealing with unemployment and misery at home: others, such as Joynes, H.H. Champion and Morris himself, were impelled by disgust at imperialist policies in Egypt, Africa and Ireland: others, such as Hyndman and Shaw, were impelled in part by their belief that the capitalist system was coming to the end of its term. Once an organized propaganda was afoot, it attracted to it a few of the old guard who had survived the apathy of the previous decade. It gathered refugees like Scheu and Lessner.[1] Here and there old Chartists, and an occasional Owenite, joined in. Wherever there existed any centre of unorthodox thought, recruits might be won for Socialism. They might come from a Secular Society, or from among the members of one of the old Republican Clubs of the 1870s. In a hundred ways, men were taking the first step towards Socialism–Tom Mann reading Carlyle, Ruskin and *Progress and Poverty,* John Burns studying a battered copy of *The Wealth of Nations* in Nigeria, Henry Hyde Champion, the artillery officer, seeing the facts of imperialism for himself in Egypt. In every town and village, the workers faced the facts of exploitation in their daily lives and while a thousand might be beaten down in the struggle, still one, by some miracle of will and courage, might find his way through.

What tool of analysis can be brought to bear to explain the conversion to Socialism of Tom Barclay, the Leicester pioneer? He came from an Irish background, the poorest of the poor. His first recollection was "one of intense fear. . . a little child alone in the upper room of a hovel".

> "What a monotonous childhood! No toys, no picture-books, no pets, no going 'ta-ta'. No carpet on the uneven brick floor, no mat, no wall-paper; what poverty! There was neither doctor nor midwife present at my birth. . I have heard mother boast that she never needed a midwife. She was very hardy, brought up in the wilds of the 'county Mayo, God help us!' After all, why shouldn't a woman be able to bring forth like cats and cows and other mammals?"[2]

[1] For Frederick Lessner, see his *Sixty Years in the Social-Democratic Movement* (1907). A veteran of the struggles of 1848 and succeeding years, he was extremely active in the First International, and a close friend and confidant of Marx and Engels.

[2] Tom Barclay, *Memoirs and Medleys: The Autobiography of a Bottle-Washer.*

Why not indeed? And why should not children like Tom Barclay, brought up in a "two-roomed crib", the window "not six feet off from the muck hole and the unflushed privies", grow up to be brutes for the service of Capital in their turn? His father, a rag-and-bone man (without even a handcart), his mother leaving the children alone in the house while she went out to sell pen'norths of fire-lighting—he himself was dedicated to the service of Progress at the age of eight, turning a wheel all day for one and sixpence a week. But Tom Barclay was an "oddity". He devoured every book that came his way, he bought or begged a pencil and became a talented draughtsman—a scholar, a writer and a Socialist. From a similar background of Irish Catholicism and poverty another "oddity", Tom Maguire, was to emerge while still in his teens to become the first propagandist of Socialism in the city of Leeds.

The Socialist propaganda brought to such people as these exactly what it had brought to William Morris—hope. Wherever the aspirations for life stirred among the workers—the clear-headed hatred of capitalism, the thirst for knowledge, beauty and fellowship—the Socialist converts might be won. Such converts might seem "oddities", it is true: but it is by such "oddities" as these that history is made.

CHAPTER II

THE FIRST PROPAGANDA

I. "All for the Cause"

MORRIS was one of the very first of the pioneers. "It must be understood that I always intended to join any body who distinctly called themselves Socialists", he wrote to Andreas Scheu in September, 1883,

> "so when last year I was invited to join the Democratic Federation by Mr. Hyndman, I accepted the invitation hoping that it would declare for Socialism, in spite of certain drawbacks that I expected to find in it; concerning which I find on the whole that there are fewer drawbacks than I expected."[1]

When he took out membership of the Federation in January, 1883, an attempt was still being made to build it on the lines of an alliance of Radical Clubs. The adoption in the summer of 1883, of the pamphlet, *Socialism Made Plain,* resulted in the withdrawal by some of the Radicals of their support. At the same time, a new Executive was elected which included firm Socialists like Joynes and Champion, Scheu, James MacDonald, and William Morris as Treasurer. Belfort Bax was brought on to the Executive in the autumn, and in January, 1884, *Justice,* the organ of the Federation, was first launched. During 1884 the sale of this paper, open-air propaganda, a public debate between Charles Bradlaugh and Hyndman, lecturing tours by Morris—all these began to draw public attention to the existence of a Socialist movement in Britain, and brought the formation of a few provincial branches. In the last week of December, 1884, when the propaganda seemed at last to be well under way, the Executive of the S.D.F. split in two: and Morris, with the majority, resigned

[1] *Letters,* p. 188.

to form the Socialist League. In less than two years Morris had become one of the two or three acknowledged leaders of the Socialist movement in England.

This result was as unexpected to Morris as it was to his new comrades. Of course, the pioneers were aware that they had won a notable convert. "Morris", Hyndman recalled, in a generous tribute on his death, "with his great reputation and high character, doubled our strength at a stroke, by giving in his adhesion."[1] "It was a curious situation for Morris", George Bernard Shaw—who had heard him discuss the matter—recalled:

> "He had escaped middle age, passing quite suddenly from a circle of artistic revolutionists, mostly university men gone Agnostic or Bohemian or both, who knew all about him and saw him as much younger and less important than he really was, into a proletarian movement in which, so far as he was known at all, he was venerated as an Elder... Once or twice some tactless ghost from his past wandered into the Socialist world and spoke of him and even to him as Topsy. It was soon morally booted out in miserable bewilderment for being silly and impudent..."[2]

Some of the pioneers (if Bruce Glasier's recollections can be trusted) regarded Morris with an awe which was near to being sickly. To them he seemed like a figure in romance, coming from—

> "the wonderful world... of poetry and art in which he and his companions, Rossetti, Burne-Jones, and Swinburne, lived their Arcadian lives, and from which, like a prince in a fairy story, he appeared to be stepping down chivalrously into the dreary region of working-class agitation."[3]

"The small minority of us who had any contacts with the newest fashions in literature and art", Shaw recalled,

[1] *Justice,* October 6th, 1896. [2] May Morris, II, p. xi.

[3] John Bruce Glasier, *William Morris and the Early Days of the Socialist Movement* (1921), p. 20.

"knew that he had become famous as the author of... *The Earthly Paradise* which few of us had read, though that magic line 'the idle singer of an empty day' had caught our ears somehow. We knew that he kept a highly select shop in Oxford Street where he sold furniture of a rum aesthetic sort, and decorated houses with extraordinary wall-papers... And that was about all."[1]

In however much respect Morris might be held, it did not follow that he would assume a position of political leadership in the movement. Most organizations have notabilities who lend the authority of their names to the movement: who occasionally chair a meeting, deliver an address, or sit on the platform at an annual meeting. Morris must have seemed well suited to this role. As Treasurer his known integrity and his own deep pocket would be invaluable. As a poet and artist of national reputation, he would be able to give supporting fire on the middle-class flank of the movement. For a man who was notoriously busy, this was all that could be expected.

In fact, on joining the Federation, Morris told Hyndman that he was ready to do whatever work lay to hand, as a rank-and-filer under Hyndman's lead. Hyndman had accepted this offer of allegiance with serene self-confidence, while the young Shaw in the background smiled grimly to himself, "measuring at sight how much heavier Morris's armament was".[2] But neither of them understood the full implications of these simple words.

Morris was not a man given to polite turns of phrase or to rhetoric. All his life it had been his business to *make* things. Whether tiles or tapestry or paper, no detail was too trivial to catch his attention. Now that he had decided that it was necessary to make a revolution, he set about the business in the same manner. First, it was necessary to find out through study and experience *how* a revolution was made. Next, it was necessary to get down to the details of making it, "turning neither to the right hand nor to the left hand till it was done". Questions of his own comfort or dignity were irrelevant.

[1] May Morris, II, p. xiii. [2] *Ibid.*

When he sold *Justice* in the streets or spoke at open-air meetings, he did not do it as a romantic gesture, or because he liked doing it: but simply because it had to be done, and, provided that he could do the job, he saw no reason why he should be excused.

But Morris's words had deeper implications even than this, and of a kind which Hyndman—and certainly Shaw—were never fitted to understand. Morris brought to the movement all the enthusiasm of the convert whose whole life had served as a preparation for conversion: but he also brought something which the youthful convert or individualist in revolt can only learn through experience—an understanding of the subordination of individual differences of outlook and temperament essential to the growth of the movement. Morris's vision of the discipline and organization necessary if the propaganda of Socialism was to take effective form was clearer than that of any of the earliest pioneers. It was a theme of his first Socialist poems:

"There amidst the world new-builded shall our earthly deeds abide,
Though our names be all forgotten, and the tale of how we died.

"Life or death then, who shall heed it, what we gain or what we lose?
Fair flies life amid the struggle, and the Cause for each shall choose."

It was a repeated theme of his first lectures. "By union I mean a very serious matter", he said in a lecture of 1883:

"I mean sacrifice to the Cause of leisure, pleasure and money, each according to his means: I mean sacrifice of individual whims and vanity, of individual misgivings, even though they may be founded on reason, as to the means which the organizing body may be forced to use: remember without organization the cause *is* but a vague dream, which may lead to revolt, to violence and disorder, but which will be speedily repressed by those who are blindly interested in sustaining the present anarchical tyranny which is misnamed Society: remember also that no organization is possible without the sacrifices I have been speaking of; without obedience of the necessities of the Cause."[1]

[1] "Art and the People", May Morris, II, pp. 404-5.

This vision of "the Cause" was Morris's special, and his most permanent, contribution to the British Socialist movement, and it was, in part, his growing conviction that such self-sacrificing organization could never be built up under Hyndman's autocratic leadership, that forced him into prominence, and precipitated the split in December, 1884.

II. "So I Began the Business. . ."

Although, in 1883, there were foreshadowings of this future conflict, they were of little importance. Morris at the outset attached himself to the most active propagandists within the councils of the Federation. After one of the first meetings which he attended, he wrote that one of the members "spoke hugely to my liking; advocated street-preaching. . . as the real practical method: wisely to my mind. . ."[1] This mood grew within him as the year grew older. In a lecture of this year he asked, "How is the change to be brought about?"

> "I say it is the plain duty of those who believe in the necessity of social revolution, quite irrespectively of any date they may give to the event, first to express their own discontent and hope when and where they can, striving to impress it on others; secondly to learn from books and from living people who are willing. . . to teach them, in as much detail as possible what are the ends and the hopes of Social Revolution; and thirdly to join any body of men which is honestly striving to give means of expression to that discontent and hope, and to teach people the details of the aim of Constructive Revolution. . ."[2]

In February and March he was busy with the second duty. The literature of Socialism in English was ridiculously small. Not even the *Communist Manifesto* was in print. The only work of scientific Socialism which Morris could obtain without difficulty was the French edition of *Capital*: and the

[1] Mackail, II, p. 97.

[2] "Art and the People", May Morris, II, pp. 403-4.

effect of his study of it is obvious in all his writing—the sudden understanding of the central fact of class struggle, the sharpening of all his historical analysis. At the same time, he was reading works of Robert Owen, whom "he praised... immensely",[1] and, in September, 1883, he was again reading books by Cobbett: "such queer things they are, but with plenty of stuff in them".[2] In August, 1884, when it had become clear to him that he might be forced to challenge the leadership of Hyndman, he wrote in anxiety to Andreas Scheu:

> "I feel myself weak as to the Science of Socialism on many points: I wish I knew German, as I see I must certainly learn it. Confound you chaps! What do you mean by being foreigners?"[3]

and enquired for the name of some German comrade who could read the classics of Socialism with him in English.

Study (he had said) must come not only from books, but also from "living people". "I have just been reading *Underground Russia*", he wrote to his daughter Jenny, in May, 1883. "It is a most interesting book, though terrible reading too."[4] Its author, Sergius Stepnaik, became one of the refugee colony in England, and Morris later came to know him well. Not only the refugees whom he met and conversed with in London, but also their nameless comrades, imprisoned or working illegally in Russia, Germany and Austria, came to exercise a powerful hold on his imagination. "Is Socialism a dream?" he asked in a lecture of 1883, and answered:

> "It is no dream but a cause; men and women have died for it, not in the ancient days but in our own time: they lie in prison for it, work in mines, are exiled, are ruined for it: believe me when such things are suffered for dreams, the dreams come true at last."[5]

[1] Mackail, II, p. 97.
[2] *Letters*, p. 183.
[3] *Ibid.*, pp. 211-12.
[4] *Ibid.*, p. 172.
[5] "Art and the People", May Morris, II, p. 403.

Morris was soon to know many refugees. Among them were Stepniak and Prince Kropotkin: Frederick Lessner, who had marched with the Chartists in 1848, had returned to Germany and been imprisoned with great brutality before escaping to England once again; and Andreas Scheu who, from 1883 to 1885, was one of Morris's closest colleagues. Scheu, an Austrian Socialist of the "Left", had escaped from persecution in Vienna in 1874: had later found work in Edinburgh (where he introduced the young bookbinder, Robert Banner, to the Socialist movement): and had returned to London in 1882. A tall, impressive man with a black beard, he became one of the best known of the early Socialist orators, with an impassioned and fluent delivery. His character was not free from vanity: but, in the 1880s, his enthusiasm was unquestionable. As a furniture-designer, he was one of the few of Morris's colleagues who took an informed interest in the aims of the Firm: and their acquaintance had ripened before the end of 1883 into warm friendship.

The first duty of revolutionists, Morris said at this time, was "to express their discontent and hope when and where they can". "Discontent and hope"—the words were carefully chosen. Middle class in origin, comfortable in his own surroundings, his revolt against capitalism stemmed from moral revulsion rather than direct experience of poverty and oppression. He put the matter in its simplest terms in a letter to C.E. Maurice:

"In looking into matters social and political I have but one rule, that in thinking of the condition of any body of men I shall ask myself, 'How could you bear it yourself? what would you feel if you were poor against the system under which you live?' I have always been uneasy when I had to ask myself that question, and of late years I have had to ask it so often, that I have seldom had it out of my mind: and the answer to it has more and more made me ashamed of my own position, and more and more made me feel that if I had not been born rich or well-to-do I should have found my position *un*endurable... Nothing can argue me out of this feeling, which I say plainly is a matter of religion to me: the contrasts of rich and poor are unendurable and ought not to be endured by either rich or poor."[1]

In his first year as a propagandist, Morris felt that he did best to confine his arguments to those fields where his own experience gave him most authority. Hyndman and others, he felt, were better qualified than he to explain the principles of Socialism. His first lecture after joining the Federation, delivered in Manchester in March, 1883, under the title of "Art, Wealth, and Riches", was an attack upon capitalist society more specific and outspoken than any he had made before: but it stopped short of any specific declaration of Socialist doctrines:

"What is to amend these grievances? You must not press me too close on that point. I believe I am in such a very small minority on these matters that it is enough for me if I find here and there some one who admits the grievances; for my business herein is to spread discontent. I do not think that this is an unimportant office; for, as discontent spreads, the yearning for bettering the state of things spreads with it. . ."[2]

The lecture called down the wrath of angry correspondents and leader-writers upon his head. The *Manchester Examiner and Times* received the lecture with "mingled feelings", denounced Morris for being "unpractical", and for being so successful in his avowed aim—the making of people discontented. The *Manchester Weekly Times* (which had had several days' breathing space to unmingle its feelings) reproved him with lofty patronage, hoping "that he will reconsider his ideal, and have something less impracticable and less discouraging to say to us the next time".[3] One indignant correspondent declared that Morris had raised "another question than one of mere art". This was too much for

[1] *Letters,* p. 176.

[2] *Works,* Vol. XXIII, p. 159.

[3] *Manchester Examiner and Times,* March 7th, 1883; *Manchester Weekly Times,* March 10th, 1883.

Morris—as yet inexperienced in the typical reactions of the bourgeois Press. "Sir", he replied, "It was the purpose of my lecture to raise another question than one of 'mere art' ":

"It may well be a burden to the conscience of an honest man who lives a more manlike life to think of the innumerable lives which are spent in toil unrelieved by hope and uncheered by praise; men who might as well, for all the good they are doing to their neighbours by their work, be turning a crank with nothing at the end of it. . .

"Over and over again have I asked myself why should not my lot be the common lot. My work is simple work enough; much of it, nor that the least, pleasant, any man of decent intelligence could do. . . Indeed I have been ashamed when I have thought of the contrast between my happy working hours and the unpraised, unrewarded, monotonous drudgery which most men are condemned to. Nothing shall convince me that such labour as this is good or necessary to civilization."[1]

In the chorus of protest, one sympathetic voice was heard:

"It is a long time since I read anything upon art that has gratified me so much. . . Although I never saw him, I felt that we were companions."[2]

It was signed, "An Artisan".

So, in his first Socialist lecture, the pattern of his future reception was laid down. After each lecture there would follow indignant letters to the local papers, and measured reproofs upon the "unpractical" poet in the editorial columns. The Victorian middle class dearly loved a Reformer whose ideals were too dream-like ever to take practical shape. But the chorus of "unpractical", "misguided idealist", "poet-upholsterer", and so forth, swelled to a crescendo the moment that Morris had found a *practical* remedy to the evils which he had before attacked, and had proclaimed himself to be a member of the *practical* revolutionary movement. In October, 1884, the London *Echo* delivered a characteristic editorial rebuke:

[1] *Letters*, pp. 165-6.

[2] *Manchester Examiner and Times*, March 19th, 1883.

"Mr. Morris. . . is not content to be heard merely as a voice crying in the wilderness. . . He will be content with nothing less than the propagation of his ideas by means which must result in a social revolution. To that end he has allied himself with a body with the aims of which, we must charitably suppose, he is only in imperfect sympathy. Judging him by the company he keeps, he would disturb the foundations of Society in order that a higher artistic value may be given to our carpets. . .

"We are a manufacturing nation. We produce in order that we may sell to other countries. . . The first thing is to exist; then to exist in as much comfort as possible; then to provide ourselves with luxuries. . . Mr. Morris has pitched his theories of life too high."[1]

On this occasion Morris replied, protesting, amongst other things, at "the assumption. . . that I care only for Art and not for the other sides of the Social Questions I have been writing about", and also asserting his complete support for the S.D.F.: "I have had my full share in every step it has taken since I joined it, and I fully sympathize with its aims."[2]

"Discontent and hope", the "relation of Art to Labour"[3] – these were the burden of Morris's lectures until the summer of 1884.[4] These lectures, with great variety of illustration and vigour of expression, followed a similar pattern. First Morris examined in some fresh and striking manner the reality of life and of labour in capitalist society. Next, he presented by contrast the vision of true society, creative and responsive to beauty, and called his listeners to action in the struggle to achieve this vision. "Misery and the Way Out", for example, commenced with a careful discussion of the reasons for discontent in every class of society, and continued with an

[1] *Echo,* October 1st, 1884. [2] *Ibid.,* October 7th, 1884.

[3] See Morris to Charles Rowley, a well-known Manchester reformer, October 25th, 1883: "I have only one subject to lecture on, the relation of Art to Labour: also I am an open and declared Socialist, or to be more specific, Collectivist. . ." (*Letters,* p. 189).

[4] The main lectures he was offering at this time were "Useful Work versus Useless Toil", "Art and Labour", "Misery and the Way Out", and "How We Live and How We Might Live": contributions to *Justice* included, "Art or No Art?", "The Dull Level of Life", "Individualism at the Royal Academy", and "Work in a Factory as it Might Be".

analysis of the causes of discontent.

"Though it is futile to cast blame on any individual of the richer classes. . . I yet want to impress the fact upon you that as classes you and they are and must be opposed to each other. Whatever gain you add to your standard of life, you must do at their expense, and they will and must resist it to the utmost of their power. . . The whole of the domination of the upper classes is founded on deliberate injustice; and that injustice I want you to feel, because when you once feel that you are slaves. . . then the emancipation of labour is at hand: I know that in a country and time like our own, people do not readily feel that slavery: if you were treated with obvious violence, were liable to be tied up and whipped, or to have your ears cut off at the bidding of your masters; nay, if you had to go to the Police Office for a passport to go from Southwark to Hammersmith, it would soon be a different thing; you would soon be in the streets, I hope, expressing your feelings in something stronger than words."[1]

But suppose you had a fine standard of life—he continued—and it was torn from you—*then* you would revolt, or else submit to being a slave. This *is* what has been done to you, at your birth—"and alas! you have got used to it; you are contented". And so the lecture rose to its climax:

"It is to stir you up not to be contented with a little that I am here to-night: you will not get the little if you are contented with it: you *must* be either slaves or free. . ."[2]

In April he was lecturing to a Radical Club in Hampstead: in May to a sympathetic audience at the Irish National League rooms in Blackfriars' Road. In May, also, he was "driven into joining" the Executive of the Federation.[3] Then lecturing engagements began to come thick and fast, not only to small groups in London, but—before the summer of 1884—to many provincial centres, among them Manchester (again), Leicester, Birmingham, Bradford, Edinburgh, Leeds, and Blackburn.

[1] Brit. Mus. Add. MSS. 45333. [2] May Morris, II, p. 159-60.
[3] *Letters*, p. 172.

Sometimes the request came from an individual or two or three Socialists struggling to form a branch: sometimes from some other body interested in hearing the Socialist case. At several of these centres he was the first speaker to address a large public meeting on behalf of the new cause.

At some time in 1883 the Federation decided to follow the pioneering work of the Labour Emancipation League, and take a hand in the open-air propaganda. Morris's own part can be read in *The Pilgrims of Hope:*

"Until it befel at last that to others I needs must speak
(Indeed, they pressed me to that while yet I was weaker than weak.)
So I began the business, and in street-corners I spake
To knots of men. Indeed, that made my very heart ache,
So hopeless it seemed; for some stood by like men of wood;
And some, though fain to listen, but a few words understood;
And some but hooted and jeered: but whiles across some I came
Who were keen and eager to hear; as in dry flax the flame
So the quick thought flickered amongst them: and that indeed was a feast.
So about the streets I went, and the work on my hands increased;
And to say the very truth betwixt the smooth and the rough
It was work and hope went with it, and I liked it well enough."

By the summer of 1884 the Socialist open-air meetings by the Reformer's Tree in Hyde Park, or in Regent's Park, were well established. *Justice* was sold, and even statesmen strolled over sometimes to hear Morris or Hyndman or Jack Williams or John Burns holding forth.[1] A vivid picture of Morris at one such meeting in Victoria Park (in 1885) is given in Tom Mann's *Memoirs:*

"He was a picture on an open air platform. The day was fine, the branches of the tree under which he was speaking spread far over the speaker. Getting him well in view, the thought came, and has always recurred as I think of that first sight of Morris—'Bluff King Hal'. I did not give careful attention to what he was saying, for I was chiefly

[1] See Lee, *op. cit.*, p. 66.

concerned to get the picture of him in my mind, and then to watch the faces of the audience to see how they were impressed. . . Nine-tenths were giving careful attention, but on the fringe of the crowd were some who had just accidentally arrived, being out for a walk, and having unwittingly come upon the meeting. These stragglers were making such remarks as: 'Oh, this is the share-and-share-alike crowd'; 'Poverty, eh, he looks all right, don't he?' But the audience were not to be distracted by attempts at ribaldry: and as Morris stepped off the improvised platform, they gave a fine, hearty hand-clapping which showed real appreciation."[1]

Meanwhile Morris was serving his apprenticeship to other forms of propaganda. Edward Carpenter, who—from his first reading of Hyndman's *England for All*—had become an enthusiastic Socialist convert, donated £300 for the launching of *Justice*, "The Organ of the Social Democracy", the first weekly Socialist paper. James MacDonald has given a vivid picture of the enthusiastic and united meeting at which Hyndman announced the new project:

"He began in the ordinary business tone; then growing warmer, he declaimed against anonymous commercial journalism, and described the power we should have in a paper of our own. Raising his voice he declared that humbug, political, social and scientific, would be exposed, art was to be emancipated (here Morris nearly shook his shaggy head off with approving nods) and the workers of the world would be united by means of a great free, independent Press!"[2]

Since *Justice* could only be run on a weekly deficit, Morris was soon reaching deep into his pocket. The paper was advertised by street-sales, and on several week-ends Hyndman in his frock coat, Morris in his soft hat and blue suit, Champion, Joynes, Jack Williams and other working-class comrades took it out in the City and on the Strand. In March, 1884, on the first anniversary of Marx's death, Morris took part in his first public procession:

[1] Tom Mann, *op. cit.*, pp. 48-9. [2] *Justice*, January, 1914.

"I was loth to go, but did not dislike it when I did go: brief, I trudged all the way from Tottenham Court Rd. up to Highgate Cemetry (with a red-ribbon in my button-hole) at the tail of various banners and a very bad band to do honour to the memory of Karl Marx *and* the Commune: the thing didn't look as absurd as it sounds, as we were a tidy number, I should think more than a thousand in the procession, and onlookers to the amount, when we got to the end, of some 2 or 3 thousand more. . ."[1]

They were refused entrance to the cemetery, "of course", by a heavy guard of police, and adjourned to some waste ground, where speeches were made (one being by Dr. Aveling) and the International was sung.

In general, the propaganda in these two years was heavy going, in the face of apathy and insult. Only on one occasion, in early 1884, did the Federation make serious contact with the broad masses of the industrial workers. The occasion was the great Lancashire cotton strike in February and March. James MacDonald and Jack Williams were sent up to Blackburn as agitators. They issued bills calling a meeting to be addressed by "delegates from London", and filled the largest hall with 1,500 of the strikers:

"They waited patiently while Morris and Joynes and Hyndman spoke, to hear the message the delegates had brought them about their own particular business. . . Their interest was aroused in the message of Socialism. . . and the meeting was a tremendous success."[2]

Nearly 100 joined the Federation, a branch was formed, and Morris was able to comment in a letter, "all likely to do well there". In fact, from this time onwards the Federation maintained its foothold in Lancashire.

In the spring of 1884, it seemed indeed that "the Cause" was gaining ground. A remarkable band of men were

[1] *Letters,* p. 195.

[2] James MacDonald, "How I Became a Socialist", *Justice,* July 11th, 1896; and *Justice,* February 23rd, 1884.

gathered together: Hyndman, Burrows, Quelch and Joynes; Champion, a determined organizer; Bax, whom Morris dubbed the "philosopher of the movement"; Scheu, an impressive orator; John Burns (a new recruit) wielding increasing influence among his fellow trade unionists; William Morris himself. The first contacts had been made with the workers of the industrial North. There was a feeling of confidence within the small organization, and excitement at every new recruit. "The Day is Coming", William Morris wrote, and he was unafraid at the prospect of bloodshed. "Commercialism, competition, has sown the wind recklessly, and must reap the whirlwind", he wrote in October, 1883: "it has created the proletariat for its own interest, and its creation will and must destroy it: there is no other force which can do so."[1] In November, 1883, he wrote of Socialism to the *Standard*:

> "It is true that before this good time comes we shall have trouble, and loss, and misery enough to wade through; the injustice of past years will not be got rid of by the sprinkling of rosewater; the price must be paid for it."[2]

Despite his own "religious hatred" of all war and violence,[3] he sounded a call to battle:

> "Come, then, let us cast off fooling, and put by ease and rest
> For the CAUSE alone is worthy till the good days bring the best.
>
> "Come, join in the only battle wherein no man can fail,
> Where whoso fadeth and dieth, yet his deed shall still prevail.
>
> "Ah! come, cast off all fooling, for this, at least we know:
> That the Dawn and the Day is coming, and forth the Banners go."

[1] *Letters*, p. 190.

[2] *Standard*, November 22nd, 1883. The opening paragraphs of the letter are included by Mr. Henderson in *Letters*, p. 191, but the final sentence is omitted.

[3] The phrase is used in a letter to T.C. Horsfall early in 1883, and quoted in Mackail, II, p. 98.

III. "Oh, it is monstrous"

This kind of stuff, of course, was a long way beyond a joke. The man had been reproved in moderate terms by the editor of the *Manchester Examiner.* He had been called to task more sternly by the Master of University College, Oxford. He had been shown his error, reminded of the public school code which governed middle-class life ("you can carp at the masters in the prefects' room, if you like, but don't let the Lower Fourth hear you"). Now there was little that could be done but to blacken his character and ignore him. "We believe that Mr. Morris contributes 1s. a week towards enlightening the world as to the aims of the Social Democratic Federation", declared the London *Echo* (inaccurately), when Morris had had the temerity to reply to its original reproof. "Not much is to be apprehended from contributions of these amounts. . ."[1] "His utterances are curiously ineffectual", remarked the *Saturday Review* on January 10th, 1885, in an editorial which sums up so well two years of the expression of the "mingled feelings" of the capitalist Press that it may be taken as his formal notice of public expulsion from the precincts of St. Grundy's, "since he left off poetry, which he understood, and took to politics, of which he knows nothing".

> "People. . . may have faintly hoped that Mr. Morris would give. . . some new lights on that very difficult point of conscience and conduct, the fact of a capitalist and 'profit-monger' denouncing capitalists and profit-mongers without. . . making the least attempt to pour his capital into the lap of the Socialist Church, or to divide his profits weekly with the sons of toil who make them."

And so to the final magisterial sweep of the cane: "the intellectual disaster of the intelligence of a man who could once write *The Earthly Paradise*". Similar sentiments were voiced by George Gissing through the medium of a character in his novel, *Demos,* published a couple of years later

[1] *Echo,* October 8th, 1884. See above p. 310.

("Westlake" was a character drawn intermittently from Morris):

"Now here is an article signed by Westlake. You know his books? How has he fallen to this? His very style has abandoned him, his English smacks of the street corners, of Radical clubs. The man is ruined; it is next to impossible that he should ever again do good work, such as we used to have from him. The man who wrote 'Daphne'! Oh, it is monstrous!"

Much of this Morris had expected, for some of it he did not care tuppence—but, nevertheless, some of it *did* sting. As far as the general run of criticism went, Morris usually ignored it, unless he saw an opportunity for explaining more clearly some point in the Socialist case. But the attack on his own position as an employer caused him some uneasiness. It was initiated by a correspondent in the *Standard* in November, 1883, and drew from Morris a prompt reply:

"Your correspondent implies that, to be consistent, we should at once cast aside our position of capitalists, and take rank with the proletariat; but he must excuse my saying that he knows very well that we are not able to do so; that the most we can do is to palliate, as far as we can, the evils of the unjust system which we are forced to sustain; that we are but minute links in the immense chain of the terrible organization of competitive commerce, and that only the complete unrivetting of that chain will really free us. It is this very sense of the helplessness of our individual efforts which arms us against our own class, which compels us to take an active part in the agitation which, if it be successful, will deprive us of our capitalist position."[1]

A day or two later he was writing to Georgie Burne-Jones:

"I have been living in a sort of storm of newspaper brickbats, to some of which I had to reply: of course I don't mind a bit, nor even think the attack unfair."[2]

[1] *Letters,* p. 191. [2] *Ibid.,* p. 191.

A prompt answer had come from his own workers at Merton Abbey, who "are very sympathetic, which pleases me hugely", and seven of whom had insisted on forming the Merton Abbey branch of the Democratic Federation. But, for all his self-assurance, Morris was by no means satisfied with his reply, especially when the question was renewed, from allies as well as enemies.

For example, among Morris's acquaintances was Thomas James Cobden-Sanderson (the Cobden was borrowed from his wife, a daughter of the famous Richard) who had recently decided to Renounce Society, and go in for a Simple Life. Morris, who always had time for any intellectual who had artistic abilities and a sincere dislike of Podsnappery, helped him to start work as a bookbinder (and also gave him his first commission, the binding of his copy of *Capital*). "Annie Cobb. S.", Morris remarked good-humouredly, "is a very unregenerate person with a furious fad towards vegetarianism, in which I see no harm, if it didn't swallow up more important matters."[1] At any rate, the Cobb. S's were among those who saw fit to badger Morris about his personal affairs. "Morris came to see me...", Cobden-Sanderson entered in his Diary on January 16th, 1884:

> "We told him we thought he ought to put his principles into practice in his own case: that his appeal would be much more powerful if he did so. He said he was in a corner and could not, that no one person could; that, to say the truth, he was a coward and feared to do so; that there was his wife, and the girls; and how could he put it upon them? . . . Dear old Morris, he would be happier if he could put his ideas into practice."[2]

Morris had already made a serious sacrifice to "the Cause", raising money from the sale of some of the most treasured early books in his private collection.[3] There is reason to

[1] *Letters*, p. 193.

[2] *The Journals of Thomas James Cobden-Sanderson.*

[3] Mackail, II, p. 87. "*You* have no revolution on hand on which to spend your money", he wrote to Ellis, his publisher, in May, 1883 (Mackail, II, p. 101).

believe that in the early months of 1884 he very seriously considered taking a further step: according to Scheu (who was one of his closest confidants at this time) he intended to sell his business and live with his family upon £4 a week: and had he not sunk his lifework as an artist into the Firm, he might well have done so. But on June 1st, 1884, his mind was at last decided against this plan: and the long letter which he wrote to his closest friend, Georgie Burne-Jones, was the result of a decision only reached after long deliberation.

The argument turned on the question of profit-sharing within the Firm. ("What is it", he asked on another occasion but "feeding the dog with his own tail?") In fact, some limited form of profit-sharing was already in operation in the Firm,[1] although not extended to the whole business. Morris's own share of the profits in the past year had been about £1,800, his literary income £120:

> "Now you know we ought to be able to live upon £4 a week, and give the literary income to the revolutionary agitation; but here comes the rub, and I feel the pinch of society, for which society I am only responsible in a very limited degree. And yet if Janey and Jenny were quite well and capable I think they ought not to grumble at living on the said £4, nor do I think they would."

Evidently Janey was opposed to the scheme, and Jenny's continuing illness weighed upon Morris. But even supposing he were to live upon this income, the £1,600 surplus profit would amount only to a bonus of £16 a year when divided among the hundred workers. Compared with the average ratio of profit to wages in a normal business, the profits of the Morris Firm were remarkably small, several incompetents were employed out of goodwill, and the majority of workers were receiving wages higher than "the market price". Even supposing the profits to be distributed to be larger, Morris could not see that any principle would be served:

[1] See the account of Thomas Wardle in May Morris, II, p. 603.

"Much as I want to see workmen escape from their slavish position, I don't at all want to see a few individuals more creep out of their class, into the middle-class; this will only make the poor poorer still."

And so he brought his argument to a conclusion:

"Here then is a choice for a manufacturer ashamed of living on surplus value: shall he do his best to further a revolution of the basis of society. . . which would turn all people into workers, as it would give a chance for all workers to become refined and dignified in their life; or shall he ease his conscience by dropping a certain portion of his profits to bestow on his handful of workers. . . if he *can* do both things let him do so, and make his conscience surer; but if. . . he must choose between the furthering of a great principle, and the staunching of 'the pangs of conscience', I should think him right to choose the first course: because although it is *possible* that here and there a capitalist may be found who could and would be content to carry on his business at (say) foreman's wages, it is *impossible* that the capitalist class could do so: the very point of its existence is manufacturing for a profit and not for a livelihood. . ."[1]

The decision was clearly a difficult one for Morris to take. Parts of this letter (so clear on questions of general principle) have the air of a reluctant rationalization of a position with which he was not wholly satisfied, since in the result it meant that he could maintain his own privileged standard of life among comrades in extreme poverty. And for this reason he was always ready to reach into his pocket whenever he was asked.

Once the decision was taken, however, Morris—as always—dismissed the argument from his mind. He did not attempt a detailed public defence of his position. Once he had straightened the matter out with Georgie he seemed to be satisfied: "certain things occurred to me which being written you may pitch into the fire if you please". Thereafter—

[1] *Letters,* pp. 197-9. Morris wrote another extremely clear letter on the question of profit-sharing to Emma Lazarus (April 21st, 1884), published in *The Century Magazine,* 1886.

although in the press of his Socialist activities the day-to-day management of the Firm passed more and more into the hands of Thomas Wardle—he maintained a constant supervision over the conditions of the workers. Many commentators left accounts of the sense of freedom, cleanliness and light in the Merton Abbey Works, and of the beauty of its surroundings.[1] "Here is none of the ordinary neat pomposity of 'business premises'", wrote one contemporary. "We turn through doors into a large, low room, where the hand-made carpets are being worked. It is not crowded. In the middle sits a woman finishing off some completed rugs; in a corner is a large pile of worsted of a magnificent red, heaped becomingly into a deep-coloured straw basket. The room is full of sunlight and colour." Close to the workshops Morris had his own studio, overlooking the gardens and the River Wandle, from which he would frequently come out from his designing to give advice on the details of the manufacture—

> "an extra ounce of indigo to strengthen the dye, an additional five minutes' immersion of threads in the vat, a weft of colour to be swept through the warp in a moment of inspiration, a dappling of bright points to lighten some over-sombre hue in the grounding of a carpet. . ."

In the words of one who worked here, wages were raised:

> "to the highest which each particular product would afford. He substituted piece work founded on the advanced rates of wages for the time work wherever the occupation permitted it, thus giving the workman a greater liberty as to the disposal of his time. . . Piece workers. . . could then occasionally knock off for an hour's work in the garden—the garden having been allotted in sections to the piece workers. . . Any objection or claim made by the workman was listened to as if it came from an equal and decided according to the equity of the case."

"No one", the account concludes, "having worked for

[1] Aymer Vallance, *William Morris, His Art, His Writing and His Public Life*, pp. 124 ff.

Mr. Morris would willingly have joined any other workshop." [1]

IV. Letters and Articles

In the first days of his enthusiasm, Morris attempted to convert many of his old Liberal friends. After successive failures, he abandoned the attempt, and—since they no longer shared the same central interests—he and they began to drift apart.

Philip Webb, it is true, with his grave appraisal of Morris's greatness, fell quietly into the Socialist movement: while Charlie Faulkner jumped in with both feet, set to work to organize an Oxford branch, and would have been ready to finish the job at once with dynamite if Morris had given the word. Burne-Jones detested the new turn of events, while William De Morgan, the potter, who had backed up Morris in the E.Q.A. was equally disgusted. "I was rather disconcerted", he wrote—

> "when I found that an honest objection to Bulgarian atrocities had been held to be one and the same thing as sympathy with Karl Marx, and that Morris took it for granted that I should be ready for enrolment."[2]

But to the end of his life Morris accepted it as one of his major responsibilities to serve as a propagandist on the middle-class wing of the movement. To any serious inquiry he was patient and sympathetic: sometimes writing letters which ran into many pages in order to enter into the doubts of his questioner. His letters to Georgie Burne-Jones, in particular, show him taking endless pains, as though he were determined to keep open at least one road of human understanding with his own past.

The hardy perennial among the questions which were put to Morris concerned the relation of the individual man of the

[1] MS. account by a member of the Firm, Brit. Mus. Add. MSS. 45350.

[2] Mackail, II, p. 120.

middle-class, with goodwill and lofty motives, to the historical concept of the class war. How could Morris associate with Socialists who denounced the capitalists as a class? Was he not aware that many manufacturers were kindly, good-natured fellows, with the interests of their workpeople at heart? Could he not understand that his cultivated friends were as distressed at the sight of poverty as he was himself? Was he not aware of the excellent motives animating the middle-class reformers, in their various philanthropic schemes? Again and again in the next few years, but especially in this first year and a half of activity, Morris strove to make the answer clear in private letters, lectures and articles. "As to what you say about employers and employed in Lancashire", came the weary reply to one questioner—

> "it seems to me to point to our disastrous system of production, because after all the masters and middlemen are of the same blood as the men; it is their *position* therefore which turns good fellows into tyrants and cheats, in fact *forces* them to be so."[1]

"A society which is founded on the system of *compelling* all well-to-do people to live on making the greatest profit out of the labour of others, must be wrong", he wrote to T.C. Horsfall in September, 1883:

> "Of course I do not discuss these matters with you or any person of good will in any bitterness: but there are people with whom it is hard to keep one's temper; such as the philistine middle-class Radicals; who think, or pretend to, that now at last all is for the best in the best of all possible worlds."[2]

A month later he was explaining to the same correspondent that he agreed "that the rich do not act as they do in the matter from malice".

[1] Morris to Birchall, November 7th, 188?, Brit. Mus. Add. MSS. 45347.
[2] *Letters*, p. 182.

"Nevertheless their position (as a class) forces them to 'strive' (unconsciously most often I know) to keep the working men in ignorance of their rights and their power."

And so—with a flaring up of the impatience he had first shown in his "Manifesto to the Working Men" at the time of the Eastern Question—he brought his second letter to T.C. Horsfall to an end:

"Though here and there a few men of the upper and middle classes, moved by their conscience and insight, may and doubtless will throw in their lot with the working class, the upper and middle-classes as a body will by the very nature of their existence, and like a plant grows, resist the abolition of classes. . . I do not say that there is not a terrible side to this: but how can it be otherwise?. . . For my part I have never under-rated the power of the middle-classes, whom, in spite of their individual good nature and banality, I look upon as a most terrible and implacable force: so terrible that I think it not unlikely that their resistance to inevitable change may, if the beginnings of change are too long delayed, ruin all civilization for a time."[1]

This theme Morris pursued in 1884, not only in private correspondence, but also in articles in *Justice*. The recent publication of the findings of the Royal Commission on the Housing of the Poor had directed attention to the appalling condition of the slums, and the efforts of Octavia Hill and others to find some remedy. Here Morris found a text to show the futility of even the best intentioned attempts to relieve the squalor of capitalist society. "As long as there are poor people they will be poorly housed", he pointed out:

"Understand this clearly—as long as labour, that is the lives of the strong and deft men, is a *commodity* which can only be bought when it yields a profit to the non-worker, we cannot be allowed to use the earth to *live on* like men; it is all wanted to *work on* like machines and just as much of the produce of our work will be given to us as will keep the *machines* going."[2]

[1] *Letters*, p. 190. [2] *Justice*, July 19th, 1884.

"What we should press upon" these well-intentioned reformers, he declared in a later article on "Philanthropists",

> "is that they should set a higher ideal before them than turning the life of the workers into that of a well-conducted reformatory or benevolent prison; and that they should understand that when things are done not *for* the workers but *by* them, an ideal will present itself with great distinctness to the workers themselves. . ."[1]

And so to the next two hardy perennials: was it not dangerous to stir up the workers with discontent, without first raising their standard of education? Was Morris not deliberately encouraging violent and bloody revolt? When posed by Georgie Burne-Jones, these questions brought forward a considered answer:

> "If these were ordinary times of peace I might be contented amidst my discontent, to settle down into an ascetic hermit of a hanger-on; such a man as I should respect even now: but I don't see the peace or feel it; on the contrary, fate, or what not has forced me to feel war, and lay hands on me as a recruit: therefore do I find it not only lawful to my conscience but even compulsory on it to do what in times of peace would not perhaps be lawful. . . if I am wrong, I am wrong, and there is an end of it: I can't expect pardon or consideration of anyone—and shan't ask it."[2]

The means by which Socialism will be brought about, he wrote to a young sympathizer in July, 1884, are:

> "First, educating people into desiring it, next organizing them into claiming it effectually. Whatever happens in the course of this education and organization must be accepted coolly and as a necessary incident, and not disclosed as a matter of essential principle, even if those incidents should mean ruin and war. I mean that we must not say, 'We must drop our purpose rather than carry it across this river of violence'. To say that means casting the whole thing into the hands of chance,

[1] *Justice*, December 20th, 1884. [2] *Letters*, p. 200.

and we can't do that: we *can't* say, if this is the evolution of history, let it evolve itself, we won't help. The evolution will force us to help: will breed in us passionate desire for action, which will quench the dread of consequences."[1]

"I cannot assure you", he told the Leicester Secular Society, in January, 1884, "that if you join the Socialist Cause,

"you will for ever escape scot-free from the attacks of open tyranny. It is true that at present capitalist society only looks on Socialism in England with dry grins. But remember that the body of people who have for instance ruined India, starved and gagged Ireland, and tortured Egypt, have capacities in them, some ominous signs of which they have lately shown, for openly playing the tyrant's game nearer home. . ."[2]

Not all these questions came from hostile or philistine quarters. Some of Morris's friends were genuinely anxious to enter into his views, but halted in alarm when they saw the consequences that must flow from them. Some of their alarm was of a warm and personal nature. Morris, they could see, was changing before their own eyes. Georgie Burne-Jones wrote to him in August, 1883, in anxiety about his poetry. His answer was friendly but firm. He could not feel his poetry to be of any great value, "except as showing my sympathy with history and the like":

"Poetry goes with the hand-arts I think, and like them has now become unreal: the arts have got to die, what is left of them, before they can be born again. You know my views on the matter; I apply them to myself as well as to others."

This would not prevent him from writing poetry any more than from doing pattern work, from "the mere personal pleasure" of the work: "but it prevents my looking at it as a sacred duty", while his grief over the illness of his daughter

[1] *Letters,* p. 207. [2] *Works,* Vol. XXIII, p. 214.

Jenny disquieted him too much to take such pleasure in any writing.

"Meantime the propaganda gives me work to do, which, unimportant as it seems, is part of a great whole which cannot be lost, and that ought to be enough for me. . ."[1]

Further enquiries brought a reply to Georgie the next month, "I *cannot help* acting in the matter, and associating with any body which has the root of the matter":

"It may ease your kind heart respecting me, that those who are in the thick of it, and trying to do something, are not likely to feel so much of the hope deferred which hangs about the cause as onlookers do. . ."[2]

By the beginning of 1884 "the Cause" was absorbing more and more of his attention: one friend remarked, "he can talk about little else, and will brook no opposition". Casual and superficial discussions on Socialism "became less and less possible".[3] The easy-going evenings at Kelmscott House, when discussion roamed from topic to topic, became less frequent, although they sometimes recurred. On June 1st, 1884, Morris was writing–once again to Georgie Burne-Jones:

"I cannot deny that if ever the D.F. were to break down, it would be a heavy thing to me, petty skirmish though it would make in the great war. Whatever hope or life there is in me is staked on the success of the cause: I believe you object to the word: but I know no other to express what I mean. Of course I don't mean to say that I necessarily expect to see much of it before I die, and yet something I hope to see."[4]

[1] *Letters,* p. 180. [2] *Ibid.,* p. 182. [3] Mackail, II, pp. 120-1.
[4] *Letters,* p. 200.

V. An Incident at Hyde Park

A final picture can be given of Morris's part in the early propaganda. The occasion was the great demonstration of Radical working men, called in Hyde Park on Monday, July 23rd, 1884, by the London Trades Council, when the House of Lords had rejected the Third Reform Act which introduced the County Franchise. The tide of Radical feeling was rising high: the call for the abolition of the House of Lords (and also for municipal government for London) was raised as an immediate issue: while seventy-three-year-old John Bright was demanding the severe limitation of the Lords' right of veto.

Meanwhile the Socialist open-air propaganda was making some progress: Burns and Jack Williams had attracted large audiences to Hyde Park on previous Sundays. The S.D.F. decided not to participate in the demonstration alongside the Radicals, but to set up a separate stall to advertise Socialism among the tens of thousands in the Park. Morris sent a detailed account of the events of the day to Andreas Scheu.

A dozen unemployed workers from the East End were mustered with a cart, a red flag, and a *Justice* poster, to distribute handbills, and to sell at a discount the new Manifesto of the Federation as well as the current number of the paper. The Manifesto went well, but *Justice* went more slowly. "Some dozen" members of the Federation, including Morris, Hyndman and Champion, went together to the Park, "where we had agreed to hold a meeting if we could after the Platform Meetings were over; we had no platform among the others and took no part in the procession; this as a matter of course". There they were joined by Joseph Lane and a few others of the Labour Emancipation League, with their banners: and by John Burns, Jack Williams, and others of the Federation. They took their stand on a small mound, and Champion opened the meeting, handing over "a fairish crowd" to Hyndman, who was "pretty well received, though there was a good deal of hooting when he attacked Fawcett by name".

When Burns took over, the crowd had swelled to four or five thousand, "much too big to be manageable I could clearly see":

> "However Burns began very well and was a good deal cheered till in an unlucky moment he began to abuse J. Bright whom of course our Franchise friends had been worshipping all day. So then they fell to hooting and howling, but Burns stuck to it... The malcontents began to take us in flank and shove on against the speakers; then whether our people were pushed down... or whether they charged down hill I don't rightly know, but down hill they went in a lump banners and all; good-bye to the latter by the way. I stuck to the hill, because I saw that some fellows seemed to be going for Burns, and... I was afraid he might be hurt: so I bored through the crowd somehow and got up to him and saw a few friends about us... However off the hill we were shoved in spite of our shoulders. But at the bottom of the hill we managed to make a ring again and Burns began again and spoke for 3 or 4 minutes, but... there was another ugly rush which broke up our ring... I was insulted by one of our friends, a German of the Marylebone branch I think, telling me in his anxiety for my safety that I was *an old man* and lugging at me to get me away..."

Seeing that Burns was safe, Morris—after making "some remarks to some of the knots of Mr. Bright's lambs"—which no doubt would have been unprintable even if they had been preserved—went home. Jack Williams and one or two others "kept their ground and spoke till nightfall, departing with cheers".[1] "I don't find our friends were either dispirited or ill-tempered at the affair: but I think we ought to guard against such incidents in the future by having some organized body guard round the speaker when we speak in doubtful places."[2]

The incident shows the Socialists taking part in an important action and mustering perhaps two or three dozen firm supporters as their total strength in the heart of London—this with the assistance of the Labour Emancipation League. Second, it shows the Socialists deliberately setting

[1] *Letters*, pp. 208-9. [2] *Ibid.*, p. 210.

themselves athwart the current of feeling of working-class Liberalism, taking no part in the procession for the County Franchise—"as a matter of course"—and singling out its idols for attack by name.

Was this tactic wise? Ought they to have taken part, alongside the Liberal working men, in a fight for the County Franchise, and the abolition of the House of Lords, and by their participation shown the way forward to the broader perspective of Socialism? Nearly every one of the Socialists who took part in the Hyde Park fray would have given an emphatic, "No". Among the pioneers at the meeting was Sam Mainwaring, an engineer and early member of the Labour Emancipation League. "I was at the Hyde Park Franchise demonstration", Mainwaring later recalled, "at which John Burns referred to Bright as a silver-tongued hypocrite":

> "This was enough for the radicals of that day; our banners. . . were torn and broken up, and some of us were being run to the Serpentine for a ducking. Morris fought like a man with the rest of us, and before they had taken us half way to the water we had succeeded in making a stand, and I remember Morris calling on Burns to finish his speech. Being on level ground, and our opponents still fighting, Burns said he wanted something to stand on. That day we had only our first pamphlet, 'Socialism Made Plain', of which Morris had a large bag-full at his side. These we placed on the ground in a heap, and Burns mounted and continued his speech, while Morris, and a dozen more of us, were fighting to keep back the more infuriated of the people. Some of our friends found fault with Burns for using language to irritate the crowd, but Morris's opinion was that they would have to be told the truth, and that it was as well to tell them first as last."[1]

[1] *Freedom*, January, 1897.

CHAPTER III

THE SPLIT

I. The Theory of Socialism

THE Hyde Park Franchise meeting was held at the end of July. In August Morris was writing in a private letter:

"The time which I have foreseen from the first seems to be upon us, and I don't see how I can avoid taking my share in the internal conflict which seems likely to rend the D.F. into two or more. More than two or three of us distrust Hyndman thoroughly: I have done my best to trust him, but cannot any longer. Practically it comes to a contest between him and me. . . I don't think intrigue or ambition are amongst my many faults; but here I am driven to thrusting myself forward and making a party within a party. However I say I foresaw it, and 'tis part of the day's work, but I begin to wish the day were over."[1]

Clearly Morris was already reconciled to the split which was to take place in December: and had been thinking over the possibility for some time before.

Little can be understood of this first serious schism unless it is constantly borne in mind that the movement was in its very earliest stages. On the most general questions of theory—"What is Socialism?"—it is true that there were few differences of opinion in 1884:

"Let us state in the briefest possible way what socialism means to some of us. (1) That there are inequality and misery in the world; (2) that this social inequality, this misery of the many and this happiness of the few, are the necessary outcome of our social conditions; (3) that the essence of these social conditions is that the mass of the people, the working class, produce and distribute all commodities, while the minority of the people, the middle and upper classes, possess these commodities; (4) that this initial tyranny of the possessing class over the producing class is based on the present wage system and now maintains

[1] Mackail, II, pp. 125-6.

all other forms of oppression, such as that of monarchy, or clerical rule, or police despotism; (5) that this tyranny of the few over the many is only possible because the few have obtained possession of the land, the raw material, the machinery, the banks, the railways—in a word, of all the means of production and distribution of commodities. . . (6) lastly, that the approaching change in 'civilised' society will be a revolution. . . The two classes at present existing will be replaced by a single class consisting of the whole of the healthy and sane members of the community, possessing all the means of production and distribution in common. . ."[1]

The authorship of the passage matters little (it is by Edward and Eleanor Marx-Aveling) since with varying emphasis, Hyndman, Morris (with an additional clause on the arts), and most active Socialists in 1884 would have accepted the definition. Apart from the Henry George-ites on one fringe of the movement, and a handful of Anarchists on the other, all Socialists accepted a certain body of principles which to-day would be known as "Marxist" but which at the time went under no other name than "Socialism". Only a minority of the Socialists, it is true, had read any of Marx's work, but the number included a majority of the effective leaders of the movement—among them Hyndman, Bax, Morris, Shaw, Scheu, Banner, Harry Quelch, Joynes, Mahon, the Avelings, and some of the early Fabians and Christian Socialists. It is true that a challenge was developing among the very small group of Fabians, which first became explicit in October, 1884, with an article by the Rev. P.H. Wicksteed in *To-day* criticising Marx's theory of value. But until 1886 the explicit differences between the Fabians and other Socialist groupings were less ones of theory than of "temperament and character".[2] "The Fabians", Shaw wrote to Scheu, in October, 1884,

[1] Edward and Eleanor Marx-Aveling, *Shelley's Socialism.* Although privately printed in 1888, this simple exposition well sums up the generally agreed principles of 1884.

[2] *The Fabian Society. . .*, by G. Bernard Shaw, Fabian Tract No. 41 (1892). Shaw continues: "When I myself, on the point of joining the Social-Democratic Federation, changed my mind and joined the Fabian instead, I was guided by no discoverable difference in program or principles, but solely by an instinctive feeling that the Fabian and not the Federation would attract the men of my own bias and intellectual habits. . ."

"are a body of middle-class philanthropists who believe themselves to be Socialists. I took advantage of this erroneous impression to induce them to adopt and print my manifesto... It is, of course, meant for distribution among the middle-class. I do not see why the tail of the middle-class, which constitutes a numerous and partly educated proletariat, should not be worked a little."[1]

When the split took place, both parties asserted their acceptance of Marxist theory. "We uphold the purest doctrines of Scientific Socialism", Morris declared two weeks after the split, identifying his views with those of Marx and Engels:[2] while Hyndman, on his side, made repeated claims to be the English inheritor of Marx's mantle. The progress of the Democratic Federation had been one of ever closer approximation to the acceptance (at any rate in the abstract) of Marxist theory. *Socialism Made Plain,* the pamphlet of 1883, after setting forward a number of Radical demands, had gone forward to an outright attack on the capitalist class—

"the loan-mongers, the farmers, the mine-exploiters, the contractors, the middlemen, the factory lords... who... turn every advance in human knowledge, every further improvement in human dexterity, into an engine for accumulating out of other men's labour and for exacting more and yet more surplus value out of the wage-slaves they employ. So long as the means of production... are a monopoly of a class, so long must the labourers on the farm, in the mine, or in the factory sell themselves for a bare subsistence wage."

This analysis was repeated with increasing clarity and wealth of historical illustration during 1883 and 1884, in pronouncements of the Federation, articles in *Justice,* in Hyndman's *Historical Basis of Socialism in England,* and above all in the *Summary of the Principles of Socialism,* published in the spring of 1884 over both Morris's and Hyndman's

[1] G.B. Shaw to Andreas Scheu, October 26th, 1884, Scheu Correspondence, Int. Inst. Soc. Hist.

[2] Interview in the *Daily News,* January 8th, 1885.

names. And the conclusion that flowed from this analysis was equally agreed and understood. "Whatever Socialism may lead to", Morris wrote to a young correspondent in July, 1884,

> "our aim, to be always steadily kept in view, is, to obtain for the whole people, duly organized, the possession and control of all the means of production and exchange, destroying at the same time all national rivalries."[1]

Hyndman, Bax, Aveling, Shaw—all would have agreed.

II. Socialist Strategy

If there was agreement as to the general aims of Socialism, this does not mean that there were no theoretical differences in the early movement. On the contrary, whenever the strategy and tactics necessary for the achievement of Socialism or the exact form of Socialist institutions were discussed, it was usual to find that there were as many viewpoints as there were people in the room. The pioneers were, at this time, the merest amateurs at revolutionary politics. An understanding of Socialism had come to them with the force of an intellectual or emotional conversion: the poverty of East London, Gladstone's "damned little wars", the Irish question, the atrocities exhibited in the Royal Academy—all seemed in a flash to fit into the same pattern, to be explained in a completely consistent manner by the central fact of the class struggle, the irreconcilable interests of the bourgeoisie and the proletariat. The next thing to do was to work for "the Revolution". So clear and simple did the matter appear to some of the pioneers that it seemed only necessary to go to the street-corners and explain it to the workers, and they would be ready to rise. Britain was already losing her privileged economic position—only let the crisis deepen, and the thing would be done.

But how was it to be done? Only twelve years before, the

[1] *Letters,* p. 207.

workers of Paris had organized their own Government. For all the pioneers the Commune was a constant source of inspiration, "a torch lighting us on our way towards the complete emancipation of labour":[1] for some of them it seemed a pattern and forecast of the English Revolution. The half-expressed theories of insurrection based upon the Commune gave birth to a feeling that "the Day" might well be more imminent than appearances suggested. "We are approaching the end of the century", Hyndman remarked with dark suggestiveness at the conclusion of *The Historical Basis of Socialism in England* (1883):

> "1889 is the centenary of the great French Revolution. The ideas of the enfranchisement of mankind from capitalist domination are everywhere abroad among the working men. In these days, when communication is so rapid and news spreads so fast, simultaneous action has a cumulative effect, economical, social, and political. . ."

For the pioneers such words were full of emotive overtones—the international proletarian revolt might begin at any point and spread throughout the world:

> "In all probability England will go first—will give the signal, though she is at present so backward: Germany with her 700,000 Socialists is pretty nearly ready: France, sick of her republic of stock-jobbers and pirates, is nearly as far on. . . Austria is ready any moment. . . America is. . . finding out that mere radicalism is bringing her into a *cul de sac.* Everywhere the tale is the same. . . The old party politics are being openly jeered at. . . I have heard the G.O.M. mentioned in crowded meetings of working men without a cheer being raised for him, over and over again within the last month. . . You may be sure the thing is moving, though of course I make no prophecies as to the beginning of the end. . ."[2]

The author is William Morris, and the date is November, 1884.

[1] "The Socialist Platform—No. 4". *A Short Account of the Commune of Paris* by E. Belfort Bax, Victor Dave and William Morris (Socialist League, 1886).

[2] *Letters,* p. 217.

But there was a gap between the Paris Communards of 1871 and the London Radical working men, disgusted with Gladstone's parliamentary compromise with the Tories on the Reform Act of 1884. Some early Socialist writings give point to Shaw's criticism of the "enthusiasts who mistake their own emotions for public movements."[1] The problem for the pioneers was that of bridging the gap between their new-found faith and the political movements of the masses. But about the real lives and aspirations of the workers many of them knew little: to Joynes the workers were the heroes and martyrs of Freiligarth's songs: to Bax they were the anti-thesis to the bourgeois thesis: to Aveling they were (at least for a brief period) the source from which complex algebraical equations illustrating surplus value could be drawn: to Shaw they were one part heroic dynamitard, and three parts duffers and dupes: to Hyndman they were the raw material of Revolution who—never quite conscious agents of history themselves—would under the leadership of himself and his few trusted companions be the dark force which would bring down Cabinets: to Morris they were the artisans of Merton Abbey, good fellows enough, who had only to be got to listen to reason—until the end of 1884 he had never even entered a house in the East End.

The pioneers were impatient. The moment they were awaiting, the revolutionary moment, was the time when the two classes, bourgeoisie and proletariat, would stand opposed to each other, face to face. Any policy which tended to delay this moment was one which gave assistance to the enemy. Even trade unions, in Hyndman's view, served only to mask the antagonism of classes:

"Trade Unionists are, all told, but a small fraction of the total working population. They constitute, in fact, an aristocracy of labour who, in view of the bitter struggle now drawing nearer and nearer, cannot be said to be other than a hindrance to that complete organisation of

[1] Fabian Tract No. 41.

the proletariat which alone can obtain for the workers their proper control over their own labour."[1]

Limited reforms were looked upon by most Socialists in 1884 with intense distrust. On the one hand they were delusory: a simplication of economic theory, the "iron law of wages", led to the belief that whatever concessions the workers won they must inevitably lose in one form or another, unless they were wrung from one section of the workers at the expense of another.[2] On the other hand they were "palliatives"—sops to the workers, bribes to buy off revolution. What did the Irish Question matter? Or the abolition of the House of Lords? Or the struggle for the Eight-hour Day? "The Revolution" would answer all.

The issue of "palliatives" provoked some of the first dissension within the movement. Several members of the Council, including Champion and (later) Aveling, held that the "Stepping Stones" adopted in 1882 should serve as the centre of an agitation, which would bring the Socialists into contact with the Radicals, and educate the workers in Socialist ideas: others, like Scheu and Joseph Lane (who joined the Council in August, 1884) rejected them outright as a mere trifling with the people.[3] The attitude to this question of both Morris and Hyndman was (for different reasons) ambiguous.

[1] Hyndman, *The Historical Basis of Socialism in England,* p. 287.

[2] See article by Hyndman, "The Iron Law of Wages", *Justice,* March 15th, 1884.

[3] In an article in *Commonweal* shortly after the split, Lane denounced the "stepping stones" of the "Democrats". Of the Eight-hour Day: "We, as Socialists, of course condemn long hours, but the essential thing we condemn is the capitalist making a profit out of our labour at all... It is the whole wages system we contend against." School feeding: "If children are entitled to one free meal, they are entitled to all their meals free. We hold that they should be fed, clothed, sheltered and educated free by the community." Of workers' dwellings: "With the overthrow of the competitive system... large towns will disappear." (Some comfort, this, to those in the slums.) Of cumulative taxation of large incomes: "Under a proper system of society we should have no large incomes." In conclusion: "It is possible that the governing classes might make a show of legislating in the direction of these palliatives; their doing so would certainly put off the revolution... True Socialists... should not take up such catch cries... There is no half-way house in the matter..." (May, 1885).

The ambiguity of Morris's attitude arose primarily from confusion. In his public lectures of 1884 he was taking pains to hammer home the central lesson that no partial reforms whatsoever could serve as a *substitute* for Socialism:

"The palliatives over which many worthy people are busying themselves now are useless: because they are but unorganized partial revolts against a vast wide-spreading grasping organization which will, with the unconscious instinct of a plant, meet every attempt at bettering the condition of the people with an attack on a fresh side; new machines, new markets, wholesale emigration, the revival of grovelling superstitions, preachments of thrift to lack-alls, of temperance to the wretched; such things as these will baffle at every turn all partial revolts against the monster we of the middle class have created for our own undoing."[1]

Several of the demands of the S.D.F.—in particular that for decent housing for the workers—lay very close to Morris's heart: but in a letter to Bruce Glasier in 1888, he referred to "the 'stepping stones' of the S.D.F., *which I always disagreed with*. . . since I don't believe in their efficacy".[2] As early as August, 1883, Morris was writing to Georgie Burne-Jones:

"Small as our body is, we are not without dissensions in it. Some of the more ardent disciples look upon Hyndman as too opportunist, and there is truth in that; he is sanguine of speedy change happening somehow, and is inclined to intrigue and the making of a party; towards which end compromise is needed, and the carrying of people who don't really agree with us as far as they will go. . . I. . . think the aim of Socialists should be the founding of a religion, towards which end compromise is no use, and we only want to have those with us who will be with us to the end."[3]

In January, 1884, he was writing to his daughter, Jenny:

"We had a good quarrel last night telling each other our minds pretty plainly. . . the real subject in dispute was really whether or no

[1] "Art and Socialism", *Works*, Vol. XXIII, p. 208.
[2] Glasier, *op. cit.*, p. 192. [3] *Letters*, p. 181.

we could drive the matter by means of supporting the parliamentary programme of the Radicals: of course I say no. Mr. Scheu made an excellent speech on my side. . ."[1]

But both these passages refer rather to interventions in the current political scene than to the Federation's own demands, of one of which, the Eight-hour Day, Morris was writing with some enthusiasm in July—"the most important thing to press upon the notice of the people. . . it is of all our stepping stones at once the most possible to carry within a reasonable time, and the most important. . . all the more so because it would at once become an international affair."[2] In November his position was reversed: at last "the thing is moving":

> "Like enough it will come with attempts at palliatives: tubs to the whale cast out first by one party then the other: every one of which we shall take without misgiving, for the better the condition of the working class grows, the more capable they will be of effecting a revolution. Starvelings can only riot."

But then, these attempts would be bound to fail: good housing—"a bourgeois government cannot deal with it". The Eight-hour Day "is good as a cry, but again how can a bourgeois government ever think of that?"[3]

A striking example of this confusion was found in the actions of Morris's own branch of the Federation.[4] In the latter half of 1884—and in the next year or two—the questions of the Dis-establishment of the Church and of Irish Home Rule were in the forefront of Radical agitation: the

[1] *Letters*, p. 193. [2] *Ibid.*, p. 205. [3] *Ibid.*, p. 217.

[4] The Hammersmith Branch of the Democratic Federation was formed on June 14th, 1884. It started with eleven members, one of whom—a Ruskinite—soon resigned. Thereafter the Committee met either once or twice a week, and lectures were held either fortnightly or weekly. Morris was present at 21 of the 27 meetings up to the end of the year: and his absences were probably all to be accounted for by "duty". Twenty-nine new members were won during the same period. Emery Walker was the Secretary of the Branch. (Minutes of Hammersmith S.D.F., Brit. Mus. Add. MSS. 45891.)

Federation—with Morris's wholehearted support—had expressed its strong sympathy with the cause of Irish independence, and taken some part in the agitation: on the other hand, when the two demands were included in the Federation's official *programme* Morris regarded them as "ineptitudes". His branch at Hammersmith promptly resolved that any statement by the S.D.F. on these two questions was "superfluous. . . the general feeling of the meeting being that details of this kind were redundant."[1] At exactly the same time an agitation broke out among the Hammersmith Costermongers, who were threatened by the Board of Works with eviction from their kerbstone market site: the Hammersmith Branch came to their aid, Morris wrote an eloquent article for *Justice* on their claims, and reported to Scheu, "we, the S.D.F. have been helping them and gaining credit and recruits. . ."[2] If only Morris had taken to heart the lesson of the Hammersmith Costermongers—to support the workers in their struggle for limited ends, and to show them thereby that (in his own words) "we are striving to make them gain a better living for themselves—themselves now living, not the generations a thousand years to come"[3]—then many of the wasteful errors of the next few years might have been avoided.

If Morris's attitude was confused, Hyndman's was ambiguous for another reason. On the one hand, Hyndman was from the outset one of the most uncompromising and doctrinaire of the Federation's speakers. Morris deplored his "perpetual sneers at, and abuse of the radicals, who, deluded as we must think them, are after all the men from whom our recruits must come."[4] On the other hand (in the view of his opponents) Hyndman's attitude to political activity was deeply influenced by the agitations of Bradlaugh and even of Dr. Kenealy in the extraordinary "Tichbourne Case" in the

[1] Morris to Scheu, *Letters,* p. 211. Hammersmith Minutes, September 24th, 1884.

[2] *Letters,* p. 212. [3] *Ibid.,* p. 206.

[4] Morris to Thompson, *Letters,* p. 228. Morris himself had written several appeals to the Radicals in *Justice* in 1884.

1870s. "He had the intention", recalled Scheu, "as he often put it unceremoniously, of bringing down the Government by the creation of a democratic workers' party, and forcing it [the Government] by threats to carry out his wishes."[1] Such an intention was consistent with a half-concealed feeling of contempt for the workers. At one moment he set forward the "palliatives" as a cry to rally discontent: at another he spoke with utter contempt of such half-measures. The "stepping stones" were the carrot for the donkey: and the donkey was the people.

Hyndman rarely gave the impression of wanting to conduct a serious and sustained fight for any of the "stepping stones". But they—or any other issue which arose in the political scene—would serve for a useful temporary peg on which to hang an agitation, to advertise the Federation and himself: not with the intention of using it for the education of the workers in Socialism, but in order to build up a loyal mass following who could be called upon when the next agitation arose. Already he had visions of entering the field like the Irish party: of holding both political parties to ransom with his following. For such a policy it was necessary that there should be some figurehead—a Bradlaugh or a Parnell: and who was more suited for this than he, Hyndman himself? *"I am sure that the split was unavoidable"*, Morris wrote to Joynes on Christmas Day, 1884:

"Hyndman can accept only one position in such a body as the S.D.F., that of master... You must not suppose that this is a matter of mere personal likes and dislikes: the cause lies much deeper than that. H. has been acting throughout (to my mind) as a politician determined to push his own advantage (if you please along with that of the party) always on the look out for anything which could advertise the party he is supposed to lead: his aim has been to make the movement seem big; to frighten the powers that be with a turnip bogie which perhaps he almost believes in himself: hence all that insane talk of immediate forcible revolution, when he knows that the workers in England are not

[1] Scheu, *op. cit.*, Part III, Ch. V.

even touched by the movement; hence the founding of branches which melt away into mere names, the neglect of organization for fruitless agitation; and, worst of all, hence discreditable intrigue and sowing of suspicion among those who are working for the party. Amidst such elements as this I cannot and will not work. . ."[1]

And one of the most serious results of the consequent split was that Morris in disgust at Hyndman's tactics was driven into the impossible "purism" which coloured his outlook for the next five years.

III. Dissension Begins

Throughout the disputes which preceded the split, one point became clear time and again: Hyndman's critics were convinced that he was guilty of dictatorial behaviour in all the Federation's affairs. On June 22nd, 1884, Engels wrote to Kautsky:

"Hyndman is thinking to *buy up* all the little movement here... Himself a rich man, and in addition having at his disposal resources supplied by the very rich artist-enthusiast but untalented politician Morris... he wants to be the sole master... Hyndman is a skilful and good business man, but a petty and hard-faced John Bull, possessing a vanity considerably in excess of his talent and natural gifts. . ."[2]

Hyndman is "a *pushful* party chief. . . a clever fellow" he had written earlier in the year.[3]

In the summer of 1884 the two factions within the Executive Council began to crystallize. Prominent in opposition to Hyndman was Andreas Scheu, who had come into collision with Hyndman's submerged Jingoism. "On every possible

[1] May Morris, II, p. 590.

[2] *Labour Monthly,* September, 1933. The letter continues: "Bax and Aveling have most excellent intentions, but everything has gone to pieces, and those literateurs alone cannot do anything. The masses still will not follow them."

[3] *Ibid.* Also: "Bax is fine, but still rather green; Aveling good, but too busy to swot up economics—a subject entirely foreign to him."

occasion", Scheu recalled, "Hyndman... related how... Gladstone mocked at the appeal of the... Federation because it contained the name of a foreigner (Andreas Scheu), which proved that the basic ideas of the social-democratic propaganda could not be wholly home-grown."[1] On the Executive Hyndman was visibly impatient at each intervention by Scheu, who may (perhaps) have regarded the young British movement with an air of patronage. Since Scheu, on his side, was not devoid of vanity, a bitter feud grew up between the two men, in which Morris's sympathies were drawn to the Austrian's side. Scheu, in turn, pressed Morris forward to assume a position of leadership in opposition to Hyndman.

Morris's instinct at first was to patch up the division on the Executive, and get on with the real work. "I had Bax here last night", he wrote to Scheu (who left London for Edinburgh early in July, 1884), "and begged him to be more 'politic' ":

"To be 'politic' and not able to say exactly what one thinks is a beastly curse, and makes one hate the infernal bourgeois more for driving one to such stupidity in carrying on the war against him: but I cannot yet forgo the hope of our forming a Socialist *party* which shall begin to act in our own time, instead of a mere theoretical association in a private room with no hope but that of gradually permeating cultivated people with our aspirations."[2]

In response to a further plea from Scheu, Morris wrote on July 18th:

"I know enough of myself to be sure that I am not fit for the rudder; at least not yet; but I promise to take my due share in all matters, and steadily to oppose all jingo business; but, if I can, with coolness, or I shall be bowled over, since I have not got hold yet of the strings that tie us to the working-class members; nor have I read as I should have. Also my habits are quiet and studious and if I am too much worried by 'politics', i.e. intrigue, I shall be no use to the cause as a writer... If in the long run I am pushed into a position of more

[1] Scheu, *op. cit.*, Part III, Ch. V. [2] *Letters,* p. 202.

importance, I will not refuse it from mere laziness or softness. . ."[1]

If Engels was to complain in his letters during the next two years at "these muddle-headed people [who] want to lead the English working class", he certainly had abundant justification: but Morris, for his part, knew well that he was an "untalented politician". "What we want is real leaders themselves working men, and content to be so till classes are abolished", he had himself written in August, 1883.

IV. The Executive and "Justice"

In July matters gathered rapidly to a head. During the previous two years Joseph Lane and the Labour Emancipation League had continued their agitation in the East End, but, owing in part to their mistrust of Hyndman, and in part to their dislike of coming in "under discipline",[2] they had refused to affiliate to the Democratic Federation. It was agreed, however, that the L.E.L. should send delegates to the Annual Conference of the Federation, at the beginning of August, with a view to affiliation. Joseph Lane, together with Scheu, spent the night before the Conference at Morris's house: and, from this time, he was for several years to exercise some influence over Morris's political views.[3]

The Conference took several steps of great importance. First, the Federation became known henceforward as the Social-Democratic Federation (S.D.F.), with an explicitly Socialist programme: the attempt to keep the organization partly within the extreme "left" of the Radical movement was finally abandoned. The Object of the S.D.F. was declared to be:

"The Socialization of the Means of Production, Distribution and Exchange to be controlled by a Democratic State in the interests of the

[1] *Letters*, pp. 203-4.

[2] Morris to Scheu, July 18th, 1884, Scheu Correspondence, Int. Inst. Soc. Hist.

[3] Joseph Lane to Ambrose Barker, 1912, Nettlau MSS., Int. Inst. Soc. Hist.

entire community, and the complete Emancipation of Labour from the domination of Capitalism and Landlordism, with the establishment of Social and Economic Equality between the Sexes."

For its Programme it took over, almost without alteration (and as the price of affiliation), five of the first six points of the Programme of the L.E.L. (equal direct adult suffrage: "direct legislation by the people": a National Citizen Army in place of a Standing Army—the people to decide on Peace or War: free secular education: and free administration of Justice).

Another step of some importance was taken when Hyndman was displaced as President of the S.D.F. In the view of Lane and Scheu, a "truly democratic party" would have no personal President at all, the Executive Council ("a chosen elite") electing a different Chairman at each session. Despite an unsuccessful attempt by Hyndman's supporters to reinstate him at the next Executive meeting, it seemed that Hyndman's opportunities for dictatorship were gone.

Finally, the opposition to Hyndman on the Executive Committee was strengthened by the election of Joseph Lane and of Eleanor Marx and Edward Aveling. For several weeks it appeared that Hyndman would no longer assert his old dominance. But the presence on the Executive of the last two brought renewed bitterness. Hyndman regarded them as the emissaries of Engels (the "foreign" influence again), and seems also to have been jealous of Aveling's evident ability, which challenged his position as theoretician of the movement. Aveling, a Vice-President, and leading publicist of the National Secular Society, had come under bitter attack from his old colleagues when, shortly after the Bradlaugh-Hyndman debate, he declared for the Socialist side. His step of joining the Federation was taken at the same time as he and Eleanor Marx decided to live together. His looseness in money affairs (later to become notorious) made it possible for Bradlaugh to accuse him of "irregularities" with regard to the accounts of the N.S.S. (an accusation which, it seems, Bradlaugh could not substantiate)[1] and to demand his expulsion as Vice-President of the Society. Aveling then resigned from the N.S.S., whereupon Hyndman demanded his resignation from the Executive of the S.D.F. as well. "I want to keep Aveling if we can", Morris wrote to Scheu on September 8th: "The worst of it is that Aveling is much disliked by many of our best men, Lane for instance. . ." And, a week later, "Aveling is undoubtedly a man of great capacity, and can use it too".[2] The row blew over, once Aveling had made a public disclaimer of Bradlaugh's charges, but the bitterness remained.

On both sides there were men totally incapable, or, at the best, inexperienced in subordinating their personal feelings in the interests of unity. The dispute began to exercise a fascination of its own, to the expense of serious business. On one side, Lane and (despite the disclaimers in his own *Reminiscences*) Bax were particularly quarrelsome:[3] on the other, Hyndman appeared to be determined to create bad blood with the Avelings. By October the atmosphere at Council Meetings was becoming intolerable. "Altogether matters are going very badly with them", Engels wrote to Kautsky on October 20th:

> "Last Tuesday Madame Lafargue was present at a meeting of the Council of the S.D.F.; they were squabbling over some trifle, but so furiously that the words 'damned liars' were scattered freely about."

The Council had become, in the words of Morris, "quite honey-combed with distrust and jealousies."[4] Six days later

[1] Morris to Scheu, September 8th, 1884, and September 13th, 1884. Morris thought it unlikely that Bradlaugh "in his character of Solicitor's clerk" would have brought a completely groundless charge against Aveling (Scheu Correspondence, Int. Inst. Soc. Hist.).

[2] Morris to Scheu, September 8th, 1884 and September 13th, 1884.

[3] Morris to Scheu, September 28th, 1884, Scheu Correspondence, Int. Inst. Soc. Hist.: "Bax is in a very rash state at present—wants to hurry on a quarrel, which I disagreed with. . ."

[4] Morris to Joynes, December 25th, 1884, May Morris, II, pp. 588-9.

Shaw sent a graphic account to Scheu of the state of the S.D.F. Executive, as he saw it from outside. Ever since Hyndman's attempt to "elbow" Aveling off it ("Aveling being a man to be thrown out of the window or shaken hands with cordially, as the case might be, but not such a fool as to let himself be elbowed out") the bad blood had continued in being, between "the Marx-Aveling party and the Hyndman party". Aveling, in Shaw's view, was sounder than Hyndman, since he placed great emphasis on the need for political education in the movement, while Hyndman would only ply the membership with "stimulants":

> "What we have got at Palace Chambers now is a great deal of agitating, very little organizing (if any), no educating, and vague speculations as to the world turning upside down in the course of a fortnight or so. Aveling. . . is on for educating, but he is hard up, heavily handicapped by his old associations and his defiance of Mrs. Grundy in the matter of Eleanor Marx, personally not a favourite with the world at large, and quite excluded from all influence in the management of Justice."[1]

Morris (it seemed to him) "wanders along between Hyndman and Aveling rather uncertainly": and this may perhaps be taken as a tribute to the neutrality which Morris was still seeking to preserve in all but his private letters to Scheu.

Striking confirmation both of Hyndman's arbitrary tendencies and of the impossible situation on the Council can be found in two letters written by Hyndman to Morris at this time in connection with the control of *Justice*. Started with Carpenter's money, and financed largely by Morris,[2] the paper was in the hands of Hyndman as Editor, and under his sole control. "All this time", wrote Morris, there were "sorenesses against the conduct of the paper. . . which were irritating the quarrel, and the question was stirred as to the control of the executive over it. . . H. was determined to resist it."[3] "It is,

[1] G.B. Shaw to Scheu, October 26th, 1884, Scheu Correspondence, Int. Inst. Soc. Hist.

[2] See Annual Report in *Justice*, August 9th, 1884. [3] May Morris, II, p. 588.

of course, impossible"—he wrote to Morris on November 27th—"to recognize any right on the part of the present Executive to claim control over a journal which has been made what it is by the extra-ordinary efforts of a few persons. . ." Indeed, rather than that this should happen—Hyndman implied—it would be better that the paper should be closed altogether. Neither Carpenter nor Morris should subsidize it longer. Hyndman himself could no longer give the same time to it—"the toil and the anxiety has, as you know, been very severe indeed for me". Should the paper cease publication,

> "We can retire with flying colours. But I am sure you would not wish that a paper which has stood so high and stands so high to-day should be handed over to a body of men who could certainly not, as a body, handle it, or be placed in the hands of others who might use its reputation to further their own ends."[1]

This "body of men" was Hyndman's own executive! Morris appears in reply to have suggested some compromise: the Executive should have at least some right of veto over the material printed. Hyndman, replying on December 8th, was quite specific:

> "Dear Morris,
>
> "I think I made the position of myself and those who have worked *Justice* into its present proud position quite plain this morning. Neither I nor they intend to submit to the 'control' of the Executive Committee of the S.D.F. in regard to what goes into the paper. Such a system has always meant and must always mean ruin; and it is worth notice that the change is specially wanted by the very persons—Dr. Aveling and Mrs. Aveling—who, owing to Bax's disastrous weakness, ruined *To-day* by their prejudices and advertising puffery of themselves.[2] Joynes is well aware of that I am sure—knows it to his cost in

[1] Brit. Mus. Add. MSS. 45345.

[2] See Engels' opinion (to Kautsky) June 22nd, 1884: "Hyndman. . . has done everything possible to ruin *To-day*. Bax, who put money into it, has erred in his calculations and will quickly be ruined." Eleanor Marx had contributed notes on the international movement to the early numbers, and Aveling two rather poor one-act "curtain-raisers". Possibly this is what Hyndman meant by "advertising puffery".

fact. But the best Council possible cannot manage a journal such as *Justice*. . ."

Hyndman was ready to consider one concession: the Committee might "*say*, if they wish" if they disagreed with an edition. He would even be prepared to hand over the Editorship to any man whose honesty and competence "we all trust": or to stop the paper: or to continue it as it was. BUT—he swept to his rhetorical conclusion:

"Without a spark of personal feeling in the matter, I cannot consent to sacrifice my own work and that of others (including yourself. . .) to what is a wholly unworkable and hopeless arrangement, suggested by people who have never done the paper any good whatever.

"Yours very truly,
"H.M. Hyndman."[1]

So that was that! Clearly Hyndman felt no love for Bax or Aveling. Equally clearly he had no time for his own Executive and (for some reason which is by no means clear) regarded *Justice* almost as personal property. On the evidence of these two letters alone the charges against him can be sustained.

Whoever it was that was shouting "damned liars" in the Executive, it was not—despite the immediate picture brought to mind—William Morris. Even at this point he had hopes of acting the part of peace-maker. There was one matter he meant to fight, it is true. A member of the Executive, W.J. Clark, had made charges of self-seeking against Hyndman in conversation with other Council members: and Hyndman had moved his expulsion. Morris thought Clark had behaved foolishly in talking so freely: but he was not the only one guilty of factionalism: "certainly Messrs. Frost, Champion and Hyndman had"—"probably we all had".[2] Yet this need not necessarily split the Federation. On the question of *Justice*, Morris was prepared to put it off to the next Annual Conference.[3] He

1 Brit. Mus. Add. MSS. 45345.
2 Morris to Thompson, *Letters*, p. 226.
3 Morris to Joynes, May Morris, II, p. 589.

even managed to force a grin at Hyndman, who "can't help it, you know. I really begin to think he *will* be Prime Minister before he dies".[1] But at this critical stage in the quarrel—in the second week of December—he paid a visit to Scotland which brought him back in a towering rage, and for the next two weeks the British Socialist movement was at war within itself.

V. The Scottish Land and Labour League

The S.D.F. was in reality a London organization. Morris told Engels at the time of the split that the entire London strength was less than 400, and there were not 100 supporters in the provinces.[2] Genuine branches existed at Battersea (where John Burns was hard at work), Clerkenwell, Marylebone (where Lane and his friends had done hard pioneering), Croydon, Tottenham, Hammersmith—perhaps at one or two other centres: the Westminster branch enrolled the unattached: at Birmingham John Sketchley was Secretary of a group: at Blackburn something still survived from the agitation of the previous year: at Bristol something was stirring: at one or two other centres where Hyndman or Morris had lectured, a few copies of *Justice* were sold and nuclei were forming.

The first stirrings in Scotland showed themselves, not in Glasgow, but in Edinburgh. Andreas Scheu had worked there at the turn of the decade, and had set afoot discussions on Socialism among the Secularists and some Radicals: he had met there Robert Banner, the book-binder, who had become an enthusiastic convert, and who had later followed him to London. When Scheu returned to Edinburgh in July, 1884, he found a small but vigorous propaganda was already under way. The leading spirit was a very young engineer, John Lincoln Mahon, of Irish stock. However erratic Mahon might later prove to be, he gave way to no one in his early fervour. By June, 1884, he had already thrown up his job and launched

[1] *Letters,* p. 218. [2] Engels to Bernstein, December 29th, 1884.

an ambitious venture—"The Social Reform Publishing Company"—for the supply of advanced Social Literature,[1] which by the end of August had ended in faulure.[2] Thenceforth he became, for nearly ten years, a floating agitator in the movement.

From Mahon Scheu learned that the S.D.F. "as an organization did not stand a chance in Scotland."[3] There, indeed, a mass agitation was already in being: its centre not on the Clyde, but in the barren Western Highlands and the Isle of Skye. The forcible depopulation of the Highlands (for the benefit of Scottish lairds and English sportsmen) had not ended with the "Clearances": less spectacular, but quite as callous and tyrannical, they had continued throughout the century, until the crofters were driven to the point of despair. In 1882 the crofters in Skye were goaded into virtual revolt: and the spark set the whole Highlands aflame.[4]

Many of the Lowland workers were still close to their Highland origins: moreover, Henry George's theories were at that very time coming into the forefront of the attention of the Radicals. A Georgeite Scottish Land Restoration League was formed, whose aim was "to Restore the Soil of Scotland to the people for whom it was intended, and to remove this great shame and crime from the land we love". On its first Executive were several who later became prominent in the Socialist movement, including Shaw Maxwell, and a young architectural draughtsman, John Bruce Glasier (himself the son of an island crofter), who was to become a leading Socialist propagandist in Glasgow. The League at once became a more formidable force than its English associate. At the Glasgow Franchise Demonstration of September 6th, several thousand of the processionists wore the cards of the League on their hats: 85,000 leaflets and pamphlets were

[1] *The Christian Socialist,* June, 1884. [2] *Letters,* p. 213.

[3] Scheu, *op. cit.,* Part III, Ch. V.

[4] See Alexander Mackenzie, *The History of the Highland Clearances* (1883), pp. 407-517.

distributed ("the total weight of which was over 10 cwt.")[1] At the General Election next year five League candidates were put up in the Clyde area, Shaw Maxwell polling over 1,000 votes in Blackfriars, Glasgow; while Dr. G.B. Clark (at one time a member of the First International) was elected as a crofters' candidate in Caithness.

In these circumstances, Scheu and Mahon took the decision not to form an Edinburgh Branch of the S.D.F., but to form a native organization, the "Scottish Land and Labour League", which could affiliate to the Federation. Morris did not like the new name at first, and foresaw trouble: "It will be looked on here as a secession I am afraid; and whatever may be the discouragements I don't like to think that we have done nothing in London, and must throw the whole thing to the dogs, and begin again. . ."[2] But the expected row blew over: the League was accepted as an affiliate at the August Annual Conference. Despite the prominence given to the land in the League's objects, the Manifesto of the League (drawn up in October) was addressed almost exclusively to the industrial workers and might indeed have been open to criticism more for neglecting to include a specific paragraph relating to the crofters' struggle, than for breaking with the general line of propaganda of the S.D.F. Nevertheless, the slight acknowledgement to national feeling brought immediate returns: Scheu made propaganda visits to Glasgow and the West of Scotland "with good success": and in Edinburgh the League began to gather strength.

But the old enmity between Hyndman and Scheu still smouldered under the surface. A small Branch of the S.D.F. had been formed in Glasgow in the summer of 1884, including Bruce Glasier and a stonemason, W.J. Nairne. In October Hyndman officially inaugurated the Branch with a highly successful lecture to an audience of 1,200 in the Albion Hall. Glasier, although later he was to become an uncompromising

[1] See account in *The Christian Socialist,* October, 1884.
[2] Morris to Scheu, July 18th, 1884, *Letters,* p. 203.

Morris partisan, found the lecture "brilliant and convincing. . . I enjoyed it greatly":

> "Racy, argumentative, declamatory, and bristling with topical allusions and scathing raillery, it was a hustings masterpiece. . . The reverberating note, in feeling if not in phrase, was 'I accuse, I expose, I denounce'. He seemed to look round on the civilized world and see there nothing but fraud, hypocrisy, oppression, and infamy on the part of the politicians and money-mongers on the one hand, and on the other only wooden-headed ignorance, stupidity, and servility on the part of the working class. . . He was jauntily cynical. . . 'I am an educated middle-class man. I derive my living from the robbery of the workers. I enjoy the spoil. . . and the workers are content. . . Why therefore should I object to their slaving for my enjoyment if they themselves don't!' Yet nevertheless there was in his protagonism a fiery and even fanatical zeal. He appealed for better things—for justice and democracy—for a new system of politics and economics. . ."[1]

Glasier's account is good—it was this sharp and incisive denunciation, this air of a man who knew the capitalist world inside-out and could give all the answers, which won Hyndman his loyal following among the workers groping their way towards Socialism. Hyndman (it seemed) knew his facts: there was nothing of the dreamer about him: anyone could see where he stood.

The Edinburgh League sent a deputation to Glasgow, presumably to propose collaboration between the two bodies on the lines of the "Scottish Land and Labour League". "The Glasgow Branch demurred, as they had full right to do, and some of the members seemed to have written to Hyndman for *orders* as to what to do."[2] Hyndman did not trouble to consult the Executive of the Federation: instead he wrote a letter attacking Scheu in what Morris "was compelled to call a treacherous manner". Hyndman took his stand upon grounds of rigid Marxist orthodoxy: Scheu, he declared, was an

[1] Glasier, *op. cit.*, p. 29. I have slightly "doctored" the quotation by cutting out the uncomplimentary reflections which Glasier read back into the speech.

[2] Morris to R. Thompson, *Letters*, p. 227.

anarchist ("'Anarchist' by the way is a kind of sacramental word with H.", Morris remarked),[1] a friend of Johann Most, he had tried to destroy the organization of the German comrades and would do the same in Scotland if the comrades were not cautious of such foreigners, "in short saying just what the writer thought would injure Scheu the most with the Glasgow people."[2]

It was at exactly this moment that Morris arrived in Scotland. On the Saturday he lectured for the League in Edinburgh, in a handsome club-room hired and decorated with the aid of £100 from a wealthy sympathizer, and although he learned something of the friction from his Chairman, the Rev. Dr. John Glasse, he went on to Glasgow the next day confident that he could "set matters right".[3] His Lecture here was given, not for the Branch, but under the auspices of the Sunday Lecture Society, to an audience of about 3,000. Once again Bruce Glasier has left an account of the meeting:

> "He was then fifty-one years of age, and just beginning to look elderly. His splendid crest of dark curly hair and his finely textured beard were brindling into grey. His head was lion-like, not only because of his shaggy mane, but because of the impress of strength of his whole front. . . I noted. . . the constant restlessness of his hands, and indeed of his whole body, as if overcharged with energy."

The audience gave him "an exceedingly friendly and respectful reception".

> "He read his lecture, or rather recited it, keeping his eye on the written pages, which he turned over without concealment. . . Every now and then [he] walked to and fro, bearing his manuscript. . . in his hand. Occasionally he paused in his recital, and in a 'man to man' sort of way explained some special point, or turned to those near him on the

[1] Morris to Scheu, December 6th, 1884, *Letters,* p. 218.

[2] Morris to R. Thompson, *ibid.,* p. 227. Scheu cites the damaging letter as being written to Moses MacGibbon, December 9th, 1884.

[3] See *Letters,* p. 219.

platform for their assent... Of the lecture itself I only remember that it seemed to me something more than a lecture, a kind of parable or prediction, in which art and labour were held forth, not as mere circumstances or incidents of life, but as life or the act of living itself. As we listened, our minds seemed to gain a new sense of sight, or new way of seeing and understanding why we lived in the world..."[1]

The description is deliberately pointed by Bruce Glasier, to contrast the manner and attitude of Hyndman and of Morris. But the point is well made. It is not difficult to see why working men and craftsmen like Glasier himself, whose interests were in artistic and intellectual fields, should come to Morris's side: and, equally, not difficult to see why some of the most earnest of the working-class comrades should distrust Morris as a dreamer, and gravitate to Hyndman's party.

After the meeting the explosion took place—the explosion which was not only the occasion for the disastrous split in the British Socialist movement, but which also gave birth to a story which has been used for two generations to dissociate the names of Morris and Marx. Morris, accompanied by James Mavor and Bruce Glasier, crossed the city to the room above a warehouse off Gallowgate (no £100 donations here!) where the Branch held its meetings. He found the comrades were torn in two by the London quarrel. Nairne, the Secretary, greeted Morris "frigidly", and said "he supposed Comrade Morris would like to say a few words". After some general remarks and some "careful words" on the friction, Morris was open to questions. Nairne, according to Bruce Glasier, in the only account of the meeting which exists, "immediately... proceeded to heckle him, much as he might have done an avowed opponent of Socialism":

"Morris showed no resentment, but answered the questions quite good-naturedly, and it was evident that the meeting felt drawn towards him, though the greater number... were, as I knew, ranged with Nairne on the Hyndman side.

[1] Glasier, *op. cit.*, pp. 23, 26.

"On his rising to go, Nairne, as a sort of parting shot, put to him the question: 'Does Comrade Morris accept Marx's theory of value?' Morris's reply was emphatic. . . 'I am asked if I believe in Marx's theory of value. To speak quite frankly, I do not know what Marx's theory of value is, and I'm damned if I want to know.' Then he added: 'Truth to say, my friends, I have tried to understand Marx's theory, but political economy is not in my line, and much of it appears to me to be dreary rubbish. But I am, I hope, a Socialist none the less. It is enough political economy for me to know that the idle class is rich and the working class is poor, and that the rich are rich because they rob the poor. That I know because I see it with my eyes. I need read no books to convince me of it. And it does not matter a rap, it seems to me, whether the robbery is accomplished by what is termed surplus value, or by means of serfage or open brigandage. The whole system is monstrous and intolerable, and what we Socialists have got to do is to work together for its complete overthrow, and for the establishment in its stead of a system of co-operation where there shall be no masters or slaves, but where everyone will live and work jollily together as neighbours and comrades for the equal good of all. That, in a nutshell, is my political economy and my social democracy.' "[1]

Leaving the meeting—once again in the company of Glasier and James Mavor—Morris remarked good-humouredly on the stairs:

" 'Our friend Nairne was putting me through the catechism a bit after your Scottish Kirk-Session fashion, don't you think? He is, I fancy, one of those comrades who are suspicious of us poetry chaps, and I don't blame him. He is in dead earnest, and will keep things going, I should say.' "[2]

Despite the fact that this account is vivid and in character, it must be said that it is unreliable as serious evidence (see Appendix II). In view of Morris's own anxiety about his reading at this time (see p. 306), he was not likely to have implied that study was unnecessary; nor is it likely that he would have ridiculed the Marxist theory of value, when in his own lectures of this period he was taking such pains to

[1] Glasier, *op. cit.*, pp. 31-2. [2] *Ibid.*, p. 33.

explain it in the simplest language. At the time when Glasier wrote this account he was a strenuous opponent of Marxism, and—whether consciously or unconsciously—he may have touched up the account to meet his own change of views. But, undoubtedly, some such outburst took place, and it followed these general lines. Morris was very conscious of his own disabilities in the field of political economy: "I want statistics terribly", he had written to Scheu the previous August. "You see, I am but a poet and artist, good for nothing but sentiment."[1] Moreover, he was enraged at Hyndman's "sacramental" dogmatism, which seemed to be the means he was employing to throw suspicion upon all those who were not ready to accept his personal leadership. *"What we Socialists have got to do is work together"*—these words are the key to the outburst. Certainly Morris himself, as he made his way back to London, was quite oblivious to the fact that he had set in motion a legend that the root of the dissension lay in his rejection of Marx's theory of value: rather, he was filled with fury at this new example of Hyndman's intrigue.

> "The spectacle of the discord so deliberately sown among these new recruits fairly swept away all doubt in my mind as to what was necessary to be done; I saw that the dispute *must* come off, and that it must be fought on the true grounds, namely resistance to H's absolutism."[2]

He had made up his mind to declare himself, and to have the whole matter out.

VI. Resignation

Immediately on his return, the "cabal" was formed, comprising the Avelings, Morris, Bax, Joseph Lane, Sam Mainwaring, Robert Banner, Clark and Mahon (who had now come to London, bringing with him evidence of Hyndman's intrigue). On December 16th the preliminary round was

[1] *Letters,* p. 212. [2] Morris to Joynes, May Morris, II, p. 589.

fought out, the expulsion of Clark being rejected by the Executive by nine votes to seven.[1] Champion, Quelch, Jack Williams, James Murray, Herbert Burrows and John Burns moved to Hyndman's side. All the suppressed bitterness and intrigue of the past few months came into the open. On the 18th Morris was writing:

> "The question only is now whether we shall go out of the S.D.F. or Hyndman: we are now only fighting for the possession of the name and the adherence of the honest people who don't know the ins and outs of the quarrel. On Tuesday next we move confidence in Scheu, and the paper *Justice* is to be handed over to the executive under a joint editorship excluding Hyndman: if these are carried I don't see how the beggar can stay in the Federation. All this is foul work: yet it is a pleasure to be able to say what one thinks at last. . ."[2]

Morris was rejoicing to be rid of Hyndman with his incurable "politician-nature": "what a pleasure not to have to shake hands with H. again", he wrote,[3] and—again—"he cannot change his nature and be otherwise than a jingo and a politician even if he tries."[4]

Under the pressure of this tide of feeling, Morris forced upon the "cabal" a policy which may well have been a serious mistake. He himself loathed such rows to the point of cowardice: the Tuesday debate (the 23rd) he reported "came off to the full as damned as I expected. . . It was a piece of degradation, only illumined by Scheu's really noble and skilful defence. . . the rest. . . mere backbiting, mixed with some melancholy and to me touching examples of faith." "However, Saturday, I *will* be out of it", he announced:

> "Our lot agreed beforehand, being I must say moved by me, that it is not worth fighting for the name of the S.D.F. and the sad remains of *Justice* at the expense of a month or two of wrangling: so as Hyndman considers the S.D.F. his property, let him take it. . . and try if he can really make up a bogie of it to frighten the Government, which I really

[1] See *Letters*, pp. 219-20. [2] Morris to his wife, *ibid.*, p. 221.
[3] Morris to Scheu, *ibid.*, p. 221. [4] *Ibid.*, p. 229.

think is about all his scheme; and we will begin again quite clean-handed to try the more humdrum method of quiet propaganda. . ."[1]

Saturday evening, the 27th, *did* see the end. The meeting lasted over four hours. Hyndman "had packed the room with his adherents, who were very noisy", while members of the L.E.L. were kept outside. "People who were not on the Executive spoke all on Hyndman's side." The vote was then taken, giving the "cabal" a majority of ten to eight. Thereupon Morris—to the surprise of the meeting—read out the prepared resignation of the majority:

"Since discord has arisen in the Council owing to the attempt to substitute arbitrary rule therein for fraternal co-operation, contrary to the principles of Socialism, and since it seems to us impossible to heal this discord, we, the undersigned, think it better in the interests of the cause of Socialism to cease to belong to the Council, and accordingly hand in our resignations.

"William Morris	E. Belfort Bax
Edward Aveling	John L. Mahon
Robert Banner	S. Mainwaring
J. Lane	W.J. Clark
Eleanor Marx-Aveling	J. Cooper."

The unexpected resignation—Morris thought—"seemed to win us favour". The majority withdrew, and went to Aveling's rooms to discuss their plans for the future. Ambrose Barker, who was one of the L.E.L. members waiting outside, still remembered seventy years later the tone of voice in which Morris said: "That's that."[2]

On the morning of the 27th, Aveling and Morris had called on Engels, at his suggestion, to discuss their plans. Already the "cabal" had decided on their next steps, and the name of their weekly paper, the *Commonweal.* Engels said that "we were weak in *political* knowledge and journalistic

[1] Morris to Georgie Burne-Jones, *Letters,* pp. 222-3.

[2] *Ibid.,* pp. 223-6, gives the account to Georgie Burne-Jones and to Andreas Scheu.

skill", and advised that the paper should commence as a monthly. Morris accepted the advice reluctantly. Two days later Engels wrote a long letter to Bernstein in which he described the intrigues of Hyndman ("a political adventurer and Parliamentary careerist") and Morris's exposure of them in detail:

> "Thereupon the majority resigned from the Federation. . . *because the whole Federation was really nothing but a swindle.* Those who resigned were Aveling, Bax, and Morris, the only honest men among the intellectuals—but men as unpractical (two poets and one philosopher) as you could possibly find. In addition, the better of the known workers. . . They want to act in the London branches; they hope to win the majority and then let Hyndman carry on with his non-existent provincial branches. Their organ will be a little monthly journal. Finally, they will work on a modest scale, in proportion to their forces, and no longer act as though the English proletariat were bound to act as soon as a few intellectuals became converted to Socialism and sounded the call."[1]

Morris, who had finally brought matters to a head, felt himself bound to prove his good faith by working wholeheartedly to found the new body: "though I think you will believe me when I say I am utterly free from ambition", he wrote to Joynes on Christmas Day, "I cannot merely stand out of the movement; I feel myself forced in the teeth of all kinds of discomfort, and even shame perhaps, to do my best in it."[2] In the next few days he wrote many letters, to the provincial branches, and to personal friends. "We have formed another body, the Socialist League", he wrote in one:

> "It begins at all events with the distinct aim of making Socialists by educating them, and of organizing them to deal with politics in the end;. . . it expects single-heartedness from its members and fraternal co-operation, and. . . it will not suffer any absolutism amongst it."[3]

[1] Engels to Bernstein, December 29th, 1884, *Labour Monthly,* October, 1933.
[2] May Morris, II, p. 591. [3] Morris to R. Thompson, *Letters,* p. 229.

In another he wrote that "our immediate aim should be chiefly educational":

"to teach ourselves and others what the due social claims of labour are. . . with the view to dealing with the crisis if it should come in our day, or of handing on the tradition of our hope to others if we should die before it comes. . ."[1]

So absorbed was he in the problem of ridding the movement of Hyndman's leadership that he scarcely seems to have noticed that he was being impelled by events into the position of being one of the most notable Socialist leaders in Britain himself. Once or twice in the sound and fury of the dispute he paused for a moment of self-questioning. "This morning I hired very humble quarters for the Socialist League", he wrote to Georgie Burne-Jones from his office in Merton Abbey the day after the split:

"We meet to inaugurate the League to-morrow evening. There now, I really don't think I have the strength to say anything more about the matter just now. I find my room here and a view of the winter garden, with the men spreading some pieces of chintz on the bleaching ground, somewhat of a consolation. But I promise myself to work as hard as I can in the new body, which I think will be but a small one for some time to come. . ."[2]

A week before he had paid a lightning visit to Chesterfield to discuss the dissension with Edward Carpenter. The peace of the Millthorpe small-holding contrasted seductively with the wrangles of London:

"I listened with longing heart to his account of his patch of ground, seven acres: he says that he and his fellow can almost live on it: they grow their own wheat, and send flowers and fruit to Chesterfield and Sheffield markets: all that sounds very agreeable to me. . . Whiles I think, as in a vision, of a decent community as a refuge from our mean

[1] Morris to Carruthers, May Morris, II, p. 594. [2] *Letters,* p. 224.

squabbles and corrupt society; but I am too old now, even if it were not dastardly to desert. . ."[1]

The vision of "a decent community as a refuge from our mean squabbles" was to grow in his imagination, giving that air of a "compensation-world" which permeates so many parts of *News from Nowhere.* Meanwhile he turned the temptation aside, and got down to the job ahead. "I will never tell you in my letters that I am in bad spirits even when I am", he wrote to Scheu. "But in truth I am now in good fair working spirits, not very sanguine but quite determined. . ."[2]

VII. The Aftermath

This was not just a quarrel in a closed debating society: it was a split—and, as it proved, a real, long-lasting and bitter split—in the British Socialist movement. It was all very well for Morris to declare—as he did at a future meeting of the Hammersmith Branch—

"that we met as friends and we wanted agreement and that he hoped as soon as possible we should bury the hatchet. He had nothing to say against his former associates but he disagreed with their tactics. He thought that the Socialist League would work without hostility to the S.D.F."[3]

But "the Cause" was not likely to be furthered by splitting up the energies of the handful of propagandists in two different organizations working fraternally in different directions. Hyndman himself, when writing his self-righteous reminiscences twenty-seven years later, declared that the split had "set the movement back fully twenty years":

"I cannot exonerate Morris and his group from the responsibility of having done more to hinder the progress of genuine Socialism in

[1] *Letters,* p. 223. [2] *Ibid.,* p. 226.

[3] Hammersmith Minutes, January 18th, 1885.

England than any people who have ever opposed it or been connected with it."[1]

What basis was there in his charge?

First, supposing that the charge of retarding the movement was true, Hyndman had only himself to blame. Nearly every one of the accusations brought against him by Morris and Engels at the time of the split were proved true in the light of future events—the political intrigue of the 1885 elections: the manner in which he exploited the unemployed agitation in 1886 and 1887: his dogmatic and authoritarian approach to questions of theory and leadership: the jingoism of his "Big Navy" policy before the Great War: his role in the war itself, and his repudiation of the Russian Revolution. Only one accusation—of personal self-seeking—was never sustained. He was an adventurer by temperament and a politician by background, which meant—as Morris summed up correctly—"waiting about to see what can be made of the political situation, if perhaps at the best one may attain to a sort of Bismarckian State Socialism."[2] Supremely self-confident himself, he saw the question of leadership as a matter of loyalty to himself and his Executive. If only the workers could be won to follow, *he* would look after the leading: the workers were the club which he would swing.

But a second question arises. Even if the split was unavoidable, were the tactics of the majority of the Council correct? On this question Morris himself was to have doubts, only three weeks after the event. "I know and knew that our resignation would throw us into the background at first", he wrote to Joynes:

"I mention this because I am responsible for that step: I hope it was not too much because I felt personally that I could not keep up the quarrel, as I certainly could not as far as I myself am concerned."[3]

[1] Hyndman, *Record of an Adventurous Life*, p. 360.

[2] *Letters*, p. 228.

[3] Morris to Joynes, January 18th, 1885. Brit. Mus. Add. MSS. 45345.

In fact, once the quarrel broke into the open, Morris's actions were dictated far less by policy than by passion. He and the "cabal" allowed themselves to be outwitted and out-manoeuvred by Hyndman. The issues upon which they joined battle were either (like the W.J. Clark affair) dictated by Hyndman, or else—like the final motion of censure on Hyndman—ones of personality rather than principle. Once the battle was joined, everything became coloured by Morris's temperament.

Morris's one instinct was to bring the matter to a decision. It was he who—despite Bax's warnings—pushed the "cabal" into pledging themselves to secede, *even if they controlled the Council.*[1] "Of course we did right to resign," he tried to re-assure himself the day after the split:

> "The alternative would have been a general meeting, and after a month's squabble for the amusement of the rest of the world that cared to notice us, would have landed us first in a deadlock and ultimately where we are now. . ."[2]

But that month of squabbling, painful as it would have been, might—if the majority had picked their ground carefully—have transformed the situation. Instead, by their precipitateness they alienated not only those honest members of the Executive who were still under Hyndman's spell,[3] but also the majority of the Federation's membership.

The fact is that to the membership the whole thing appeared as a mystery. They knew nothing of the history of the dispute: and the majority, by refusing to submit it to a general meeting, seemed afraid to consult them. Hyndman was quick to seize his advantage, and the minority issued a

[1] See Bax, *op. cit.*, p. 80. [2] *Letters*, p. 224.

[3] Morris seems to have thought well of Champion ("Of whose singleness of purpose I [do not] have the slightest doubt"), Williams (an "innocent"), and Burns (despite his "usual claptrap style"). Fitzgerald and Quelch ("the stupid!") he seems to have regarded as loyal to Hyndman beyond recall, while he called Burrows "a bad beast".

counter-statement calling a general meeting, opening the minutes of the Council to general inspection, and expressing the opinion–

"that in leaving the control of the Executive Council in the hands of a minority accused by them of not acting in accordance with the principles of Socialism, the majority have not fulfilled their duty to those who elected them to the Council."[1]

It almost seems as if Morris, in his fury, had forgotten that the S.D.F. had a membership.

The split was unavoidable. But Morris and the majority allowed themselves to be provoked into taking action on the wrong issues and in the wrong way. Three months before Morris himself had seen this danger clearly, and had warned Scheu and Bax of it:

"At present there is no definite cause of quarrel which those outside the quarrelling parties could understand as anything more than a squabble; and the result would be that the S.D.F. with its present elements minus a few of the best, who would be left out in the cold, would be the representative of Socialism in England."[2]

In the result, not only was Hyndman left in the position of strength, but the split was, of necessity, an ugly, ragged split, rather than a clean break. Rather than clarifying any principles at stake, it confused them further. It divided friends and left opponents in each other's midst. It prepared the way for further splits and secessions in both bodies; and the Socialist League was doomed to further dissension from the start.

[1] Lee, *op. cit.*, p. 70.

[2] Morris to Scheu, September 28th, 1884, Scheu Correspondence, Int. Inst. Soc. Hist.

CHAPTER IV

THE SOCIALIST LEAGUE, 1885-1886: "MAKING SOCIALISTS"

I. The Provisional Council

THE Socialist League was founded on December 30th, 1884. "Fellow Citizens", began the splendid Manifesto which Morris had drafted,

> "We come before you as a body advocating the principles of Revolutionary International Socialism; that is we seek a change in the basis of Society—a change which would destroy the distinctions of classes and nationalities."

A Provisional Council was formed, whose members added their names to the Manifesto. And the new party was launched—"Earth's newest planet wheeling through the night".

How fitted was the Provisional Council for its responsibility? Of the signatories to the Manifesto, several were to play only a minor part in the League, and need only be mentioned in passing—W. Bridges Adams, W.J. Clark, J. Cooper, W. Hudson, James Mavor of Glasgow and Edward Watson. E.T. Craig, by reason of his age, and Faulkner (Oxford), Maguire (Leeds) and Scheu (Edinburgh), by reason of their distance from London, were unable to take part in regular Council meetings. Even with these names subtracted, the Council appears as an able and determined group.

Heading the list were Edward and Eleanor Aveling. Dr. Aveling was one of the most brilliant of the younger intellectuals who joined the movement. In 1880 he was the rising star of the Secularists, a brilliant scientist with a Fellowship at University College, London, and a member of the London School Board, for Westminster. Born in 1851, he was in 1883 already the author of nearly a score of books and pamphlets on Secularism and Darwinism. When he became converted to Socialism by studying *Capital* early in 1884, he accepted Marxism as being in the strictest sense a science. Darwin and Marx became his twin masters, the one master in biological, the other in social, science. His understanding was schematic rather than creative. Marxism he regarded as a set of irrefutable factual discoveries in the field of economics, rather than as an historical method of analysis. But this tendency towards inflexibility was a less serious hindrance to the early movement than his notoriously erractic moral conduct. The facts of this unhappy matter are difficult to establish. But one important fact cannot be burked. Aveling acquired a reputation in the movement so unsavoury that not only the man himself, but also the principles which he espoused were brought under suspicion.

George Bernard Shaw later wrote of Aveling as an "agreeable rascal":

> "He was quite a pleasant fellow who would have gone to the stake for Socialism or Atheism, but with absolutely no conscience in his private life. He seduced every woman he met, and borrowed from every man."

Shaw drew from him the character of Dubedat in *The Doctor's Dilemma,* and Edouard Bernstein, the German Social-Democrat, who was on close terms with the Avelings during these years, said that the portrait, though "somewhat retouched", was close to life.[1] "Nearly everyone who had

[1] *My Years of Exile,* p. 162: "Shaw gave Dubedat nearly all the characteristic attributes of Edward Aveling: his passion for having everything of the best; the assured and shameless manner in which he borrowed, in order to pay for his pleasures, the scanty cash of even the poorest of his acquaintances; his gift of fascinating the ingenuous, and, in particular, women, by his lyrical and aesthetic affectations and flirtations... these are the characteristic features of the man for whom Eleanor Marx sacrificed herself as completely in real life as Mrs. Dubedat sacrificed herself for her husband in the play. And the deliberate blindness and deafness of Mrs. Dubedat in respect of all that was said to the detriment of her husband is precisely the counter-part of the obstinacy with which Eleanor Aveling, despite all her painful experience of her chosen comrade, continued to believe in him..."

dealings with him," said Henry Salt, who also knew him in the early days, "even those who were on the friendliest of terms, found themselves victimized, sooner or later, by his fraudulence in money matters." In revolt against all bourgeois conventions, Aveling did not replace them by any new moral concern, but simply filled the vacuum with his own egotism: and, like other "agreeable rascals" of the same sort, he ended his life as a disagreeable rogue.

"It is easy to set him down as a scoundrel", wrote Salt,

> "but in truth he was an odd mixture of fine qualities and bad; a double-dealer, yet his duplicities were the result less of a calculated dishonesty than of a nature in which there was an excess of the emotional and artistic nature, with an almost complete lack of the moral."[1]

When he had left university, he had become the manager of a company of strolling players. Later, he became established as a dramatic critic (under the name, "Alec Nelson"), and he wrote several "curtain-raisers" and one-act plays. He and Eleanor were among the small circle in the late 1880s who first perceived the importance of Ibsen, and encouraged the first stirrings of the "new drama" in England. There is no doubt that Aveling included within his contradictory personality exceptional ability, a good measure of courage and of artistic perception. It is likely that his personal weaknesses were exaggerated in the malicious gossip of political enemies; and the working-class leader who knew him best, Will Thorne, wrote of his part in the early movement with admiration, despite his own close knowledge of the tragic circumstances of the Avelings' last years.[2] "How said has life been all these years", Eleanor wrote shortly before her suicide in 1898:

> "I realize. . . more and more, that wrong behaviour is simply a moral sickness, and that the morally healthy. . . are not qualified to judge the

[1] H.S. Salt, *Seventy Years Savages,* p. 80.

[2] Will Thorne, *My Life's Battles* (1925).

condition of the morally sick. . . There are people who lack a certain moral sense just as others are deaf or short-sighted or are in other ways afflicted. And I begin to realize the fact that one is as little justified in blaming them for the one sort of disorder as for the other. We must strive to cure them, and if no cure is possible, we must do our best. I have learnt to perceive this through long suffering—suffering whose details I could not tell even to you—but I have learned it, and so I am endeavouring to bear all these trials as well as I can."[1]

No apology need be made for the role in the English Socialist movement of Eleanor Marx herself. In 1880, when Edouard Bernstein first met her, she was "a blooming young maiden of twenty-four",

"with the black hair and black eyes of her father, and an exceptionally musical voice. She was unusually vivacious, and took part, in her sensitive and emotional manner, in our discussions of party matters. With much greater devotion than her two elder sisters, Tussy, as Eleanor was called by her friends and her family, had dedicated herself to the Socialist movement."[2]

In her early twenties, Eleanor had a consuming desire to be an actress, which she strove to hide from her father, who was already ailing and in need of attention. After her father's death she was forced to abandon her dramatic career, and took a post in a boarding-school. She was soon active in the young movement, writing International Notes for *To-day,* helping Engels with her father's papers, and (in 1884) going on the Council of the S.D.F. She was drawn towards Aveling, it seems, by their common work in "the Cause", their shared interest in drama, his sensitive, intelligent and unconventional manners. Since Aveling was already married (although long separated from his wife) she decided to proclaim openly their free marriage. "Our union cannot. . be a legal one", she wrote to the young Scottish engineer, J.L. Mahon, as yet unknown to her, in order to forestall the slander of enemies:

[1] Bernstein, *op. cit.,* p. 164. [2] *Ibid.,* p. 159.

"It is a true and real one none the less. We are doing no human being the smallest wrong. . . We have both felt that we were justified in setting aside all the false & really immoral bourgeois conventionalities, & I am happy to say we have received—the only thing we care about—the approbation of our friends and fellow socialists."[1]

"My London is a little Paris", Engels wrote to Bernstein,[2] and among those who approved and defended the unorthodox arrangement from Hyndman's criticisms was William Morris.

It was largely through the Avelings that Engels maintained contact with the English movement. Engels, now living in his house in Regent's Park Road, was (in the eyes of one young English Socialist) "a tall, bearded, vigorous, bright-eyed and genial septuagenarian. . . hospitable, fond of good living, and blessed with a sense of humour".[3] He had little time to take part in English affairs. The death of Marx, in March, 1883, had thrown upon him tremendous responsibilities, and he ordered his life by strict routine. "Every day, every post"—Aveling recalled after his death—"brought to his house newspapers and letters in every European language, and it was astonishing how he found time, with all his other work, to look through, keep in order, and remember the chief contents of them all."[4] Correspondence and polemical writings, new editions or translations of his own or Marx's books, above all, work on Marx's papers—every day these kept him busy until the small hours, with only a break for a stroll through Regent's Park after lunch, and an hour or two with a friend after his evening meal. Only on his famous Sunday evenings was his house thrown open to his friends—refugees from Germany, Russia, Austria, visitors from America and France. Bax was a frequent visitor at Engels's house, and entertained the table with his solemn paradoxes. Aveling, as the husband of "Tussy", was naturally another close friend. Engels seems, in the 1880s, to

[1] See first edition, p. 860.
[2] Bernstein, *op. cit.*, p. 162.
[3] W.S. Sanders, *Early Socialist Days*, p. 80.
[4] "Engels at Home", in the *Labour Prophet*, September, 1895.

have taken little notice of Aveling's reputation in private life. Whatever rumours of Aveling's behaviour reached his ears, he seems to have passed over as youthful vagaries. Eleanor he regarded almost as his own daughter, and if Aveling was her choice, he was prepared to support her against the criticisms of society.

This problem of personal relationship had a part in the complex of factors confusing the Socialist movement of the 1880s. "On account of Aveling", Bernstein recorded, "many people kept away from Engels's house."[1] Whether Morris was among these it is not clear. It is, on the face of it, unlikely. Morris and Engels had discussions before the "Split", and they met on more than one occasion afterwards. Both men always spoke of each other with respect, and Engels regarded Morris's medievalism "with good-humoured toleration".[2] Both time and temperamental differences prevented their becoming intimate, and Morris did not attend Engels's Sunday evenings simply because this was his own busiest evening—either lecturing up and down the country, or at the head of his own circle at the Hammersmith Branch.

One point, however, should be made clear. The charge thrown at Engels by Hyndman—that the "Grand Lama of Regent's Park Road" was ceaselessly intriguing in the English movement—cannot be sustained. He did not pretend to be leading any section of the movement, or to have his own party within it. For a moment, in 1885, it is true that by writing in *Commonweal* he publicly identified himself with the Socialist League. But as soon as dissension appeared within the League he withdrew into the background again, taking the attitude that until the movement had become clarified and the men had become sorted out, his own intervention would only add to the conflict. If he was approached for advice, no matter if the enquirer was Bax or Morris or Mahon, he was prepared to give it. In his letters to the comrades abroad (and especially his

[1] Bernstein, *op. cit.*, p. 202.

[2] *Labour Prophet*, September, 1895. See also Bernstein, *op. cit.*, p. 206.

personal friends) he gave his opinions on the development of the movement, and recounted sympathetically the actions of the Avelings, who were most closely in his confidence. But (inescapable as was the situation in which he was placed) it was without doubt a disaster that Aveling was so close to him, and that he should have gained the reputation of being the "leader" whom (in Bax's words) Engels wished to "foist" upon the English movement.

However, the tragedy of 1898 (when the marriage ended in Eleanor's suicide) should not be read back into the events of the 1880s. Until 1887 Morris valued the Avelings as among the best comrades in the leadership of the League. Month by month Eleanor contributed her record of the International movement to *Commonweal,* her own contacts and those of Engels being drawn upon to the full. Aveling shared the editorship of the paper with Morris for the first year, and Morris admired his command of Scientific Socialism, both as a lecturer and writer. The Avelings took part in the struggle for free speech at Dod Street, and it was Morris's protest at the rough-housing of Eleanor which led to his own arrest. Political issues rather than personal matters may account for the coldness growing up between Morris and the Avelings in 1887: although it cannot account for Morris's angry reference to Aveling, in September, 1887, as a "disreputable dog".

Two others of the Provisional Council were frequent visitors at Engels's house—old Frederic Lessner, the survivor of 1848 and E. Belfort Bax. Bax's introduction to the Socialist movement has already been described. From his pen came the first serious critiques by an English Marxist of a score of problems in religion, ethics, and social morality: in the years between 1885 and 1895 he published *The Religion of Socialism, The Ethics of Socialism, Outlooks From the New Standpoint* and *Outspoken Essays,* as well as some studies in the French Revolution and half a hundred articles in Socialist periodicals. In particular, all the work he did in collaboration with Morris was of a high order, especially the series of articles in *Commonweal,* "Socialism From the Root Up".

May Morris has given a warm picture of Bax and her father at work together on their editorial duties in the study at Kelmscott House:

"Bax with his fine regular features and bushy moustache. . . tall and thin, in his black velveteen coat, sitting in a comfortable armchair by the fire, smoking, with perhaps a glass at his elbow: my Father. . . short and square and blue-clad, sitting at the writing-table, his splendid head bent over the paper, with perhaps a dry grin on his face at a vagary of Bax's—it was thus they did. . . the *Commonweal* make-up. . ."[1]

But there *was* something funny about Belfort Bax. The truth is that he was an owl. There was a good deal in him of the music-hall professor—the sudden fits of utter abstraction, the completely unpractical cast of mind, the essential lack of proportion which revealed itself in a blank absence of the sense of humour. His best work was done when Morris was at his elbow to bring him down to earth with a bang out of his naive ruminations. Bax alone of the early Marxists (if we except Morris) seemed to have a really flexible understanding of the historical method of Marxism. But, time and again, his pronouncements seem to be strangely off the point. The real bull's-eye of his target was the Victorian middle-class family. His articles on imperialism kept on plunging off after the spectacle of hypocrisy, rather than the fact of exploitation. When the Trafalgar Square Riots took place Morris—on the front page of *Commonweal*—was wrestling with the essential political implications of the outbreak, while in the inner pages Bax was having the time of his life using the incident as a text for a long and triumphant article on the importance of the event as an "exposure of the abject cowardice of the English middle-classes *en bloc*". The opening paragraph will serve as a fairly good example of the difficulties of his style:

"Nothing strikes the Bourgeois mind with a keener sense of horror than the 'lamentable', (as he calls it) destruction of property. Misery

[1] May Morris, II, p. 173.

and starvation in times like the present, are part of the natural order of things, very unfortunate, very deplorable, perhaps, but inevitable, and even useful as affording the well-to-do classes an opportunity of posing as the charitable benefactors of the distressed. Besides, is not the traditional founder of that religion which is often described as one of the bulwarks of our 'social order', reported to have given utterance to the dictum, 'the poor ye have always with you'? But the fracture of plate-glass windows, the destruction or alienation of respectable tradesmen's stock, and in a wholesale manner too, no this verily is not in the bond which knits society together; this is entirely out of the nature of Bourgeois law and order, and hence to be bewailed as a calamity."[1]

This lack of proportion in Bax's outlook sometimes took ludicrous forms. Where Morris could suggest his disgust of the philistinism and joylessness of the middle class in a few savage strokes of the pen, the subject had for Bax a peculiar sort of fascination. He inspected bourgeois conventions in the light of a solemn and literal child-like reason, as if he were analysing the habit of some species of slug. He took up an attitude to the "Woman Question" which Morris and most of his contemporary Socialists could only find laughable. "Looked at from the ordinary point of view", he said,

"It is quite clear that considering the fact that the female population of England is in excess of the male by about a million, female suffrage, in spite of its apparent embodiment of the principle of equality, really means, if it means anything at all (which may be doubtful) the handing over of the complete control of the state to *one* sex."[2]

In repeated writings and conversations he rode this hobby-horse of the Bourgeois raising "the female sex into a quasi-privileged class", commiserating the working man,

"whose wife, to all intents and purposes, now has him completely in her power. If dissolute or drunken, she can sell up his goods or break

[1] *Commonweal*, March, 1886, "Looting, Scientific and Unscientific."

[2] *The Religion of Socialism*, p. 117.

up his home at pleasure, and still compel him to keep her and live with her to her life's end. There is no law to protect *him.* On the other hand, let him but raise a finger in a moment of exasperation against this precious representative of the sacred principle of 'womanhood', and straightway he is consigned to the treadmill. . ."[1]

Of the other members of the Provisional Council, there is less to be recorded. John Lincoln Mahon and Joseph Lane have already been introduced. Sam Mainwaring, an engineer with a "quiet, dignified bearing", was an early member of the L.E.L. "He was full-bearded, like Morris", recalled Tom Mann. "After attending propagandist meetings William Morris frequently walked back with Mainwaring, and it was said of them that they looked like the skipper and the first mate of a ship."[2] Charles Mowbray, who was imprisoned in 1887 after an unemployed demonstration at Norwich, and, later, came to play a dubious role on the Anarchist wing of the movement, seems to have left little record of his own introduction to Socialism. Thomas Binning was a London compositor, and a trade unionist of twenty years' standing in 1885. He became employed full-time by the League on the publication of *Commonweal,* and, later, he was Father of the Chapel at the Kelmscott Press. In 1885 and 1886 he was the League's foremost propagandist on trade union questions.

Frank Kitz was even more of a "veteran" of the movement than was Joseph Lane: indeed, in the early 1870s, he was once accused of being "the only Socialist in London".[3] He was (recalled Glasier) "a rebel by temperament rather than Anarchist by philosophy". A dyer, who was sometimes employed at Morris's Merton Abbey Works, a bold and humorous open-air speaker—"a bluff, breezy chap, fond of his beer

[1] *The Religion of Socialism,* p. 116. When a woman fell off Clifton Suspension Bridge without breaking her neck, Bax (to Morris's delight) pointed out in all seriousness that this proved that woman was a lower organism; man would have been killed (May Morris, II, p. 174)

[2] Tom Mann, *op. cit.,* p. 47.

[3] *Commonweal,* August Supplement, 1885.

and jolly company".[1] As the only English member of the Rose Street Club with a fluent command of German, he had been in the thick of this strange atmosphere of international conspiracy at the end of the 1870s. According to one account, in the early 1880s he had formed a small circle for the making of explosives. In the first years of the League, Kitz was ebullient and impetuous, "a fine burly figure, with a mass of light brown curly hair, blue eyes, rather heavy features, a pleasant, jolly smile."[2] His occasional contributions to the *Commonweal* are full of wrath against the capitalist class, and equally full of detailed knowledge of the real misery of the people of East London. More than one of his articles, detailing the iniquities of the system, ends with an open cry for vengeance.[3] "I have made Kitz's acquaintance lately", Morris wrote to Joynes early in 1885:

> "Like most of our East-enders, he is certainly somewhat tinged with anarchism or perhaps one may say destructivism; but I like him very much: I called on the poor chap at the place where he lived, and it fairly gave me the horrors to see how wretchedly off he was; so it isn't much to wonder at that he takes the lines he does."[4]

This "destructivist" tinge to the views of Kitz, Lane and their following in the Labour Emancipation League, was to prove of increasing importance within the Socialist League. Extreme individualism—the desire to dispense with party discipline and serious forms of organization—they inherited in part from the ultra-Jacobin tradition. The workers' struggle against the machinery of the bourgeois State had passed, among some of Bronterre O'Brien's followers, into a struggle against the State itself—the police, law courts, Parliament—as

[1] Glasier, *op. cit.*, p. 128.

[2] Obituary notice signed "J.M." (probably J.L. Mahon) in *Justice*, January 20th, 1923.

[3] e.g. Kitz's article, "Bastille, Bourgeoisie, and Bumble", in *Commonweal*, November, 1885.

[4] Morris to Joynes, February 3rd, 1885, Brit. Mus. Add. MSS. 45345.

instruments of coercion and class rule. In the late 1870s the apathetic misery of the East End had made the methods of the Nihilists in Russia, and the threats uttered by Most over the bar at the Rose Street Club, seem an effective—even a realistic—way of striking at capitalism. Such men as Kitz hoped that agitation in the slums and among the unemployed might provoke a revolutionary uprising as overwhelming as their visions of the Paris Commune.

The presence of some of these attitudes in the minds of such men as Lane and Kitz helps to explain why the League was later to become a nursing-ground for Anarchism. It helps to explain why the League was launched with a marked list to the Left, in contrast to Hyndman's list to the opportunism of the Right: why, when Morris shifted his weight towards the Anarchist side, the list at once became dangerous: and why, when he removed his influence altogether, the acrobatics of the rest of the crew soon had the craft capsized. But, while several of the Leaguers had a slight knowledge of Anarchist theory,[1] it would be wrong to think of the "Anarchists" within the League in 1885 and 1886 as the conscious advocates of certain theoretical positions. They were class-conscious workers in revolt against intolerable conditions, hostile to Hyndman's top hat and frock coat, earnest in their desire to get a real revolutionary propaganda afoot, and attracted to William Morris by his own enthusiasm and his evident hatred of the middle class. Years afterwards—despite the fact that Morris, in his last years, broke decisively with them—both Frank Kitz and Joseph Lane paid warm tributes to his memory. William Morris had "none of the meanness and bitterness which the horrible competitive system implants in all of us", wrote Lane—with perhaps a self-critical glance at his own quarrelsome part in the early movement. "Morris was one of nature's noblemen, and I never expect to see his like again."[2]

[1] In the recollection of the late Mr. Ambrose Barker, Joseph Lane and his circle were aware of the writings of Kropotkin, Bakunin, and of Benjamin Tucker, in America, as early as 1885.

[2] Lane to Ambrose Barker, 1912, Nettlau Collection, Int. Inst. Soc. Hist.

II. The League's Policy

The weeks immediately following the "Split" were confused. The Provisional Council, installed in their new premises, found themselves without a membership—without even a list of the Secretaries of the Branches of the S.D.F. Within a few weeks firm affiliations could be recorded from several London branches, from the Labour Emancipation League, the Scottish (Edinburgh) Land and Labour League, and Branches at Leeds and Oxford. Several Council members urged the League to embark forthwith on a struggle to win over or destroy the remaining S.D.F. Branches. Scheu called for a Manifesto denouncing "the party of Jingoism and Boss-ship at Westminster".[1] Hyndman and the rump of the S.D.F. Executive issued a statement of their case, and from Leeds on January 11th, 1885, Tom Maguire sent a desperate plea for a "counterblast" from the League:

> "Our work is at a standstill. The confidence of our members is necessarily growing weaker and the whole movement cannot be other than in a state of compromise. . A dignified silence just now counts for nothing against the Jesuitical activities of pronounced opponents."[2]

In response to this pressure a dignified statement was issued on January 13th, over the names of the ten resigning members of the S.D.F. Executive.

The delay in issuing this statement was not only due to scruples against carrying on a public dog-fight within the movement. It was due, at least in part, to differences among the Provisional Council as to the actual questions of principle involved in the "Split" and as to the policy of the new body. Morris's first public statement (in an interview with the *Daily*

[1] Scheu to Provisional Council, January 4th, 1885, S.L. Correspondence, Int. Inst. Soc. Hist.

[2] Tom Maguire to Secretary, S.L., January 11th, 1885, S.L. Correspondence, Int. Inst. Soc. Hist.

News, January 8th, 1885) would probably, it is true, have won the assent of all the Provisional Council. He stressed his view that the new party must be a party of *cadres*, with a high level of theoretical understanding, ready to play a leading part in any revolutionary movement of the masses. The occasion for the split, he said, was Hyndman's "arbitrary rule" and tendency to "political opportunism tinctured with Jingoism". The League took its stand for revolutionary and scientific Socialism, as opposed to this opportunism on the one hand, and to reformism on the other:

> "There are many people who will admit the justice of the Socialist criticisms of the present state of society, and are prepared to do all they can for the working classes than can be done *for* the working classes and not *by* them."

Hyndman's methods—he implied—would bring about a "mechanical revolution". By contrast with this—

> "I want an educated movement. Discontent is not enough, though it is natural and inevitable. The discontented must know what they are aiming at. . . My belief is that the old order can only be overthrown by force; and for that reason it is all the more necessary that the revolution. . . should be, not an ignorant, but an intelligent revolution. What I should like to have now, far more than anything else, would be a body of able, high-minded, competent men, who should act as instructors of the masses and as their leaders during critical periods of the movement. It goes without saying that a great proportion of these instructors and organizers should be working men. . . I should like to see 2,000 men of that stamp engaged in explaining the principles of rational, scientific Socialism all over the kingdom."

"The whole movement here is only a phantom", Engels was to write to Sorge in January, 1886, "but if it is possible to draw into the Socialist League a kernel of people who have a good theoretical understanding, much will be gained for a genuine mass movement, which will not be long in coming." Morris would have assented to this judgement.

On the other hand, in the statement issued by the seceding

members of the S.D.F. Executive on January 13th, several phrases foreshadow future differences within the League. The occasion for the "Split" is described in the same terms—Hyndman's arbitrary rule, political opportunism and jingoism—but the conclusion drawn is sharper than in previous statements. The tendency to opportunism is denounced on the grounds that it "would have involved us in alliances, however temporary, with one or other of the political factions, and would have weakened our propagandist force by driving us into electioneering", which might, in turn, have deprived the movement of some of their leaders, "by sending them to our sham parliament, there to become either nonentities, or perhaps our masters, and it may be our betrayers".[1] The educational role of the propaganda is stressed, the importance of building up a party of *cadres,* but—once again—in sharper terms:

> "Our view is that such a body in the present state of things has no function but to educate the people in the principles of Socialism, and to organize such as it can get hold of to take their due places, when the crisis shall come which will force action on us."

This phrasing, increasingly to be repeated in Morris's writings, is worth some attention. The revolutionary movement is looked upon from two aspects: a small educated propaganda on the one hand, a spontaneous rising provoked by misery on the other: in the final event "the crisis" arises—one sharply-defined revolutionary moment (like the Commune)—when the Socialist *cadres* will master the spontaneous mass movement and steer it through to Socialism.

Shortly after the "Split", the Provisional Council adopted a draft Constitution, which almost certainly was brought forward by the Avelings and represented Engels's view as to the correct policy of the League:

[1] The Statement, published as a leaflet, is reprinted in full in Tom Mann, *op. cit.,* pp. 45-6.

"1. Forming and helping other Socialist bodies to form a National and International Socialist Labour Party.

"2. Striving to conquer political power by promoting the election of Socialists to Local Governments, School Boards, and other administrative bodies.

"3. Helping Trade-Unionism, Co-operation, and every genuine movement for the good of the workers.

"4. Promoting a scheme for the National and International Federation of Labour."

The rejection of this Constitution[1] is an indication of the defeat of the Avelings on the Provisional Council, and the complete conversion of William Morris to the "purist" and anti-parliamentary position. As early as February, 1885, J.L. Mahon, as Secretary of the League, informed the Leeds Branch that joining the League involved renouncing "the political opportunism and State Socialism of the S.D.F.",[2] and, it was implied, the renunciation of parliamentary or local electioneering. In July, 1885, Morris defined his own position in *Commonweal:*

"I should like our friend to understand whither the whole system of palliation tends—namely, to the creation of a new middle class to act as a buffer between the proletariat and their direct and obvious masters; the only hope of the bourgeois for retarding the advance of Socialism lies in this device. Let our friend think of a society thus held together. Let him consider how sheepishly the well-to-do workers to-day offer themselves to the shearer; and are we to help our masters to keep on creating fresh and fresh flocks of sheep? What a society that would be, the main support of which would be capitalists masquerading as working men! Shall the ultimate end of civilization be the perpetual widening of the middle classes? I think if our friend knew as well as I do the terrible mental degradation of our middle classes, their hypocrisy, their

[1] This Constitution, provisionally adopted after the Split, was dropped from the revised Constitution adopted at the First Annual Conference. Later, it reappears in the North of England Socialist Federation (see p. 464) and the Hoxton Labour Emancipation League in 1888. A copy is preserved in the British Library of Political and Economic Science.

[2] Report of J.L. Mahon to the Provisional Council, February 8th, 1885, S.L. Correspondence, Int. Inst. Soc. Hist.

cowardice, their joylessness, it would scare him from attempting to use their beloved instrument of amelioration—Parliament.

"It is a new Society that we are working to realise, not a cleaning up of our present tyrannical muddle into an improved smoothly-working form of that same "order", a mass of dull and useless people organized into classes, amidst which the antagonism should be moderated and veiled so that they should act as checks on each other for the insurance of the stability of the system.

"The real business of Socialists is to impress on the workers the fact that they are a class, whereas they ought to be Society; if we mix ourselves up with Parliament we shall confuse and dull this fact in people's minds instead of making it clear and intensifying it. The work that lies before us at present is to *make Socialists,* to cover the country with a network of associations composed of men who feel their antagonism to the dominant classes, and have no temptation to waste their time in the thousand follies of party politics. If by chance any good is to be got out of the legislation of the ruling classes, the necessary concessions are much more likely to be wrung out of them by fear of such a body, than they are to be wheedled and coaxed out of them by the continual life of compromise which 'Parliamentary Socialists' would be compelled to live, and which is deadly to that feeling of exalted hope and brotherhood that alone can hold a revolutionary party together."[1]

III. Fighting Imperialism

Morris possessed to the full his own share of the historical sense, which he called "the new sense of modern times".[2] His Socialist poems were consciously the poems of the pioneers of a new world. He knew that the trivial or serious episodes of the early Socialists would at some time be a subject of history. And towards the end of 1887 he sat down some hurried "Notes on Propaganda" as a guide to the future historian. It is interesting to see the events which he singled out as important:

"The propaganda went on briskly", the sheet of notes begins. "On the First of February 1885 appeared the first number of the *Common-*

[1] "Socialism and Politics", July Supplement, 1885.

[2] From Morris's Preface to Robert Steele's *Medieval Lore* (1893) (reprinted in May Morris, I, pp. 286-9).

weal. . . In the March number appeared an admirable article by F. Engels—which attracted much attention. . . The wretched commercial-piratical war in the Soudan drew our attention somewhat at this time. . . A series of lessons on Socialism explaining the works of Carl Marx were given during these months."[1]

The first number of the *Commonweal* was indeed an event of importance. In contrast to *Justice,* the paper was declared to be "The Official Organ of the Socialist League", the Editor and Sub-Editor (Morris and Aveling) acting "as delegates of the Socialist League, and under its direct control". The first number carried the Manifesto, articles by Bax, Aveling, Lane, and Craig, Eleanor Aveling's "Record of the International Movement", news of the movement in Britain, and Morris's "March of the Workers":

"Hark the rolling of the thunder!
Lo the sun! and lo, thereunder
Riseth wrath, and hope, and wonder,
And the host comes marching on."

The second number, in March, must surely have been one of the most remarkable issues of any British Socialist periodical. An Editorial by Morris, articles by Bax, Stepniak, George Bernard Shaw, Paul Lafargue, Frank Kitz and Aveling were capped by three outstanding items: Eleanor Marx-Aveling's "Record" included messages greeting the formation of the League from Bebel, Liebknecht, Vaillant, Lafargue, Leo Frankel, Kautsky, Pierre Lavroff, Stepniak and Domela Nieuwenhuis: Morris contributed his "Message of the March Wind", which was to serve as the prelude to *The Pilgrims of Hope:* and Engels contributed his remarkable article, "England in 1845 and in 1885", which was later included in his Preface to the English edition of *The Condition of the Working Class in England in 1844.*

It is unfortunate that Engels was not able to contribute

[1] Brit. Mus. Add. MSS. 46345.

more frequently to *Commonweal*. Certainly, this article had a very marked influence upon Morris, as his references to it, and the echoes of it in his articles and lectures of 1885 and 1886 reveal. In his article Engels traced the causes of the decline of Chartism and Socialist organization in England to the supremacy of British capitalism in the world market between 1850 and 1875, showed how these conditions gave birth to a skilled aristocracy of labour protected by strong Trade Unions, while leaving the East End as "an ever-spreading pool of stagnant misery and desolation, of starvation when out of work, and degradation, physical and moral, when in work". Even the masses of the workers, Engels argued, had benefited in limited and temporary ways from Britain's industrial monopoly: "with the breakdown of that monopoly the English working-class will lose that privileged position", the article concluded. "And that is the reason why there will be Socialism again in England."

> "War in the world abroad a thousand leagues away,
> While custom's wheel goes round and day devoureth day.
> Peace at home!—what peace, while the rich man's mill is strife,
> And the poor is the grist that he grindeth, and life devoureth life?"[1]

so wrote Morris. And in many articles and lectures Bax and Morris drew the implications from these facts, and pointed clearly to the new character of British imperialism. Lecturing at Oldham in July, 1885, on "The Depression of Trade", Morris based his argument upon Engels' article:

> "We have said, 'Buy this or—take a bayonet in your belly!' People don't want the goods we offer them, but they are poor and have to buy something which serve their turn anyhow, so they accept. . . Their own goods, made slowly and at a greater cost, are driven out of the market, and the metamorphosis begins which ends in turning fairly happy barbarians into very miserable half-civilized people surrounded by a

[1] *Pilgrims of Hope*, Section 3.

fringe of exploiters and middle-men varied in nation but of one religion—'Take care of Number One.' "[1]

Bax had written for the first number of *Commonweal* one of his very best (and briefest) articles—on "Imperialism *v.* Socialism", underlining the words of the League's own Manifesto: "The markets of the world are being competed for with an eagerness never before known." Pointing to the numerous colonial wars in Asia, North and Central Africa, and Polynesia, he declared:

"Such wars must necessarily increase in proportion to the concentration of capital in private hands, i.e. *in proportion as the commercial activity of the world is intensified, and the need for markets becomes more pressing.* Markets, markets, markets! Who shall deny that this is the drone-bass ever welling up from beneath the shrill bawling of 'pioneers of civilization', 'avengers of national honour', 'purveyors of gospel light', 'restorers of order'. . ."

Morris, in his lecture on "Commercial War" delivered a few months later, went even further, and pointed to a change in the character and intensity of the imperialist rivalry of his time. The wars against backward peoples, he said,

"are by no means a new manifestation of this decade. . . but there is something in the way in which it is set about, which to my mind shows. . . that the great commercial system is shaking. . . You cannot fail to have noted the frequency and persistency and bare-faced cynicism of these wars of exploitation of barbarous countries amongst all European nations these last few years; and next as far as we are concerned we are not contented with safe little wars against savage tribes with whom no one but ourselves wanted to meddle, but will even risk wars which may or indeed must in the long run embroil us with nations who have huge armies who no more lack the 'resources of civilization' than ourselves."[2]

In February, 1885, the skirmishes and intrigues in Egypt and the Soudan culminated in the fall of Khartoum and the

[1] Brit. Mus. Add. MSS. 45333. [2] *Ibid.*

death of General Gordon, and the Press turned on its floods of emotion, lamentations over the death of the "Christian Hero" and cries for vengeance, "ready-made from the great vats in Fleet Street and Printinghouse Square".[1] The Provisional Council threw itself athwart the current of Jingoism, distributing in London a thousand copies of a defiant Manifesto: "Citizens, if you have any sense of justice, any manliness left in you, join us in our protest against the wicked and infamous act of brigandage now being perpetrated for the interest solely of the 'privileged' classes of this country. . ." It is typical of the early propaganda that the Leaguers sought less to make common cause with other opponents of the war, than to expose their half-heartedness and to draw the lesson of the character of imperialism from the events. On February 24th a meeting was convened by the Peace Society in the Memorial Hall, with Thomas Burt in the chair. "The promoters of the meeting were half-hearted in their speeches", Mahon reported in *Commonweal,* "and seemed afraid to say anything that would hurt the Government, while the market-hunters, who instigated the war, were allowed to go unscathed." In consequence a Socialist League rider was proposed to the general peace solution, declaring:

> "That this meeting, consisting mainly of working men, is convinced that the war in the Soudan was prompted by the capitalist class, with a view to the extension of their fields of exploitation. And we admit that the victory gained by the Soudanese was a triumph of right over wrong won by a people struggling for their freedom."

The rider was carried with enthusiasm.[2] The same rider was proposed and carried at further meetings, although with more difficulty. On April 2nd a really large peace meeting was held at St. James's Hall, with Bradlaugh in the Chair, and Professors Beesly and Thorold Rogers among the speakers. Once again the speakers, with the exception of Thorold

[1] *Manifesto of the Socialist League on the Soudan War,* four-page leaflet, 1885.
[2] *Commonweal,* April, 1885. Notes by J.L. Mahon, League Secretary.

Rogers, were lukewarm, and avoided any discussion of the underlying causes of the war: once again the League put forward a rider, to which Morris and Mowbray were delegated to speak:

> "And that this meeting believes that the invasion of the Soudan has been prompted solely by the desire to exploit the country in the interests of capitalists and stock-jobbers; and warns the working classes that such wars will always take place until they (the workers) unite throughout the civilized world, and take their own affairs into their own hands."

Bradlaugh announced that he would allow the mover and seconder of the rider five minutes each, and (according to the *Daily News*) William Morris then rose and said:

> "He was convinced that no war had ever been undertaken by the English people that had been more unpopular with the English people than the war in the Soudan. [Cheers.] That was rather a strange thing. The whole English people made the war, and the whole English people condemned it. Why was that? Because they were forced into the war. And who forced them into it? The masters of the English people. And who were their masters? Those capitalists and stock-jobbers of whom he had just spoken, and who could not exist as a class without this exploitation of foreign nations to get new markets. . ."

At this point Morris was called to time by the Chairman, and a lively altercation took place. Morris protested that he had only been allowed two minutes, and Bradlaugh refused to let him continue unless he spoke in the seconder's time. Morris was finally forced to withdraw, and after Mowbray had seconded, Annie Besant had opposed and John Burns had tried to fight his way to the platform, the rider was rejected.[1] Three weeks later the League held their own "well-attended" meeting at the South Place Institute with Morris in the chair. Edward and Eleanor Aveling, Joseph Lane, E.T. Craig, Frank Kitz, Mow-

[1] *Daily News,* April 3rd, 1885: *Commonweal,* May, 1885, Monthly Report (signed W.M.)

bray and Scheu, together with John Burns and H.H. Champion of the S.D.F. were among the speakers. "Comrade Shaw", billed to speak, was not present, finding some objection to the resolutions, and also because "I am G. Bernard Shaw, of the Fabian Society, member of an individualist state, and therefore nobody's comrade."[1]

In the agitation for Irish Home Rule which swept England from 1885 to 1887 the Socialist League took its place side by side with the Radical agitation against the Coercion Bill of the Liberal Government, but took pains to make it clear that it was marching to a different step. "To the Irish", wrote Morris in *Commonweal,* "as to all other nations, whatever their name and race, we Socialists say, Your revolutionary struggles will be abortive or lead to mere disappointment unless you accept as your watchword, WAGE-WORKERS OF ALL COUNTRIES UNITE!"[2] "The Socialist League", Morris noted, "has taken part in all the demonstrations organized by the Irish party, pointing out at the same time that the only real hope of the Irish workmen was that of all workmen throughout the world: Socialism."[3] But, to the ordinary Radical, the League's emphasis must have seemed to have been only upon the second point. In January, 1886, a leaflet was produced, "Home Rule and Humbug", supporting the demand for Irish independence, but turning the whole issue to the Socialist demand, "You must be free from RENT!" Morris went to lecture in Dublin, and wrote in *Commonweal:* "It is a matter of course that until the Irish get Home Rule they will listen to nothing else":

> "I fear it seems likely that they will have to go through the dismal road of peasant proprietorship before they get to anything like Socialism; and that road in a country so isolated and so peculiar as Ireland, may be a long one. . ."[4]

[1] G.B. Shaw to Secretary, S.L., April 13th, 1885, S.L. Correspondence, Int. Inst. Soc. Hist. For the full letter, see J.O. Baylen, "G.B. Shaw and the Socialist League", *International Review Social History,* VII (1962), p. 431.

[2] *Commonweal,* October, 1885.

[3] "Notes on Propaganda", Brit. Mus. Add. MSS. 46345.

[4] *Commonweal,* May 8th, 1886, "Socialism in Dublin and Yorkshire".

In July, 1886, in his regular *Commonweal* "Notes" Morris was analysing (with his usual close eye for detail) the results of the Home Rule Election in which Gladstone had suffered defeat ("To investigate the chances of the elections in detail is rather the business of an election-agent than a human being. . ."). After his customary attack on the "shuffling and intriguing self-seekers" who made up the parliamentary candidates, and on the voters who "consider that when they have voted for the candidate provided for them they have fulfilled all the duties of citizenship", he prophesied that the victors would make a fresh attempt to divide the Irish into "moderates and irreconcilables":

". . . The Irish will be divided indeed, like the familiar demon in the old fable, cut by his unhappy employer into two unmanageable devils; and the more unmanageable will not be asking for a mere Dublin parliament, but will be claiming his right to do something with the country of Ireland itself, which will make it a fit dwelling-place for reasonable and happy people."

Imperialism—this was understood from the very first by Morris and the Leaguers to be the deadliest enemy to internationalism and to the cause of the people at home. The facts of imperialist oppression were ever-present in Morris's mind, and it was from the instruments of this oppression that he once drew one of his most striking images of the reality of the class-struggle underlying the apparent peace of capitalist society. "Do not be deceived by the outside appearance of order in our plutocratic society", he warned:

"It fares with it as it does with the older forms of war, that there is an outside look of quite wonderful order about it; how neat and comforting the steady march of the regiment; how quiet and respectable the sergeants look; how clean the polished cannon; neat as a new pin are the storehouses of murder; the books of the adjutant and sergeant as innocent-looking as may be; nay, the very orders for destruction and plunder are given with a quiet precision which seems the very token of a good conscience; this is the mask that lies before the ruined cornfield and the burning cottage, the mangled bodies, the untimely death of worthy men, the desolated home."[1]

[1] *Works,* Vol. XXIII, p. 186, "Art under Plutocracy" (November, 1883).

IV. The Membership and Commonweal

The fight against Imperialism was taken up with enthusiasm by the Leaguers. But they felt their most serious work to lie elsewhere—in maintaining the propaganda, by means of open-air and public meetings, the sale of *Commonweal,* the distribution of leaflets and sale of pamphlets. William Morris and J.L. Mahon wrote hundreds of letters, from the office of the League, to inquirers and possible contacts of the movement. The message of Socialism was spread from Farringdon Road as far as Lerwick in the Shetlands, while from outlying villages occasional letters of encouragement were received. "I shall go heartily in to support its principles", wrote an agricultural worker from a village in North Berwick,

> "and hope we shall be at a level with the aristocracy before the close of this century. . . This is an agricultural district, & I think if the people had time to consider what Socialists went in for there could be a strong branch formed in this district. But the people are working from 5 in the morning till 7 at night & have not much time to consider much. . ."[1]

The message was sometimes spread by unusual means. A "travelling musician", Joseph Williamson, distributed thirty leaflets a day on his tramps through the Midlands. Charlie Faulkner claimed to have converted the Norwegian Captain and Second Mate of his ship on a trip to Sweden in August, 1885. He also won over a Radical Club in Oxford to the League. "It makes me feel fresh again", he wrote, "to be aiming at something in which I can feel an interest after the miserable, dreary twaddle of university life."[2] Among the letters were several expressing "unbounded admiration & esteem" for William Morris. Fred Pickles, the author of one, and a pioneer of the Bradford Branch of the League, wrote in terms which well express the sympathies and outlook of many

[1] S.L. Correspondence, Int. Inst. Soc. Hist.

[2] *Ibid.,* C.J. Faulkner to Secretary, S.L., February 1st, 1885.

of those who were to become prominent in the League:

> "I am what Mr. Morris would term a 'slave of the Desk' for a firm of Machine Makers (bitterly opposed even to Trade Unions) & I am certain that if they had any idea I sympathized with Socialism I should very soon. . . be unemployed.
>
> "I am a lover of Art, Poetry & Nature, but the major portion of my days have to be spent on a stool, writing 'To Goods', 'By Cash', without end. Outside the Office window I can see nothing but smokey chimneys & ugliness almost unbearable & six yards from my seat is a horribly smelling stream *literally blacker* than the ink I am now writing with."[1]

From Leicester there came an order for *Commonweal* signed, "Thomas Barclay, Wage Slave". "I will do my best to push it among my class. But it is hard. They are ignorant, selfish, apathetic. . ."[2] So the letters poured in—from exceptional manual and agricultural workers, from "slaves of the Desk", from old Owenites and young intellectuals: only the active trade unionists and co-operators were conspicuous by their absence.

The *Commonweal* was the main medium of communication with this variegated membership. It was, indeed, a remarkable paper. Appearing as a monthly (with supplements) from February, 1885, to May 1st, 1886, it then commenced as a weekly: and shortly after this Bax replaced Aveling as sub-editor. Almost every issue included at least one major contribution from Morris. During 1885 *The Pilgrims of Hope* appeared in monthly instalments: during 1886 and 1887 his series of articles with Bax, "Socialism from the Root Up", appeared side by side with *A Dream of John Ball.* From Morris's pen also came articles on art, labour and occasional careful analyses of the political situation and the aims of the Socialists; while in the greater number of issues he contributed the "Signs of the Times", "Notes", or Editorial, which commented in detail upon the political and social scene. Even with-

[1] S.L. Correspondence, Fred Pickles to Secretary, S.L., February 16th, 1885.

[2] *Ibid.*, Thomas Barclay to Secretary, S.L., June 25th, 1885.

out Morris's contributions, the paper would rank among the best of Socialist journals at least until 1888 or 1889. Articles by Bax, the Avelings, Scheu, Sketchley and a score of others were of a high quality.

On the other hand, as a Socialist paper it had serious weaknesses. It never seemed to reconcile the twin tasks of a theoretical journal and a popular propaganda weekly. In fact, Morris seems to have hoped to make it serve both functions. As early as July, 1885, the paper came under criticism as being too difficult and theoretical for general sale. Morris seems to have been worried by the criticism, since he declared at the end of the Annual Conference that "he was very anxious that the literary character of the paper should be maintained. He, for one, could not offer to the workers what he did not himself think good. The journal must be Socialistic."[1] It was the change to the weekly paper which made the dual functions no longer easily compatible. To fill eight solid pages of print a week, more and more long articles were commissioned or accepted: moreover, a great number of these were on interesting side-issues—material far more useful for a monthly journal than for propagandist sales.

Whatever weaknesses there were in this early Socialist propaganda, it was slowly but certainly taking effect. The presence of a Socialist movement was being advertised: it was being noticed in the Press: the ideas of the "share-and-share-alike crowd" were being discussed in the workshops and the Radical clubs. Tom Mann in his engineering shop in 1885 felt that "something was buzzing". For the movement to get out of its infant stage, it was necessary for the Socialists to make contact, not with a few exceptional workers (the authors of the packages of poetry which poured into the *Commonweal* office), but with wider sections of the working class. This is the reason why it was so important that the Socialists took to the streets and the parks. This is also the reason why the authorities felt it was important to drive them back into the

[1] *Commonweal*, August Supplement, 1885.

private rooms and lecture halls from which they had come. And this is the reason why the Socialists, if they were to become a force, had no alternative but to defy the police and stay in the streets in the face of intimidation. The resulting struggles, which continued in London and the provinces until the end of the decade, were the most important form of advertisement for Socialism at this stage of the propaganda.

V. The Fight for Free Speech

The Socialist pioneers took to the street corners with enthusiasm. In 1885 and 1886 Morris led the League into a friendly rivalry with the S.D.F. as to which could keep open the greatest number of open-air pitches in London. Even in the depth of winter, a few of the stands were kept going. The audience did not, of course, gather of its own accord. Regularity, persistence, good speakers, the attention of the police, hecklers in the crowd—all or some of these conditions were necessary before a really good open-air pitch could be established. Often branches were discouraged by disappointing results on a first or second attempt, and had to wind up their courage anew before beginning again. Sometimes it took months before a really suitable site could be found. For all these reasons, Morris—although by no means a gifted outdoor speaker[1] —felt that it was his duty to take a lead in the work by personal example: and to the end of his life it was the outdoor stand which seemed to him the *real* platform of the propaganda.

Morris would go with a few members of the League, James Tochatti or Bernard Shaw (one of the most brilliant of the

[1] Most accounts agree that Morris was an indifferent outdoor speaker. "Anyone can be a public speaker if he only pegs away sufficiently at it", Morris said himself (Compton-Rickett, *op. cit.,* p. 233). Bernstein voices the general opinion on his speaking, indoor and outdoor, when he says: "He could express his ideas in a very arresting manner, but this when speaking to a comparatively small circle in an unconstrained gossiping tone. Rhetoric was. . . not natural to him; his whole nature was. . . anti-rhetorical" (*My Years of Exile,* p. 206).

open-air propagandists, and the best at handling the hecklers) to the stands of the Hammersmith Branch, at Walham Green or Hammersmith Bridge, where audiences of up to 500 were sometimes won. His long-established Sunday breakfasts with the Burne-Joneses were now cut short, and Morris would set off for his duty with a "simplicity which. . . was fine to see". "I am not over inclined for my morning preachment at Walham Green", he wrote once to Georgie,

"but go I must, as also to Victoria Park in the afternoon. I had a sort of dastardly hope that it might rain. Mind you, I don't pretend to say I don't like it in some way or other; like it when I am on my legs, if I flow."[1]

Like it or not, he drove himself on with it: in his provincial lecturing tours he was not only ready to fit in open-air meetings, but insisted that the comrades should arrange to hold them. "Next time I come it had better be later in the year when the weather is more possible", he wrote to Glasier in Glasgow in 1888. "I had a good deal of time on my hands which I might have used for open-air work."[2]

The first serious attack by the police was upon the International Club, in Stephen's Mews, on May 9th, 1885.[3] Very soon the weary round of prosecutions for "obstruction" began in earnest. The centre of interest shifted to Dod Street in Limehouse, where the S.D.F. were using a long-established open-air site of Radical and religious bodies. Several cases of "obstruction" were brought against S.D.F. speakers, and Jack Williams, refusing to pay his fine, was sentenced to a month's hard labour. The League formally offered its help to the S.D.F.—an offer which was warmly accepted. Support among the London Radical Clubs was aroused, and the Defence Committee was transformed into a Vigilance Committee with the powerful backing of the East London United

[1] *Letters*, p. 194. [2] Glasier MSS., April 16th, 1888.
[3] See *Commonweal*, June, 1885.

Radical Club, as well as of the Fabian Society (whose delegate was Annie Besant) and various smaller societies.[1] On Sunday, September 20th, 1885, a great crowd was drawn to Dod Street, and addressed by Hyndman and John Mathias (a prominent Radical) from one end of the street, and by Mahon and Kitz from the other. A resolution was moved protesting against the recent prosecutions. It was only after the meetings had been declared closed, and the crowd was dispersing, that the police suddenly struck, arresting two banner-bearers with some brutality, and seizing others in the crowd.

The scene next day in the Thames Police Court, presided over by a magistrate named Saunders, later became notorious in the Socialist movement. Eight members of the crowd were accused of resisting the police or of obstruction, including Mowbray, Kitz, Mahon and Lewis Lyons, a tailoring worker. Their attitude was defiant. Mahon declared:

> "He went along with others with the distinct intention of holding a meeting there, and, of course, going to prison if he were arrested and charged, and thousands went and would go again with the same intention."[2]

The attitude of Saunders, the magistrate, was scandalous throughout. When Aveling gave evidence on behalf of the accused, Saunders told him that he had broken the law by attending and speaking at the meeting himself, since any such meeting was an "obstruction":

> "DR. AVELING [said] he spoke himself, as he should do again next Sunday.
>
> "MR. SAUNDERS: I advise you not to, or else you will find yourself locked up.
>
> "DR. AVELING: I shall speak there each Sunday till I am locked up."

[1] Circular among S.L. Correspondence, Int. Inst. Soc. Hist.

[2] *Daily News,* September 22nd, 1885.

Eleanor followed suit. The police singled out Lyons for their special favours, at least one of them (as was incontestably shown upon his later appeal) perjuring himself right, left and centre. Saunders capped the whole with a vindictive summing-up, followed by a sentence of two months' hard labour upon Lyons, and 40*s*. or one month upon the remainder. The sentence called forth cries of "Shame" from the spectators, who included Morris, and "a rush of police was made at those in court". According to Aveling's account, the police–among whom the perjured constable was prominent–"commenced an assault upon all and sundry", and in particular upon Eleanor. "William Morris, remonstrating at the hustling and thumping, became at once the chief thumpee. There has rarely been seen anything more brutal than the way in which two or three able-bodied young men fell upon the author of what one of the newspapers called the 'Paradise League'." Morris threatened to summons the police, and promptly found himself under arrest.[1]

The sequel took place two hours later, when the author of *The Earthly Paradise,* "who had been arrested for alleged disorderly conduct was placed at the bar." A constable declared that after the sentence was passed he–

"was endeavouring to restore quiet when the prisoner, who had called out 'Shame', hissed, became very violent, and struck him on the chest and broke the strap of his helmet. . .

"MR. MORRIS: I give a direct negative to that. I certainly did not hit him.

"MR. SAUNDERS: Have you any witnesses?. . .

"MR. MORRIS: I do not know whether there is any one here who saw it. . . I quite confess that when I heard the sentences passed on the prisoners my feelings got the better of me, and I did call out 'Shame'. . . Then this policeman came and distinctly hustled me. When you are pushed you naturally push again, but that is not resisting the police, I turned round and remonstrated with the policeman, but I distinctly assert that I never raised my hands. He was very rough, and I am quite prepared to bring a charge of assault against him.

[1] *Commonweal,* October, 1885.

"MR. SAUNDERS: What are you?

"PRISONER: I am an artist, and a literary man, pretty well known, I think, throughout Europe.

"MR. SAUNDERS: I suppose you did not intend to do this?

"PRISONER: I never struck him at all.

"MR. SAUNDERS: Well, I will let you go.

"PRISONER: But I have not done anything.

"MR. SAUNDERS: Well, you can stay if you like.

"PRISONER: I don't want to stay.

"He was then liberated, and on getting into the street was loudly cheered by the crowd who had gathered there."[1]

It was indeed an unlucky moment for the police when they singled out Morris for arrest. The scene, of course, was a three days' wonder. No amount of editorials taxing Morris with his "indiscretion" or worse could hide the fact that the police persecution was both unjust and inequal. *Funny Folks* carried a cartoon of the police blacking Morris's boots. The dovecots of literature were thrown into a flutter. "Do you see the report of the row the Socialists have had with the police in the East End?" George Gissing wrote to his brother:

"Think of William Morris being hauled into the box for assaulting a policeman! And the magistrate said to him: 'What are you?' Great Heavens!. . . Alas, what the devil is such a man doing in that galley? It is painful to me beyond expression. Why cannot he write poetry in the shade? He will inevitably coarsen himself in the company of ruffians.

"Keep apart, keep apart, and preserve one's soul alive—that is the teaching for the day. It is ill to have been born in these times, but one can make a world within the world."[2]

"The man who wrote 'Daphne'! Oh, it is monstrous!"

The police attack at Dod Street, and the incident of Morris in the Thames Police Court, together did a power of good. The

[1] *Daily News,* September 22nd, 1885.

[2] To Algernon Gissing, September 22nd, 1885 (*Letters of George Gissing to his Family*).

first enraged the feeling of Radicals and Socialists alike. "I am prepared to come armed [next week], and should I be arrested and abused to defend myself as best I can", wrote Robert Banner from Woolwich.[1] The second tickled people's sense of humour, and helped to bring more Radicals behind the Vigilance Committee. Between 30,000 and 50,000 turned up the next Sunday at Dod Street, and Aveling fulfilled his pledge, addressing the crowd together with Hyndman, Shaw, John Burns and leading Radicals. The police, for fear of alienating the whole Radical movement, kept at a discreet distance.

Repercussions of the Thames Police Court incident were felt even as far afield as America, one correspondent writing:

> "The news of Morris's arrest has reached us, and we take that to be the best thing that has happened for a long time. That very day an attempt to suppress free speech was made here, and a League for its defence promptly formed."[2]

Morris's comments on this "best thing" are not recorded. Certainly he saw its humorous side:

> "There was a funny scene in the police station where they charged me, the inspector and the constable gravely discussing whether the damage done to the helmet was 2*d.* or 1½*d.*"[3]

In public he made no comment, but set about the defence of Lyons, making use of attacks upon himself in the Press as an excuse for sending letters on Lyons's case. In private he loathed the notoriety of the whole business. On another occasion, says Shaw,

> "when he had been desperately uncomfortable at a police court, going bail for some of the comrades, I found him rubbing it all off by reading

[1] R. Banner to Secretary, S.L., September 21st, 1885, S.L. Correspondence, Int. Inst. Soc. Hist.

[2] *Commonweal*, November, 1885, Eleanor Marx-Aveling's International Record.

[3] *Letters*, p. 239.

The Three Musketeers for the hundredth time or so. On one such occasion his co-bailsman was Bradlaugh, and he envied the assurance with which that platform athlete ordered everyone about and dominated the police staff as if he had been the Home Secretary. He was nothing of a bully in spite of his pathological temper, and when physical courage came under discussion said: 'I am a funkster; but I have one good blow in me."[1]

If the Socialists had hoped that the Dod Street affair would settle the matter, they were disappointed. "This summer", Morris noted for 1886,

"we were much annoyed by the police who persisted in interfering with our open-air meetings... in the course of the legal proceedings... it was made clear that the law could so be wrested as to make impossible *any* meeting on public ground not specially set apart... Our open-air meetings nevertheless went on briskly: the stations being very numerous."[2]

The persecution was active in the provinces as well, and was certainly part of a national campaign of intimidation.[3] Morris was throughout prominent in the struggle, as bailsman, witness, speaker, and propagandist in the *Commonweal*. The unemployed riots of February, 1886, preluded a fresh bout of prosecutions. Arrests were almost a weekly occurrence, and bail was in constant demand. Sam Mainwaring recalled a prosecution of Kitz in the early days:

"I went to the office of the S.L. in Faringdon Road, and informed the members—who were having a social evening at the hall—of the arrest, and that we wanted bail. Carruthers and Morris left at once with me, and when we arrived at West Ham Police Station I introduced them

[1] G.B. Shaw in the *Observer*, November 6th, 1949.

[2] "Notes on Propaganda", Brit. Mus. Add. MSS. 46345.

[3] The Glasgow comrades commented on "the inordinate regard for the public convenience in the way of keeping vacant pieces of ground and spacious street corners free for the passage of hypothetical vehicles, which our presence invariably excites in the mind of the local policeman" (*Annual Report of the Glasgow Branch of the Socialist League*, May, 1887).

to the inspector on duty as the sureties for Kitz's appearance on the following Monday.

"The officer put the question: 'What is your name?' Our comrade answered, 'William Morris'.

" 'What are you?' queried the officer. But before Morris could reply to this question, Carruthers stepped up to the desk, and in a vehement manner said: 'Don't you know? Why, this is the author of *The Earthly Paradise*.'

"Morris turned to his friend with an astonished look and said: 'Good heavens, Carruthers! You don't expect a *policeman* to know anything about *The Earthly Paradise*, do you?' And, turning to the inspector, said: 'I am a shopkeeper, carrying on business in Oxford Street.' "[1]

Morris knew that his presence embarrassed the police, and made them a little hesitant in their attentions. Consequently, he made a point of taking the platform in the danger-spots himself. Probably the most serious contest in London in 1886 was at Bell Street, Edgware Road, where for nearly two years the Marylebone comrades had been keeping open a pitch. The police seemed determined to make a test case. They chose a site which, unlike Dod Street, was not in the heart of the East End, and where they could get various chemists, publicans and respectable tradesmen to issue complaints. Although the Socialists kept the pavements clear of crowds, plain-clothes men and police agents stood in the footway and refused to move when requested by the speakers. One man, the Socialists alleged in open court, was actually paid by the police to issue complaints. Everything indicated that the police were out for a real "kill": and when, after the first court case, Mainwaring of the League and Jack Williams, the fearless champion of free speech of the S.D.F., addressed a large meeting on July 11th, twenty or thirty mounted police were stationed conspicuously in surrounding streets. Both men were summoned and—instead of being fined summarily by the magistrate—they were committed for trial at the Middlesex Sessions. Sam Mainwaring later recalled with admiration Morris's part in the ensuing struggle:

[1] *Freedom*, January, 1897.

"When we all thought that a long term of imprisonment would be the result, he volunteered to speak in the interval between the committal and trial; and, when reminded of the general impression that imprisonment would be the result, he simply said, 'Well, it will be another experience, and we must not allow the fear of consequences to interfere with our duty.' "[1]

Accordingly, he took the stand at Bell Street the next Sunday, and delivered a characteristic speech:

"After adjuring the people to keep quiet and orderly in the event of the police interfering, he said that he had come to Marylebone to maintain the right of the Socialists to speak in the streets in the same way that people holding other opinions were allowed to do. . . He was impelled to talk to them that morning because the present condition of things was a bad one. He had been asked by a lady the other day why he did not talk to the middle-class. Well, the middle-class had their books with plenty of leisure to read them; the working-classes had no leisure, no books. [At this point Chief Inspector Shephard appeared outside the crowd, and said that he could not get in. This was false, however, and the inspector was immediately made way for by the people, who groaned him heartily as he approached the speaker. Having come to Morris he told him to desist, which Morris refused to do, on which the inspector took his name and address. . .] The middle and upper classes were enabled to live in luxury and idleness on the poverty and degradation of the workers. There was only one way in which this state of things could be altered—society must be turned downside up. A true society meant to every one the right to live, the right to labour, and the right to enjoy the fruits of his labour. The useless class must disappear, and the two classes now forming society must dissolve into one whole useful class, and the labour class become society. In conclusion, he appealed to them to do all they could for the Cause; to educate themselves, to discuss the social question with their fellows, and prepare themselves for the great social revolution."[2]

The speech lasted half an hour, and was heartily cheered, and a summons for obstruction was duly issued.

[1] *Freedom.* See Morris to Carruthers, March 25th, 1886: "I rather expect to learn one more new craft—oakum-picking to wit; though I assure you I don't want to—far from it" (*Letters,* p. 251).

[2] *Commonweal,* July 24th, 1886.

There is no doubt that Morris's intervention embarrassed the magistrate. Mainwaring, who—while still under a writ for the previous case—had officiated for a minute or two at Morris's meeting, came before the court on the same day (July 24th) and his case (like that of Williams) was sent up to the Sessions. But Morris, the magistrate said, "as a gentleman would at once see, when it was pointed out to him, that such meetings were a nuisance, and... would desist from taking part in them." He thought a fine would meet the case—1*s.*! In the event, both Williams and Mainwaring were fined £20, plus a surety for good behaviour of £50; and Williams, as in his previous case, refused to pay and was imprisoned for two months. "The Judge was abhominable", Morris wrote to his daughter. "You would have thought that our friends had at least committed a murder under aggravated circumstances—so bitter an advocate he was against them."[1] The Radicals, alarmed by the February riots, were far slower to come to the defence of the Socialists than at the time of Dod Street, and Morris took them to task. "This is their [the 'reactionists'] revenge for Dod Street", he warned: "their counter-stroke in the war for the free expression of opinion." He pointed to the tendency of the middle classes to take offence at *all* "unseemly" behaviour in the streets, irrespective of opinion:

> "I have noted of late years a growing impatience on the part of the more luxurious portion of society of the amusements and habits of the workers, when they in any way interfere with the calm of their luxury; or to put it in plainer language a tendency to arrogant petty tyranny in these matters. They would, if they could, clear the streets of everything that may injure their delicate susceptibilities... They would clear the streets of costermongers, organs, processions, and lecturers of all kinds, and make them a sort of decent prison corridors, with people just trudging to and from their work."[2]

Temporarily—and as far as London was concerned—the battle for the street corners and the parks was won. It was

[1] *Letters,* p. 257.

[2] "Free Speech in the Streets", *Commonweal,* July 31st, 1886.

won, not by abstract legal decisions or the "liberal tradition", but by the fearlessness of the comrades who came before the courts. It was won, even more, by the persistence of the Socialists. The meetings simply went on, irrespective of the cases. Despite the Bell Street decision, the Marylebone Branch resumed their meetings on a new site at once. Morris himself was busy in August keeping the propaganda going:

"I had a brisk day yesterday. . . though no policeman's hand touched my sacred collar. I went from the Grange to Walham Green where we had a good little meeting attentive and peaceable, back then to the Grange & dinner and then away Eastward Ho to Victoria Park rather sulky at having to turn out so soon after dinner. Though Victoria Park is rather a pretty place (dirty though) and lots of trees. Had a good meeting there also—spoke for nearly an hour altogether in a place made noisy by other meetings near, also a band. . ."[1]

The police had certainly not thrown in their hand. 1887 was to see a frontal attack on the right of meeting in Trafalgar Square. But they were more cautious in their petty local provocations. And there is no doubt that Morris's part in the fight for free speech was an important influence in winning popular sympathy to the Socialist side.

VI. The S.D.F. and the Unemployed Riots

Throughout 1885 and 1886 relations between the S.D.F. and the League were in a fluid state. Apart from the unity of Dod Street relations between the Councils of the two bodies were never good. In May, 1885, the S.D.F. were spreading the tale that the Socialist League,

"was composed entirely of middle-class men, who had no real interest in the workers; that they were not Socialists at all, but anarchists and revolutionists; and that they were all at loggerheads with each other, and were only held together by the influence of William Morris."[2]

[1] *Letters*, p. 258.
[2] Thomas Ewing (Manchester Socialist Union) to William Morris, May 9th, 1885, S.L. Correspondence, Int. Inst. Soc. Hist.

Scheu, Bax, Lane and others, for their part, were equally bitter in their hostility to Hyndman. Morris used his influence to prevent public attacks on the S.D.F. in *Commonweal:* while John Burns and Jack Williams, on their side, were always ready to co-operate with the Leaguers in the fight for free speech, and remained on friendly terms with Morris. Much of the propagandist work done by both bodies was of the same kind, and outside London it was often a toss-up whether provincial bodies affiliated to the S.D.F. or League, or, like the societies in Manchester and Sheffield, remained independent of both. Indeed, there was little reason why the membership of both bodies should not have been drawn into even closer relations if it had not been for the election scandal of November, 1885.

The S.D.F. had put up two propaganda candidates in this first election under the new Reform Act—Jack Williams and Fielding in Hampstead and Kennington. They polled twenty-seven and thirty-two votes respectively. This was bad enough—but worse followed. It leaked out (and was admitted by the Federation) that the candidatures had been backed by "Tory gold": moreover, Hyndman visited Joseph Chamberlain and threatened him with more Socialist candidatures in opposition to the Liberals if he did not promise to support the Eight Hours Bill in the next session. Every word in the statement of the seceders from the Federation seemed to be justified.

The scandal destroyed at a blow the goodwill established between the Socialists and Radicals in the Dod Street affair. Moreover, it exposed the puny strength behind Hyndman's grandiose phrases. Several of the League's Council were filled with "gratified spite",[1] and sought to profit from the S.D.F.'s discomfiture. Scheu became convinced that Hyndman was "a paid agent of the Tories (or liberal-reactionists) for the purpose of bringing Socialism into discredit with the masses".[2] Bax

[1] G.B. Shaw to Andreas Scheu, December 17th, 1885, Scheu Correspondence, Int. Inst. Soc. Hist.

[2] Andreas Scheu to H.H. Sparling (Secretary, S.L.), December 13th, 1885, S.L. Correspondence, Int. Inst. Soc. Hist.

drafted a resolution, against which Morris protested in vain,[1] viewing "with indignation the action of certain members" of the S.D.F. in "trafficking with the honour of the Socialist party", and expressing sympathy with those members who "repudiate the tactics of the disreputable clique concerned in the recent nefarious proceedings".[2] Beyond this, no comment was made in *Commonweal.*

The League's own part in the General Election was confined to the distribution of a new leaflet, *For Whom Shall We Vote?* The leaflet was drafted by Morris,[3] and became adopted for standard use in subsequent elections, since—whatever the issue of the election—the League's policy was the same: "DO NOT VOTE AT ALL!"

> "When those who govern you see the number of votes cast at each election growing less and less, and note at the same time the growth of Socialist bodies... terror will fill their souls, and they must... either use violence against you, which you will learn how to repel, or quail before you and sit helpless... until the time will come when you... will step in and claim your place, and become the new-born Society of the world."

Here, it is clear, is one reason why the majority of those who resigned from the S.D.F. in disgust at Hyndman's intrigues did not throw in their lot with the League. And here, also, are grounds for Engels's complaint to Liebknecht early in 1886:

> "Bax... and Morris are strongly under the influence of the anarchists. These men must pass through this *in corpore vile.* They will get out of it somehow, but it is certainly fortunate that these children's ailments are passing before the masses come into the movement. But so far they are obstinately refusing to come in... You will not bring the numerous working class as a whole into the movement by sermons..."[4]

[1] G.B. Shaw to Scheu, December 17th, 1885, Scheu Correspondence, Int. Inst. Soc. Hist.

[2] *Commonweal,* January 1st, 1886.

[3] William Morris to Chairman, Council of S.L., November 9th, 1885, Int. Inst. Soc. Hist.

[4] Engels to Sorge, April 29th, 1886, *Labour Monthly,* November, 1933.

But—in the meantime—the S.D.F. had taken part in something a good deal more arresting than "sermons". Champion, Burns, Tom Mann and others had for some time been conducting an agitation among the unemployed in the East End. A meeting called in Trafalgar Square for February 8th, 1886, by a curious gang of "Tory Fair Traders" was the occasion for a counter-demonstration of the unemployed called by the S.D.F. Both bodies met in the Square, and a part of the crowd was addressed by Burns, Williams, Champion, Hyndman and Sparling of the League—all of them with a touch of revolutionary bluster which both Morris and Engels thought overdone. In the sequel, the Socialists led the crowds up Pall Mall for a further meeting in Hyde Park. There was some jeering from the clubs. The unemployed retaliated with stones and window-smashing, and then a good deal of indiscriminate damage and looting took place, in which Morris's own shop was lucky to escape.

The next two days of dark, foggy weather were full of monstrous rumours. "If MESSRS. BURNS and HYNDMAN are not arrested already, they ought to be arrested this morning", thundered *The Times* editorial the next day. "No misplaced fear of making martyrs of them ought to stand in the way of their punishment." Its news column for the 10th began: "In the West End yesterday there was something little short of panic. . ." Its editorial declared: "There has been nothing like a panic. . ." Its news column for the following day: "London was yesterday thrown into a state of utter panic. . ." Rumours flew round that the East End was marching through the fog towards the West. All the submerged class-fears and hatred of the bourgeoisie suffered nearly a week of naked exposure.[1] The tradesmen put up their shutters as far afield as Hammersmith and Kilburn. Queen Victoria wrote furious letters to her Home Secretary. 1848 was mentioned in solemn tones. "Sir", one gentleman who had had the misfortune of getting his eye-glasses and carriage windows smashed in the rioting, wrote to *The Times:*

[1] For a sensitive analysis of the significance of this moment, see Gareth Stedman Jones, *Outcast London* (Oxford, 1971).

"I am a subscriber to various charities and hospitals, which I shall discontinue. I have always advocated the cause of the people. I shall do so no more."[1]

But those whose eye-glasses and windows were still intact took a different view. The Mansion House Fund for the unemployed rocketed overnight. Fresh fuel was added to the flames by unemployed demonstrations in Birmingham, Norwich and other centres, and rioting in Leicester. The authorities in Glasgow found work for 895 unemployed in *one day* when the news of the Trafalgar Square riots came through. The middle and upper classes throughout the country reacted as if they had suddenly discovered a foreign army camping in their midst. Charity organizations were thrown up like defence works. "Princess Christian", reported *The Times* on February 12th,

"in view of the extent of the distress in Windsor, is very anxious to organize some cheap dinners for children, and has invited several ladies to assist in carrying out this benevolent object."

The denunciation of the Socialists was unmeasured, even Thomas Hughes (a one-time "Christian Socialist") contributing a shameful letter to *The Times* in which he called them indiscriminately "notorious ruffians", and demanded "a year or two's oakum picking" for "Messrs. Hyndman & Co."[2] By the time his letter was published, summonses had already been served on Hyndman, Champion, Williams and Burns.

The Socialists, indeed, were partly fooled themselves into thinking that they were seeing (in Morris' words) "the first skirmish of the revolution".[3] Hyndman and Champion gave an interview to the *Pall Mall Gazette* in which they spoke of disappearing for six months, and then reappearing "in a much more serious fashion."[4] The state of tension remained at a

[1] *The Times*, February 10th, 1886.
[2] *The Times*, February 17th, 1886. [3] *Commonweal*, March, 1886.
[4] *Pall Mall Gazette*, February 22nd, 1886.

critical point for several weeks. The police, as if to revenge their failure of the 8th, repeatedly attacked peaceful meetings. At a monster demonstration in Hyde Park called by the S.D.F. on February 21st the police (according to *The Times* report) "were compelled to draw their batons and use them without mercy on all who encountered them." One man ridden down by a mounted policeman "received shocking injuries to his face, but it is probable that the rioters will not seek medical assistance. . . for fear of detection."[1]

The Trafalgar Square riots were a sudden test of Morris's ability as a Socialist leader, and also of the sincerity of his revolutionary opinions. Scarcely a month before, the Leaguers had denounced Hyndman & Co. as a "disreputable clique". Moreover, Morris disliked Hyndman's attitude to the unemployed agitation, suspecting that he exploited their misery in an opportunist manner, and put forward unrealistic demands for relief which could only raise false hopes. With the hysteria of the Press, the alarm of middle-class friends,[2] and waverings within the ranks of the Socialist League, it might have been easy for him to dissociate the League from the events of February 8th, and stand aside from the line of fire. A garbled account of a speech at the Hammersmith Liberal Association, which appeared in the *Daily News* on February 11th, and which suggested that he thought the S.D.F. a "dangerous" body and was himself shocked by the riots, provided him with this opportunity. He rejected it with contempt, writing to the *News* to contradict its report, and adding:

> "Under present circumstances I am very loath to be misunderstood: especially. . . when members of the Social Democratic Federation are threatened with prosecution for accidents that accompanied their performance of a duty which I myself have frequently to perform. . ."[3]

[1] *The Times,* February 22nd, 1886.

[2] See his reassuring letter to Edward Burne-Jones, *Letters,* pp. 247-8.

[3] *Daily News,* February 12th, 1886.

On the previous day he had written at greater length to reassure the Rev. John Glasse at Edinburgh:

"As to Monday's riot, of course I look at it as a mistake to go in for a policy of riot, all the more as I feel pretty certain that the Socialists will one day have to fight seriously because though it is quite true that if labour could organize itself properly the enemy could not even dream of resisting, yet that organization could not possibly keep pace with the spread of discontent which will accompany the break-up of the old system... Yet I do not agree with you that Monday's affair will hurt the movement. I think it will be of service: any opposition to law and order in the streets is of use to us, *if the price of it is not too high*... For the rest an English mob is always brutal at any rate until it rises to heroism. Altogether taken I think we must look upon this affair as an incident of the Revolution, and so far encouraging: the shop wrecking was partly a grotesque practical joke (quite in the English manner) at the expense of the upper classes..."[1]

The riots marked for him a break in the docility of the London workers since the Reform demonstrations of 1866—"the surprise of people in finding that the British workmen will not stand everything is extreme."[2] The Council of the League expressed "heartiest sympathy" with the members of the S.D.F. facing prosecution, and Morris himself went bail for Williams and John Burns. That action was in itself sufficient to declare his position.

In the March number of *Commonweal* he made a careful assessment of the situation. His initial analysis was much the same as in his letter to Glasse:

"What was the meaning of it? At bottom misery, illuminated by a faint glimmer of hope, raised by the magic word SOCIALISM, the only hope of these days of confusion. That was what the crowd represented, whatever other elements were mingled with it."

[1] Morris to Glasse, February 10th, 1886, *Unpublished Letters*, p. 2.

[2] *Letters*, p. 251. Morris himself had written to F.S. Ellis shortly before the riots (December 26th, 1885): "As to the British working man, to say truth—he could hardly be faster asleep than he is now... I sometimes fear he will die asleep, however hard the times grow, like people caught frozen" (Mackail Notebooks, Walthamstow MSS).

Some "palliative measures" would, he thought, come of it. Also, "We may be suppressed; practically at least, if not formally":

"Now I should like to say a few words with the utmost seriousness to our comrades and supporters, on the policy of the Socialist League. I have said that we have been overtaken unprepared, by a revolutionary incident, but that incident was practically aimless. This kind of thing is what many of us have dreaded from the first, and we may be sure that it will happen again and again while the industrial outlook is what it is. . . It is above all things our business to guard against the possible consequences of these surprises. At the risk of being misunderstood by hot-heads, I say that our business is more than ever *Education*. . .

"It is too much to hope that the *whole* working class can be educated in the aims of Socialism in due time, before other surprises take place. But we *must* hope that a strong party can be so educated. Educated in economics, in organization, and in administration. To such a body of men all the aspirations and vague opinion of the oppressed multitudes would drift, and little by little they would be educated by them, if the march of events would give us time; or if not, even half-educated they would follow them in any action which it was necessary to take.

"To forge this head of the spear which is to pierce the armour of Capitalism is our business, in which *we must not fail*."

In the absence of such a party, a spontaneous revolt (he continued) would—even if it carried a small Socialist group to power—soon succumb to the counter-revolution:

"The educational process, therefore, the forming a rallying point for definite aims is necessary to our success; but I must guard against misunderstanding. We must be no mere debating club, or philosophical society; we must take part in all really popular movements when we can make our own views on them unmistakeably clear; that is a most important part of the education in organization.

"Education towards Revolution seems to me to express in three words what our policy should be. . ."

Morris fully understood that the tactics of Hyndman were premature. But however "purist" he might be in his theoretical leanings, he viewed events as a revolutionary must do, as they were, and not as he would have liked them to be. "The rudest and most unsuccessful attempts at revolution are better", he wrote two months later, than "the periods of quietude" when the workers "learn a dull contentment with their lot":

"With all genuine revolutionary attempts... we must sympathize and must at the least express that sympathy, whatever risks its expression may subject us to; and it is little indeed if we can do no more than that."[1]

To Georgie Burne-Jones he privately expressed the hope that the "ferment" would sink down again:

"I have often thought that we should be overtaken by the course of events—overtaken unprepared, I mean. It will happen again and again: and some of us will cut sorry figures in the confusion... Things industrial are bad—I wish they would better: their doing so would not interfere with our propaganda, and would give us some chance of getting at working men with intelligence and some share of leisure. Yet if that will not come about, and the dominating classes *will* push revolution on us, let it be! the upshot must be good in the end. If you had only suffered as I have from the apathy of the English lower classes (woe's me how low!) you would rejoice at their awakening, however ugly the forms it took. As to my capacity for leadership in this turmoil, believe me, I feel as humble as could be wished; yet after all it is my life, and the work of it, and I must do my best."[2]

This feeling of his personal inadequacy was always with him:

"I wish I were not so damned old. If I were but twenty years younger. But then you know there would be the Female complication somewhere. Best as it is after all."[2]

[1] *Commonweal*, May 1st, 1886. Editorial by Morris and Bax.

[2] *Letters*, p. 248.

[3] Morris to Edward Burne-Jones, *ibid.*, p. 248.

VII. The League in 1886

The League's support for the S.D.F. in this moment of crisis, the common fight of the two bodies for the freedom of the streets during the summer, co-operation in the annual meeting for the celebration of the Commune—all these augured well for joint action in the future. But Hyndman and the old guard of the L.E.L. were irreconcilable. Morris approached the S.D.F. with the suggestion that the Trafalgar Square meeting on August 29th, 1886, to greet Jack Williams on his release from prison after the Bell Street incident should be a joint affair. From his Olympian heights Hyndman replied in aggrieved tones. Morris *himself* would be welcome as a speaker at the *S.D.F.* meeting (this was one of several attempts by the S.D.F. to "capture" Morris from the League):

"Any ill-feeling that may have existed—as of course I thought not unjustifiable—on my part is *quite* at an end. The reasons our people have for declining joint action with the Socialist League are however sufficient. . .

"At Dod Street there was a distinct breach of faith, and much mischief was made. Then your body passed a resolution and published it in all the capitalist press denouncing us as a 'disreputable gang'. We nevertheless took part in the Commune affair at South Place when every effort was made by Lane the Chairman to snub our men and we were prevented as far as possible from selling our paper in the Hall. After our trial at the Old Bailey one of the men who came up with you the other night—who is always very careful to keep himself out of danger, I notice—denounced Burns, Champion, Williams and myself as 'cowards' in your own rooms. This statement was received with cheers. . . Wherever it has been at all possible your people have tried, as at Hull, Croydon, Hackney, Paddington, and now at Clerkenwell, to break up our Branches. . . Some of these attempts, of which I am sure you are not cognisant, have been of the meanest and dirtiest character.

"All this while, too, two at least of your members, Mahon, now at Leeds, and Aveling, have never lost a chance of vilifying members of our body in the American and other foreign Press. . . How. . . *can* we make common cause with people who are perpetually calling us all liars, rogues, intriguers, etc.? From first to last we have refrained from attacking the League in any way. . ."

The letter then embraced Hyndman's grievances against the Fabians, and Fitzgerald's Socialist Union, and concluded:

"If men act altogether in an anti-Socialist sense surely the mere fact that they call themselves Socialists does not render it incumbent upon other Socialists, who have been throughout the injured party, to run the risk of further insult."[1]

Humph! No mention of the fact that the two comrades Williams and Mainwaring had spoken together at Bell Street, been tried together, and that Morris and Hyndman had together gone to give witness on their behalf. The differences seemed to Morris "preposterously petty", Hyndman "stiff and stately, playing the big man, and complaining of being ill-treated by us, which was a Wolf and Lamb business". "Well, I think I have done with that lot. Why will people quarrel when they have a serious end in view?"[2] In Glasgow, too, the old friction continued, and Morris wrote wearily to Glasier: "I'm sorry to hear about the S.D.F. I thought some of those I saw were good sort of chaps. However, you must take their place now."[3] A comrade in Farnham wrote to *Commonweal* early in 1887:

"We Socialists in small towns or villages. . . feel especially the need of unity and good-feeling, [and] cannot but deplore and feel ashamed of this bad-blooded rivalry, which makes the Cause look ridiculous, and gives occasion to the common enemy to laugh in his sleeve at us. . . It must be comic. . . to witness the complacent swagger of *Justice*, and the occasional mutter of the *Commonweal*, as of some sulky boy who has been teased by his fellows."[4]

What, in fact, had the League achieved in its first two years?

In terms of membership, a slow but gradual increase was to be recorded. Starting with a handful of supporters in January,

[1] Brit. Mus. Add. MSS. 45345. [2] Mackail, II, pp. 162-3.

[3] Glasier MSS., February 3rd, 1887.

[4] *Commonweal*, February 5th, 1887: this comrade was George Sturt, who was to write the great *The Wheelwright's Shop*.

1885, it had climbed by the Annual Conference in July to a membership of about 230, with branches at Hammersmith, Bloomsbury, Merton Abbey, Stratford, North London, Leeds, Bradford, Oxford, and a central branch for the unattached. The Labour Emancipation League was still affiliated, but its Mile End and Stratford branches merged in the League, and only its branch at Hoxton remained independent. The Scottish Land and Labour League had branches at Glasgow and Edinburgh. Of the first number of *Commonweal* 5,000 copies had been sold, but thereafter the circulation dropped to a regular average fluctuating between 2,000 and 3,000.[1] During the next twelve months new branches were opened at Manchester, Oldham, Leicester, Marylebone, Mile End, South London, Dublin, Birmingham, Croydon, Norwich, Hackney and Clerkenwell. At the Annual Conference in June, 1886, nineteen of these branches were represented, and of the five which sent no delegates, only one, Stratford, appears to have been inactive. Not one branch had totally lapsed: moreover, the Scottish Land and Labour League appeared now to be maintaining an existence *alongside* League branches in Edinburgh and Glasgow. No figures were published of the total membership of the League, but Engels (who was well informed) told Bebel in April, 1886, "at the very most the two organizations [S.D.F. and S.L.] have not 2,000 paying members between them nor their papers 5,000 readers".[2] The League could claim half of this readership, and perhaps 600 or 700 of the members.[3]

[1] Sales of *Commonweal* (Hammersmith Minutes) 2,400, March 21st, 1886; 2,600, July 25th, 1886; 2,600 ("a decrease"), August 7th, 1887.

[2] *Marx-Engels Sel. Cor.*, p. 448.

[3] See also H.M. Pelling, *The Origins of the Labour Party*, p. 47 (note). Dr. Pelling refers to "an undated statement of the League signed by J.L. Mahon, and probably referring to summer 1886", which gives the total membership as 393. But since Mahon was no longer Secretary in 1886, this statement must refer to some date in 1885. Membership of the League seems to have progressed from 230 in July, 1885; 393(?), autumn, 1885; 550, January, 1886, to 600 to 700 members in the summer of 1886; but, as Dr. Pelling points out, some of these members were not paid up, and branch membership quotas were not received regularly at Farringdon Road.

In July, 1886, Mahon brought the Hull members of the S.D.F. into the League: and, before the end of the year, further branches were opened at Ipswich, Bingley, Fulham, Hamilton (in the Lanarkshire mining area), Mitcham, and Lancaster. Until the Annual Conference of May, 1887, the League's membership was climbing, and—on the basis of delegation at the Conference—it would seem to have come near to the 1,000 mark. At this Conference new branches were represented from Walsall and North Shields, but those at Stratford, Oldham, Manchester, Marylebone, Mile End, South London, Dublin, Birmingham and Fulham seem either to have merged into other branches or to have lapsed. By the second half of 1886 the League was certainly being outstripped in membership by the S.D.F. in London, the Midlands and Lancashire, and only in Norwich, West Yorkshire and Scotland was it holding or gaining ground. In London at the end of 1886 Hyndman was crowing over the dead body of the League, provoking an unusually angry response from Morris in a private letter to Glasier:

> "As to what he says about the League in London, that be damned! As a party of principle, we are not likely to number as many members as an opportunist body; but we have several solid and increasing branches here. A good South London branch... we Hammersmith chaps have formed a Fulham one now flourishing; Hackney is not bad; Hoxton is good; Mile End is being reorganised: North London is much improved; Bloomsbury is very much so; Mitcham has been set on its legs by Kitz; Croydon is sound, though somewhat sleepy. Of course we ought to do much more, but we are suffering from the lack of energetic initiative men, who are not overburdened with work and responsibilities."[1]

The reluctance of "energetic initiative men" to join the League in 1886 and 1887 can be traced to a number of causes. The leadership of the League was lacking in unity, vigour and organizational ability. The Council was torn by dissension, not only on important political issues, but also upon the most

[1] Glasier, *op. cit.*, p. 187.

trivial questions of personality. Resignations took place almost monthly. In November, 1885, Joseph Lane resigned "from the Council of the League called Socialist" because an offer by a friend to put up a brass plate outside the League's offices had been negatived.[1] In the same month Henry Charles, J.L. Mahon and two others resigned (with better grounds) because Council meetings were "a sheer waste of time", and in protest at "the unwarranted and extravagant expenditure of money by the Council", defrayed chiefly by Morris.[2] At the same time, useful Council members like Frank Kitz and Robert Banner were prevented from attending "owing to want of work, and of course want of money."[3] Finally, in June, 1886, Thomas Binning, in a notable letter of resignation, brought a serious list of accusations against the Council and its proceedings. Meetings, he declared, were disorderly and inconclusive. The League was without either discipline or serious organization. Its affairs were largely dominated by a London faction:

> "I earnestly hope the League is not going to degenerate into a mere Quixotic debating society for the discussion of philosophical fads. I care not how angelic may be the theories of Anarchists or Anarchist-Communists. I contend that the real solid basis of the Revolutionary movement is the economic question... If the League means business let it not waste time in metaphysical subtleties such as the precise shade of difference between 'Rules' and 'Arrangements', etc."[4]

If the centre was indeed as weak as this, there is no cause for wonder that progress was slow.

It should be recalled, however, that Morris held control over *Commonweal*, and into its pages none of these squabbles were allowed to enter. The paper served as a link with a genuine

[1] Joseph Lane to Council, S.L., November 2nd, 1885, S.L. Correspondence, Int. Inst. Soc. Hist.

[2] *Ibid.*, J.L. Mahon to Council, S.L., October 19th, 1885: R. Beckett (Secretary, North London Branch) to Council, December 28th, 1885, etc.

[3] *Ibid.*, R. Banner to Secretary, S.L., April 23rd, 1885.

[4] *Ibid.*, T. Binning to Council, S.L., June 3rd, 1886.

movement both in London and the provinces which deserved a much better leadership than it got. Moreover, it would be an error to pass judgement on the League on the evidence of the proceedings of its London Council alone. The dramatic events of these two years were taking place, not in 75 Farringdon Road, but at the open-air pitches and in the small rooms where Socialist ideas were first reaching the workers. In Leeds, for example, the propaganda was driven forward by Tom Maguire, who was scarcely twenty years old.

This highly gifted young worker picked up a copy of *The Christian Socialist* from the Secular Hall bookstall in 1883. In 1884 Maguire formed a small branch of the S.D.F., and soon made his influence felt. On friendly terms with J.L. Mahon, and a warm admirer of Morris, he brought the eight or ten Leeds Socialists across to the League in January, 1885. Every Sunday open-air meetings were held, at which Maguire was pursued with the "utmost spite" by a section of the Irish Catholics. "We shall live their narrow fury down",[1] he wrote confidently to the Council in September, 1885: and nothing could drive Maguire and his comrades from the streets. Numbering twenty at the most early in 1886, the branch was a centre of propaganda which extended to many points in the West Riding: twice a month four or five of the branch would mix propaganda and pleasure, tramping through the South Yorkshire coalfield or the Dales, holding meetings and selling literature on the way.

Similar ardour was to be found in the early days of the branch at Norwich. The leading spirit here was Fred Slaughter, a young man with a small income which enabled him to run a café as a centre for the movement. Early in 1885 he promoted "The Norwich Pioneer Class for the discussion of Socialism", from which eleven members were drawn to found a branch of the League. A visit from Morris, a correspondence in the Press, and the accession of two able speakers, C.W. Mowbray (from London) and the young Fred

[1] *Tom Maguire: a Remembrance* (1895), p. xiii.

Henderson (from Bradford), brought additional support. As at Leeds, the Norwich Leaguers carried their propaganda to the countryside,

> "and on Friday nights our members have tramped the six miles along a bad road in all kinds of weather, always sure of finding the room filled with men anxious to hear the new gospel. . ."

in the village of St. Faith's.[1] The Norwich Leaguers drove hard for working-class support and headed the unemployed agitation. By Easter, 1886, the branch was drawing audiences of 1,000 to its open-air meetings in the Market Place. From this time onwards, for the next twelve months, its membership rose rapidly.

Leeds and Norwich were among the most successful branches. In other centres, enthusiastic propaganda gave way under the pressure of poverty, apathy or victimization. Edinburgh, which started early in 1885 with a meeting over 500 strong, and a nominal membership of fifty, was reduced to five or six active members in December of the same year. Two if its best speakers, Scheu and A.K. Donald, had left the city. The Secretary was complaining of the apathy of "the mob", and of Edinburgh as the "home of Whiggery and orthodoxy". The branch was crippled by lack of money, and urgently requested another visit from "Mr. Morris, from whose last appearance here we profited to the extent of about 30*s*."[2] At Glasgow the story was more hopeful, and Edinburgh was to see a great improvement in 1887. But at Leicester, after an initial burst of enthusiasm, a similar tale of set-backs was reported: "We, the officers. . . have done all we could to get meetings & members. . . but have got nothing but debts

[1] MS. Notes on the History of Norwich Socialist League, written about 1888, among Nettlau Collection, Int. Inst. Soc. Hist.

[2] J.A. Tait (Secretary, Edinburgh S.L.) to Secretary S.L., December 21st, 1885, S.L. Correspondence, Int. Inst. Soc. Hist. Tait states in this letter that the local Branch of the S.D.F. after a temporary success during the autumn during a visit from J. Hunter Watts was now also reduced to three, four, or six regulars.

for our pains."[1] Money due to the League for *Commonweals* could not be sent in, since the branch had local debts which must be settled first, so that its enemies "could not taunt us with that matter". From Nottingham came a cancellation of an order for the paper: "we are not in a position to bear any loss, being all working men and many out of work."[2] At Huntingdon several workmen "would become members of the League, only they are afraid of their employers. Men in Huntingdon dare not express their honest opinion, in such a hot-bed of Toryism."[3]

It was, however, the *political* weakness of the League which was the prime factor in discouraging its own membership. What did the Leaguers do? The answer is only the propaganda of meetings and the written word. The occasions when the League came into real prominence in 1886 were the result, not so much of its own propaganda, as of the oppression of the police or the agitation of the S.D.F. There was a constant danger of degeneration of several kinds. In the proletarian branches of the East End, "purism" could easily pass into anarchism and bloodthirsty phrase-mongering. Morris was puzzled by these groups. "On Sunday I went a-preaching Stepney way", he wrote to Georgie Burne-Jones in May, 1885. The visit "intensely depressed" him, lecturing to twenty people in a small and dirty room among "the vast mass of utter shabbiness and uneventfulness":

> "It took the fire out of my fine periods, I can tell you: it is a great drawback that I can't *talk* to them roughly and unaffectedly. Also I would like to know what amount of real feeling underlies their bombastic revolutionary talk when they get to that. I don't seem to have got at them yet—you see this great class gulf lies between us. . ."[4]

[1] *Ibid.*, Copeland to Secretary, S.L. (n.d.).

[2] *Ibid.*, J. Proctor Hardie (Secretary, Nottingham and District Social-Democratic League) to Secretary, S.L., March 5th, 1886.

[3] *Ibid.*, E. Boyle to Secretary, S.L., December 7th, 1886.

[4] *Letters*, p. 237.

Morris's fight against reformism and opportunism could easily overbalance into the "bombastic talk" satirized by Gissing in *Demos:*

> "Half measures. . . can only result in delaying the Revolution. . . Away with these palliatives; let us rejoice when we see working men starving and ill-clad, for in that way their eyes will be opened. The brute who gets the uttermost farthing out of the toil of his wage-slaves is more a friend to us and our cause than any namby-pamby Socialist. . ."

This satire was by no means wide of the mark where Kitz and some of the growing anarchist section were concerned. Moreover it found a counterpart among friends of Morris, like Charlie Faulkner of Oxford (dubbed by the *Oxford Magazine* an "alehouse anarchist") who wrote to Lane on behalf of the Oxford Branch in May, 1887, that they had—

> "refused to have anything to do with Parliamentary action. . . The opinion was almost unanimous against having anything less than Revolution. The very idea of mere reform is to keep the present institutions going. For my own part I think all such movements as '8-hours a day' are just as reactionary as allotment schemes. The passing of such measures would, I dare say, take off the immediate pressure and so far would of course have the effect of checking the socialistic movement. It is the Tories who, if they had any brains, would promote such half-hearted legislation. . ."[1]

Branches of the League were also weakened simply by boredom. Again and again they were formed with enthusiasm: sallied out into the streets and sold the *Commonweal:* and then, caught in the endless round of open-air pitch, *Commonweal* sales, lectures, with no prospect of any change until the "Revolution", members began to drop out. Where the branches kept a continually expanding propaganda combined with social activities, they held their membership and were held together by a really remarkable spirit of comradeship. "Our business",

[1] C.J. Faulkner to Joseph Lane, May 18th, 1887, Brit. Mus. Add. MSS. 46345.

related Alf Mattison, "was to make Socialists: to go on making 'em until we had roped in all the human race. In some old way or other our ideal Common-wealth would then come about. . ."[1] But even the finest enthusiasm was bound to flag, especially in London where propaganda outings to the East End had little charm.

Morris's own branch at Hammersmith provides an example of the difficulties imposed on the League by its own purism. From its formation (as a branch of the Democratic Federation) in June, 1884, until the end of 1886, no fewer than 117 members were posted, and of these one only resigned formally. Yet, in August, 1886, only forty members were paid up and in "good standing", while its Annual Meeting in March, 1887, had to be adjourned because only twelve were in attendance—and when it was resumed in April the attendance was nine.[2] But at the same time, the open-air propaganda was going briskly, with audiences of 200 and more at Walham Green in the worst winter months, and good sales of *Commonweal*, while the regular Sunday evening lectures in the Hammersmith clubroom were well attended.

Since the propaganda was largely "educational" (and it was clear that the "Revolution" was not imminent) the League seemed rather safer to some of the timid than the S.D.F. Discussions tended to become abstract and detached from events. Moreover, when a lecture was to be held every week, it could not deal with the same fundamental principles again and again. Between October, 1886, and October, 1887, there was a marked tendency for the Hammersmith branch to include more cultural subjects among their lectures, and to fetch in outsiders more frequently.[3] Gissing (an unfriendly observer) who was visiting branches of the League for "copy"

[1] *Leeds Weekly Citizen*, October 4th, 1929. [2] Hammersmith Minutes, *passim.*

[3] Lecturers at Hammersmith over this period included G.B. Shaw (several times), Graham Wallas (Education), Sidney Webb (Economic Rent), Bax (The New Ethic), Walter Crane (The Architecture of Art), Ernest Rhys (The New Poetry), Mrs. Bland, Hubert Bland and Sidney Olivier, as well as League speakers on more immediate topics.

in 1886, noted the tendency in Hammersmith:

"The people who occupied the benches were obviously of a different stamp from those... at the Hoxton meeting place. There were perhaps a dozen artisans of intensely sober appearance, and the rest were men and women who certainly had never wrought with their hands... Of the men other than the artisans the majority were young, and showed the countenance which bespeaks meritorious intelligence rather than ardour of heart or brain... It needed but a glance over this assembly to understand how very theoretical were the convictions that had brought its members together."[1]

Engels wrote to Bebel in August, 1886: "Still practically nothing doing",

"... as many sects as heads... The S.D.F. has at any rate a programme and a certain discipline, but it has absolutely no support among the masses... The League is passing through a crisis. Morris... has fallen headlong over the phrase 'revolution' and become a victim of the anarchists. Bax is very talented and understands something—but after the fashion of philosophers has concocted his own form of socialism which he takes for the true Marxist theory and does a lot of damage with it. However, this is an infantile disease in his case and will pass, it is only a pity that this process is being gone through in public. Aveling is forced to work so hard for his daily bread that he also is not able to do much studying; he is the only one I meet regularly."[2]

At the end of November, 1886, Engels wrote to Sorge that "the labour movement is beginning here, and no mistake", but the Socialist League "has embarked on a dogfight with the anarchists and has no time to take an interest in the living movement going on under its very nose". That dog-fight was to go on for two years. And when it was finished with, the League was to all intents and purposes a dying organization.

[1] G. Gissing, *Demos,* Ch. XVII.

[2] Engels to Bebel, August 18th, 1886, *Labour Monthly,* December 1933.

VIII. William Morris, Agitator

One fact stands beyond question in these two years of propaganda—the personal example of William Morris. In October 1886 he wrote to Georgie Burne-Jones, in a humorous reference to Lane and his party, who rejected all leadership on principle:

> "In spite of all the self-denying ordinances of us semi-anarchists, I grieve to have to say that some sort of leadership is required, and that in our section I unfortunately supply that want."[1]

His official position was that of Treasurer (until his place was taken by Philip Webb) and Editor of *Commonweal.* The League had no Chairman, and the paid full-time Secretary was an executive officer. If anyone was to keep a constant check on all decisions, give advice to branches, and shape a consistent policy, it had to be Morris.

He did it without complaint. It is absolutely impossible to understand how he found time for all his activities, at the same time keeping some supervision over the Firm, and (before the end of 1886) launching on a translation of Homer. In these two years he wrote *The Pilgrims of Hope, A Dream of John Ball,* and the first part of *Socialism From the Root Up:* articles, notes and editorials for *Commonweal:* he delivered something like 120 lectures, about fifteen of which (at the least) were written out in long-hand and are permanent contributions to Socialist theory: he attended the weekly Executive Council meeting of the League, the Ways and Means Committee, and goodness knows how many other meetings besides: he made tours of the provinces, breaking new ground, and consolidating old branches—Dublin, Scotland, Yorkshire and Lancashire, the Potteries, East Anglia and a dozen other centres. He was present at sixty out of the ninety-nine meetings of the *Committee* of the Hammersmith

[1] Mackail, II, p. 149.

Branch, at some of which only two or three others troubled to attend: and in addition was often in the Chair at the Sunday evening lectures—if he was not lecturing elsewhere himself. He spoke at scores of open-air meetings, chaired them, carried the banner, sold literature, took round the hat for collections. He acted as a sandwichman, between placards advertising *Commonweal.* He gave a hand with the smallest mechanical details of office or branch organization, and wrote basketfuls of correspondence. He edited *Commonweal.* He attended the police-courts. He drew up balance-sheets, and subsidized the movement with his money. He helped with social evenings, gave readings of his own work or wrote special poems, entertained speakers, and made personal contacts with people sympathetic to the movement.

" 'Tis all meeting and lecture, lecture & meeting with a little writing interspersed", he wrote to his daughter Jenny. [1] Successive biographers have lamented this waste of Morris's energies. They need not have troubled. Morris himself gave the answer to them, when, lying on his back crippled with gout after the Dod Street affair, Georgie Burne-Jones tried to persuade him to give up his active propagandist work:

> "You see, having joined a movement, I must do what I can while I last, that is a matter of duty... All this work I have pulled upon my own head, and though in detail much of it is repulsive to the last degree, I still hold that I did not do so without due consideration. Anyhow, it seems to me that I can be of use, therefore I am impelled to make myself useful...
>
> "You see, my dear, I can't help it. The ideas which have taken hold of me will not let me rest: nor can I see anything else worth thinking of. How can it be otherwise, when to me society, which to many seems an orderly arrangement for allowing decent people to get through their lives creditably and with some pleasure, seems mere cannibalism; nay worse... is grown so corrupt, so steeped in hypocrisy and lies, that one turns from one stratum of it to another with hopeless loathing. One must turn to hope, and only in one direction do I see it—on the road to Revolution: everything else is gone now..."[2]

[1] *Letters,* p. 255. [2] *Ibid.,* pp. 241-2.

CHAPTER V

THE SOCIALISTS MAKE CONTACT WITH THE MASSES, 1887-1888

I. "Staying power is what we want"

1887 and 1888 are the years of the confluence of the small clear-water stream of Socialist theory with the broad waters of the labour movement. Everywhere there were eddies, back-waters, cross-currents. Although Socialist opinion was spreading rapidly during these years, there was no comparable increase in the membership of either the S.D.F. or the Socialist League. Indeed, one consequence of the penetration by the Socialists of the mass movement was the disintegration of the two Socialist bodies themselves. One after another some of the most gifted propagandists—H.H. Champion, John Burns, the Avelings, Tom Mann, J.L. Mahon, Tom Maguire, and many others—were being forced by events to loosen their organizational ties with the Federation or the League in order to make contact with the working class in their own organizations. By contrast, the dogmatism of the S.D.F. and the anarchist-tinged purism of the League were increasingly forming a back-water aside from the direct currents of the mass movement. And William Morris, although one of the few men respected on nearly every side of the Socialist Movement, was finding himself reduced to being the prisoner of an Anarchist tail.

Already by the early months of 1887, some of Morris's first fervour had spent itself, and he looked on the prospect ahead with foreboding. He did not abate the work of the propaganda. But he had come to realize more of the forces pitted against it. The "Revolution" seemed less and less likely to occur in his own life-time. Early in February he took a short holiday ("I don't know what a long one means")[1] at Rottingdean, and

[1] See Mackail, II, p. 172.

wrote an article, "Facing the Worst of It", for *Commonweal,* which he felt to be somehow unsatisfactory.[1] "Though we Socialists", he wrote, have "full faith in the certainty of the great change coming about, it would be idle. . . to prophesy. . . the date. . . and it is well for us not to be too sanguine, since overweening hope is apt to give birth to despair if it meets with. . . disappointment". Two forces, he said, were making for Socialism–first, the inner disintegration of capitalist society, which although it is now "sweeping onward to the sea of destruction. . . yet it may itself create checks–eddies. . . in which we now living may whirl round and round a long time". At the same time,

> "although commercial ruin *must* be the main stream of the force for the bringing about revolution, we must not forget the other stream, which is the *conscious* hope of the oppressed classes, forced into union. . ."

Most of the article was given up to an analysis of the ways in which "the onward course of capitalistic commerce to its annihilation" might be delayed, and he took a view more sober and far-seeing than most of his contemporaries. The three main possibilities he felt to be:

> "1st. The lessening of stocks and consequent slight temporary recovery; 2nd, A great European war, perhaps lengthened out into a regular epoch of war; and 3rd, The realization of the hopes of important new markets, which hopes are the real causes of hostility between nations."

Apart from these three–recurrent and temporary trade recovery, war, and the opening of fresh markets–Morris referred to "more speculative possibilities. . . which would lead to more ruin and suffering than even those. . ."

These three possibilities, Morris felt, were not without

[1] *Socialist Diary,* Brit. Mus. Add. MSS. 45335: "Did. . . an article for *Commonweal* which. . . was weak, long and no use."

opportunities for the Socialist, if the other current, that of conscious and organized hope could be brought to hasten the downfall of capitalism.

A great European war would "give a great stimulus to trade while it lasted; just as if half London were burned down, the calamity would be of great service to those who were not burned out". But, Morris reminded the comrades, "only the most short-sighted of the capitalists can pray for war in the times we are now in... because behind the brilliant 'respectable' war stands its shadow, revolution".

> "And yet though they may dread war, still that restless enemy of the commercial system, the demon which they have made, and is no longer their servant but their master, forces them into it in spite of them; because unless commerce can find new capacities for expansion it is all over... the one thing for which our thrice accursed civilization craves, as the stifling man for fresh air, is *new markets;* fresh countries must be conquered by it which are not manufacturing and are producers of raw material, so that 'civilised' manufactures can be forced upon them. *All wars now waged, under whatever pretences, are really wars for the great prizes in the world market.*"

From these three possibilities, Morris envisaged a fourth—a labour movement subsidized by the pickings of imperialism and war and content with limited reform. "The claims of non-Socialist workmen go little beyond the demand for a bigger ration, warmer coat, and better lodging for the slave; and even Socialist workmen, I think, are apt to put their claims too low." The job of organized Socialists under all conditions, he urged, was to "aid the *conscious* attacks on the system by all those who feel themselves wronged by it":

> "It is possible that we may live to see times in which it will be easier than now for the labourer to live as a labourer and not as a man, and there is a kind of utilitarian sham Socialism which would be satisfied by such an outcome of times of prosperity. It is very much our business to meet this humbug by urging the workers to sustain steadily their due claim to that fullness and completeness of life which no class system can give them."[1]

[1] "Facing the Worst of It", *Commonweal*, February 19th, 1887.

The article voiced a mood less apocalyptic than that of "The Day is Coming". "I am glad to hear that you are getting *solid* up there", Morris wrote to Glasier, of the Glasgow branch, in January, 1887. "Staying power is what we want, the job before us being so egregiously long." "What I am on the look-out for is the *staying* qualities", he re-emphasized in April, 1888, although he added: "I believe we shall yet make a good fist at it even while we live."[1] Faced with the long perspective of struggle ahead, Morris placed even more emphasis upon Socialist education—the formation of a band of comrades, proof against any seduction they might meet with on the way.

II. "Jonah's View of the Whale"

"I am writing a diary", Morris wrote early in 1887 to his daughter, Jenny, "which may one day be published as a kind of view of the Socialist movement seen from the inside, Jonah's view of the whale, you know. . ."[2] The diary runs from the end of January to April, 1887.[3] Day by day Morris's part in the movement is recorded—the round of lectures, open-air meetings, committees—and some of the reasons for his discouragement when he wrote "Facing the Worst of It" are made plain.

The diary opens on January 25th:

> "I went down to lecture at Merton Abbey last Sunday: the little room was pretty full of men, mostly of the labourer class: anything attacking the upper classes directly moved their enthusiasm; of their discontent there could be no doubt or the sincerity of their class hatred; they have been very badly off there this winter, and there is little to wonder at in their discontent, but with a few exceptions they have not yet learned what Socialism means. . ."

[1] Morris to Glasier, January 27th, 1887, April 16th, 1888, Glasier MSS.

[2] Mackail, II, p. 169.

[3] Brit. Mus. Add. MSS. 45335. Some passages were published by Mackail, II, pp. 169-80.

Again and again the same note is struck. On January 27th he spoke at a meeting of the Hammersmith Radical Club called to condemn new evictions in the Highlands. The room was crowded and his speech was well received, but—he comments:

"I thought the applause rather hollow as the really radical part of the audience had clearly no ideas beyond the ordinary party shiboleths, and were quite touched by Socialism: they seemed to me a very discouraging set of men, but perhaps can be got at somehow: the frightful ignorance and want of impressibility of the average English workman floors me at times."

On February 4th he was at another Radical Club, this time at Chiswick, where he was called upon to open a debate on the Class War before an audience of twenty, which swelled later to forty:

"The kind of men composing the audience is a matter worth noting, since the chief purpose of this diary is to record my impressions on the Socialist movement. . . The speakers were all either of the better-trade workmen or small tradesmen class. . . My Socialism was gravely listened to by the audience but taken with no enthusiasm; and in fact however simply one puts the case for Socialism one always rather puzzles an audience: the speakers. . . were muddled to the last degree; but clearly the most intelligent men did not speak. . . I was allowed a short reply in which I warmed them up somehow: this description of an audience may be taken for almost any other at a Radical Club. . . The sum of it all is that the men at present listen respectfully to Socialism, but are perfectly supine and not inclined to move except along the lines of radicalism and trades unionism. . ."

The same week the Hammersmith Branch re-started their open-air meetings:

"I spoke alone for about an hour, and a very fair audience (for the place which is out of the [way]) gathered curiously quickly; a comrade counted a hundred at most. This audience characteristic of small open-air meeting also quite mixed, from labourers on their Sunday lounge to 'respectable' people coming from Church: the latter inclined to grin: the working men listening attentively trying to understand, but mostly failing to do so: a fair cheer when I ended, of course led by the 3 or 4 branch members present. The meeting in the evening poor. . ."

On Saturday, February 12th, he notes: "I have been on League business every night this week till to-night." On Monday he was at the weekly Council meeting of the League—"peaceable enough & dull". On Tuesday he took the chair at a joint meeting of Socialists and Anarchists of various groups to protest at the threat of a European war. The Anarchist followers of Kropotkin refused to participate.

"on the grounds that Bourgeois peace is a war, which. . . is true enough: but of course the meeting was meant to be a protest against the Bourgeois whether in peace or war, and also to keep alive the idea of a revolt behind the bourgeois and Absolutist armies if a war did happen."

On Wednesday he was lecturing at a schoolroom in Peckham High Street "for some goody-goody literary society or other". However, the meeting of about 100 was "quite enthusiastic" and 30*s.* were collected for the *Commonweal* printing-fund. On Thursday he was at the Ways and Means Committee of the League: "found them cheerful there on the prospects of *Commonweal.* I didn't quite feel as cheerful as the others, but hope it may go on." On Friday he returned to the Chiswick Radical Club, to conclude the debate opened on the previous Friday. Sunday he was once again at the open-air post, speaking in a very cold north-east wind to about sixty people: and in the evening was lecturing at the Hammersmith League Clubroom on "Medieval England".

This is a typical week of his London propaganda, the days being spent in writing for and editing *Commonweal,* correspondence, the affairs of the Firm, and—as a stolen luxury—a spell of work on the Homer. Visits to the struggling League branches were rarely encouraging. On Sunday, February 13th, he visited the new Branch in Mitcham:

"Spoke extemporary to them at their club-room, a tumble-down shed opposite the grand new workhouse built by the Holborn Union: amongst the woeful hovels that make up the worse (and newer) part of Mitcham, which was once a pretty place with its old street and greens and lavendar fields. Except a German from Wimbledon (who was in the chair) and two others who looked like artisans of the painter or small builder type, the audience was all made up of labourers and their wives: they were very quiet and attentive except one man who was courageous from liquor, and interrupted sympathetically; but I doubt if most of them understood anything I said; though some few of them showed that they did by applauding the points. I wonder sometimes if people will remember in times to come to what a depth of degradation the ordinary English workman has been reduced; I felt very downcast amongst these poor people in their poor hutch whose opening I attended some three months back (and they were rather proud of it). There were but about 25 present: yet I felt as if I might be doing some good there: the branch is making way amongst a most wretched population."

On Sunday, March 13th, he visited the Hoxton Branch (Labour Emancipation League), and "rather liked it".

"A queer little no-shaped slip cut off from some workshop or other, neatly whitewashed, with some innocent decoration obviously by the decorator member of the branch: all very poor but showing signs of sticking to it: the room full of a new audience. . . all working men except a parson in the front row, and perhaps a clerk or two, the opposition represented by a fool of the debating club type; but our men glad of any opposition at all. I heard that our branch lecture was a wretched failure. The fact is our branch, which was very vigorous a little time ago, is sick now; the men want some little new thing to be doing or they get slack in attendance. I must try to push them together a bit. . ."

The next Tuesday week he was lecturing on "Feudal England" at the Hammersmith Radical Club: "9 people for audience! the fact is this is a slack time for lectures." On Sunday, March 27th, he had a better audience, but still felt dissatisfied:

"I gave my 'Monopoly' at the Borough of Hackney Club, which was one of the first workmen's clubs founded, if not the first; it is a big

Club, numbering 1,600 members: a dirty wretched place enough, giving a sad idea of the artizan's standard of comfort: the meeting was a full one, and I suppose I must say attentive, but the coming and going all the time, the pie-boy and the pot-boy was rather trying to my nerves: the audience was civil and enclined to agree, but I couldn't flatter myself that they mostly understood me, simple as the lecture was. This was a morning lecture, over about 2 o'clock: I went afterwards. . . to the Hackney Branch as I had to speak at the 'free-speech demonstration' in Victoria Park: dined on the way off 3*d.* worth of shrimps that I bought in a shop & ate with bread & butter & ginger beer in a coffee shop, not as dirty as it looked from outside."

It is a curious and moving situation. Morris was trying to fill the role of the active agitator, and yet his reputation as a poet and artist and his class background were standing in his way. To some degree he did not understand the people he most wanted to reach. Until he became a Socialist he had viewed the working class from a distance. His grasp of Socialist theory had led him to see the workers as the revolutionary force within society—the men who were Chartists, Communards, and from whom the Socialist Party must be built. But he was no romancer, and as he made these long journeys by underground and by horse-tram into the most depressed regions of the East End, the intellectual and spiritual deprivation of the workers weighed upon his senses. The impoverishment of the lives of the people of the East End evoked in him feelings, not of patronage, but of shame: "a sense of shame in one's own better luck not possible to express—that the conditions under which they live and work make it difficult for them even to conceive the sort of life that a man should live."[1]

He struggled hard to express his meaning in the simplest terms. Preparing a talk for the Mitcham branch ("a rather rough lot of honest poor people"), he commented: "I shall have to be as familiar and unliterary as I can."[2] If he caught

[1] "Facing the Worst of It", *Commonweal,* February 19th, 1887.

[2] Morris to his daughter, Jenny, February 18th, 1887, Brit. Mus. Add. MSS. 45339.

himself parading his own knowledge, he was severely self-critical. But he preferred to regard his audiences as his intellectual equals rather than to suggest the least shade of condescension. His lectures were simple in expression, but his manner was to deal in broad historical generalizations, which were strange to the average Radical working-class audience.

As an agitator, Morris could not help but be an amateur. This does not mean that his profound and imaginative lectures were wasted. Born agitators like Tom Mann and John Burns, skilled open-air speakers like Maguire and Mahon, learned much of their Socialist theory, and gained something of their vision, from them. But the lectures were not suited for agitation among the masses. Morris's ideas could only reach the broad working-class movement through the medium of translators.

III. The Northumberland Miners

The test of the League's maturity came in its reaction to the industrial struggles in the first months of 1887—and, in particular, to the great miners' strikes in Lanarkshire and in Northumberland. The Council of the League was not indifferent to industrial battles in the first two years of its existence: but it regarded them in the main as opportunities for general Socialist propaganda. In September, 1886, a Strike Committee was set up, and in its first eight months, 23,000 leaflets were distributed in strike centres. The strikers may, it is true, have sometimes been at a loss to decide whether they were being approached by enemies or friends. "Fellow Workers", declared the League's standard strike leaflet:[1]

> "You are now on strike for higher wages or against a reduction in your already small wage. Now, if this strike is but to accomplish this object and nothing more, it will be useless as a means of permanently bettering your condition, and a waste of time and energy, and will

[1] *Strikes and the Labour Struggle,* issued by the Strike Committee of the Socialist League (1886).

entail a large amount of suffering on yourselves, your wives and families, in the meantime.

This must have seemed suspiciously like the bosses' line. But the League had encouragement to offer as well:

"If, on the other hand, you intend to make this a starting-point for a complete emancipation of the labourers from the thraldom of the capitalists, by bringing about the solidarity of the workers—employed and unemployed, skilled and unskilled—if you intend to learn why we the wealth-producers are poor, and what is the remedy,—then we Socialists welcome you as comrades... But if you are looking for a small betterment of your own condition only—if you are content to attempt to fight this question with your sectional trades' unions—then we feel that it is a duty that we owe to our class and to you to show you that it is a hopeless fight."

The hopelessness of the fight was then explained for a good part of the leaflet, and a positive alternative suggested. This was the old recipe of the purists in the League: first, education in Socialism: second, the organization of a great federation of labour (national and international) in preparation for the Day:

"Then when the crisis comes they will be able to rise as one man and overthrow this system of exploitation, and all class-hatred will cease and men live federated together as brother workers the world over."

"UNION among ALL workers" was becoming the slogan of the Leaguers, and the one aim set before all trades unionists was the General Strike for Socialism. To such mere incidents on the way to this goal as the bitterly-fought miners' strikes in S. Wales, Scotland and Northumberland, many of the Leaguers gave only absent-minded sympathy. "You must incessantly aim at... *common action among all workers*", the Glasgow Branch declared in a Manifesto at the time of the strike of the Lanarkshire miners:

> "*When the Miners resolve to demand an advance, let it be understood that, should it not be conceded, every riveter would lay down his hammer, every joiner his plane, every mason his trowel.* Let it be known that every railway guard, porter, signalman, and driver folded his arms; that every baker refused to make his dough, every cook refused to make dinner, and every maid refused to wait at table... One day, or at most two days, of this paralysis would bring the holders of capital and spoilers of labour to their senses and their knees. *One general strike would be sufficient... This perfectly fair, impartial, and non-confiscatory policy should commend itself to all reasonable people.*"

Having put forward this impartial, non-confiscatory policy for reasonable people to meditate upon, they advised the miners "not to lose either heart or head", not to indulge in "deeds of aimless violence", and asked them to recognize that their present struggle was "but a prelude" to the "great Revolution".[1]

The irony of the situation lies in this: already in 1887 sections of the workers were showing marked signs of sympathy with the Socialists. In February, 1887, when the Glasgow Branch called a demonstration on the Green in support of the striking Lanarkshire miners, over 20,000 attended: the miners' leaders spoke from the same platform as the Leaguers: a collection for the miners of £23 was taken. On a subsequent Sunday the Edinburgh League and S.D.F. followed suit, before an audience of 12,000.[2] Further collections were made by the League in other parts of the country, and relations between the miners and the Socialists improved with great rapidity. But the League did not learn from its experience. The Glasgow demonstration was only a flash in the pan. The miners went back, and soon the League was back to its old exhortations—Utopian in form, but in actual effect and tone defeatist. A branch of the League had been formed with brilliant prospects in the mining town of

[1] *Manifesto of the Glasgow Branch of the Socialist League to the People of Scotland* (1887).

[2] See *Annual Report* of the Glasgow Branch (May, 1887), pp. 4-50.

Hamilton during the strike, forty miners enrolling at the first meeting: but when Morris visited it in April it was already in a dismal state:

"We went to Hamilton", he noted in his diary, "the centre of the coal-mining district: the miners had gone in on a sort of compromise, but were beaten in point of fact: so it is hardly to be wondered at that this was a depressing affair: we met in an inn parlour some members of the Branch which seems to be moribund, and they would scarcely say a word and seemed in the last depths of depression: the hall, not a large one, was nothing like full: it was a matter of course that there was no dissent, but there was rather a chilly feeling over all."

Among those present were the Secretary and President of the Hamilton miners, who actually moved and seconded the resolution in favour of Socialism which the meeting carried unanimously.[1] Morris appears to have failed to realize either the importance of the possibilities opened up by this foothold in the coalfields or the gravity of the defeat.

It was the ambiguity of the League's attitude to industrial matters which was decisive in causing its failure in 1887 and 1888 to organize the opinion in favour of Socialism which was spreading among the workers. The impossibility of preaching purism to workers engaged in bitter class struggles was illustrated clearly in the dilemma of the young agitator J.L. Mahon. After resigning from the Council at the end of 1885, Mahon was replaced as Secretary of the League by H. Halliday Sparling. Returning to Leeds and to Hull (where he swung the S.D.F. branch into the League), he was "systematically boycotted by the employers" and barred from his work as an engineer.[2] In January, 1887, he started a tour of the Midlands and the North, still a convinced partisan of the "anti-parliamentary" side. The Socialists of Nottingham he ridiculed as "mere politicians. . . anxious to shine on School boards or town councils: with perhaps vague & distant dreams of parliament." In the first fortnight of February he went on to

[1] *Commonweal*, April 16th, 1887. [2] *Hull Critic*, July 26th, 1890.

Lancashire, held some successful propaganda meetings, and made friendly contact with local branches of the S.D.F.: the futility of carrying the London quarrel into the provinces began to work in his mind. His ready reception the next week from the chain-makers on strike at Cradley Heath and Walsall, and among the Derbyshire miners, strengthened his feeling that the movement outside London was on the eve of great advances.

> "Socialism should be before the miners & iron workers *now* of all times. Durham or Northumberland are more important than 20 Londons. . . I suppose it will be too much to expect Londoners to see the importance of anything outside the area of their abominable fogs."[1]

Meanwhile, a bitter strike of the Northumberland miners—provoked by lock-outs by the mine-owners in an attempt to enforce a 12½ per cent. reduction in wages—was in progress. Early in March Mahon visited Newcastle, and he decided to stay. John Williams and J. Hunter Watts of the S.D.F. had arrived several days before, and the propagandists found they could work "quite harmoniously" together. Mahon reported that the miners were coming to Socialist meetings in "great crowds", the smallest meetings being four or five hundred strong, the largest up to 2,000. "A county demonstration in favour of Socialism is being arranged", he reported, and "steps for founding an organization in the northern counties are going rapidly forward."[2]

> "Next Sunday, a conference will be held in Newcastle, and miners from a number of collieries and towns of Northumberland and Durham will attend. As members of the Socialist League and Social Democratic Federation have worked equally hard in the district, it would be unwise to force one organization on to the exclusion of the other. . . My own opinion is that a local society, say the North of England Socialist

[1] J.L. Mahon to S.L. Council, February 19th, 1887, S.L. Correspondence, Int. Inst. Soc. Hist., and *Commonweal*, March 12th, 1887.

[2] J.L. Mahon to S.L. Council, March 19th and 26th, 1887.

Federation should be formed and issue its own rules, etc. That both London parties and papers should be treated exactly alike, while no official connection should be formed with either. When the reunion and consolidation of the Socialist movement takes place, the local body could join the reunited forces. . . In 1888 the United Socialists could hold their first conference in Newcastle-on-Tyne. . ."[1]

Mahon, hearing that Hyndman was coming up to speak at the miners' county demonstration on Easter Monday, sent an urgent message requesting that Morris also should come. Morris was at the time conducting a propaganda tour of his own in Scotland, under the auspices of the Glasgow Branch, but he agreed reluctantly to break his journey at Newcastle on his return. His tour had been a fair success, with the exception of the damp reception by the dispirited miners at Hamilton, and he had himself made some contact with the rising mood of the people. He had had several good meetings in Glasgow, and useful ones in Dundee, Edinburgh and Paisley.[2] On Saturday, April 9th, he took part in a propaganda outing to Coatbridge, speaking on a cinder-tip to an audience of about sixty miners and steel-workers to the accompaniment of a Salvation Army meeting and a cheap-jack selling linoleum and wall-papers: "all this we did by star and furnace light, which was strange and even dreadful": but the meeting put him in good heart, from the earnest attention of some of the miners.[3] The next day, before leaving for Newcastle, he spoke at a very successful open-air meeting on Glasgow Green, where Socialist and anti-coercion resolutions were passed before an audience of over 1,000. He noted in his diary:

"The audience quite enthusiastic. The Glasgow Branch is in good condition apparently, are working hard, & getting a good deal of support. There are some very nice fellows amongst them; they are a good deal

[1] J.L. Mahon to S.L. Council, April 2nd, 1887.

[2] There is a full account of this propaganda trip to Scotland in his *Socialist Diary,* and anecdotes from it are recounted in Glasier, pp. 72-83, "A Propaganda Outing". See also *Letters,* pp. 269-71, and *Commonweal,* April 16th, 1887.

[3] *Letters,* p. 271; *Socialist Diary;* Glasier, *op. cit.*

made up of clerks, designers, & the like, and rather under the thumbs of their employers or they would be able to do more. Kropotkin's visit has turned them a little in the Anarchist direction, which gives them an agreeable air of toleration, and they are at present quite innocent of any parliamentary designs. The feeling amongst the working men about is certainly in favour of Socialism; but they are slack in joining any organization as usual; still, the thing is taking hold."

Morris arrived at Newcastle on Sunday, April 10th, and was met by Mahon and Donald: by chance they ran into Hyndman, "who I suspect was not over-pleased to see me, as the S.D.F. have been playing a rather mean game there": "after seeming to agree that neither organization should press itself on the miners [the S.D.F.] has been trying to bag them after all". The next morning they set off for the collieries: Morris and Donald were entertained in a miner's cottage in Seghill, while Mahon—who had planned the demonstration with energy and skill—busied himself with preliminary arrangements. Morris was impressed by all he saw: by his host, "a tall strong man, his face wrecked by an accident which had blown out one eye and damaged the other", a "kindly intelligent man", talking with "that queer Northumbrian smack"; by his host's description of the issues of the strike; by the good-temper and hospitality of the miner's wife and daughter; by the house, "as clean and neat as a country cottage", and by the other houses he passed which were equally so, although "they are most woful looking dwellings of man, and the whole district is just a miserable backyard to the collieries". Leaving Seghill they went by train to Blyth, where a considerable crowd was awaiting them. Morris mounted a trolly and made an impromptu speech for about forty minutes. "Then we set off, rather a draggle-tailed lot because we couldn't afford a paid band. . . as we plodded on through the dreary (O so dreary) villages, & that terrible waste of endless back-yard, we could see on our left hand a strip of the bright blue sea, for it was a beautiful sunny day." After about three miles they joined another contingent with band and banner, and "soon swelled into a respectable company" of about 2,000 strong. After a six-mile march they reached the meeting-field and found two strong contingents already there, and "groups of men and women. . . streaming up the field from all about". Soon the crowd was many thousands strong, with contingents from all the mining villages around. "It was a very good meeting", Morris noted. "The audience listened intently and were heartily with us." "We spoke from one waggon, Fielding of the S.D.F. in the Chair, then Mahon, then me, then Hyndman, then Donald." The mood of the crowd was something new in Morris's experience, "orderly & good-tempered", but militant and swiftly responsive. When (at the opening of the meeting) the reporters in a waggon beside the speakers got out their notebooks, the miners threatened to "put them out. . . unless they promise to put all down!" "There were many women there", Morris noted, "some of them very much excited: one (elderly) when any obnoxious person was named never failed to chorus it with 'Put him out!' " The front ranks of the audience sat and squatted on the ground, to let the others see and hear, and the whole scene became deeply marked in Morris's memory—the desolate "backyard" to the collieries, the earnest faces of the miners, "the bright blue sea forming a strange border to the misery of the land."[1]

Morris, his enthusiasm set afire, made one of the best impromptu speeches of his life. Here at last he was speaking as he wanted to speak, as a leader of the Socialists addressing the workers—not as the distinguished curiosity and man of letters lecturing to an audience partly drawn by his artistic reputation. The speaker's plank on the waggon was "rather perilous": "I was for simply coming to the front without mounting on the plank but some of them sung out from the side, 'If yon man does na stand on the top we canna hear him!' " Someone turned up a notice board on a pole for him to lean on. "It was very inspiriting to speak to such a crowd of eager & serious

[1] The account of the Northumberland demonstration is given in the *Socialist Diary; Letters,* pp. 271-4; *Commonweal,* April 16th and 23rd, 1887; *Newcastle Chronicle,* April 12th, 1887.

persons", he noted. "I did pretty well and didn't stumble at all." The speech (as reported in the *Newcastle Chronicle*) may be quoted at length:[1]

"Mr. Wm. MORRIS, of London, [said]: Sometimes. . . when he was addressing meetings of his countrymen he was in doubt whether the whole of those whom he was addressing were discontented. He thought he need not have any particular doubt about the audience at that meeting. He hoped there was not a person on that ground who for one reason or another was not discontented with the life he or she lived. They were connected with a great struggle. Into the details of the strike he would not enter. He quite understood that they were at present in such a position that they could scarcely live at all. Their struggle was for a position in which they would be able to live a life which people called tolerable. (Hear, hear). He did not call the life of a working man, as things went, a tolerable life at all. When they had gained all that was possible under the present system, they still would not have the life which human beings ought to have. (Cheers). That was flat. What was their life at the best? They worked hard day in, day out, without any sort of hope whatever. Their work was to work to live, in order that they might live to work. (Hear, hear, and 'Shame'.) That was not the life of men. That was the life of machines. That was the way in which capitalists regarded them. . . Even supposing he did not understand that there was a definite reason in economics, and that the whole system could be changed, he should still stand there in sympathy with the men present. . . If the thing could not be altered at all, he for one would be a rebel against it. (Cheers.)"

The miners had only one choice, Morris said. They must either rebel, or be slaves. When the workers were organized throughout the country, and demanded Socialism with one voice, the masters might give in peacefully:

"He admitted there was another thing they might do. If there was such a thing as a general strike, he thought it was possible that the masters of society would attack them violently—he meant with hot shot, cold steel, and the rest of it. But let them remember that they (the men) were many and the masters were few. It was not that the masters could attack them by themselves. It was only the masters with

[1] The report is reliable, since Morris noted in his diary that it was almost verbatim.

a certain instrument, and what was that instrument? A part of the working classes themselves."

Here Morris caught sight of the four or five policemen who had been sent to the meeting (a strange contrast with the multitudes of police set on to pester the small open-air meetings in London), and began to "chaff [them] rather unmercifully":

"Even those men that were dressed in blue with bright buttons upon them and white gloves"—Morris continued, to the accompainment of cries of "Out with them"—"and those other men dressed in red, and also sometimes with gloves on their fingers, what were they? Simply working men, very hard up, driven into a corner and compelled to put on the livery of a set of masters." (Hear, hear, and prolonged hooting.) (Here the "blue-coats beat an undignified retreat" according to a *Commonweal* reporter.) "When these instruments, the soldiers, and sailors, came against them and saw that they were in earnest, and saw that they were many—they all knew the sufferings of the workers—what would happen? They would not dare obey their masters. The cannon would be turned round, the butts of the muskets would go up, and the swords and bayonets would be sheathed, and these men would say 'Give us work: let us all be honest men like yourselves.' "

Then Morris, veering back to the old prescription of the League, told the miners that they must organize not for a partial victory, but a *true* victory:

"Not a little more wages here and leave to work six days instead of four. He wished they only worked two days and got the same wages or more. Six days a week for the work they had to do was a great deal too much for men of ordinary body and strength. What, he asked, was a life of real happiness? Work for everybody who would work. For him who would not they could not say that Society had rejected him: he had rejected Society. The masters had rejected Society. He wished that the men might have a life of refinement and education and all those things which made what some people called a gentleman, but what he called a man. (Cheers.) That was the victory he wished them. Nothing short of that would be victory. And yet every skirmish on the road and every attack on the position of the masters brought them nearer. They must go on until all the workers of the world were united in goodwill and peace upon earth. (Loud cheers.)"

Morris, Donald and Mahon hurried off from the meeting to catch the Newcastle train, had "a bite and a drop" in the station refreshment-room, and went on to Ryton Willows, a recreation ground by the side of the Tyne—"a piece of rough heathy ground. . . under the bank by which the railway runs: it is a pretty place and the evening was lovely". "Being Easter Monday, there were lots of folks there with swings and cricket and dancing & the like." Here, among the merry-go-rounds and the holiday-makers, another meeting was held:

> "I thought it a queer place for a serious Socialist meeting, but we had a crowd about us in no time and I spoke, rather too long I fancy, till the stars came out and it grew dusk and the people stood and listened still, & when we were done they gave three cheers for the Socialists, & all was mighty friendly and pleasant: & so back we went to supper and bed, of which I for one was glad enough. . ."

"I guess I tried their patience", Morris noted in his diary, "as I got 'lectury' and being excited went on & on. . ." The next morning he felt "very well & brisk". "There is no doubt of the success (which may be temporary) which we have made in those northern mining districts." He returned to London full of a new enthusiasm, and reached the weekly Council meeting in time to propose a Hyde Park meeting in aid of the Northumbrian miners. His proposal was accepted. But the return to London was like a dousing of cold water over his hopes. "Got to the Council in time to come in for one of the usual silly squabbles about nothing", he noted in the privacy of his diary. "I spoke the next Sunday at Beadon Road and couldn't help contrasting our Cockneys much to their disadvantage with the northerners. . ." In fact, the Socialist League was at the very moment when the masses were beginning to listen to its message entering a phase of savage internal dispute: and was becoming less and less competent to give leadership to the movement which it had played a part in setting in motion.

IV. The Third Annual Conference

From the time of the Second Annual Conference of the League in the summer of 1886, the Council had been divided on the issue of parliamentary action. In November, 1886, a sub-committee was appointed, comprising Mahon and Lane, from the "anti-parliamentary" side, and Bax and Binning, from the "parliamentary", to draft an agreed policy statement. The sub-committee failed to agree (as might have been expected) both on the parliamentary issue, and on the League's attitude to the Eight Hours agitation. By the end of 1886 there were "two separate parties" formed on the Council, and squabbles were continuous.

At first, Morris confided in his diary he had hoped to act the part of peacemaker:

> "I may as well say here that my intention is if possible to prevent the quarrel coming to a head between the two sections, parliamentary and anti-parliamentary, which are pretty much commensurate with the Collectivists and Anarchists: and this because I believe there would be a good many who would join the Anarchist side who are not really Anarchists, and who would be useful to us: indeed I doubt if, except one or two Germans, etc., we have any real Anarchists amongst us: and I don't want to see a lot of enthusiastic men who are not very deep in Socialist doctrines driven off for a fad of the more pedantic part of the Collectivist section. . ."

But his attempt to heal the split was unsuccessful. On March 21st, he noted:

> "Council meeting short and confused: the two parties bitter but not inclined to do much since the Conference comes off so soon. . . I am certainly feeling discouraged about the League: between them they will break it up, I fear, and then the S.D.F. will be the only practical body here; which I don't like the idea of, as its advertising tactics make it somewhat ridiculous. I shall move at the Conference that the question of parliament or non-parliament be deferred for a year. The Fabians. . . have issued their parliamentary league manifesto: I don't mind this if they like to try it. But the S.L. going parliamentary would be a misfortune."

After the next Council meeting, on March 28th, Morris's despondency had deepened: "Whatever happens, I fear. . . that as an organization we shall come to nothing though personal feeling may hold us together." When he left London for his Northern propaganda tour, Lane was planning to canvass the branches on the anti-parliamentary side, and the efforts to secure a genuine compromise seemed to have failed.

Lane fired his opening salvo by reading at a meeting of London members of the League his *Anti-Statist, Communist Manifesto,* which he claimed was a "minority report" from the sub-committee, and which (in Morris's opinion) "turned out to be a long lecture not at all fit for its purpose, and which would have been damaging to us anti-parliamentarians if it had gone to the Branches. . . a vote was taken as to whether the Council should be advised to print it. . . and it was carried that it should not be. I voted in the majority."

> "We revolutionary socialists"—declared Lane—"desire to organize ourselves in such a manner as to render politics useless and the powers that be superfluous. . . We aim at the abolition of the State in every form and variety. . . We are Atheists in point of philosophy. . . Anti-Statists in point of politics. . . Communists as regards the economic development of human society. . . We are free communists as opposed to the state communists. . ."

The Manifesto also embraced free love:

> "It is hardly necessary for us to add that we fight against (on the same principle of the abolition of private property), the institution of the family, such as it exists nowadays. Thoroughly convinced partisans of the free union of the sexes, we repell the thought of marriage. . ."

On the one hand, there were ultra-revolutionary phrases:

> "We do not believe in the advent of the new order for which we are struggling by means of legal and pacific methods, and that is why we are revolutionary socialists. The study of history has taught us that the noblest conquests of man are written on a blood-stained book. To give birth to justice, humanity suffers a thousand tortures. . ."

On the other hand, Lane rejected both the Anarchist "propaganda by deed" and all methods of political and industrial struggle. "It appears hard"—he commented—"to call meetings of the unemployed, and tell them that they cannot be permanently benefited until the Revolution, and that they must starve in the meantime." But still, this was the truth which the Anti-Statist Communist must tell them. Equally, the struggle for the Eight Hours' Day was useless and delusive. The trade unions were "little better than Benefit Societies. . . helpless in the meshes of capitalism":

> "With the practical break-down of Trades Unions, Socialism springs forth and says the day for this unequal and losing battle between the bloated capitalist and the starving workman for a mere increase or to prevent a decrease of wage is past. Today and from henceforth, the battle is by the workers as a whole, for the destruction of monopoly and tyranny of every description. . ."

And for means, Lane had only one solution to offer—education.

The inner politics of the months before and after the Third Annual Conference of the League on May 29th, 1887, are confused in the extreme. One or two general comments may be made. Already the first signals could be seen of that re-awakening of the masses which was soon to give birth to the New Unionism among the unskilled, and was to lead to the formation of the I.L.P. Indeed, as early as May, 1887, it seemed to Engels that there was "an immediate question of organizing an English Labour Party with an independent class programme".[1] It must have been as a result of his advice that, on the League's policy sub-committee, Bax, Binning and, later, Mahon, were seeking to draw up a policy which might serve as the basis of such a Party. But Engels (while giving

[1] Engels to Sorge, May 4th, 1887, *Labour Monthly,* December, 1933: "It is now an immediate question of organizing an English Labour Party with an independent class programme. If it is successful, it will relegate to a back seat both the S.D.F. and the Socialist League, and that would be the most satisfactory end to the present squabbles. . ."

this advice) was too occupied to give time to considering the *manner* in which the theoretical battle should be fought. He did not think that he was directing the tactics of a Marxist group within the League. The leadership of this group was, in fact, in very inexperienced hands. Chief spokesman of the "parliamentarians" on the Council was A.K. Donald, a young Edinburgh intellectual, a man who appears to have inspired little confidence in the movement, and who had a knack of enraging both Morris and the "anti-parliamentary" group. Aveling's reputation was—perhaps unknown to Engels—sinking fast in 1887.[1] The weaknesses of Bax have already been discussed, and throughout the dispute he made no serious theoretical contribution to it. Indeed, not one piece of serious polemic came from the pen of *any* of the "parliamentary" group before the decisive vote at the Annual General Conference.

They were not alone in this. Morris's most considered statement on the matter, "The Policy of Abstention", was first delivered after the Conference, and Lane's *Manifesto* was certainly not representative of the views of the "anti-parliamentary" group as a whole. In the result, the struggle cannot be regarded as a responsible political controversy, since more depended upon questions of personality and on juggling with the voting strength of the branches, than upon clear issues of conviction.

Bax's branch, Croydon, opened the fight by tabling a motion for the Annual Conference, amending the Constitution to include the sentence: "Its objects shall be sought to be obtained by every available means, Parliamentary or otherwise."[2] Morris countered it with a resolution from Hammersmith:

"That whereas there is some difference of opinion among the members of the Socialist League as to whether it be right and expedient

[1] It was in 1887 that Mahon declined to work with Aveling on personal grounds (see p. 468) and (in September) that Morris referred to Aveling as "that disreputable dog".

[2] *Report of the Third Annual Conference of the Socialist League,* p. 12.

to put forward agitation in Parliament and through Parliamentary candidates as a means of Propaganda, and whereas the League has hitherto refrained from doing so; and also seeing that the principle work of the League must always be steadily educating the people in the principles of Socialism, the question of agitating for and by Parliamentary means be not considered at this Conference and be deferred for one year."[1]

He wished this resolution to be regarded as a genuine attempt at the reconciliation of the two sections. But it is clear that the resolution begged the question in its phrasing. On May 19th he was writing to the Rev. John Glasse (of the Edinburgh Branch) that "the parliamentary people are looking like driving matters to extremity, which means driving me out of the League if they succeed. I am quite ready to let the matter rest if they will really leave it alone. . "[2] This is not as fair as it seems, since "leaving it alone" would mean leaving the purist position of the League unchanged. It seems that Glasse was by no means satisfied with Morris's letter, and he drew from him a further and more considered one on May 23rd:

"My position as to Parliament and the dealings of Socialists with it, I will now state clearly. I believe that the Socialists will certainly send members to Parliament when they are strong enough to do so: in itself I see no harm in that, so long as it is understood that they go there as rebels, and not as members of the governing body prepared by passing palliative measures to keep 'Society' alive. But I fear that many of them will be drawn into that error by the corrupting influence of a body professedly hostile to Socialism: & therefore I dread the parliamentary period (clearly a long way ahead at present) of the progress of the party: and I think it will be necessary always to keep alive a body of Socialists of principle who will refuse responsibility for the action of the parliamentary portion of the party. Such a body now exists in the shape of the League, while germs of the parliamentary side exist in the S.D.F., Fabian, & Union. . ."

[1] Hammersmith Minutes, March 27th, 1887.

[2] *Unpublished Letters,* p. 4.

Those who wanted parliamentary action within the League would, he suggested, be better advised to join one of the other bodies, "for whom I for my part feel a complete tolerance, so long as they are not brought *inside* ours". If the internal dispute continued, Morris felt, "the League will sooner or later be broken up".

"All this has nothing to do with the question of Collectivism or Anarchism; I distinctly disagree with the Anarchist principle, much as I sympathize with many of the anarchists personally, and although I have an Englishman's wholesome horror of government interference & centralization which some of our friends who are built on the German pattern are not quite enough afraid of, I think."[1]

In the week before the Conference both sides were lobbying hard, and Morris was definitely lobbying with the anti-parliamentary group. In March he was looking to a compromise; in May for some reason the tactics of the parliamentary group had touched him to the raw. Mahon had declared for the parliamentary side, and was doing his utmost to swing the Scottish and Northern branches over. But it seems to have been the behaviour of A.K. Donald which most aroused Morris's ill temper. Whatever the reasons, two days before the Conference he was writing urgently to Bruce Glasier as to the necessity of delegates being present from Glasgow to vote on the anti-parliamentary side:

"I apprehend that your people don't understand the situation: if the parliamentary resolution is carried *the League will come to an end:* that is certain: & I shall invite you & some few honest men to form a new organization. Between you and me the members of the parliamentary party are behaving so ill that I should feel it a relief to be no longer associated with them, though I can put up with a good deal."[2]

Mahon, striving to form his North of England Socialist Federation, was being constantly asked by the Northumber-

[1] *Unpublished Letters,* pp. 6-7.

[2] Morris to Glasier, May 27th, 1887 (Glasier MSS.). See also *Letters,* p. 291.

land miners the difference between the outlook of the S.D.F. and the League. If the major tactical difference were in the attitude to Parliament, there is little doubt which organization the miners would prefer to join. The purisms which seemed reasonable in Farringdon Road, were irrelevant where a mass movement was already under way. It seemed to Mahon essential that the League should alter its policy without delay if it was to have any chance of gathering the fruits of its own propaganda. When the Annual Conference met it had before it not only the Croydon and Hammersmith resolutions, but also a long one from Mahon, which may well have been drafted with Engels's assistance, and which at last really went to the root of the matter, presenting a positive new orientation of the whole League propaganda:

> "Whereas the primary duty of the Socialist party is to educate the people in the principles of Socialism and to organize them to overthrow the capitalist system: This Conference lays down the following line of policy for the guidance of the executive and branches of the Socialist League:—That every effort be made to penetrate the existing political organizations with Socialism; that all possible help be given to such movements as trades'-unionism, co-operation, national and international labour federation, etc., by which the working classes are trying to better their condition; that Parliament, municipal and other local-government bodies, and the contests for the election of members to them, be taken advantage of for spreading the principles of Socialism and organizing the people into a Socialist Labour Party; that while we share the common aspirations of the wage-earners to win better terms from the capitalist, we steadily insist that their complete economical emancipation can only be effected by transforming the society of to-day into a co-operative commonwealth."

On the afternoon of the Conference, Morris opened in conciliatory mood, withdrawing the Hammersmith resolution when it did not meet with unanimous approval. A further anti-parliamentary resolution (from Glasgow) was rejected, without any attempt on Morris's part to give it support. Mahon, however, pressed his resolution forward, Bax withdrawing in his favour. Morris and Faulkner then moved an uncompromising anti-parliamentary amendment which, after prolonged discussion, won the day by seventeen votes to eleven.

Defeated in the voting, the parliamentary group declined to stand for the Council. As Engels pointed out to Sorge, in reality very little had been settled, and (perhaps less fairly)—

> "the decisive circumstance was Morris's threat to leave the League if any kind of parliamentary struggle be recognised in principle. And as Morris covers the weekly £4 deficit of the *Commonweal*, that outweighed all else by far."

But the day after the Conference, the parliamentary group met in private and took further decisions. According to a circular issued later by their opponents, Edward Aveling occupied the Chair, and Eleanor Aveling, Mahon, Bax, Donald, Binning, Utley and others were present. An organized faction within the League was set up, and a Treasurer and Secretaries appointed. It was agreed that they should join the Labour Emancipation League (an affiliate of the League) and use it as an organizing centre for the parliamentary supporters.[1] Engels's emphasis (in a letter to Sorge) was slightly different: "Our people now want to organize the provinces, and after three or four months to call an extraordinary congress to overthrow the decision."[2]

It was a curious reversal of the old positions. The Labour Emancipation League, formed by Lane and Kitz, and a breeding ground of the "leftists", had now become absorbed into the Socialist League proper: but a branch still existed at Hoxton, and it had passed under the control of the parliamentarians. As an affiliated organization, the L.E.L. was only loosely controlled by the Council of the S.L., and yet had full voting powers at the Annual Conference. The plan appears to

[1] *To the Members of the Socialist League,* a handbill issued by J. Lane and F. Charles in preparation for the Annual Conference of 1888.

[2] Engels to Sorge, June 4th, 1887, *Labour Monthly,* December, 1933.

have been that the London parliamentarians should strengthen the L.E.L., while in the provinces Mahon, Donald and others should develop similar Socialist organizations—the North of England Socialist Federation and the Scottish Land and Labour League—connected only loosely with the parent body. But the plan was faulty in several respects. It could only be operated by breaking with any pretence of party discipline or loyalty within the Socialist League, and embarking on a policy of intrigue and factionalism, rather than open controversy. It left the Council of the League more firmly than ever in the hands of the anti-parliamentarians, who were now aided by men of more pronounced Anarchist views, such as F.C. Slaughter ("Fred Charles") and David Nicoll.[1] From Morris's point of view, the tactics of the parliamentarians appeared uncomradely, and the breach between them and his "centre" group was embittered.

Whatever judgements are made, much of this was inevitable from the first. It was the outcome of the confused manner in which the first "Split" took place in December, 1884. "No movement absorbs so much fruitless labour as one which has not yet emerged from the status of a sect"—this was Engels's comment—"At such times everything turns to scandalmongering." Nor was Engels much perturbed at the defeat:

> "It follows that our people, in face of the imminent outbreak of a *bona fide* labour movement, are not tied to an organization which claims to lead the whole movement... In the provinces the workers are everywhere organizing local Leagues (Socialist). They have a colossal contempt for anything coming from London."[2]

[1] David Nicoll, Librarian and Propaganda Secretary of League, 1887-8.

[2] Engels to Sorge, June 4th, 1887, *Labour Monthly*, December, 1933, Engels's optimistic picture of developments in the provinces might perhaps have been a little coloured by the enthusiastic reports of J.L. Mahon.

V. The Policy of Abstention

Just as in the months following the "Split" of December, 1884, Morris continued to debate the issues in his mind. His immediate reaction to any contact with "things parliamentary" was emotional rather than carefully considered. His disgust at a Parliament of Podsnaps had been nourished in him during his early revolt, encouraged by Dickens and John Ruskin, intensified by his experiences during the "Eastern Question" agitation. Parliament (in his mind) was a word synonymous with sharp-tactics, intrigue, false promises: it was the "great myth" of modern capitalism, the greatest barrier to the advance of revolutionary ideas. His position before the Annual Conference he summed up thus:

> "We should treat Parliament as a representative of the enemy... We might for some definite purpose be forced to send members to Parliament *as rebels*... but under no circumstances to help to carry on their Government of the country... and therefore we ought not to put forward palliative measures to be carried through Parliament, for that would be helping them to govern us."[1]

After the Annual Conference he made a more serious attempt to present an alternative to parliamentary action, in a new lecture, "The Policy of Abstention", first delivered at Hammersmith at the end of July, 1887, and afterwards read to private meetings of Socialists in several places.[2] In this he sought to characterize two possible Socialist policies—the policy of parliamentary action, and that of abstention. Advocates of the first, he said, "believe in what may be called a system of cumulative reforms... carried out by means of Parliament and a bourgeois executive". They hoped to elect sufficient Socialists to Parliament to transform it from "a mere instrument in the hands of the monopolizers of the

[1] Morris to Glasier, May 19th, 1887, Glasier, *op. cit.*, p. 193. For the misdating of letters in Glasier and in Henderson, *Letters*, see first edition, p. 540 n.2.

[2] Hammersmith Minutes, July 31st, 1887; Morris to Glasier, July 27th, 1887.

means of production, into a body which should destroy monopoly". The policy of abstention he characterized in greater detail:

"This plan is founded on the necessity of making the class-struggle clear to the workers, of pointing out to them that while monopoly exists they can only exist as its slaves: so that Parliament and all other institutions at present existing are maintained for the purpose of upholding this slavery; that their wages are but slaves' rations, and if they were increased tenfold would be nothing more: that while the bourgeois rule lasts they can indeed take part in it, but only on the terms that they shall do nothing to attack the grand edifice of which their slavery is the foundation. Nay more than that: that they are asked to vote and send representatives to Parliament (if 'working-men' so much the better) that they may point out what concessions may be necessary for the ruling class to make in order that the slavery of the workers may last on: in a word that to vote for the continuance of their own slavery is all the parliamentary action that they will be allowed to take under the present regime: Liberal Associations, Radical clubs, working men members are at present, and Socialist members will be in the future, looked on with complacency by the government classes as serving towards the end of propping the stability of robber society in the safest and least troublesome manner by beguiling them to take part in their own government. A great invention, and well worthy of the reputation of the Briton for practicality—and swindling! How much better than the coarse old-world iron repression of that blunderer Bismark. . ."

"The Policy of Abstention", he continued, "is founded on this view":

"That the interests of the two classes, the workers and the capitalists are irreconcilable, and as long as the capitalists exist as a class, they having the monopoly of the means of production, have all the power of ordered and legal society; but on the other hand that the use of this power to keep down a wronged population, which feels itself wronged, and is organizing for illegal resistance. . . would impose such a burden on the governing classes as they will not be able to bear; and they must finally break down under it, and take one of two courses, either of them the birth of fear acting on the instinct to prolong and sustain their life which is essential in all organisms. One course would be to try the effect of wholesale concessions. . . and this course would be almost certain to have a partial success; but I feel sure not so great a success in delaying revolution as it would have if taken with the expressed agreement of Socialist representatives in Parliament: in the latter case the concessions would be looked upon as a victory; whereas if they were the work of a hated government from which the people were standing aloof, they would be dreaded as a bait, and scorned as the last resource of a tyranny growing helpless. The other course. . . would be stern repression. . . of the opinion and aspirations of the working classes as a whole: for in England at least there would be no attempt to adopt this course until opinion was so grown and so organized that the danger to monopoly seemed imminent. In short the two courses are fraud and force, and doubtless in a commercial country like this the resources of fraud would be exhausted before the ruling class betook itself to open force."

Supposing the policy of abstention were to be adopted, what did it imply in immediate tactics? First, the preaching of the principles of Socialism as widely as possible. "The real business of us propagandists", Morris suggested, "is to instil this aim of the workers becoming the masters of their own destinies, their own lives". Once this was done, the workers should be organized through trade unions in "a vast labour organization—the federation according to their crafts. . . of all the workmen who have awoke to the fact that they are the slaves of monopoly". The one overriding aim of these unions should be the overthrow of capitalism, and the establishment of Socialism. All their tactics before achieving this victory should be looked upon "as so much necessary work. . . to enable them to live till they have marched to the great battlefield":

"Let them settle. . . what wages are to be paid by their temporary managers, what number of hours it may be expedient to work; let them arrange for the filling of their military chest, the care of the sick, the unemployed, the dismissed: let them learn also how to administer their own affairs."

But Morris sketched only the general outline of this plan: "time and also power fails me to give any scheme for how all this could be done".

The problems of the building of such a Federation being

thus glossed over (and Morris never returned to them in any detail) he advanced to the point at which the labour organization was already established and powerful. The result would be the open and "conscious opposition of the two powers, monopolist authority and free labour", and this, in turn, could not fail to lead on to a revolutionary situation; whereas the policy of parliamentary socialism would enable the monopolists–

"to detach a portion of the people from the people's side, to have it in their midst helpless, dazed, wearied with ceaseless compromise, or certain defeat, and yet to put it before the world as the advanced guard of the revolutionary party, the representative of all that is active or practical of the popular party."

The policy of abstention might be supplemented, he suggested, by creating a truly popular centre outside Parliament ("call it the labour parliament if you will"), deliberating at the same time, and whose decrees will be obeyed by the people "and not those of the Westminster Committee". Its weapons of enforcement would be those of the strike, co-operation, and the boycott: above all, it would be continually educating the people in the administration of their own affairs. The plan of parliamentary action, by contrast, he prophesied would develop along the following lines:

"Starting from the same point as the abstentionists they have to preach an electioneering campaign as an absolute necessity, and to set about it as soon as possible: they will then have to put forward a programme of reforms deduced from the principles of Socialism. . . they will necessarily have to appeal for support (i.e. votes) to a great number of people who are not convinced Socialists, and their programme of reforms will be the bait to catch these votes: and to the ordinary voter it will be this bait which will be the matter of interest, and not the principle. . . So that. . . The Socialist members when they get into Parliament will represent a heterogenous body of opinion, ultra-radical, democratic, discontented non-politicals, rather than a body of Socialists; and it will be their opinions and prejudices that will sway the action of the members in Parliament. With these fetters on them the Socialist members will have to act, and whatever they propose will have to be a mere matter of compromise: yet even those measures they will not carry: because long before their party gets powerful enough to form even a formidable group for alliance with other parties, one section or other of ordinary politicians will dish them, and will carry measures that will pass current for being the very thing the Socialists have been asking for; because once get Socialist M.Ps., and to the ordinary public they will be the representatives of the only Socialists. . . So it will go on till either the Socialist party in Parliament disappears into the advanced Democratic party, or until they look round and find that they, still Socialists, have done nothing but give various opportunities to the reactionists for widening the basis of monopoly by creating a fresh middle-class under the present one, and so staving off the day of the great change."

He admitted a further possibility—that the Socialists in Parliament by good fortune or intrigue should capture power; but in this case it would not be a conscious revolution, since the people would have been "ignorantly betrayed into Socialism" instead of achieving it by their own conscious efforts; and, hence, a counter-revolutionary movement would quickly triumph.[1]

This lecture contains Morris's most considered reflections during his anti-parliamentary period; and although he repeated them in a hundred different ways, he did not substantially modify them until 1891 or 1892. Already in September, 1887, he was identifying his real theoretical opponents as being among the Fabians, and this despite the fact that Shaw was a close personal friend. "The attitude of Shaw. . . and his Fabians is very difficult to get over", he wrote to Glasse. "They are distinctly pushing forward that very useful association of lecturers as the only sound Socialist Body in the country: which I think is nonsense":

"I admit, and always have admitted, that at some future period it may be necessary to use parliament mechanically: what I object to is *depending* on parliamentary agitation. There *must* be a great party, a

[1] The lecture is published in full in May Morris, II, pp. 434-52.

great organization outside parliament actively engaged in reconstructing society and learning administration whatever goes on in the parliament itself. This is in direct opposition to the view of the regular parliamentary section as represented by Shaw, who look upon parliament as *the* means; and it seems to me will fall into the error of moving earth & sea to fill the ballot boxes with Socialist votes which will not represent Socialist *men*."[1]

If he could not win the Socialist movement as a whole to his view, still he believed it necessary for the League to exist alongside the parliamentary movement, keeping alive the propaganda of "principle". Increasingly between 1887 and 1890 he came to see the role of the League as being educational and propagandist within a larger Socialist movement. He was opposed to the amalgamation of the various Socialist groupings, but strongly in favour of joint action wherever possible. "Let those meet together who agree and like each other, however few they are", he wrote to Glasier in January, 1888:

"And not entangle themselves by joining bodies in which they must either quarrel or suppress part of their genuine opinions. In meantime the various bodies can always unite for specified purposes, and are much more likely to do so effectively if they are not always wrangling about their differences... The *party* cannot possibly be coterminious with one organization in it, or indeed with all the organizations together."[2]

Such reflections were forced upon him increasingly in the next two years by the gradual disintegration of the League. In July, 1887, the circulation of *Commonweal* was in the region of 2,800 and Morris gave a general estimate of League membership at about 700.[3] In December, 1887, the

1 Morris to Glasse, September 23rd, 1887, *Unpublished Letters,* pp. 7-8.

2 Glasier MSS., January 28th, 1888.

3 Based on Morris's statement to Glasier, July 27th, 1887 (Glasier, *op. cit.,* p. 194), that 1½*d.* a week from each member of the League would cover the weekly loss of £4 on *Commonweal.* This would give an exact figure of 720 members. The voting strength at the Annual Conference was twenty-eight, with at least one branch (Leicester) unrepresented; an analysis would give six full fifties, and twenty-three parts of fifty. Taking an average of twenty per branch, this would give about 760 members.

Commonweal sales still stood at 2,850, but in June, 1889, the number "sent out" (not necessarily sold) had fallen to 2,331.[1] The sharpest decline came after the Fourth Annual Conference in May, 1888, but a general decline may be presumed over the whole period. This decline is a fair index of the general activity of the League, since the bulk of *Commonweal* sales were in conjunction with the open-air propaganda. The Hammersmith Branch recruited over forty new members in 1887 (nearly all in the second half of the year), and it was conducting a vigorous open-air propaganda. But the lectures were of an increasingly intellectual character[2] and the Fabians (among them Hubert Bland, Shaw, Graham Wallas, Sidney Webb and Sydney Olivier), were becoming more popular among the members.

Hammersmith was a lively Branch, which put out new off-shoots (Fulham, Acton, North Kensington, Notting Hill) right to the end. Morris was always prodding forward new activities, in which he took his full share himself.[3] Few of the other Branches were gaining ground. Glasgow, although active in its propaganda, persistently failed to pay its full capitation dues to the central Council, and sometimes failed to return cash for *Commonweals* sold. Norwich, which claimed a membership of over 150 at the Third Annual Conference (May 29th, 1887), had fallen below 100 at the Fourth (May 20th, 1888): nevertheless, its propaganda was very much more vigorous than most. The Leeds Branch, which—together with the small Bradford Branch—was gaining influence in the working-class movement of the West Riding, still could

[1] *Weekly Letter to Secretaries of Socialist League branches*, June 20th, 1889 (among papers of Hammersmith Society, Brit. Mus. Add. MSS. 45893).

[2] Among lectures between December, 1887 and June, 1888 were "Peasant Life in Italy" (E. Carpenter), "The Origins of the Ornamental Arts" (Morris), "Copyright" (Shaw), "The Policy of Ancient Peru" (Beasley), and "Social Science 2,200 Years Ago" (Graham Wallas).

[3] E.g. Of seventy-two ordinary branch meetings between December, 1887 and September, 1888 (average attendance eleven), Morris was present at fifty-two; in addition, he spoke at many of the 150 open-air meetings held by his branch in the same period, and (when not lecturing elsewhere himself) was usually in the chair at the regular Sunday-night lecture. (Hammersmith Minutes, *passim.*)

not seem to climb above the charmed figure of thirty or forty members.[1] Morris's private letters of the summer of 1887 are profoundly discouraged. "I cannot say that I have encouraging news from London", he wrote to Glasier on July 23rd, 1887:

"I am afraid that our parliamentary friends if they cannot get their way will at any rate break up the League. . . It is but right and proper to let you know how things really are; and you must remember that the parliamentarians are only running their heads into a sack; they have no chance of beating the S.D.F. because that has been in existence so long that it has got that best of all titles 'prescription'. The Ps will if they please succeed in breaking up the League, but they will not succeed in founding another body. Their mistake is not joining the S.D.F. at once: they might raise its tone, or else get so many supporters in it that they could secede later on when they had done all that could be done in it.

"All that we Londoners can do is to try to keep up the old status of the League as long as possible and altogether if possible; to be as little controversial as we can help and to push on London Propaganda: though of course these wretched intrigues stop us very much, and make us dreadfully short-handed. If after all our struggles we are beaten we must then begin again, as a sort of 12 or even 6 apostles: but I am now more than ever determined that I will not go into the humbug business and promise people political successes and economical relief which I *know* we have no power to win for them. Our Hammersmith Branch is doing pretty well: very well as far as half a dozen members are concerned: and all we of any character are really working like niggers at it. . ."[2]

The decisive failure was in the provinces. Bradford, Edinburgh, Glasgow, Hamilton, Hull, Ipswich, Lancaster, Leeds, Leicester, North Shields, Norwich, Oxford and Walsall (thirteen in all) were represented at the Annual Conference in 1887: at the Conference in 1888 only eight provincial branches sent delegates (although at least one other effective branch, Leeds, was still active), and Hamilton, Hull, Lancaster and

[1] Notebooks and papers of Alf. Mattison.

[2] Glasier MSS. It is not certain whether this letter should be 1887 or 1888, but internal evidence suggests 1887.

North Shields had disappeared. After this date, it is true, the League occasionally promoted new branches, or gained affiliations from independent societies, at such various places as Yarmouth, Southampton, Wednesbury and Bristol. But, with the possible exception of Yarmouth, these did not constitute stable new propagandist centres. Propagandist visits to the South Wales coalfields, by Mainwaring and Kitz, resulted in good meetings but in no new branches. The foothold in Lancashire (in Manchester) was maintained, but the S.D.F. had the cotton towns to itself.

The reasons for this disintegration of the League in the provinces are not far to seek. The rising tide of the mass movement did not appear as a sudden desire amongst the workers for Socialism in the abstract, but as a taughtening mood of militancy in their fight for industrial and political objectives, combined with a new receptiveness to Socialist propaganda. The decision of the Third Annual Conference on parliamentary action had immediate repercussions: the Socialists of Clay Cross refused to affiliate to the League as a result,[1] and the Secretary of the Nottingham Socialist Club who had been trying to persuade his members to affiliate, wrote of his disappointment, and mentioned rumours of "general dissatisfaction" in the League and of a crisis in the Norwich branch.[2] *Commonweal* was out of touch with the working-class movement, and was difficult to sell: where branches were small and poor, unsold copies became a burden. "2/3rds of our members are out of work or on short time", wrote the Secretary of the Leicester branch in January, 1888, complaining that only a dozen of their quota could be sold.[3] "We cannot sell the *Commonweals*", he wrote in March, "simply because our members have no work and no money".[4]

[1] R. Unwin to Secretary, S.L., September 18th, 1887, S.L. Correspondence, Int. Inst. Soc. Hist.

[2] *Ibid.,* A. Clifton to Secretary, S.L., June 7th, 1887.

[3] *Ibid.,* J. Fowkes to Secretary, S.L., January 18th, 1888.

[4] *Ibid.,* J. Fowkes to Secretary, S.L., March 1st, 1888.

The fact that there *was* a potential readership for a lively Socialist paper, in touch with events in the labour movement, is indicated by the progress of the *Labour Elector,* Keir Hardie's *Miner,* the *Cotton Factory Times,* and (in 1889) the *Yorkshire Factory Times.* The League was not failing through the apathy or opposition of the working class. It was being left behind and isolated by its own purism, and for this failure William Morris must bear a part of the blame.

VI. John Lincoln Mahon

The career of J.L. Mahon in the last six months of 1887 illustrates the dilemmas of the League and of the movement. Returning to Northumberland after the Third Annual Conference, Mahon put into effect his policy of organizing a North of England Socialist Federation independent of both League and S.D.F. The Federation's Programme followed that of the draft constitution of the Socialist League, with one significant change—participation in parliamentary, as well as local elections was advocated. (Mahon sent on a copy to Engels, who gave his general approval.[1]) In the rules it was laid down that the Socialist League and S.D.F. should be treated "on equal terms of friendship and equality."[2] Branches might be formed "in any district in the North of England."

The first results of the Federation were good, although when Mahon told Engels that it had "about twenty branches" he was probably exaggerating. The S.D.F. now had several of its own branches in Newcastle and Gateshead, and Tom Mann came up as organiser at the end of May, working amicably enough with the Federation, whose branches were in the coal-field.[3] With the prospects of success opening before him Mahon began in earnest to "have ideas".

[1] The full correspondence between Mahon and Engels is published in Appendix II in the first edition of this book.

[2] *Commonweal,* June 25th, 1887.

[3] See Dona Torr, *Tom Mann and His Times* (1956), pp. 242-51.

Mahon was a capable propagandist. But he seems to have been an incapable organiser,[1] with rather more vanity than is proper in a man of twenty-four. ("I wish", he wrote in one letter to Engels, "our young lecturers could be got to pay more attention to these facts"). "He has more cheek and less chin than any man in the movement", Morris once said of a comrade who was almost certainly Mahon.[2] To Mahon himself he wrote: "I have always thought that though you were good at propaganda, you had a knack of setting people by the ears."[3] And later, when Mahon had broken with the League, Morris wrote in sorrow to Glasse:

> "I like him. . . and when I last saw him had no doubt of his sincerity: but I think as I always thought that as things are the career of a professional agitator is not good for him, & I am afraid that he will do nothing else now. . . Somehow he has (though a good natured fellow enough) a fatal gift of breeding squabbles, I scarcely know how. . . When he was up in London he used to have 'ideas' from time to time, which always ended in a quarrel."[4]

The exchanges between Mahon and Engels in June and July 1887 are of exceptional interest. In his first letter, of June 14th, Mahon sketched out a policy which some elements in the movement were in fact to follow in the next five years, and which was to lead to the formation of the I.L.P. in 1893:

> "I really think that here amongst the miners & iron works Socialism will take its first firm hold on the masses of the people. . Our real immediate foes are the Trades Union Leaders. We must fight these fellows in their own stronghold. We must lay down a policy & line of action for Socialists to persue *inside* the Unions, foster a Socialist ring there & get the leaders driven out."

[1] He had resigned after a few months as the first Secretary of the League, under pressure and as a result of his own "shortcomings": see R. Page Arnot, *William Morris, the Man and the Myth* (1964), pp. 51-2. This study publishes in full the letters from Morris to Mahon—letters not available to me for the first edition of this book.

[2] James Leatham, *William Morris, Master of Many Crafts* (1908), p. 115.

[3] R. Page Arnot, *op. cit.*, p. 71. [4] *Ibid.*, p. 90.

His perspective was to "amalgamate the various little organizations on one broad definite political platform." He deprecated further secessions from the S.D.F. or League, and advocated the formation of an unofficial group "of influential people from all the organizations." Only "a good & overwhelming force from the provinces" would be able to silence the London factions or bring the London leaders together. The North of England Socialist Federation and a (revived) Scottish Land and Labour League were steps in implementing this strategy. A.K. Donald was to keep the former going in Northumberland while Mahon went on a ten week missionary tour in Scotland. Engels was invited to make a financial contribution to this propaganda.[1]

Mahon's proposals appear very reasonable, and they won Engels's general assent. But the dividing line between political manoeuvring and intrigue, in this delicate situation, was very fine. To Engels—and no doubt to the parliamentary section of the League—Mahon offered this perspective; but it would seem that he was telling to Morris a different story. The independent North of England Federation was a necessary stratagem, forced upon him by the need to avoid a confrontation in the North with the S.D.F. He called upon Morris and the League to support him financially, while insisting upon his own independence of action.[2] Morris temporised, and handled the problem with genial patience, publishing Mahon's reports and advertisements in *Commonweal* ("I don't want to make the *Commonweal* sectional so I will probably put them in"), and finally blowing up when Mahon failed to return money for *Commonweals* sold—presumably because he was

[1] See first edition of this book, pp. 861-3.

[2] It is clear from Morris's letters to Mahon in R. Page Arnot, *op. cit.*, pp. 67-73, that this support was withheld. The League's "Strike Committee" thought it "inadvisable" to keep Mahon as an emissary in the North, and Morris told Mahon that he would give money only through the League's Treasurer, i.e. for objects approved by the League's Council.

applying the funds to his own keep.[1] "I am vexed," he wrote at the end of July, "that the road to *organisation* should lie through the breaking up of the League, and the snuffing out of *Commonweal.*"[2]

Meanwhile Mahon was receiving, through the hands of A.K. Donald, some subsidy from the Bloomsbury Branch and the League's parliamentarians. Mahon was himself a very recent convert to the parliamentary side, and he already had a reputation for sudden changes of front. Yet his policy demanded the building of a new centre of personal influence within the movement, and hence could not be divorced from his own reputation and stability. When Engels was applied to by Mahon for money, his reply was (on the face of it) correct. With the work of propaganda amongst the industrial workers in the provinces he thoroughly sympathised, but—while encouraging Mahon—he mildly rebuked him for experimenting with fresh organizations: "there has been in my opinion already too much impatience in what is called by courtesy the Socialist movement in England". As for funds for the propaganda,

> "I am quite willing to contribute my share. But the means for this must be got together & distributed by some *English* Committee, & as far as they are to come from London, by a *London* Committee. I shall speak to the Avelings about this & give them my contribution."[3]

It is clear that Engels was placing his subsidy in the hands of the League's parliamentary faction.

[1] *Ibid.,* pp. 68-71; Morris to Mahon, July 30th, 1887: "It seems to me as if this were dis-organisation rather than organisation. Of course I admit that you acted for what you thought the best: but lord! if we all take to the same game why should we take to an organisation at all? This is anarchism gone mad."

[2] *Ibid.,* p. 72. It is clear from Morris's correspondence in these months with Glasse, Mahon and Glasier that he was working exceedingly hard on *Commonweal*—not only in the editorial department but also in pushing circulation, raising funds and trying to get sellers to pay their debts. This constant preoccupation added to his irritation with the parliamentary section, who did little for the paper except criticise it: he also believed (*ibid.,* p. 67) that Aveling wished to get it out of his hands.

[3] First edition, p. 864.

This faction, however, was evidently suffering from its own tensions. Certain of these arose from a long-familiar problem: the position in the movement of Edward Aveling. Mahon visited London in July, and had conversations with Aveling and with Engels. In a letter to Engels of July 21st, he summarised the outcome of the latter meeting:

> "I understand that your financial help to the provincial propaganda will only be given on the conditions that I treat Aveling with the fullest confidence, consult him in all party matters & regard him as an essential person in the movement. You insist upon a clear understanding in this matter & therefore I am compelled to say bluntly that I *do not* accept these conditions."

But—as was again becoming very familiar—no particular charges were brought against Aveling. Engels demanded that these be brought ("If you decline to work along with Aveling on *public* grounds, you are bound to come out with them"), and Aveling wrote to Mahon demanding to know why he wished to "shove me out of the movement". Mahon's reply was formal and evasive:

> "As I am not *breaking off* any relations with you, nor making any attack upon you, but simply *refusing an invitation* to work with you I don't see why I should be called upon to formulate any charges. Nor do I see what good could come of it if I did, and I have never said that I had any to make."[1]

It is a most complex and confused situation. By the summer of 1887 Aveling's reputation in the movement had—as Eleanor Marx's biographer notes—fallen "very low indeed". The Aveling's recent lecture-tour of the United States as guests of the Socialist Labour Party of America had ended in bitter public controversy, turning upon Aveling's luxurious tastes and excessive expenses: but even these accusations, upon close examination, appeared to be unproven, and Engels could comfort himself with the reflection that all came from

[1] First edition, pp. 866-9.

Aveling's "weakness for poetic dreaming. . . Well, I still remember the time when I was just such a noodle." The suggestion that Eleanor could have been associated in any "swindle" on the working class provoked him to a defensive paternal fury: "I have inherited from Marx the obligation to stand by his children as he would have done himself, and to see, as far as lies in my power, that they are not wronged."[1] And other accusations against Aveling had a way of disappearing into rumour, insinuation, innuendo, which Engels could dismiss as the fabrications of political enemies. Some part of these probably arose from Aveling's financial expedients and his willingness to exploit the movement;[2] others from his exploits in borrowing money on all sides which (Shaw later wrote) "have grown into a Homeric legend";[3] and others from the rumours of his sexual infidelities—rumours which were never particularised for obvious reasons. For Aveling hid from all criticism behind Eleanor, and any blow aimed at him must strike at Eleanor first. In June 1887, only a few weeks before Mahon refused to work with Aveling, Mme Guillaume-Schack, a visitor to Engels's house, broke off relations with him on the grounds that she could no longer meet Aveling who had "committed discreditable acts" and had been slandering Eleanor. But when Engels "summoned her to particularize and prove" there was "nothing but gossip, insinuations, infamies" and suggestions that " 'the credit of my house' must suffer if I take responsibility for Edward". As always, Engels placed his loyalty to Eleanor first: Mme Schack's accusations were dismissed as the provocations

[1] See the judicious assessment of this episode in C. Tsuzuki, *The Life of Eleanor Marx* (Oxford, 1967), Chapter VI.

[2] In January 1886 Morris had written to Mahon: "Aveling—hem hem! he has been behaving more than queerly to the Woolwich people about some science lessons he was to have given there. They however couldn't quite make a hanging matter of it, and weak attacks strengthen the object of them. . .": R. Page Arnot, *op. cit.*, p. 56.

[3] Tsuzuki, *op. cit.*, pp. 308-9.

of the Anarchists and the gossip of "pious bourgeois women."[1]

Confronted by Mahon's unexplained refusal to work with Aveling, Engels was puzzled and exasperated:

> "Of all the various Socialist groups in England, what is now the 'opposition' in the League, was the only one with which so far I could thoroughly sympathize. But if that group is allowed to fall to pieces from mere personal whims and squabbles, or from mutual suspicions and insinuations which are carefully kept away from the light of day, it can only dissolve into a number of small cliques held together by personal motives, and utterly unfit to take any sort of lead in a really national movement. And I do not see on what grounds I should sympathize with any of these cliques more than with another, or with the S.D. federation or any other body."[2]

This may seem a correct enough response, in its way. But Engels's motivation was very much less his political judgement than his personal loyalty to Tussy. He had been warned again and again, and—with few sources of information about the English movement except those which came through the Avelings and their friends—he was being wilfully blind. If Mahon was right that the only way out of the wrangling of the London factions lay through building a new centre for political influence attached to no section, then he was also right that it would have been harmful to have identified Aveling as one of the main leaders of a movement for Socialist unity. In insisting that Aveling be "essential" and be consulted "in all party matters", Engels was imposing an arbitrary and personal condition. While pretending not to meddle in English matters, he was in fact meddling in an ineffectual, ill-informed and damaging way. Ageing, in trouble with his eyes, surrounded with the demands of Marx's manuscripts, the problems of the German party, international concerns, the concerns of Marx's extended political family,

[1] F. Engels, Paul and Laura Lafargue, *Correspondence* (Moscow, 1959), pp. 45-6.

[2] First edition, p. 867.

Engels simply had no time to exert an informed influence within the English movement. He should therefore have watched his own impatient reactions with more self-criticism, and have restrained himself from exerting an *un*informed influence. The impatience, the pressure of work, and the self-satisfied assumption of authority can all be felt in a comment upon Morris of the previous September:

> "Morris is a settled sentimental socialist; he would be easily managed if one saw him regularly a couple of times a week, but who has the time to do it, and if you drop him for a month, he is sure to lose himself again. And is he worth all that trouble even if one had the time?"[1]

But Morris was worth, perhaps, as much "trouble" as was Edward Aveling.[2] Engels's lofty dismissal of "small cliques held together by personal motives" ill became a man whose own "party", in its British influence, might be described in exactly this way.

At this point Mahon struck off on his own. In July he had discussions with H.H. Champion and others in London,[3]

[1] Engels to Laura Lafargue, September 13th, 1886, in *Engels-Lafargue Correspondence,* II, p. 370. As Page Arnot has remarked (*op. cit.,* p.40): "in none of his correspondence after the death of Marx does Engels give unqualified praise to any Briton, middle class or working class. Outside the circle of the Marx family, there is no Englishman or Scotsman for whom Engels has really a good word to say."

[2] In January 1886 Morris commented on Aveling: "I wish he would join Hyndman and let them have a hell of their own like the Texas Ranger." In the summer of 1887, when it became apparent that the Aveling group were refusing to accept the decision of the Third Annual Conference, and were forming a continuing opposition, he wrote to Mahon: "In no spirit of hostility I recommend the parliamentary section of the League to join the Federation." By October 1887 he saw the threat of renewed disruption within the League as coming from the "Marxist" section, writing to Mahon: "I am in hopes we shall yet turn our backs on our quarrels; only there is not one back but Bax who is being steeped in the Marxite pickle over at Zurich who I fear will want some sitting on when he returns. It would be very foolish to let him embroil everything again merely to get a compact adherence to the German Social Democrats." R. Page Arnot, pp. 56, 70, 74. For Bax's close contacts with Engels in August 1887, see *Engels-Lafargue Correspondence,* II, p. 58.

[3] See first edition, p. 553 n.l and (for Champion) H.H. Pelling, "H.H. Champion", *Cambridge Historical Journal,* VI, 1953.

and he then went North, to act as agitator for the Scottish Land and Labour League for the next six months. "A great deal of hard propagandist work must be done yet before we can call ourselves a party at all," he wrote to Engels at the conclusion of the Aveling incident. "In the meantime, I wish only to be of service to the cause in doing such part of that work as I can."[1] His work for the Land and Labour League immediately provoked suspicion within the Glasgow branch of the League. "I am afraid Mahon has taken post to the Devil," Morris wrote to Glasier on July 23rd (possibly after some news of the Champion-Mahon meeting had come to his ears): "which is a pity, as I am sure he is sincere; but, O so weak!"[2] But Morris tried to prevent the burning of any bridges. He published in *Commonweal,* through August and September 1887, a series of articles from Mahon, which represent a serious attempt to work out the policy learned from Engels in terms of British conditions.

In fact Mahon was one of the first to write and think in a creative way about the Labour Movement as a whole, rather than the propaganda within it of a strict Socialist theory. "Socialism", wrote Mahon in *Commonweal* ("A Labour Policy", August 27th), "is simply [the] most advanced stage of the labour movement," the most conscious expression of the class struggle which already existed in spontaneous forms:

> "The Socialist party has no interests in antagonism to other labour organisations... Trades' unionism means securing to the workers a larger share of the fruits of their labour; Socialism means securing to the workers the full fruits of their labour. Co-operation means checking the shopkeeping section of the traders from cheating the people; Socialism means stopping all sections of traders from cheating the people. Therefore, there cannot be any antagonism between these movements and the Socialist movement. Socialism embraces all other Labour movements, and the very gist of the Socialist policy is to combine all sectional Labour movements into one solid array..."

[1] First edition, p. 869.

[2] This ill-advised comment evidently came to Mahon's ears: but when he wrote to Morris complaining of it, in September, Morris appears to have forgotten that he had made it: see R. Page Arnot, *op. cit.,* p. 72.

On October 8th, in an article on trade unionism, he came out in flat opposition to the purism of the League. The Trades Union Congress of September, 1887, had seen the first serious challenge to the old Lib-Lab leadership. Keir Hardie had come into sharp opposition to Broadhurst. The fight for the Eight-hour Day was winning widespread support and (while Tom Mann and John Burns were championing this fight within the engineers) generally speaking both the S.D.F. and the League were standing aside from the agitation, and ignoring the importance of the new militancy within the unions. Mahon, touring the industrial centres of Scotland, could see the futility of this policy:

"Socialism... is on its trial! the Socialists generally must soon choose between broadening the lines of their movement so as to include the practical aspirations of the working class, or becoming a mere group of factions, preaching, it may be, pure enough principles, but preaching them to the winds and exercising no real influence with the masses. My view of the matter is... that the method of Socialist propaganda must not be merely, or mainly, preaching rigidly pure principles which the masses of the people *cannot* grasp, but taking hold of the working-class movement as it exists at present, and gently and gradually moulding it into a Socialist shape."

Socialists—Mahon declared—should without any further delay enter the fight of the unions, struggle to get elected to trades councils, to send Socialists to the T.U.C., and organize a group to combat the "Burt and Broadhurst gang". One of his last contributions to *Commonweal* (on October 15th, 1887), was a forthright appeal to the miners in Conference at Edinburgh. There is no doubt that with his defection in December, the League lost one of their best theorists.

They also lost one of their best agitators. Wherever he went this year, Mahon seemed to have "green fingers". Small Socialist organizations sprang up in his wake. Glasgow was a regular branch of the League, but Edinburgh was still in affiliated relationship, as the Scottish Land and Labour League, and through this organization Mahon conducted his propaganda, forming new branches which were only in loose association with the League's Council. Since he was operating with the support of the Edinburgh comrades (while Glasier and the Glasgow Branch looked on him with distrust), his propaganda was largely in the east—Forfarshire, West Fife, Aberdeen and Dundee. Within a very few weeks he had actually formed branches with a fair membership at Arbroath, Carnoustie and Lochee in Forfarshire, Cowdenbeath and Dysart and Gallatown in Fife, while by the end of October he had formed firm branches at Aberdeen and Dundee, and opened up new centres at Galashiels, Lochgelly and West Calder.

These successes were so striking (and in such marked contrast with Glasgow, which could only keep the Hamilton branch going with difficulty) that they give cause for reflection. In some places, as in the mining villages of West Fife, Mahon was on virgin territory: and yet found the miners willing to enroll in tens and twenties at the first or second open-air meeting. It was only necessary for him to put round hand-bills advertising his meetings, to get a large and eager audience. He succeeded where the Leaguers were failing in Lanarkshire because he took the trouble really to discover the aims and grievances of the workers whom he was addressing, and because he presented the case for Socialism in straightforward, practical terms.

Socialism reached Aberdeen with a spectacular episode in the fight for free speech which illustrates both Mahon's ability and the ready reception of the people. For some time a radical Unitarian minister, Mr. Webster, had been giving his support to Socialist ideas. Young James Leatham had been writing some articles with a Socialist slant which came to Mahon's notice. He wrote to the author (then unknown to him) asking if he would be prepared to make arrangements for a series of open-air meetings in Aberdeen. Leatham agreed:

"Mahon arrived on a fine harvest Saturday afternoon. He was only a year or two older than myself, but sported a small Swinburnian beard of sanguine hue, his fine head of red-gold hair was topped by a broad-brimmed soft black hat, and he carried, besides his satchel, two large bundles of pamphlets. . . He was a fine specimen of a type with which I was afterwards to have considerable experience.

"In Aberdeen's great historic square, Castle Street, that same evening, as Chairman of a large gathering, I delivered the first avowed Socialist speech ever given in [that] arena.

"Mahon. . . was an experienced outdoor speaker—robust but leisurely. . .—and he gripped his audience at once with simple, pungent, sentences such as: 'You sing about your bonnie Scotland and your heather hills. It's not your bonnie Scotland. It's not your heather hills. It's the landlord's bonnie Scotland. It's the landlord's heather hills. And if you want enough earth to set a geranium in you've got to pinch it.' "[1]

There was a large and responsive audience, which the police—by chivvying the speakers—succeeded in swelling. A few names were handed in at the end of the meeting of people willing to form a Socialist branch.

The next day (Sunday) further meetings were held, which culminated in the arrest of Mahon for lecturing on politics on the Lord's Day. This served as a splendid advertisement for Socialism. On Monday evening there was a packed protest meeting in the hall of the Friendly Societies, with the president of the Trades Council in the chair. A hostile journalist, who described the audience as being "of a low nature" and the Land and Labour League as a "newly-emerged abortion", was nevertheless favourably impressed by Mahon's presence:

"His long wavy hair comes down on the right side over a high broad forehead. His eyes are somewhat shifting, save when he concentrates all his passion in some argument—they are then fixed and keen. His red beard does not completely hide his lower jaw which recedes far and is the worst feature in an otherwise interesting and powerful face. Mahon is of middle height, of spare build and has a slight stoop—in form, altogether a typical factory-worker. . . His speech is on the whole logically arranged. . . His illustrations are capital and entirely suited to

[1] *The Gateway*, November, 1941.

his audience."[1]

In the result—and by skilful defence by himself and his Aberdeen friends—Mahon obtained an acquittal. There were further well-attended open-air meetings, leading on to the formation of a branch which continued in the next year or two to grow in numbers on the curious basis of affiliation to the League, while adopting the programme of the S.D.F. In view of Mahon's subsequent failures as a propagandist and organiser, the honours of this encounter should in fairness be granted to him.

Mahon's term as a League agitator came to an end in December 1887. He had appointed himself to this role, and he must have been living on the proceeds of collections, literature sales, and occasional donations from the Edinburgh branch and possibly from H.H. Champion. As a result of his refusal to consult Aveling "in all party matters" the parliamentarians of the League had sent him no assistance. He wrote to Engels in January 1888:

> "For the last twelve months I have been agitating on workhouse rations. . . I shall carry it on for another couple of months & if I can't get a half decent living by then I shall return to making my living in the factory—the sublime enjoyments of which can only be appreciated properly after experiencing the untold hardships and humiliations of the life of a Socialist Agitator."[2]

Morris and the official League had also refused him assistance. Morris clearly felt that Mahon was ill-suited to his self-appointed mission, warning him, in kindly terms, not to "become a hack of any party" nor to live on the movement by—"well, by cadging". "It's all very well for a time, at some special crisis to do as you have been doing", but:

[1] *Northern Figaro,* October 8th, 1887.

[2] First edition, p. 870. Tom Mann in Newcastle, at about this time, was experiencing the same hardships and humiliations. He had been forced to sell his violin, his telescope and his books, and bitterly resented being accused of being "a paid agitator": See Dona Torr, *op. cit.,* pp. 244-6.

> "I don't like the idea of professional agitators, & think we ought to be able to do without them: but at any rate no *loose* organisation can manage with them; they must be employed either by a well organised body, or by some private person, and be either kept in very strict order, or be perfectly free to go their own ways."[1]

Mahon certainly had felt himself free to do that, and in December, 1887, with the support of H.H. Champion he had moved his propaganda campaign across to the West of Scotland. Here he immediately quarrelled with the members of the Glasgow Socialist League, who complained that "J.L. Mahon. . . has been with us during the past week, and has attempted to suppress the name Socialist League in everything he has done for us."[2] "The Glasgow chaps fairly quarrelled with him," Morris wrote to Glasse. "I don't know all the story, but judge. . . that he, knowing the turn of mind of our friends there, unnecessarily irritated them."[3] To Glasier he wrote in private:

> "As for Mahon. . . I don't know all the circumstances, but it was clear to me that he had been rather playing for his own side of things, so I had to write as I did write, though without any wish to exacerbate the quarrel. . . Yes, I think that Champion is going all awry with his opportunism. . . I cannot believe, however, that he is a self-seeker, and so hope that he will one day see the error of his ways."[4]

Mahon retired to his old centre in Northumberland. The North of England Socialist Federation still maintained a paper existence, but the great miners' strike had been defeated, and organized anti-Socialist propaganda had made some headway. Several branches had, in Mahon's absence, linked officially with the League, the comrades at North Shields requesting in

[1] R. Page Arnot, *op. cit.*, pp. 68-70, 71.

[2] G. McLean (Sec., Propaganda Committee, Glasgow S.L.) and four others to Secretary, S.L., December 2nd, 1887: Int. Inst. Soc. Hist.

[3] R. Page Arnot, *op. cit.*, p. 90. [4] Glasier MSS., December 21st, 1887.

August, 1887, "to be properly connected with the Central Socialist League under Mr. Morris' Socialism".[1] The branches were working under the greatest difficulty, without political leadership, or secretarial experience. Blyth was forced to reduce its order of *Commonweal* to twelve in the autumn, "as the pits are working short time and cannot get sale for them". East Hollywell, at the end of November, cancelled their order altogether: "the pits are working so bad and so small wages. . . we might make another Effort soon".[2] The most effective organizer in the area in the previous six months had been Tom Mann of the S.D.F., who—while centred on the S.D.F. branches in Newcastle—had lent a fraternal hand to keeping the branches in the coalfields alive. Mahon and Tom Mann found that they were both looking in the same direction. Mann and John Burns were canvassing the possibility of amalgamating the best elements among the Socialists, launching a general Socialist newspaper, and thus cutting the movement free of the disastrous influence of Hyndman, who—despite what Morris called his "sham terrorist tactics"[3] —was ridiculing the engineer's demand for the "palliative" of an Eight-hour Day. Both Mann and Mahon were thinking less of a strict Socialist propaganda than of a Labour Party under Socialist leadership: and Mahon now saw the need for electing "three or four Socialist M.P.s. . . who could put Socialism in this country on a different footing. . . and weld the party together."[4] It seemed the height of folly that Mann and Mahon should be working in opposed organizations. Mahon swallowed his pride and rejoined the S.D.F., bringing whatever remained of the North of England Socialist Federation with him into formal union. "I suppose you know that Mahon has definitely joined the S.D.F.", Morris wrote to Glasier in January 1888,

[1] Secretary, North Shields, to Secretary, S.L., August 22nd, 1887, S.L. Correspondence, Int. Inst. Soc. Hist.

[2] *Ibid.*, Secretary, East Holywell, to Secretary, S.L., November 28th, 1887.

[3] Glasier, *op. cit.*, p. 190.

[4] First edition, p. 870. In a few month's time Mahon was to be supporting Keir Hardie's electoral intervention at Mid-Lanark: see R. Page Arnot, pp. 74-5.

"which makes me grin somewhat considering the energy with which he once attacked it. However, I am not going to quarrel with him: though I am sincerely sorry that for the present he is chiefly of use as an example of. . . political intrigue. He certainly has a genius for setting people by the ears. . . I still hope there is some sincerity in him, though it is clear that there is no stability."[1]

VII. The Jingo Jubilee

In the summer of 1887 only one campaign of the London Leaguers really seemed to arouse their ready enthusiasm—the campaign against Queen Victoria's Jingo Jubilee. This was real red meat for the old ultra-Radical leftists like Frank Kitz: it provided the Anarchists with an opportunity to take a bash at the State: and all elements of the League were able to unite in some effective anti-imperialist propaganda. Comrade Kitz was in his element, and proposed the sending up of balloons laden with Socialist literature on Jubilee Day.[2] The Queen was well known to be both an arch-imperialist and an arch-enemy of Socialism. She was also suspected, among the old Leftist core, of being an arch-fraud and the mother of an illegitimate child whose father was the notorious John Brown. As the supreme symbol of bourgeois sham and fraud, she presented them with a full-size target.

The Jubilee of 1887 may be taken as the inauguration of the "modern" concept of royalty. Although the Republican sentiment of the early 1870s had long subsided as an effective political force, it was still alive among the Radicals, and among the people generally indifference towards royalty was the rule. Now the stage-managers of the monarchy cast the Queen for the three roles which she and her successors have played ever since. First, the Crown was to serve as a symbol of imperial unity. Properly speaking, it was Disraeli who hatched this idea in 1876, when he proclaimed the Queen "Empress of India". But 1887 was a Jingo Jubilee in good earnest.

[1] Glasier MSS., January 28th, 1888.

[2] Hammersmith Minutes, June 19th, 1887. The Hammersmith Branch turned down the proposal.

Maharajas and African tribal chiefs were paraded in the streets, as at a Roman triumph. As a climax to the imperial celebrations, no less than 23,000 prisoners in Indian jails (some of them political offenders) were released. Morris had an apt comment in his regular *Commonweal* notes on this piece of "Jubilee flunkeyism":

> "To some people it will reveal depths of tyranny undreamed of before. Here is a dilemma for our Jubileeists: 'If it was dangerous to the public that these men should be at large, why do you release them?. . . If you can safely release this host of poor miserable tortured people, why did you torture them with your infernal prison?' "[1]

Second, the occasion was used (as it is always used) to provide pageants to distract the people from their own problems—in this case, from the severe depression year of 1887. The Romans at least doled out some bread with their circuses. This one was different. The people had to pay for their flag-wagging. But the Jubilee was not all made up of ardour and enthusiasm, as the official historians suggest. The unemployed and the working-class movement in many towns stood like a rock against the mass-produced hysteria. The *Commonweal* assiduously gathered the reports. At a public meeting in Llanelly "Her Majesty's name was received with groans and hisses". The Neath Town Council refused to pay for celebrations. The Cardiff Trades Council refused "to do anything in the shape of servile admiration of a well-paid servant of the State". At Bristol a large open-air meeting was held in the centre of the city on Jubilee day, addressed by Socialists and trade unionists, at which two militant Republican resolutions were carried with enthusiasm.[2] In some parts of the country, at least, the League was swimming with the stream.

Third, the monarchy was employed as a focal point for all the humbug, "respectability", and orthodox herd instincts

[1] *Commonweal*, February 26th, 1887. [2] *Ibid.*, June 25th, 1887.

which can be employed to prop up bourgeois rule. In brief, the Crown was to be used as an occasion for jingoism, circuses and guff, as it has been used ever since, and of the three, Morris found the guff the most distasteful. "The powers that be", he wrote in his *Commonweal* notes,

> "are determined to use the opportunity to show what a nuisance the monarchy and court can be as a centre of hypocrisy and corruption, and the densest form of stupidity."[1]

The Leaguers set themselves athwart the insidious gathering pressure of orthodox emotion, distributing on Jubilee Day a leaflet in Kitz's style which included the words:

> "The discovery of gas, electricity, steam-driven locomotives and machinery and the vast extension of commerce, is all to be mixed up with the deification of a mean old woman who has had as much to do with inventions or art as the man in the moon."[2]

On June 25th, 1887, the week after the main pageantry, Morris summed up his impressions in *Commonweal:*

> "Socialists feel of course that the mere abolition of the monarchy would help them little if it only gave place to a middle-class republic; such a one, for example, as that which butchered so many thousands of citizens at Paris in 1871... Nevertheless, now the monstrous stupidity is on us... one's indignation swells pretty much to the bursting-point... We must not after all forget what the hideous, revolting, and vulgar toomfoolery in question really means nowadays..."

After recalling the position of the Crown in feudal times, when the monarch—for good or ill—has at least "to do the deeds of men and women, however faulty or perverse, and not the deeds of a gilt gibbiestick", Morris considered the role of the Crown in his own time, describing the Jubilee as "a set of

[1] *Commonweal*, June 18th, 1887.

[2] *Socialists and the Jubilee. A Word on the Class War* (Socialist League handbill).

antics. . . compared with which a corobboree of Australian black-fellows is a decent and dignified performance." The monarchy no longer represented the "extinct superstitions" of feudalism and the divine right of kings,

> "but commercial realities rather: to wit, jobbery official and commercial, and its foundation, the Privilege of Capital, set on a background of the due performance of the conventional domestic duties: in short, the representation of the anti-social spirit in its fulness is what is required of it.
>
> "That is the reason why the career of the present representative is. . . so eminently satisfactory. It has been the life of a respectable official who has always been careful to give the minimum of work for the maximum of pay. . . All this. . . it has performed in a way which has duly earned the shouts of the holiday-makers, the upholsterers, firework makers, gasfitters and others who may gain some temporary advantage from the Royal (but shabby) Jubilee Circus, as well as the deeper-seated applause of those whose be-all and end-all is the continuance of respectable robbery."

And yet from all this farce, Morris extracted some comfort:

> "Even this vulgar Royal Upholstery procession, trumpery as it is, may deepen the discontent a little, when the newspapers are once more empty of it, and when people wake up, as on the morrow of a disgraceful orgie, and find dull trade all the duller for it, and have to face according to their position the wearisome struggle for riches, for place, for respectability, for decent livelihood, for bare subsistence, in the teeth of growing competition in a society now at last showing its rottenness openly."

VIII. "Bloody Sunday"

The bourgeoisie could not lay on a Jubilee every month to provide a target for League propaganda. But more serious trouble was gathering. Throughout the spring and summer months the mood of the London unemployed had been rising. The S.D.F. had put forward demands for immediate relief and public works, and had led a number of successful demonstrations—a great Church Parade at St. Paul's, a counter-demonstration to the Lord Mayor's Show, smaller church parades and deputations to the local authorities in the East End and many other centres. Although individual Leaguers had helped in the agitation, Morris and the Council had held aloof. Morris applauded the major demonstrations and some of the local agitation, as drawing attention to the misery of the unemployed, but he suspected Hyndman of using the agitation for opportunist ends—on the one hand holding out prospects of relief to the starving men which a capitalist State would never grant, and on the other using their misery to advertise the S.D.F. and to brandish as a stick of sham insurrection at the Government.[1]

Some colour was lent to Morris's view by the retirement of both John Burns and H.H. Champion from the agitation in the summer of 1887 (both of whom had become dissatisfied with Hyndman's attitude), and according to Shaw, "the result was that the unemployed agitation was left almost leaderless at the moment when the unemployed themselves were getting almost desperate". Early in the winter of 1887,

> "the men themselves, under all sorts of casual leaders, or rather speech-makers, took to meeting constantly in Trafalgar Square. . . The shop-keepers began to complain that the sensational newspaper accounts of the meetings were frightening away their customers and endangering the Christmas quarter's rent. On this the newspapers became more

[1] For the S.D.F.'s part in the unemployed agitation, see Lee, *op. cit.*, pp. 125-30. Morris's comments in his *Diary* are published in part in Mackail, II, pp. 175-6, and conclude: "If a riot is quite spontaneous it does frighten the bourgeois even if it is but isolated; but planned riots or shows of force are no good unless in a time of action, when they are backed by the opinion of the people and are in point of fact indications of the rising tide. . ." Of a torchlight procession organized by the Clerkenwell and Marylebone branches of the S.D.F. in commemoration of the "riots" of 1886, Morris noted: "a stupid thing to do unless they had strength and resolution to make a big row, which they *know* they have not got." On the other hand, Morris took part in several unemployed demonstrations, both in Hammersmith and in London (see Vallance, *op. cit.*, p. 341), and Joseph Pennell recollected one church parade from Trafalgar Square to Westminster Abbey: "An enormous crowd began to pour out of the Square down Parliament Street. . . On they came, with a sort of irresistible force, . . . and right in front—among the red flags, singing with all his might the 'Marseillaise'—was William Morris. He had the face of a Crusader, and he marched with that big stick of his, as the Crusaders must have marched" (quoted in *Labour Leader,* October 10th, 1896).

sensational than ever; and those fervid orators who preserve friendly relations with the police began to throw in the usual occasional proposal to set London on fire simultaneously at the Bank, St. Paul's, the House of Commons, the Stock Exchange, and the Tower. This helped to keep the pot boiling; and at last the police cleared the unemployed out of the square. . ."[1]

Shaw's account, despite its mock cynicism, seems to be pretty close to the mark. At least one *agent provocateur* was unearthed in the subsequent court proceedings, and it is clear that the relatively unorganized nature of the agitation gave the police the opportunity, for which they had been watching, of forcing a showdown on the issue of free-speech in the Metropolis.

James Allman, an unemployed worker on the Council of the League, took a leading part in the agitation, but again in a haphazard way. "Returning from a meeting held early in October to protest against the murder of our Chicago comrades", relates Allman, he and three other Socialists passed through the Square, and seeing the unemployed gathered without leaders or purpose, determined that they and other unemployed Socialists would conduct a series of organized meetings:

"The first meeting was held next morning, the speeches being delivered from one of the seats and beneath the shadow of a black banner upon which the words 'We will have work or bread' were inscribed in large white letters. The result of this meeting was a series of daily assemblages in the same place. . . Day by day the sansculotic workless multitude met, marched, and spoke, and daily their numbers increased."[2]

On one occasion, Allman recounted, while the injury was still fresh in his mind:

[1] G.B. Shaw, *The Fabian Society: What It has Done and How It has Dont It* (Fabian Tract No. 41, 1892), pp. 7-10.

[2] "The Truth About the Unemployed, By One of Them", *Commonweal*, November 26th, 1887.

"The processionists were proceeding towards Stepney Green via Strand and City, when, opposite Charing Cross Station, the police suddenly pounced upon them, seized and smashed up their black banner, and dispersed the procession. Strange to say, though, the red flag remained, and from that day till quite recently was borne before the procession. The black banner, representing the dark prospects of unemployed workmen, and borne in our parades as an appeal to the commiseration of the wealthy and a symbol of despair, was torn from us. . . But the red flag, the emblem of sturdy revolt, remained with us, and henceforth we marched in the wake of the flame-coloured flag. . ."

Strange, indeed! But it would not have been so strange to Allman and the unemployed if they had realized that the police were deliberately provoking them into an insurrectionary temper.

Morris and the Council of the League smelled danger, but took refuge in their old purism. They passed a resolution on the Unemployed Question which was definitely flabby:

"That the Socialist League do maintain officially the continuance of that policy of non-intervention pursued by it up to the present; and though it can prohibit no individual members. . . from participating in unemployed agitation, it cannot undertake to support, either morally or pecuniarily, any member whose participation. . . leads him into difficulties."[1]

This was backed up, on October 29th, by a Manifesto of the Council, signed by H.A. Barker, the Secretary, but certainly

[1] *Commonweal*, October 22nd, 1887. The Glasgow Branch passed a vigorous protest against this resolution, which it accused of giving the impression of "callousness or indifference". Glasier, in a well-argued covering letter (October 24th, 1887), said he had found it "no easy task to maintain the principle that we cannot secure any adequate amelioration of the condition of the unemployed under the existing system". The comrades had maintained that "cases of *absolute starvation* must have to the living generation a claim above all abstract principles". In Glasgow the City Council had a large fund for "the common good" and unreclaimed land on which to give employment to the unemployed, and the comrades urged an agitation for the employment of direct labour ("without middlemen or contractors") on socially useful tasks. Such measures, so far from weakening Socialist support among the unemployed, "would be of immense advantage as means of creating a sympathy and interest in our propaganda if we took the lead in the matter. . . as in the case of the Lanarkshire miners' strike". S.L. Correspondence, Int. Inst. Soc. Hist.

written by Morris. While expressing sympathy with the unemployed, and demanding (in an off-hand way) immediate relief, the Manifesto urged the futility of asking the capitalist State to provide outdoor relief, since—while such relief might be given—the result would only be to throw more workers out of employment:

> "While the present State lasts. . . there is no remedy possible for this huge misery and wrong. Must we Socialists tell this, then, to starving men seeking victuals and shelter for the passing day? Yes, we *must* tell it them. . . to give them lying and delusive hopes of a decent livelihood which they have no chance of obtaining is not doing them a service. . . There is no salvation for the unemployed but in the general combination of the workers for the freedom of labour—for the REVOLUTION. . ."

Premature rioting would bring no relief—and here Morris showed that he had seen through the police tactics, and had real and genuine cause for anger at Hyndman's opportunism:

> "Once for all, unless we Socialists are prepared to organize and lead such disturbances, and carry them through to the bitter end, we are bound, under penalty of being justly blamed for egging on people to do what we dare not heartily take part in, to point out to the unemployed what would probably be the results of a riot. . ."

The riot, Morris declared, would be repressed with ease, unless part of a general revolutionary movement of the whole working class. Moreover, the brutal attacks at present being made by the police upon the unemployed demonstrations (against which the statement made a vigorous protest) "are made with the deliberate intention of forcing them into riot in order to give the authorities an excuse for another step in the suppression of free speech".

The Manifesto was negative on the one hand, prophetic on the other. The mood of the authorities was a great deal sterner than it had been when they were taken unawares by the riots of 1886. Gladstone and the old Liberal Party had been defeated on Home Rule, and the Tory-Liberal Unionist

Government was forcing coercion upon Ireland, and in a mood to destroy Socialism at home. Bismarck's anti-Socialist laws had attracted favourable attention in England, and the judicial murder of the Anarchists in Chicago (the long public preparations for which were going on throughout October and November, until their execution on November 11th) had emboldened reactionaries to preach openly from the text, "Go thou, and do likewise". On the day after the Chicago executions, and the day before "Bloody Sunday", *The Times* published a remarkable editorial, denouncing the public petitions throughout the United States for clemency to the Anarchists as a "mischievous practice... an unparalleled amount of illegitimate pressure": complaining at the "lax discipline which enabled Lingg [who committed suicide] to disappoint the hangman": and commending,

> "the sternness of Americans in repressing offences against law and order... American police... do not wait to read a Riot Act... They take little reck of the right of public meetings... They carry revolvers, and use them without mercy when they see signs of resistance... Judges and juries draw no distinction between incendiaries of the platform and the Press, and the men who do their dirty work. These things, which happen in the freest Republic in the world, may suggest... whether there is anything so essentially incompatible with the liberty of the subject in the methods, in many respects milder, which are the objects of... vehement denunciation..."

in Ireland, and (as the events of the next day were to show) in Britain as well. "If the people of the United States do not hesitate when order is persistently disturbed to restore it with a strong hand, why should we be afraid to give effect to the general will?"[1]

The brutal assaults of the police upon the unemployed demonstrators were no mere fictions of the imaginations of Allman and the Council of the League. Throughout October repeated assaults and arrests were made upon the demon-

[1] *The Times*, November 12th, 1887.

strators. On October 17th, 18th, and 19th, Trafalgar Square was cleared by charges of mounted police and the plentiful use of the baton. In the first week of November meetings were being held daily in the Square, and on November 4th, when the Square was once again cleared, the red flag was at last taken. On November 8th Sir Charles Warren banned all further meetings in the Square, on the pretext that it was Crown property. By now the best of the Radicals were alarmed. *Reynolds* and the *Pall Mall Gazette* (under the editorship of W.T. Stead) were championing the cause of free speech and exposing the worst cases of provocation and framed-up charges of the police. Morris wrote to the *Pall Mall Gazette* proposing a Law and Liberty League, to defend the rights of free speech. The Metropolitan Radical Association and several prominent individuals—Annie Besant, W.T. Stead, Cunninghame Graham, the Rev. Stewart Headlam—took up the issue with vigour. The Radicals and the Irish called for a demonstration in Trafalgar Square on November 13th, to protest against Coercion and the treatment in prison of the Irish M.P. O'Brien. It was an emergency decision, driven forward by Stead, under the slogan: "To the Square!" Scarcely three days were left for preparations, but—as at Dod Street—the Radicals and the Irish turned out in their thousands on the day.

The events of November 13th have gone down in history as "Bloody Sunday". For action of *this* kind—the keeping of the streets and squares free for the work of propaganda—Morris and the Council of the League had no hesitation. The demonstrators—Radicals, Irish National League, and Socialists—formed up at various points in the east, before rallying for the procession to the west. Morris joined the contingent on Clerkenwell Green. According to *The Times'* report, the contingent was made up of "respectable artisans", and was addressed from a cart by Morris and Annie Besant, in speeches of a "determined character":

"Mr. William Morris. . . proceeded to say that wherever free speech was attempted to be put down, it was their bounden duty to resist the attempt by every means in their power. He thought their business was to get to the Square by some means or other, and he intended to do his best to get there whatever the consequences might be. They must press on to the Square like orderly people and good citizens. Mr. Morris's views were evidently the views of most of those he was addressing, and met with not a little applause. . ."

According to another report, he also added some advice as to how to deal with the police:

"When the procession was passing through the streets, those behind must not fall back, no matter what happened to those in front. This, he added, amid laughter, would only be offering 'passive resistance' to the authorities. He hoped they would shove the policemen, rather than hit them, for the policemen were armed and they were not. . ."[1]

It is clear that he had a better idea of what was to be expected than most of the good-humoured but earnest crowd massing around the cart. But what took place far surpassed even his worst expectations. The main body of the foot police and the military (armed, and with twenty rounds apiece) lined the sunken part of the Square, while the mounted police and contingents of foot police guarded the outlying approaches. The defence, Morris wrote in the next issue of *Commonweal,* "was ample against anything except an organized attack from determined persons acting in concert and able to depend on one another". The Clerkenwell contingent of upwards of 5,000, which had marched in good order to within a quarter of a mile of the Square, was attacked as it was entering St. Martin's Lane:

"It was all over in a few minutes: our comrades fought valiantly, but they had not learned how to stand and turn their column into a line, or to march on to the front. Those in front turned and faced their rear, not to run away, but to join in the fray if opportunity served. The police struck right and left like what they were, soldiers attacking an enemy. . ."

[1] *The Times,* November 14th, 1887.

The Socialist League banner was torn from the hands of a determined comrade, Mrs. Taylor. Flags were torn from the hands of the processionists, "and their staves broken by the police laying them down. . . and jumping on them". The band instruments were captured, and—Morris recounted:

> "All that our people could do was to straggle into the Square as helpless units. I confess I was astounded at the rapidity of the thing and the ease with which military organization got its victory. I could see that numbers were of no avail unless led by a band of men acting in concert and each knowing his own part."

Morris himself was in the centre of the police attack. He had been walking in the middle of the column beside Shaw, but—anticipating trouble—he had gone to the head of the procession, "where he saw the rout at its most striking moment".[1] "I shall never forget how quickly these unarmed crowds were dispersed into clouds of dust", he wrote to Andreas Scheu. "I found myself suddenly alone in the middle of the street, and, deserted as I was, I had to use all my strength to gain safety."[2] By some means he entered the Square and witnessed the last act of the assault.

The other columns had met with even more brutality before they reached the Square. Cunninghame Graham, the aristocratic Radical-Socialist M.P. for N.-W. Lanark, headed an attack on the police cordon with John Burns. Graham's head was cut open, and a neutral observer reported:

> "After Mr. Graham's arrest was complete one policeman after another, two certainly, but I think no more, stepped up from behind and struck him on the head from behind with a violence and brutality which were shocking to behold. Even after this, and when some five or six other police were dragging him into the Square, another from behind seized him most needlessly by the hair. . . and dragged his head back, and in that condition he was forced forwards many yards."[3]

[1] Account of G.B. Shaw, quoted by Vallance, *op. cit.,* p. 338.

[2] Scheu, *op. cit.,* Part III, Ch. VI.

[3] *Remember Trafalgar Square* (*Pall Mall Gazette* "Extra"). Account by Sir E. Reed, M.P.

Even the foreign Socialists were appalled at the behaviour of the "British bobby". The Radicals were angry and astonished, "but by no means strung up to fighting pitch", commented Morris. The many stragglers on the edges of the Square were treated to another demonstration of "firmness", in the calling out of the soldiers, the reading of the Riot Act by "a sort of country-gentleman-looking imbecile", and the totally unnecessary appearance of a regiment of Guardsmen with fixed bayonets, who proceeded to clear the Square. Seventy-five arrests were made: 200 people were treated in hospital for injuries, and countless scores more bore the marks of "law and order" to their homes: three sustained fatal injuries.[1]

The reactions of the various parties were immediate. In the police stations the prisoners were kept from sleeping by the "Hurrahs!" and choruses of "Rule Britannia" of the victorious police. *The Times* blossomed into a leader which far exceeded its "mingled feelings" of February, 1886, and which (not that it mattered) completely contradicted the accounts of its own reporters:

> "Putting aside mere idlers and sightseers. . . and putting aside also a small band of persons with a diseased craving for notoriety. . . the active portion of yesterday's mob was composed of all that is weakest, most worthless, and most vicious of the slums of a great city. . . no honest purpose. . . animated these howling roughs. It was simple love of disorder, hope of plunder, and the revolt of dull brutality against the rule of law. . . morbid vanity. . . greed of gain. . . hound. . . ignorant. . . debased. . . ranting. . . pernicious incitements. . . nauseous hypocrisy. . . ringleaders. . . criminals."[2]

On the 15th it reported "great rejoicings all over London, especially in the West End":

> "If this meeting had been permitted, no other meetings, even if they had been held day and night, could have been put down."

[1] W.B. Curner and Connell died soon after Bloody Sunday; another victim, Harrison, died after a lingering illness. Linnell received his injuries on another occasion.

[2] *The Times*, November 14th, 1887.

The authorities consolidated their victory by swearing in special constables and trying to recall the panic of 1848. On the next Sunday mounted police galloped up and down the Square, pursuing irresolute and straggling crowds, and an innocent by-stander, a Radical law-writer named Alfred Linnell, was ridden down and sustained fatal injuries. Sentences of hard labour, ranging from one month to a year, were doled out on largely perjured evidence. Two months after the affair John Burns and Cunninghame Graham were awarded the relatively mild sentence of six weeks.

The Gladstonian Liberals maintained a shameful complicity of silence—only Bradlaugh resuming his old championship of the rights of free speech. Among the Radicals and Socialists reactions were altogether different. Morris's feelings were ones of fury from the start. "Harmless citizens were. . . beaten and trodden underfoot; men were haled off to the police courts and there beaten again", he wrote in his Notes on the year, 1887, after he had had time to check the evidence.[1] In *Commonweal* he wrote, "Sir Charles Warren. . . has given us a lesson in street fighting", and stressed the need for crowd drill and discipline:

> "The mask is off now, and the real meaning of all the petty persecution of our open-air meetings is as clear as may be. No more humbug need be talked about obstruction. . . The very Radicals have been taught that slaves have no rights."[2]

Cunninghame Graham, as might be expected, took his own lesson thoroughly to heart. Whilst a captive in the Square, he saw plenty to cause reflection:

> "I saw repeated charges made at a perfectly unarmed and helpless crowd; I saw policemen. . . under the express order of their superiors, repeatedly strike women and children. . . As I was being led out of the

[1] Brit. Mus. Add. MSS. 46345.

[2] "London in a State of Siege", *Commonweal*, November 19th, 1887.

crowd a poor woman asked a police inspector... if he had seen a child she had lost. His answer was to tell her she was a 'damned whore', and to knock her down..."

The main result of the brutality, in his opinion, was "to make the Liberal Party as odious and as despised as the Tory Party in the Metropolis". Three men killed (one of them a well-known local Radical leader),[1] hundreds wounded and bruised, three hundred arrested, many imprisoned—and the great Liberal Party that was crying out against Irish Coercion did—nothing. "I expected"—wrote Graham—"that it would be thought as cruel and tyrannical to break up a meeting at which thousands of Irishmen were to be present, in London as it would be in Ireland".

"I thought that freedom of speech and the right of public meeting were facts in themselves, about which politicians were agreed. I did not know the meanness of the whole crew even at that time. I was not aware that freedom of speech and public meeting were nothing to them but stalking-horses to hide themselves behind, and under cover of which to crawl into Downing Street. I soon found, however, that the Liberal party was a complete cur, that what they excelled in doing was singing, 'Gloria Gladstone in excelsis', and talking of what they intended to do in Ireland..."[2]

Thousands of London Radical working men shared his views.

This new unity between the Radicals and the Socialists found its complete and victorious demonstration in the solemn public funeral of Alfred Linnell. Morris, together with Annie Besant, W.T. Stead, and others in the Law and Liberty League, played a prominent part in preparing the ceremony. Despite the poor weather, the people—Radicals, Irish, and Socialists—turned out in their tens of thousands, in the greatest united demonstration which London had seen. "It was a victory",

[1] William B. Curner, a prominent Deptford Radical and Secularist, was buried with public ceremony on January 7th, 1888, William Morris's "Death Song" closing the proceedings.

[2] *Commonweal*, November 10th, 1888.

wrote Morris, "for it was the most enormous concourse of people I ever saw; the number incalculable; the crowd sympathetic and quite orderly."[1] Cunninghame Graham, Annie Besant, W.T. Stead, Herbert Burrows, Frank Smith (of the Salvation Army) and William Morris were the pall-bearers: on the hearse were the flags of the Irish, Socialists and Radicals, and a shield with the lettering, "KILLED IN TRAFALGAR SQUARE". As the enormous procession moved behind a band playing the "Dead March" to Bow Cemetery, the streets were lined with vast crowds of sympathizers, and the police were greeted with cries of "That's your work!" They reached the graveside at about half-past four, with the light already failing in the rain, so that the Rev. Stewart Headlam read the burial service by the light of a lantern. "The scene at the grave", Morris wrote, "was the strangest sight I have ever seen, I think. It was most impressive to witness; there was to me something aweful (I can use no other word) in such a tremendous mass of people, unorganized, unhelped, and so harmless and good-tempered."[2] First, Mr. Tims, of the London Liberal and Radical Federation, spoke to the crowd. Morris followed, speaking with great simplicity and under the stress of strong feeling:

"There lay a man of no particular party—a man who until a week or two ago was perfectly obscure, and probably was only known to a few... Their brother lay there—let them remember for all time this man as their brother and their friend... Their friend who lay there had had a hard life and met with a hard death; and if society had been differently constituted from what it was, that man's life might have been a delightful, a beautiful one, and a happy one to him. It was their business to try and make this earth a very beautiful and happy place. They were engaged in a most holy war, trying to prevent their rulers... making this great town of London nothing more than a prison. He could not help thinking the immense procession in which they had walked that day would have the effect of teaching a great lesson. He begged them to do their best to preserve order in getting back to their homes, because their enemies would be only too glad to throw

[1] Glasier, *op. cit.*, p. 190. [2] Mackail, II, p. 193.

a blot upon that most successful celebration; and they should begin to-morrow to organize for the purpose of seeing that such things should not happen again."[1]

"He threw his whole soul into his speech", recorded one witness. "There was fearful earnestness in his voice when referring to the victim we had just laid to rest. He cried out, 'Let us feel he *is* our brother.' The ring of brotherly love in it was most affecting."[2] The London organizer of the Irish National League and Harry Quelch of the S.D.F. followed—the latter forcing his Socialist views a little sharply upon the mourners. The light was growing very dim as the crowd sang Morris's "Death Song" to the music of Malcolm Lowson, and with Walter Crane's design of a mounted policeman attacking the people on the front of the sheet:

"We asked them for a life of toilsome earning,
They bade us bide their leisure for our bread;
We craved to speak to tell our woeful learning:
We come back speechless, bearing back our dead.
Not one, not one, nor thousands must they slay,
But one and all if they would dusk the day.

"They will not learn; they have no ears to hearken.
They turn their faces from the eyes of fate;
Their gay-lit halls shut out the skies that darken.
But, lo! this dead man knocking at the gate.
Not one, not one, nor thousands must they slay,
But one and all if they would dusk the day."

Quietly the great crowd dispersed from the cemetery. Morris walked back in the rain with the comrades, deeply moved, and musing to himself. "Well, I like ceremony", he finally said.

For many weeks Morris was busy with the Law and Liberty League, and was lecturing by choice upon "Trafalgar Square"

[1] *Commonweal*, December 24th, 1887.

[2] MS. reminiscences of H.A. Barker in the Walthamstow Collection.

in different parts of the country.[1] He was bitterly attacked in the Press for his part in the Linnell funeral. But at the same time he gained, for the first time in his political agitation, real stature and affection in the eyes of the Radical London masses. It was perhaps in these days, more than at any other time, that he laid the basis for the love—almost veneration—in which he was held by great sections of the Labour movement at the time of his death. It is true that he did not regard the Radical-Socialist alliance as anything more than a temporary unity upon a limited issue. In some ways he even regarded the work of the Law and Liberty League as a distraction from the essential work of the Socialist propaganda.[2] But where the unity existed he valued it: he understood and respected both the motives of his new allies and the limits of his agreement with them: when he acted with the Radicals, or spoke at combined meetings, he respected their prejudices and spoke upon the cause they had in common. He was looked on from all sides—S.D.F. and Radical alike—as a spokesman and arbiter. By contrast, Hyndman, who had never ceased to wither the Radicals with his scorn, saw the agitation as only one more platform from which to retail the red meat of his own brand of Socialist theory, irrespective of the occasion or the audience. On February 19th, 1888, Morris went down to Pentonville Jail early in the morning to greet John Burns and Cunninghame Graham and other prisoners on their release from their sentences. In the evening he helped to serve tea at a social in their honour, in which the Irish and the Radicals joined. The next evening a great public meeting was held to greet them, with Michael Davitt, the Irish leader, in the Chair, and William O'Brien (the Irish M.P. whose imprisonment had

[1] See Morris to Glasse, March 2nd, 1888: "I don't think the Glasgow people have chosen a good subject: who cares about history? I think I shall refuse to give it them. I think I might make Trafalgar Square the subject of the lecture at Edinburgh. I notice that out of London people are quite ignorant of the subject" (Glasse MSS).

[2] See Glasier, *op. cit.*, p. 190, where Morris writes (December 21st, 1887): "I shall be glad to let the *Pall Mall Gazette* go on its way now. . . Ordinary meetings have been somewhat neglected for these bigger jobs."

been the occasion for the calling of the demonstration on November 13th), Annie Besant, John Burns, Cunninghame Graham, W.T. Stead, Hyndman and Morris as the speakers—a considerable victory, Morris thought, since "it will mean no less than an acknowledgement by the Irish party that they are the allies of the London discontent & Trafalgar Square".[1] The hall was crammed, the audience at the height of excitement and taking their mutual differences in good humour until Hyndman rose. He began by attacking the cowardice of the Liberal party, and the Liberal M.Ps. for not being present: then suddenly he swung round upon twelve Radical M.Ps., who—while certainly not conspicuous for their part in the earlier agitation—had at least made a tardy gesture of solidarity by accepting an invitation to sit on the platform, and—Morris afterwards remarked—"we were therefore prepared to accept their repentance I suppose."[2] "The sight of those twelve Radical M.Ps.", Hyndman later wrote,

> "who had never done anything for the unemployed nor helped our fight for free speech in any way, stirred my anger, and turning on them I asked: 'What on earth are these men doing here?' "[3]

And thereupon he began to direct his scorn upon their individual shortcomings, until one of the restive Radicals broke from the audience with a cry of "You infernal firebrand!" and rushed at the platform with the apparent intention of knocking Hyndman down. The meeting broke up in scrimmages and disorder, with Morris's speech undelivered. Its break-up signaled the end of the unity of Trafalgar Square.

The episode of Bloody Sunday affected Morris's imagination powerfully. It marked also a perceptible change in his outlook and perspectives. "Up to this time", Bax records, "he had more or less believed in the possible success of a revolutionary outbreak on the part of the populace of our

[1] *Letters*, p. 280. [2] May Morris, II, p. 268.
[3] Hyndman, *Record of an Adventurous Life*, pp. 323-4.

great cities." Bax was attending the German Social-Democrat Congress in Zurich at the time:

"He wrote me a letter. . . telling me that he had always recognized the probability of any scratch body of men getting the worst of it in a rough-and-tumble with the police, not to speak of the military, yet he had not realized till that day how soon such a body could be scattered by a comparatively small but well-organized force. . . When I had come back to London, he vividly described to me how, singly and in twos and threes, his followers began for a few moments to make a show of fight with the police, and how in vain he tried to rally them to effect a determined dash as a united body on. . . Trafalgar Square itself. . . This incident certainly had a strong effect in making Morris pessimistic as to the success of any popular civil rising under existing circumstances. . ."[1]

Shaw, also writing after Morris's death, was even more emphatic:

"If the men who had had the presumption to call themselves his 'comrades' and 'brothers' had been in earnest about cleaning and beautifying human society as he was in earnest about it, he would have been justified in believing that there was a great revolutionary force beginning to move in society. Trafalgar Square cured him and many others of that illusion."[2]

Most of Morris's biographers have accepted the evidence of these two friends, and especially that of Shaw, without question—and even embroidered on it, in the sense that it is suggested that after Bloody Sunday Morris passed out of the revolutionary phase of his political convictions into one of reformism or Utopian idealism.

It must be said that both Bax and Shaw misunderstood the effect of Bloody Sunday—and that, in the case of Shaw at least, the misunderstanding was wilful. Shaw was, perhaps, reluctant to admit that it was Bloody Sunday which saw the parting of the political ways between him and Morris. Until this time they had been close colleagues in the movement: and, indeed, they remained on friendly terms until Morris's

[1] Bax, *op. cit.*, pp. 87-8. [2] Vallance, *op. cit.*, p. 339.

death. Morris had been among the first to recognize the genius of Shaw's early novels.[1] He rejoiced in his company, and the wit with which he scourged their common enemy, the Bourgeois. Shaw was—and remained—the most popular outside lecturer at the Hammersmith Clubroom, and one observer recalled,

> "there were few prettier sights than to see the rugged Saxon viking and the daring Celtic sabreur on the same platform. If you imagine a father and son deeply attached to one another—the elder man warmly admiring yet at times questioning the adroit cleverness of his boy, and the younger man eager to suppress himself and his sardonic humour when touched by a genuine regard for the dignity of his sire—you can picture Morris and Shaw together."[2]

In the years between 1884 and 1887, Shaw had refused to join either Federation or League, finding various reasons to justify his own intellectual vanity and eclecticism. Later he declared that he had remained uncommitted because he felt more at home among the middle-class milieu of the Fabians.[3] His failure to throw in his lot with the League in 1885, and subsequent failures to support it on important occasions,[4] must have been a disappointment to Morris. Yet it should not be supposed that Shaw's services to the movement at this time were unimportant. Apart from his important fact-finding work with the Fabian Society, he addressed hundreds of meetings for the S.D.F., League, Radical Clubs, and other bodies, and sometimes took part in the League's open-air propaganda. William Morris was the one man whom Shaw in his maturity respected without reserve, and to the end of his life he always wrote of Morris with quite unusual

[1] See G.B. Shaw, "William Morris as I Knew Him", Preface to May Morris, II, p. xii.

[2] *Labour Leader,* October 10th, 1896.

[3] Fabian Tract, No. 41 (1892), pp. 9-10.

[4] For example, the League wished him to be their protagonist in debate with Bradlaugh, but Shaw made so many difficulties about the wording of the resolution to be debated that it was impossible to continue.

warmth and humility. Morris's influence upon him was perhaps the most positive and enduring of any other influence in his adult life.

It was *Shaw,* however, and not Morris, who thought himself cured of "illusions" by Bloody Sunday, and his comments upon Morris's reactions are clouded by his own. The two men had marched in the column together, but had separated shortly before the attack of the police. A few days later Shaw sent his comments to Morris:

"The women were much in the way. The police charged us the moment they saw Mrs. Taylor. But you should have seen that high-hearted host run. Running hardly expresses our collective action. We *skedaddled,* and never drew rein until we were safe on Hampstead Heath or thereabouts. Tarleton found me paralysed with terror and brought me on to the Square, the police kindly letting me through in consideration of my genteel appearance. On the whole, I think it was the most abjectly disgraceful defeat ever suffered by a band of heroes outnumbering their foes a 1,000 to 1."

Shaw next objected to an article in *Commonweal* by Sparling (who now—married to May—was Morris's son-in-law)—not because it was revolutionary, but because if it got him into gaol it would do no good. Since Sparling's article was a fairly inoffensive parable, Shaw was probably criticizing in a roundabout way Morris's own comments in his article: "London in a State of Siege". He continued:

"I object to a defiant policy altogether at present. If we persist in it, we shall be eaten bit by bit like an artichoke. They will provoke; we will defy; they will punish. I do not see the wisdom of that until we are at least strong enough to resist 20 policemen with the help of Heaven and Mrs. Taylor.

"I wish generally that our journals would keep their tempers. If Stead had not forced us to march on the Square a week too soon by his 'Not one Sunday must be allowed to pass' nonsense, we should have been there now. It all comes from people trying to live down ['up' deleted] to fiction instead of up to facts."[1]

[1] Brit. Mus. Add. MSS. 45345.

Five years later it was *Shaw,* once again, who looked back on this "defeat" as a turning-point for British Socialism:

> "Insurrectionism, after a two year's innings, vanished from the field. . . In the middle of the revengful growling over the defeat at the Square, trade revived; the unemployed were absorbed; the *Star* newspaper [which the Fabians for a brief season "captured"] appeared to let in light and let off steam: in short, the way was clear at last for Fabianism."[1]

In his most famous Fabian essay (written in September, 1888) he paid his parting tribute to the views of Morris, declaring his sympathy for those "enthusiasts" who refused to believe in the slow and cowardly course of winning Socialism through vestries and Parliament, and who still aimed at establishing the new society with one revolutionary stroke. The course he chose—he argued—was less heroic, but was inevitable. Such an "army of light" as Morris and the revolutionary Socialists envisaged "is no more to be gathered from the human product of nineteenth-century civilization than grapes are to be gathered from thistles. . .".[2] From the outset Shaw's fine intellectual fury against capitalism had been blunted by his lack of faith in the conscious, revolutionary efforts of the proletariat. He saw the workers (as he was to describe them in *Major Barbara*) as corrupted and demoralized by capitalism. Bloody Sunday he took as confirmation of his disillusion.

Morris knew all about Fabianism—that chip off the old utilitarian block. He had thought it all out for himself several years before Shaw had started reading Henry George—in the days of the old National Liberal League—and he had become a Socialist because he did not like the thought. He knew, and publicly acknowledged, that "in economics Shaw is my master",[3] but he also knew that Fabianism led in the end to

[1] Fabian Tract No. 41.

[2] *Fabian Essays* (1889), p. 201. See also Alick West, *A Good Man Fallen Among Fabians,* pp. 34-47.

[3] May Morris, II, p. xx.

"deadlock" and that it bred the kind of moral evasions and class attitudes which he abhorred. Morris's reactions, both at the time of Bloody Sunday and in the months that followed, had little in common with those of Shaw. In what sense, then, did the episode mark a change in his outlook?

Trafalgar Square confirmed for Morris the train of thought which he had first started in his article, "Facing the Worst of It" at the beginning of the year. Throughout 1887 he had been abandoning his hopes of a speedy revolution; after 1887, to all intents and purposes, he had abandoned any hope of seeing Socialism in his own lifetime. Bloody Sunday showed him not so much the weakness of the people as the true face of reaction. He saw not only the mounted police and the batons; he also saw the complicity of almost the entire capitalist Press, the treachery of the professed advocates of freedom in Parliament and public life. He saw the need not only for organization, but for a vast increase in Socialist understanding on the part of the people, if a revolutionary movement were to stand any chance of success. Moreover, he saw the effect upon Shaw and others of his comrades of the "defeat": he saw the turn towards Fabianism and gradualism, the spread of disillusion in revolutionary organization and tactics: he foresaw the whole story ahead of him, of blind alleys, betrayals and failure. In so far as this foresight damped his earlier optimism, and even made him feel less urgency in his own part in the propaganda, Shaw and Bax were right.

But this implied not a modification of his theory, but a change in his perspectives. There is no need to speculate about the effect upon him of his experiences during these months: they are written into every page of the remarkable chapter of *News from Nowhere,* "How the Change Came". They are implicit in the date suggested for the beginning of the Revolution—1952—a date which many of his comrades thought unduly pessimistic and which he himself would never have conceived in 1885. The first events of the Revolution are drawn from the main tendencies and events of November, 1887: the vacillating Government, the clever young General

(Sir Charles Warren), the betrayal of the Press (worst of all in the Liberal *Daily News*), the horror of the people and their counter-demonstrations (Linnell's funeral), the excitement of the young reactionaries who at last had something to do when the General Strike was proclaimed (comparable to the reactions of the young aristocrats enrolled as special constables after Bloody Sunday). The events take a different pattern in 1952 because the workers are more determined, better organized in their Federation of labour (despite repeated corruption of its leadership by opportunists and time-servers), and because there are younger determined Socialist cadres at work among the rank-and-file organizations of the masses, who in the struggle gain in ability and influence. After 1887 Morris more and more saw his work in this long-term perspective: whatever vagaries the movement as a whole might pass through, he saw the need for the establishment of a school of Socialist theory which would survive the failures and errors of opportunism. In the year before his death he re-affirmed once more his conviction that sooner or later a moment of climactic revolutionary confrontation must come:

"I have thought the matter up and down and in and out, and I cannot for the life of me see how the great change which we long for can come otherwise than by disturbance and suffering of some kind... Can we escape that? I fear not. We are living... in an epoch when there is combat between commercialism, or the system of reckless waste, and communism, or the system of neighbourly common sense. Can that combat be fought out... without loss and suffering? Plainly speaking I *know* that it cannot."[1]

IX. Exit the Bloomsbury Branch

"I am not in a good temper with myself", Morris wrote to Georgie Burne-Jones in March, 1888:

"I cannot shake off the feeling that I might have done much more in these recent matters than I have; though I really don't know what

[1] "What We Have to Look For" (March 30th, 1895), Brit. Mus. Add. MSS. 45334.

I could have done: but I feel beaten and humbled. Yet one ought not to be down in the mouth about matters; for I certainly never thought that things would have gone on so fast as they have in the last three years; only, again, as opinion spreads, organization does not spread with it. . ."[1]

Morris could never fool himself for long. Now he was coming to a realization that the League had little future as a mass Socialist organization, and that he himself had failed as a propagandist leader. Somehow his organization and his ideas were being left outside the general line of advance of the broader movement. During the early months of 1888 he did not slacken in the least in his propaganda work: in March he paid a visit to Scotland, touring some of the new centres which had been opened by Mahon, encouraging the comrades and leaving them in good heart; *Commonweal* now, more than ever, was filled with his lectures and political notes. But, gradually some of his older interests were coming to reclaim more of his attention—the Anti-Scrape, preparations for the first Arts and Crafts Exhibition, the Firm, and the first of his prose romances—*The House of the Wolfings*. The incessant faction fights and squabbles among his comrades was beginning to wear down his patience.

Early in 1888, when the reverberations of Bloody Sunday had scarcely died away, dissension broke out once again in the League. The Bloomsbury Branch, which included Edward and Eleanor Aveling, A.K. Donald, the two Binnings and most of the active London "parliamentary" Leaguers, had continued an active and semi-independent existence. It had played an important part in the agitation among the Radical Clubs after Bloody Sunday and had greatly increased its membership during the year. In April, 1888, it had united with the local S.D.F. to run two candidates for the Board of Guardians elections. There had been one or two minor quarrels between the two sections: but the angry faction fights of the previous year had died down. They revived when the branch put down a resolution for the Fourth Annual Conference:

[1] *Letters*, p. 280.

"That the Conference... take measures to call a meeting of all Socialist Bodies to endeavour to arrive at a scheme for the federation of the various Socialist organizations."

Morris thought the resolution to be "nonsense"—a mere symptom of faction.[1] In the 1890s he was to change his mind on this question. But in 1888 he thought that unity was valuable only on specific issues and he read the resolution as implying (in effect) the merging of the League once more in the S.D.F. Further resolutions from the Bloomsbury Branch raised once again the issue of parliamentary and municipal electioneering, and attempted to establish the principle of a National, rather than a London, Council for the League—a proposal resisted by the majority on the grounds of impracticability and expense.

In general, the dispute followed the same lines as in 1887. Once again the parliamentarians failed either to raise the quarrel to a serious theoretical level, or to find common cause with Morris and his group against the increasing Anarchist influence. This was the more serious in that the Anarchists, who in 1887 had represented a sentiment rather than a party, had now become an effective, organized and coherent group.

It was clear as early as 1885 that the errors of the "Lefts" were breeding tendencies towards Anarchism within the League. But the declared Anarchists—few in numbers and mostly foreign refugees of Johann Most's old circle—had been scattered either in tiny intransigent organizations of their own, like the "Autonomie Group", or—like Mrs. Wilson and her small following in the Fabian Society—within other Socialist bodies. Prince Kropotkin's arrival in England in the spring of 1886 resulted in the formation of a small "Freedom Group", publishing its own monthly paper (*Freedom*) which was sold at open-air meetings, alongside *Commonweal* by members of League branches in London, Glasgow and Norwich.

[1] See account in Glasier, *op. cit.*, p. 47.

Throughout 1887 Kropotkin's influence gained ground within the League. To the Leftists thirsting for the revolution Kropotkin's was a name to conjure with—Scientist and Adventurer, "Apostle of Revolutionary Socialism". "The life of this remarkable man is itself a prophecy of a new and nobler civilization", declared a handbill of the Glasgow Branch:

> "PRINCE KROPOTKIN has stepped down from his place beside the imperial throne to fraternise with the poor and the oppressed. He has faced imprisonment and death in behalf of the cause of the people. After escaping by a remarkable strategem from a Russian Prison. . . he came to Western Europe to associate himself with the struggle of the workers. In 1882 he was thrown into a French prison. . . Whilst in prison, Prince Kropotkin,—whose scientific and literary attainments are as remarkable as his humane sympathies,—occupied himself in writing scientific and literary essays. . ."

The tone of the handbill is worth noting—for it was Kropotkin's romantic history even more than his writings which brought him support within the League. His was a name which could fill any hall. His great reputation, pleasant manners, and the note of high-toned idealism which was the main message of his *Appeal to the Young,* were exactly calculated to appeal to those earnest and self-educated comrades who had come to Socialism by way of Ruskin's *Munera Pulveris* and Morris's Lectures on Art, or who had been nurtured on the ethical idealism of the militant Secularists.

The decisive factor in turning the League in an Anarchist direction, however, was not Kropotkin's teaching but the great and inspiring example of the Chicago Anarchists, whose brutal judicial murder on the eve of Bloody Sunday had both shocked and inspired Socialists of every opinion. For months the shameful proceedings of a brutal and prejured "justice" had dragged themselves out before the horror-struck Leaguers—seeming to their eyes as if they were a grotesque magnification of the petty perjuries and brutalities familiar to them in the British courts. The case exhibited to the full what William

Morris termed "that spirit of cold cruelty, heartless and careless at once, which is one of the most noticeable characteristics of American commercialism".[1]

"... a country with universal suffrage, no king, no House of Lords, no privilege as you fondly think; only a little standing army chiefly used for the murder of red-skins; a democracy after your model; and with all that a society corrupt to the core, and at this moment engaged in suppressing freedom with just the same reckless brutality and blind ignorance as the Czar of all the Russias uses."[2]

The heroic bearing of the Chicago victims inclined many members of the Socialist League to listen with respect to the Anarchist case—and even to look with sympathy upon acts of terrorism and political assassination on the continent of Europe. From the time of the execution of the Chicago Anarchists, the small Anarchist movement in Britain, took on for several years a more determined and serious character. A pamphlet on the trial was widely sold by the Leaguers and biographies of the martyrs were published in *Commonweal*. The influence of their example did not reach its climax until November, 1888, when Lucy Parsons, the heroic widow—a woman of American-Indian origin, of striking beauty, and a moving speaker—addressed a series of commemorative meetings in London, Edinburgh, Glasgow, Ipswich and Norwich, largely organized by the League. But early in 1888 it is possible to identify a declared Anarchist group among the leadership of the League, and distinct from the old "Leftists", such as Joseph Lane, Frank Kitz and Sam Mainwaring. Most prominent amongst this group were Charles Mowbray, the London tailoring worker who had come into prominence after receiving a vindictive sentence of nine months' hard labour after addressing a meeting of Norwich unemployed who had later sacked a butcher's shop; "Fred Charles" (F.C. Slaughter), also of Norwich; David J. Nicoll, a young man with a very

[1] *Commonweal*, September 24th, 1887.

[2] "Whigs, Democrats and Socialists" (*Signs of Change*, 1888, pp. 42-3).

small independent income—a highly-strung and unstable intellectual, who gave up most of his time to the propaganda of the London League, and helped to compile an excellent weekly "Revolutionary Calendar" for *Commonweal;* and among other Londoners, H. Davis, Tom Cantwell and J. Tochatti, a tailoring worker and very active propagandist in the Hammersmith Branch.

The real victory in the League's Fourth Annual Conference was won, not by Morris and the anti-parliamentarians, but by this small Anarchist section. Morris, in his alarm at the vision of reformism, overbalanced backwards into their arms. On the eve of the Conference, Glasier, who was staying with Morris at Hammersmith, found him looking forward to the proceedings "without anger, but with a sense of depression". The activities of the Bloomsbury Branch he regarded as "a sheer faction racket".[1] Donald and his friends had clearly forfeited all Morris's respect, and he doubted not their policy so much as their intentions and motives. On the following day (May 20th) discussion continued for nearly twelve hours. At the end of the day the Bloomsbury resolutions were all rejected by large majorities, the Conference adopting amendments from the Hammersmith Branch which urged "cordial co-operation" (as opposed to "formal federation") with other Socialist bodies, and which evaded the old issue of parliamentary action. Morris then rose "and made a deeply earnest appeal for unity and good-will".[2] But the split was beyond healing. The parliamentarians refused once again to stand for election to the Council: and a Council was appointed which showed a clear majority of "Leftists" (including Kitz, Lane, Mainwaring, Sparling, Philip Webb[3] and Morris himself), with two of the pronounced Anarchist wing—Tochatti and Charles. Morris seconded a resolution

[1] Glasier, *op. cit.,* pp. 47 ff.

[2] Glasier, *op. cit.,* p. 50, and *Report of the Fourth Annual Conference of the Socialist League, passim.*

[3] Philip Webb was now Treasurer of the League, but was inactive during much of 1887-8 owing to illness.

recommending the Council "to take steps to reconciliate or, if necessary, exclude the Bloomsbury Branch from the... League". "The damned business is over at least for another year", Morris said, as he and Glasier went back on the bus to Hammersmith. But he was by no means satisfied with the outcome: "We have got rid of the parliamentarians, and now our anarchist friends will want to drive the team. However, we have the Council and the *Commonweal* safe with us for at least a twelve-month, and that is something to be thankful for."[1] A week later he wrote to Glasier: "We... yesterday *suspended* (not dissolved) the BL[oomsbury] B[ranch] until they should withdraw their stupid defiance... I don't want to dissolve them if they would give us some pledge of peace."[2] Charges against the branch, tabled by Mainwaring, included the fact that some members held joint membership of the S.D.F., and that Mahon (still a member of the branch) had conducted a "largely political" propaganda in the North of England, and had acted as election agent for Keir Hardie in Mid-Lanark. But it was a melancholy reflection upon the level which the dispute had now reached that the actual occasion of the branch's suspension lay not in any question of principle, but in the fact that its members had "sold publicly in the streets" an "illustrated squib" lampooning Morris and his following.[3]

The breach was final, and the independent Bloomsbury Socialist Society was formed. A few days later, the Labour Emancipation League (Hoxton) withdrew its affiliation. On June 9th, 1888, *Commonweal* published a new policy statement of the League's Council, drafted by Morris, which reaffirmed the League's rejection of parliamentary action, and declared once again that "the education of the vague discontent... of the workers into a definite aim, is the chief

[1] Glasier, *op. cit.*, p. 122.
[2] Glasier MSS., May 29th, 1888.
[3] The MS. of Mainwaring's motion in the Nettlau Collection, and reference to it in the Council's *Weekly Letter to Branches*, May 14th, 1888; also extract from the Minutes of the Council, June 4th, 1888, suspending the Bloomsbury Branch on account of "this insult to the League" (Int. Inst. Soc. Hist.).

business of the Socialist League".

It was an inglorious conclusion to a dispute which was of serious importance to the British labour movement. Morris in the previous twelve months—despite his contact with the Radical masses in the agitation for the right of public meeting—had fallen even further out of touch with working-class opinion. Keir Hardie's election fight at Mid-Lanark was scarcely allowed to soil the pure pages of *Commonweal.*[1] Throughout the dispute Morris had persisted in equating parliamentary action with opportunism, careerism and political corruption. Many times after the break with his old comrades he felt doubts as to the wisdom of his own position. At the end of July, 1888, he expressed them to Georgie Burne-Jones:

> "I am a little dispirited over our movement in all directions. Perhaps we Leaguers have been somewhat too stiff in our refusal of compromise. I have always felt that it was rather a matter of temperament than of principle; that some transition period was of course inevitable, I mean a transition involving State Socialism and pretty stiff at that; and. . . towards this State Socialism things are certainly tending, and swiftly too. But then in all the wearisome shilly-shally of parliamentary politics I should be absolutely useless: and the immediate end to be gained, the pushing things a trifle nearer to State Socialism, which when realized seems to me but a dull goal—all this quite sickens me. . . Preaching the ideal is surely always necessary. Yet on the other hand I sometimes vex myself by thinking that perhaps I am not doing the most I can merely for the sake of a piece of 'preciousness.' "[2]

Meanwhile, if any of the Anarchists within the League had hoped to find a convert in Morris for their last redoubt of individualism, they would have been swiftly disillusioned if they had glanced over his shoulder in his leisure moments; for

[1] Almost the only reference to this famous election fight in Morris's correspondence is in a letter to his daughter May, March 26th, 1888, referring to Mahon: "He is on some electioneering job or trying to be: for a candidate (labour) who is going to contest Mid-Lanark" (Brit. Mus. Add. MSS. 45341). For a good account of the circumstances of the Mid-Lanark election, see H.M. Pelling, *op. cit.,* pp. 68-73.

[2] *Letters,* p. 291.

they would have found him busy on the manuscript of *The House of the Wolfings,* written "to illustrate the melting of the individual into the society of the tribes"--and in its pages a rediscovery of that social sense which Victorian "self-help" had brought near to extinction everywhere except in the centres of working-class life.

For five years William Morris had been in the very forefront of the Socialist propaganda in England—setting the fire aflame in new centres, patiently explaining this or that point of theory, encouraging the doubters, putting himself in the van of scores of actions, bringing his own special qualities of vision and enthusiasm to the new movement, spending his own energies without thought. The last two years, in particular, had seen an unending series of committees, lectures, articles and editorial work, open-air meetings and correspondence, which he had undertaken without complaint. Was it all to end in a faction-fight within his own party, and alongside it the birth of a new movement, Socialist in name but Radical and opportunist in reality? Whatever he may have said, by way of encouragement to his comrades, by the summer of 1888 Morris knew that somehow he and the pioneers had failed in their aim of building a revolutionary party. And from that time onward he looked increasingly across the intervening years to a future in which he never lost confidence.

CHAPTER VI

THE LAST YEARS OF THE SOCIALIST LEAGUE

I. "The League Don't Get On"

"Up at the League, says a friend, there had been one night a brisk conversational discussion, as to what would happen on the Morrow of the Revolution. . .

"There were six persons present, and consequently six sections of the party were represented, four of which had strong but divergent Anarchist opinions. One of the sections, says our friend, a man whom he knows very well indeed, sat almost silent at the beginning of the discussion, but at last got drawn into it, and finished by roaring out very loud, and damning all the rest for fools; after which befell a period of noise, and then a lull, during which the aforesaid section, having said good-night very amicably, took his way home by himself to a western suburb. . ."

AND so the opening of *News from Nowhere* gives us an authentic description of the League, as Morris, with humorous self-criticism, saw it in its last two years of half-effective existence.

During the previous two years, Morris had been working with every faculty strained to the extreme. Perhaps this had brought upon him a nervous and creative fatigue, as well as physical exhaustion. As early as 1884 he had expressed the fear to Andreas Scheu that if he were to become too involved in " 'politics', i.e., intrigue" he would be "no use to the cause as a writer".[1] Events had forced him into prominence, and in the first flush of successful propagandist activity, in 1885 and 1886—the years of *The Pilgrims of Hope* and *A Dream of John Ball*—political action and imaginative vitality had each reinforced the other. But 1887 and the first months of 1888—the period of faction squabbles within the League—saw a flagging of his creative powers and even a certain narrowing of his responses as revealed in his private letters. "I had three

[1] *Letters*, p. 204.

very good days at Kelmscott", he wrote to Georgie Burne-Jones in September, 1887:

> "Once or twice I had that delightful quickening of perception by which everything gets emphasised and brightened, and the commonest landscape looks lovely: anxieties and worrits, though remembered, yet no weight on one's spirits—Heaven in short. It comes not very commonly even in one's younger and brighter days, and doesn't quite leave one even in the times of combat. . ."[1]

But pressure of work, anxieties about the League, made these moments rare in 1887. He was becoming a stranger at Kelmscott Manor, visiting the Oxfordshire countryside only for rare and rapid visits when the work at the League allowed him.

After the Annual Conference of 1888, for the first time since 1884, he allowed himself to relax. Early in August he took part in a strenuous long week-end of propaganda with the Norwich Branch.[2] Then, in the middle of August, he went down to Kelmscott and lingered there through September until October, completing *The House of the Wolfings,* making his first investigations into the art of printing, busying himself with the affairs of *Commonweal,* the Anti-Scrape and the Firm. The easing of months of tension seemed to bring with it a re-awakening of his dormant senses. He wrote about family affairs, cooking and fishing, to his daughter Jenny:

> "There are two tall hollyhocks (O so tall) by the strawberries, one white, one a very pretty red. . . Woke up this morning to a most splendid but very stormy sunrise. The nights have been fine, and the moon rises her old way from behind the great barn. . ."[3]

"Her old way"—there is an unmistakable sense of something which had been forgotten, beginning once again to return. "I

[1] *Letters,* p. 275.

[2] For an account of the Norwich visit, see *Letters,* pp. 294-5, and *Commonweal,* August 25th, 1888 ("Socialist Work in Norwich", by Morris). See also Fred Henderson's reminiscences in Groves, *Sharpen the Sickle,* pp. 100 ff.

[3] *Letters,* p. 297.

saw an owl last night", he wrote to another friend, "come sailing along, and suddenly turn head over heels and down in the grass; after a mouse I suppose: such a queer action I never saw."[1] Small indications, perhaps: and yet the foretaste of that flooding sense of "the earth and the growth of it and the life of it" which pervades *News from Nowhere* and the serene peace of the last prose romances.

The obvious failure of the League, and the change in Morris's perspectives which followed Bloody Sunday, led him to feel less urgency in the immediate details of the day-to-day struggle for Socialism—or, at least, less confidence that he himself had an urgent practical part to play. He had come to realize that he was (as Engels had called him several years before) "an untalented politician". The tide seemed to him to have set in the direction of Fabianism. In August, 1888, he wrote privately to Georgie Burne-Jones:

> "I am prepared to see all organized Socialism run into the sand for a while. But we shall have done something even then, as we shall have forced intelligent people to consider the matter; and then there will come some favourable conjunction of circumstances in due time which will call for all our active work again. If I am alive then I shall chip in again, and one advantage I shall have, that I shall know much better what to do and what to forbear than this first time. . ."[2]

The larger background to Morris's change in perspective was in his growing realization of the resources of monopoly capitalism and of imperialism. During 1888 there was a good deal of discussion in Socialist circles, Fabian and Marxist alike, of the phenomenon of the growing trustification of American Big Business, and Morris made frequent reference to it in his *Commonweal* notes. But it was the scramble for markets in Africa which claimed his closest attention. On July 28th, 1888, Belfort Bax published in *Commonweal* a brief and excellent summary of the struggle for the partition of Africa: England in the South; Germany in the Cameroons;

[1] *Letters*, p. 297. [2] *Ibid.*, p. 294.

Portugal on the East Coast; various powers in Zanzibar; England, France, and Italy in the North:

> "Few people probably realize what the opening up of Africa means. It means this: *untold* mineral, vegetable, and animal wealth placed at the disposal of the modern commercial system; a new world of markets; *limitless* cheap labour; practically *boundless* territories for emigration. . ."

Bax's article was unusually lucid, factual and direct. His conclusions were tentative. Africa, he suggested, was now the *mainstay* of European capitalism, and he confessed the "dread possibility" of world capitalism "taking a new lease of life" from this new field of exploitation. His last words were ominous:

> "It is quite conceivable. . . that the present stage should be prolonged in a slightly changed form even for another century. . ."

There is no doubt that Morris read these words carefully and pondered them many times. Indeed, he took the unusual step of singling out the article for special comment in his "Notes". To Bax's pessimistic outlook he put forward a counter-suggestion: "whether the accelerated pace which the impulse of huge new markets would certainly give to competitive commerce would not go far to neutralize the advantages of capitalism of 'opening up' Africa". The "practical moral" which he put before the comrades was certainly not defeatist:

> "It is not our business merely to wait on circumstances; but to do our best to push forward the movement towards Socialism, which is at least as much part of the essence of the epoch as the necessities of capitalism are. Whatever is gained in convincing people that Socialism is right always, and inevitable at last. . . will not be lost again, though it may be obscured for a time, even if a new period of prosperity sets in by leaps and bounds. . ."

Meanwhile, the continued disintegration of the League added to his depression. A series of letters written to Bruce

Glasier in the second half of 1888 describe the process. Edinburgh, and the branches of the Scottish Land and Labour League founded the previous autumn by Mahon, were dismayed by the anti-parliamentary victory, and were supporting the formation of a Scottish Labour Party. "Don't be as factious as we are in London", Morris wrote on May 29th. "If the S.L.L.L. insists on the parliamentary game, let it remain as it is and don't affiliate to it, but work with it cordially from outside." "I for one. . . should be only too glad to see the whole quarrel drop, on the grounds of letting each branch do as it pleases *as a branch*", he wrote again on August 15th, after hearing that the S.L.L.L. was adamant on the parliamentary issue. The Annual Conference had recommended that *Commonweal,* if still running at a serious deficit, should become once again a monthly, and Morris discussed the prospect:

> "True, it would be a defeat; but we must get used to such trifles as defeats, and refuse to be discouraged by them. Indeed, I am an old hand at that game, my life having been passed in being defeated; as surely every man's life must be who finds himself forced into a position of being a little ahead of the average in his aspirations."

The letter reported "something of a slack in the direct propaganda at present; but the big world is going on at a great rate. . . towards the change, and I am sure. . . that steady preachment of even a dozen men. . . will make steady progress for the cause".[1]

Two weeks later the story was even less hopeful. Only the branches at Hammersmith and Glasgow seemed to be making headway. Elsewhere, in London, "the few who take an interest are pig-headed and quarrelsome":

> "The East End agitation is a failure; the sale of Commonweal falls off. . . which of course was inevitable after the business of the Con-

[1] Glasier MSS. For the Scottish Labour Party, see H.M. Pelling, *op. cit.,* pp. 73 ff.

ference. . . a great deal of the excitement of our East End Leaguers was the result of 'indoor' agitation, i.e. quarrelling amongst ourselves, and the Parliamentarians having gone off the excitement has gone with them, and the excited friends withal. Now all this does not discourage me simply because I have discounted it; I have watched the men we are working with and know their weak points, and knew that this must happen. One or two of them are vainglorious humbugs; a good many are men who. . . cannot argue, and have only impulsive feelings based on no sort of logic, emotional or otherwise, and fall back when there is nothing exciting going on. . . With all this the worst of them are no worse than other people; mostly they are better, and some very much better; so that supposing we broke up the band, any new band we got together would be composed of just the same elements. Therefore the only thing is to be patient and try to weld together those that are work-worthy."

On one point the letter expressed confidence: "We are quite determined here at Hammersmith to keep things going if no one else will."[1]

The London and provincial branches kept the open-air stands going, and still held street sales of *Commonweal.* There was even an apparent accession of strength during the year—at Manchester a new recruit, Leonard Hall, pressed forward the propaganda; the Leicester Branch, led by Tom Barclay, showed renewed vigour; and the Nottingham and Sheffield Socialist Societies entered into closer fraternal alliance. But all the industrial "bite", the sharp presentation of class issues on the industrial front, which had once come from the pens of Binning and Mahon, was absent from the pages of *Commonweal.* The paper was full of padding, and some of the articles were detached and academic, others vague with revolutionary romanticizing. Everywhere the tale was the same: the burden of propaganda carried on the shoulders of a dozen or half a dozen comrades, while within each branch Anarchist influence was growing. As early as November, 1887, Mowbray had complained from Norwich of the conduct of Fred Henderson, "who claims to be the 'Leader' of the Anarchist Group. . . it is

[1] Glasier, *op. cit.,* pp. 194-5.

uphill work for me to crush this confounded 'Upas Tree' of no organization as preached by F.H."[1] Within a twelve-month the roles were reversed, Fred Henderson joining Mahon in his efforts to found a Labour Party, Mowbray a leader of the Anarchists on the League Council! Even at Leeds Anarchist influence, led by Samuels, was becoming felt: while at Leicester Tom Barclay (inclined towards Anarchist-Communism himself) was complaining that he and another comrade frequently conducted large open-air meetings in the City centre without the support of any members of the branch. At Hammersmith the Sunday lectures were popular enough: but the weekly branch meeting was rarely attended by more than ten comrades, and the Sunday open-air stands at Hammersmith Bridge and Walham Green were manned by seven or eight "regulars", including Morris himself. Throughout the remaining months of the year the return of *Commonweal* to a monthly seemed imminent: "I say 3 quires seems but a little to sell in the Commercial Capital of Scotland"; Morris scrawled across the top of a stiff financial letter to Glasier in September.[2] By the end of the year each branch of the League seemed to be going on its own independent way. No serious joint campaign or common purpose—Commune Celebrations and Chicago Commemorations apart—served to knit the League together from now until its final end. If it had not been for *Commonweal,* and Morris's letters and occasional propaganda tours, the League would have had no real identity at all.

No identity, no discipline, no common conviction or direction—but none the less (or, perhaps, *because* of these things) it could be a happy hunting ground for factions and "indoor" agitators, exhibitionists and even police spies. On December 15th, 1888, Morris was writing wearily to Glasier:

[1] C.W. Mowbray to Secretary, S.L., November 10th, 1887, S.L. Correspondence, Int. Inst. Soc. Hist.

[2] Glasier MSS.—another *very* stiff financial letter, beginning "People up here are getting impatient about your slackness in paying up. . ." For some reason, Glasier tacked on the protest about the small sale of *Commonweal* to a letter of another date (Glasier, *op. cit.,* p. 191). Naturally, he did not publish any of the letters in which Morris admonished him for financial laxity.

"... I am sorry to say that up here we have by no means got rid of our quarrels in getting rid of the Bloomsbury Branch: there seems to be a sort of curse of quarrelling upon us. The Anarchist element in us seem determined to drive things to extremity and break us up if we do not declare for Anarchy—which I for one will not do... Hammersmith remains satisfactory... but is getting into bad odour with some of our fiercer friends, I think principally because it tacitly and instinctively tries to keep up the first idea of the League, the making of genuine convinced Socialists without reference to passing exigences of tactics... I find that living in this element is getting work rather too heavy for me. It is lamentable that Socialists will make things hard for their comrades..."

"After all", he concluded, "all this... is but one corner of the movement, which really taken as a whole and looked at from some way off is going on swimmingly..."[1] But he found little real comfort in this reflection. The possible curtailment or end of *Commonweal* discouraged him as much as any falling off in the League, since he had always prided himself that it was one of the foremost Socialist papers in the world. "There is no doubt that the death of the *Weal* would be a great discouragement to the party both at home and abroad", he wrote to Glasier on January 21st, 1889:

"The truth must be faced, the 'Communists of the League' are in a very weak position in the Socialist party at present. We have been much damaged both by parliamentaries & Anarchists, & I don't think we are strong enough to run a paper; although, numbers apart, there is something to be said for us."[2]

By the spring of 1889 he had abandoned all hope for the League, and held on only for the sake of old loyalties and friendships, and for the sake of keeping *Commonweal* in being. Of his immediate circle of friends, Charlie Faulkner, of the old Oxford "Brotherhood", had been struck down by a lingering mortal illness, which cast yet another shadow upon Morris's mind. Emery Walker, the Secretary of the Hammersmith Branch, was busy with the new Arts and Crafts Society,

[1] *Letters*, p. 304. [2] Glasier MSS. and Glasier, *op. cit.*, p. 198.

and had less time to spend upon the League. Philip Webb was still at his side, but more through loyalty than through conviction. Joseph Lane had been incapacitated by illness, and in 1889 withdrew from the League altogether after some final difference of opinion. Frank Kitz now Secretary of the League, was active enough, but his natural impulsive "leftism" had put him into the hands of the Anarchist section. For some time Andreas Scheu (although an occasional contributor to *Commonweal*) had withdrawn from prominent activity. He was travelling for Jaeger, and "had begun to express disappointment" in the workers. Robert Banner had never been prominent in League affairs, and had confined his work to Woolwich. Belfort Bax had rejoined the S.D.F., although remaining on terms of friendship with Morris, J.L. Joynes had long been ill and in retirement. Edward Carpenter still assisted the Sheffield Socialist Society (and was to attend the International Congress in the summer) but his preoccupations were moving away from the political field. Old E.T. Craig was confined to bed. The Avelings, Binning and old Fred Lessner, the veteran of 1848, had gone with the Bloomsbury Branch, although Lessner at least remained in touch with Morris at Hammersmith. Of the others who were prominent with him in the pioneering days, or who had signed the original Manifesto of the League, only Mainwaring, Mowbray and Tom Maguire of Leeds remained.

"As to the movement", Morris wrote to Glasier on March 19th, 1889,

"between you and me the League don't get on—except like a cow's tail, downwards. Up here there is a great deal of quarrelling (in which I take no part), the basis of which is that some of them want the paper made 'more revolutionary', i.e., they want to write the articles themselves (which they can't do), and to do a little blood and thunder without any meaning, which might get *me* into trouble but couldn't hurt them. . . I am now paying for the League (including paper) at the rate of £500 a year, and I cannot stand it; at Whitsuntide I must withdraw half of that, whatever may happen: which will probably be the end of *Commonweal* followed by the practical end of the League. A little while ago this would have seemed very terrible, but it does not trouble me much now. Socialism is spreading, I suppose on the only lines on which it could spread, and the League is moribund simply because we are outside those lines, as I for one must always be. But I shall be able to do just as much work in the movement when the League is gone as I do now. . . Meantime, it is a matter of course that I shall do what I can to put off the evil day for *C'weal*. . ."[1]

Morris was speaking no more than the truth. The puzzle is, not that he left the League at the end of 1890, but that he did not leave it eighteen months before. Almost the entire financial burden was now upon his shoulders: and after £1,000 damages had been mulcted from him in a libel action early in 1888, he had been forced to limit his propaganda visits to the provinces, and to cover the expenses of his Scottish visit by a professional engagement. "This perhaps seems to you unpoetic", he wrote to Glasier:

"I think you once before reproached me with this failing: so I will remind you that I have a remarkably good appetite and that I shall probably have another thirty years (unless the Lord cuts me short) and that I can't reasonably expect to be kept at her Majesty's expense for above two or three of those years."[2]

Now, with the constant disapproval of his wife, and his long neglect of the Firm, this drain on his pocket could not be allowed to continue. At Whitsun, 1889, he made his first cut by bringing his "salary guarantee" to an end.[3]

[1] Glasier, *op. cit.*, p. 201. I presume the letter to have been written in 1889 and not 1890 (as dated by Glasier).

[2] Glasier MSS., January 28th, 1888.

[3] *Weekly Letter to Secretaries of Socialist League Branches,* June 20th, 1889. Morris informed Glasier in a letter of March 19th, 1889 (Glasier, *op. cit.*, p. 201) that he was then paying for the League and *Commonweal* "at the rate of £500 a year". From various papers, treasurer's statements, etc., preserved with the Hammersmith Minutes, I calculate that in 1889 Morris was paying on the average £1 4*s.* a week rent of League office: £1 a week salary guarantee (withdrawn at Whitsun) and £4 a week to meet the *Commonweal* deficit (average expenditure £9 10*s.*, average receipts £5 10*s.*). In addition, there were regular "exceptional" subsidies to make up salaries, special leaflets, publications, Hammersmith activities, etc. The League income came largely from literature sales, collections, and donations, and the branch monthly contributions were by now pitiful: on October 8th, 1890, they dropped to the sum of 1*s.* 8*d.* for the week.

Even more true was his judgement that the League (apart from *Commonweal*) was becoming a restraint upon his work for the cause. If Donald had irritated and angered him by his methods of intrigue, the leading spirits among the Anarchists seemed to provoke him to contempt. "Outside the Hammersmith Branch", he wrote in April, 1889,

"the *active* (?) members in London mostly consider themselves Anarchists, but don't know anything about Socialism and go about ranting revolution in the streets, which is about as likely to happen in our time as the conversion of Englishmen from stupidity to quickwittedness."[1]

Donald and Mahon were making troublesome flanking attacks, drawing away a few good supporters. Finally, in June the Annual Conference was once again upon him, and he wrote in irritation to Glasier, asking for a Glasgow delegate:

"It may be of importance to send a good man; since I believe there will be an attempt to get on to the Council a majority of stupid hobbldehays who call themselves anarchists and *are* fools, and to oust Kitz from the Secretaryship as he forsooth is not advanced enough for them. If this were to succeed it would break up the League. I and, I think, most of the others who were worth anything would walk out. . ."[2]

As it turned out, the Fifth Annual Conference was a meek and mild affair compared with the previous two. "Harmony permeated the meeting", declared an official report. "At no previous Conference. . . were Liberty, Fraternity and Equality so practically set forth."[3] Only twelve branches sent delegates, as opposed to twenty-one the year before.[4] Kitz retained the Secretaryship, and Morris the Editorship of *Commonweal,* with the addition of Nicoll as an Assistant Editor. The Anarchist section on the Council were strengthened by the

[1] Glasier, *op. cit.,* p. 202.
[2] Glasier MSS., June 5th, 1889.
[3] *Commonweal,* June 15th, 1889.
[4] London branches: Hammersmith, Clerkenwell, St. George's-in-the-East, North London, East London. Provincial: Glasgow, Edinburgh, Norwich, Leicester, Yarmouth, Oxford, Manchester.

election of H. Davis, Samuels, and John Turner. For the first time the names of Mainwaring, and Lane did not appear on the Council. Morris's own group was reduced to himself, Philip Webb, Sparling (an unreliable ally), and Sam Bullock and H.B. Tarleton of the Hammersmith Branch. This was a sad decline in quality from the Provisional Council of 1885.

To all serious intents, the old Socialist League was at an end.

II. The New Unionism

The S.D.F., as well as the League, was encountering difficulties in 1888 and 1889. The "Tory Gold" incident had blown over, it is true, and the S.D.F. had made more progress, especially in South Lancashire, where Tom Mann had come as organizer after leaving Newcastle in the Spring of 1888. Morris made a lecture tour of the district in December, 1888—visiting Manchester, Liverpool, Bolton, Blackburn, Rochdale, and also Charles Rowley's Sunday Society at Ancoats.[1] In Manchester he stayed with his friend, J. Hunter Watts, and was impressed by the quality and enthusiasm of the S.D.F. rank and file. But elsewhere (London excepted) the S.D.F. was by no means as firmly established as Hyndman liked to claim. Many of its branches passed through the same vicissitudes as did those of the League. According to charges made by Edouard Bernstein in June, 1889, the circulation of *Justice* had shrunk in the previous months from over 4,000 to "barely 1/3rd of that number". "There are branches which never go through the formality of a meeting, and large industrial towns where never a copy of the paper is read."[2] If these charges were true, the sales of *Justice* had fallen below those of *Commonweal*—for Frank Kitz, the League's Secretary, was still "sending out" over 2,000 copies in June, 1889. Hyndman's dictatorship (in his own words, "my. . . contempt for un-

[1] An account of the tour was given by Morris in an article, "In and About Cottonopolis", *Commonweal*, December 15th, 1888.

[2] E. Bernstein, *The International Working Men's Congress of 1889: a Reply to the 'Manifesto' of the S.D.F."* (1889).

educated and undisciplined democracy")[1] was alienating his best members; and his sectarianism, just as much as Morris's purism, was hampering Socialist participation in the Eight-hour agitation and the New Unionism. In June, 1888, Tom Mann was writing to John Burns: "Nationally I have lost hope as regards S.D.F., tho' I am sanguine concerning one or two districts."[2] There was no more harmony on its Executive than on the League's Council. John Burns was feeling "very depressed about the immediate future of the movement. Am convinced that we have dissipated nearly all our energy in the wrong direction and upon the wrong man."[3] "The S.D.F. as a national body representative of the workers", he noted in his diary in August, 1888, "must be remodelled not to say merged in other bodies ere it does practical work."

Nothing seemed to be able to break down the jealousies and differences in London. Outside London and Glasgow, the members of League, S.D.F. and independent Socialist Clubs, might work together amicably enough. But every attempt to build up formal unity broke down, or brought to birth yet one more faction. Champion, who had left the S.D.F., had incurred the high displeasure of Hyndman for sounding out the possibilities of amalgamation, which could only be accomplished by detaching Hyndman's following from him. He and Mahon had worked together in the Scottish Land and Labour League propaganda at the end of 1887: and, after playing a prominent part in promoting Keir Hardie's fight at Mid-Lanark early in 1888, they had assisted in forming the

[1] Hyndman, *Further Reminiscences* (1912), p. 144.

[2] Six months earlier (December 31st, 1887) Tom Mann had written to Burns: "I'm glad to know so many London comrades are in favour of Amalgamation. . .", and was suggesting Annie Besant as Editor of a general Socialist newspaper (Brit. Mus. Add. MSS. 46286).

[3] Diary of John Burns for 1888, Brit. Mus. Add. MSS. 46310.

Scottish Labour Party. Together with Tom Mann and John Burns, Champion launched, in the same year, *The Labour Elector*;[1] J.L. Mahon, also, was now acting as a free-lance, having brought most of the Scottish Land and Labour League into the Scottish Labour Party. Late in 1888 he wrote *A Labour Programme,* which contained a clear blue-print for the I.L.P. Mahon's debt to Engels can be seen on every page of this pamphlet–in the broad, unsectarian approach, the understanding of the labour movement, and of the educative role of political and industrial action. On the other hand, Mahon, in his flight from doctrinaire theory, was beginning to slide down the opposite slope of belief in "spontaneity": throughout the pamphlet there runs a half-spoken contempt for theory, and an acid and unfraternal treatment of his old comrades, whom he believed to be over-academic and doctrinaire.[2] The workers, wrote Mahon, "want their every-day lives made easier, and in the meantime the mass of them will only do what will lead to that in some tangible way". If Joseph Lane wished to make the sole slogan of the movement "Educate!", Mahon would seem to have preferred only "Organize!"

In conformity with his *Labour Programme* he promoted early in 1889 the "Labour Union", whose objects were:

> "The Emancipation of Labour from the control of the monopolists, and the realization of a State based on co-operative principles, in which the workers will have the wealth they create and idlers will have no place.

[1] For Champion's activities in this period, see H.M. Pelling, *op. cit.,* pp. 59 f.

[2] *A Labour Programme,* by J.L. Mahon (Labour Platform Series, No. 1, 1888), p. 77: "Political education. . . does not consist of mere talking. There is nowadays a small school of doctrinaire academic politicians who think they are advancing the political education of the people merely by trying to spread a knowledge of formulas and theories. . ." See also the jibes at the "non-political Socialists", p. 63.

"To aid present movements for improving the social condition of the people."

To these objects—far vaguer than those of the North of England Socialist Federation of 1887—was added a whole string of immediate reforms, taken from current Radical programmes.

It is doubtful whether the "Labour Union" was ever much more than a paper organization, and certainly Mahon's influence was of much less importance than that of Champion and Tom Mann. In immediate practical terms its chief impact must have been as nuisance value to Morris and the League. "A great deal of our trouble comes from Messrs. Donald and Mahon", Morris wrote to Glasier in April, 1889, "who have been rather clever at pulling us to pieces, but could do nothing towards building up even their own humbugging self-seeking party."[1]

Six years of active propaganda, hundreds of converts, many thousands of people influenced—and yet the political Socialist movement was split into a hundred fragments: the Socialist Union and North of England Socialist Federation dead; the League and the S.D.F. declining in membership; here a "Labour Union" and there an independent Socialist Club; in Hull a "Freiheit Group" and in Battersea a Labour League; in Bristol a Socialist splinter group brooding over *Munera Pulveris* and the ethics of the new life; in Chelsea a Social Democratic Club, issuing red leaflets headlined, "TO HELL WITH TRADE-UNIONISM".[2] What had happened to all the years of enthusiasm and sacrifice? To the winter mornings when John Burns and his wife went month after month at three and four o'clock to the dock gates? To the eager faces of the

[1] Glasier, *op. cit.*, p. 202. I presume this letter to be wrongly dated by Glasier.

[2] The handbill continues: "It is manifest that it is a matter of urgency that trade unionism be at once and without reverence deposited in Gehenna. When it has been got rid of, the workers will join a union wide enough to include them all, and that has for its aim the Social Revolution. They will RALLY ROUND THE RED FLAG. . ." etc. etc.

Northumberland miners at their Easter rally? To the months spent by Mahon tramping the Scottish coalfields? To the massed crowds watching Linnell's funeral after "Bloody Sunday"? To the thousands of *Justices* and *Commonweals*, the thousands of open-air meetings on street corners and village greens, held by the pioneers?

"No movement absorbs so much fruitless labour as one which has not yet emerged from the status of a sect", Engels had written to Sorge in June, 1887. But now at last these labours were beginning to bear fruit, and the movement of ideas (which cut off from action was beginning to assume so many exotic hothouse shapes) was to be transformed into a movement of men. The Eight Hours' Campaign, which Tom Mann had been championing within the Socialist movement since 1886, the strike of the Bryant and May's match-girls, and the strikes of tram-men and seamen, were heralding those great events of 1889 and 1890, which, willy-nilly, forced the most active and resolute Socialists in the direction of unity. In March, 1889, the Gasworkers' and General Labourers' Union had been formed by the Socialist Will Thorne, with the help of Eleanor Aveling, John Burns and Tom Mann. By the summer it had attracted widespread attention, and won its first victories without even a strike. The "unorganizable" unskilled workers were stirring everywhere. It was a time when one Socialist, active and determined, giving assistance to the unskilled workers, was worth twenty discussing revolutionary tactics in their private clubrooms.

At Leeds the Socialist Leaguers took note. "We are endeavouring to organize the unskilled labourers in all branches of industry in the town", they reported laconically in *Commonweal* on July 6th, 1889, "since the aristocrats of labour take no steps in organizing them." Thereafter they went "off the air", sometimes for weeks at a time. It was a dramatic story, which might have been repeated in every town in the country (as it was in several) if only the Socialists had come through the previous six years with a united party, however small. Since 1884, when Tom Maguire, still in his teens, had joined the Democratic Federation, and had started to preach the word at "the popular spouting place", Vicar's Croft, the small League branch had kept up an unceasing propaganda. The Leaguers had opened their own clubroom; sold *Commonweal;* gone on propaganda outings; held joint activities with the branches at Bingley and Bradford. William Morris had paid them a successful visit; Edward Carpenter was often with them; when Annie Besant had visited them, their clubroom was smashed up by an angry mob inspired by Catholic priests. Maguire never spared himself. He earned a pittance as a photographer, and was often without work. His *Machine-Room Chants* and occasional verse in Socialist papers stand out from other Socialist versifying at the time by reason of their greater range and realism.

In 1889 he was only twenty-four, but six years of agitation had brought him to early maturity. Although the Leeds branch of the League still stood at a membership of about thirty, Maguire and Tom Paylor, Fred Corkwell, W. Hill and Alf Mattison were now well known among the workers of Leeds—crazy, crack-brained Socialists, perhaps, but there was no doubting their sincerity—and there was truth in what they said. In the early summer of 1889 they began to draw bigger and bigger crowds to Vicar's Croft—600, 800, even 1,000. Then, at the beginning of July, some builders' labourers who were at the meeting, began to discuss their grievances. Like the London dockers, they were paid at the rate of 5*d.* an hour. "Comrades Sweeney and Paylor. . . took the matter up and urged the men to form a Union". The next Sunday, July 30th, 3,000 labourers came to the spouting-place: Maguire, Paylor, Hill and Sweeney addressed them: 200 names were handed in; in the afternoon the Socialist League clubroom was crowded out; a provisional committee was elected; it decided at once to strike for ½*d.* an hour; a general meeting was held, and the proposal was agreed to unanimously.

This was six weeks before the great dockers' strike set the movement of the unskilled aflame throughout the country.

The builders' labourers used the League clubroom as their campaign centre. Maguire and Paylor gave constant advice and leadership. The Leaguers organized collections, and meetings 3,000 and 4,000 strong became frequent on Vicar's Croft. The small master-builders capitulated first: later the big contractors were forced to their knees. "The resolute attitude of the men from the first", wrote Maguire,

> "the comparative absence of 'scabs', and the successful conducting of the struggle have won the admiration of skilled workmen, whose unions. . . have never carried through so unanimous and uncompromising a strike."[1]

"Throughout this struggle", Alf Mattison recalled, "Maguire worked like a Trojan, and for a long time afterwards remained the adviser and general helper of the Union."[2] On the eve of the Dock Strike complete victory was celebrated. A strong and permanent union of the "new" type had been formed.

After this there was no respite. The Leeds Socialists had been transformed in a month from being a curious sect into being the advisers and leaders of the unskilled workers of Leeds. The great Dock Strike, under the leadership of John Burns, Tom Mann and Ben Tillett, repeated the same thing on a vast scale for the "submerged" population of the East End. Tens of thousands of men struck under Socialist leadership, and marched repeatedly in disciplined order through the heart of London. The "criminal classes" of bourgeois fiction and of *The Times'* leading articles proved themselves, not the *sans-culottes,* rioters and assassins of the poems of David Nicoll and the Anarchist wing of the League, but "working men". The men who had fought at the dock gates for work, slept ten in a room in the rotting tenements, dropped exhausted from an hour or two of labouring: these men regained their manhood. "The coals we blew upon were working men", wrote John Burns,

[1] "Notes on the Leeds Labourers Strike", *Commonweal,* August 10th, 1889.

[2] *Tom Maguire: a Remembrance,* p. xiv.

"oppressed, beaten down; but working-men still, who had it in them to struggle and to fight for their daily bread... I have been in the thick of starving men, with hundreds of pounds about me (they knowing it), and not a penny have I lost. I have sent men whom I did not know, for change of a gold piece, and have never been cheated of a penny. Not a man through all the weeks of that desperate Strike ever asked me for drink money..."[1]

The dockers, wrote Morris after they had won,

"have shown qualities of unselfishness and power of combination which we may well hope will appear again before long... They have knocked on the head the old slander against the lower ranks of labour, and shown that... these men can organize themselves at least as well, and be at least as true to their class, as the aristocracy of labour. No result of the strike is more important than the effect it will have as a blow against class jealousy amongst the workers themselves..."[2]

Their example had set the whole East End on the move, and all the "sweated" trades were seething with discontent.

Meanwhile, official League and official S.D.F. alike looked on with a certain lofty detachment, mixed with expressions of sympathy, and also a certain element of suspicion aroused by the widespread middle-class support for the strikers. Every worthwhile branch of the League, including Hammersmith, held meetings and made collections in the dockers' support, and the most active London agitators, chiefly of the Anarchist wing (for Nicoll had now been for some time Secretary of the Propaganda Committee), went down to the dock gates to distribute "tons" of literature and make revolutionary speeches. But their support was from outside, rather than from within. The concept of *building* the workers' organizations, leading and organizing their struggles, as John Burns, Tom Mann, Eleanor Aveling and Tom Maguire were doing, was strange to them. In October, 1889, the League's Council issued a statement which was surely the most pitiful in all its years of existence:

[1] *The New Review,* October, 1889. [2] *Commonweal,* September 21st, 1889.

"In answer to numerous enquiries, the Executive Council. . . desires to express its opinion that members of the League do not in any way compromise their principles by taking part in strikes, but asks them not to let the revolutionary propaganda suffer thereby."[1]

How did William Morris react to these great movements, which Engels was hailing as the re-birth of the English working class? When the builders' labourers' strike was afoot at Leeds, Morris was attending the International Congress in Paris (see p. 535). On his return, he went down to Kelmscott, where he remained for the first fortnight of the dock strike. From there he sent down his usual "Notes" to *Commonweal,* which sadly underestimated the great event, expressing the need for a "general combination" of the workers (as if this could come about, of itself, without such events as were at that very time in progress) and of the necessary failure of strikes which did not, for exceptional reasons, have the backing of public opinion.[2] Returning to London at the end of August he found the Leaguers "in a great state of excitement about the strike, the importance of which I had not at all understood in the country. . . I thought that perhaps our folk a little exaggerated the importance of it, as to some of them it seemed that now at last, the revolution was beginning. Whereas indeed it began before the Mammoth ended, and is now only going on."[3] Hopes of speedy revolution apart, he now recognized the importance of the strike. "However it ends, it will have been by far the most important one of our times. . ."[4] Next week the whole of his *Commonweal* notes were devoted to the strike, under the title, "The lesson of the Hour". His attitude was far more positive ("This is a revolt against oppression. . . this is a strike of the poor against the rich"), although still carrying a savour of the old detachment, i.e. the concept that the strike was something *apart* from the Socialist movement. He returned to the theme the next week, and gave a necessary

[1] *Commonweal,* October 12th, 1889.
[2] *Ibid.,* August 24th, 1889.
[3] *Letters,* p. 317.
[4] *Ibid.,* p. 316.

warning to those Socialists who had been deluded into mistaking the degree and nature of middle-class support for the strikers:

> "These strikes are not less dangerous to the supremacy of the landlords and their abettors than the Trafalgar Square incidents, but more dangerous. There is only one reason why Burns is not going to Pentonville this time, and why the streets are not cleared by the bludgeon, and if necessary by the bayonet, and that is because the rulers of this happy land are afraid to do it. The men are too many and too desperate, and their miserable condition has really impressed itself on a large part of the non-political middle classes; and... above all, their brother-workers are really in active sympathy with the strikers."[1]

At last he understood that the strike (together with the revolt within the older trade unions, voiced once again in the attacks on Broadhurst at the Trades Union Congress) was leading in the direction of the general combination of labour the League had advocated for so long—towards a "far wider and more generous association of the workers... inspired with Socialistic feeling". On the victory of the strikers, he summed up the issues of the struggle in a way which suggested that he was moving rapidly away from his early purist attitude to the trades unions:

> "Although mere combination amongst the men, with no satisfactory ulterior aim, is not itself Socialism, yet it is both a necessary education for the workers, and it is an instrument which Socialism cannot dispense with..."

Still, however, he underestimated the importance of the issues around which the new unions must be built: the "dockers' tanner" aroused his indignation as a "precarious mere-subsistence wage for the hardest of hard work". He still gave the impression of brushing aside the justice of the workers' immediate demands, and of looking forward impatiently to the time when the dockers should have learnt the irreconcilable

[1] *Commonweal*, September 14th, 1889.

opposition of capitalists and workers, and should be compelled to use their new organization for—

> "its one real use, the realization of Socialism, to which undoubtedly this strike has been a step, as part of the labour struggle, as part of the attack on our enemy—Capitalism."[1]

Meanwhile Tom Maguire and his comrades in Leeds, the Leaguers in Bradford, Sheffield, Manchester and one or two other provincial centres—these men were plunged up to the neck in the work of organizing section after section of the unskilled. Had Morris been surrounded by comrades of that quality in London, he might have taken up an even more positive attitude. But the active Leaguers in London were now a poor bunch: it is difficult to find, in 1889, more than a handful of active trade unionists among them. The reaction of some of the Anarchist section to the Dock Strike was altogether different from that of Morris. It indicated to them that the workers were on the eve of a rising; that *Commonweal* should speak more often and more plainly of the barricades; even that the time was near when dynamite should be put in the people's hands. Except in Hammersmith, Morris withdrew more and more from the active propaganda in despair.

III. The Second International—and the Fabians

It was in 1889 that William Morris began consistently to define his political position among the contending Socialist factions by the term which he maintained to the end of his life, "Communist". What did he mean by the word?

He meant, in the first place, to identify himself with the recognized Communist tradition: the *Communist Manifesto* of 1848; the Communists of the Paris Commune; the

[1] *Commonweal*, September 21st, 1889.

revolutionary theory of Marx and Engels.[1] In the second place, he meant to dissociate himself emphatically from several sections of the English movement: from the Fabians; from the Anarchists inside and outside the League; and from the "Social-Democracy" of Hyndman, which—while making use of the name and some of the teachings of Marx he suspected of both opportunism and reformism. In the third place, he wished it to denote acceptance of the revolutionary road of struggle as opposed to the road of gradual "evolution" (and, until 1892, he insisted that this must include acceptance of the "anti-parliamentary" position); and, further, to denote acceptance of certain points of principle in the organization of the society of the future. Three controversies served to crystallize his views during 1889—the calling of the International Congress in Paris, the struggle with Fabianism; and the contest with the Anarchists within the League.

At the same time as Hyndman was writing in *To-day* of Marx as "the Aristotle of the Nineteenth Century" he was bitterly opposing the calling of the International Socialist Working-Men's Congress which was being promoted by leading European Marxists—among them Bebel, Liebknecht, Bernstein and Lafargue—and which had Engels's full support. The French Possibilists (engaged in similar parliamentary manoeuvring to that which Hyndman denounced mercilessly in Broadhurst and Burt) were convening a rival Congress, on terms which would have excluded the French Marxists (and, possibly, other European Socialist Parties) from attending. By contrast the "Marxist" Congress (which was to be the foundation Congress of the Second International) was declared open to all Socialist and working-class representatives.

Hyndman associated himself with the Possibilist Congress,

[1] E.g. see *Commonweal*, June 18th, 1887, where Morris, in a review of Kempner's *Common-sense Socialism*, remarks approvingly: "It is worth while to note apropos of the attempt some persons make to draw a hard and fast line between Socialism and Communism, that Mr. Kempner uses the latter word in the sense that it is used in the 'Manifesto' of Marx and Engels of 1847. A Communist is with him one who advocates the communisation or nationalisation of the raw material and instruments of labour and distribution."

partly from personal pique, in revenge at the Avelings' part in the split in the S.D.F., and from opposition to Engels, the "Grand Lama of Regent's Park Road."[1] It was a sorry business, since if the S.D.F. had taken a different attitude, a magnificent united delegation might have attended the Paris Congress from Britain. Morris associated himself with the "Marxist" Congress from the start; and other signatories from Britain included Cunninghame Graham, Keir Hardie (for the Ayrshire Miners' Union), and Tom Mann and H.H. Champion (for the newly-formed Labour Electoral Association). Alongside Hyndman was Annie Besant, now active in the Fabian Society, and making public attacks both on Marxist theory and the Socialist League.

Frank Kitz and William Morris were delegated to the Congress from the Council of the League, while several of the branches sent their own delegates. Delegates were assembled from nearly every European nation, and from America: their "earnestness and enthusiasm", wrote Morris, "was very impressive". The formal proceedings of the Congress provoked his impatience. Differences of opinion were aggravated by bad organization, and various trifling matters—the Parisian delegates chatted together when the French speeches were concluded, so that Eleanor Marx-Aveling and the other translators could not make their voices heard: two days were spent in discussing possible fusion with the Possibilist Congress, so that insufficient time was left for the discussion of resolutions: delegate after delegate exceeded his permitted time. A number of anti-parliamentary resolutions (including one from Frank Kitz) were left undiscussed. On the final day, when Morris (with Kitz and Tarleton) was visiting his favourite cathedral, Rouen, a well-known Italian Anarchist from London, Dr. Merlino, created a disturbance. He had put down a long-winded Anarchist resolution which was not discussed; and when protesting, he was ruled out of order by the Chairman and forcibly expelled, to the accompainment of the with-

[1] *Justice,* April 1st, 1893.

drawal of the remaining delegates of the League. Morris, returning from Rouen, was informed of the incident, and registered a formal protest on behalf of his comrades. In loyalty to his own delegates, he had no alternative. But, as far as this incident went, the clamour raised by the Anarchists about "suppression of opinion" was mostly bally-hoo. Dr. Merlino was out to provoke an incident of exactly this kind; he represented no important organization, and, since he had popped up a day or two before at the Possibilist Congress with the same resolution, he could hardly lay much claim on the delegates' time.

That was the negative side of the Congress. Thereafter, Kitz, Merlino & Co. fanned the flames of dissension for as long as they could—a controversy in which Morris refused to take part. The overall effect of the Congress Morris felt to be positive—"a successful demonstration at the least". He himself had presented the report from England: while (on his insistence) Keir Hardie had presented a second report from the "parliamentary side".[1] The selection by the international committee (among whom the German Marxists greatly predominated) of Morris as the English spokesman, together with the enthusiastic reception he received from the delegates, was a clear indication of the great standing which his name held at this time in the European and American Socialist movement. Edward Carpenter has left a description of Morris speaking from the rostrum:

> "After the glib oratorical periods of Jules Guesde and others, what a contrast to see Morris. . . fighting furiously there on the platform with his own words (he was not feeling well that day), hacking and hewing the stubborn English phrases out—his tangled grey mane tossing, his features reddening with the effort! But the effect was remarkable. Something in the solid English way of looking at things. . . made that speech one of the most effective in the session."[2]

[1] Morris's contribution is given in full in the *Protocol* of the Congress, published in Paris (1889) and in a German translation by Liebknecht (Nuremburg, 1890).

[2] *Freedom*, December, 1896.

Since the main point on the agenda concerned labour legislation and the international fight for the Eight-hour Day (the value of which Morris—still holding to his belief in the Iron Law of Wages—doubted),[1] Morris's contribution was outside the main current of the debate. It was in the social events and informal meetings that he felt the spirit of fraternity and internationalism found its best expression, and, on his return, he summed up his general impression:

> "Such gatherings are not favourable for the dispatch of business, and their real use is as *demonstrations*, and. . . it would be better to organize them as such. . . Two or three great public meetings should be held. . . opportunities should be given for the delegates to meet each other in social and conversational meetings, and. . . there should be no voting, no 'playing at Parliament'. This is my wisdom after the event. . ."[2]

If the Paris Congress had found Morris (apart from his anti-parliamentary views) standing alongside the European Marxist parties, he was at the same time dissociating himself without compromise from the Fabian and Anarchist positions. His disagreements with the Fabians dated back for several years: but, at that time, the issues had been befuddled by the "parliamentary" question, and the character of Fabianism, already implicit in the social make-up and outlook of the Society, had not yet emerged as explicit theory. Although several of the Fabian lecturers were content to confine themselves to valuable research, and to polite propaganda, Shaw—whom Morris declared to be "one of the clearest heads and best pens that Socialism has got"[3] —was as ready to go on to the street-corners or into the Radical Clubs as was Morris himself.

[1] Morris quoted with approval the gibe of one Anarchist historian: "Apropos of palliation by legislation on labour, he said: 'When I was a Collectivist I was taught the Iron Law so well by Marx and Liebknecht, that I cannot forget it now I am an Anarchist' " (*Commonweal*, August 3rd, 1889).

[2] See Morris, "Impressions of the Paris Congress", *Commonweal*, July 27th, and August 3rd, 1889. F. Kitz, August 10th, 1889, and correspondence in ensuing issues.

[3] *Commonweal*, January 25th, 1890.

It was after Bloody Sunday that Fabianism began to emerge as an important influence within the Socialist movement. "We are all Socialists now", Sir William Harcourt had declared; and John Morley, in his *Life of Cobden,* had pointed to state interference in industry and municipal government as examples of "Socialistic" legislation. "I am a Socialist because I am a believer in Evolution", Annie Besant had written in 1886:

> "The State has interfered with factories and workshops, to fix the hours of labour, to insist on sanitary arrangements, to control the employment of the young. Land Acts and Ground Game Acts, Education Acts and Shipping Acts, Employers' Liability Acts and Artisans' Dwellings Acts, crowd our Statute book. Everywhere the old ideas of free contract, of non-interference, are being outraged by modern legislation. . ."[1]

A few more and bigger Acts, the implication was, and Socialism would have evolved—without struggle, revolution, or serious inconvenience. The enemy was no longer the capitalist class, but outworn theories of *laisser faire,* backed up by pockets of vested interest and entrenched privilege. Wicksteed and Shaw had already "overthrown" Marx's theory of value. Morris, who knew he was an amateur in economic theory, had put up little resistance. Now, in 1888 and 1889, the Fabian lecturers began to dispense with the theory of the class struggle: or, rather, to employ the concept as a figure of speech when describing the struggles of the oppressed in the past, but to deny its application to Britain in the future.

But here they met with greater difficulties—the writings of Morris were thrown across the way. In disputing Marx's economic theory, they had only Hyndman and Aveling to encounter, neither of whom were accomplished masters of the theory themselves. But Morris's breadth of knowledge, his profound historical understanding, were without equal in the Socialist movement; and every page of his Socialist

[1] Annie Besant, *Why I Am a Socialist* (n.d.).

writing served as a demonstration of the process of the class struggle. Typically, the Fabians failed to challenge his position: instead, they made a *détour*. In the autumn of 1888 Morris's first collection of Socialist lectures, *Signs of Change,* was published. The unsigned review in *To-day,* now the Fabian journal (although still mis-titled the "Monthly Magazine of Scientific Socialism") is worth quoting at length:

"Mr. William Morris is about the only Socialist who can write with the pleasing certainty that his literary productions will be read; and, therefore, there lies upon him a weight of responsibility from which all we ordinary scribblers are delightfully free. Unfortunately the burden sits but airily on his brawny shoulders, and his utterances on the platform are apt to smack too much of the 'hare-brained chatter of irresponsible frivolity'. When such deliverances are made to a Socialist audience, who knows him and who overlooks the eccentricities of the lecturer in its liking for the man... the amount of harm done is a minus quantity. But when he takes to publishing his views it is a different matter; for many of them are such as... to render Socialism a subject of mockery to sane men and women. For instance we gather from the little volume before us (a) that the author *desires* to bring about a civil war (p. 46),[1] and to create suffering for the purpose of intensifying discontent (p. 48),[2] and rejoices in the fact that the Socialists are still only a sect and not yet a party (p. 52).[3] Now we have no hesitation in saying that if once the hard-headed English workmen... came to believe that these ideas of Mr. Morris's were in any degree representative, the present by no means un-brilliant prospects of Socialism in England would vanish like a dream... and all the good work of the last few years would be worse than undone. Happily no such mistake is likely to be made... for the rapid conversion of so many of our writers and lecturers to political methods has left Mr. Morris almost alone in the possession of his peculiar views. The

[1] For Morris's words, see p. 542.

[2] "Semi-State-Socialistic measures", said Morris, might "entangle commerce in difficulties, and so add to discontent by creating suffering". Morris was demonstrating that, whichever road was taken, the downfall of capitalism was inevitable: and was arguing *against* these "semi-Socialistic" measures and in favour of the direct revolutionary road.

[3] Morris declared: "I think it is quite possible that Socialism will remain a sect till the very eve of the last stroke that completes the revolution... And is it not sects, bodies of definite, uncompromising principles, that lead us into revolutions? ... They may give birth to parties, though not parties themselves.

effect of this change has been immensely to raise his value of us. Just in proportion as the importance of the active propagandist declines so does the value of the poet and artist appreciate. Some of Mr. Morris's best services to Socialism may be seen in the Arts and Crafts Exhibition in Regent Street, some of his worst in the volume before us."

The line of argument is important, since upon this kind of "interpretation" a whole school of explaining-away-of-William-Morris was founded. No open and frank controversy; no attempt to meet Morris's arguments and defeat them fairly; the only time when his views are referred to they are falsified; and the bulk of the criticism given over to insinuation, philistinism and condescension, so that the reader may emerge with a picture of a brawny, lovable and irresponsible man, with "eccentricities" and "peculiar views", of much more value to the Socialist movement designing tapestries than preaching Socialism. And yet, perhaps the Fabian critic did not care *quite* so much about culture as he suggested, for the review continued:

"On the historic and art critical essays in it. . . we would venture humbly to protest that things artistic are hardly in quite so parlous a state as Mr. Morris appears to think. . . The fact is that when our Socialist artists and critics set about wailing over the 'Decline of Art' they use the term in much too restricted a sense. . . The age which has produced Dickens and George Eliot, Balzac, Thackeray, Zola and George Meredith, has little to fear from comparison with any of its predecessors. Of course the fact that we have good music and good landscapes, good novels and good portraits, is no reason why we should have hideous public buildings and drawing-room decorations which set the teeth on edge; but it is a reason why we should not be perpetually whining, however tunefully, about the 'Decline of Art'. To sum up, Socialists will do well to buy Mr. Morris's latest book for they will derive thereupon much pleasure and some profit, but they had better keep it to themselves and not lend it to their, as yet unconverted, acquaintances."[1]

It is hardly conceivable that Morris can have read this review without a passing twinge of bitterness. *Signs of Change*

[1] *To-day*, November, 1888.

was one of his greatest achievements, the point of confluence of the moral protest of Carlyle and Ruskin and the historical genius of Marx, backed by Morris's own lifetime of study and practice in the arts and in society. It is a book written, not by a lovable clown or childlike craftsman, but by a profoundly serious, cultured and responsible man. These Fabian lecturers—several of them had been drawn to the movement by his propaganda and example; he had helped them to clarify their minds, had invited them repeatedly to the Hammersmith Clubroom, had made them known in the movement. If he differed with them, he did so on points of principle which he made abundantly clear. This kind of philistine attack was to be expected from the declared enemies of the movement. But must it now come from within as well?

The *Fabian Essays* published in 1889 show many variations of emphasis. But throughout them all, two central points were becoming blurred: the economic basis of exploitation in capitalist society, and the irreconcilable interests of the bourgeoisie and working class—points upon which all the Socialist pioneers of 1883 and 1884 had been in agreement. Morris did not deny the possibility of winning reforms within the fabric of capitalism: indeed, he had always prophesied that such reforms—"tubs to the whale"—would be offered by the capitalist parties themselves as a means of staving off revolution, and raising a privileged section of the working-class. But, if these reforms were far-reaching enough, he thought, they might well weaken capitalism itself, thereby intensifying, rather than diminishing, class antagonisms, and bringing about a revolutionary crisis. It was precisely this conjecture, in his lecture *Whigs, Democrats and Socialists,* originally delivered at a Conference convened by the Fabian Society in June, 1886, which had aroused the indignation of the anonymous reviewer. Those who think they can deal with the capitalist system in a "piecemeal way", he had declared,

"very much underrate the strength of the tremendous organization under which we live. . . Nothing but a tremendous force can deal with this force; it will not suffer itself to be dismembered, nor to lose anything which really is its essence without putting forth all its force in resistance; rather than lose anything which it considers of importance, it will pull the roof of the world down upon its head. For, indeed, I grant these semi-Socialist Democrats that there is one hope for their tampering piecemeal with our Society; if by chance they excite people into seriously, however blindly, claiming one or other of these things in question, and could be successful in Parliament in driving it through, they would certainly draw on a great civil war, and such a war once let loose would not end but either with the full triumph of Socialism or its extinction for the present. . ."[1]

During the second half of 1889 Morris seems to have prepared only one new major lecture, and it is no accident that this should have been entitled "The Class Struggle". In May, 1889, he had been reading Edward Bellamy's *Looking Backward,*[2] which was receiving widespread attention in England. In June he reviewed the book in *Commonweal,* and the train of thought was started which led to his writing *News from Nowhere.* Bellamy pictured the transition to Socialism as one of pacific inevitability. Looking back from the year 2000, he pictured the great American trusts growing to the point where they controlled the entire economic life of the nation: at which point, when "public opinion had become fully ripe", the great corporations and syndicates handed over the industry and commerce of the country to "a single syndicate representing the people".[3] The "red-flag Socialists", so far from leading the struggle for this State syndicate, had hindered the march of evolution by frightening people with their propaganda. The reception accorded to this book, combined with many other pointers of the time—the first electoral success of London Socialism (returning John Burns to the L.C.C.), the changed tone of the capitalist Press towards the dock strike, the social reforms increasingly

[1] *Signs of Change* (1888), p. 46.

[2] Morris to Glasier, May 13th, 1889 (Glasier, *op. cit.,* p. 198): "I suppose you have seen. . . 'Looking Backward'. . . Thank you, I wouldn't care to live in such a cockney paradise as he imagines."

[3] *Looking Backward,* Ch. V.

advocated by such different men as Joseph Chamberlain, Lord Randolph Churchill, A.J. Mundella, Cardinal Manning and Jesse Collings, made it seem all the more important to Morris that Socialists should keep the main point—the essential antagonism of the classes—steadily before the workers. "At present", he wrote, "it is fashionable for even West-End dinner-parties to affect an interest" in Socialism, while "a certain tincture of Socialism. . . is almost a necessary ingredient. . . in a novel which aims at being at once serious and life-like".[1] Moreover, the gradual revival in trade after 1887 was providing conditions once more in which it was possible for limited reforms to be won. All these circumstances help to explain why Morris returned with such insistence to the essentials of Socialist theory in his lecture.

According to a report in the *Leeds Mercury* (March, 1890), Morris began by insisting that—

> "in the phrase 'the class struggle' was involved not merely what was now called Socialism, but the whole of the progress of mankind from savagery to civilization. . . Seven or eight years ago. . . before Socialists began to make a stir. . . nobody, unless he had studied Socialism from a continental point of view, had any idea that there was or could be any possibility of change in the economical relations of men. . ."

Those Radicals who admitted the suffering of many of the workers attributed these, not to "the essentials of their position, but to the accidental defects of some of the men themselves":

> "It was supposed that it was possible for a painstaking, careful, and perhaps rather stingy working man to raise himself out of the working class and become a member of the dominant class."

Such a view, Morris said, implied "an entire ignoring of anything like classes in the community. . . This view had been roughly shaken":

[1] "Looking Backward", *Commonweal*, June 22nd, 1889.

"It was now admitted... that the workers were a class apart, that they had definite claims on society, and that those claims involved the bettering of the whole class of workers as a class."

This carried with it the realization that society must somehow be altered, and that this alteration would necessarily be "in the direction of Socialism".

Next he spoke of certain "evasions" already becoming popular:

"The practical form which those evasions took was to try and push another class between the propertyless workers and their employers, to get more and more people interested in the present rights of property, so that there might be a broader basis for property to stand on."

Among examples he pointed to the cry of "peasant proprietorship" in Ireland: the allotment system for the farm labourers, "founded on the idea that when an agricultural labourer had been working as hard as he could all day he would be fit to give the dregs of his bodily capacity to cultivating a little bit of land for himself"; co-operative schemes; and "efforts such as those of the young gentlemen who were setting to work to teach art and history to the starvelings of the East of London". Also among the "evasions" he listed the movement for the limitation of the hours of labour—"a good thing in itself", but a dangerous red herring if it was put forward as a *substitute* "for the actual rights that he [the working man] could claim as the producer in society".

"All that sort of thing", he continued,

"did not mean Socialism, nor any approach to it, because Socialism was this: that people shall work for themselves and administer for themselves, and that every State shall include the whole people, and not be composed of two classes."

Such "evasions" were really "the last resource of the monopolists", although in fact, he added (with some ambiguity), if they were carried "they would better enable the working class to carry Socialism through".

No doubt there was confusion at this point—a standing apart from the day-to-day struggle. But the burden of Morris's lecture was that in the course of the fight for limited gains it was the first duty of Socialists to make the character of the class struggle more, rather than less, clear. Any real or enduring improvement in the worker's life, he declared, could only be won "by carrying this class struggle, which had been going on for centuries, to the bitter end—by abolishing classes altogether". This could be achieved only by the overthrow of the "useless" classes, and the ownership by the "useful" classes of the means of production and this, in turn, could only be won by the *conscious* rebellion of the working class. This rebellion need not be one of riot and bloodshed,

> "if they ever did rebel in that sense of the word, they would be driven to do so: they would not begin using brute force, but their masters would use it, and the people would be obliged to defend themselves, and he hoped they would do it well. . ."

Rebellion, as he used the word, meant, rather—

> "the attacking of privilege at all points, the constant harassing of the monopolist capitalists by strikes and Trade Unions, the sacred boycott, bold speech where necessary, and the endurance of fine and imprisonment—these things perhaps might do what musketry could not do. . ."

No longer did he look forward so confidently—as he had done two years before—to the General Strike as the decisive blow. "What was the hinge that Labour depended upon at present?" he asked:

> "Coal-mining. They therefore knew how they could enforce their claims. . . by a strike of the coal-miners of the United Kingdom, backed by all the intelligence of labour. That was one of the possible instruments of the rebellion which was perhaps not so far ahead of us."[1]

[1] *Leeds Mercury*, March 26th, 1890.

This was certainly at the opposite pole from Fabianism. Moreover, Morris's emphasis upon the industrial struggle was more concrete here than it had been in "The Policy of Abstention" in 1887. In the *Commonweal* for January 25th, 1890, Morris contributed a long review of the recently published *Fabian Essays* and joined issue closely and in matters of detail with the Fabian falsification of the class struggle in history. He began by regretting that the book had not been produced three years before, when the writers' economic understanding was still in the service of the revolutionary movement,

"whereas a large part of the present volume is given up to the advocacy of the fantastic and unreal tactic which the Fabian Society has excogitated of late... The result is that the clear exposition of the first principles of Socialism, and the criticism of the present false society (which latter no one knows how to make more damaging than Mr. Bernard Shaw, *e.g.*) is set aside for the sake of pushing a theory of tactics, which could not be carried out in practice; and which, if it could be, would still leave us in a position from which we should have to begin our attack on capitalism over again..."

Directly he singled out Sidney Webb as the "leader in this somewhat disastrous move. He seems to enjoy all the humiliations of opportunism, to revel in it...". Webb's "Historical" Essay had completely dismissed the class struggle from the centre of the stage, and replaced it with the now-familiar pieties about State regulation of industry (including the registration of hawkers, playing-card makers, pawn-brokers, etc., etc.) quietly ousting the anarchy of unchecked competition. "Slice after slice has gradually been cut from the profits of capital... Slice after slice has been cut off the incomes from rent and interest by the gradual shifting of taxation..." Capitalism (in the imagery of the ball-room) was performing an "irresistible glide into collectivist Socialism": "He is so anxious" (Morris commented on his "rollicking opportunism")—

"He is so anxious to prove the commonplace that our present industrial system embraces some of the machinery by means of which a Socialist system *might* be worked... that his paper tends to produce the impression of one who thinks that we are already in the first stages of socialistic life..."

Logically, wrote Morris, Webb's "municipal Socialism" might seem to work; "yet *historically* it may do nothing of the kind: the highly centralized municipal administration of the Roman Empire did not in the least alter the economic basis of chattel slavery". Webb's "historic" basis of Socialism he found to be unhistoric, inaccurate, and misleading. For example,

"his history only begins at the period just before the great industrial revolution of the eighteenth century... Mr. Sydney Webb has ignored the transition period of industry which began in the sixteenth century with the break up of the Middle Ages, and the shoving out of the people from the land. The transition is treated of by Karl Marx with great care and precision under the name of the 'Manufacturing Period' (workshop period we might call it), and some mention of it ought to have been included in Mr. Sydney Webb's 'history'..."

The importance of this omission (apart from the ignorance or deliberate evasion of Marx's work, which Morris drew attention to) lay in the blurring of the distinctive character of capitalism, the essential basis of capitalist exploitation, and the replacement of it by a generalized and ill-defined concept, "industrialism". In the stage before the "industrial revolution" the workers were already subject to capitalist exploitation: they "had a world market behind their backs though they were unconscious of it; the goods were made for profit, not primarily for use".[1] Conversely, Morris argued, Socialism did not necessarily imply large-scale industrialism as an essential condition of its existence.

Webb's mistake, Morris declared, was "to over-estimate the importance of the *mechanism* of a system of society apart

[1] In a new lecture, "The Development of Modern Society", published in instalments in *Commonweal* in July and August 1870, Morris returned to the theme of the pre-industrial genesis of capitalism: see especially August 16th, 1890.

from the *end* towards which it may be used". This error he found present in the other essayists, in particular Graham Wallas:

> "Socialism is emphatically not merely 'a system of property-holding', but a complete theory of human life, founded indeed on the visible necessities of animal life, but including a distinct system of religion, ethics, and conduct, which, . . . will not indeed enable us to get rid of the tragedy of life. . . but will enable us to meet it without fear and without shame."

Annie Besant's Essay he dismissed with a polite snort, as "State Socialism. . . in its crudest form", but he reserved some friendly words for Hubert Bland and especially for Shaw:

> "His criticism of the modern capitalistic muddle is so damaging, his style so trenchant, and so full of reserves of indignation and righteous scorn, that I sometimes wonder that *guilty*, i.e. non-Socialist, middle-class people can sit and listen to him. If he could only forget the Sydney-Webbian permeation tactic. . . what an advantage it would be to us all! He would encourage his friends thereby; and as to his enemies—could he offend them more than he does now?"

Here came the great parting of the ways in the modern Socialist movement. Morris's article, despite its many excellent thrusts, was not one of his best. It was written at a time when other interests were commanding his main attention and as if his mind had been dragged back unwillingly to the subject. But still—how much more open, fraternal and responsible than the anonymous Fabian sneers! Thereafter the Fabians left Morris alone: perhaps they could not answer his objections; perhaps they did not wish to draw attention to them. From time to time they co-operated with each other, and after Morris's death Shaw made a half-hearted attempt to claim him for the Fabians—an attempt which his intellectual integrity forced him to abandon in his later years. The Fabians were navigating the hard-headed British workman towards the "by no means un-brilliant future" of the "Welfare State": and they left behind them "the Revolution" and William

Morris with his "peculiar views".

IV. Morris and the Anarchists

"Such finish to what of education in practical Socialism as I am capable of I received. . . from some of my Anarchist friends, from whom I learned, quite against their intention, that Anarchism was impossible. . ."—so Morris was to write in *Justice* five years later.[1] This "education" was of two kinds—theoretical and practical.

The theoretical controversy between Morris and the Anarchists need not claim much attention. Morris was never seriously interested in theoretical Anarchism, despite his liking for Kropotkin, and consequently he never really exerted his mind to controvert the Anarchist positions. Throughout the "parliamentary" struggle within the League and the campaign of sympathy with the Chicago Martyrs, he had taken care to differentiate his own position from Anarchism. In April, 1889, a comrade named James Blackwell had written to *Commonweal* to initiate a discussion on "Communist-Anarchism", quoting with sympathy some resolutions of the Spanish Anarchists:

> "1. By Anarchism we understand a social state in which there is no necessity for government. . . Whilst the principle of authority exists, there will be no guarantee for the liberty of all members of society. The principle of authority. . . always degenerates into tyranny. . .
>
> "2. Since we recognize that a society will never be completely Anarchist whilst there remains in it the least authoritarianism or subjection, we must also recognize as a guarantee of liberty the abolition of the principle of private property and of the exploitation of man by man. . ."[2]

The next month, Morris took up the discussion. With an eye to the disintegrating unity of the League, he sought to subdue

[1] "How I Became a Socialist", *Justice,* June 16th, 1894.

[2] *Commonweal,* April 13th, 1889.

all polemical spirit, and seek for points of agreement rather than differences:

"I will begin by saying that I call myself a Communist, and have no wish to qualify that word by joining any other to it. The aim of Communism seems to me to be the complete equality of condition for all people; and anything in a Socialist direction which stops short of this is merely a compromise. . . a halting-place on the road. . . Communism also will have to keep itself free of superstition. Its ethics will have to be based on the recognition of natural cause and effect, and not on rules derived from *a priori* ideas of the relation of man to the universe or some imagined ruler of it; and from these two things, the equality of condition and the recognition of the cause and effect of material nature, will grow all Communistic life."

"If freedom from authority means the assertion of the advisability or possibility of an individual man doing what he pleases always and under all circumstances, this is an absolute negation of society, and makes Communism. . . impossible". Even in Communist society, differences of opinion would arise (examples of which he gave) which must be settled by the vote and authority of the majority: so far as possible this "authority" would take the form, not of force, but of "that something. . . made up of the aspirations of our better selves, . . . the *social conscience* without which there can be no true society". This social conscience, he declared in a subsequent correspondence, should act as a check to all tendencies towards arbitrary authority. "Without that, there can be no society; and further. . . man without society is not only impossible, but inconceivable."[1]

On one point Morris acknowledged his sympathy with the "Anarchist-Communist" position—by temperament he was opposed to a great industrial civilization, centred on large towns, and he looked forward impatiently to the re-emergence in Communist society of a life based upon small communes and villages. But he took pains to differentiate this speculative

[1] See *Commonweal*, May 18th and August 17th, 1889, for Morris's contributions to the correspondence.

question from more essential matters of Socialist theory: indeed, it was from this region that he drew one of his examples of the necessity for individual submission to collective decisions, as it affected *his* temperament:

"I have always believed that the realization of Socialism would give us an opportunity of escaping from that grievous flood of utilitarianism which the full development of the society of contract has cursed us with; but that would be in the long run only; and I think it quite probable that in the early days of Socialism the reflex of the terror of starvation, which so oppresses us now, would drive us into excesses of utilitarianism. . . So that it is not unlikely that the public opinion of a community would be in favour of cutting down all the timber in England, and turning the country into a big Bonanza farm or a market-garden under glass. And in such a case what could we do, who objected 'for the sake of life to cast away the reasons for living', when we had exhausted our powers of argument? Clearly we should have to submit to authority."

Once again it is possible to see how this controversy (like the reflections caused by reading *Looking Backward*) were urging his mind towards the creation of *News from Nowhere.*

Of the *practical* exucation which Morris received at the hands of the Anarchists, a good deal has already been said. Anarchist theory tended in the direction of the liquidation of all organization, not only in the society of the future, but also in the struggle for its realization. James Blackwell quoted with approval from the Spanish resolutions, the demand that "no statutes or rules of conduct" be imposed upon the organization: "to each individual, to each group. . . is left the study and the means which they will find most suitable to secure the triumph of Anarchism". The utmost that could be permitted was a "Centre of relations and statistics", without initiative, leadership, or disciplinary powers. Morris, for fear of breaking up the League completely on the parliamentary issue, had tolerated the tendency towards virtual autonomy in the branches. Now the tendency began to become marked within the branches as well. Rival groups contended for leadership, and the Anarchists—so opposed to organization in general—organized factions a great deal more effectively than the weakened and bewildered anti-parliamentary Communists. When without official position, they constituted an opposition: when with official positions they had an excuse for inactivity. "I am quite mad at the carelessness of our *Weal* Secretary... in not sending the money regularly", Bruce Glasier wrote in February, 1890, to Frank Kitz, the League Secretary:

> "He is unfortunately an Anarchist... and fails to see the reasonableness... of duly accounting to his London comrades month by month."[1]

Possibly this was just a humorous excuse—a shaft aimed at Kitz himself—since the Glasgow Branch had always been backward in its finances. But there was more than a grain of truth in it, and the disintegration of the League went on apace.

V. Artistic and Intellectual Colleagues

There was one small section of the public among whom Morris's views were making some headway in the last two years of the League. A small number of young intellectuals, students and artists were attracted towards the Socialist movement—less by Morris's arguments than by his personal example. The Hammersmith Clubroom was the centre of this intellectual life. It became even fashionable for the young *avant-garde* to pay at least one visit to the converted outhouse; and there was competition to be among those invited by Morris to supper with a few of the comrades after the meeting. "Something—none of us knew how to define it, but we called it generally the Capitalist System... was wasting life for us and we were beginning to realize as much"—so H.G. Wells, a science student at the time, recalled. "Socialism was then a splendid new-born hope... Wearing our red ties to

[1] Brit. Mus. Add. MSS. 46345.

give zest to our frayed and shabby costumes we went great distances through the gas-lit winter streets of London and by the sulphureous Underground Railway, to hear and criticize and cheer and believe in William Morris, Bernard Shaw, Hubert Bland, Graham Wallas and all the rest of them, who were to lead us to that millennial world." He recalled them lecturing in the Hammersmith outhouse; Graham Wallas, "drooping, scholarly, and fastidiously lucid"; "a lean young Shaw", "a raw aggressive Dubliner. . . with a thin flame-coloured beard beneath his white illuminated face"; and William Morris, who—

> "used to stand up with his back to the wall, with his hands behind him when he spoke, leaning forward as he unfolded each sentence, and punctuating with a bump back to position."[1]

Morris did not always relish this attention, especially when it came from those who were interested only in getting a glimpse of the picturesque author of *The Earthly Paradise* and manager of the Firm. Sometimes visitors of this sort got more than they bargained for, when they presented some anti-Socialist cliché in the discussion. "What he could not stand was smug respectability and cant", one working-class member of the Hammersmith League recalled:

> "If an opponent came forward, however illiterate, but with honest purpose, Morris was delighted; he was just the reverse with hypocritical criticism."[2]

What "just the reverse" implied has become proverbial—Morris's great rages were more rare than has sometimes been

[1] H.G. Wells, *Experiment in Autobiography.*

[2] Reminiscence of R.A. Muncey in *The Leaguer,* October, 1907. See also Rowley, *Fifty Years of Work Without Wages:* "It was delightful to watch his patience when the same old questions were asked by labouring men, or his vehemence when flooring some well-to-do jabberer—often a mere *rentier,* who assumed he was advocating robbery."

suggested, but when they came they were not quickly forgotten, as at least one volume of Victorian reminiscences testifies:

> "His thick curly hair was massed above his forehead and always in confusion because of his habit of running his hands through it in moments of excitement, and oftener than not he was excited. He was weak on argument. In amiable mood, his retort to straying sheep might be, 'My comrade does not believe it in his heart.' But, as a rule, he lost his temper and said nasty things. At one long-remembered meeting he worked himself up to the verge of apoplexy, calling his opponent every possible bad name, lost his voice in the process and did not recover it all evening. . ."[1]

Not all the visitors came from mere curiosity or fashion. Morris was intensely concerned to build up a nucleus of intellectuals, identified heart and soul with "the Cause", and wherever he found ardour and integrity he extended his friendship. The young W.B. Yeats, self-absorbed and self-dramatizing, was one of those who found his way to the League's Clubroom. Morris quickly found him out; invited him frequently to supper; and meeting him by chance in the street praised his recently-published *Wanderings of Usheen* saying, "You write my sort of poetry"—and would have said more "had he not caught sight of a new ornamental cast-iron lamp-post and got very heated upon the subject". To the young poet, Morris, with his "spontaneity and joy", was "chief of men". "No man I have known was so well loved; you saw him producing everywhere organization and beauty, seeming, almost in the same instant, helpless and triumphant." Even in late life, Yeats paid him the finest possible tribute—"if some angel offered me the choice, I would choose to live his life. . . rather than my own or any other man's". But, for all this, Yeats stubbornly repelled the principles he taught. His Socialist strivings ended abruptly:

[1] E.R. Pennell, *Life and Letters of Joseph Pennell*, Vol. I, pp. 158-9.

"The attitude towards religion of almost everybody but Morris, who avoided the subject altogether, got upon my nerves, for I broke out after some lecture or other with all the arrogance of raging youth. They attacked religion, I said... and yet there must be a change of heart and only religion could make it. What was the use of talking about some new revolution putting all things right, when the change must come... with astronomical slowness... Morris rang his chairman's bell, but I was too angry to listen, and he had to ring it a second time before I sat down. He said that night at supper, 'Of course I know there must be a change of heart, but it will not come as slowly as all that. I rang my bell because you were not being understood'. He did not show any vexation, but I never returned after that night..."[1]

This was inevitable, perhaps. Yeats could not be at home in the company of blunt working-class comrades like the one who told him to his face that "I had talked more nonsense in one evening than he had heard in the whole course of his past life". But the anecdote reveals Morris's discernment: from the casual and shallow intellectual, the complacent cliché about a "change of heart" never failed to arouse his wrath; but coming on the flood of Yeats's nervous rage, he understood the sincerity and hatred of utilitarian values which flung the objection forth.[2]

It must have been sad to Morris to have seen so many pass through the movement, like Yeats, as birds of passage; or, like Wells, inclining their attention to the sophistries of the Fabians. There were a few intellectuals in the provinces who gave the League constant support. John Glasse at Edinburgh, R. F. Muirhead, lecturer in Mathematics at Glasgow University and active propagandist, and Raymond Unwin, the architect, at Chesterfield—a frequent contributor to *Commonweal.* Apart from these few, one group only could be relied upon to give him support: and it was held together only in part by Socialist principle, in part by affection for the man, and in part by common artistic interests and activity. Chief among them were Philip Webb, Walter Crane (whose pen and brush was always at the service of the movement) and Emery

[1] W.B. Years, *Autobiographies* (1926), pp. 183-4.

[2] See P. Faulkner, *William Morris and W.B. Yeats* (William Morris Society, 1962).

Walker, Secretary of the Hammersmith Branch and close colleague of Morris in the Kelmscott Press: among younger men were Cobden-Sanderson, the binder, Catterson-Smith, the engraver, and Sir Sydney Cockerell. Around them, again, was a larger group of men and women, many of whose names have been notable in the history of the visual arts in this century, who were more or less influenced by his ideas.

Several among this group of friends were far from being revolutionaries. Morris no longer regarded his work in the Firm as a part of the "holy warfare" against the age, and there is evidence that in the Eighties he looked askance at tendencies towards preciousness within the "arts and crafts" movement which his own example had helped to engender, and at those who tended to turn the movement into a sufficient end in itself. "Morris. . . began to talk about my prices. . .", Cobden-Sanderson noted in his diary some months after he had taken to book-binding (on "Janey's" advice) as a means of spiritual salvation:

> "[He] thought my work too costly; bookbinding should be 'rough'; did not want to multiply the minor arts(!); went so far as to suggest that some machinery should be invented to bind books."[1]

That was a clout from an unexpected quarter! No doubt there was something in "Cobden-S.'s" subjective motivations, his desire to turn the League into a Socialist Charity Organization Society, and his "cosmic" mooning, which rubbed up the bristles on Morris's back. Cobden-Sanderson retaliated in the privacy of his diary, June 1st, 1888:

> "At Croydon the other day Morris and Belfort Bax sniffed at Land Nationalization as not going to the root of things. Simple people! Does their own 'League' then, go within measurable distance of it?"

On November 8th he was grumbling at Morris's insistence upon calling "the social movement" the "war of classes". By

[1] *The Journals of T.J. Cobden-Sanderson,* entry for March 21st, 1885.

March, 1891, his Socialism had taken a thoroughly cosmic turn:

> "I feel that Socialism wants extricating from the ideas of property, ownership, possession, etc., and establishing as a co-operative effort to build up a beautiful humanity. . ."

What could Morris do with material like this?

As a matter of fact, he did little beyond extend his goodwill towards every genuine and seriously-intended project initiated by younger men, some of whom had no sympathy with his Socialist opinions, but acknowledged his authority as the leader of the artistic movement to which they belonged. The Art Workers' Guild (founded in 1884), the Arts and Crafts Exhibition Society (first launched in 1888) and the "unofficial" but widely representative Art Congresses at Liverpool (1888) and Edinburgh (1889) were all promoted with Morris's sympathetic advice and co-operation rather than active initiation.[1] Once they were under way, he gave these projects his services: he lectured for them, wrote articles, and did committee-work. He encouraged them in their guerrilla warfare against the Royal Academy and all its works. The Edinburgh Art Congress of October, 1889, was even looked upon in the Press as a Socialist demonstration, with papers delivered by Walter Crane, Cobden-Sanderson, Emery Walker and Morris himself,[2] and its effect upon many young artists and architects was deeper and more lasting than Morris would have recognized.

In the last two years of the League these activities claimed more of his attention. But—with the exception of his work for the "Anti-Scrape", which he now resumed with enthusiasm—his participation was qualified, as if he was withholding some of his energies. "You understand that I would

[1] See Mackail, II, pp. 196 f., and Morris, "Talk and Art", *Commonweal*, December 22nd, 1888.

[2] See Glasier's full account, *op. cit.*, pp. 84-94; *Letters*, pp. 319-20; Mackail, II, pp. 225-6.

not have gone merely for the Art gammon and spinach", he wrote to Glasier of a professional lecture which he delivered in Glasgow early in 1889: "but it was an opportunity of seeing you chaps free of expense."[1] And to Glasse he wrote later in the year: "I would not have thought of going to the Art Congress unless I had hoped to have been some use to our Scotch Comrades."[2] The majority of the papers at the Congress he found "monumentally dull":

> "It goes without saying that, though there were people present who were intent on playing the part of Art-philanthropists, all the paper readers, except the declared Socialists, showed an absurd ignorance of the very elements of economics; and also. . . the general feeling was an ignoring of the existence of the working class except as instruments to be played on. . ."[3]

The "Art-philanthropists" annoyed him most—who thought of art as "a kind of mumbo-jumbo fetishism for the working class"—"Just the sort of tommy rot that curates talk about religion at mothers' meetings, and Oxford professors say about education at Cutlers' Feasts."[4] Only two features redeemed the Congress: the fact that "we managed to get a good deal of Socialism into our discourses"; and the warm response of the audiences of workmen to whom he and the other Socialists gave papers on the technique of their crafts.

In truth, Morris had lost serious hope of any widespread revival of any of the arts within capitalist society; and there is no evidence at all to suggest that in these years he was turning back to art as an alternative to political action. His own art he thought of as a source of enjoyment and relaxation, and as he saw that the League had failed, and began to feel age coming upon him, he allowed himself to indulge in his own pleasures more and more. But he thought of his art as a private indulgence, not as a public act. When, three years after the Edinburgh Congress, Glasier wrote to invite him to do an art

[1] Glasier, *op. cit.*, p. 198. [2] *Unpublished Letters*, p. 14.
[3] *Commonweal*, November 9th, 1889. [4] Glasier, *op. cit.*, p. 89.

lecture in Glasgow, Morris refused:

> "I am the less troubled at not being able to give the art lecture as I am rather sick of putting matters before people, which they cannot attend to under the Present State of things—let 'em turn Socialists!"[1]

VI. The "Hobbledehoys" Triumph

Morris's incredible energy was at last beginning to show signs of flagging. "I am about from pillar to post very much in these days", he wrote to the ailing Joynes on November 28th, 1889,

> "which to you who are so kept in may seem jolly, but to me is not so. I find that people will insist in looking on me as a young man, and expect work out of me accordingly. I shall have to turn round on them soon if they don't look out."

"The movement is going on curiously now, it seems to me", the letter continued:

> "So many of our hopes in small matters overthrown; and on the wider scale of things going on so much faster than we dared to hope."[2]

His writing was occupying much of his time: *The Roots of the Mountains* was finished in 1889, and *The Story of the Glittering Plain* written early in 1890. In 1890, also, he was revising for re-publication some of his earlier poems, collecting and revising the *Poems By the Way*, preparing translations for the Saga Library, and studying typography as a prelude to founding the Kelmscott Press. Above all, it was in 1890, in this mixed mood of temporary despondency and profounder hope, that he made his greatest imaginative contribution to "the Cause": for it was in this year that *News from Nowhere* was issued in instalments in *Commonweal*.

This was work and enough for any ordinary man in his full

[1] Glasier MSS., October 11th, 1892. [2] Brit. Mus. Add. MSS. 45345.

strength, and—while he continued his work for *Commonweal,* frequent lectures, open-air meetings and committee-work for the League and his own branch—the volume of this work fell off perceptibly in 1890. Every month brought fresh signs of the break-up of the League. In the autumn of 1889 the Edinburgh Branch amalgamated with the local branch of the S.D.F., and formed (together with other surviving outposts of Mahon's propaganda for the Scottish Land and Labour League) the Scottish Socialist Federation. There remained in being as effective branches of the League outside of London the branches at Glasgow, Leicester, Norwich and Yarmouth—all under Anarchist influence; the branches at Leeds, Bradford, Manchester and Aberdeen—all of a firm "parliamentary" persuasion, and acting in effect as independent societies; and a few scattered groups at Walsall, and elsewhere. In February, 1890, Glasier was writing from Glasgow to Frank Kitz of the "downright apathy of our members".[1] In Leeds, Bradford, Manchester and Aberdeen the tale was quite otherwise, for here the Leaguers had been swept into the forefront of the gathering organization of the unskilled and semi-skilled. At Leeds the strike of the builders' labourers had been victorious and a union with 900 members had been formed. Maguire, Paylor, Alf Mattison and others were advising and organizing the gas-workers, the tailoresses, Jewish clothing workers, and many other groups. The Leaguers at Bradford—among them Bland, Minty and the young F.W. Jowett—were active in the same work and extending their influence among the textile workers on the eve of the great strike at Manningham Mills. There was no more time to spend on factional squabbles in the League.[2]

Had the London Leaguers taken a similar part in the organization of the unskilled, then Morris's last years might have taken a somewhat different course. As it was, the

[1] Brit. Mus. Add. MSS. 46345.

[2] For a fuller account of these developments see my "Homage to Tom Maguire", in A. Briggs and J. Saville (eds.), *Essays in Labour History* (1960).

Yorkshire movement brought no additional strength to the Council of the League. Indeed, both the League and *Commonweal* were becoming a hindrance to Maguire and his friends in their work. "Here we have *Commonweal*!" one miners' agent in Scotland had thundered at a meeting a year or two before,

> "The *largest* Socialist paper in the country! Edited by William Morris, the greatest poet, painter, designer, and art critic of the age! Cram full of news about the labour struggle in America, France, Germany, Italy, and Russia! Tells you how you are robbed and who robs you! Tells you what the Social Revolution means, how it can be brought about, and when it will be brought about! Stirring labour songs. . . Only a few copies left!"[1]

In 1889 with the *Labour Elector* in the field this line of sales-talk was not so impressive: nor did the contents of the paper go far to justify it. "*Commonweal* sold well", it was reported in October 1889, at a great demonstration in Halifax of gas-stokers and supporters. But the gas-stokers were given, as the main political article in this number, a frothy "address" by Frank Kitz, which turned its back (with much revolutionary bluster) upon the new unionism, and urged the provincial comrades to "sally into the villages and fields with the cry of 'Back to the Land'."

No wonder the Leeds comrades began in 1888 (rather guiltily) to take copies of Keir Hardie's *Miner;* no wonder they turned to Champion's *Labour Elector* and took a part in the work of the *Yorkshire Factory Times* (founded in 1889, with one of its reporters, Ben Turner, a young official of the General Union of Textile Workers, joining the Leeds League). Only loyalty to William Morris held them in the Socialist League at all; Tom Maguire, in particular, felt the closest affinity with Morris's outlook, and he was perhaps the ablest socialist leader in the North. He and his friends were willing to

[1] J. Bruce Glasier, "Humours of Propaganda", *Commonweal*, October 28th, 1888.

remain, technically, within the League until Morris himself was driven out. In March 1890, when Morris lectured in Leeds on "The Class Struggle", Maguire and Paylor officiated at the meeting. But only a few weeks later the branch finally fell apart.

The occasion was the violent termination of the great Leeds gas strike, in a shower of brickwork and masonry poured over a railway bridge on to a convoy of blacklegs, and a pitched battle in the streets by strikers and their wives against the soldiers and police. Throughout these events Maguire kept his head like a mature leader, rather than a young man of twenty-four, and piloted the strike to victory. Meanwhile, the Anarchist party within the branch, led by H.B. Samuels, aimed a blow at his rear. In July Maguire wrote of the dissension of Edward Carpenter:

> "There has been such a rumpus raised by a few demented Anarchists here—since the gas-riots—that it has become impossible for us to work together any longer. As usual with Socialists when they fall out, all kinds of personal attacks and insinuations have been the order of the day. . . I have withdrawn from the club since I find it more than my nerves can stand to be continually warring with a parcel of raving fools in public and private over matters which are the outcome of personal feelings and not principle. Perhaps the real issue. . . is which of the two courses is the correct one to take bearing in mind the events of the gasworkers' struggle. Those of us who had to do with the gasworkers, in response to the men's wishes and in accordance with our ideas of policy, considered a Labour Electoral League should be formed, and accordingly this was done.
>
> "Our Anarchist friends, who were conspicuous by their absence in the gas fights, joined issue with us at once, attacked not only the League but ourselves, and finally told the people that no policy should be entertained but physical force. Now, while I believe in the *use* of physical force when necessary I think it is midsummer madness to advocate it on the public platform, and it is unlikely, as it would be undesirable, for the people to resort to it until other means had been tried and found wanting. I admit the Labour Electoral move is not all to be desired, but it seemed the next immediate step to take in order to keep the Labour unions militant, and to emphasize the conflict of the workers and the employers. . ."

As for the rest, the Anarchists remained in possession of the remnants of the branch, and "if our Anarchist friends can make the Leeds folk into revolutionists no one will be more pleasantly surprised and mightily satisfied than yours fraternally, T. Maguire".[1] Except for the turn towards parliamentary action, which Morris was not yet ready to countenance, events at Leeds foreshadowed Morris's own virtual ejection from the League a few months later.

At Aberdeen a few Leaguers were playing an equally prominent part in the new unionism; while in Manchester, Leonard Hall, no older than Maguire, and also of great ability, was leading the Leaguers in similar struggles.[2] Meanwhile, in London, two groups of ex-Leaguers were striving to bring part of the unskilled movement under their leadership. Mahon, Donald and Binning strove to set their "Labour Union" afloat on the tide of new unionism, and claimed the credit for forming the Coal Porters' Union in September, 1889. Next they turned to the London postmen, but their confident attempt to organize from the outside one of the most difficult trades in the country ended in total disaster in July, 1890, with the failure of the strike at Mount Pleasant and the victimization of scores of workers. Neither Mahon nor Donald ever recovered their reputation in the South after this fiasco; and (however much their errors were exaggerated by their enemies within and without the movement) there is no doubt that a heavy responsibility for the failure of the strike rested upon them, since their amateurish conduct of the affair, and their innate tendency to intrigue, gave colour to the suspicions and dissensions sown by their opponents among the ranks of the workers.[3]

[1] *Tom Maguire: a Remembrance*, p. xi-xii.

[2] Leonard Hall, born 1866, was the son of Dr. Spencer Hall. "Cast on his own resources" at the age of thirteen, he worked as a railway porter, deck-hand, and in the U.S. as a farmhand and docker before returning to Manchester in the late 1880s. See *Labour Prophet*, February, 1894. For the Manchester League, see also "Revolutionary Reminiscences" by "J.B.S." in *Co-operative News*, August 5th, 1905.

[3] For an unsympathetic account of Mahon's part in this unfortunate business, see Swift, *A History of Postal Agitation* (1900), pp. 203 ff.

The work of the Avelings and of the Bloomsbury Socialist Society was far more constructive. On August 7th, 1889, Engels wrote to Sorge:

> "There are now prospects here for the development of a live socialist organization which will gradually cut the ground from under the feet of the S.D.F. or absorb it. The Socialist League is no good at all. It consists wholly of anarchists, and Morris is their puppet. The plan is to get up agitation for the Eight Hour day in the democratic and radical clubs—our recruiting grounds here—and in the trade unions, and also organize a demonstration on May 1st, 1890."

"The plan" succeeded better than his most optimistic hopes. Eleanor Marx-Aveling, as counsellor to the gas-workers and friend to Will Thorne, was already in the heart of the "new unionism". As Engels was writing, the Dock Strike was beginning to set the whole East End on the move. The Bloomsbury Socialist Society directed its main efforts in the first months of 1890 towards bringing the widest possible section of London workers to carry out the decision of the Paris Congress to observe May Day as a day of international demonstration of the solidarity of labour in the demand for a legal Eight-hour Day. Stage by stage the "New Unions", the small skilled unions, and, finally, the London Trades Council, in which the old skilled unions were still predominant, gave their support to the plan. So impressive was the unity achieved in the campaign that the Avelings took the leading part in promoting a "Legal Eight Hours and International Labour League", with wide trade union affiliation, whose first object was "the formation of a distinct Labour Party" to obtain the limitation of hours of labour and improvement in the factory acts and electoral laws.

Official League and official S.D.F. stood apart from the campaign: the S.D.F. through Hyndman's hostility to the Paris Congress and its decisions; the League out of characteristic purism. Morris, and the League in general, were heartily in agreement with an international May Day, as a day of international solidarity and Socialist demonstrations; but they declared the eight-hours' question to be a secondary issue, raised by the London organizers to undue prominence. Moreover, they declared inflexibly for May 1st—the day when the German workers had declared their decision to demonstrate—whereas the London Trades Council could only be brought to support the demonstration if it were to be held on the first Sunday in May, the 4th. For the sake of this principle, which they held to honestly in the belief that they were acting true to international fraternity, they rejected the chance of sharing in the leadership of one of the greatest British working-class demonstrations since the last days of Chartism. And, in the result, two May Days were held in London in 1890: a gathering of several thousand under the banner of the League at Clerkenwell Green on the 1st; and the demonstration, over 100,000 strong, at Hyde Park on May 4th, of which Engels exclaimed in delight—"the grandchildren of the old Chartists are entering the line of battle."[1] Well might Engels, deeply moved by this revival for which he had waited impatiently for forty years, grumble at the League,

> "which looks down on everything which is not directly revolutionary (which means here in England... everything which does not limit itself to making phrases and otherwise doing nothing) and the Federation, who still behave as if everyone except themselves were asses and bunglers, although it is only due to the new force of the movement that *they* have succeeded in getting some following again. In short, anyone who only looks at the surface would say it was all confusion and personal quarrels. But *under* the surface the movement is going on... and the day is no longer far off when this mass will suddenly *find itself*... and when that day comes short work will be made of all the rascality and wrangling."[2]

One thing, at any rate, was clear after this May Day—the League was no longer fit to give leadership to any section of the British workers. Only fourteen delegates were present at

[1] See *Marx-Engels Sel. Cor.*, p. 469.

[2] Engels to Sorge, April 19th, 1890, *ibid.*, p. 468.

the Sixth Annual Conference, held on May 25th, 1890. The "Anarchist-Communists" were triumphant all along the line: they elected their own group in a solid bloc onto the Executive Council leaving Morris isolated with Webb and two of the Hammersmith Branch: and (a note on the Conference adds) "the delegates were saved the trouble of confirming any new rules, as the late Council had sense enough to make none".[1] Greatest triumph of all, William Morris and Sparling were ejected from the editorship of *Commonweal,* and Kitz and Nicoll elected in their place.[2] Morris endured the proceedings with a mixture of good humour and contempt. Questioned closely about his financial statement as Treasurer, he finally remarked, with a shade of bitterness, "Well, Mr. Chairman, I can't see that it matters a damn; for I receive £10 in one hand, and with the other I pay out £50."[3] As the room thickened with tobacco smoke and revolutionary bluster, he busied his hands with flower-patterns and lettering on his agenda-paper, in the end flinging himself back in his chair and growling, "Mr. Chairman, *can't* we get on with the business? I want my TEA!" At tea he sat next to Tom Barclay of Leicester, and gave relief to his suppressed irritation in literary criticism. Barclay spoke of Meredith. Morris dug his fist into his palm and declared vehemently: "Meredith! He tweaks you by the nose; he makes me feel I'd like to punch his head!"[4] At ten the Conference broke up, and the Hammersmith group went back on the underground. For a few moments they stood on the embankment and watched the lights and traffic on the Thames. "The wind's in the

[1] *Commonweal,* May 31st, 1890.

[2] The inner history of this event is given in a letter from H.H. Sparling to R. Steele: "You know how 'Weal has been running? At a dead loss of £7 a week for some time, all of which has fallen upon Morris. At the Conference the proposal was made it should become a monthly and this we strongly supported. But the 'Ballyhooley' section out-voted us and said that if they had the whole conduct of the paper they would make it go. . . So Kitz and Nicoll were elected. . . so ends a five-year record" (June 2nd, 1890, Brit. Mus. Add. MSS. 45345).

[3] May Morris, II, p. 324.

[4] Tom Barclay, *Memoirs and Medleys: The Autobiography of a Bottle-Washer.*

West", said Morris. "I can almost smell the country."[1] Perhaps *News from Nowhere,* Kelmscott and Ellen, were in his mind. "He found himself musing on the subject-matter of discussion, but still discontentedly and unhappily. 'If I could but see a day of it', he said to himself; 'if I could but see it!' " It is in this very mood that *News from Nowhere* was begun.

For one of the first times in his life, Morris seemed to procrastinate. He dropped out of League activity, he absorbed his attention in other work; he seemed to postpone a decision which he knew to be inevitable. "I have been somewhat worrited by matters connected with the League", he wrote to a friend in July; "but somehow or other I don't seem to care much."[2] In this frame of mind, Morris might have remained a member of the League for many more months if the Anarchists had shown the least desire for compromise. But the degeneration of the League was going on at an astounding rate. An East London and a West-end Anarchist-Communist Group were formed within the League itself. The "moderate" Anarchists—in the main followers of Prince Kropotkin—were being out-blustered by a curious assortment of cranks and fire-eaters: Malatesta, the stormcock of Anarchism and inheritor of Bakunin's conspiratorial mantle, was back in England and had joined the League. In the wake of the conspirators came the police-spies, sent in in part from genuine alarm at the terrorist complexion of the movement, and in part with the aim of using this handful of political eccentrics to discredit the Socialist movement as a whole.

Little over a month after Morris had lost control of *Commonweal,* Nicoll was in full swing. The issue of July 12th, 1890, was a real snorter. In his Editorial Nicoll called upon a "No Rent" Campaign to start without delay: half a dozen comrades "well barricaded" in a house might hold law and order at bay for weeks. Kitz wrote a long Appeal to Soldiers. Nicoll, in his "Notes", greeted the police strike with the cry, "the whole Governmental machine is going to

[1] May Morris, II, p. 325. [2] Mackail, II, p. 231.

pieces. Even the practical middle-class man is beginning to ask, 'Are we on the verge of a Revolution?' " The instalment of *News from Nowhere* ("Hampton Court") seemed strangely our of place. Samuels capped the issue by sending in an account of the attack upon the blacklegs in the Leeds gas-strike which invited the attention of the public prosecutor. "If the people had only the knowledge", he wrote, "the whole cursed lot would have been wiped out. As the horses and men picked themselves up, it was seen that many were bruised and bleeding, but, alas! no corpses to be seen." Reluctantly Morris, who as technical owner and publisher of the paper, was liable to all prosecutions, took up his pen to write to Nicoll:

"I have been looking at this week's *Commonweal*, and I must say that I think you are going too far: at any rate further than I can follow you. You really must put the curb upon Samuels's blatant folly, or you will *force* me to withdraw all support. I never bargained for this sort of thing when I gave up the editorship.

"I look upon you as a sensible and friendly fellow, and I am sure that you will take this in a friendly spirit as it is meant to you... Please understand that this is meant to be quite private, and do your best not to drive me off. For I do assure you that it would be the greatest grief to me if I had to dissociate myself from men who have been my friends so long and whom I believe to be at bottom thoroughly good fellows."[1]

For a week or two Nicoll was a shade more discreet. But the whole League in London (outside of Hammersmith) was becoming a fanatic's playground. A solemn "Revolutionary Conference" was held at the Autonomie Club on August 3rd, at which four provincial and six London branches of the League were represented, together with a dozen high-sounding groups of foreign refugees. The Conference was "most successful". "All red-tapeism and quasi-authoritarianism were banished." The only thing actually decided by the Conference

[1] *Letters*, pp. 324-5. Nicoll later alleged in a pamphlet entitled *The Greenwich Mystery: "Letters from the Dead"* (1898) that Samuels was a police agent.

appears to have been the agreement to dispense with a Chairman, or "any such quasi-constitutional official". The aim of the Conference was to secure United International Action in the event of a European Crisis. Mowbray declared that in this event, "he would do his best to get the groups called together for consultation; but as to preliminary steps he should form himself into a committee of one. In the event of a crisis at home, the first thing to do was to fire the slums and get the people into the West-end mansions." Kitz returned to his old nostrum: "We should preach to the thieves, the paupers, and the prostitutes. . . The first act of the Revolution ought to be to open the prison doors." Malatesta delivered himself of a fiery speech, advocating the seizure of property in general. Pearson (Freedom Group) advocated "individual guerrilla warfare. . . We should recognize individuality." Kant (Sheffield Socialist Society) said: "We wanted to know where the gatling guns and other instruments of destruction were kept, so that we might find them when wanted." Miss Lupton "believed in assembling the people in the streets". But she did not go far enough for the delegates: "There must be leaders—(some cries of 'No')—but they must arise when the time came. Leadership was necessary—(renewed dissent)—but we must not plan it." Mrs. Lahr "thought we should do our utmost to get among the soldiers." Nicoll "thought the General Strike meant the Social Revolution. It was not necessary to tell everybody *so;* all revolutions hitherto had been made by minorities. A General Strike would mean the streets thronged with desperate hungry crowds ready for anything, and that would mean the Revolution."[1]

Commonweal was now an Anarchist organ. Morris contributed his last "Notes on News" (which he had written week in, week out, with only a few intervals, for over five years) on July 26th. He was at Kelmscott Manor a good deal in the late summer and early autumn, and (with the exception of *News from Nowhere,* the last instalment of which was published on

[1] *Commonweal,* August 16th, 1890.

October 4th) he contributed nothing to the paper during September and October. On November 1st he suddenly vented his spleen upon General Booth and the Salvation Army, in an article entitled "Workhouse Socialism". Two weeks later he sent in his final article—"Where are We Now?"—and the breach was complete.

The break, when it came, was so unadvertised that Glasier, in Glasgow, knew nothing of it for a fortnight. Some final folly of Nicoll's provided the last straw, and "Where are We Now?" was "meant. . . as a 'Farewell' ". "I never wait to be *kicked* downstairs", Morris wrote to Glasier:

> "We have borne with it all a long time; and *at last* have gone somewhat suddenly. For my part I foresaw all this when we allowed the Bloomsbury branch to be expelled. They deserved it, for it was that pig of a Donald who began it all; but they being out, it was certain that the Anarchists would get the upper hand. . .
>
> "Personally, I must tell you that I feel twice the man since I have spoken out. I dread a quarrel above all things, and I have had this one on my mind for a year or more. But I am glad it is over at last; for in good truth I would almost as soon join a White Rose Society as an Anarchist one; such nonsense as I deem the latter. . .
>
> "Good-bye, and don't be downcast, because we have been driven to admit plain facts. It has been the curse of our movement that we would lie to ourselves about our progress and victories. . ."[1]

Just over a month before Morris had given an interview to *Cassell's Saturday Journal,* in which he said nothing of disagreements with his comrades, but was at particular pains to put himself within the Marxist tradition (Appendix II). At the same time his attitude to the S.D.F. was more than usually conciliatory. But, when Hyndman wrote to invite him to contribute once again to *Justice,* he met with a friendly refusal: "I have come to the conclusion that no form of journalism is suited to me. . . I want to pull myself together after what has been, to me at least, a defeat. . ."[2] With

[1] Glasier, *op. cit.,* pp. 203-5.

[2] Hyndman, *Record of an Adventurous Life,* p. 361.

Glasier, it is true, he discussed the possibility of a *general* Socialist paper, embracing all sections: but it was a prospect far removed in the future. "For the rest", he concluded, "speaking and lecturing as much as sickened human nature can bear are the only things as far as I can see. . ."[1]

The Hammersmith Branch was only too ready to accept Morris's lead. In October it had registered an official protest at an article of Nicoll's on the (imaginary) "No Rent" movement, in which he had advocated the defence of his (imaginary) house by five resolute comrades with "bricks, stones, and hot water".[2] Pursuant to this resolution it had appointed a deputation to meet the League Council, and its unsatisfactory reception provided the actual occasion of the breach.[3] On November 21st, the Branch officially severed its connection with the League, and was renamed the "Hammersmith Socialist Society", with Emery Walker as Secretary. The North Kensington Branch seceded in the following week.[4] A letter of explanation was sent out to all remaining branches and groups (Glasgow, Oxford, Manchester, Norwich, Leicester and Yarmouth in the provinces; and East London, North London, Streatham and the "Commonweal Group" in London), declaring the intention of the Branch to carry on its propaganda independently, since—had they remained within an Anarchist-dominated League—"a great part of our time, which should be spent in attacking Capitalism, would have to be spent in bickering with our own comrades."[5]

The Hammersmith Branch, in the summer of 1890, was 120 strong—and yet Morris thought it might well be "as

[1] Morris to Glasier, December 16th, 1890 (Glasier, *op. cit.,* p. 206).

[2] *Commonweal,* October 18th, 1890; Hammersmith Minutes, October 24th, 1890.

[3] Hammersmith Minutes, October 31st and November 7th, 1890.

[4] *Ibid.,* December 5th, 1890.

[5] Published in full in Mackail, II, pp. 239-40. List of branches in Hammersmith papers.

numerous as all the rest of the League."[1] If these figures are correct, then the League had sunk in 1890 *below* its membership at the time of the First Annual Conference in 1885. Morris had reason to wonder, "Where are We Now?"

VII. "Where are We Now?"

The seeds of dissolution had been within the League from its very birth. Hyndman's opportunism and arbitrary methods had provoked their opposites in Morris's purism and inattention to party discipline. "It was partly Morris's fault that the Anarchists gradually won the upper hand in the Socialist League", Andreas Scheu, who had come back into activity in 1889 and 1890, wrote many years later:

> "He was too good-natured and too tolerant towards his opponents. His indulgence was often painful to witness, and was bound to lead to a complete break, since his manner drove away the more serious elements, and opened the door to all sorts of doubtful characters."[2]

The comment is just. The S.D.F.—for all Hyndman's many failings, had a definite leadership, discipline of a sort, and engaged in clearly defined political campaigns. Morris was not a successful political leader. He took too much upon himself, and was unable to develop a responsible leadership around him. His experiences in the S.D.F. and his own temperamental dislike of bickering and intrigue led him to appease the Anarchists until the whole fabric of the League had become rotten. He allowed the League to become totally dependent upon himself financially, and then was unable to refuse each additional demand for a subsidy, for fear he should seem to

[1] Glasier, *op. cit.,* p. 204. The annual report of the Hammersmith Branch, in the summer of 1890, reported a membership of 120, nearly double that of the previous year, and attributed this rate of recruiting to the vigorous open-air propaganda, at which an average of audience of 300 had been built up (Hammersmith papers).

[2] Scheu, *op. cit.,* Part III, Ch. V.

be tieing policy to his purse-strings. The failure of the League was at least in part his own failure.

A good deal of this Morris understood at the end of 1890, and he came to understand more before he died. He did not make the mistake of confusing his own grievous personal set-back with a defeat for the movement as a whole. Indeed, the remarkable thing about his "Farewell" article for *Commonweal* is the degree to which he was able to stand outside of the affairs of the League, and judge his own endeavours in an impersonal light, "Men absorbed in a movement", he commenced his article, "are apt to surround themselves with a kind of artificial atmosphere which distorts the proportions of things outside, and prevents them from seeing what is really going on." By contrast, he sought to look round and note the way the movement was affecting the people as a whole.

First, he looked back down the seven years since "Socialism came to life again in this country". "Few movements surely have made so much progress during this short time... as Socialism has done":

> "What was it which we set out to accomplish? To change the system of society on which the stupendous fabric of civilization is founded, and which has been built up by centuries of conflict with older and dying systems, and crowned by the victory of modern civilization over the material surroundings of life.
>
> "Could seven years make any visible impression on such a tremendous undertaking as this?"

The pioneers themselves were little more than a "band of oddities":

> "Who were the statesmen who took up the momentous questions laid before England of the nineteenth century by the English Socialists? Who were the great divines who preached this new gospel of happiness from their pulpits? Who were the natural philosophers who proclaimed their hope and joy at the advent of a society which should at last use their marvellous discoveries for the good of mankind?
>
> "There is no need to take pen in hand to write their names. . ."

And yet, despite the smallness and oddity of the band, the pioneers had succeeded in impressing "the idea of Socialism deeply on the epoch... The shouts of triumph over the glories of civilization which once drowned the moans of the miserable... have now sunk into quavering apologies for the existence of the horrors and fatuities of our system." This impression had been made, despite all the failings of the Socialists themselves:

"We have between us made about as many mistakes as any other party in a similar space of time. Quarrels more than enough we have had; and sometimes weak assent for fear of quarrels to what we did not agree with.

"There has been self-seeking amongst us, and vainglory, and sloth, and rashness; though there has been at least courage and devotion also. When I first joined the movement I hoped that some working-man leader, or rather leaders, would turn up, who would push aside all middle-class help, and become great historical figures. I might still hope for that, if it seemed likely to happen, for indeed I long for it enough; but to speak plainly it does not so seem at present."

Yet, despite all this, the very decay of capitalist society had prepared the soil for their propaganda, and helped it to bear fruit.

Next, he turned to analyse his feelings of disappointment as to the general tendency of the movement:

"When we first began to work together, there was little said about anything save the great ideals of Socialism; and so far off did we seem from the realization of these, that we could hardly think of any means for their realization, save great dramatic events which would make our lives tragic indeed, but would take us out of the sordidness of the so-called 'peace' of civilization. With the great extension of Socialism, this also is changed. Our very success has dimmed the great ideals that first led us on; for the hope of the partial and, so to say, vulgarised realization of Socialism is now pressing on us."

Discussion within the movement now turned less on ends, and more and more upon differences of method. Two methods he singled out for criticism: first, the anarchist bluster of riot and partial revolt, which he dismissed in a few words: second, "our old acquaintance palliation, elevated now into vastly greater importance than it used to have, because of the growing discontent, and the obvious advance of Socialism". This second tendency he discussed in more detail:

"The whole set [of] opinion amongst those more or less touched by Socialism. . . is towards the New Trades' Unions and palliation. Men believe that they can wrest from the capitalists some portion of their privileged profits. . . That [this] could only very partially be done, and that the men could not rest there if it were done, we Socialists know very well. . ."

In the end, thought Morris, the legal Eight Hours' Day might be won, but would bring "next to no results either to men or masters". "No permanent material benefit *can* accrue to [the workers] until Socialism has ceased to be militant, and is merged in the new society":

"For the rest, I neither believe in State Socialism as desirable in itself, or, indeed, as a complete scheme do I think it possible. Nevertheless some approach to it is sure to be tried, and to my mind this will precede any complete enlightenment on the new order of things. The success of Mr. Bellamy's book, deadly dull as it is, is a straw to show which way the wind blows. The general attention paid to our clever friends, the Fabian lecturers and pamphleteers, is not altogether due to their literary ability; people have really got their heads turned more or less in their direction."

All these signs, it seemed to Morris—the growing discontent, the great strikes, the stirring of new ideas—pointed in the same direction:

"This time when people are excited about Socialism, and when many who know nothing about it think themselves Socialists, is the time of all others to put forward the simple principles of Socialism regardless of the policy of the passing hour.

". . . In saying this I am speaking for those who are complete

Socialists—or let us call them Communists. I say for us *to make Socialists* is *the* business at present. . ."

While the new unionists, and (with an eye on Samuels & Co.?) "disturbance-breeders", might do some good from which the movement would benefit, "we need not and cannot work heartily with them when we know their methods are beside the right way":

"Our business, I repeat, is the making of Socialists, i.e. convincing people that Socialism is good for them and is possible. When we have enough people of that way of thinking, *they* will find out what action is necessary for putting their principles in practice. Until we have that mass of opinion, action for a general change that will benefit the whole people is *impossible.* Have we that body of opinion or anything like it? Surely not. . . Though there are a great many who believe it possible to compel their masters. . . to behave better to them, and though they are prepared to compel them. . . all but a very small minority are not prepared *to do without masters.* They do not believe in their own capacity to undertake the management of affairs, and to be responsible for their life in this world. When they are so prepared, then Socialism will be realized; but nothing can push it on a day in advance of that time.

"Therefore, I say, make Socialists. We Socialists can do nothing else that is useful, and preaching and teaching is not out of date for that purpose; but rather for those who, like myself do not believe in State Socialism, it is the only rational means of attaining to the New Order of Things."[1]

In truth, between 1889 and 1892 Morris was both discouraged and bewildered at the turn the movement was taking, despite all his enthusiasm at the spirit of the unskilled themselves, and this final article shows him at his lowest ebb of confidence. Unspoken, but behind the article all the time, is the devastating comment which he made to Bruce Glasier in a letter of October, 1890:

"As to League affairs; I have really been a good bit out of them. I don't think there is much life in it anywhere except at our Branch. . .

[1] *Commonweal,* November 15th, 1890.

The whole movement has taken the turn which might have been expected, towards unideal & humdrum 'gradual improvement', i.e. towards general deadlock and break-up. That's all right but of course it goes slow; and meantime I sometimes rather feel sick of things in general. The humbug which floats to the top in all 'branches of intelligence' is such a damned greasy pot of scum."[1]

Here Morris's real feelings are given open expression. On every side of him, he could see "Fabianism" gaining ground, which could only lead (as he thought) to a "State Socialism" on the models framed by Annie Besant and Edward Bellamy—a bureaucratic extension of Fabian "municipal Socialism", without any fundamental change in social relationships. "An article in the *Star* the other day carried the 'We are all Socialists now' about as far as that stale piece of cant could be carried", he burst out in his *Commonweal* "Notes" in February, 1890:

" 'We have had municipal Socialism for fifty years', said its writer. Have we indeed? It must be a valuable article, then, considering how it has abolished all the evils of which Labour has to complain!... Whereabouts is this municipal Socialism? I should like to find out. I think it must be Socialism for the rich; that is the reason why we cannot find it out..."[2]

In one sense, Morris had a prophetic insight into the character of the emergent theory of twentieth-century Social-Democracy. The pioneers of the 1880s had had a wide influence; but they had failed to achieve the objective which Engels had set in 1883—that of forming a nucleus of theoretically advanced Socialists who would succeed in mastering the mass movement when it arose. But, deep as was his insight into the character of Fabianism, his conclusions in "Where are We Now?" pointed towards an aggravation of the disease rather than a cure. "This... is the time of all others to

[1] *Letters,* p. 328. Glasier excised this passage from his published version (Glasier, *op. cit.,* p. 208).

[2] *Commonweal,* February 1st, 1890.

put forward the simple principles of Socialism *regardless of the policy of the passing hour*"—the tone of this implies an independent propaganda of pure Socialism *outside* the mass labour movement, rather than a propaganda of both theory and practice within the workers' own organizations. Engels's advice throughout these years was different in emphasis: he urged the Socialists (in Lenin's words) to carry on their activities "*right in the heart* of the proletarian masses", to "throw off their narrow sectarianism *at all costs* and *affiliate* to the labour movement in order *politically to shake up* the proletariat." Morris's attitude to the first May Day is symbolic of his confusion at this time. He was still placing far too much emphasis upon the inculcation of Socialist theory in the abstract; far too little upon the educative role of the struggle itself. Engels, by contrast, stressed repeatedly the importance of practical experience. He and Marx (he wrote in 1888):

"entirely trusted to the intellectual development of the working class, which was sure to result from combined action and mutual discussion. The very events and vicissitudes of the struggle against capital, the defeats even more than the victories, could not help bringing home to men's minds the insufficiency of their various favourite nostrums, and preparing the way for a more complete insight into the true conditions of working class emancipation."[1]

In January, 1890, writing of the English and American workers, he was even more specific:

"... they go their own way. One cannot drum the theory into them beforehand, but their own experience and their own blunders and the evil consequences of them will soon bump their noses up against theory—and then all right."[2]

Morris cannot be accused, like Hyndman, of having reduced Marxism to a series of narrow texts and dogmas. But in other

[1] Preface to the 1888 edition of Samuel Moore's translation of the *Communist Manifesto*.

[2] Engels to H. Schlüter, January 11th, 1890, *Marx-Engels Sel Cor.*, p. 464.

respects his attitude at this time falls under Engels's criticism. To "make Socialists" while holding aloof from the New Unionism was simply a policy of self-destruction.

The source of Morris's strength and inspiration was at the same time a cause of his political weakness. The depth of his hatred of capitalism made him inclined to denounce all partial reforms as compromises or betrayals. The clarity of his vision of Socialist society made him impatient of any advances which savoured of the re-organization or "improvement" of capitalism. Above all, he feared the penetration of the Socialist movement by the values and outlook of the middle class. He had at times a prophetic insight into the hypocrisy and self-seeking, betrayal and opportunism, which might bewilder and corrupt the labour movement of the future.

This—and this only—was the reason why he urged, again and again during the years of the League, the necessity for "making Socialists". It was not through some desire to rest in a world of beautiful impracticable idealism. His advice sprang directly from the need which he saw ever before him, to build a nucleus of "convinced Socialists", a tradition of revolutionary Socialist theory, which might either master the movement or survive the errors of reformism into a future phase of revolutionary action.

CHAPTER VII

TOWARDS A UNITED SOCIALIST PARTY, 1890–1896

I. The Kelmscott Press

"I AM not going to retire", Morris wrote to Glasier on December 16th, 1890. "We Hammersmith-ers will. . . be eager to join in any arrangement which would bring us together." Certainly, Morris did not think of his defeat as the signal for his withdrawal from active propaganda. Rather, he felt that in breaking with the Anarchists he had untied his hands for co-operation with the general movement. Before deciding the form which this co-operation might take, he wanted time to take new bearings. Meanwhile, he turned to organizing the half of the League that remained in the new Hammersmith Socialist Society.[1]

The "Rules" and "Statement of Principles" of the Hammersmith Society were ratified on January 2nd, 1891. It was declared:

> "That the object of the Society shall be the spreading of the principles of Socialism, especially by Lectures, Street-Meetings, and Publications, and its funds be applicable to that object only."[2]

The "Statement of Principles", drafted by Morris, was of a very general character, and marked a low ebb in his usually vigorous style. The new society, it declared, could only be won "by the conscious exertions of those who have learned to know what Socialism is". Both Anarchism and Parliamentarianism were disclaimed, but little was put in their places other than the general aim of "making Socialists"—

> "by putting before people, and especially the working-classes, the elementary truths of Socialism; since we feel sure. . . that in spite of

[1] The last sound Branch—Aberdeen—followed Hammersmith out (Hammersmith Minutes, January 9th, 1891).

[2] Hammersmith papers.

the stir in the ranks of labour, there are comparatively few who understand what Socialism is. . ."

But there was no attempt in the Statement to represent the Society as holding to the only pure and true Socialist doctrine, or to set it forward as a rival *national* centre to Fabians or S.D.F. Morris was temporizing.

If Morris refused to acknowledge that he was beaten, it would be foolish to minimize the bitterness of his defeat. "I have got to rewrite the manifesto for the new Hammersmith Society", he wrote on December 9th—"and that I must do this very night: it is a troublesome and difficult job, and I had so much rather go on with my Saga work."[1] Now, as before, his reflex when faced with disappointment was to plunge himself into other work. The volume of his writing had been growing throughout the previous eighteen months. In the summer of 1890 he had embarked upon the Kelmscott Press in earnest. Now, in January, 1891, his preparations were complete: a cottage was rented close to his Hammersmith home, and the Press was installed.

Notwithstanding this new interest, which was to sustain him for the rest of his life, suddenly, in February, 1891, Morris's health collapsed. More than once before attacks of gout had followed hard upon the heels of some disappointment, and it is reasonable to connect this most serious illness of all with the failure of the League, and with his distress at a new turn for the worse in the condition of his daughter, Jenny. His illness was more grave than has generally been realized, and it may have represented the first onset of the diabetic condition from which he died. In the middle of March, May Morris wrote to Glasier that Morris was still too ill to write: he was "terribly low-spirited", and anxiety over his daughter Jenny had "terribly upset my Father's nerves". On March 27th, her husband, Halliday Sparling, was writing:

[1] Mackail, II, p. 240.

"Morris is on the mend. . . is now quite cheerful, which is an immense gain. Part of the time he was fearfully depressed, and talked about dying. . . He will write when he can hold a pen comfortably." [1]

By April he was back at his work: "It is a fine thing to have some interesting work to do, and more than ever when one is in trouble—I found that out the other day."[2] In May, June and July he spent much time at Folkestone, convalescing from his own illness, and keeping company with Jenny who was recovering from hers. But he was by no means fit. On July 29th he was writing to Georgie: "I am ashamed to say that I am not as well as I should like, and am even such a fool as to be rather anxious. . ."[3] In August he went with Jenny for a holiday in France (on "doctor's orders"): despite his impatience at being taken from his work with the Press, he was refreshed by the journey, writing lengthy architectural commentaries to Emery Walker and Philip Webb.[4] "I have given myself up to thinking of nothing but the passing day and keeping my eyes open", he wrote from France.[5] It was not until the autumn that he was fit enough to take up his work with the Press once again.

The illness left its mark. It is only necessary to compare a photograph of Morris in the late 1880s with one in his last years to see how rapidly he must have aged between 1890 and 1893. No longer did he have that excess of energy which had enabled him to do the business of half a dozen ordinary men. A new mood of resignation was growing upon him. His temper was becoming more equable, his outbursts of rage more rare. He knew that he would not see Socialism in his own life-time. He knew that as a practical leader of the movement he had failed. He had given the best of his mind and energies to the "Cause", and now, when he must have known that he had not many more years to live, he allowed himself to enjoy his pleasures. Once again he attended sales

[1] Glasier MSS. [2] Mackail, II, p. 256. [3] *Letters,* pp. 338-9.
[4] *Ibid.,* pp. 341 ff. [5] Mackail, II, p. 261.

of manuscripts and early printed books, and added to his collection. Both his last prose romances and his work with the Kelmscott Press were undertaken in this mood.

The Kelmscott Press, about which much has already been written by experts,[1] was founded in a different spirit from that in which the original Firm had been launched thirty years before. Morris now had no thought of reforming the world through his art, and little thought of reforming contemporary printing and book production. Indeed, he did not seek to justify his pleasure in any way. The Press was simply a source of delight and relaxation, in which his craft as designer and his craft as a writer both found expression. His son-in-law, Halliday Sparling, who was closely associated with the venture, described the Press as "a personal experiment to see what could be done *at his own expense* in the way of producing a decent book".[2] It was his intention at first neither to publish nor to sell the books, but only to work at the designing of type and at printing as a private hobby. In the outcome, the high cost of his experiments made it essential that he should recoup some of his losses by publishing a limited edition of each work. The prices of the books were prohibitive for the general public. "When he has paid a high price for his paper", Frank Colebrook recalled,

> "hand-made from the linen shirts of certain peasants; when he has used black ink at about 10 shillings a pound; when he has designed his three types and had them cut; when he has paid fair wages to his workmen, from whom he does not require a longer week than 46½ hours—nor,

[1] See Vallance, *op. cit.*, pp. 376 f.; Mackail, II, pp. 247 f.; William Morris, "The Ideal Book" (May Morris, I, pp. 310-17); *Three Papers on William Morris*, ed. Holbrook Jackson (Shenval Press, 1934); *The Kelmscott Press and William Morris, Master-Craftsman* (1934), by H. Halliday Sparling; *An Annotated List of All the Books Printed at the Kelmscott Press*, by Sir Sydney Cockerell (Hammersmith, 1898); *A Note by William Morris on His Aims in Founding the Kelmscott Press Together with a Short History and Description of the Press* (1898), by Sir Sidney Cockerell; *De la Typographie et l'harmonie de la Page imprimée. William Morris et son influence sur Les Arts et Métiers* (1898), by C. Ricketts & L. Pissarro.

[2] H.H. Sparling, *op. cit.*, p. 77.

indeed, bind them down to any specified time—he is not able to sell the product of all this for a less sum."[1]

As each new book came off the Press, he dissipated any possible profit by distributing copies among his closest friends. "You see. . . I do the books mainly for you and one or two others", he wrote to Philip Webb in August, 1894.[2] With the exception of one small job for the new London County Council, Morris executed no outside orders at the Press. The atmosphere of the place was rather that of a studio than of a business. Entering the Press once, Morris found the foreman, Mr. Bowden, "in the depth of dismay". A long deal slab with dozens of page formes on it had collapsed, and all the type was pied. Morris regarded the disaster with equanimity. "Oh then," he remarked, "this is what you call 'pie'. . . Ah well, we must put it straight. I came up to tell you that you must take a holiday on May 1st, Labour Day. . ."[3]

In October, 1892, Morris cancelled an engagement to lecture in Glasgow, writing: "At present the absolute *duties* of my life are summed up in the necessity for taking care of my wife and daughter. . . My *work* of all kinds is really simply an amusement taken when I can out of my duty time."[4] The Kelmscott Press proved to be the perfect form of creative relaxation for him in his last years, since he could continue with his designing even when in poor health or confined to bed. The scale of his work was so costly, and his favourite Gothic type was so unfamiliar, that his work could not have an immediate influence upon popular book production. "Morris's achievement", in the view of Gerald Crow,

"is more conspicuously that of having awakened general interest in the production of volumes beautiful in every feature (including an appropriate type and an insistence upon well-proportioned margins), than of having contributed to type-design as an independent and

[1] Frank Colebrook, *William Morris, Master Printer*, p. 10. [2] *Letters*, p. 361.
[3] Frank Colebrook, *op. cit.*, p. 30. [4] Glasier MSS.

specialised art."[1]

This stimulus to general interest provided by the Press was probably the greatest single factor in the revival of fine printing, both in England and in Europe, in succeeding years.

So, with his work at the Press, visits to Kelmscott Manor, work on the prose romances and his translations, and occasional propaganda for the Socialist movement or for Anti-Scrape, he passed his last few years. The intense nervous energy which had sustained him through the 1880s was flagging, and was giving way to a note of peace unknown in his life before, and given expression in some verses written for his old bed at Kelmscott Manor in the summer of 1891:

"I am old and have seen
Many things that have been;
Both grief and peace
And wane and increase.
No tale I tell
Of ill or well,
But this I say,
Night treadeth on day,
And for worst and best
Right good is rest."

II. Goodbye to the Anarchists

Despite his recent illness, from which he had scarcely recovered, Morris was present at London's May Day in 1891. He spoke, not at a splinter meeting as in the year before, but at the main demonstration of May the Third. Aveling was Chairman of his platform, and Cunninghame Graham, Shaw, and Harry Quelch (of the S.D.F.) spoke beside him, while Engels, a spectator, sat on the platform. This was symbolic of the direction of his last years of work for the "Cause".

For the greater part of the next year, his activities were

[1] Gerald Crow, *William Morris, Designer* (1934), p. 101.

limited to his own society at Hammersmith. It was certainly in a healthy state. A regular audience of between forty and seventy attended its Sunday lectures. In addition a monthly discussion meeting was held, and at the weekly business meetings, which Morris usually attended,[1] twenty and more members were regularly present. Throughout the year, summer and winter, the open-air stands were kept open, with a regular audience of 300 at the Hammersmith Bridge site. Morris was still a frequent open-air speaker, sometimes carrying the banner and platform himself to the Bridge or to the Latimer Road arches. With *Commonweal* now a monthly Anarchist broadsheet, the Society sought for another paper to sell at their propaganda meetings. *Justice* was passed over in favour of the *Labour Leader* (Keir Hardie's paper), and then for Burgess's *Workman's Times*. Early in 1892 both of these were given up in favour of Robert Blatchford's more forthright Socialist paper, the *Clarion*. Meanwhile, in October, 1891, the Society commenced publication of a small four-page monthly, the *Hammersmith Socialist Record*.

The Hammersmith Socialist Society provided a platform where every opinion within the movement could find expression. Lecturers in 1891, 1892 and the first three months of 1893 included Morris (eight times), Hyndman (twice), Keir Hardie (February, 1893), Shaw (three times), Scheu, Stuart Headlam, Bax, Graham Wallas, Carruthers, Edouard Bernstein, Shaw Maxwell, Robert Banner, Sidney Olivier, Stepniak, Herbert Burrows, D.J. Nicoll, Tom Mann and many others. In October, 1891, the Society took some provisional steps towards giving support to a candidate of the Chelsea S.D.F. in the School Board elections, but relations were later broken off. Slowly Morris was beginning to shed his purist attitudes, and to revive in spirit.

Ever since that day of bright sunshine in April, 1887, when Morris had addressed the striking Northumbrian miners, he

[1] Of seventy-five business meetings between January, 1891, and June, 1892, Morris was present at forty—a high percentage if his illness and his visit to France are taken into account (Hammersmith Minutes).

had been particularly responsive to events in the coalfields. Here he had gained a sense of the tremendous power of the organized workers in action. In the London streets he saw only the fragments, "ground down by the life of our easy-going hell". The great strikes of 1890 had won his immediate enthusiasm. Now, in 1892 and 1893, further great strikes in the coalfields helped him to complete his own "education". In his comments of 1890 he well understood the miners' *power;* but he suggested that their *knowledge* "of what to claim" must come from the independent Socialist propaganda outside their own ranks. In April, 1892, writing in the *Hammersmith Socialist Record,* he expressed clearly for the first time the importance of the educative role of the struggle itself. After pointing to the half-hearted "Lib.-Lab." leadership of the miners, he continued:

> "The conduct of the labour war under its present purblind guidance and weak organization will teach the workers by hard necessity. Their very mistakes will force them into looking into the facts of their position; their gains will show them how wretchedly they live still; their losses will show them that they must take the responsibility of their labour and lives on their own shoulders. They will learn that there is no necessity for masters, and therefore that the masters need not be paid at the dire price to the workers of their foregoing all the pleasure and dignity of life. And then they will use the power which all are now beginning to see that they have got, and true Society will be born."

If Morris was coming closer towards Engels's position, events were placing a gulf between him and his former comrades of the League. After November, 1890, the remaining "Leftists", such as Kitz, Tochatti and Mainwaring, were quickly swamped by the pronounced Anarchists. The innate tendency of the Anarchists towards the liquidation of all organization ensured that the League, as a national organization, did not survive after February, 1891. Morris, before leaving, had paid up all debts to the end of 1890, leaving the type, plant and copyright of *Commonweal,* without any liabilities, in the hands of the Council. For a month or two, indeed, he seems to have hoped that the Hammersmith Society might continue selling the paper at their own propaganda meetings.[1] But it was obvious within a few weeks that this would be impossible. Angry replies to "Where are We Now?" by Dr. Creaghe (of Sheffield) and Charles Mowbray in the issue of November 29th revealed only too clearly that Morris had got out of the League only just in time. Creaghe advocated "really revolutionary action" to "show our contempt for what is called private property":

"Every man should take what he requires of the wealth around him, using violence whenever necessary, and when dragged before his enemies he should tell them plainly that he has done what he knows to be right. . ."

"I feel confident", wrote Mowbray, "that a few determined men. . . could paralyse the forces of our masters." The means, he suggested, were "gatlings, hand-grenades, strychnine, and lead. . . Everywhere there are signs of the *bloody* conflict which is about to take place between the workers and their masters." Dynamite, above all, was the weapon for revolutionaries: "the people could carry it around in their pockets. . . and destroy whole cities and whole armies." Thereafter *Commonweal* became once again a monthly: in February, 1891, it was announced as the property of the newly-formed "London Socialist League"; in May it was subtitled, "A Revolutionary Journal of Anarchist Communism". The formation of the London League did not mean the complete extinction of all provincial support: groups of Anarchists still persisted in Walsall, Leicester, Glasgow, Norwich, Hull, Leeds, and, above all, Sheffield. Rather, it signified an intensification of the process by which every Anarchist constituted himself into "a committee of one".

[1] Discussing a possible general Socialist newspaper with Glasier on December 16th, 1890, he wrote: "I would do nothing in it as long as. . . *Commonweal* exists; I would rather support that if I could" (Glasier, *op. cit.*, p. 206).

"Hurrah! for the kettle, the club, and the poker
Good medicine always, for landlord and broker. . ."

So carolled D.J. Nicoll and the "moderate" section of the old League (Mainwaring, Mowbray, John Turner and W.B. Parker) when advertising a "No Rent" meeting in July, 1891, on a handbill headed "MURDER!"[1] In the next few years a rash of Anarchism was to appear in one major city after another. It took all sorts of shapes and colours: there was the sober group around Kropotkin and Edward Carpenter, which published *Freedom;* there was the studious and restrained old friend of Morris, the tailor, James Tochatti, who lived at Carmagnole House, Railway Approach, Hammersmith, and who (after 1893) edited *Liberty;* there was the old Autonomie Club, in Windmill Street, where foreign refugees hatched real conspiracies: the Jewish Anarchist Club in Berners Street; the Scandinavian Club, in Rathbone Place; the Christian Anarchists, the Associated Anarchists, the Collectivist Anarchists, Socialist Anarchists, the followers of Albert Tarn and those of Benjamin Tucker. Papers published, on blue paper, red paper, and toilet paper, ranged from the *Anarchist, Commonweal, Alarm* and *Sheffield Anarchist,* to the *Firebrand, Revenge, British Nihilist* and Dan Chatterton's *Atheistic Communistic Scorcher.*

It would be impossible to understand the vagaries of sincere and self-sacrificing Socialists like Sam Mainwaring, James Tochatti and Fred Charles,[2] unless one fact is recognized: the Anarchist groupings were now deeply penetrated by spies, and deliberately used by *agents-provocateurs* to discredit the wider movement. In France this process went so

[1] W.C. Hart, *Confessions of an Anarchist* (1906), p. 41.

[2] Associates of these three men always spoke very highly of their personal qualities, e.g. for Mainwaring, see Tom Mann, *Memoirs,* p. 47: for Fred Charles, see Carpenter, *My Days and Dreams,* p. 132: "No surrender or sacrifice for the 'cause' was too great for him; and as to his own earnings [as clerk]... he practically gave them all away to tramps or the unemployed." Nicoll paid a similar tribute to Charles's generosity and single-heartedness in *The Walsall Anarchists.*

far that one Anarchist journal was actually subsidized by the police. It is doubtful whether the British police ever troubled to go so far as this, but undoubtedly by 1890 they were learning from their Continental colleagues that the Anarchists could create dissension far out of proportion to their small numbers. In 1890 the Anarchist Leaguers were physically driven off by the dockers, after bringing their red flag and their bluster to a dockers' demonstration.[1] In Sheffield, Leeds, Nottingham and other cities, the Anarchist Communists aroused disgust among the workers by advocating immediate forcible actions, or the "propaganda by deed". The fact that prosecutions were infrequent needs no explanation. It was in the interests of the police to prosecute only when their agents had succeeded in manufacturing a "conspiracy" which would provide a Nine Days' Wonder in the Press.

Such an occasion was reached in February, 1892. The agent in this case was Auguste Coulon, who had been connected with the French Possibilists, had worked for a few months within the Social Democratic Society in Dublin, and had come to England, joining the North Kensington Branch (an off-shoot and close relation of the Hammersmith Branch) of the League in January, 1890. He posed as a militant Anarchist; wrote stirring and convincing "International Notes" for *Commonweal;* and visited the Hammersmith Branch frequently, selling copies of *L'Indicateur Anarchiste,* a terrorist manual (compiled, it is said, by a French detective) containing instructions on the making of bombs and dynamite. He joined the Autonomie Club, and imposed upon the noble Anarchist refugee, Louise Michel, who was running a school in Fitzroy Square. As Louise Michel's assistant he appeared to other Anarchists to be above suspicion.

[1] *Commonweal,* August 30th, 1890. The incident reveals the whole truth about the futility of the League in its last days: "Several of our comrades attended the Dockers' Demonstration... At this meeting we had a strange experience. A meeting was started by us, and some reference made by us to the fact that the New Unionism was due to the work of the Socialists, but that now those who have benefited by their work shrink from the name of Socialist, and would wear anything but red as a badge, the dockers intolerantly refused to hear this lecture and broke up the meeting."

In 1891, after Morris had left the League, Coulon got to work in earnest, and there is no doubt that he had assistants in his work. He approached Nicoll to commence the "propaganda by deed" (theft), but was rebuffed. He won the confidence of Fred Charles, accompanied him to Sheffield, where, with Dr. Creaghe, he published some numbers of the *Sheffield Anarchist.* In July, 1891, he found his way to Walsall, where he got into touch with a tiny Socialist Club of Anarchist complexion, and got on to friendly terms with John Westley, a brush-manufacturer, and the Secretary, Deakin, who worked in an iron foundry. Returning to London, he sent a French Anarchist refugee, Victor Cailes, down to Walsall, asking the comrades to look after him and find him some work. A few weeks later a letter reached Cailes, signed "Degnal", and including a sketch of a bomb which he was asked to manufacture. Cailes wrote to Coulon, who informed him that the request was authentic, and that the bombs were being made for use by the Russian Nihilists. Cailes and Fred Charles, who was now in Walsall, agreed to do what they could.

Meanwhile, Coulon was hard at work in London. In August, 1891, a "Revolutionary Conference" was held in the Jewish Anarchist Club in Berners Street. Coulon was present, advocating the formation of chemistry classes, to study the making of explosives; and several such groups of "mere boys" were formed. Nicoll, the Editor, and Mowbray, the publisher of *Commonweal,* were invited to join, but both (on their own evidence) declined. Nevertheless, they allowed Coulon to continue writing his "International Notes", in which he showered praise on every terrorist attempt abroad. "No voice speaks so loud as Dynamite", he wrote in December, 1891, "and we are glad to see it is getting into use all over the place." His example was infectious; other comrades tried to outdo him by the fury of their bluster. In the last months of 1891 the *Commonweal* advocated theft, train-robbery, assassination, the sacking of warehouses and of jewellers' shops and indiscriminate terrorism. Later, even Nicoll came to understand how he had been duped:

"Thus the great conspiracy was worked up. Violent paragraphs in *The Commonweal,* a book on explosives in the Press [Johann Most's latest production], the bombs at Walsall, Nitro-Glycerine in the hands of a mere child in London. *Voilà* the widespread conspiracy of which Mr. A. Young, the council for the Treasury, spoke in an awestruck tone at the commencement of the case. Coulon understood his trade. . ."[1]

So it was that the great Walsall Anarchist Case was sprung on the public in February, 1892. Coulon, in December, 1891, and January, 1892, sent urgent messages to Deakin to *hurry up.* Jean Battola, an Italian shoemaker, was sent from London to Walsall to get the bomb. From this time onwards, the Walsall group were shadowed. Deakin, sent by Cailes with a bottle of chloroform to London, was shadowed to the Autonomie Club, where he was arrested. The arrest of Fred Charles, Cailes, Westley, Battola and another Walsall anarchist implicated in the bomb manufacture, Ditchfield, followed in the early days of January. Coulon, denounced by his colleagues, disappeared into hiding in London; his brother admitted in an unguarded moment that Coulon had for two years been in the pay of the police. In prison, Deakin was brought to confess the whole "conspiracy" after the police had staged the voices of a bogus "confession" of his supposed comrades in the next cell. The authorities took their revenge. Despite the fact that all evidence pointed to Coulon as the real instigator, despite the fact that there was no evidence of any overt act beyond the making of the bomb which Charles and Deakin seem genuinely to have believed was meant for Russia, and despite the fact that the defence solicitor, Thompson, extracted from Chief-Inspector Melville the admission that he "had paid lots of Anarchists money",[2] savage sentences of ten years' penal servitude were passed on Charles, Cailes and Battola; five years on Deakin; while only Westley and Ditchfield were acquitted.

The Press had their Nine Days' Wonder, and used the

[1] D.H. Nicoll, *The Walsall Anarchists—Trapped by the Police.*

[2] *Birmingham Daily Post,* February 10th, 1892.

occasion to the utmost. Nicoll rushed to the defence of his comrades with a mixture of courage and stupidity. He published in *Commonweal* on April 9th, 1892, an article ("Are these men fit to live?"), which could hardly fail to be interpreted as inciting to the murder of the Judge in the Walsall Case, and of Chief Inspector Melville. On April 18th, the police raided the *Commonweal* office, effectively suppressing a number of the paper which exposed Coulon's part in the "conspiracy". Nicoll and Mowbray were arrested, and held jointly responsible for the article of April 9th: "You will be sorry to see", Morris wrote to his daughter on the 21st, "that Nicoll and Mowbray, two of our old comrades, have got into trouble with the *Commonweal.* It was very stupid of Nicoll, for it seems that he stuck in his idiotic article while Mowbray was away, so that the latter knew nothing of it. I think Mowbray will get off. I am sorry for him, and even for the *Commonweal.*"[1] Mowbray's wife had died a day or two before the arrest, and he was refused permission to attend the funeral, until Morris came before the Court and entered into surety for him for £500.[2] In the event, Nicoll was sentenced to eighteen months' imprisonment. With all his faults, he was no coward, and he succeeded in carrying on the fight for Fred Charles and his other comrades from prison.

It was one thing for Morris to come to the aid of an old comrade in distress. But it was of the first importance that he should not appear to condone the Anarchist folly which had been so deliberately engineered to discredit the Left. In the *Hammersmith Socialist Record* for May, 1892, he made his position plain enough:

"It is difficult to express in words strong enough the perversity of the idea that it is possible for a minority to carry on a war of violence against an overwhelming majority without being utterly crushed. There is no royal road to revolution or the change in the basis of society. To make the workers conscious of the disabilities which beset them; to make them conscious of the dormant power in them for the removal of

[1] Mackail, II, p. 238. [2] Vallance, *op. cit.*, p. 357.

these disabilities; to give them hope and an aim and organization to carry out their aspirations. Here is work enough for the most energetic; it is the work of patience, but nothing can take the place of it. And moreover *it is being done,* however slowly, however imperfectly."

In February, 1893, when he delivered before the Hammersmith Society a lecture on "Communism", he turned aside to emphasize the same point:

"As to the attempt of a small minority to terrify a vast majority into accepting something which they do not understand, by spasmodic acts of violence, mostly involving the death or mutilation of non-combatants, I can call that nothing else than sheer madness. And here I will say once for all, what I have often wanted to say of late. . . that the idea of taking any human life for any reason whatsoever is horrible and abhorrent to me."[1]

The immediate effect of Walsall upon the remaining old Leaguers, who were not frightened out of the movement, was to make them suspect any and every colleague, and thereby to loosen their organization and make its penetration by spies all the more easy. "Down with the Politicians!" declared a leaflet issued in support of *Commonweal:*

"In the struggle which is near at hand *any weapon* is justifiable, but we must beware of *traitors and spies. . .* trust your life in *no* man's hands. Keep your own secrets; *individual initiative* will paralyze the efforts and successfully defy the political pimps who seek to entrap you."

This was not Frank Kitz's work—he had pulled out some time before, burning the minute books of the League when he left.[2] Nor is it in the style of Mainwaring or Tochatti, who were both, in their own ways, responsible men. *Commonweal* now appeared over the name of an old member of the League

[1] Morris prepared two lectures on Communism in 1892 and 1893. One was published after his death as Fabian Tract No. 113, and in *Works,* Vol. XXIII. The other is in Brit. Mus. Add. MSS. 45334.

[2] Information from the late Mr. Ambrose Barker.

Council, T. Cantwell, and with unsigned articles. "The day when a Government depot of ammunition", declared an article entitled "Revolution and Physical Force" on August 6th, 1892, "can be safely and suddenly made to vanish into the hands of those who will use it in self defence. . . the prestige of the State will have received a shock from which it will find it hard to recover." How true!

The *name* "Commonweal" persisted off and on for several more years, but the old League was splitting into smaller and smaller factions. Nicoll, on his release from prison, engaged in bitter polemic with his old comrades, who would not permit him to resume the editorship of the paper.[1] He was now a pathetic figure; he surrounded his life in imaginary conspiracy, and his conversation returned again and again to the subject of police spies. To his credit, he never gave up the fight for his imprisoned comrades. He resumed the editorship of a spasmodic *Commonweal*, hawking it at meetings to gain a wretched livelihood. Later, he sold pitiful, child-like stories scrawled in coloured crayons, in return for which old comrades and sympathizers gave him donations, until his life ended in St. Pancras Workhouse in 1919.[2]

The remaining Anarchist Communists scattered in different directions, Kitz, Turner, Mainwaring and Tochatti all playing a more sober part on the extreme left-wing of the movement.[3] Once more Morris went into Court to help one of his old comrades—this time Tom Cantwell, who had been charged with "soliciting the murder of members of the Royal

[1] See David Nicoll, *The Greenwich Mystery* and *The Ghosts of Chelmsford Jail*, strangely earnest and unbalanced accounts of persecution and treachery.

[2] Recollections of the late Mr. Ambrose Barker, and Guy Aldred, *Dogmas Discarded*, II, pp. 67-8.

[3] Frank Kitz remained active on the extreme left wing of the movement until shortly before his death in 1923, at the age of about seventy-four; his last years were spent in poverty (obituary in *Justice*, January 20th, 1923). John Turner was well-known for his work as Secretary of the Shop Assistants' Union. Sam Mainwaring removed to Swansea in 1891, formed the Swansea Socialist Society, and later returned to London, where he died while addressing an open-air meeting on Parliament Hill Fields on September 29th, 1907 (Mann, *Memoirs*, p. 47). Tochatti edited *Liberty* in the 1890s.

Family".[1] Only with Tochatti, at Hammersmith, did he remain on friendly personal terms. In December, 1893, Tochatti asked Morris to write an article for his *Liberty*. During the previous two years a series of Anarchist outrages had taken place on the Continent; in 1892 Ravachol was arrested after several explosions in Paris; in October, 1892, the Mayor of Chicago was assassinated, an attempt was made to blow up the Spanish Cortes, and a bomb was placed in front of the offices of the Carmaux Mining Company. In 1893, at Barcelona, a bomb was thrown in the Liceo Theatre, killing about twenty of the audience; in Paris a bomb was thrown in the French Chamber of Deputies by August Vaillant; and, late in the year, there were further incidents in Spain and Italy. These were the circumstances in which Morris replied to Tochatti on December 21st, 1893:

"I do not remember having promised to contribute to your paper, though I do remember promising to write a pamphlet for you. In any case however considering the attitude which some anarchists are taking up about the recent anarchist murders, and attempts to murder, I could not in conscience allow anything with my name attached to it to appear in an anarchist paper, (as I understand yours is to be) unless you publish in said paper a distinct repudiation of such monstrosities.

"Here I might make an end, but since we have been in friendly association, I will ask you if you do not think you ought for your own sake as (I should hope) a person holding views which may be reasonably argued about ['against' deleted], to repudiate the use of means which can bring with them nothing but disaster to the cause of liberty. For your own sake and for those who honestly think that the principles of anarchy are right. For I cannot for the life of me see how such principles, which propose the abolition of compulsion, can admit of promiscuous slaughter as a means of converting people."[2]

[1] Several days after Carnot was assassinated in Paris, the Prince and Princess of Wales opened Tower Bridge (June 29th, 1894). Cantwell and Charles Quinn held an open-air meeting near the bridge, selling a pamphlet, *Why Vaillant Threw the Bomb*. When arrested, Cantwell, the compositor of *Commonweal*, had letters on him showing the paper to be on its last legs (*The Times*, July 31st and August 1st, 1894).

[2] First published in A. Compton Rickett, *William Morris: A Study*. The MS. in the Walthamstow collection.

Tochatti gave the repudiation Morris asked for, and Morris, in his turn, fulfilled his part of the bargain by allowing him to print "Why I am a Communist" in *Liberty,* and, later, to reprint it as a pamphlet. In May, 1895, Tochatti secured from Morris a further article for *Liberty,* "As to Bribing Excellence".[1]

In 1894 the first pathetic action of the Anarchists in England took place—a French member of the Autonomie Club, Martial Bourdin, blew himself up on his way to destroy (it was supposed) the Royal Observatory at Greenwich. As for Morris, his final opinions on the Anarchist movement were given in an interview with *Justice* on January 27th, 1894:

> "I regard it as simply a disease—a social disease caused by the evil conditions of society. I cannot regard it in any other light. Of course, as a Socialist I regard the Anarchists—that is, those who believe in Anarchism pure and simple—as being diametrically opposed to us."

"You are not opposed to insurrectionary methods simply because they are insurrectionary?" he was asked: and he replied:

> "No, but because they are inexpedient. Here in England, at any rate, it would be simply madness to attempt anything like an insurrection. . . Anarchism, as a theory, negatives society, and puts man outside it. Now, man is unthinkable outside society. Man cannot live or move outside it."

III. The Rejection of Purism

"What do you think of the L.C.C. election?" Morris asked Glasier, in March, 1892:

> "I am pleased on the whole. It is certainly the result of the Socialist movement, and is a Labour victory, as the affair was worked by the Socialist and Labour people. . . Of course, I don't think much of gas-

[1] Published in May Morris, II, pp. 524-7.

and-water Socialism, or indeed of any mere mechanical accessories to Socialism; but I can see that the spirit of the thing is bettering, and in spite of all disappointments I am very hopeful."[1]

In the elections the Progressives—an alliance of the London Liberal and Radical Union, the Metropolitan Radical Federation, trade unions, nonconformist bodies, and Fabians—had won the victory, with six Fabian candidates (including the twenty-four-year-old ex-Leaguer, Fred Henderson) securing election. The S.D.F., which had conducted an independent campaign, had secured some fair-sized votes. Slowly the propagandist work of ten years was beginning to take solid organizational form. In the North, the I.L.P. was taking shape, and the independent labour unions were coming into being. In London the Fabians were the first Socialist grouping to win any effective following of voters. In the previous year over 25,000 copies of the cheap edition of *Fabian Essays* had been sold. In Hammersmith they were making a determined effort to establish a strong group, and very possibly Shaw and his friends hoped that Morris's disillusion in the League would throw him into their arms. Notable converts were made: Halliday Sparling (once as extreme a Leftist as the League contained), Sam Bullock (the Editor of the *Hammersmith Record*), Ernest Radford, Walter Crane, A. Beasley and (later) May Morris herself—all prominent members of the Hammersmith Socialist Society. In the provinces, too, in the two years preceding the formation of the I.L.P., remarkable events were taking place in the Fabian Society. Old Leaguers—Leonard Hall in Manchester, Tom Maguire and Alf. Mattison in Leeds—had, in default of any other organization, joined the Society, and were promoting working-class groups in their areas. During 1893 nearly all these working-class provincial groups were absorbed into the I.L.P.

In the *Record* for August, 1892, Morris commented at

[1] *Letters,* p. 349.

greater length on the general development of the movement, as evidenced by the General Election, in which Keir Hardie was returned for West Ham, John Burns for Battersea, and J. Havelock Wilson (the seamen's leader) for Middlesbrough. In addition, thirteen "Lib.-Lab." candidates had been returned; Ben Tillett, fighting both Liberal and Conservative at East Bradford, had come within a few hundred of victory; and on Morris's home ground at Hammersmith, Frank Smith, standing as independent Labour, had polled 3,718 against the Conservative's 4,387. Morris withdrew none of his previous comments upon the institution of Parliament—"an institution. . . which would be a permanent and striking failure, if it were the business of parliament *to do anything;* but which, as it is the business of parliament *to do nothing,* must be considered a very fair success". Once again, he spoke of "the cowardice, irresolution, chicanery, and downright lies in action, which after a little swamp all parliaments". But the election itself he thought remarkable for one thing, "the weight that the instincts of the working men *as working men* have had in the polling". The Labour Party of three would be able to do nothing: but their election was "significant of the change which is coming over working-class opinion; for they *must* be looked on by everyone not blinded by party politics as a protest against the organized hypocrisy of the two great (?) political parties. . .":

"For us Socialists this obvious move forward of the class-feeling is full of real hope; for we cannot doubt that it is the result of the last ten years of Socialist agitation. . . Now once more it is incumbent on the Socialists whose ideas of Socialism are clear, who know what they are aiming at, to clear the essentials of Socialism from the mere passing accidents of the new form of the struggle between labour and capital. It is our business to show the workers that the essential thing is not an improved administrative machinery. . . not a more perfect form of joint-stock enterprise than at present. . . not a system of understanding between masters and men which would rain wages when the markets were good. . . not mere amelioration of the condition of certain groups of labour, necessarily at the expense of others. . . not to level down and level up till we are all of us sharing in a poor life, stripped of energy, without art, research or pleasure... But that the essence of our aim is the destruction of property of all kinds, by means of the organization of work *for the benefit of the workers only, and each and all of them...* Rise of wages, shortening of hours of labour, better education, etc., all these things are good, even in themselves; but unless they are used as steps towards equality of condition, the inconvenience they will cause to the capitalists will be met by changes in the markets, and in the methods of production, which will make the gains of the workers mere names..."

Close as these expressions were to his earlier views, they mark a definite stage in the evolution of his opinions. Now, for the first time, he was prepared to acknowledge the importance of the fight for limited gains, of "steps" on the road to Socialism, provided that they were fought for with a revolutionary aim kept steadily in view. In his first lecture on "Communism", he at last retracted from his anti-parliamentary position:

"I am no great lover of political tactics; the sordid squabble of an election is unpleasant enough for a straightforward man to deal in: yet I cannot fail to see that it is necessary somehow to get hold of the machine which has at its back the executive power of the country, however that may be done. And that the organization and labour which will be necessary to effect that by means of the ballot box will be little indeed compared with what would be necessary to effect it by open revolt..."[1]

It was not easy for him. His direct contacts with the North were now few. At Whitsun, 1892, Alf. Mattison of Leeds called at the Clubroom, and Morris, hearing that an old Leeds Leaguer was there, paced the garden with him for an hour, questioning him closely about events in Yorkshire, the New Unionism, and the position of Tom Maguire.[2] The *Clarion* helped him to understand the change that was in the air. But in his own Society he was still at a disadvantage. On the one

[1] Brit. Mus. Add. MSS. 45334.

[2] Notebooks of Alf. Mattison and *Labour Echo,* November, 1896.

hand, there was a group of comrades who had learned their "anti-parliamentarism" so thoroughly at his feet that they had come to accept it as an inflexible doctrine for every circumstance. On the other, the parliamentary members of the Society were already being drawn into Fabian channels. He had no desire to fight the matter to an issue within his own Society, only to emerge at the end with a new sect of Morrisian parliamentary revolutionaries! His own position now approximated more closely to that of the S.D.F., so far as theory was concerned, than at any time since 1885. But, had he swallowed his own pride (as he was ready to do), and rejoined the Federation, the Hammersmith Society would have fallen into two or more parts in a matter of weeks. More important than this, he could see how the arrogant, dogmatic tone bred into the membership of the S.D.F. by ten years of Hyndman's leadership and of isolation from the mass movement, was actually holding back the cause. In December, 1889, Engels had written to Sorge:

> "Here in England one can see that it is impossible simply to drill a theory in an abstract dogmatic way into a great nation, even if one has the best of theories, developed out of their own conditions of life... The movement has now got going at last... But it is not directly Socialist, and those English who have understood our theory best remain outside it: Hyndman because he is incurably jealous and intriguing, Bax because he is only a bookworm."[1]

The Federation, he wrote next year, "still behave as if everyone except themselves were asses and bunglers." In April, 1891, he was writing of Hyndman:

> "He proves how useless a platform is—theoretically correct to a large extent—if it does not show understanding of how to fasten on to the real needs of the people."

In the most important parts of the movement, the New Unionism, and the Eight Hours' agitation, many S.D.F.

[1] Engels to Sorge, December 7th, 1890, *Marx-Engels Sel. Cor.*, p. 460.

members were active, "but it is precisely those who are being drawn away from the particular influence of Hyndman, and treat the S.D.F. as a purely secondary matter". "People who pass as orthodox Marxists", Engels wrote in June, 1891, "have turned our ideas of movement into a fixed dogma to be learnt by heart. . . [and] appear as pure sects."[1]

Morris echoed his words. "I sometimes have a vision of a real Socialist Party at once united and free", he wrote to Glasier in March, 1892:

> "Is it possible? Here in London it might be done, I think, but the S.D.F. stands in the way. Although the individual members are good fellows enough as far as I have met them, the society has got a sort of pedantic tone of arrogance and lack of generosity, which is disgusting and does disgust both Socialists and Non-Soc."[2]

A great Socialist working-class party, "at once united and free". It was his old dream at the founding of the League: now it was to become a central preoccupation for the rest of his life. If he was an "untalented politician" (and knew it): if he could scarcely persuade the twenty-odd most active members of the Hammersmith Socialist Society to follow his lead; nevertheless, he was gradually becoming aware that he exercised enormous influence within the young Socialist movement. Ever since the days of "Bloody Sunday" his reputation had continued to grow, despite his dwindling following in the League. *His* propaganda (as often as not) had been the first to be heard in this great town and that city; every group of Socialists included some who had been converted by his words, his poems, or his *Signs of Change;* his *News from Nowhere* (published in a cheap edition in 1891) was selling more widely than any other of his Socialist writings, and was making his name widely known among the workers of America and on the Continent.

[1] *Ibid.,* April 8th and June 10th, 1891, *Labour Monthly,* April, 1934.

[2] Glasier, *op. cit.,* p. 207.

If with every year that passed Morris's stature grew greater in the eyes of the working-class movement, startling confirmation of his great reputation among his own class came when, on Tennyson's death, he was "sounded" by a member of the Cabinet (with Gladstone's approval) to become the next Poet Laureate.[1] "What a set of ninnies the papers are about the Laureateship", Morris wrote to Glasier on October 11th, 1892, when speculation was rife: "Treating it with such absurd solemnity! Bet you it is offered to Swinburne. Bet you he takes it. . ."[2] Some hint of the matter reached the Press, and Blatchford sent a *Clarion* reporter down to Kelmscott House. First, Morris was questioned about his work with the Firm:

" 'It is a shoddy age', he cried. 'Shoddy is King. From the statesman to the shoemaker all is shoddy!'

"I concealed my boots under the table. . .

" 'Then you do not admire the commonsense John Bull, Mr. Morris?'

" 'John Bull is a STUPID, UNPRACTICAL OAF.' "

The reporter ("Quinbus Flestrin") changed the subject:

" 'What do you think of Manchester, Mr. Morris?'

"The Poet started as if he had been stung, drew his pipe from his mouth, blew a gargantuan cloud, and after a pause, as if he were seeking a fitting expression, exclaimed, 'Manchester is a big ——.' "

The subject was changed again:

" 'I see it was said in the *Daily Chronicle* that you had been offered the Laureateship.'

" 'The very idea!' he replied. 'As if I could possibly accept it. A PRETTY PICTURE I should cut: a Socialist Court Poet!' And his laugh was good—exceedingly good to hear."[3]

[1] Mackail, II, p. 287. But Gladstone rejected the idea anyway, finding that Morris was "an out and out Socialist", while he was warned by Lord Acton that he was a Communist "with unpleasant associations": see M.P. Pariser, "The Poet Laureateship, 1892", *Manchester Review*, VIII, Winter 1958-9, p. 226.

[2] *Letters*, p. 352.

[3] *Clarion*, November 19th, 1892.

Among his friends, Morris pictured himself with joy, "sitting down in crimson plush breeches and white silk stockings to write birthday odes in honour of all the blooming little Guelphings and Battenbergs that happen to come along!"[1]

It was in such ways as this that the new generation of the Labour Movement of the Nineties made their acquaintance with Morris, fashioning a picture made up of humour, affection and deep respect. For ten years the capitalist Press had cast doubts upon his moral honesty or mental sanity. If the question, "How can you be a 'capitalist' *and* a Socialist at the same time?" had been asked once, it had been asked a thousand times. "This modern Moses of Socialism", wrote the *Primitive Methodist Quarterly Review* in July, 1892, "prefers the ease and luxury of commercial Egypt to the arduous and risky labour of leading the hosts to their promised land." But the mud had refused to stick. The rank and file of the Socialist movement might disagree with Morris's tactics and misunderstand his theory; they might be amused at his manners, and mistrust the luxuries of the Firm; but one fact was known throughout the movement: Morris was incorruptible.

Morris's long and steadfast refusal to become engaged in the bitter polemics which were such a common feature of the early movement, or to allow the columns of *Commonweal* to be used for personal attacks upon any section of the Socialist movement, was now beginning to bear fruit. In these last years, from 1892 to 1896, Morris stood *above* the movement—not in the sense of standing apart from it, but in the sense of comprising in his own person a point of unity above the divisions. He could write for the *Labour Prophet* (the organ of the Labour Church) although it was known that he had no interest in religion; or for *Liberty* without being accused of returning to Anarchism; or for *Justice* without bringing down on himself an attack from the *Labour Leader;* or he could lecture to the Fabians without being accused by Hyndman of

[1] H.H. Sparling, *op. cit.*, p. 7.

treachery to the cause. This was in part, it is true, because he was no longer so closely engaged in the day-to-day struggle of the movement. But this very disengagement meant that he could work for the unity he so much desired with better effect.

IV. An Approach to Unity

In December, 1892, the Hammersmith Socialist Society held a discussion on the subject: "Is it now desirable to form a Socialist Federation?" The question was answered in the affirmative, and approaches were made at once to the two effective Socialist organizations in London—the S.D.F. and the Fabian Society. On December 18th, the Society appointed a special sub-committee, including Morris, "to promote the alliance of Socialist organizations in Great Britain". From the outset, Morris advocated an alliance of autonomous bodies, rather than proposing the merging of bodies so recently in opposition to each other. By mid-January, 1893, a joint committee of the Hammersmith Society and S.D.F. was meeting, which resolved:

> "It is advisable that an alliance should be established of all avowed Socialist organizations in the British Isles with the object of taking united action whenever possible without infringing on the autonomy of any organization represented."[1]

At the same time the Fabian Society agreed to join the "Alliance" on these very general terms. Unexpected opposition came from Morris's own Society, which passed a resolution on February 10th, advocating the calling of a Conference of all Socialist societies by the narrow margin of fifteen to eight.

In a sense, the move towards unity was made from the wrong end. Instead of seeking to build up unity in action upon common issues of importance, Morris was seeking the

[1] Hammersmith Minutes, January 13th, 1893.

acknowledgement of a general agreement upon points of Socialist theory—where disagreement was most bitter. It was largely a tribute to Morris's own position that the Committee succeeded in achieving anything. Five delegates were appointed from each of the three societies: Morris was elected Chairman, Sydney Olivier Treasurer, and Hyndman, Morris and Shaw were appointed to draw up a joint Manifesto. Later Hyndman, characteristically, claimed the Manifesto as his own production; Shaw, more circumstantially, attributed the original drafting to Morris:

> "In drafting the manifesto Morris had taken care to give some expression to both the Fabian policy and the Social Democratic Federation policy. Hyndman immediately proposed the omission of the Fabian programme of municipal Socialism, and its explicit denunciation. . . I was equally determined not to endorse the policy of the S.D.F. Morris soon saw that we were irreconcilable. There was nothing for it but to omit both policies and substitute platitudes that any Church Congress could have signed."[1]

"The result was, I believe, a complete agreement between the three of us, though we did not formally express it, that the Manifesto was beneath contempt."[2] "It was the only document any of the three of us had ever signed that was honestly not worth a farthing."[3]

So much for Shaw's opinion. Unfortunately, it is Shaw's opinion, which is not worth a farthing, since—the week after Morris died—he convicted himself out of his own mouth of bad faith in the whole proceedings. "I did not believe in the proposed union", he wrote, "and, in fact, did not intend that it should be carried out if I could help it."[4] The *Manifesto of English Socialists,* which was issued on May 1st, 1893, bears the mark of both Morris and Hyndman, but very

[1] May Morris, II, pp. xxxv-xxxvi.
[2] G.B. Shaw to Emery Walker, July, 1912. Brit. Mus. Add. MSS. 45347.
[3] May Morris, II, p. xxxvi.
[4] *Clarion,* October 10th, 1896.

little of Shaw. So far from containing "platitudes that any Church Congress could have signed", it succeeded in presenting a platform which would (if accepted in good faith) have committed the Fabian Society to a statement of revolutionary principles a good deal more explicit than they desired. As far as the drafting of unity on paper went, Morris had won a success, and had nailed down Shaw and his friends to definitive statements from which they soon sought to wriggle free. A comparison of the Fabian "Basis" and the *Manifesto* makes this clear enough:

"The Fabian Society consists of Socialists.

"It therefore aims at the re-organization of Society by the emancipation of Land and Industrial Capital from individual and class ownership, and the vesting of them in the community for the general benefit...

"The Society... works for the extinction of private property in Land... and for the transfer to the community of the administration of such industrial Capital as can conveniently be managed socially..."

In every third word is an imprecise definition, a qualification evasion. "Re-organization" as opposed to revolutionary change; "emancipation", not of the working class, but of "Land and Industrial Capital"—to be "vested in" the community, not to be owned and controlled by the producers; the community to "administer" "such industrial Capital" (not means of production) "as can conveniently be managed". Here are the words of the *Manifesto:*

"Municipalization... can only be accpeted as Socialism on the condition of its forming a part of national and at last international Socialism, in which the *workers* of all nations... can federate upon a common basis of the *collective ownership* of the great means and instruments of the creation and distribution of wealth...

"On this point all Socialists agree. Our aim, one and all, is to obtain for the whole community *complete ownership and control of the means of transport, the means of manufacture, the mines, and the land.* Thus we look to put an end for ever to the wage-system, to sweep away all distinctions of class, and eventually to establish national and international communism...

"To this end it is imperative on all members of the Socialist party to gather together their forces in order to formulate a definite policy and force on its general acceptance."

From its opening paragraphs, in Morris's manner, in which it urged the need for co-operation among all genuine Socialists, to its final pages in which it set forward definite steps for immediate campaigning,[1] and urged the necessity of Socialists constituting themselves "into a distinct political party with definite aims, marching steadily along our own highway", the *Manifesto* was both more constructive and more specific than Shaw, and the historian of the Fabian Society (Edward R. Pease) suggest.[2] It is clear enough why "it was deemed advisable" by Shaw and Olivier to withdraw from the Committee in July.[3]

"Whatever other people do, we the Hammersmith people must be careful to make as little quarrel with either party as we can help", Morris wrote to Emery Walker on August 9th, 1893, after the Fabian secession. "More and more at any rate I want to see a due Socialist party established."[4] But, if Shaw had been playing false, Hyndman was obstructing unity in a far more important direction. For, in January, 1893, the Independent Labour Party had held its first Conference in Bradford, and emerged confidently on the British scene. "You will find", Tom Maguire wrote to Edward Carpenter in November, 1892:

"that this new party lifts its head all over the North. It has caught the people as I imagine the Chartist movement did. And it is of the people—such will be the secret of its success. Everywhere its bent is

[1] The main immediate measures advocated were: An Eight-hour Law: Prohibition of all Child Labour; Equal Pay for Equal Work; A Minimum Wage in State Services; Abolition of Sweating; Universal Male and Female Suffrage; Payment for all Public Service.

[2] See E.R. Pease, *History of the Fabian Society*, p. 202.

[3] *Eleventh Annual Report of... the Fabian Society*, p. 11.

[4] May Morris, II, p. 353.

Socialist because Socialists are the only people who have a message for it. . ."[1]

Maguire had a right to rejoice. His active mind and resolute leadership had done more than any other individual in the West Riding to pilot the newly-emerged mass movement into this form. Several other old Leaguers were prominent at the first Conference of the I.L.P., among them J.L. Mahon and A.K. Donald (supported, back-stage, by H.H. Champion). Other old Leaguers present included Jowett and Pickles of Bradford, Alf. Mattison of Leeds, while in 1894 Leonard Hall of Manchester went onto the Executive.

What was Morris's attitude to the I.L.P.? Why did the Joint Committee not include their representatives? "I really think we must have taken it for granted that the I.L.P. did not rank as a Socialist body", Shaw wrote, when trying to answer this question.[2] Once again, Shaw's recollection played him false. Hyndman declared in his reminiscences that it was Morris's hope that the I.L.P. *would* be drawn in. It can hardly be a coincidence that in February and March, 1893, the Hammersmith Socialist Society invited Keir Hardie and Shaw Maxwell (twice) to speak on their aims.[3] The real cause lay in the unmeasured hostility of Hyndman and his following to the new party. "There is occasionally a cry for a united Independent Labour Party", *Justice* declared while the Conference was sitting:

"A really independent labour party must be a Social-Democratic party. Outside Social-Democracy there is no basis for a labour party."[4]

[1] *Tom Maguire: a Remembrance*, p. xii.

[2] G.B. Shaw to May Morris, April 24th, 1913, Brit. Mus. Add. MSS. 45347.

[3] Hammersmith Minutes, February, 1893, J. Keir Hardie, "The Labour Movement"; Shaw Maxwell, "Programme of the Labour Party"; March, 1893, Shaw Maxwell, "Aims and Objects of the Labour Party".

[4] *Justice*, January 14th, 1893.

Engels, who declared his support for the tendency of the new party (and who approved Aveling's action in taking a seat on its Executive), came in for a special round of abuse:

> "Why is it that he carefully secludes himself, Grand Lama-like, in the Thibetan fastnesses of Regent's Park Road, as if he were qualifying for the post of a Socialist Mahatma?"[1]

J.E. Dobson, of the S.D.F., who was a secretary of the Joint Committee, later crossed over to the I.L.P., where he declared the truth of the matter:

> "When the Hammersmith Socialist Society, under William Morris, called for a united conference, the I.L.P. was left out, because in the eyes of the S.D.F., the I.L.P. was not a Socialist party, although the Fabians were included. He personally [Dobson] had met with nothing but censure when he proposed that the I.L.P. should be admitted. . ."[2]

So ended Morris's most earnest attempt to promote a united party—with the Fabians frightened off by their own *Manifesto,* and Hyndman resolutely closing his eyes to the very existence of the I.L.P.

V. Mature Theory

It was the question of leadership, of the absorption into the mass movement of a clear, revolutionary theory—which was the constant theme of Morris's last years. Unity in itself was not enough. The united party must be a *Socialist* party. The workers "need education; they want to be shown what to demand, and how to do so. This is the task of us

[1] *Justice,* April 1st, 1893. Hyndman's editorial in the same issue complained: "At his little Paris Commune meeting in the supper-room of the Communistische Arbeiter-Bildungs Verein. . . the other night, Frederick Engels proclaimed that this same Party [the I.L.P.] with his special favourite [Aveling] at the head, would sweep on to victory for the petty Marxist clique."

[2] *Report of the Sixth Annual Conference of the I.L.P.* (1898), p. 34.

Socialists. . ." Morris wrote in May, 1893.[1] He distrusted the "intensely electioneering" tactics of the new I.L.P., and had reservations about Keir Hardie, Robert Blatchford and its general leadership. Engels who shared this distrust, placed his confidence in the power of the mass movement to silence the petty ambitions of the leaders. "Socialism has penetrated the masses in the industrial districts enormously in the past years and I am counting on these masses to keep the leaders in order."[2] Morris did not share this confidence. While he now recognized the educative role of the struggle, he feared that the revolutionary theory might be submerged, rather than absorbed in the mass movement. The propaganda of theory, he repeatedly insisted, must not be neglected, but should rather be redoubled; although he now saw that it must come from within the movement, or in friendly alliance with it, rather than from a purist sect outside.

His article in the *Labour Prophet* for January, 1894, put the matter most clearly. It was still the business of Socialists to make Socialists, he began:

> "Socialism has begun to take hold of the working classes, and is now a genuine working man's movement. That is a fact, the importance of which it is impossible to overrate. But, on the other hand, the movement is taking a different form from what many, or most, of us supposed it would; a thing which was, in fact, inevitable, and which is so far encouraging that it is one of the signs of the genuineness and steadfastness of the movement. I mean, there is nothing in it of conscious and pedantic imitation of former changes—the French Revolution for instance. Abstract theories are not much in favour; less than they should be, perhaps, though time will surely mend that. As yet there is no formulated demand for a great, sudden, and obvious recasting of society. . . but there is a steady set towards a road which will infallibly lead us to a society recast in a Socialistic mould.
>
> "The instinct towards Socialism is awake, and is forcing the working classes into what we now see to be the right, because it is the only course. And though as yet it may not be more than an instinct with the

[1] Morris to J. Edwards, May 5th, 1893 (*Labour Prophet,* July, 1893).

[2] *Marx-Engels Sel. Cor.,* p. 507.

great mass of the workers, yet we must remember that it is headed by a great number of men (I am not speaking of those technically called 'leaders') who are declared Socialists, and who understand at least what may be called work-a-day Socialism. All this makes our advance much greater than we had any right to expect to come out of the then condition of things ten years ago... The first act of the great Class War has begun, for the workmen are claiming their recognition as citizens...

"But great as the gain is, our responsibilities as Socialists have increased in proportion to it. In the earlier stage of the movement they were simple indeed. Socialism was a theory in this country, an ideal held by a little knot of enthusiasts and students, who could give little reason for their hope of seeing it realized, save the irresistable force with which its truths had taken hold of their minds and hearts. The working classes were not in the least touched by it...

"I say our duties were simple... To preach Socialism, in season and out of season, where we were wanted, where we were tolerated, where we were *not* tolerated, that was all we had to do... No other action was possible to us than trying to convince people, by talking, that Socialism was right and possible.

"This has still to be done, and will always be necessary till Socialism is realized... But now... other action... is forced upon us by the growing... practical acception of the theory of Socialism. The workers have started to claim new conditions of life which they can only obtain at the expense of the possessing classes; and they must therefore *force* their claims on the latter...

"To speak plainly, there are only two methods of bringing the necessary force to bear: open armed insurrection on the one hand; the use of the vote, to get hold of the executive, on the other. Of the first method they are not even thinking: but the second they are growing more determined to use day by day, and it is practically the only direct means. And it must be said that, if they are defeated in their attempt, it means the present defeat of Socialism: though its ultimate defeat is impossible."

Thus Socialists were set (Morris wrote) a twofold task. First, they must provide the theory of the struggle: if they failed in this, they were abandoning their duty of giving direction to the spontaneous movement of the workers. Second, they must participate alongside the workers in all forms of the labour struggle, including parliamentary and municipal elections:

"It is certainly our business, then, to make that struggle as strenuous as possible, while we at the same time hold up before the workers the ideal that lies ahead of the present days of conflict."

It was precisely this period of transition, this "troublesome and wearisome action", which he felt to be a difficult one. "The number of declared and instructed Socialists is small in proportion to the general movement", and herein he noted both a source of danger, and an especial reason for Socialist unity.

This article contains the clearest practical embodiment of Morris's changed views, which found many expressions in his lectures and writings between 1892 and 1894: notably in two lectures on "Communism", his lecture, "What Is: What Should Be: What Will Be", and his letters to the *Sun* and the *Daily Chronicle* ("The Deeper Meaning of the Struggle"—reprinted as a leaflet by the Hammersmith Socialist Society) on the great coal lock-out of the autumn of 1893. Morris had never, even in his most intransigent "anti-parliamentary" period, denied that *at some stage* Socialists might enter parliament to seize control of the executive power: now, with important qualifications, he accepted the necessity of following the parliamentary road. The lectures, written for close discussion among the Socialists, and not for general publication, are more hesitant in tone than the letters and the article in the *Labour Prophet.* The workers, he declared in "What Is: What Should Be: What Will Be"—

"are beginning to be discontented. What they see is that they might be better off; that they might get higher wages and less precarious work, more leisure, more share in public advantages, and as a means to all these things some direct share in the national talk-shop. All this they will try for, and will get the formula thereto made into law within a certain time. Now I firmly believe that it is an illusion to think that they can have the reality of any of these things without their gaining the beginnings of Socialism. . . but I also believe that things have now gone so far, that the lesser claim above mentioned. . . will lead to the greater; though it will be through many blunders and disappointments: and the road will be long."

The parliamentary road was not the road of his choice; but the workers had chosen it, and—

"I do not fail to appreciate the necessity for immediate action, and I now see that this parliamentary action must be and will be: so let us do our best in it, not merely [as] working men members but [as] Socialists."

The lecture was now jotted rapidly in note form, and only the outline survives:

"Ought to have working men in order to break down the habit of class members, but get good men and good for the purpose where you can. And let them be under good party discipline. This party must be and will be, but I fear will be somewhat long in coming: but when it is formed, then the advance to Socialism will be speedy."[1]

In his well-known lecture on "Communism", delivered to the Fabian Society in 1893, his new understanding of the dual role of practical and theoretical struggle found its maturest expression. It is a lecture which should be read as a whole, in the light of the situation and of his changing views; here there is space only to summarize the leading lines of the argument:

"I am driven to the conclusion that those [i.e. immediate] measures . . . *are* of use toward the education of the great mass of the workers; that it is necessary in the present to give form to vague aspiration. . . Taking up such measures, directly tending towards Socialism, is necessary also in getting working people to raise their standard of livelihood. . . Lastly, such measures, with all that goes towards getting them carried, will train them into organization and administration. . . But this education by political and corporate action must. . . be supplemented by instilling into the minds of the people a knowledge of the aims of socialism, and a longing to bring about the complete change which will supplant civilization by communism. . . The measures. . . are either make-shift alleviations. . . or means for landing

[1] Brit. Mus. Add. MSS. 48334.

us in the new country of equality. And there is a danger that they will be looked upon as ends in themselves."

If Morris now saw the importance of the practical struggle, he knew that his own abilities cast him for a role on the theoretical wing of the movement. In 1892 he had been revising with Bax the series of articles which they had written for *Commonweal*, "Socialism From the Root Up". Now, in 1893, they were published in book form as *Socialism: Its Growth and Outcome*. The original *Commonweal* chapter on "Socialism Militant" was totally rewritten. A new prominence was given to the industrial struggle. By contrast with the position in 1883 (Bax and Morris wrote):

"There is in it less of the mere dispute between two parties to a contract admitted as necessary by either, and more of an instinct of essentially opposed interests between employers and employed."[1]

They declared their approval for the immediate demands voiced by the most militant section of the movement: the legal eight-hour day, the minimum wage and maximum price. Municipal reform received favourable mention. The mass movement set in motion by the New Unionism, they were careful to point out, was a movement "not of *Socialists*, but of men moved by the growing *instinct towards Socialism*". The traditional discrepancy, or even antipathy, "in all democratic fermentations. . . between the theoretic movement. . . and the actual popular or working-class struggle" might still be traced. But its end had been signalled in 1847, with the publication of the *Communist Manifesto*, and in the new movement:

"The workmen are not unwilling to accept the theorists as leaders; while the theorists fully and frankly recognize that it is through the instinctive working-class movement towards the bettering of life, by whatever political-economic means, that their ideal of a new society must be sought."

[1] Morris and Bax, *Socialism, Its Growth and Outcome* (1893), p. 271.

In short, while it was essential that the theory should be "always kept before the eyes of the mass of the working-classes", lest the continuity of the struggle should be broken, or the movement should be misdirected, yet at the same time "it is no less essential that the theorists should steadily take part in all action that tends towards Socialism, lest their wholesome and truthful theories should be left adrift on the barren shore of Utopianism".[1] It is "a matter of course" that Socialism would not appear one day by some sudden catastrophe, "that some Monday morning the sun will rise on a communized state which was capitalistic on Saturday night". Armed revolt or civil war was not the main, or the major, means of achieving the revolution, although it "may be an *incident* of the struggle, and in some form or another probably will be, especially in the latter phases of the revolution". But these latter phases would only be reached through "the gradual shifting of the opinions and aspirations of the masses", through the industrial and political struggles already outlined. At the same time, Morris and Bax did not suggest a gradual Fabian "glide" into the new society, but, rather, after long preliminaries of education and struggle, a sharp, qualitative break:

> "The first real victory of the Social Revolution will be the establishment not indeed of a complete system of Communism in a day, which is absurd, but of a revolutionary administration whose *definite and conscious aim* will be to prepare and further, in all available ways, human life for such a system—. . . an administration whose every act will be of set purpose with a view to Socialism."[2]

VI. Reconciliation with the S.D.F.

In *Justice* in January, 1894, Morris made his position even more clear. It is a sign of his generosity that he was ready to retract his old differences with Hyndman. "Present circum-

[1] Morris and Bax, *Socialism, Its Growth and Outcome* (1893), pp.278-9.
[2] *Ibid.*, p. 285.

stances", he said,

"go to prove the wisdom of the S.D.F. in drawing up palliative measures. . . Mean and paltry as it seemed to me,—and does still, as compared with the whole thing,—something of the kind is absolutely necessary."

The immediate need was to create "a strong party", "a party with delegates in the House of Commons, which would have complete control over those delegates". This insistence upon the subordination of the parliamentary party to the discipline of the party as a whole is of the greatest importance, and Morris deliberately stressed it as a point of demarcation between the revolutionary and the reformist use of Parliament. Such a group of delegates would win concession after concession until the point of crisis would be reached. But Morris made it clear that there was nothing inherently holy in the constitutional machinery itself, nothing "undemocratic" in employing extra-parliamentary means. It was a matter of tactics, deduced from the conditions of the movement in Britain.

"You cannot start with revolt—you must lead up to it, and exhaust other means first. I do not agree that you should abstain from any act merely on the grounds that it would precipitate civil war, even though the result of the civil war were problematical, so long as the initial act was justifiable. But with the tremendous power of modern armies, it is essential that everything should be done to legalise revolt. As we have seen [at Featherstone, where Yorkshire miners were fired on in 1893] the soldiers will fire upon the people without hesitation so long as there is no doubt as to the legality of their doing so. Men do not fight well with halters round their necks, and that is what a revolt now would mean. We must try and. . . get at the butt end of the machine-gun and the rifle, and then force is much less likely to be necessary and much more sure to be successful."[1]

The interview in *Justice* marked a definite turn by Morris

[1] *Justice*, January 27th, 1894.

towards the S.D.F. Blatchford, in *Clarion,* was calling upon him to take his rightful position in the leadership of the I.L.P. He refused, for several reasons. He knew that neither his health nor his abilities suited him for active leadership. Such propaganda work as he could still do in London was obviously done better for his own Society or the S.D.F. than for the I.L.P. He had turned his back upon the Fabians ever since their withdrawal from the Joint Committee. The blather by which they tried to represent the smallest piece of administrative machinery or the least "Lib.-Lab." victory, as a portent for the advance of something they called "Socialism" earned his brief contempt: "Was it true that Shaw" (he asked the *Justice* interviewer) "said the other day that there was a party of fifteen already in the House of Commons? If I had been there I should have asked him to name them."[1] As far as Morris was concerned there was a party of one—Keir Hardie; and about him he had doubts, although he told Glasier next year that he felt "his fight for the unemployed has had something great in it".[2] Blatchford he "rather liked the looks of." "You see", he wrote to Leatham of Aberdeen, who had now joined the S.D.F., "you must let a man work on the lines he really *likes.* No man ever does good work unless he likes it: evasion is all you can get out of him by compulsion."[3] But, while he now accepted the need for a revolutionary parliamentary struggle, the absorption of the I.L.P. in electioneering and its neglect of theory disturbed him. In his own Society a contest was being waged, on the issue of whether or not to enter candidates to the joint "Progressive" list for the Vestry and Board of Guardians elections. The "Progressives" won, and Bullock and Morris's daughter, May, were among the candidates. Morris duly voted; but the election (in December, 1894) left him "lethargic and faint-hearted". "I

[1] *Justice,* January 27th, 1894. The 1892 election had returned Keir Hardie, John Burns, and J. Havelock Wilson, together with eleven Lib.-Labs. Perhaps the fifteenth in Shaw's mind was Michael Davitt, the Irish Land Leaguer, who was later unseated.

[2] Glasier, p. 137.

[3] May Morris, II, p. 340.

dare say you think me rather lukewarm about the affair", he wrote to Georgie Burne-Jones—

> "but I am so depressed with the pettiness and timidity of the bill and the checks and counterchecks with which such an obvious measure [the new Local Government Act] has been hedged about."

Eight candidates were successful for the Board of Guardians, but the Vestry candidates were defeated: "You see all through London the middle class voted solid against us; which I think extremely stupid of them, as they might well have got credit for supporting an improved administration."[1] The enthusiasm expended by some of his colleagues upon capturing a part of the liberal vote was "tommy-rot" which left him cold.[2]

Therefore it was with the S.D.F. that he identified himself most closely in 1894 and 1895. He would not join the organization, so long as he felt that his influence might contribute towards bridging the split in the movement. Moreover, in the first full article which he wrote for *Justice* ("How I Became a Socialist", June 16th, 1894), he inserted a humorous reference to his own difficulties with *Capital,* and an insistence upon the importance of cultural questions to the Socialist movement: both very salutary rebuffs to the doctrinaire and mechanical outlook of some of the S.D.F. But, as the known party of revolution, he felt his place to be at its side: he contributed poems and occasional articles to *Justice:* he spoke from the S.D.F. platform on the May Day of 1894. In February, 1894, he spoke for George Lansbury, S.D.F. candidate at Walworth, in a by-election.[3] In March, 1894, he made a propaganda visit to Manchester under the auspices of the local branch of the S.D.F., speaking both in the Free Trade Hall and at an open-air meeting near Trafford Bridge. Leatham has left a description of this last

[1] Mackail, II, pp. 308-9.

[2] Entry in his diary for February 15th, 1895, Brit. Mus. Add. MSS. 45410.

[3] *Justice,* February 24th, 1894.

act of open-air propaganda in the North. "The last time I saw Morris", he wrote,

"he was speaking from a lorry pitched on a piece of waste land close to the Ship Canal. . . It was a wild March Sunday morning, and he would not have been asked to speak out of doors, but he had expressed a desire to do so. and so there he was, talking with quiet strenuousness, drawing a laugh now and then from the undulating crowd, of working men mostly, who stood in the hollow and on the slopes before him. There would be quite two thousand of them. He wore a blue overcoat, but had laid aside his hat; and his grizzled hair blew in wisps and tumbles about his face. . . In spite of the bitter cold of the morning, scarcely a man moved from the crowd; though there was comparatively little fire or fervour in the speech, and next to no allusion to any special topic of the hour. Many there were hearing and seeing the man for the first time; most of us were hearing him for the last time; and we all looked and listened as though we knew it."[1]

In 1895 he spoke again for George Lansbury and in the General Election of the same year, he was invited by the South Salford S.D.F. to become their parliamentary candidate (another "PRETTY PICTURE!"). He agreed to go to Burnley and speak in Hyndman's support. There he publicly declared (according to Hyndman): "In 1884 Hyndman and I had a great quarrel, and I have to say this: that he was quite right and I was quite wrong."[2] If indeed he said this, then generosity could have been taken no further.[3]

His last full lecture-notes which have survived are dated March 30th, 1895, and the lecture entitled "What We have to Look For". He started, as in other late lectures, by contrasting the early days of the movement, when the Socialists were no more than a sect, with the present labour movement, with its vague aspirations towards Socialism. Then he looked into the future. He could not, however he looked at the matter, see

1 James Leatham, *William Morris, Master of Many Crafts* (1908), pp. 124, 127-8.

2 Hyndman, *Record of an Adventurous Life*, pp. 361-2.

3 Morris headed the subscription list for Hyndman's fight at Burnley, and gave the largest individual subscription to Lansbury's fund, *Justice*, July 13th, and 20th, 1895.

any final resolution of the class struggle "otherwise than by disturbance and suffering of some kind". "I believe that the very upward movement of labour. . . will have to be paid for like other good things, and that the price will be no light one." Then, once again, he struggled with the vision of reformism which had haunted all his Socialist propaganda. His friend, John Carruthers, had written a pamphlet (issued in 1894 by the Hammersmith Society) in which he made a masterly exposure of the way in which limited measures of nationalization, and in particular the nationalization of the railways, might make the machinery of exploitation more efficient, without endangering the existence of the capitalist system.[1] Morris took due note of this, as he did also of the prevailing set of opinion in hostility to serious theory within the I.L.P. Here are the questions which he put to the new movement:

"I should above all things like to have a genuine answer to this question; setting aside all convention, all rhetoric and flummery, what is it that you want from the present labour movement? Higher wages; more regular employment? Shorter working hours—better education for your children—old age pensions, libraries, parks and the rest. Are these things and things like them what you want? They are of course, but what else do you want? If you cannot answer the question straightforwardly I must say you are wandering on a road the outcome of which you cannot tell. . .

"If you *can* answer it, and say Yes, that *is* all we want: then I say here is the real advice to give you: Don't meddle with Socialism: make peace with your employers, before it is too late, and you will find that from them and their Committee, the House of Commons, you will get such measure of these things as will probably content you. . . If this is all you want, work with your employers. . . consider their interests as well as your own. . . make sacrifices to-day that you may do well to-morrow, compete your best with foreign nations. . . and I think you will do well. I cannot indeed promise you that you will bring back the prosperity of the country. . . but you may well stave off the breakdown, which in these last years does really seem to be drawing near, and at any rate you will make the best of what prosperity there is left us as *workmen* and according to their standard of life.

[1] See J. Carruthers, *Socialism and Radicalism* (1894).

"If that is all you want, how can we who are not workmen blame you? . . . I must own that sometimes when I am dispirited I think this is all that the labour movement means: it doesn't mean Socialism at all, it only means improvement in the condition of the working classes: they will get that in some terms or another—till the break up comes, and it may be a long way ahead. And yet. . . imperfect, erring, unorganized, chaotic as that movement is, there is a spirit of antagonism to our present foolish wasteful system in it, and a sense of the unity of labour as against the exploiters of labour which is the one necessary idea for those who are ever so little conscious of making toward Socialism."

By example, he pointed to the astonishing reception of "Comrade Blatchford's" *Merry England:*

"The thousands who have read that book must if they have done so carefully have found out that something better is possible to be thought of than the life of a prosperous mill-hand. . . Self-respect, happy and fit work, leisure, beautiful surroundings, in a word, the earth our own and the fullness thereof, and nobody really dares to assert that this good life can be attained to till we are essentially and practically Socialized."

Finally, some words on the need for a united party:

"My hope is. . . that we shall do so much propagandist work, and convert so many people to Socialism that they will insist on having a genuine Socialist party. . . and they will not allow the personal fads and vanities of leaders (so-called) to stand in the way of real business."

Until that party should be firmly formed, "we" (the Hammersmith Socialist Society) "had better confine ourselves to the old teaching and preaching of Socialism pure and simple, which I fear is more or less neglected amidst the. . . futile attempt to act as a party when we have no party".[1] On the back of the final page were jotted some notes to jog his memory when he replied to the discussion:

[1] Brit. Mus. Add. MSS. 45334.

"Tochatti—to use our recruits when we've got them.
"Mordhurst—the unemployed.
"Unknown—Henry George and co-operation.
"Bullock—giving up the problem.
"Unknown clergyman—rather more depressed than I."

On May Day, 1895, Morris was again on the S.D.F. platform.[1] In *Justice* he contributed an article, in which he took up the same theme as in "What We have to Look For"—the difference between the revolutionary and reformist roads. "To the Socialist", he stressed, "the aim is not the improvement of condition but *the change in position* of the working classes." Of the reformist road he said, "I think it will be taken, I fear not wholly unsuccessfully":

"The present necessities of working people are so great that they must take what they can get, and it so hard for them in their miserable condition to have any vivid conception of what a life of freedom and equality can give them that they can scarcely, the average of them, turn their hopes to a future which they may never see."

"And yet if that future is not to be indefinitely postponed they must repudiate this demi-semi-Socialism":

"Again and again it must be said that in this determination we shall be justified when the working-classes make it their determination; and. . . the first step towards this consummation is the union in one party of all those in the movement who take that view of the movement, and not merely the gas and water and improved trade union view. The view not of improved condition. . . for the workers but of essentially changed position."[2]

It is a moving situation. Morris was depressed because he saw the future too plain. He saw the movement he had helped to form, the charlatans and parliamentary cheap-jacks who would betray it, and lead it for secondary or personal ends. When he had first thrown in his lot with the "Cause", he had told Hyndman that he desired only to *serve* the movement, in

[1] *Daily News,* May 2nd, 1895. [2] *Justice,* May Day Special, 1895.

whatever manner he could be of use. Now, in 1895, Bruce Glasier visited him for the last time. He questioned Glasier closely about the I.L.P. and the movement in the North:

"He listened to my *apologia* attentively, sitting back in his chair smoking, keeping his eyes fixed on me reflectively while I spoke."

Glasier painted a picture of Keir Hardie and the I.L.P. in glowing terms. When he turned to leave,

"I remember that at the gate he held my hand longer than was his custom, and said, 'I have been greatly cheered by what you say about Keir Hardie and the Labour movement. Our theories often blind us to the truth.' Then, laying his hand on my shoulder, he said, 'Ah, lad! if the workers are *really* going to march—won't we all fall in.' "[1]

VII. The Last Year

In 1895, five years had passed since the founding of the Kelmscott Press. Morris's grey beard and hair were shading into white. From the autumn of 1892 until early in 1895 he had enjoyed a recovery of health. A letter of Halliday Sparling's, at Christmas 1892, reveals him at his favourite relaxation:

"... We are all here at Kelmscott... except Mrs. Morris, who had to go to Italy for the winter. Shaw is also here, amusing himself by pasting into a scrap-book all the Press-notices of his play... Morris has just gone off to try for a pike, having vainly endeavoured to get either Shaw or myself to share his fishing enthusiasm... He is extremely well & hearty."[2]

To the active Socialists, Morris still seemed "one of the most get-at-able men around London." He was a well-known figure in the Hammersmith streets, or in the Underground Railway, where "armed with books and wearing a soft crowned felt hat

[1] Glasier, *op. cit.*, p. 139.

[2] H.H. Sparling to E. Radford, December 24th, 1892, Radford MSS.

and Inverness cape. . . he made his presence fully known by the loud cheery tones in which he discussed art, literature, or politics with his companions."[1] But, although he scarcely noticed it himself, he was in a position of some intellectual isolation during his last years. As he walked up and down the aisle in the Kelmscott Clubroom, one observer thought he had "the air of a rather melancholy sea-captain on the quarter-deck".[2] Few of the intellectuals who gathered there had any real understanding of his profound revolutionary aspirations. Wilfred Scawen Blunt saw something of him in these last years, and interpreted Morris's faint air of melancholy as disillusion in Socialism.[3] The workers who saw him bare-headed by the Manchester Ship Canal knew better. But the story of Morris's "disillusion" was beginning to go the rounds among the intelligentsia, gathering force as all stories do which people want to believe.

Absorption in work and family made his contacts fewer. He was writing, in odd moments, *The Wood Beyond the World, The Well at the World's End, The Water of the Wondrous Isles,* and (in his last year) *The Sundering Flood.* When illness made him sleepless he would rise at dawn to continue his writing. From 1893 onwards he was co-operating with A.J. Wyatt in a version of Beowulf and other early English poetry. He was busy in the experiments which always gave him such pleasure, learning old processes for making the paper and ink to be used at the Kelmscott Press. From 1893 onwards he found ceaseless relaxation in the designing and production of the great Kelmscott Chaucer: "My eyes! how good it is!" he said, when the first page was complete.[4] When his old friend Magnússon visited him in his last year, and praised the Chaucer, Morris rejoined with enthusiasm: "It is not only the finest book in the world, but an undertaking that was an absolutely unchecked success from beginning to

[1] *Labour Leader,* October 10th, 1896.

[2] F.M. Ford, *Return to Yesterday,* p. 110.

[3] See Blunt, *My Diaries,* Part One, pp. 28, 65, 70.

[4] Mackail, II, p. 284.

end."[1] At the same time, Morris was still executing occasional designs for the Firm; and he was working once again with Magnússon—this time on a translation of the *Heimskringla.* Some contact he maintained outside the Hammersmith Socialist Society and the colleagues in his artistic work by attending, occasionally, the "Socialist Supper Club" and, more regularly, the Committee of Anti-Scrape. Indeed, his public work for this Society increased in his last four years. In 1893 he took a prominent part in resisting drastic proposals for the restoration of the spire of Great St. Mary's, Oxford. In 1894 he was resisting a proposed addition to Westminster Abbey, which he described as "in a special degree the work of the *people* of the country in past times". In 1895 he was protesting, as one "born and bred in its neighbourhood", at the destruction of the special character of Epping Forest by the wholesale felling of hornbeams: "this strange, unexampled, and most romantic wood" was, he urged, in danger of being turned into a commonplace park or golf course.[2]

Thereafter came a spate of protests: at the proposed restoration of the Royal Tombs in Westminster Abbey; at the rebuilding, in red brick, of a lock-keeper's cottage by the Thames Conservators in the grey stone village of Kelmscott; of the restoration of the cathedrals of Rouen, Peterborough, Chichester. More often than not the protests met with failure: the inroads of commercialism into the countryside could not be checked. Seeing, in August, 1895, a favourite barn transformed with a zinc and iron roof, he felt "quite sickened":

> "That's the way all things are going now. In twenty years everything will be gone in this countryside, which twenty years ago was so rich in beautiful buildings: and we can do nothing to help it or mend it. The world had better say, 'Let us be through with it and see what will come after it!' Meanwhile, I can do nothing but a little bit of Anti-Scrape. . . Now that I am grown old and see that nothing is to be done, I half

[1] *Cambridge Review,* November 26th, 1896.
[2] See *Letters,* pp. 354, 358, 363-9, and Mackail, II, pp. 314 f.

wish that I had not been born with a sense of romance and beauty in this accursed age. . ."

It is not clear whether it was this reflection, or some personal incident, which provoked the wry reflection in his same letter to Georgie:

"I was thinking. . . how I have wasted the many times when I have been 'hurt' and (especially of late years) have made no sign, but swallowed down my sorrow and anger, and nothing done! Whereas if I had but gone to bed and stayed there for a month or two and declined taking any part in life. . . I can't help thinking that it might have been very effective. Perhaps you remember that this game was tried by some of my Icelandic heroes, and seemingly with great success. . ."[1]

By the summer of 1895 it was evident that Morris's strength was gradually failing. He could no longer take strenuous walks, and even his favourite relaxation of fishing had lost its charm. "It is sad", Burne-Jones (now, to Morris's disappointment, *Sir* Edward)[2] wrote in the autumn, "to see even *his* enormous vitality diminishing."[3] During the work of the Press they had been much together, Burne-Jones falling in with delight with all Morris's projects. His admiration for Morris (despite his abhorrence of Socialism) was still that of his Oxford days. "Morris will be here to-morrow", he wrote in 1891–

"strong, self-contained, master of himself and therefore of the world. Solitude cannot hurt him or dismay him. Such strength as his I see nowhere."[4]

Now, as Morris saw the end drawing near, a wistful note came into their long relationship. One day, while the work on the

[1] *Letters*, p. 374.

[2] It is related (Stirling, *op. cit.*, p. 210) that on the evening previous to Burne-Jones receiving his baronetcy he dined with Morris, but was too nervous to inform his friend. The subject was never mentioned between them thereafter.

[3] *Memorials*, II, p. 268. [4] *Ibid.*, p. 216.

Chaucer was going on apace, and a Kelmscott Malory and Froissart were dimly projected ahead, Morris remarked to his friend: "The best way of lengthening out the rest of our days now, old chap, is to finish off our old things."[1] If he had admitted, two years before, in "The Deeper Meaning of the Struggle", that he felt that his own art was only "a survival of the organic art of the past", yet still his service for the Socialist cause had rid him of his old sense of guilt at his own self-indulgence. "I am afire to see the new designs", he wrote to Burne-Jones—"and as to the age, that be blowed!"[2] He had not lost his delight at "the beauty of the earth", but a letter written to Georgie in November from Rottingdean, shows an intermingling of reminiscence and regret for his passing strength:

> "I started out at ten and went to. . . a chalk pit near (where you took me one hot evening in September, you remember), and I walked on thence a good way, and should have gone further, but prudence rather than weariness turned me back. They were ploughing a field at the bottom with no less than ten teams of great big horses: they were knocking off for their bever just as I came to them, and seemed very jolly, and my heart went out to them, both men and horses."[3]

Two months later, walking back from his last meeting of Anti-Scrape, a friend who noted his weakness, commented politely that it was the worst time of the year. "No; it ain't," he replied, "it's a very fine time of the year indeed: I'm getting old, that's what it is."[4]

In the summer months of 1895 his Socialist activity had dropped off to the very minimum: infrequent attendance at the Hammersmith Clubroom and the Socialist Supper Club. Now, as if with deliberate effort, he picked up some of the old threads: he would at least nail the lie that he was turning from Socialism before he died. On September 15th he was

[1] *Memorials*, p. 268. [2] Mackail, II, p. 319.
[3] *Letters*, p. 378. [4] Mackail, II, p. 320.

lecturing at Hammersmith; on October 6th he was Chairman for Shaw for the last time; on October 30th, at the request of Hines, the old League propagandist and chimney-sweep, he visited Oxford and inaugurated the Oxford Socialist Union before a large and enthusiastic audience; in December he lectured again, and took the chair for the last time for his old friend Bax.[1] On December 28th he made his last open-air speech—in a foggy drizzle outside Waterloo Station. The occasion was the funeral of Sergius Stepniak. A speaker who preceded him said that Stepniak, in his later years, had abandoned his revolutionary outlook and become an advocate of Fabianism. When Morris's turn to speak came, he had no hesitation in refuting the slander:

> "This is a lie—to suggest that Stepniak had ceased to be a revolutionary. He died as he had lived, a revolutionary to the end."[2]

"I have *not* changed my mind on Socialism", Morris wrote to an American correspondent on January 9th, 1896. On January 3rd, he attended the New Year's meeting of the London S.D.F. at Holborn Town Hall. He was received with tumultuous applause. George Lansbury moved a resolution of international fraternal greetings, and William Morris came forward as seconder. He congratulated the S.D.F.,[3] and then—it was the time of the Jameson Raid—he turned to the subject which had first brought him into the movement, imperialism:

> "As far as Africa was concerned [he said] there was a kind of desperation egging on all the nations to make something of that hitherto undeveloped country; and they were no doubt developing it with a vengeance. (Laughter and cheers). When he saw the last accounts about

[1] Hammersmith Minutes.

[2] R. Page Arnot, *William Morris: a Vindication*, p. 21. For a report of the funeral, at which Keir Hardie, John Burns, Eleanor Marx-Aveling, and Kropotkin also spoke, see *The Times*, December 30th, 1895.

[3] *Labour Leader*, January 25th, 1896, quotes Morris as describing Hyndman's election campaign at Burnley as a "remarkable event". "As he was not a member of the S.D.F. he could praise them for holding aloft the real flag of revolution."

the Transvaal he almost wished he could be a Kaffir for five minutes in order to dance around the 'ring'. (Laughter and cheers.) He thought it was a case of a pack of thieves quarrelling about their booty. The Boers had stolen their land from the people it had belonged to; people had come in to help them 'develop' their stolen property, and now wanted to steal it themselves. (Laughter and cheers.) The real fact, however, that we had to deal with was that we lived by stealing—that was, by wasting—all the labour of the workmen."[1]

On January 5th he lectured for the last time in the Clubroom. His subject was "One Socialist Party", but the notes of his lecture have not survived.

His active work for the movement was now over. The next day he entered in his diary, "Could not sleep at night: got up and worked from 1 to 4 at Sundering Flood".[2] On January 31st he spoke, for the last time in public, at a meeting of the Society for Checking the Abuses of Public Advertising. He began to be anxious that he would not live to see the finished Chaucer: "I'd like it finished to-morrow", he said: "Every day beyond to-morrow. . . is one too many."[3] In February the existence of diabetes, and complicating conditions, was confirmed. "I don't feel any better: so weak", he noted in his diary at the end of the month. He was working on a new prose romance, *Kilian of the Close,* whose hero was touched with his own mood: "On a day when the sun was just set, he sat in his hall by the fire under the luffer, turning over uncheery thoughts in his mind. It was midmost March, and the wind swept up the bent and clattered on the hall-windows and moaned in the wall-nook, and the night drew on and seemed entering the wall from the grey world without as if it would presently tell him that there should never be another day." By the end of April he seems to have recognized that his life was over. "My dear fellow", he wrote to Philip Webb, "it was very kind of you to write to me and to want to know how I

[1] *Justice,* January 11th, 1896.
[2] Diary for 1896, Brit. Mus. Add. MSS. 45411.
[3] Mackail, II, p. 322.

am. Well, I am not getting on; I say that in all calmness: I am afraid I am rather weaker than stronger. . ."[1] And to Georgie he wrote from Kelmscott Manor: "Down in this deep quiet, away from the excitements of business and callers, and doctors, one is rather apt to brood, and I fear that I have made myself very disagreeable at times."[2] It was in this frame of mind that he set himself to write an article for the special May Day number of *Justice.* Once again he summoned up his mental energies, writing with his old fire, revealing that profound quality of moral insight which marks his best passages at once as "William Morris". There can be no doubt that he intended the article as a final testament to the movement.

What wonder that he chose as his theme "imperialism"? Imperialism—which had brought him to Socialism; imperialism—fomenter of wars and last hope of capitalism drawing to its end; imperialism—corrupter of the moral health of the labour movement, already entering into it like a spreading stain. Even the S.D.F. was not free from its taint, as Morris, from his long association with Hyndman, well knew. In January, 1896, the S.D.F. Executive had issued a Manifesto in which Hyndman's disastrous "Big Navy" policy (which Morris and Engels had detected beneath *England for All* in 1883, and which later led him directly into his capitulation in the First World War) was shadowed forth:

> "To the adequate increase of our Navy no reasonable man can object. The navy is not an anti-democratic force, and can scarcely be used for aggression under present conditions. The Atlantic and the Pacific are now our Mediterranean Sea, and a nation like ours. . . cannot afford to take such risks in the future as we have taken in the past."[3]

Many still think, Morris wrote:

> "that civilization will grow so speedily and triumphantly, and production will become so easy and cheap, that the possessing classes will

[1] *Letters,* pp. 382-3. [2] *Ibid.,* p. 382.
[3] *Justice,* January 18th, 1896.

be able to spare more and more from the great heap of wealth to the producing classes. . . and all will be peace and prosperity. A futile hope indeed, and one which a mere glance at past history will dispel. For we find as a matter of fact that when we were emerging from semi-barbarism, when open violence was common, and privilege need put on no mask before the governed classes, the workers were not worse off than now, but better. In short, not all the discoveries of science, not all the tremendous organization of the factory and the market will produce true wealth, so long as the end and aim of it all is the production of profit for the privileged classes. . .

"The capitalist classes are doubtless alarmed at the spread of Socialism all over the civilized world. They have at least an instinct of danger; but with that instinct comes the other one of self-defence. Look how the whole capitalist world is stretching out long arms towards the barbarous world and grabbing and clutching in eager competition at countries whose inhabitants don't want them; nay, in many cases, would rather die in battle, like the valiant men they are, than have them. So perverse are these wild men before the blessings of civilization which would do nothing worse for them (and also nothing better) than reduce them to a propertyless proletariat.

"And what is all this for? For the spread of abstract ideas of civilization, for pure benevolence, for the honour and glory of conquest? Not at all. It is for the opening of fresh markets to take in all the fresh profit-producing wealth which is growing greater and greater every day; in other words, to make fresh opportunities for *waste;* the waste of our labour and our lives.

"And I say this is an irresistible instinct on the part of the capitalists, an impulse like hunger, and I believe that it can only be met by another hunger, the hunger for freedom and fair play for all, both people and peoples. Anything less than that the capitalist power will brush aside. But that they cannot; for what will it mean? The most important part of their machinery, the 'hands' becoming MEN, and saying, 'Now at last we will it; we will produce no more for profit but for *use,* for *happiness,* for LIFE."[1]

It was generally known that Morris was coming to the end of his life. From Germany, Liebknecht sent his last fraternal greetings:

[1] *Justice,* May Day Special, 1896. Reprinted in part in May Morris, II, pp. 361-3.

"It is a great debt which I owe to your country. The twelve years of exile I spent there gave me my political education. And your working classes have been my teacher. . .

"*Au revoir,* dear Morris! My wife, who translated your splendid *News from Nowhere,* sends her love. . ."[1]

His Sunday morning visits to Georgie and Ned Burne-Jones at the Grange were now discontinued—one February Sunday in the middle of breakfast he had leant his forehead on his hand, and Burne-Jones had written in alarm: "It is a thing I have never seen him do before in all the years I have known him."[2] In June he was convalescing in Folkestone: "I toddle about, and sit down, lean over the chains, and rather enjoy it, especially if there are any craft about."[3] He still had energy to explode to Philip Webb about the hideous ribbon-development along the coast—"But 'tis an old story!" The Hammersmith Socialist Society continued the work in his absence; the unbroken series of Sunday lectures went on; and candidates were put up, in alliance with the I.L.P., for the vestry elections. But attendance at business meetings had fallen to an average of twelve; and throughout the whole summer, from May to October, only five open-air meetings were held—a falling-off which revealed only too clearly how dependent the Society was upon the driving force of its founder.

In August, 1896, Burne-Jones was writing to Swinburne, describing the progress on the Chaucer: "I abstained from decorating certain of the Canterbury Tales. . . Morris has been urgent with me that I should by no means exclude these stories from our scheme of adornment—especially he had hopes of my treatment of the Miller's Tale, but he ever had more robust and daring parts than I could assume."

"It has been a wretched sight all this year to see him dwindling away. . . I am old and though I work away it is with a heavy heart

[1] Brit. Mus. Add. MSS. 45346. [2] *Memorials,* II, p. 277.
[3] Morris to Philip Webb, June 14th, 1896, *Letters,* p. 383.

often, as if it didn't matter whether I finished my work or not. . ."[1]

In July Morris had been recommended by his doctors and friends to take a sea voyage. He had a yearning to return to the North, and chose to go to the coast of Norway and as far as Spitzbergen. He was already "so ill and weak that is impossible for me to do any work".[2] "I am going with what amount of hope I can muster, which varies, to say sooth, from a good deal to very little", he wrote to Swinburne, when sending him a copy of the at-last-completed Chaucer.[3] It seemed possible that he might have to make the journey alone; but at the last moment his old Socialist friend, John Carruthers, was able to join him. Hyndman visited him before he left, and recalled that he said:

> "If it merely means that I am to be laid up for a little while it doesn't so much matter, you know; but if I am to be caged up here for months, and then it is to be the end of all things, I shouldn't like it at all. This has been a jolly world to me and I find plenty to do in it."[4]

The journey was not a success, and aroused none of his old enthusiasm: although he appeared to pick up a little in his health.[5] On his return in mid-August it was clear that he was gravely ill—too ill to be removed to Kelmscott Manor, as he desired.

From Norway he had sent a telegram of greetings to the International Socialist Workers' Congress in London, at which Tom Mann and Keir Hardie gave fraternal addresses, but which in its result was dominated by the Anarchists. Now he was too weak to do more than design a few letters for the Press, and to dictate a conclusion to *The Sundering Flood.* "Come soon",

[1] Edward Burne-Jones to Algernon Swinburne, August 8th, 1896, Brotherton Collection, Leeds University.

[2] Morris to A.J. Wyatt, July 13th, 1896, *Letters,* p. 384.

[3] *Letters,* p. 384.

[4] *Justice,* October 6th, 1896.

[5] MS. recollections of the journey, by John Carruthers, are preserved in Brit. Mus. Add. MSS. 45350, but recount little of interest.

he wrote to Georgie, "I want a sight of your dear face".[1] To Glasier he wrote, on September 3rd, in a pitifully shaky hand:

> "So many thanks to you for your kind notes. I am really very ill but am trying to get better. . . Fraternally, W.M."[2]

"Morris is dying slowly", Cobden-Sanderson wrote in his diary, shocked for a moment, out of his own self-absorption:

> "It is an astonishing spectacle. He sits speechless waiting for the end to come. . . Darkness. . . soon will envelop all the familiar scene, the sweet river, England green and grey, Kelmscott, Kelmscott House, the trees. . . the Press, the passage, the Bindery, the light coming in through the windows. . . the old books on the shelves. . . 'But', he said to Mary de Morgan, 'but I cannot believe that I shall be annihilated.' "[3]

In his weakness, his strong emotional control was relaxed. When Georgie said something of the life of the poor, he broke into tears. Arnold Dolmetsch brought his virginals to the house, and at the opening phrase of a pavan and galliard by Byrd Morris cried out with joy, and, after the pieces had been repeated, was so moved that he could bear no more. He took the greatest delight in some illuminated manuscripts, lent to him from the Dorchester House library. On October 3rd, near the age of sixty-three, he died peacefully: almost his last words were, "I want to get mumbo-jumbo out of the world". His family doctor pronounced with "unhesitation" that "he died a victim of his enthusiasm for spreading the principles of Socialism". Another doctor had a different diagnosis: "I consider the case is this: the disease is simply being William Morris, and having done more work than most ten men."[4]

So often had the Socialists met with Jane Morris's disapproval that they feared to intrude upon her at the funeral

[1] Mackail, II, p. 332. [2] Glasier MSS.

[3] *Journals of T.J. Cobden-Sanderson*, entry for September, 1896.

[4] Mackail, II, p. 336.

at Lechlade. The Hammersmith comrades were there, of course; and a few others–John Burns and Jack Williams, Walter Crane, Kropotkin and some foreign refugees. Perhaps the absent comrades were mistaken. Certainly Cunninghame Graham, old comrade of "Bloody Sunday", half aristocratic adventurer and half Socialist, thought they were. Morris had liked the man: but–he had complained–"he's too bloody politeful".[1] In the *Saturday Review* next week Graham threw politeness to "the North-West Wind":

> "Seen through the gloom at Paddington. . . were gathered those whom England had sent forth to pay respects to the most striking figure of our times.
>
> "Artists and authors, archaeologists, with men of letters, Academicians, the pulpit, stage, the Press, the statesmen. . . all otherwise engaged.
>
> "Philanthropists agog about Armenia, Cuba, and Crete, spouting of Turks and infidels and foreign cruelties, whilst he who strove for years for Englishmen lay in a railway waggon. . .
>
> "So we reached Oxford, and found upon the platform no representatives. . . and no undergraduates to throng the station. True, it was Long Vacation; but had the body of some Bulawayo Burglar [Cecil Rhodes] happened to pass, they all had been there. . . Sleeping but stertorous, the city lay girt in its throng of jerry buildings, quite out of touch with all mankind, keeping its sympathy for piffling commentators on Menander. . ."

There was no mere rhetoric here: for Cunninghame Graham broke down next week, while speaking at a memorial meeting, and was unable to continue. But, for all that, the final ceremony was not unfitting. The coffin was borne to the church in an open haycart, festooned with willow-boughs, alder and bullrushes. Among the small group of mourners were his close friends, like Ned Burne-Jones, workmen from Merton Abbey, the villagers from Kelmscott, and members of the Art Workers' Guild. "Inside the church was decorated for a

[1] See A.S. Tschiffeley, *Don Roberto.* Cunninghame Graham's opinion of Morris was that he was like "a bull bison surrounded by a pack of wolves."

harvest festival, the lamps all wreathed with ears of oats and barley, whilst round the font. . . lay pumpkins, carrots, and sheaves of corn." Throughout the whole day there raged the storming wind from the north.

It was not to be expected that the Hammersmith Socialist Society would survive his death. Some members were Fabians, some art workers drawn by Morris's influence alone, some inclined towards the I.L.P. or the S.D.F. The Clubroom had to be vacated, anyway, for Jane Morris would hardly have wished it to remain in their hands. In November, readings were given from "Monopoly" and *A Dream of John Ball.* Thirty-six members were present at the special meeting which agreed to discontinue the activities which Morris's energies had driven forward for over twelve years. On December 11th the last lecture was delivered, and the Clubroom, where every Socialist leader in Britain must have spoken, was closed.

"Well do I remember that grey October morning", recalled Alf. Mattison, the Leeds engineer and Leaguer, "when—amid the rattle of riveters' hammers [and] the whirl of machinery. . . a fellow shopmate, who shared my admiration for William Morris, shouted the sad news to me through the tube-plate of a boiler. . . that he, the inspirer of my youthful ideals, had passed away."[1] Hundreds and thousands of workers, comrades known and unknown to Morris, sorrowed at the news. In Portland Gaol, Fred Charles, still serving his long sentence for the "Walsall Case", met Edward Carpenter with tears in his eyes.[2] The Hammersmith comrades, who had spoken side by side with him so often at Hammersmith Bridge, discussed him on their way to the funeral:

> "Kindly but choleric, the verdict was, apt to break into fury, easily appeased, large-hearted, open-handed, and the 'sort of bloke you always could depend on. . .' "[3]

[1] Papers of Alf. Mattison. [2] *Freedom,* December, 1896.
[3] Cunninghame Graham, "With the North-West Wind", *The Saturday Review,* October 10th, 1896.

"The greatest man that ever lived on this planet", wrote one of them afterwards, a postal worker.[1] "He is my greatest human topic", wrote Leatham, of Aberdeen.[2] "To me he was the greatest man in the world", wrote Glasier: and in his diary, on the day he heard the news he entered: "Socialism seems all quite suddenly to have gone from its summer into its winter time. William Morris and Kelmscott House no more!"[3]

Justice and *Freedom* wore black, but it was Blatchford in *Clarion* who voiced the mood of the thousands:

"I cannot help thinking that it does not matter what goes into the *Clarion* this week, because William Morris is dead... He was our best man, and he is dead...

"I have just been reading the obituary notices in some of the London papers, and I feel sick and sorry. The fine phrases, the elaborate compliments, the ostentatious parade of their own erudition, and the little covert sneers at the Socialism Morris loved: all the tawdry upholsteries of these journalistic undertakers seems like desecration... Morris was not only a genius, he was a *man.* Strike at him where you would, he rang true."

If he had failed to bring unity in his life, yet in the moment of his death the whole Socialist and progressive movement stood united in sympathy. From the *Labour Prophet* to *Freedom,* from Edward Carpenter to Cunninghame Graham and Harry Quelch, the same heartfelt tributes came. "We have lost our greatest man", wrote "Marxian" in the *Labour Leader.* "He was really our greatest man", Blunt noted in his diary. Resolutions came from every quarter in the next few days: from the Walthamstow Branch of the Navvies and General Labourers' Union and from the Christian Socialist Union; from a mass meeting of cab-drivers in Trafalgar Square, addressed by John Burns; and from a hundred other parts of the labour movement. One tribute, from a Lancashire branch

[1] R.A. Muncey, in *The Leaguer,* October, 1907.
[2] *The Gateway,* January, 1941. [2] Glasier, *op. cit.,* p. 141.

of the S.D.F., may stand for all:

"Comrade Morris is not dead there is not a Socialist living whould belive him dead for he Lives in the heart of all true men and women still and will do so to the end of time."[1]

[1] Mackail, II, p. 347.

PART IV

NECESSITY AND DESIRE

NECESSITY AND DESIRE

I. Architecture, Machinery and Socialism

WILLIAM MORRIS'S theoretical insights as to the relations between art and labour are revealed in the course of historical and descriptive exposition, rather than schematically in any single book; and they must be reconstructed from many scattered references. We have already seen how profoundly Morris was influenced as a young man by John Ruskin's "The Nature of Gothic", and how he was later forced to develop Ruskin's theories to justify his own actions in the early years of the Anti-Scrape. These theories were brought to their conclusion in 1883 or 1884, after his reading of *Capital* and his active participation in the Socialist movement, and—in the several dozen lectures and articles written from that time to his death—he altered them in no important principle.

These theories were developed, from origin to conclusion, in relation to the architectural and associated arts (among which Morris sometimes included the art of printing, as well as the lesser decorative arts), and Morris scarcely attempted to apply them in detail to the "intellectual" arts. Morris himself was often at pains to make this distinction. "Art" meant, to him, the visual arts, and the popular arts "might all be summed up in that one word Architecture":

> "They are all parts of that great whole, and the art of house-building begins it all: if we did not know how to dye or to weave; if we had neither gold, nor silver, nor silk; and no pigments to paint with. . . we might yet frame a worthy art that would lead to everything, if we had but timber, stone, and lime, and a few cutting tools to make these common things not only shelter us from wind and weather, but also express the thoughts and aspirations that stir in us. Architecture would lead us to all the arts. . ."[1]

[1] "The Beauty of Life", *Works,* XXII, pp. 73-4.

In a more general sense, he distinguished the Intellectual and the Decorative arts: the first "addresses itself wholly to our mental needs", the second is always "but a part of things which are intended primarily for the service of the body":

> "In all times when the arts were in a healthy condition there was an intimate connexion between the two kinds of art. . . The highest intellectual art was meant to please the eye. . . as well as to excite the emotions and train the intellect. It appealed to all men, and to all the faculties of a man. On the other hand, the humblest of the ornamental art shared in the meaning and emotion of the intellectual. . . the best artist was a workman still, the humblest workman was an artist. This is not the case now—"

and the sharp division between the professional "artist" and the wage-earning workman was one of the sources of his ever-welling indignation against industrial capitalism.[1]

His theory of the architectural arts was firmly based upon those sections of "The Nature of Gothic" which described the relationship of the medieval craftsman to his society and to the tradition. "A man at work", wrote Morris—

> "making something which he feels will exist because he is working at it and wills it, is exercising the energies of his mind and soul as well as of his body. Memory and imagination help him as he works. Not only his own thoughts, but the thoughts of the men of past ages guide his hands; and, as a part of the human race, he creates. If we work thus we shall be men, and our days will be happy and eventful."[2]

Not only does he create "as a part of the human race", but as a member of a definite society, with its own local traditions, its own conditions of labour and social commands; and we have seen how Morris, in successive lectures to the Anti-Scrape, examined these conditions in medieval society, and the gradual destruction of the creative initiative of the craftsman in the architectural arts, first in the profit-making workshop,

[1] "Art Under Plutocracy", *ibid.*, pp. 165-6.

[2] "Useful Work *versus* Useless Toil", *Signs of Change*, p. 144.

second in developed industrial capitalism. It must be emphasized (since Morris's own repeated emphasis has been ignored or misunderstood by so many commentators) that he did not indict industrialism *as such* for degrading the craftsman to a machine, but capitalism, the production of goods *primarily for profit and not for use.* Indeed, in more than one lecture he referred to the eighteenth-century workshop system as being a blacker and more degrading period for the workman than the factory system of the nineteenth-century which at least provided the possibility of the lightening of toil which production for profit, specialization and repetition-work had already rendered hateful and mechanical.

Although based in the first place upon Ruskin, it is untrue to suggest (as a critic does) that Morris's views are in the main "the orthodox Ruskinian view of the history of architecture", reiterated without significant development.[1] Rather, we have in the best of these articles and lectures a fusion of Ruskin's finest moments of moral-artistic insight, of Morris's lifetime of historical study, and of the economic and social analysis of Marx. Where Ruskin had jabbed an indignant finger at capitalism and had often (guided by Carlyle's wrath at the "cash-nexus") indicated, in the worship of Mammon, the source of its degradation and horror, Morris was able in page after page of coherent and detailed historical exposition to reveal in the very processes of production, the common economic root both of capitalist exploitation and of the corruption of art.

Morris knew perfectly well that there had been exploitation of a vicious kind in feudal, as well as in capitalist society. Therefore, he was at pains to explain (with great attention to the details of the productive process) how it was that feudal society was compatible with the "freedom" of the craftsman *as* craftsman, and with the flourishing of the architectural arts. "The ancient buildings of the Middle Ages", he wrote many times, were "the work of the associated labour and thought of the *people,* the result of a chain of tradition unbroken

[1] Graham Hough, *The Last Romantics* (1949), p. 93.

from the earliest ages".[1] "There is not an ancient city in the East or West", he declared:

"that does not bear some token of their grief, and joy, and hope. From Ispahan to Northumberland, there is no building built between the seventh and seventeenth centuries that does not show the influence of the labour of that oppressed and neglected herd of men. No one of them, indeed, rose high above his fellows. There was no Plato, or Shakespeare, or Michael Angelo amongst them. Yet scattered as it was among many men, how strong their thought was, how long it abided, how far it travelled!"[2]

The State, then as now, was based on robbery, which "was carried out quite crudely, without any concealment or excuse, by arbitrary taxation or open violence".[3] On the other hand, he suggested, the medieval craftsmen—

"worked shorter hours than we do. . . and had more holidays. They worked deliberately and thoughtfully as all artists do. . . the unspoiled country came up to their very doors. . . All their work depended on their own skill of hand and invention, and never failed to show signs of that in its beauty and fitness."[4]

Like Carlyle he stressed that feudal bonds were "theoretically at least, personal rights and personal duties" and not the impersonal bonds of the commercial market. More of the co-operative ethic was to be found in feudal society than in capitalist, and (again in theory) usury, forestalling, and re-grating were offences against the law.[5]

Under such conditions the labour of the mason, weaver and smith was a source of interest and pleasure to himself, and the product of his labour was fitting and beautiful. With capitalist production,

"the creation of surplus value being the one aim of the employers of labour, they cannot for a moment trouble themselves as to whether the

1 May Morris, I, p. 189.
2 "The Art of the People", *Works,* XXII, pp. 31-2.
3 "The Hopes of Civilization", *Signs of Change*, p. 86.
4 *Commonweal*, May Supplement, 1885. 5 *Signs of Change,* pp. 86 f.

work which creates the surplus value is pleasurable to the worker or not. In fact in order to get the greatest amount possible of surplus value out of the work... it is absolutely necessary that it should be done under such conditions as make... a mere burden which nobody would endure unless upon compulsion."[1]

The system of wage-slavery, crowned by the industrial revolution, destroyed both the attractiveness of labour for the craftsman and the beauty of the product,

"by lengthening the hours of labour: by intensifying the labour during its continuance; by the forcing of the workmen into noisy, dirty crowded factories; by the aggregation of the population into cities and manufacturing districts... by the levelling of all intelligence and excellence of workmanship by means of machinery... All this is the exact contrary of the conditions under which the spontaneous art of past ages was produced."[2]

Nevertheless, by destroying the attractiveness of labour, capitalism lays on the backs of the workers one more burden too intolerable to be borne. It was necessary that the medieval craftsmen, struggling against their oppressors, "should struggle upwards till they formed a middle-class and created commerce with its proletariat doomed to ceaseless unattractive dull labour... Nevertheless, it is that proletariat only that can make good the claim of workmen to their share of art, without which no art can live long." "The price which commercialism will have to pay for depriving the worker of his share of art will be its own death."[3]

Upon this central historical argument, developed with a wealth of illustration, there hung a hundred further lines of thought. The Renaissance appeared to Morris as the watershed: being at one and the same time the period of the flowering of individual genius from the traditions of the past, and the beginning of the degeneration of that tradition in the architectural arts, and of the division between the workman

[1] *Commonweal*, June Supplement, 1885.
[2] *Ibid.*, May Supplement, 1885.
[3] *Ibid.*, May Supplement, 1885.

and the professional artist, the article of use and the "work of art".[1] Fundamental to his outlook, was his view that "neutrality is impossible in man's handiwork": a product must either be actively beautiful or actively ugly; "a house, a knife, a cup, a steam engine... anything that is made by man and has form, must either be a work of art or destructive to art".[2] He hated the "utilitarian" economy, not because its products were *useful,* but because "the word instead expresses... a quality pretty nearly the opposite of useful, and means something which is useful for nothing save squeezing money out of other people's necessities".[3] The "utilitarian" he saw, in capitalist society, as always the ally of "makeshift"–the production of shoddy, substitute, *ersatz;* and also of the useless and debased "luxury" articles, stimulated by advertising and an artificially fostered demand. The vast majority of the products of modern industry he placed within one or the other category, with the exception of the machines ("for the making of makeshifts") and "instruments made for the destruction of wealth and the slaughter of man, on which indeed wonderful ingenuity almost amounting to genius is expended".[4]

For Morris, who found both his rest and his satisfaction in his own work, the reduction of labour by capitalism to hateful drudgery appeared as a culminating horror. From Daniel Defoe he borrowed a quotation which he prefixed to one of his lectures:

> "And the men of labour spent their strength in daily struggling for bread to maintain the vital strength they labour with: so living in a daily circulation of sorrow, living but to work, and working but to live, as if daily bread were the only end of a wearisome life, and a wearisome life the only occasion of daily bread."

[1] See May Morris, II, pp. 629-30, I, p. 281; *Works,* XXII, pp. 56, 389.
[2] "The Socialist Idea in Art", *Works,* XXIII, p. 255.
[3] "Makeshift", May Morris, II, p. 474.
[4] *Ibid.,* p. 475.

He broke sharply with Carlyle's doctrine that "all labour is noble". "It has become an article of the creed of modern morality", he wrote, "that all labour is good in itself—a convenient belief to those who live on the labour of others."[1] "If I were to work ten hours a day at work I despised and hated, I should spend my leisure I hope in political agitation, but I fear—in drinking."[2] From his study of the architectural arts in the Middle Ages he drew his most famous "precepts". First, "Art is Man's expression of his joy in labour".[3] Second, "Nothing should be made by man's labour which is not worth making, or which must be made by labour degrading to the makers".[4] Third, that the only healthy art is "an art which is to be made by the people and for the people, as a happiness to the maker and the user".[5] "I have looked at this claim by the light of history, and my own conscience", he declared in one of his best-known passages—

> "and it seems to me. . . a most just claim, and that resistance to it means nothing short of the denial of the hope of civilization. This then is the claim: *It is right and necessary that all men should have work to do which shall be worth doing, and be of itself pleasant to do; and which should be done under such conditions as would make it neither over-wearisome nor over-anxious.* Turn that claim about as I may. . . I cannot find that it is an exorbitant claim; yet. . . if Society would or could admit it, the face of the world would be changed."[6]

But such a claim, as Morris had discovered several years before he read Marx, was revolutionary: it could not be granted by capitalism. However high-sounding the appeals to "progress" and the "public welfare", Morris detected under each fresh advance of industrial capitalism one sole motive—the extraction of fresh profit, with the accompanying destruct-

[1] "Useful Work *versus* Useless Toil", *Signs of Change,* p. 141.
[2] "Making the Best of It", *Works,* XXII, p. 115.
[3] "Art under Plutocracy", *ibid.,* XXIII, p. 173.
[4] "Art and Socialism", *ibid.,* p. 205.
[5] "The Art of the People", *ibid.,* XXII, p. 47.
[6] "Art and Socialism", *ibid.,* XXIII, p. 194.

ion of the beauty of nature and the treasures of the past. "No man of sense and feeling", he wrote, "would dare to regret such losses if they had been paid for by new life, and happiness for the people. But there is the people still as it was before, still facing for its part the monster who destroyed all that beauty, and whose name is Commercial Profit".[1] Opposing the railway to the Lake District, he said "as things go now... [it] is not a question of the convenience of the Amblesiders, or the pleasure of the world in general, but the profit of a knot of persons leagued together against the public... under the name of a railway company".[2] The slums of Glasgow he described as "a most woeful abode of man, crying out from each miserable court and squalid, crowded house for the abolition of the tyranny of exploitation".[3] So long as the search for profit dominated economic life, so long would that beauty be desecrated which Morris regarded as one of the sources of artistic inspiration:

> "Until the contrast is less disgraceful between the fields where beasts live and the streets where men live, I suppose that the practice of the arts must be mainly kept in the hands of a few highly cultivated men..."[4]

It might be possible to alleviate the present, to "make the best of it", to restrain and check the ravages of commercialism. A public demand for simple and solid craftsmanship might be fostered even within capitalist society, according to his often-repeated precept: "Have nothing in your houses which you do not know to be useful or believe to be beautiful."[5] But the tendency of modern commercialism would persist: to make, on the one hand, self-conscious objects of ornament for display and, on the other hand, to confine those articles of genuine fitness and beauty, produced more by accident than

[1] "The Aims of Art", *Signs of Change,* p. 134.
[2] *Commonweal,* February 25th, 1887. [3] *Ibid.,* July 10th, 1886.
[4] "The Lesser Arts", *Works,* XXII, p. 25.
[5] "The Beauty of Life", *ibid.,* p. 76 f.

design, to the kitchen. The claim, when phrased in positive terms—

> "Every man willing to work should be ensured: First, Honourable and fitting work; Second, A healthy and beautiful house; Third, Full leisure for rest of mind and body,"[1]

could only be achieved in a Socialist society.

There is a very widespread opinion, both among those who approve and those who oppose Morris's views, that he was an uncompromising enemy of all machinery as such, and that his chief motive in becoming a Socialist lay in an Utopian desire to return to a society of handicraftsmen—a feudal society, with social equality somehow replacing the feudal hierarchy of class. This view has been fostered in many minds by a reading of *News from Nowhere* unrelated to the conditions of its creation and to the specific statements on this issue in Morris's other writings.

In fact, Morris makes his views on this matter perfectly clear in his lectures. Capitalism, not machinery, has reduced the workman to "an appendage of profit-grinding", reducing the mill-hand, for example, to being "as much a part of the factory where he works as any cog-wheel or piece of shafting is". The horror, for Morris, was not in the factory system itself, but in its subjugation to profit-grinding in its working conditions and social organization. "The socialization of labour which ought to have been a blessing to the community has been turned into a curse by the appropriation of the products of its labours by individuals."[2] "Our epoch", he said, "has invented machines which would have appeared wild dreams to the men of past ages, and of those machines we have as yet *made no use*." The real *human* use to which machines ought to be put is in the saving of labour: capitalism uses them "to reduce the skilled labourer to the ranks of the unskilled. . . to

[1] "Art and Socialism", *Works*, XXII, p. 210.
[2] "A Factory as It Might Be", May Morris, II, p. 136 f.

intensify the labour of those who serve the machines", and to create a growing army of unemployed.[1]

With Socialism the role of machinery is transformed:

> "The manufacture of useless goods, whether harmful luxuries for the rich or disgraceful makeshifts for the poor, having come to an end, [we shall still be] in possession of the machines once used for mere profit-grinding but now used for saving human labour."[2]

"In short, we should be the masters of our machines and not their slaves":

> "It is not this or that tangible steel and brass machine which we want to get rid of, but the great intangible machine of commercial tyranny which oppresses the lives of all of us."[3]

Not only will machinery be useful in alleviating those forms of heavy and unattractive labour (such as coal-mining) to which (at the time Morris was writing) it had scarcely been seriously applied, on the grounds that it did not "*pay*": but it will also prove to be the essential instrument for the realization of the new society. In Morris's words, it will,

> "when the worker-class, the proletariat, is full grown be the instrument which will make socialism possible by making possible the equalisation of labour as applied to the necessities of life, and will thereby leave open to men the higher field of intellectual effort."[4]

When we are equal, he wrote in one of his last articles, "there will be no fear then of our doing nothing but dry utilitarian work":

[1] "Useful Work *versus* Useless Toil", *Signs of Change,* p. 169.

[2] "A Factory as It Might Be", May Morris, II, pp. 136 f.

[3] "Art and Its Producers", *Works,* XXII, p. 352.

[4] Lecture at Oldham on "The Depression in Trade" (1885), Brit. Mus. Add. MSS. 45334; E.D. Lemire, *Unpublished Lectures of William Morris,* pp. 129-30.

"Have we not our wonderful machines to do that for us?. . . What are the said machines about now that the mass of the people should toil and toil without pleasure? They are making profits for their owners, and have no time to save the people from drudgery. When the people are their owners—then we shall see."[1]

Not only would the role of machinery be transformed in Socialist society, but the factory itself:

"This very factory system, under a reasonable order of things (though to my mind there might still be drawbacks to it), would at least offer opportunities for a full and eager social life surrounded by many pleasures."

The factory would be a "centre of intellectual activity",[2] and,

"besides turning out goods useful to the community, will provide for its own workers work light in duration, and not oppressive in kind, education in childhood and youth, serious occupation, amusing relaxation. . . leisure. . . beauty of surroundings, and the power of producing beauty which are sure to be claimed by those who have leisure, education and serious occupation."[3]

On the other hand, "it may be allowable for an artist, that is one whose ordinary work is pleasant and not slavish, to hope that in no factory will all the work. . . be mere machine-tending".[4] There must be variety of labour as well as leisure:

"If the work be specially rough and exhausting. . . I must take turns in doing it with other people; I mean I mustn't, for instance, be expected to spend all my working hours always at the bottom of a coal-pit."[5]

Even repetitive labour would be "made attractive by the consciousness of usefulness":

[1] "As to Bribing Excellence", *Liberty*, May, 1895.
[2] "Useful Work *versus* Useless Toil", *Signs of Change*, p. 166.
[3] "A Factory as It Might Be", May Morris, II, p. 137.
[4] *Ibid.*
[5] "How We Live and How We Might Live", *Signs of Change*, p. 27.

"It is most certain that labour may be so arranged that no social relations could be more delightful than communion in hopeful work; love, friendship, family affection, might all be quickened by it; joy increased, and grief lightened by it."[1]

But the arduous or boring character of the labour should be borne in mind in assessing the social value of the product: and if the product was inessential and the cost in wearisome labour high, then society would have to do without it. The doing away of "all antagonism between town and country" Morris thought a necessary consequence of Socialism, though the actual way in which this would happen would rest with the future.[2] The factory itself, surrounded by gardens and of pleasant and fitting architecture, would provide facilities not only for technical and liberal education, but for the pursuit of music, drama, and the fine arts. With the death of competition, "no new process, no details of improvements in machinery, would be hidden from the first enquirer"; and the high technical knowledge of the workers "would foster a general interest in work and in the realities of life, which would surely tend to elevate labour and create a standard of excellence in manufacture".[3] Finally, it went without saying that a Socialist society would employ its scientific genius in finding means of eliminating smoke and filth, in disposing of rubbish and waste, and in preventing industry from blackening and despoiling the countryside.

This, then, is an exact statement of the position as Morris saw it when he set forward the matter carefully in his political lectures. But he made no bones about the fact that by temperament he had a strong dislike to all machinery, except those primitive kinds which could not perform their work unless the craftsman's "hand was thinking". The intricacies of machinery, the great constructional achievements of the

[1] "Why Not?", *Justice,* April 12th, 1884.
[2] *Socialism: Its Growth and Outcome,* p. 316.
[3] "A Factory as It Might Be", May Morris, II, pp. 137 f.

nineteenth century, evoked little response in him; he was not excited by a sense of power or wonder at their potentialities. That this was, in part, a matter of his own background and temperament he recognized.[1] In part, the source of his objection was more profound. As he once declared, "I believe machines can do everything—except make works of art".[2] This reservation he always kept to the fore:

> "I believe that the ideal of the future does not point to the lessening of men's energy by the reduction of labour to a minimum, but rather to the reduction of *pain in labour* to a minimum."[3]

He thought it likely that in the transitional stage of Socialism machinery would be greatly developed; "the reflex of the terror of starvation, which so oppresses us now, would drive us into excesses of utilitarianism."[4]

> "For the consolation of artists I will say that I believe indeed that a state of social order would probably lead at first to a great development of machinery for really useful purposes... but after a while [people] will find that there is not so much work to do as they expected, and then they will have leisure to reconsider the whole subject; and if it seems to them that a certain industry would be carried on more pleasantly as regards the worker, and more effectually as regards the goods, by using hand-work rather than machinery, they will certainly get rid of their machinery, because it will be possible for them to do so."[5]

In sum, when men have mastered their material needs, "they will doubtless turn themselves and begin to find out what it is

[1] Lecture, "What Is: What Should be: What Will Be" (1893?). "The most obvious way of using machinery... would seem to be to use it for the prevention of drudgery and not otherwise... I have a kind of an idea that the time will come when people will rather overdo their hatred of machinery, as perhaps I do now." Brit. Mus. Add. MSS. 45330.

[2] "Art and Beauty of the Earth", *Works,* XXII, p. 166.

[3] Review of *Looking Backward, Commonweal,* June 22nd, 1889.

[4] Letter to Comrade Blackwell, *ibid.,* May 18th, 1889.

[5] "How We Live and How We Might Live", *Signs of Change,* p. 33.

they really want to do".[1]

Morris never posed this question as one of practical theoretical importance. He knew perfectly well that:

> "We cannot turn our people back into Catholic English peasants and Guild craftsmen, or into heathen Norse bonders, much as may be said for such conditions of life."[2]

He saw the matter as a choice to be made after the transitional stage of Socialism, when men might either work greatly reduced hours with improved machinery and satisfy their creative faculties in their leisure;[3] or might decide to return to handcrafts in certain fields—textiles, pottery, metal-work, and possibly agriculture[4]—for the pleasure of creating art in their daily labour. When that choice came (as it had already come in *News from Nowhere*) he hoped that men would choose "to keep life simple, to forgo some of the power over nature won by past ages in order to be more human and less mechanical, and willing to sacrifice something to this end."[5] Machinery would then be used "for the prevention of drudgery and not otherwise".[6] In no case would it altogether disappear. One is reminded of Shaw's story of accompanying Morris through the Merton Abbey works. Directing attention to a dull and mechanical task he "dared to say": "You should get a machine to do that." "I've ordered one", was Morris's reply.[7]

[1] "The Aims of Art", *Signs of Change*, pp. 132 f. [2] *Letters*, p. 206.

[3] This appears to have been Morris's view in his last years. See, for example, his article in *Liberty*, February, 1894, "Why I am a Communist": "A Communal Society would bring about a condition of things in which we should be really wealthy, because we should have all we produced, and should know what we wanted to produce; that we should have so much leisure from the production of what are called 'utilities', that any group of people would have leisure to satisfy its cravings for what are usually looked on as superfluities, such as works of art, research into facts, literature, the unspoiled beauty of nature; matters that to my mind are utilities also. . ."

[4] See "The Aims of Art", *Signs of Change*, p. 136; May Morris, II, p. 462.

[5] "The Society of the Future", May Morris, p. 466.

[6] Brit. Mus. Add. MSS. 45330. [7] *Observer*, November 6th, 1949.

II. Theories of Art

So far we have been concerned with Morris's theories as they relate to the practice of the architectural and allied arts, and the labour of the workman. Before leaving these theories, we must enquire how far Morris fashioned a coherent aesthetic–a theory of the nature of art and of its value among other human activities. Moreover, we have still to examine his attitude to the "intellectual" arts and to the creative problems of the individual artist.

Morris found it difficult to ask himself seriously the question, "Does art have any value?" His own pleasure in creative work was so intense that he found it difficult to conceive of anyone without an artistic sense. It was, to him, like eyesight, hearing, touch; and the deprivation of thousands of workers of the full development of this sense filled him with rage.[1] Nevertheless, the question was forced upon him, and he attempted to answer it, by describing his own feelings, and by interpreting the past.

On the one hand, there was the Ruskinian formula, "Art is the expression of man's joy in labour". Viewed from this aspect (the satisfaction of the artist or craftsman) Morris regarded art (but the lesser decorative arts in particular) as the pleasurable exercise of physical, intellectual and emotional faculties. He drew a parallel directly from nature:

> "The horse in his natural state delights in running, and the dog in hunting, while in the elementary conditions of savage human life, certain ceremonies, and adornments of weapons. . . point to a sense of pleasure and dignity even in the process of the acquisition of food. . . It was from this turning of a necessary work into amusement that definite art was finally born."[2]

As "Barbarism began to give place to early Civilization, this

[1] See *Commonweal*, May Supplement, 1885: "For my part, having regard to the general happiness of the race, I say without shrinking that the bloodiest of violent revolutions would be a light price to pay for the righting of this wrong."

[2] *Socialism: Its Growth and Outcome*, pp. 301-2.

solace of labour fell asunder into duality. . . and art became incidental and accessory on the one side and independent and primary on the other".[1] Nevertheless, the relationship between the two kinds of art will always persist, and neither can be sick for long without affecting the health of the other.

On the other hand, Morris viewed art from a different aspect. On several occasions he described the "Reverence for the Life of Man. . . [as] the foundation of all art". On another,

> "Art is man's embodied expression of interest in the life of man; it springs from man's pleasure in his life; pleasure we must call it, taking all human life together, however much it may be broken by the grief and trouble of individuals. . ."[2]

Again, he speaks of "the sense of beauty in the external world, of interest in the life of man as a drama, and the desire of communicating this. . . to our fellows" as "an essential part of the humanity of man".[3] The arts "are man's expression of the value of life, and also the production of them makes his life of value".[4] "Eager life while we live. . . is above all things the Aim of Art", he wrote in another place.[5] It was implicit in his view that the arts had an enobling influence, a potent moral influence:

> "Stories that tell of men's aspirations for more than material life can give them, their struggles for the future welfare of their race, their unselfish love, their unrequited service: things like this are the subjects for the best art. . ."[6]

And he declared:

> "I will say, without pretending to give a definition, that what I mean by an art is some creation of man which appeals to his emotions

[1] May Morris, II, p. 168, and *Works,* XXII, p. 151.
[2] *Commonweal,* April Supplement, 1885. [3] May Morris, II, p. 408.
[4] *Ibid.,* I, pp. 266-7. [5] "The Aims of Art", *Signs of Change,* p. 140.
[6] "Some Hints on Pattern-designing", *Works,* XXII, p. 176.

and his intellect by means of his senses. All the greater arts appeal directly to that intricate combination of intuitive perceptions, feelings, experience, and memory which is called imagination. All artists. . . have these qualities superabundantly, and have them balanced in such exquisite order that they use them for purposes of creation."[1]

This is a description rather than a definition, although the terms used to describe imagination show that Morris was aware of the complexity of the artistic process. It is true, and in a profound sense, that "all worthy schools of art. . . [are] the outcome of the aspirations of the people towards the beauty and true pleasure of life."[2] But such words as "beauty", "pleasure", and "aspiration" are signposts only to further assumptions which Morris never discussed.

Morris leant too heavily upon arguments derived from the decorative arts when dealing with art as a whole. He knew little or nothing about recent discoveries as to the active social agency of certain arts in the life of primitive peoples: the carving on the bone handle of a knife cannot explain to us the function and meaning of the ritual dance. Moreover, in the second part of his descriptive definition, he erred by divorcing art from the historical process as a whole. One might be tempted to exclaim: "Art *would have been* this had it not been for class society, art *will be* this with the abolition of classes." But Morris has not emphasized sufficiently the ideological role of art, its active agency in changing human beings, its agency in man's class-divided history. It is true that these considerations are never absent when Morris treats the history of architecture or pattern-designing in detail. But in the "intellectual" arts he did not see the matter so clearly.

It is perhaps too extreme a judgement to say (as one sympathetic critic has said) that Morris's aesthetics "were of the standard Pre-Raphaelite brand". It is difficult to point to any such "standard brand", and Morris, with his great historical understanding, could not be confined within it. But

[1] "The Lesser Arts of Life", *Works,* XXII, pp. 235-6.
[2] "The Deeper Meaning of the Struggle," *Letters,* pp. 355-7.

several of his favourite terms—and, in particular, "beauty" and "pleasure"—carry the associations gained in Morris's early romantic revolt. In this area of artistic theory the illusions of his youth clung most closely and were the hardest to shake off. His view of "beauty" was coloured to the end by the romantic search for the "ideal": art must be either epic or heroic, or "beautiful" in the sense of sweet, easeful, decorative, soothing. He stoutly maintained the view that it was impossible for the painter to create this "beauty" without beautiful models in the life and society around him,[1] and therefore—

> "those only among our painters do work worth considering, whose minds have managed to leap back across the intervening years, across the waste of gathering commercialism, into the later Middle Ages... Anyone who wants beauty to be produced at the present day in any branch of the fine arts, I care not what, must be always crying out 'Look back! look back!' "[2]

This was in part a reflection of his own practice in the arts. *The Earthly Paradise, Love Is Enough,* even *Sigurd the Volsung,* show little of that imaginative and intellectual contest with reality which marks the greatest creative achievement. "Pleasure"—the word Morris had borrowed from Ruskin—was a deceptive doctrine, especially when applied to the "intellectual" arts. He carried the analogy between the pleasing exercise of the craftsman's energies further than can be justified. While he shook off the romantic concept of "inspiration", he tended to assume that all worth-while art had an easy and almost spontaneous birth, whatever problems of execution might later intervene.

Some illustration of his attitude may be found in his own literary and artistic taste. Here he maintained a strong predisposition towards late medieval art on the one hand, and

[1] See May Morris, I, p. 305, Lecture on "The English Pre-Raphaelites", where he argues that the artist's imagination must naturally take "the raiment of some period in which the surroundings of life were not ugly but beautiful."

[2] *Ibid.,* pp. 239-40.

saga and epic on the other. He could never forget that the Renaissance was the time "when Europe first opened its mouth wide to fill its belly with the east winds of commercialism".[1] "The great men who lived and glorified the practice of art in those days were the fruit of the old, not the seed of the new order of things", he declared,[2] thereby denying by implication that bourgeois individualism made any addition to man's consciousness. Because the Renaissance marked in his view the beginning of the degeneration of the architectural arts, he attempted to fit the "intellectual" arts into the same pattern of interpretation. The literature of the eighteenth century, he held, "lacks all imaginative qualities", and its painting reveals little but "cleverness, readiness and confidence", while its verses which "insult the name of poetry" were filled with a "hatred of imagination and humanity".[3] Always he returned with relief to the architecture and art of the thirteenth and fourteenth centuries: "the loveliest, brightest, and gayest of all the creations of the human mind and hand".[4]

Although Morris made token references to the great artists and writers of the past four hundred years, his references were without warmth. "Shakespeare", Shaw remarks, "was not in the Morris movement, which was strongly anti-rhetorical."[5] When he was invited, in 1885, to set down his "Best Hundred Books", he selected fifty-four: the first thirty-seven were made up of ancient and traditional writing, the sagas, and a few classical and medieval works; in the remaining seventeen he included six English poets—Shakespeare, Blake ("the part of him which a mortal can understand"), Coleridge, Shelley, Keats and Byron; seven novelists—Bunyan, Defoe, Scott, Dumas, Victor Hugo, Dickens and George Borrow—and the works of Ruskin and Carlyle. The omissions are significant—Marlowe, Ben Jonson, Milton ("the union in

[1] "Art and Industry in the Fourteenth Century", *Works,* XXII, p. 389.
[2] "The Beauty of Life", *ibid.,* p. 56.
[3] May Morris, II, p. 631.
[4] "Feudal England", *Signs of Change,* p. 73.
[5] May Morris, II, p. xxxiii.

his works of cold classicism with Puritanism (the two things which I hate most in the world) repels me so that I *cannot* read him"), the eighteenth-century novelists, Wordsworth (whom, Shaw says, he hated for his piety), let alone the major European novelists and poets.[1] He was aware of the greatness of Balzac and Tolstoy, but he seems to have read them with difficulty—even distaste. He was moved to fury by the attempt to ban Zola for "obscenity": *Germinal* he thought to be "part of a true picture of the life which our civilization forces on labouring men", but he clearly did not regard this as a fit subject for "art".[2] He praised Ibsen's *Doll's House* as "a piece of the *truth* about modern society clearly and forcibly put", and jeered at the horror of "the respectable critics":[3] indeed, he found in Ibsen "another token of the new dawn". But, for all that, it is clear that he felt little real enthusiasm. Henry James, like Meredith, aroused in him little but impatience: he was "the clever historian of the deadliest corruption of society, the laureat of the flirts, sneaks, and empty fools of which that society is mostly composed, and into whose hearts (?) he can see so clearly".[4] He accused him of total insensitivity to the people: he looked on the "working-classes as an useful machine", and "has not imagination enough to realize the fact that the said machine is composed of millions of men, women, and children who are living in misery". The impressionists Morris considered to be openly at enmity with beauty, and "drifting into the domain of empirical science": nevertheless, he recognized their honesty and eagerness of purpose—"the public would be quite wrong in supposing them to be swayed by mere affectation".[5] In sum, he was out of sympathy with many of those trends in the arts in his own time which now command our attention or respect.

Morris tried his hand at formal literary criticism only once

[1] See May Morris's Introduction to *Works,* XXII.
[2] See *Commonweal,* August 25th, 1888.
[3] *Ibid.,* June 22nd, 1889.
[4] *Ibid.,* December 15th, 1888.
[5] May Morris, I, p. 243.

or twice in his life, and it must be counted a misfortune that he did not make more effort to order and discipline his responses than he did. He recognized this weakness in himself, and expressed it in 1877, when refusing nomination to the Chair of Poetry at Oxford University.

"It seems to me that the *practice* of any art rather narrows the artist in regard to the *theory* of it; and I think I come more than most men under this condemnation... I have a peculiar inaptitude for expressing myself except in the one way that my gift lies. Also... I have a lurking doubt as to whether the Chair of Poetry is more than an ornamental one, and whether the Professor of a wholly incommunicable art is not rather in a false position..."[1]

As Morris stressed, "I never set up for a critic". His feeling that art should be a "solace", an expression of "pleasure", led him to underestimating the agency of art in history. This was paralleled in his responses by a lack of enthusiasm for the painful, the tragic (unless in terms of epic and saga), and a definite dislike of introspective and subjective art.[2] This does not mean that he evaded suffering in his life: his actions must disprove this. But he did avoid the contemplation of suffering in art: he had a surfeit of it in his daily experience, and he tended to turn to art for repose or even for escape. It would be after some painful experience, some sordid exposure in the law courts during the propaganda, that (Shaw relates) Morris would return home and lose himself in the pages of Dumas or Dickens or *Huckleberry Finn.*[3] In general, Morris was blind towards the

[1] *Letters,* p. 85.

[2] See *Letters,* p. 280. Morris, writing to Georgie Burne-Jones, comments on his reading of *War and Peace,* and is clearly comparing it in his mind with Stepniak's tales of the Russian nihilists and revolutionaries: "There seems to be a concensus of opinion in these Russian novels as to the curious, undecided turn of the intellectual persons there: Hamlet... should have been a Russian, not a Dane. This throws some light on the determination and straightforwardness of the revolutionary heroes and heroines there; as if they said, 'Russians must be always shilly-shally, letting I dare wait upon I would, must they? Look here then, we will throw all that aside and walk straight to death." See Sergius Stepniak, *Underground Russia.*

[3] See Shaw's Introduction to May Morris, II, and *Observer,* November 6th, 1949.

great achievements of bourgeois realism. He knew these works existed, he recognized that they were great, but they moved no enthusiasm in him: and this blind-spot robs his general theory of the arts of some of its value.

An interesting parallel can be seen between Morris's weaknesses in political theory in the 1880s, and his blind-spots in the appreciation and understanding of the arts. Both sprang from the very vehemence of his revolt against capitalist society, his utter disgust at the values of his own class. The "hatred of modern civilization" which had been part of his early Pre-Raphaelite revolt had impelled him on his way to Socialism, and saved him from becoming enmeshed in many illusions from which other sincere artists of his time could not escape. On the other hand, it imbued him with a hostility to the individualist ethic of capitalist society which appears to have deadened in him all positive response to many great artistic achievements in the previous three hundred years.

This blindness was not only loss. It fostered in him an acute response to those periods of history when the people participated most in the practice of the arts. Moreover, it helped him to view the problem of the relation of the artist to his society from a social, rather than an individualist, standpoint. It is here that some of his most telling judgements on the arts were made. Repeatedly he declared that art could not thrive in the hands of a few highly-cultivated men within an utilitarian and hostile society. Rather—

> "it will be always but the blossom of all the half-conscious work. . . below it, the fulfilment of the shortcomings of less complete minds. . . it will waste much of its power, and have much less influence on men's minds, unless it be surrounded by abundance of that commoner work, in which all men once shared."[1]

The divorce of the artist from "the general sympathy of simple people weighs very heavily on him, and makes his

[1] "The Beauty of Life", *Works,* XXII, p. 55.

work feverish and dreamy, or crabbed and perverse".[1] The argument that Socialism should be opposed because it would not encourage genius received from him short shrift:

> "Do you think, as some do, that it is not ill that a hundred thousand harmless people should be boiled down on the fire of misery to make one single glorious great man? I honestly believe that there are people who are fools enough to think that. I answer plainly, great men are nourished on no such soup, though prigs may be; it is the happiness of the people that produces the blossom of genius. But even if it were so I. . . would rather have a hundred thousand happy persons than one genius made up of murder."[2]

The relation between the artist, or the craftsman, and his society was the theme of many lectures. He looked upon the history of the arts, not—as did many of his contemporaries—as the record of individual geniuses, each "inspired" and each influencing each other, but as part of wider social processes. In his first lecture (in 1877) he described the development of the arts as a natural process: "Like all growth, it was good and fruitful for awhile; like all fruitful growth, it grew into decay: like all decay of what was once fruitful, it will grow into something new."[3] Already in 1880, three years before reading *Capital,* he sensed the dialectical movement of history:

> "Ancient civilization was chained to slavery and exclusiveness, and it fell; the barbarism that took its place has delivered us from slavery and grown into modern civilization; and that in its turn has before it the choice of never-ceasing growth, or destruction by that which has in it the seeds of higher growth."[4]

But, while this dialectical understanding of change, growth and decay, was ever-present in his writing, he saw man's economic and social development always as the master-process,

[1] "Art and the Beauty of the Earth", *Works,* XXII, p. 164.
[2] May Morris, II, p. 203. [3] "The Lesser Arts", *Works,* XXII, pp. 9-11.
[4] "The Beauty of Life", *ibid.,* p. 65.

and tended to suggest that the arts were passively dependent upon social change. In the 1880s he suggested more than once that the arts must "die" with capitalist society, and could only be re-born when Socialist society had for many years been established. "The old art is no longer fertile", he wrote—

"no longer yields us anything save elegantly poetical regrets; being barren it has but to die, and the matter of moment now is, how it shall die, *with* hope, or *without* it. . ."[1] "Once again I warn you against supposing, you who may specially love art, that you will do any good by attempting to revivify art by dealing with its dead exterior. . ."[2] "For my part I believe that if we try to realize the aims of art without much troubling ourselves what the aspect of the art itself shall be, we shall find we shall have what we want at last; whether it is to be called art or not, it will at least be *life;* and, after all, that is what we want."[3]

We can see how Ruskin's challenge in *Unto This Last* was still echoing in his mind—"There is no Wealth but Life." If the source of art was "pleasure" in labour, then Socialism seemed to him the necessary precondition of its rebirth. "It is possible", he wrote,

"that all the old superstitions and conventionalities of art have got to be swept away before art can be born again; that before that new birth we shall have to be left bare of everything that has been called art; that we shall have nothing left us but the materials of art, that is the human race with its aspirations and passions and its home, the earth; on which materials we shall have to use these tools, leisure and desire."[4]

And so he still viewed the matter in one of his last and clearest statements:

"I do not believe in the possibility of keeping art vigorously alive by the action, however energetic, of a few groups of specially gifted men and their small circle of admirers amidst a general public incapable of understanding and enjoying their work. I hold firmly to the opinion

[1] "The Aims of Art", *Signs of Change*, p. 134.
[2] *Ibid.*, p. 140. [3] *Ibid.*, p. 133. [4] *Commonweal*, April Supplement, 1885.

that all worthy schools of art must be in the future, as they have been in the past, the outcome of the aspirations of the people towards the beauty and true pleasure of life... These aspirations of the people towards beauty can only be born from a condition of practical equality... I am so confident that this equality will be gained, that I am prepared to accept as a consequence of the process of that gain, the seeming disappearance of what art is now left us; because I am sure that that will be but a temporary loss, to be followed by a genuine new birth of art, which will be the spontaneous expression of the pleasure of life innate in the whole people."[1]

"Any one who professes to think that the question of art and cultivation must go before that of the knife and fork... does not understand what art means", he wrote.[2] At the end of the nineteenth century this was one of the most important lessons which an artist of his stature—and one, moreover, who had been brought to Socialism in part for the sake of art itself—could voice abroad. Morris's lectures tore down the precious veils before the Palace of Art, challenged the late romantic postures of self-conceit and self-dramatization, revealed the enormous reserves of creative energy in the people, and stimulated the discussion of cultural problems within the working-class movement. Moreover, Morris did not fall into the error of supposing that the working class could enter upon their heritage in the arts without arduous struggle to master the best traditions of the past, and to cast out the inferior traditions of commercialized culture:

"People sometimes talk as though the ordinary man in the street... is the proper person to apply to for a judgement on Works of Art. They say he is unsophisticated, and so on. Now, just let us look the facts in the face... As a matter of fact, he is not unsophisticated. On the contrary he is steeped in the mere dregs of all the Arts that are current at the time he lives. Is not that absolutely and positively the state of the case?... I am perfectly certain that in the Art of Music

[1] *Letters,* pp. 355-7 (November 10th, 1893). This important letter, "The Deeper Meaning of the Struggle", addressed to the *Daily Chronicle,* was later reprinted as a handbill by the Hammersmith Socialist Society.

[2] "How I Became a Socialist", *Justice,* June 6th, 1894.

what the 'unsophisticated' person takes to is not the fine works of Art, but the ordinary, commonplace, *banal* tunes which are drummed into his ears at every street corner. That is natural. . . There is a tendency for all people to fall under the domination of tradition of some sort; and the fine tradition, the higher tradition, having disappeared, men will certainly fall into the power of the lower and inferior tradition. Therefore let us once for all get rid of the idea of the mass of the people having an intuitive idea of Art, unless they are in immediate connection with the great traditions of times past. . ."[1]

Only on rare occasions did Morris suggest the possibility that the revolutionary working class (as opposed to the "ordinary man" in the capitalist street) might itself be the creator of new traditions and a new art:

"May we not hope that we shall not have to wait for the new birth of art till we attain the peace of the realized New Order? Is it not at least possible. . . that what will give the death-blow to the vulgarity of life which enwraps us all now will be the great tragedy of Social Revolution, and that the worker will then once more begin to have a share in art, when he begins to see his aim clear before him—his aim of a share of real life for all men—and when his struggle for that aim has begun? It is not the excitement of battling for a great and worthy end which is the foe to art, but the dead weight of sordid, unrelieved anxiety, the anxiety for the daily earning of a wretched pittance by labour degrading at once to body and mind. . ."[2]

More often he suggested the likelihood of the transitional stage of Socialism proving to be a "blank" in the arts, until the people should "take up the chain where it fell from the hands of the craft-guilds of the fifteenth century."[3] Indeed, despite his own Socialist poetry, and the importance he laid upon cultural activity in the Socialist movement, Morris repeatedly leaves the impression that he had come to regard the poetry and painting of his time (including his own) as in some way marginal activities. As early as 1882 he had expressed the

[1] "The English Pre-Raphaelite School", May Morris, I, pp. 307-8.

[2] *Commonweal*, April Supplement, 1885.

[3] "The Exhibition of the Royal Academy", May Morris, I, p. 241 (from *To-day*, July, 1884).

feeling that Swinburne's poems were "founded on literature, not on nature", and continued:

> "In these days the issue between art, that is, the godlike part of man, and mere bestiality, is so momentous, and the surroundings of life are so stern and unplayful, that nothing can take serious hold of people, or should do so, but that which is rooted deepest in reality and is quite at first hand: there is no room for anything which is not forced out of a man of deep feeling, because of its innate strength and vision.
>
> "In all this I may be quite wrong. . . I only state my opinion, I don't defend it; still less do I my own poetry. . ."[1]

III. Chants for Socialists and *The Pilgrims of Hope*

Morris's creative writing, after he joined the Socialist movement, falls into three groupings. First, the occasional propagandist poems—published as *Chants for Socialists,* in the main written for *Justice* or *Commonweal* between 1883 and 1886, and the long narrative poem, *The Pilgrims of Hope,* written for *Commonweal* in instalments in 1885. Second, *A Dream of John Ball* (1886) and *News from Nowhere* (1890), also written in instalments for *Commonweal.* And third, the late prose romances, beginning with *The House of Wolfings* (1888) and concluding with *The Sundering Flood* —finished a few days before Morris's death.

Morris did not write the *Chants* for the critics, or even for posterity, but simply for the day-to-day needs of the movement—for Hyndman's debate with Bradlaugh, for a Socialist League entertainment, for the funeral of Linnell. If they served the occasion for which they were written, then they had done the job which he intended them to do. And they *did* do this job to such a degree that it is as part of the history of the early Socialist movement that they must be judged. "Sometimes in summer-time", recalled F.W. Jowett,

> "the joint forces of Leeds and Bradford Socialism tramped together to

[1] *Letters,* pp. 158-9.

spread the gospel by printed and spoken word in neighbouring villages. And at eventide, on the way home, as we walked in country lanes or on river bank, we sang—

'What is this, the sound and rumour? What is this that all men hear,
Like the wind in hollow valleys when the storm is drawing near,
Like the rolling on of ocean in the eventide of fear?
'Tis the people marching on. . .'

And we believed they were!"[1]

Morris did not feel it to be the least an offence against his dignity, or the Purity of Art, that he should be asked to do this job. He could not understand the "art for art's sake" argument.[2] If verse written under these conditions should turn out to be ephemeral, this did not trouble him in the least. The Socialist movement stood for "life", and if his poems helped to feed this life, they found their immortality in the spirit of the movement which they helped to shape. He did not labour to create new forms. He strove simply to do the best he could with the materials which lay to his hand:

"O why and for what are we waiting? while our brothers droop and die,
And on every wind of the heavens a wasted life goes by.

"How long shall they reproach us where crowd on crowd they dwell,
Poor ghosts of the wicked city, the gold-crushed hungry hell?

"Through squalid life they laboured, in sordid grief they died,
Those sons of a mighty mother, those props of England's pride."

And the poems caught fire in the hearts of the comrades whose feelings were already high within them, and whose previous knowledge of romantic verse had accustomed them to the material which Morris used.

[1] F.W. Jowett, *What Made Me a Socialist* (n.d.).

[2] See May Morris, I, p. 200: "True, we have all of us heard discussions as to whether art should be for art's sake, should itself be its own end, or be done for a purpose—most fruitless discussions they are, I must say, mere confusion of words. You may be sure both that a real artist does his work because he likes it, and that when done 'tis a blessing to his fellows. . . Every work of art is both a good thing in itself though nobody sees it, and if seen will influence the minds and lives of men, and lead to other things scarce guessed at by those who wrought it."

With all this it may be said—without either belittling the poems or condemning them for not being what they never were intended to be—that the *Chants* cannot be said to lay the foundations of a poetry of "revolutionary realism". Look back at these verses and note both how moving and effective they are—how unquestionable in their sincerity, their horror at the waste beyond remedy; and also how much they rely upon words, images, rhythms coined in the romantic movement. The city is "wicked" and a "hell", like Shelley's "London": the lives of the workers are "squalid" and "sordid", and they are "poor ghosts" who "droop and die". The sense of "crowds" as something oppressive is present. Morris rarely expresses any sense of vitality in the working class, but only in the "Cause" itself, the hope of the future. The hatred of industrialism as such is never absent for long.

The Pilgrims of Hope provides many examples of this. At its opening stands "The Message of the March Wind"—a remarkable poem, which is fully within the tradition of late romanticism. The setting of the poem is that of pastoral peace, with its increase and fruition, and its ancient associations—the ox-yard, the grey church, the grey homes of our fathers. Into this peace comes the "March wind", which we cannot help feeling is a close relation to Shelley's "West Wind"—the "destroyer and preserver". On the one hand it tells of the city, of "unrest" and "gold", and the "haggard and grim" life of the people. On the other it tells of the "hope of the people" and "strife". Where Shelley's message is idealized to the point of abstraction—a hatred of tyranny, a generalized aspiration towards freedom—Morris's accusation against the "great city", London, commercialism, is far more specific. Its crime lies in the poverty and wearisome toil of the workers, their deprivation of any part in this pastoral beauty, and of the heritage of the arts. But the effect of the poem is not one of courage and decision in the awakened struggle. Rather, there is an undertow of regret at the passing of this peace. "Shall we be glad always?" the lovers ask. And the answer seems to come, "Hark, the wind in the elm-boughs!" This moment of love, poised before the entering of the struggle, is a sad moment: foreshadowing the loss of rest, ease of mind, beauty, even of love. The slow-moving line, "This land we have loved in our love and our leisure", scarcely conceals the nostalgia underneath. And then the sharp change of focus, to the interior so reminiscent of a scene from one of Hardy's tales of the passing of rural England:

> "Come back to the inn, love, and the lights and the fire,
> And the fiddler's old tune and the shuffling of feet. . ."

Here is a glimpse of a warm community, where the lovers are secure and at ease. The poem leaves us less with a sense of of hope than with the poignancy of loss? Surely it is no accident that it is to this idealized pastoral scene that the hero of the poem returns at last, with his love lost in the struggle, and "the half of life gone":

> "The forks shine white in the sun round the yellow red-wheeled wain,
> Where the mountain of hay grows fast; and now from out of the lane
> Comes the ox-team drawing another, comes the bailiff and the beer,
> And thump, thump, goes the farmer's nag o'er the narrow bridge of the weir."

"The Message of the March Wind" was written for the March number of *Commonweal* in 1885, at the time when Morris had thrust upon him by events the responsibility for the leadership of a section of the Socialist movement. It is perhaps not far-fetched to suggest that it gives a moment of insight into the turmoil of Morris's personal feelings at the time. It suggests to us how strong the grip of his will and his political convictions had to be over his inclinations—inclinations which rebelled at the daily struggle in the heart of industrial capitalism, and which beckoned him back to Kelmscott and the repose of his art.

Thereafter *The Pilgrims of Hope* seems to make several false starts, to be hesitant in plot and direction, until—halfway through—it finds in the Commune and the sundering of the lovers by the friend a theme which carries it through to the end. The weaknesses are obvious and need cause no surprise. The poem was written hastily in monthly instalments for *Commonweal,* and Morris did not wish it to be re-published without considerable revision.[1] But, for all this, it contains passages where the dramatic power overcomes the facility (which is sometimes downright slapdash) of the writing. Among such are the famous "New Birth"—the conversion to Socialism: the brawl at an open-air meeting and arrest of the hero: the meeting with the bourgeois war-machine in Paris; and the fine "Sending to the War", where the jingo military parade through London streets lined with poverty and unemployment gives place suddenly to the dream of the "deeds of another day":

"Far and far was I borne, away o'er the years to come,
And again was the ordered march, and the thunder of the drum,
And the bickering points of steel, and the horses shifting about
'Neath the flashing swords of the captains—then the silence after the shout—

"Sun and wind in the street, familiar things made clear,
Made strange by the breathless waiting for the deeds that are drawing a-near.
For woe had grown into will, and wrath was bared of its sheath,
And stark in the streets of London stood the crop of the dragon's teeth.
Where then in my dream were the poor and the wall of faces wan?
Here and here by my side, shoulder to shoulder of man,
Hope in the simple folk, hope in the hearts of the wise,
For the happy life to follow, or death and the ending of lies,
Hope is awake in the faces angerless now no more,
Till the new peace dawn on the world, the fruit of the people's war. . ."

The remarkable thing about *The Pilgrims of Hope* is not the weakness in construction, which might be expected, or the technical slackness bred of haste and lack of concentration, but the degree to which Morris succeeds in escaping

[1] See Buxton-Forman, *The Books of William Morris* (1897): "I could not persuade its author to reprint it; he considered it wanted more revision than he could give it at the time."

from the limitations of middle-class experience and outlook. In many touches—the reduction of the hero to a wage-labourer, his humiliation by his employer, his sufferings in unemployment—Morris succeeds in presenting capitalist society with a realism which he does not attempt in any other of his creative writings. Moreover, the poem rediscovers (although within a romantic mode) heroic values which the romantic tradition could envisage only in a stereotyped literary past of legend: Morris discloses the heroic in the everyday events of the revolutionary propaganda, and in the Commune. Even in the sad theme of the sundering of the lovers, with its obvious echoes from Morris's personal life, there is a dignity, and in particular a respect for the woman's personality and emotional identity which is alien to the conventions of Victorian romanticism.

But new attitudes, new advances in human consciousness, cannot find their complete expression in the forms of the old. In a letter of 1891 Morris remarked humourously of a poem he was writing: "My wig! but it is garrulous: I can't help it, the short lines and my old recollections lead me on. . ."[1] "My old recollections. . ."—this is an exact description of the process by which Morris, in his hasty writing, fell into the rhythms, the associations, the vocabulary of his apprenticeship to poetry. Moreover, as we have seen, Morris still clung to his Pre-Raphaelite view that art, by definition, must be "a thing of beauty", and that beauty and realism in the nineteenth century must be incompatible. It was in the year in which he wrote *The Pilgrims of Hope* that he wrote to Fred Henderson:

> "Now language is utterly degraded in our daily lives, and poets have to make a new tongue each for himself: before he can even begin his story he must elevate his means of expression from the daily jabber to which centuries of degradation have reduced it."[2]

But this special vocabulary of poetry had been fashioned by

[1] *Letters,* p. 338. [2] First edition, p. 879.

late romanticism (and most notably by Morris himself in his own middle period) to provide a dream-world of aspiration untarnished by the sordid realities, a "poetic" refuge from "the world". Clearly, it could not be adequate to give full expression to Morris's new experience and convictions.

Morris no longer saw his art as the central battlefield: if he could strike a blow there for the "Cause", so much the better. The immediate task—as he saw it—was to change life itself: he was too old, too busy, too much a romantic bred and born, to concentrate his faculties at the end of his life upon transforming his art. There would be time enough for those who came after him to do that. "If I can't be the Laureate of reading men", he remarked on one occasion, "I'll be the Laureate of sweating men." In the small Socialist movement he felt there was being built an audience of a new type, where labour and intellect, action and reflection, were no longer opposed, and where the poet (like the *scald* and *makar* of old) was regarded not as an eccentric or a fragile genius but as a craftsman with special gifts, of value to the community, exercising these gifts to please both himself and his fellows. A friend of his relates that once, in the underground, a working man recognized Morris and accosted him: "They tell me you're a poet, Mr. Morris? Well, I know nothing about poets or poetry, but I'm blooming well sure I know a *man,* and *you're* one, by God!" Morris was delighted, and said afterwards: "That's the stuff I'm working for, and, mark you, that's the stuff, too, that in the long run I'm working for in prose and poetry as well."[1]

IV. The Prose Romances

Between 1888 and the end of his life scarcely a year passed when Morris did not add one or more lengthy volume to his series of prose romances. Chief among them were *The House of the Wolfings,* and *The Roots of the Mountains,*

[1] William Sharp in *The Atlantic Monthly,* December, 1896.

written during the last years of the Socialist League: and, in succeeding years, *The Well at the World's End, The Wood Beyond the World, The Water of the Wondrous Isles,* and *The Sundering Flood.* These romances appear to present a strange contrast to Morris's active political and intellectual life. To Shaw they were "a startling relapse into literary Pre-Raphaelitism"—"nothing more nor less than the resuscitation of Don Quixote's burnt library".[1] Whatever judgement be made upon them, they certainly provide a striking example of the strange and unpredictable courses which the creative imagination will follow.

From beginning to end, Morris's writing (with the exception of *The Pilgrims of Hope*) partakes of the nature of dream. We are taken out of the world we know into a world having its existence only in the writer's imagination, with its own inner consistency and its own laws, unlike those of the real world but related distantly to them. Into this world of dream Morris was driven by his "hatred of civilization" during his youthful revolt: and ever after his imagination found its natural expression in this form. Ralph and Ursula, in *The Well at the World's End* are told by the Elder of the Innocent Folk:

> "For ye of the World beyond the Mountains are stronger and more godlike than we. . . and ye wear away your lives desiring that which ye may scarce get; and yet set your hearts on high things, desiring to be masters of the very Gods. Therefore ye know sickness and sorrow, and oft ye die before your time, so that ye must depart and leave undone things which ye deem ye were born to do; which to all men is grievous. And because of all this ye desire healing and thriving, whether good come of it, or ill. Therefore ye do but right to seek to the Well at the World's End, that ye may the better accomplish that which behoveth you, and that ye may serve your fellows and deliver them from the thralldom of those that be strong and unwise and unkind, of whom we have heard strange tales."

At the root of the dream lies this separation between the boundless desire of the heart and the poor or bitter realities

[1] May Morris, II, p. xxxviii.

of life, the thirst for waters at the world's end. But while this helps us to understand something of the character of the dream-form—the "poetic" vocabulary of *The Earthly Paradise*, the archaic diction, unworldly relationships, and leisurely hypnotic rhythms of the prose romances—it tells us by no means all.

The extraordinary thing about Morris's employment of dream lies in the wide variety of uses to which he put it. At times he used dream to build a compensation-world to which he could escape; at other times he constructed a world with values and conditions totally unlike his own, only in order to be able to criticize and understand his own the better. We should not forget that the dream was the form he chose for his realistic meditations, upon the meaning of history (*A Dream of John Ball*) and upon the quality of life in a Communist society (*News from Nowhere*). In his late years Morris consciously turned his predisposition towards dream into a means of liberating his imagination from the sordid restrictions of a society he hated. He was not ashamed of the romantic nature of his art, although he did not recommend others to imitate it. "The feeling for art in us artists is genuine", he wrote in 1893, "though we have to work in the midst of the ignorance of those whose whole life ought to be spent in the production of works of art." But the blossom of the art of the future, "I shall not see: therefore I may be excused if, in common with other artists, I try to express myself through the art of to-day, which seems to us to be only a survival of the organic art of the past. . ."[1]

The first two prose romances, *The House of the Wolfings* (1888) and *The Roots of the Mountains* (1889), employ the dream-form differently from the romances of his last four or five years. This makes them more acceptable than the others to the reader who approaches them with a literal mind. In certain respects they are more realistic: where the supernatural intervenes it is more as a manifestation of the beliefs

[1] "The Deeper Meaning of the Struggle", *Letters*, p. 357.

of the people than as an external device of the plot. The narrative flows from the action of the characters, not primarily—as in the last romances—from the tricks of magic. wood-goddesses, witches, and wierd.

Nevertheless, these romances should *not* be read with a literal mind, or Morris's intention will be misunderstood. He knew perfectly well that he could not reconstruct with accurate detail the lives of the Germanic peoples at the dawn of the Middle Ages, although such detail as he did know—of craftsmanship, custom, and circumstance—he employed to construct the special atmosphere of these two dreams. He knew well that his "Folk of the Kindreds" and "woodland carles" would not really have conversed, made love and quarrelled with the melodious courtesy which he gave to them. His intention was quite different, and was expressed in a letter while he was working on *The House of the Wolfings:* "It is meant to illustrate the melting of the individual into the society of the tribes..."[1] The dream-picture is quite consciously idealized.[2] Morris had long been fascinated by the contribution which the Germanic peoples had made toward the art and social structure of feudalism in Western Europe.[3] With his conversion to Socialism, this interest deepened and his knowledge of the life of the Germanic tribes was supplemented in his many discussions with Belfort Bax.

In *Socialism: its Growth and Outcome* Morris and Bax referred to the difference between the "impersonal state" and the "simple and limited kinship group":

> "The difference between these opposing circumstances of society is, in fact, that between an organism and a mechanism. The earlier condi-

[1] *Letters,* p. 302; Morris discussed the values of the tribal "kindred" in "The Development of Modern Society", *Commonweal,* July 19th, 1890.

[2] H.H. Sparling, *The Kelmscott Press and William Morris, Master-Craftsman,* p. 50, recounts that when a German archaeologist wrote to Morris asking him what new sources of information he had used in writing *The House of the Wolfings,* Morris exclaimed: "Doesn't the fool realize... that it's a romance, a work of fiction—that it's all LIES!"

[3] Morris's hatred for the Roman Empire found frequent expression; e.g. *Letters* p. 265; *Commonweal,* May, 1886 ("Socialism from the Root Up", I).

tion in which everything, art, science. . . law, industry, were personal, and aspects of a living body, is opposed to the civilized condition in which all these elements have become mechanical, uniting to build up mechanical life, and themselves the product of machines material and moral."[1]

It was Morris's intention in these two romances to recapture something of the organic and personal life of the tribe or folk: and (as, later, in *News from Nowhere*) he was concerned not so much with the details as with the quality of life.

The House of the Wolfings is marred by the unsuccessful combination of prose and verse, and by the intrusion of the Pre-Raphaelite maiden, the Hall-Sun. Morris is at his weakest in these two romances when treating personal relationships. His strength is found always in his treatment of social relations, in the collective life of the folk, in the Hall, at the Folk-Mote, in their labour, their battles, their ceremonies. From the opening paragraphs, we are given that strong sense of *place,* of the relation between man and his environment in his struggle with nature, which recurs in all the last romances:

"For many generations the folk that now dwelt there had learned the craft of iron-founding, so that they had no lack of wares of iron and steel, whether they were tools of handicraft or weapons for hunting and for war. It was the men of the Folk, who coming adown by the river-side had made that clearing. The tale tells not whence they came, but belike from the dales of the distant mountains, and from dales and mountains and plains further aloof and yet further."

Thiodolf's speech to the Wood-Sun is an expression of the values uniting the kindreds:

"Mine eyes are cleared again, and I can see the kindreds as they are, and their desire of life and scorn of death, and this is what they have made me myself. Now therefore shall they and I together earn the merry days to come, the winter hunting and the spring sowing, the summer haysel, the ingathering of harvest, the happy rest of midwinter,

[1] *Socialism: Its Growth and Outcome,* p. 21.

and Yuletide with the memory of the Fathers, wedded to the hope of the days to be. Well may they bid me help them who have holpen me! Well may they bid me die who have made me live!. . . I have lived with them, and eaten and drunken with them, and toiled with them, and led them in battle and the place of wounds and slaughter; they are mine and I am theirs; and through them am I of the whole earth, and all the kindreds of it. . ."

Morris's vocabulary, with its emphasis upon antiquity and the *difference* between the values of the folk and those of to-day, is an essential part of his purpose. As he becomes more sure of himself, in *The Roots of the Mountains,* the clumsy and self-conscious archaisms become less noticeable, and the vocabulary becomes melodious and consistent, sustaining the remote, impersonal and dream-like quality in which the values of the peoples can be shadowed forth. Had he been content, in this second romance, to have limited his tale to the central theme of the reuniting of the kindreds and their resistance to the invaders, treating the whole in an aloof and impersonal manner, *The Roots of the Mountains* would have stood high among his work. Unfortunately he chose to weave in and out of it his romantic love themes (not, unfortunately, without Victorian overtones), which are incompatible with the more serious intention of the whole.

Moreover, we are already aware in *The Roots of the Mountains* of the motive for writing which becomes dominant in the other late romances—that of pure self-indulgence in pleasurable reverie in which neither Morris's intellect nor his deeper feelings are seriously engaged. He had at first intended that the Bride should die during the tale, but he changed his mind, marrying her to Folk-Might, with the rationalization, "it would be a very good alliance for the Burgdalers and the Silverdalers both, and I don't think sentiment ought to stand in the way."[1] Well and good: but such repeated compromises rob the tale of its dignity and sombre interest, and reduce it

[1] May Morris's Introduction to *The Roots of the Mountains, Works,* XV, p. xi. R.A. Muncey said that Morris told him that he had written the book on a train journey to Aberdeen and back (*The Leaguer,* October, 1907).

to the level of wilful fantasy—like an imaginative child's day-dreams, set forth in noble prose, and shot through with a mature men's insight into history. The final fight for Silver-dale is described with all of Morris's clear pictorial genius; but the issue is never in doubt, neither heroes nor heroines are ever seriously endangered, it is a mere skirmish beside the day-long fight by the ford in *The House of the Wolfings.* As one critic has shown, Morris had come to have a reluctance to "suffer imaginatively".[1] From the *Life and Death of Jason* onwards, his creative writing had tended to become facile—something which engaged only half of his attention—and he had met and engaged with his age on other grounds. No doubt when he started the romance he had proposed to carry for-ward the tale of the kindreds to a further point in history; but he had fallen victim to his desire to please himself, and if he was disappointed with the book's reception he had himself to blame.

Thereafter came a series of romances: *The Story of the Glittering Plain* (1890); *The Well at the World's End* (com-menced 1892); *The Wood Beyond the World* (1894); *The Water of the Wondrous Isles* (1895); and *The Sundering Flood* (1896); as well as several shorter tales and translations. In all these romances Morris's desire to please himself is uppermost—just as the Kelmscott Press was no part of the earlier "warfare against the age" of the Firm but was a source of unashamed enjoyment to the designer. When a critic detected a Socialist allegory in *The Wood Beyond the World,* Morris was quick to disillusion him: "it is meant for a tale pure and simple, with nothing didactic about it".[2]

Approached with a mind earnestly seeking hidden truths, these romances would be unreadable. But if they are read in the same mood as that in which they were written, Morris's own pleasure is infectious. Here his mind and imagination are "free-wheeling", and his artistry in story-telling is given loose rein. All the tales move in a vague medieval setting,

[1] D. Hoare, *op. cit.,* pp. 43 ff. [2] *Letters,* p. 371.

peculiar to Morris's imagination. The intention of the tales is, above all, decorative. They are fairy-stories, legends, for which the belief of the active mind is not invited. Suffering, pain or death are passed over in a paragraph, while sensuous beauty or physical love are embroidered for whole chapters. Hero and heroine bear charmed lives, and the evil witch and baron are always worsted. If there are battles and blood, the scarlet threads look pleasant in the tapestry.

Had Morris gone soft in the head? Is this really a return to *The Earthly Paradise,* and the evasion and fear of life which lurked under it? Not in the least. Some element of relaxation, rather than refuge, from life is present: as also perhaps some element of compensation for what he had missed, as he embroidered lovers on his own regret. But the undertow of death, the sense of guilt, the oscillation between sensuous joy and horror that underlay *The Earthly Paradise* are vanquished. In only one romance is any really significant decision taken freely by hero or heroine: and that is when the hero in *The Story of the Glittering Plain* chooses to leave the Acre of the Undying and return to the land of mortality, to his kindred and his love. Striving to enter the Acre of the Undying, across deserts and mountain passes, are men who resemble the restless and unsatisfied Wanderers of *The Earthly Paradise* and upon these the story turns its back.

In these curious fairy-stories there are echoes from all of Morris's previous work.[1] But all are muted in the prevailing mood of calm and fulfilment. These are tales, not so much of desire unsatisfied, but of desire fulfilled. The water of the well at the world's end, which Ralph and Ursula drink, is not of immortality but of more abundant life. In each tale, hero and heroine start from a secure hearth and home in a society pictured with realistic detail, pass through adventures, trials

[1] For example, in *The Water of the Wondrous Isles* note the parallel between the death of the evil knight who is Birdalone's suitor and the "Haystack in the Flood"; also the image of the Kings and Queens struck dead in the postures of life which recurs in *The Earthly Paradise.*

and magic experience, but return in the end once again to their homes. Most characteristic is *The Waters of the Wondrous Isles,* with its plot formed almost like a perfect figure-of-eight: the stealing of Birdalone as a child from the town by the wood; her growth to a young maiden in the cottage by the lakeside, tending the goats and hunting in the wood; her escape across the lake, with its magic isles which figure like a repeated decorative motif; her encounter with her lover; her retirement to the City of the Five Crafts; her return across the lake; the fulfilment of her love, without marriage rite or ceremony, in the cottage where she grew up as a girl; and final return with her lover to the town of her birth. Where, in *The Earthly Paradise,* pleasure had always seemed an uneasy dream on the edge of a bitter reality, here we are always on the edge of awakening to the freshness and fulfilment of life, as when Birdalone dreams:

> "Somehow were they two, the witch and she, amidmost of the Isle of Nothing, and the witch drew close anigh her, and was just going to whisper into her ear something of measureless horror, when she awoke; and the sun was bright outside the shaded whiteness of her tent; the shadows of the leaves were dancing on the ground of it; the morning wind was rustling the tree-boughs, and the ripple of the stream was tinkling hard by. . ."

This freshness, this sense of growth in the June English countryside, of the continuity of life, is the reality beneath the romance. This is the Morris whom Yeats knew and described as the "Happiest of Poets".[1] The mournful Pre-Raphaelite ladies of earlier days have given way, in these romances to maidens who can shoot with the bow, swim, ride and generally do most things, including making love, a good deal more capably than their young men, who weep for joy so often that it is a matter of surprise that their armour does not fall to pieces with rust. Perhaps this is a sign of Morris's views on the rights of women, or a cunning way of revenging

[1] W.B. Yeats on "The Happiest of the Poets" in *Collected Works* (1908), pp. 55-70.

himself on Belfort Bax. However that may be, ever and again into these last strange romances there seems to come the figure of Ellen from *News from Nowhere,* saying: "The earth and the growth of it and the life of it! If I could but say or show how I love it!"

V. The Society of the Future

Morris's claim to importance as a political theorist rests upon two grounds. First, he was one of the earliest, and remains one of the most original and creative thinkers within the Marxist tradition in England. Second, he was a pioneer of constructive thought as to the organization of social life within Communist society.

No one familiar with Socialist theory can doubt that Morris stood within the Marxist tradition, despite certain secondary circumstances which have clouded the issue.[1] The evidence is to be found, not in coloured reminiscences or second-hand opinions, but in Morris's own political writings.

The whole of Morris's Socialist writing is rich in illustrations of the class struggle. This, indeed, was to him the point of prime importance, distinguishing revolutionary Socialism from Reformism. Referring directly to Sidney Webb and the Fabians, he wrote in 1889:

> "What is the real gate which will pull up these soft Socialists, who so long as they are allowed to steal the goose will not object to give the giblets to the poor? This is the barrier which they will not be able to pass, so long as they are in their present minds, the *acknowledgement of the class war.* The 'Socialists' of this kind are blind as to the essence of modern society. They hope for a revolution, which is not *the* Revolution, but a revolution which is to ignore the facts that have led up to it and will bring it about. . .
>
> "It is most important that young Socialists should have this fact of the class-war always before them. It explains past history, and in the present gives us the only solid hope for the future. And it must be

[1] See Appendix II and Paul Meier, *La Pensée Utopique de William Morris,* (Paris, 1972), discussed in the Postscript below.

understood that it is only by the due working out of this class-war to its end, *the abolition of classes,* that Socialism can come about. . . The middle-class semi-Socialists, driven by class instinct, preach revolution without the class struggle; which is an absurdity and an impossibility."[1]

The objection that the Socialists themselves create the class-war, he brushed aside with contempt:

"Who or what sets class against class? The whole evolution of society. That is, the existence of the classes."[2]

Morris accepted also the Marxist theory of the State. The privilege of the capitalist class, he never tired of repeating,

"is but the privilege of the robber by force of arms, is just the thing which it is the aim and end of our present organization to uphold; and all the formidable executive at the back of it, army, police, law courts, presided over by the judge as representing the executive, is directed towards this one end—to take care that the richest shall rule, and shall have full licence to injure the commonwealth to the full extent of his riches."[3]

His experience in the fight for free speech, and on "Bloody Sunday", rid him of any illusions as to the impartiality of capitalist justice, and his one Socialist play, *The Tables Turned: or Nupkins Awakened,* is a bitter satire on the procedure of the courts in these cases—the difference in the treatment of rich and poor, the perjury of the police, the stupidity and prejudice of the judge. Commenting on the aftermath of "Bloody Sunday", he wrote: "Thus at one stroke vanishes the dream of bringing about peaceably and constitutionally the freedom which we long for." If the bourgeoisie were made really afraid by the rising movement, and not merely "a little alarmed", "then we shall see suppression of indoor meetings also: suppression of associa-

[1] *Commonweal,* September 28th, 1889. [2] *Ibid.,* December 22nd, 1888.
[3] "The Socialist Ideal in Art", *Works,* XXIII, p. 263.

tion, Press prosecutions, and the like; and there is plenty of law for all that".[1]

Morris did not shrink from any of the revolutionary conclusions which flow from these principles. Above all, his writings and life reveal inflexible opposition to imperialism and chauvinism in any form. Regard, for example, his notes in *Commonweal* when war between Germany and France seemed possible:

> "If war really becomes imminent our duties as Socialists are clear enough, and do not differ from those we have to act on ordinarily. To further the spread of international feeling between the workers by all means possible; to point out to our own workmen that foreign competition and rivalry, or commercial war, culminating at last in open war, are necessities of the plundering classes, and that the race and commercial quarrels of these classes only concern us so far as we can use them as opportunities for fostering discontent and revolution; that the interests of the workmen are the same in all countries and they can never really be enemies of each other; that the men of our labouring classes, therefore, should turn a deaf ear to the recruiting sergeant, and refuse to allow themselves to be dressed up in red and be taught to form a part of the modern killing machine for the honour and glory of a country in which they have only a dog's share of many kicks and few halfpence,—all this we have to preach always, though in the event of imminent war we may have to preach it more emphatically."[2]

In one further point Morris's writing and his practice prepare us for themes made familiar by the experience of this century: in his search for the best type of organization and leadership for the revolutionary Socialist party. His views were worked out through trial and error. He came to think in terms of a party of "cadres", convinced propagandists and agitators, drawn in the main from the working class (p. 410), which would in the revolutionary period assume leadership of that class's wider organizations.[3] He stressed always that sub-

[1] *Commonweal*, January 28th, 1888. [2] *Ibid.*, January 1st, 1887.

[3] The whole process is envisaged in the chapter, "How the Change Came", in *News from Nowhere.*

ordination of "individual whims" to the collective decisions of the party (p. 304), whose leadership should not be made up of a "government and an opposition" (p. 533). Full-time organizers should be "kept in very strict order" by the party (p. 477), and should representatives be sent to Parliament or onto other bodies, it must be understood that they went not as individuals but as delegates of the party "under good party discipline" (p. 614). "I now see", he wrote to Mahon in 1886, "the absolute necessity of discipline in a fighting body, which of course in no sense resembles the Societys of the future."[1]

Morris was well aware of the dangers of speculating about the form of this future society. "It is impossible to build up a scheme for the society of the future", he wrote,

> "for no man can really think himself out of his own days; his palace of days to come can only be constructed from the aspirations forced upon him by his present surroundings, and from his dreams of the life of the past, which themselves cannot fail to be more or less unsubstantial imaginings."[2]

Nevertheless, the 1880s and 1890s were rich with speculations of this kind, and Morris made many contributions to them.

Morris's picture of the future found twofold expression: first, in many scattered references and passages in his lectures and articles; and second in *News from Nowhere.* In both places he had no intention whatsoever to make cut-and-dried prophecies, but rather to make hints and suggestions. These suggestions are not always consistent with each other: the choices before men in a Communist society (he saw) were numerous, the manifestations of their social life would take many forms. For example, he made no pretence at consistency when speculating as to the architecture of Communism. In *News from Nowhere* he leaves the suggestion that the majority

[1] R. Page Arnot, *William Morris, the Man and the Myth,* p. 62.
[2] *Socialism: Its Growth and Outcome,* pp. 17-18.

of the people live in detached villas and cottages, with here and there in the countryside a college of learning and manufacture. In other writings he dwelt more often on the idea of communal dwelling-houses, "with good public cooking and washing rooms. . . beautiful halls for the common meal. . . a pleasant and ample garden, and a good play-ground."[1] Again he proposed (especially for London) tall blocks of flats "in what might be called vertical streets", with ample privacy for each family, common laundries and kitchens, and public rooms for social gathering.[2] "Often when I have been sickened by the stupidity of the mean idiotic rabbit warrens that rich men build for themselves in Bayswater", he wrote,

> "I console myself with visions of the noble communal hall of the future, unsparing of materials, generous in worthy ornament, alive with the noblest thoughts of our time, and the past, embodied in the best art which a free and manly people could produce. . ."

"I can't see why we should think it a hardship to eat with the people we work with; I am sure that as to many things, such as valuable books, pictures. . . we shall find it better to club our means together. . ."[3] In both *News from Nowhere* and the lectures, the emphasis is upon the communal life. But (as Morris never ceased to repeat) true individualism was only possible in a Communist society, which needed and valued the contribution of each individual to the common good; and, in a society which fostered true variety, he knew that different men would choose to live in different ways.

Morris tended, in his speculations, to leap over the transitional stage of Socialism, and come to rest in fully-established Communist society. When Socialism "ceases to be militant and becomes triumphant", he wrote, "it will be Communism".[4] Following St. Simon, he emphasized

[1] May Morris, II, p. 129. [2] *Ibid.*, pp. 127-8.
[3] "How We Live and How We Might Live", *Signs of Change*, p. 31.
[4] "Communism", *Works*, XXIII, p. 271.

that "government" in a Socialist society would become increasingly rather "an administration of *things* than a government of *persons*".[1] Throughout his theoretical writings he made use of the contrast (first learned from Carlyle) of "false" and "true" society—of property relations and laws on the one hand, and human relations and morality on the other:

"That true society of loved and lover, parent and child, friend and friend, the society of well-wishers, of reasonable people conscious of the aspirations of humanity and of the duties we owe to it through one another—this society, I say, is held together and exists by its own inherent right and reason, in spite of what is usually thought to be the cement of society, arbitrary authority. . ."

Thus Communist society implied the re-establishment of the personal and voluntary bonds of society and the disappearance of the impersonal and compulsive relations based on the ownership of property and the maintenance of class rule—the re-creation of the society of "the Wolfings" shorn of its barbarity and superstition, and enriched by the culture of past ages. The "withering away of the state" assumed great importance to Morris, not (in the negative sense employed by some of his Anarchist colleagues) as the absence of all social bonds, but in the positive sense of the re-establishment at a higher level than known before of the human and personal bonds existing even within a class society.

In this respect, he sought to distinguish his views from those of the Fabian State Socialists on the one hand, and the Anarchists on the other. "Even some Socialists", he wrote, "are apt to confuse. . . the co-operative machinery towards which modern life is tending with the essence of Socialism itself."[2] From this there followed—

"the danger of the community falling into bureaucracy, the multiplication of boards and offices, and all the paraphernalia of official authority,

[1] *Letters*, p. 287. See also *Socialism: Its Growth and Outcome*, p. 289.

[2] "Communism", *Works*, XXIII, p. 275.

which is, after all, a burden, even when it is exercised by the delegation of the whole people and in accordance with their wishes."[1]

With Communism, he suggested, the central machinery of the State would disappear (except in so far as it was necessary in arranging matters of production and distribution), not because the citizens would have fewer public responsibilities, but because they would shoulder more themselves. He quarrelled with Bellamy's *Looking Backward* because it gave the impression that "the organization of life and necessary labour" would be dealt with in Socialist society "by a huge national centralization, working by a kind of magic for which no one feels himself responsible." On the contrary, he declared:

"It will be necessary for the unit of administration to be small enough for every citizen to feel himself responsible for its details, and be interested in them; that individual men cannot shuffle off the business of life on to the shoulders of an abstraction called the State, but must deal with it in conscious association with each other. . . Variety of life is as much an aim of true Communism as equality of condition, and. . . nothing but an union of these two will bring about real freedom."[2]

Writing on another occasion, he said:

"To my mind in the new Society, we should form bodies like municipalities, county-boards and parishes, and almost all practical public work would be done by these bodies the members of whom would be working at and living by their ordinary work, and. . . everybody who had any capacity for such work would have to do his share of it."[3]

Controversies in such a society would be more upon matters of fact than of conflicting interests: "Would this or that project benefit the community more?" And the existence of

[1] "True and False Society", *Works*, XXIII, p. 236.

[2] "Looking Backward", *Commonweal*, June 22nd, 1889.

[3] "What Socialists Want", Brit. Mus. Add. MSS. 45333; Lemire, *Unpublished Lectures*, p. 230.

party spirit would be impossible or ridiculous. While the federal principle would tend to assert itself in national life, there would be (on the other hand) "the great council of the socialised world" which would have "the function of the administration of production in its wider sense":

"It would have to see to... the collection and distribution of all information as to the wants of populations and the possibilities of supplying them... Also it would be its necessary duty to safeguard the then recognized principles of society; that is, to guard against any country, or place, or occupation reverting to methods of practices which would be destructive or harmful to the socialistic order, such as any form of the exploitation of labour..."[1]

Such larger federal units would be staffed by delegates from the lower federal units.

Such a society, Morris well understood, could only be reached after the transition period of Socialism, "during which people would be getting rid of the habits of mind bred by the long ages of tyranny and commercial competition...". The fundamental step was not the destruction of all personal property, but of the power for individuals to "turn it into an instrument for the oppression of others".[2] Above all, Morris constantly insisted that even the initial stages of Socialism would lead to an inconceivable transformation in *people,* in their values, relationships, and outlook:

"It is not a small change in life that we advocate, but a very great one... Socialism will transform our lives and habits, and leave the greater part of the political social and religious controversies that we are now so hot about forgotten, useless and lifeless like wrecks stranded on a sea-shore."[3]

"We shall adore what we used to burn, and burn what we used to adore."[4]

[1] *Socialism: Its Growth and Outcome,* pp. 291-2.

[2] "True and False Society", *Works,* XXIII, p. 236.

[3] May Morris, II, p. 199.

[4] "How Shall We Live Then?", *International Review of Social History,* XVI, 1971, Part 2, p. 12; cf. *Commonweal,* February 18th, 1888.

Education, whatever form it took (and few will agree wholeheartedly with the educational system in *News from Nowhere*), would itself be transformed, thus accelerating the change in people:

> "It must of necessity cease to be a preparation for a life of commercial success on the one hand, or of irresponsible labour on the other. . . It will become rather a habit of making the best of the individual's powers in all directions to which he is led by his innate disposition; so that no man will ever 'finish' his education while he is alive. . ."[1]

Everywhere the spirit of the *common* wealth—material, moral, spiritual—will become triumphant.

On one point, above all, Morris expressed himself with strong personal feeling. The division between the intellectual and the worker, the man of "genius" and the people, the manual and "brain" worker, would be finally ended. Although he is unlikely to have read it, Morris reached in his intuitive way the most important statements of Marx in *The Critique of the Gotha Programme:*

> "In a higher phase of Communist society, after the enslaving subordination of individuals under division of labour, and therewith also the antithesis between mental and physical labour, has vanished, after labour has become not merely a means to live but has become itself the primary necessity of life, after the productive forces have also increased with the all-round development of the individual, and all the springs of co-operative wealth flow more abundantly—only then can the narrow horizon of bourgeois right be fully left behind and society inscribe on its banners: from each according to his ability, to each according to his needs."[2]

[1] *Socialism: Its Growth and Outcome,* p. 317.

[2] Paul Meier in his substantial examination of Morris's political thought, *La Pensée Utopique de William Morris* (Paris, 1972), pp. 408-17 argues that Morris cannot have come upon the central themes of the *Critique of the Gotha Programme* independently: "il nous est difficile de croire qu'il ait pu s'élever tout seul à ce niveau théorique." In particular he remarks upon Morris's indebtedness to the theory of the *Critique* in his acceptance of two stages of transition to the new society—Socialism (with inequality of reward) and full communism. He points out that the manuscript of the *Critique,* written in 1875 but not

But for Morris these preconditions of Communism were in themselves primary objectives. The unity of thought and creative labour would find its realization, not only in the society as a whole, but in the life of every member of it:

"From this healthy freedom would spring up the pleasures of intellectual development, which the men of civilization so foolishly try to separate from sensuous life, and to glorify at its expense. Men would follow knowledge and the creation of beauty for their own sakes, and not for the enslavement of their fellows... The man who felt keenest the pleasure of lying on the hill-side... among the sheep on a summer night, would be no less fit for the enjoyment of the great communal hall with all its splendours of arch and column, and vault and tracery."[1]

Just as physical labour would no longer carry with it any indignity, but rather the reverse, so intellectual labour at the expense of the exercise of bodily faculties would appear as an abuse of the fullness of life.

Morris is only one of the latest in the tradition, reaching back to the ancient Greeks, where this ideal has found expression. But he was one of the first to show how it may at last be realized in a definite society. Among the ideas which influenced his young friend W.B. Yeats, this took firm root and grew to its noble expression in his poem, "Among School Children":

"Labour is blossoming or dancing where
The body is not bruised to pleasure soul,
Nor beauty born out of its own despair,
Nor blear-eyed wisdom out of midnight oil.

O chestnut-tree, great-rooted blossomer,
Are you the leaf, the blossom or the bole?
O body swayed to music, O brightening glance,
How can we know the dancer from the dance?"

published until 1891, was in the keeping of Engels, and suggests that Morris—directly or through the medium of Bax—was acquainted with its themes. This is possible. But see Postscript for further discussion.

[1] "The Society of the Future", May Morris, II, p. 467.

VI. News from Nowhere

Most of these reflections about Socialist society were made by Morris at different dates between 1884 and 1889, and show clearly the way in which he was turning over the ideas which found their full expression in *News from Nowhere,* written in instalments for *Commonweal* in 1890.

The writing of *News from Nowhere* strikes one with a sense of inevitability—it is such a characteristic expression of Morris's genius, springing so logically from his development both as creative artist and as political theorist. With unselfconscious artistry he drew, while writing, upon those personal experiences which lay ready to hand: the story begins with his awakening at his own house in Hammersmith, strangely transformed; it ends at his own house in Kelmscott, and the journey thither up the Thames was one which he had himself enjoyed.[1] When reading "How the Change Came" we are aware of Morris's experiences on "Bloody Sunday". We are aware throughout of his enthusiasm for Gothic architecture and of his life-long practice of the decorative arts. We are aware of current debates between himself and the Fabians and Anarchists. We are aware of his interest in the writings of Fourier, his enthusiasm for More's *Utopia,* and his warm response to Samuel Butler's *Erewhon.*[2] We are aware of the ever-present intention in Morris's mind to contrast the variety and simplicity of the life of "Nowhere" with the bureaucratic State Socialism (or "managerial revolution") of Bellamy's *Looking Backward,* which was then so much in vogue, and whose regimented labour battalions and tubular

[1] See Stirling, *op. cit.,* p. 120 f.

[2] May Morris testifies in several places to her father's delight in *Erewhon,* and there seems to be a clear sign of Morris's indebtedness to it in the conclusion to Ch. IX ("Concerning Love") of *News from Nowhere,* where he envisages an improvement in the comeliness and beauty of the people in a Communist society. For an excellent study of the sources of *News from Nowhere,* see A.L. Morton, *The English Utopia* (1953).

conveniences Morris dubbed "a cockney paradise".[1] Indeed, we are aware that his opposition to *Looking Backward* led him to wilful exaggeration, more than once, on the other side. Above all, we are aware of Morris's practical participation in the Socialist movement, his study of Marx, his understanding of the class struggle:

> " 'Tell me one thing, if you can', said I. 'Did the change. . . come peacefully?'
>
> " 'Peacefully?' said he. 'What peace was there amongst those poor, confused wretches of the nineteenth century? It was war from beginning to end: bitter war, till hope and pleasure put an end to it. . .' "

What a world of personal feeling underlies such passages as this!

In sum, *News from Nowhere* seems to have grown spontaneously rather than to have been constructed with careful artifice. We are aware of William Morris, writing fluently in his study in the intervals of propaganda or designing, drawing on the experience of both his public and his private life, making no attempt to disguise the intrusion of his own temperamental likes and dislikes into the narrative. Indeed, he wrote on one occasion: "The only safe way of reading a utopia is to consider it as the expression of the temperament of its author."[2]

The key to the artistic power and unity of *News from Nowhere* lies in the fact that it is a Scientific Utopia. The contradiction implied by the coupling of these two words was intuitively perceived by Morris, and was quite deliberately turned into a fruitful source of tension, underlying the whole tale.

We have already noted that the characteristic form taken by Morris's imagination was that of dream. But here we do

[1] Glasier, p. 198. Another remark provoked by *Looking Backward* is recorded by May Morris (*Works,* XVI, p. xxviii): "If they brigaded *me* into a regiment of workers, I'd just lie on my back and kick."

[2] "Looking Backward", *Commonweal,* June 22nd, 1899.

not have—as in *The Defence of Guenevere,* or *The Earthly Paradise,* or *The House of the Wolfings*—the dream-form employed to take us entirely out of our own world into a world that is strange. In both *News from Nowhere* and *A Dream of John Ball,* Morris breaks with his usual practice, and skilfully interweaves the dream and the conscious mind, counterposing realism and romance. In both, the narrative commences with humdrum everyday reality, described in a leisurely conversational way, passes into the dream of past or future, and returns at the end to the everyday world. But, unlike *The Eve of St. Agnes* of his poetic master, Keats, where the bright illusion is made more poignant by the stormy and colourless reality surrounding it, reality is allowed to enter into the heart of the dream itself, in the person of Morris the narrator; and it is reality which is made more poignant by the dream when we come back to the real world at the end.

Never for long, in *News from Nowhere,* does Morris allow us to forget this sense of tension between the real and the ideal. This is the role which he constructs for himself as narrator. As we visit London, listen to the conversations with old Hammond, hear the characters discuss problems of morality, we do not relapse into dream—we are sometimes made uncomfortably awake. We are made to question continually our own society, our own values and lives. This is why the story engages our feelings. We cannot sit back as spectators, looking at a pretty never-never land. Always we are conscious of Morris's troubled brow, his sense of not being a part of the scenes through which he moves. He is the link between our experience and the future.

Observe with what skill Morris builds up this tension. If he had made his narrator fall into some Rip Van Winkle sleep, and enter the new world with full explanations all round, to be conducted round by its inhabitants; if he had dispensed with the narrator altogether, and simply plunged us into the future; then all tension would have been lost. Instead, he allows an ambiguity to hang over the narrator throughout: he is troubled to understand how he is there himself; the other characters sense him as someone different; and this is a disturbing influence on their relationship; he has premonitions that he must return:

> "I felt rather uncomfortable at this speech, for suddenly the picture of the sordid squabble, the dirty and miserable tragedy of the life I had left for a while, came before my eyes; and I had, as it were, a vision of all my longings for rest and peace in the past. . ."

It is a complex feeling—a dream of a reality in which he dreamed—and yet it is convincing, and finds its compelling expression in his relationship with Ellen:

> "She looked at me kindly, but as if she read me through and through. She said: 'You have begun your never-ending contrast between the past and this present. Is it not so?'
>
> " 'True', said I. 'I was thinking of what you, with your capacity and intelligence, joined to your love of pleasure, and your impatience of unreasonable restraint—of what you would have been in that past. And even now, when all is won and has been for a long time, my heart is sickened with thinking of all the waste of life that has gone on for so many years.'
>
> " 'So many centuries,' she said, 'so many ages!' "

This is romanticism inverted—instead of the unsatisfied aspirations rebelling against the poverty of the present, the fulfilled aspirations reveal the poverty of the past.

"This present", "that past", the "never-ending contrast"—in truth this is a Scientific Utopia, which no one but Morris could write. The science lies not only in the wonderful description of "How the Change Came", the mastery of historical process, the understanding of the economic and social basis of Communism; it is present also in the element of realism embodied in the artistic construction of the work itself, the manner in which the world of dream and the world of reality are re-united. And yet it is still a Utopia, which only a writer nurtured in the romantic tradition could have conceived—a writer ever conscious of the contrast between the "ideal" and the "real".

At the same time, this emphasizes the fact that *News from Nowhere* must not be, and was never intended to be, read as a literal picture of Communist society. One half of its purpose is a criticism of capitalist society, the other half a revelation of the powers slumbering within men and women and distorted or denied in class society. The method demands a heightening, an idealization. Surely Morris makes this clear in his constant opposition between strife and peace? In the midst of the wasteful struggle of capitalist society he desires, above all, rest. The tale is sub-titled "An Epoch of Rest". It commences with the narrator hoping "for days of peace and rest, and cleanness and smiling goodwill". On awakening he finds his hope fulfilled. But, to complete the contrast with the "bitter war" of capitalism it is *over*-fulfilled. There is one thing lacking in "Nowhere". "I don't think my tales of the past interest them [the younger people] much", says old Hammond:

> "The last harvest, the last baby, the last knot of carving in the market-place, is history enough for them. It was different, I think, when I was a lad, when we were not so assured of peace and continuous plenty as we are now. . ."

Again, he says:

> "The spirit of the new days [is] . . . delight in the life of the world; intense and overweening love of the very skin and surface of the earth on which man dwells. . . The unceasing criticism, the boundless curiosity in the ways and thoughts of man, which was the mood of the ancient Greek. . . was gone past recovery. . ."

The lack of eager intellectual life is not only present in "Nowhere" but is underlined. Both Hammond and Ellen sense it. The "grumbler" is introduced to point it. The narrator murmurs, "Second childhood!" and the question hangs in the air, "What is to come after this?" And Ellen's last look seems to say: "You belong so entirely to the unhappiness of the past that our happiness even would weary you."

Of course Morris knew life would not be exactly like this in any real society. But the artistic method, of contrast and dream, depended upon his projecting his desires within capitalist society—his thirst for peace, for an absence of anxiety and guilt—into the future:

> "Here I could enjoy everything without an afterthought of the injustice and miserable toil which made my leisure; the ignorance and dullness of life which went to make my keen appreciation of history; the tyranny and the struggle full of fear and mishap which went to make my romance."

As A.L. Morton has written:

> "Morris's is the first Utopia which is not Utopian. In all its predecessors it is the details which catch our attention, but here, while we may be dubious about this detail or that, the important things are the sense of historical development and the human understanding of the quality of life in a classless society,"[1]

and, we might add, the contrasting impoverishment of life within capitalism.

Morris is not concerned with the mechanics of society but with the people—their relationships, their values, their pleasure in the details of life. And how remarkable his insights are, whether dealing with love, or labour, or communal life:

> " 'This is the way to put it,' said he. 'We have been living for a hundred and fifty years, at least, more or less in our present manner, and a tradition or habit of life has been growing on us; and that habit has become a habit of acting on the whole for the best. It is easy for us to live without robbing each other. It would be possible for us to

[1] A.L. Morton, *op. cit.,* p. 164. For a criticism and self-criticism of the notion of a "Scientific Utopia", see Postscript below.

contend with and rob each other, but it would be harder for us than refraining from strife and robbery. That is in short the foundation of our life and our happiness.' "

VII. Personality and Influence

What kind of a man was William Morris? Scores of anecdotes surround his memory, humorous, full of honour, grave. There is the story of the first performance of Morris's play, *The Tables Turned,* in the Socialist League hall in October, 1887. The play is a short topical extravaganza in two parts—the first, showing the sentencing of a Socialist agitator for obstruction, with the Archbishop of Canterbury and Tennyson called as witnesses, and ending with the invasion of the courtroom by triumphant revolutionaries; the second, dealing with the "rehabilitation" of "Justice Nupkins" in Socialist society. For the part of Tennyson, Shaw relates:

> "Morris took a Socialist who happened to combine the right sort of beard with a melancholy temperament, and drilled him in a certain portentous incivility of speech which... threw a light on Morris's opinion of Tennyson which was all the more instructive because he delighted in Tennyson's verse..."[1]

The part of the Archbishop he took himself, with a shovel-hat, clerical bands, and black stockings:

> "The rest he did by obliterating his humour and intelligence, and presenting his own person to the audience like a lantern with the light blown out, with a dull absorption in his own dignity which several minutes of the wildest screaming laughter... could not disturb."

According to another witness, the tension on the eve of the first performance was unbearable. The actors were packed into the wings of the small improvised stage, and—

[1] *Saturday Review,* October 10th, 1896.

"His Grace of Canterbury was packed in with the rest, in a high state of excitement. . . due, in part probably, to the fact that this was his first appearance as actor and dramatist, and also to his having 'delivered himself pretty straight' to the gentleman who was assuming the character of Justice Nupkins",

who had been taking this first night altogether too light-heartedly. The climax came, when—as Morris was making his entrance—Lord Tennyson fainted in the wings. The prompter struggled into his get-up, and Morris, aware of all that was going on, "got excited again", forgot his own part, and (with the prompter otherwise occupied) had to improvise something in the witness-box as best he could.[1]

Or there is the occasion when Morris lunched with Watts-Dunton in the Cock in Fleet Street, and the conversation got onto the Elizabethan dramatists, especially Tourneur, whom Morris denounced. "That was a loudish gent a-lunching with you yesterday", said the waiter next day to Watts-Dunton: "I thought once you was a-coming to blows".[2] Or the anecdotes of Morris's impatience with polite social intercourse, as when a curate button-holed him and remarked, "I suppose, Mr. Morris. . . you have seen a good deal of poor people?", Morris growled an assent:

"Impervious to his growing restlessness, the curate pursued his sign-song way. Finally, he asked, 'May I ask you, Mr. Morris, have you ever sat upon a Board of Guardians?' 'No, thank God!' thundered Morris. . ."[3]

Or the occasion, when Morris was being entertained to supper after giving a Socialist lecture in Leicester, and a clergyman, the Rev. J. Page Hopps remarked: "That's an impossible dream of yours, Mr. Morris; such a Society would need God Almighty Himself to manage it."

[1] "William Morris as a Playwright", by H.A. Barker, *Walthamstow Weekly Times and Echo,* November 15th, 1896.

[2] *Athenaeum,* October 10th, 1896.

[3] A. Compton-Rickett, *William Morris: A Study in Personality,* p. 28.

"Morris got up and walked round his chair, then, going across to Mr. Hopps and shaking his fist to emphasize his words, he said, 'Well, damn it, man, you catch your God Almighty—we'll have Him!' "[1]

Certain characteristics reappear in many stories. We know of his surprising energy. "When I talked to him", wrote Watts-Dunton,

"of the peril of such a life of tension as his, he pooh-poohed the idea. 'Look at Gladstone', he would say; 'look to those wise owls your chancellors and your judges. Don't they live all the longer for work? It is rust that kills men, not work.' "[2]

Those who knew him well were astonished, above all, by his ability to pass rapidly from one kind of work to another, the extent and depth of his interests, and his remarkable imaginative fertility. His son-in-law, Halliday Sparling, close associate in his work both in the League and the Kelmscott Press, has left a picture of Morris in his study:

"He would be standing at an easel or sitting with a sketchbook in front of him, charcoal, brush or pencil in hand, and all the while would be grumbling Homer's Greek under his breath... the design coming through in clear unhesitating strokes. Then the note of the grumbling changed, for the turn of the English had come. He was translating the *Odyssey* at this time and he would prowl about the room, filling and lighting his pipe, halting to add a touch or two at one or other easle, still grumbling, go to his writing-table, snatch up his pen, and write furiously for a while—twenty, fifty, and one hundred or more lines, as the case might be... the speed of his hand would gradually slacken, his eye would wander to an easel, a sketch-block, or to some one of the manuscripts in progress, and that would have its turn. There was something well-nigh terrifying to a youthful onlooker in the deliberate ease with which he interchanged so many forms of creative work, taking up each one exactly at the point at which he had laid it aside, and never halting to recapture the thread of his thought..."[3]

[1] May Morris, II, p. 221.
[2] *Athenaeum,* October 10th, 1896.
[3] H.H. Sparling, *op. cit.,* p. 37.

We are told by many witnesses of his capacity for total concentration, his almost child-like absorption in the immediate matter on hand, whether it were fishing, lecturing, or appearing as the Archbishop of Canterbury. We know of his ability to master even uncongenial work, once he had set his mind upon it. "Anyone can be a public speaker", he once said, "if he only pegs away sufficiently at it."[1] We know of his physical impatience of restraint, his vigorous gestures, his perpetual pacing of the room,[2] his irritation at the trivialities of "polite" intercourse. His acquaintance, William Sharp, summed up these characteristics well. "I never saw him at any of those literary gatherings where he might have been expected to put in an appearance", wrote Sharp:

> "His method of enjoyment was 'to do something', and it fretted him to sit long or listen long. Indeed, this physical impatience rendered him apparently more heedless to music, the theatre, lectures, than he really was, though when heart and brain were both under a spell, as when some speaker was urging in some new and vigorous way the claims of the people or. . . when a friend was reading from the manuscript of a poem. . . he would listen intently, leaning forward, with his vivid blue eyes gleaming out beneath his mass of upstanding and outstanding grizzled grey hair. . . so eagerly interested that it was possible to see the nervous life within him."[3]

Beneath the bluff, self-critically humorous exterior, there persisted (says Sharp) "a curious kind of shyness" from his youthful years.

His generosity, where his sympathies were engaged, is proverbial: indeed, in his last years his feelings of guilt at his comfortable life in the midst of poverty, made him a target for imposters as well as honest men. Several of his friends relate the constant trickle of refugees to his house, whom

[1] A. Compton-Rickett, *op. cit.*, p. 233.

[2] See Edward Carpenter in *Freedom*, December, 1896: "At meals even it would happen that he could not sit still, but, jumping up from the table and talking vehemently, would quarter-deck the room."

[3] *Atlantic Monthly*, December, 1896.

Morris helped in a prompt and liberal manner. Over and above his unceasing assistance to the propaganda, he was often giving help privately where he could. When a comrade in the Hammersmith League hurt his leg and was unemployed, Morris privately sent him £2 a week for six months until the wound was healed: there must be a score of similar unrecorded incidents. So great was his hatred of meanness that he sometimes went too far the other way, handing over money to the movement on occasions when it should have been a point of political principle for the comrades to find the money through activity. But any flavour of "commercial" dealings pulled him up short. A sculptor once asked to borrow £10 from him to buy some marble, and tactlessly offered interest. "What?" answered Morris. "Do you think I'm a damned pawnbroker?"[1]

A good deal has been written of Morris's famous "rages". Perhaps they were not so frequent as has sometimes been supposed, since Sir Sydney Cockerell, who was Secretary to the Kelmscott Press in Morris's last years, witnessed only "about half a dozen of them":

> "They were startling at the moment, but they were over in a very few minutes, and when he became calm he was like a penitent child."[2]

Shaw, on the other hand, was convinced that his rages were "pathological": they "left him shaken as men are shaken after a fit":

> "Being a great man, Morris could face and bear great trials; but on some utterly negligible provocation anything might happen, from plucking hairs out of his moustache and growling, 'Damned fool, damned fool,' to kicking a panel out of a door."[3]

He was, says Shaw, "rich in the enormous patience of the greatest artists", but went "unprovided with the small change of that virtue which enables cooler men to suffer fools

[1] R.A. Muncey in *The Leaguer*, October, 1907.
[2] *Observer*, November 19th, 1950. [3] *Ibid.*, November 6th, 1949.

gladly". In open-air speaking he was at a disadvantage through his slowness at repartee when dealing with hecklers, and "the provocations and interruptions of debate. . . infuriated Morris, especially when they were trivial and offensive (he could bear with any serious and honest utterance like an angel); so that at last the comrades when there was a debating job to be done, put it on me. . .'.[1] When once in one of his rages, Morris was capable of a flow of language not customarily found in the vocabulary of a Victorian gentleman; and sometimes seems to have revelled in the artistry of a row for its own sake. Surely no one but an artist could have conceived of those "Homeric passages" on the upper Thames near Kelmscott, when Morris would encounter on the water some "salaried minion" of the hated Thames Conservancy Board, and, leaning out of their punts, they would engage each other in colourful invective and defamation of character until they drifted out of earshot on the quiet reaches.[2]

Morris was always impatient with what he considered to be "fads", especially when they seemed to direct the attention of comrades away from essentials in the Socialist movement. True, he was thought to be a faddist himself because of his unconventional simple blue serge suit, his refusal to dress like his class. But this was not only consistent with his whole attitude to the decorative arts:[3] it was also a plain matter of convenience—he passed so rapidly from one type of work to another that he was forced to find fitting and workmanlike clothes—and almost without forethought he pioneered the saner fashions of our own century. But vegetarianism, teetotalism, "simple lifers", had little of his sympathy. "When we are a society of equals", he wrote, "we shall be able to consider all these niceties of life and to do what we think best."[4] When he was told that a young middle-class acquain-

[1] May Morris, II, p. xxxix.

[2] *Ibid.*, p. 620. On April 5th, 1890, he was writing to his wife: "We met some Conservancy men going up the water in a big punt this morning: which makes me uneasy, as I fear their bedevilling the river: they are a crying example of the evils of bureaucratic centralization" (Brit. Mus. Add. MSS. 45338).

[3] *Works*, XXII, p. 265. [4] *Commonweal*, October 6th, 1888.

tance had retired to the woods to lead a natural life, he only grinned and remarked: "Let us know when she comes out."[1] To any form of asceticism he was firmly opposed, as every page of *News from Nowhere* reveals. Simplicity did not imply deprivation of the senses, but the clearing away of a clutter of inessentials. Lecturing on "The Society of the Future", he said:

"I demand a free and unfettered animal life for man first of all: I demand the utter extinction of all asceticism. If we feel the least degradation in being amorous, or merry, or hungry, or sleepy, we are so far bad animals, and therefore miserable men. And you know civilization *does* bid us to be ashamed of all these moods and deeds, and as far as she can, begs us to conceal them, and where possible to get other people to do them for us."[2]

He could scarcely hide his disappointment if—after a public meeting—the comrades were all teetotal, and took him to have lemonade in some temperance hotel. "I'd like to ask you to have a drink", he would say to such friends. "And then he would add, as in despair: 'But you *won't* drink.' "[3]

With Yeats he found a congenial companion:

"I saw him once at Hammersmith, holding up a glass of claret towards the light, and saying, 'Why do people say it is prosaic to get inspiration out of wine? Is it not the sunlight and the sap in the leaves? Are not grapes made by the sunlight and the sap?' "[4]

Morris never attempted to disguise his disgust at Victorian Grundyism, with—

"its increasing sense of the value of moral purity among those whose surroundings forbid them to understand even the meaning of physical purity; its scent of indecency in Literature and Art, which would prevent the publication of any book written out of England or before the

[1] *Works,* XXII, p. xxiv. [2] May Morris, II, p. 457.
[3] Salt, *Seventy Years Among Savages,* p. 80. See also May Morris, I, p. 663.
[4] *Fortnightly Review,* March, 1903.

middle of the 19th century, and would reduce painting and sculpture to the production of petticoated dolls without bodies."[1]

His own life and Janey's had, perhaps, been "unconventional", and his experience led him to beware of dogmatizing on questions of personal and sexual morality. The Socialist movement of the 'eighties and 'nineties, with its sense of sudden liberation from all bourgeois conventions, was a period rife both in speculation and in unconventional practice in sexual relations; naturally there were muddles and naivities enough, but the atmosphere was healthy in so far as secretiveness and hypocrisy were replaced by open advocacy of unorthodox behaviour.

Morris did not identify himself with any "school" of thought: with Edward Carpenter, or with Joseph Lane's Anarchist-Communist "free love", nor did he bestow more than a chuckle upon Bax's solemn opinion that "many generations of rational social life" in a Socialist society would "modify" and "eradicate" "the coarser side of the sexual passion. . . by a gradual succession of inherited changes in the human organism through the medium of its social and economic surroundings".[2] His own views were set forward in public (but not pressed) in his Notes to the League Manifesto (Appendix I, p. 740), and in Chapter IX of *News from Nowhere.* The test, as he saw it, lay not in "mere theological views as to chastity", but in the happiness and fullness of life of the men and women of the future. Speaking at a League meeting in 1885 on the occasion of the *Pall Mall Gazette* exposures of prostitution in London he rounded upon the prurient Grundies of the Press:

"Two things are to be noticed," he said. "First, the children of the poor are always the victims. Second, the terrible and miserable unhappiness of the whole affair. There is much talk of immorality. Whatever is unhappy is immoral. It is unhappiness that must be got rid of.

1 *Socialism: Its Growth and Outcome,* pp. 3-4.
2 *Commonweal,* August 7th, 1886.

We have nothing to do with the mere immorality. We have to do with the causes that have *compelled* this unhappy way of living. . . There is the closest of relations between the prostitution of the body in the streets and of the body in the workshops. . . We desire that all should be free to earn their livelihood–with that freedom will come an end of these monstrosities, and true love between man and woman throughout society."[1]

In Socialist society, declared Note F to the Manifesto, "contracts between individuals would be voluntary and un-enforced by the community". "Fancy a court for enforcing a contract of passion or sentiment!" exclaimed old Hammond in *News from Nowhere,* in one of the richest chapters in that great book. While the pattern revealed in "Nowhere" is one of enduring love and friendship between two individuals, it is shown that the pattern is not uniform, and does not necessarily exclude more transient relationships (both happy and unhappy) alongside marriage. Everywhere flexibility is the keynote, in that most difficult thing to regulate, human feeling:

"There is no unvarying conventional set of rules by which people are judged; no bed of Procrustes to stretch or cramp their minds and lives; no hypocritical excommunication which people are *forced* to pronounce. . ."

Respect for authentic love, absence of deceit and constriction, are stressed:

"There need be no pretext of unity when the reality of it is gone; nor do we drive those who well know that they are incapable of it to profess an undying sentiment which they cannot really feel: thus it is that as that monstrosity of venal lust is no longer possible, so also it is no longer needed. . ."

Moreover, Socialism would effect a similar transformation in family relationships: "in opposition to the bourgeois view, we

[1] *Commonweal,* September, 1885.

hold that children are *persons,* not *property,* and so have a right to claim all the advantages which the community provides for every citizen".[1] The problem, he wrote to the Reverend William Sharman, was this: "How is it possible to protect the immature citizen from the whims of his parents?" Must the child be "under the tyranny of two accidental persons? . . . Children. . . have as much need for the revolution as the proletarians have."[2] The liberation of the woman from anxiety as to the livelihood of her children would provide the necessary pre-condition for true equality in social life:

> "Thus a new development of the family would take place, on the basis, not of a predetermined lifelong business arrangement, to be formally and nominally held to, irrespective of circumstances, but on mutual inclination and affection, an association terminable at the will of either party. . . The abhorrence of the oppression of the man by the woman or the woman by the man. . . will certainly be an essential outcome of the ethics of the New Society."[3]

In the society of the future all persons would take part in "the domestic arts: The arrangement of a house in all its details, marketing, cleaning, cooking, baking and so on. . . Whoever was incapable of taking interest and a share in some parts of such work would have to be considered diseased; and the existence of many such diseased persons would tend to the enslavement of the weaker sex."[4]

This was as far as Morris stated his views in public. An insight into his private views is given in a long letter to his old friend, Faulkner, of October 16th, 1886:

> "My dear Charley,
>
> "Thanks for your letter. It is right to 'blow off' to a friend when one is exercised. There is so much to be said on the subject of the

[1] Glasier, p. 185.

[2] Undated letter, 1886 or 1887, printed in *Labour Leader,* April 18th, 1903.

[3] *Socialism: Its Growth and Outcome,* pp. 299-300.

[4] Paul Meier, "An Unpublished Lecture of William Morris: 'How Shall We Live Then?' " *International Review of Social History,* XVI, 1971, 2, p. 14.

family that I can not attempt to state the whole of my opinion, part of which of course is only *mine* and not necessarily doctrine. But here goes for a hurried line or two.

"Copulation is worse than beastly unless it takes place as the outcome of natural desires and kindliness on both sides: so taking place there is even something sacred about it in spite of the grotesquery of the act, as was well felt by the early peoples in their phallic worship. But further man has not been contented with leaving the matter there, mere animal on one side, inexplicably mysterious on the other; but has adorned the act variously as he has done the other grotesque act of eating and drinking, and in my opinion he will always do so. Still if he were to leave off doing so, I don't think one ought to be shocked; there would still remain the decent animalism plus the human kindliness: that would be infinitely better than the present system of venal prostitution which is the meaning of our marriage system on its legal side; though as in other matters, in order to prevent us stinking out of existence, real society asserts itself in the teeth of authority by forming genuine unions of passion and affection.

"Clearly the present marriage system can only be kept up by the same means as the wages system is, i.e. the police & the army. When the wife can earn her living as a citizen, and the children are citizens with inalienable rights of livelihood there will be nothing to force people into legal prostitution or tempt them into irregular venal d^{o}, which for the rest they couldn't have, as it is simply a form of ordinary market exploitation. Husband, wife and children would all be free.

"So far as this I think all Socialists go. I should further say that the economical freedom of the family would clear away the false sentiment with which we have gilded the chain; but to my mind there would still remain abundance of real sentiment which man has evolved from the mere animal arrangement, and that this would prevent indecencies; though as to the outward form or symbol that it would take I can make no prophecies.

"Here then is in brief my views:

"1st The couple would be *free.*

"2 Being free, if unfortunately distaste arose between them they should make no pretence of its not having arisen.

"3 But I should hope that in most cases friendship would go along with desire, and would outlive it, and the couple would still remain together, but always as free people. In short artificial bolstering up of natural human relations is what I object to, though I admit that to make some ceremony or adornment of them is natural & human also.

"I think this is a reasonable view of the marriage question, & am prepared to defend it in public. Marson's view,[1] as far as I understand it, seems to be that once 2 people have committed themselves to one act of copulation they are to be tied together through life no matter

[1] See article by the Rev. C.L. Marson, "Socialists and Purity", in *Christian Socialist,* September, 1886; also *Commonweal,* October 2nd, 1886.

how miserable it makes them, their children, or their children's children. That is a superstition which I have no doubt he is sincere in holding; under our present circumstances it does not burden men of the world at all since there are plenty of whores in the market owing to our system of industrial exploitage. I think though that it weighs heavily on sensitive people endowed with real sentiment; while it degrades poor people horribly since they *must* wriggle out of it somehow. But if property were abolished such a view would not be very harmful; simply because it could not possibly be the general view: only those would hold it whom it suited, and public opinion would leave people free; though once more I believe that it would without violence and in some way that I cannot foresee, take care of the decencies; that it would adorn the subject in such a way as its knowledge of the great art of living would bid it.

"Well, I have written a longish letter after all but I thought it was only friendly to do so: as regards the policy of putting the matter forward, it is a ticklish subject, but one day or another we must face it. We must not forget that the present iniquity like all iniquities weighs much heavier on the working classes than on us because they are cooped together like fowls going to market.

"Please excuse haste, my dear fellow, as I am so hurried.

"Yours affectionately,
"William Morris."[1]

"Our modern bourgeois property-marriage, maintained as it is by its necessary complement, universal venal prostitution, would give place to kindly and human relations between the sexes," the Manifesto of the League proclaimed (see Appendix I). This drew a "very clever paper" from Shaw, in the form of a submission to *Commonweal,* which Morris, as editor, found regretfully that "we couldn't quite endorse":

"Of course I agree that abolishing wedlock while the present economical slavery lasts would be futile; nor do I consider a man a Socialist at all who is not prepared to admit the equality of women as far as condition goes—also that as long as women are compelled to marry for a livelihood, real marriage is a rare exception and prostitution or a kind of legalized rape the rule. I fancy we agree pretty much about the matter. . ."

[1] Bodleian Library, Oxford: MS Autogr. d. 21, pl. 220.

But he could not publish Shaw's piece without altering points which "would spoil the spirit of it." "Before long" the League must state its views on wedlock plainly "and take the consequences which I admit are likely to be serious." Until then the question was best left alone. It would seem that (caught between Bax's misogyny on one hand and Lane's demand for instant universal free love on the other) he found it difficult to "pluck up heart to explain the ambiguities of our sentence in the Manifesto."[1]

On questions of religious belief, Morris was (for the sake of the movement) reticent, and rarely made any public statement of a partisan nature. When he did so, he made it clear that he did not share the views of the "Christian Socialists", although he respected their position:

> "Real (I should call it ideal) Christianity has never existed at all", he wrote in one *Commonweal* controversy. "Christianity has developed in due historic sequence from the first, and has taken the various forms which social, political economic circumstances have forced on it; its last form moulded by the sordid commercialism of modern capitalism being the bundle of hypocrisies which. . . Christian Socialists condemn. When this beggarly period has been supplanted by one in which Socialism is realized, will not the system of morality, the theory of life, be all-embracing, and can it be other than the Socialist theory? Where then will be the Christian ethic?—*absorbed in Socialism.* No separate system of ethics will then be needed. . ."[2]

In private conversation he drove home the fact that organized religion was one of the strongest pillars of capitalist orthodoxy. "One night", recalled his acquaintance, Harry Lowerison,

> "Shaw, Belfort Bax and I were chatting after a lecture in the old shed in the Mall. The churches were just then a little more intolerant and reactionary than usual, and I got angry and was damning them in good set terms, when I was surprised to hear Bax, of all men, say: 'You're flogging a very dead horse, Lowerison.' Morris had come up behind me,

[1] Morris to Shaw, March 18th, 1885, Brit. Mus. Add. MSS. 50541.
[2] *Commonweal,* March 8th, 1890.

and he met Bax on the rebound with: 'Dead! the church! you mind its hoofs, Bax, *and* its teeth; neither end is safe.' "[1]

This account of his breach with the orthodoxies of Victorian morality will help us to understand the importance of his personal example in his breach with the even greater orthodoxy of class. True, Edward Carpenter and others had familiarized themselves with certain aspects of working-class life; while, at the time of the Dock Strike, middle-class "slumming" was almost respectable. But these facts re-emphasize how firmly demarked the social classes were at the end of the nineteenth century—revealing themselves not only in the class outlook of those who observed every social distinction, but also in the self-consciousness of those who deliberately ignored them. The attitude of middle-class men and women (including many of those who joined the Socialist ranks) to the working class was vitiated by half-conscious feelings—of fear, of guilt, of patronage, of contempt. In Cobden-Sanderson's *Journal* there are passages which reveal the great gulf dividing the workers from some of Morris's friends on the artistic edge of the movement:

"I am sitting at the small table in the bow window. . . hot bright sunshine on the world outside. I am going to give an hour or two to Hyndman's *Historical Basis of Socialism.* Annie darling is outside sitting under the shade of a tree reading. Blue-bottles are buzzing, and white-winged butterflies flit by. . . Through the open window. . . I look upon a wicket beyond, surmounted with jassamine. . . The wind flutters in the trees and blows refreshingly in gusts upon my cheeks. What a day! What a time! What perfection of quiet and happiness. How the world is beautiful! And now to the contrast offered in the pages of Hyndman, 'The Present Position of the City Workers'. . . It is too horrible. It is cryingly miserable. And yet here it is in tranquil print. . . Why do not the poor get up and cut the throats of all of us?"[2]

[1] Address by Harry Lowerison at the Annual Supper of the Kelmscott Fellowship, March, 1932 (typescript copy in Mattison Collection).

[2] *Journals of T.J. Cobden-Sanderson,* entry for August 2nd, 1884.

Why not, indeed? Or, at another extreme, regard the animal fear of Gissing, caught off his guard in *Workers in the Dawn:*

> "O, what a hell could I depict in the Whitecross Street of this Christmas Eve! Out of the very depths of human depravity bubbled up the foulest miasmata which the rottenness of the human heart can breed, usurping the dominion of the pure air of heaven, stifling a whole city with their infernal reek."

Then, as now, there were middle-class men and women to whom Socialism was a form of Charity Organization Society, or a passing adventure of an exhibitionist kind. There is no shade of this in Morris's attitude. On certain points of principle he broke deliberately with the customs of his class. "My dear", he wrote guiltily to one of his earnest young daughters, in 1888, "to confess and be hanged I went 2nd class to Kelmscott with your mother: we did not like to be scrowdged"[1] —revealing in this passing manner that he (and the unhappy Jane) had been in the custom of travelling third class on their way to Kelmscott. But, in general, Morris's attitude to the working class was unselfconscious and free of inhibitions. He had a greater respect for craftsmanship than he had for academic learning, and he always felt that his own craftsmanship joined him to the working people. Despite certain failures in communication, he always succeeded in impressing any working-class gathering which he addressed with his honesty of purpose. "So convinced was he of the utility of open-air propaganda", recalled Frank Kitz,

> "that he stood by my side on many a windy, inclement night at the corner of some wretched East-End slum whilst I endeavoured to gain him an audience. . . He had no feeling of contempt for those who do the rough work of the movement. . . Although his audience were at first somewhat mystified by his method of delivering his message, for he was no great orator, they gradually grasped his meaning: and as he preached to those toil-worn crowds in the gloomy East-End byways. . . he would

[1] Either to Jenny or May, September 2nd, 1888, Brit. Mus. Add. MSS. 45340.

warm to his subject, and his audience would enter into the spirit of his address."[1]

His comradeship in the "Cause" was a source of enrichment to many lives. Wilfred Scawen Blunt was astonished to find that Morris regarded women with the respect of equality:

"He was the only man I ever came in contact with who seemed absolutely independent of sex considerations. He would talk in precisely the same tone to a pretty woman as to a journeyman carpenter—that is to say, he would be interested if she had anything interesting to tell him, but not for a minute longer." [2]

With the comrades he was careful not to impose his views by force of his personal authority. Bruce Glasier's book of reminiscences is full of accounts of Morris's unselfconscious part in the casual comradeship of the movement. The same note recurs in many reminiscences. John Bedford Leno, the veteran Chartist poet, attended a lecture at Hammersmith, and was warmly welcomed by Morris: he later recalled with joy "this oasis in the desert of an old man's life."[3] Alf. Mattison, the Leeds engineer and historian of the movement, cherished as a "priceless possession" his memory of calling at Kelmscott House in 1892. After Morris had paced with him up and down the garden, interrogating him on the movement in the North, he stayed to supper after the Sunday lecture:

"What a pleasant time we had! There was Morris at the head of the table; May Morris at my side, and about six or eight more comrades. Morris was in a hearty and jovial mood. . . Tales were told and songs were sung. . . Often since that time, when the Social outlook was depressing and hope seemed fled, I have recalled that happy occasion, and under his manifold inspirations have again taken the road to Socialism—the earthly paradise of the toiling millions."[4]

1 *Freedom,* May, 1916.
2 MS. reminiscence in Brit. Mus. Add. MSS. 45350.
3 J.B. Leno, *The Aftermath* (1892), p. 86.
4 Mattison MSS.

For many comrades, these famous Sunday suppers seemed to open new windows on the wealth of life. One Hammersmith Leaguer recorded:

> "We first discussed a Socialist colony, and Morris went into every detail, with such zeal that he made us think it a project dear to his heart. He talked about the upper reaches of the Thames and about salmon fishing, about his country house, 'Kelmscott', about the folk-lore. . . and some of the doings when feasts used to take place *inside* the churches. . ."[1]

Nor should we forget the conscious efforts made by Morris to instill this spirit of comradeship into the movement, and to enrich the day-to-day struggle with an eager cultural life. "It was William Morris's great hope", wrote Edward Carpenter:

> "that these branches growing and spreading, would before long 'reach hands' to each other and form a network over the land—would constitute in fact 'the New Society' within the framework of the old."[2]

Sometimes he described this spirit as the "Religion of Socialism":

> "It has been seen over and over how a religion, a principle—whatever you may chose to call it—will transform poltroons into heroes, by forcing men to make the best of their better qualities, and making the excess of what they have got in them that is good, supply the defects of their lacking qualities. . . Let us remember that the Religion of Socialism. . . calls upon us to be better than other people, since we owe ourselves to the Society which we have accepted as the hope of the future."[3]

Here, then, are some aspects of the personality—humorous, brusque, shy, meditative, vehement by turns—which so strongly impressed all who knew him, and which has left its

[1] R.A. Muncey in *The Leaguer,* October, 1907.
[2] Carpenter, *op. cit.,* p. 125.
[3] *Commonweal,* August 28th, 1886.

permanent stamp upon the Socialist movement. So far from giving the impression of the "dreaming idealist", the impression gained by acquaintances was often the reverse. Margaret McMillan recalled his conversation:

> "He talked nearly all the time about material things, not theories or speculations, but concrete things, and failing these, news of the doings in the party. He had nothing of Hyndman's fire and storm, nothing of Hardie's mysticism. It seemed as if you could put his information in your pocket."[1]

Perhaps if there is a dominant trait it is one of deep seriousness, combined with a total absence of affectation, a constant struggle to find the most direct honesty of expression. In one of his earlier lectures he said:

> "It is good for a man who thinks seriously to face his fellows, and speak out whatever really burns in him, so that men may seem less strange to one another. . ."[2]

This is the prevailing note of his whole life. But we should beware of painting his character in black and white. "I'm a lonely chap", he once remarked, and the words recall sharply the turbulence of his romantic revolt, the arduous conflict of his middle years, the failure in his personal life, his intellectual isolation at the dawn of modern Socialism, the stresses beneath the surface of his final years of action. The French critic, Gabriel Mourey, was struck by his "strange face"—

> "Fierce, and yet at the same time overflowing with gentleness. . . the undecided *brusquerie* of the shy, the reserve of a man filled with his own thoughts and self-contained, but with sudden fits of *bonhomie* and gusts of enthusiasm which all at once fire, exalt, and transfigure him."[3]

[1] M. McMillan, *The Life of Rachel McMillan* (1927), p. 58.
[2] "The Art of the People", *Works*, XXII, p. 49.
[3] *St. James Gazette*, October, 1896.

While Morris's acquaintance, Stopford Brooke, who knew him over twenty-five years, declared:

> "His life was a wonder of work and pursuit and of intensity. His character. . . is a strange study, extraordinarily heterogeneous. People think it simple; it was amazingly complex. . ."[1]

Perhaps the truth is twofold. His character *was* amazingly complex in the strange blend of the romantic and realist, in the fires of conflict through which he had passed and which still flickered within him to the end. But in the integration of his life, the splendid unity of aspiration and action of his later years, there is the simplicity of greatness. It was this simplicity which held so much influence over his contemporaries, and drew tributes from men so diverse as Tom Mann:

> "He was to me the outstanding man among the intellectuals of the time, with a personality of so distinguished and commanding a type that I felt it a privilege to be identified with the same movement that held out such a glorious hope to the workers of the world. . ."[2]

As W.B. Yeats, in the deep romanticism of his early period:

> "He may not have been, indeed he was not, among the very greatest of poets, but he was among the greatest of those who prepare the last reconciliation when the Cross shall blossom with roses."[3]

And as George Bernard Shaw, at the end of his life:

> "With such wisdom as my years have left me I note that as he has drawn further and further away from the hurlyburly of our personal contacts into the impersonal perspective of history he towers greater and greater above the horizon beneath which his best advertised contemporaries have disappeared."[4]

[1] See *Life and Letters of Stopford Brooke* (Ed. L.P. Jacks).
[2] *Daily Worker*, March 24th, 1934.
[3] *Fortnightly Review*, March, 1903.
[4] May Morris, II, p. xl.

And, in so writing, he proved the truth of his words written forty years before, in the week when Morris was buried: "You can lose a man like that by your own death, but not by his."[1]

VIII. Desire and Necessity

What was the source of the greatness of Morris—this growing stature which he assumes in the perspective of history? His poetry alone, or his work in the decorative arts—profound though its influence was—would hardly be sufficient to establish his claim to the universal greatness suggested by Shaw. As a political organizer his efforts ended in failure. As a theorist of the arts—despite all his profound insight—he failed to construct a consistent system, and muddled his way around some central problems. Did he make any major contribution which is marked by the stamp of unquestionable originality and excellence?

The answer must be, "Yes". Morris's claim to greatness must be founded, not on any single contribution to English culture, but on the quality which unites and informs every aspect of his life and work. This quality might best be described as "moral realism": it is the practical moral example of his life which wins admiration, the profound moral insight of his political and artistic writings which gives them life. *A Dream of John Ball* and *News from Nowhere,* those two richly imaginative moralities, seem the most natural and fitting expression of his artistic genius.

Morris never sought to disguise the leading part which moral considerations played in the formation of his outlook, and in guiding his actions. He was brought to Socialism by his conscious revolt against that mechanical materialism which reduced the story of mankind to an objectless record of struggle for the survival of the "fittest", and which, in his own time, under whatever high-sounding phrases, put profit and not "free and full life" as the touchstone of value. He

[1] *Saturday Review,* October 10th, 1896.

declared, by contrast: "I *am* a sentimentalist in all the affairs of life, and I am proud of the title."[1] "I must tell you that my *special* leading motive as a Socialist is hatred of civilization; my ideal of the new Society would not be satisfied unless that Society destroyed civilization."[2] His ever-ready response to the possibilities of life, his capacity for indignation at its impoverishment in "civilized" capitalist society, was limitless. Unlike those late romantic poets who revolted once in their youth, and slumbered thereafter for years, he was in continuous volcanic eruption. Here he is writing his *Commonweal* "Notes", and catches sight of a sordid incident of Imperialism:

> "What now? Who is the civilized English Government copying now?—Genghis Khan or Tamerland? Scarcely even these; for these destroyers had their ideas stirred and their blood heated by the atmopshere of personal war and violence in which they lived, and at worst they were no hypocrites. But our black-coated, smug-visaged, dinner-party-giving, go-to-church 'scourges of God' who have not even the spirit to plead for themselves that they *are* curses and must act after their kind, who can one liken them to? For the sake of what one cannot even call a whim—for the sake of one knows not what, they must slaughter a number of innocent persons whom they are pleased to call 'the enemy. . .' "[3]

"Bah! the man of modern civilization is a sickening animal to contemplate", he breaks out on another occasion, after describing a British shooting-party in an Egyptian village.[4] General Gordon, "martyr", of the Sudan, is placed in a phrase—"that most dangerous tool of capitalist oppression, the 'God-fearing soldier'."[5] "One paper says that this task of civilizing Africa is well worthy of Modern Christianity. Surely that is undeniable. Tom Turnpenny never had a better job offered to him; 20 per cent. and the Gospel. . . are tempting indeed."[6] And so the sordid climax of capitalist "progress" is put in the perspective of history:

[1] May Morris, I, p. 147. [2] "The Society of the Future", *ibid.*, II. p. 457.
[3] *Commonweal*, December 29th, 1888. [4] *Ibid.*, April 9th, 1887.
[5] *Ibid.*, October 27th, 1888. [6] *Ibid.*, August 27th, 1888.

"O lame and impotent conclusion of that Manchester school which has filled the world with the praises of its inventiveness, its energy, its love of peace! Strange that the new Attila, the new Genghis Khan, the modern scourge of God, should be destined to stalk through the world in the gentlemanly broadcloth of a Quaker manufacturer!"[1]

Or here we have his attention caught by such a trivial incident as we might read in the Press every day of our lives. Notice how the whole of capitalist society, its legal code, its sense of values, is present in his mind as he comments on the incident:

"A citizen complained of a nuisance, in the form of a stink, in a police-court the other day, and the whole subject was thought to be very funny, the magistrate... leading off the laughter. We cannot tell... what the merits of this particular case might be; but we do know that a neighbourhood may be stunk out without a legal nuisance being established, which is indeed ridiculous enough, though not more ridiculous than most of our law. Perhaps the magistrate and his audience were laughing at English law in general. Or perhaps they thought it a preposterous joke that a well-to-do citizen should make a fuss about commerce annoying him with a mere stink when it murders so many poor people day by day. No doubt this is a joke, but I can't laugh at it. There is another explanation, which is that these laughers were such dullards that they had no conception that people might possibly restrain commerce so as to allow people to live decent lives. *That* also is no laughing matter."[2]

And so, in these casual passing notes, he revealed his astonishing insight into the self-destructive progress of captalism in its final years:

"International Capitalism and the workman a hungry machine; International Socialism and the workman a free man and the master of his own destiny—it must be one or other of these two. All the feeble compromises... will be speedily found out... by the monster which the Age of Commerce has made by dint of such mighty effort and cleverness, and which it must now feed by anything that may be handy. Honour, justice, beauty, pleasure, hope, all must be cast into that

[1] May Morris, II, p. 196. [2] *Commonweal,* June 29th, 1889.

insatiable maw to stave off the end awhile; and yet at last the end must come. . ."

Morris had seen into the heart of "the Bourgeois" and had found within it the negation of life. On one side was the comfortable hypocrisy:

"In the naivest and most unconscious way the one standard of good or. . . evil, of better or worse, is the comfort and morals of the Middle-class. . . They very naturally therefore are always fairly contented with the world as it is especially since most of them look forward to another Bourgeois world beyond. . ."[1]

On the other hand, his writings are full of forecasts of the recklessness of individualism grown desperate when its end is near. In a striking image he suggested that Albert Dürer's "Knight and Death" (a favourite of his youth) might serve as "a figurement of the doom of Blood and Iron in our own day", and of—

"the armed bourgeoisie. . . which to-day owns all that is made and all that makes, and which after a long period of that confidence of living for ever, which is the natural gift of youth and manhood, is now entering the valley of the shadow of death, and has become conscious of its coming defeat, and of the companions it has made for itself, and so rides on warily and fearfully, Crime behind it, Death before it."[2]

And yet there was hope in this as well, for—

"happily it always happens. . . in revolutions [that] the nearer the time comes for the defeat of reaction. . . the more the courage of the reactionists fails them, because they begin to be conscious that their cause has become a mere mass of found-out lies and helpless hypocrisies."[3]

[1] "The Political Outlook", Brit. Mus. Add. MSS. 45334.
[2] *Commonweal*, March 21st, 1887. [3] *Ibid.*, March 19th, 1887.

This is, indeed the prevailing note of Morris's later actions and writings—the appeal to the moral consciousness as a vital agency of social change. It is unlikely that Morris ever read *The Origin of the Family, Anti-Duhring* or *Ludwig Feuerbach,* although he may have learned something of their theme from Bax, and he would have encountered their central ideas in *Capital.* The understanding that in the fight for Socialism the age-old contradiction between the unfolding possibilities of life and their negation by class oppression, between aspiration and actuality, was at last ended; or, if not ended, at last transmuted into the contradiction between man's boundless desire and the necessary limitations imposed by his environment and nature; this came upon him with the force of an independent discovery. The whole face of the world was changed for him by this new understanding. This discovery appeared to him to give a new meaning and dignity to man's whole story. The Marxist interpretation of history made possible a great access of sympathy with the struggles of men in past times, which need no longer be viewed as a series of haphazard accidents:

"We see that the world of Europe [in the Middle Ages] was no more running round in a circle then than now, but was developing, sometimes with stupendous speed, into something as different from itself as the age which succeeds this will be different from that wherein we live. The men of those times are no longer puzzles to us, we can understand their aspirations, and sympathise with their lives, while at the same time we have no wish (not to say hope) to put back the clock. . . For indeed it is characteristic of the times in which we live, that, whereas, in the beginning of the romantic reaction, its supporters were for the most part mere *laudatores temporis acti* [praisers of past times]: at the present time those who take pleasure in studying the life of the past are more commonly to be found in the ranks of those who are pledged to the forward movement of modern life: while those who are vainly striving to stem the progress of the world are as careless of the past as they are fearful of the future. In short, history, the new sense of modern times, the great compensation for the losses of the centuries, is now teaching us worthily, and making us feel that the past is not dead, but is living in us, and will be alive in the future which we are now helping to make. . ." [1]

This passage takes us directly to the central theme of *A Dream of John Ball.* Here, in those magnificent last scenes in the Church, with the dead from the day's battle, friend and foe, lying beside him,

> "I. . . pondered how men fight and lose the battle, and the thing that they fought for comes about in spite of their defeat, and when it comes turns out not to be what they meant, and other men have to fight for what they meant under another name."

Here is Morris's reflection, from the standpoint of aspiration, upon man's unmastered history. It is paralleled in a passage of Engels's *Ludwig Feuerbach,* first published in the same year:

> "In spite of the consciously desired aims of all individuals, accident apparently reigns on the surface. That which is willed happens but rarely; in the majority of instances the numerous desired ends cross and conflict with one another, or these ends themselves are from the outset incapable of realization or the means of attaining them are insufficient. . . The ends of the actions are intended, but the results which actually follow from these actions are not intended; or when they do seem to correspond to the end intended, they ultimately have consequences quite other than those intended."

Morris declared that his main intention in writing *A Dream* had been in the dialogue of the concluding chapters,[2] and the problem debated here is whether "John Ball's" struggle and death is not a mockery in the light of the centuries of capitalism to come. The answer is two-fold: first, "John Ball", symbol of the oppressed struggling for objectives unattainable within the determined course of history, has no alternative;

1 Preface by Morris to R. Steele, *Medieval Lore.*
2 Owen Carroll, "William Morris", *Everyman,* September 23rd, 1933.

he can only achieve the dignity of manhood by rebellion—"to strive was my pleasure and my life". Second, his rebellion is given deeper meaning by its foreshadowed consummation in "The Change Beyond the Change", in which his aspirations, and those of the nameless millions he represents, will at length be fulfilled, in that day-dawn which may be "cold and grey and surly":

> "And yet by its light shall men see things as they verily are, and no longer enchanted by the gleam of the moon and the glamour of the dreamtide. By such grey light shall wise men and valiant souls see the remedy, and deal with it, a real thing that may be touched and handled, and no glory of the heavens to be worshipped from afar off. . . The time shall come, John Ball, when that dream of thine that this shall one day be, shall be a thing that men shall talk of soberly, and as a thing soon to come about. . ."

Morris did not exalt the primacy of moral factors as agents of revolutionary change:

> "No amount of preaching, of enthusiasm, or of devotion even, will induce the workers, with whom the world's future lies, to accept and to act upon mere abstract propositions of what they have a right to aspire to; necessity must push them on before they can even conceive of the future of equality and mutual good-will which we KNOW awaits them. . . Necessity only can make them conscious of this struggle."[1]

But, nevertheless, he laid the greatest stress upon their agency. "Necessity" alone would impell spontaneous riot and class-struggle, wasteful and uncertain of success:

> "If the present state of society merely breaks up without a conscious effort at transformation, the end, the fall of Europe, may be long in coming, but when it does, it will be far more terrible, far more confused and full of suffering than the period of the fall of Rome."[2]

[1] *Commonweal,* December 18th, 1886. [2] May Morris, II, p. 201.

And *conscious* effort implied not only clear theoretical understanding but also hatred for the present and love for the future. Speaking of "the two great forces which rule the world, Necessity and Morality", he declared, "if we give it all up into the hands of necessity, Society will explode volcanically with such a crash as the world has not yet witnessed."[1]

"I am not going into argument on the matter of free will and predestination; I am only going to assert that if individual men are the creatures of their surrounding conditions, as indeed I think they are, it must be the business of man as a social animal, or of Society, if you will, to make the surroundings which make the individual man what he is. Man must and does create the conditions under which he lives; let him be conscious of that, and create them wisely."[2]

"Necessity", on the one hand, he wrote, was hastening the crisis by the increasing tendency towards monopoly, and by forcing the workers into closer combination—

"and on the other hand morality, her eyes cleared by the advance of necessity, is beginning to remember the ancient legend of the first murderer, and the terrible answer to his vile sneer, Am I my brother's keeper?"[3]

"Her eyes cleared by the advance of necessity"—could there be a more dialectical expression of the interrelation between "desire" and "necessity" than this? And so to the magnificent recognition of what victory will mean:

"If we live to see the day when that slavery receives its death wound we shall regret no labour or pain that we have spent in the cause; no men that have ever lived will have been so happy as we shall be."[4]

[1] May Morris, II, p. 202.
[2] "The Society of the Future", *ibid.*, p. 456.
[3] *Ibid.*, p. 203.
[4] May Morris, II, p. 163.

Morris was not a mere muddle-headed convert to Marxism. He was a creative and original thinker, whose best work falls within the Marxist tradition. He understood that the consummation of his own romantic aspirations in the Socialist cause symbolized a historical consummation of vast significance. Socialism, he saw,

"is not a change for the sake of change, but a change involving the very noblest ideal of human life and duty: a life in which every human being should find unrestricted scope for his best powers and faculties."

All his Socialist writings returned to this point. Moreover, he actively resented the suggestion that the perception of the artist, the moral criticism of society, was irrelevant to "Scientific Socialism". In an important *Commonweal* article he criticized the attitude of such "one-sided Socialists":

"They do not see except through the murky smoked glass of the present condition of life amongst us; and it seems somewhat strange not that they should have no vision of the future, but that they should not be ready to admit that it is their own defect that they have not. Surely they must allow that such a stupendous change in the machinery of life as the abolition of capital and wages must bring about a corresponding change in ethics and habits of life. . . Is it conceivable, for instance, that the change for the present wage-earners will simply mean hoisting them up into the life of the present 'refined' middle-classes?. . . What! will. . . the family of the times when monopoly is dead be still as it is now in the middle-classes, framed on the model of an affectionate and moral tiger to whom all is prey a few yards from the sanctity of the domestic hearth? Will the body of the woman we love be but an appendage to her property? Shall we try to cram our lightest whim as a holy dogma into our children, and be bitterly unhappy when we find that they are growing up to be men and women like ourselves? Will education be a system of cram begun on us when we are four years old, and left off sharply when we are eighteen? Shall we be ashamed of our love and our hunger and our mirth, and believe that it is wicked of us not to try to dispense with the joys that accompany procreation of our species, and the keeping of ourselves alive, those joys of desire which make us understand that the beasts too may be happy? Shall we all, in short, as the 'refined' middle classes now do, wear ourselves away in the anxiety to stave off all trouble, and emotion, and responsibility, in order that we may at last merge all our troubles into one, the trouble that we have been born for nothing but to be afraid to die?"

And he concluded:

"I hold that we need not be afraid of scaring our audiences with too brilliant pictures of the future of Society, nor think ourselves unpractical and utopian for telling them the bare truth, that in destroying monopoly we shall destroy our present civilization. . . If you tell your audiences that you are going to change so little that they will scarcely feel the change, whether you scare anyone or not, you will certainly not interest those who have nothing to hope for in the present Society, and whom the hope of a change has attracted towards Socialism. . . And certainly the Socialists who are always preaching to people that Socialism is an economic change pure and simple, are very apt to repel those who want to learn for the sake of those who do not."[1]

Conversely, this was the compelling reason why Fabianism, Reformism, "semi-demi-Socialism" held no attractions for him whatsoever. Shaw got hold of a part of the truth when he attempted to answer the question, "Why did Morris not join the Fabians?":

"The answer is that he would have been more out of place in our drawingrooms than in any gang of manual labourers or craftsmen. The furniture would have driven him mad; and the discussion would have ended in his dashing out of the room in a rage, and damning us all for a parcel of half baked shortsighted suburban snobs, as ugly in our ideas as in our lives. He could be patient with the strivings of ignorance and poverty towards the light if the striver had the reality that comes from hard work on tough materials with dirty hands, and weekly struggles with exploitation and oppression; but the sophistications of middle-class minds hurt him physically. He had made his way through much opposition and ridicule; and he was a wise and great man *sub specie eternitas;* but he was an ungovernable man in a drawingroom. . ."[2]

By temperament Morris had not the least interest in "politics". He was interested in "free and full life and the consciousness

[1] "On Some 'Practical' Socialists", *Commonweal,* February 18th, 1888.
[2] May Morris, II, p. xviii.

of life".[1] He was in uncompromising rebellion against the shadow life of the Victorian middle class—its cant of individualism, "that unceasing cry of the bore and the dullard",[2] its orthodox religion, its Grundyism, its callous brutality. Morris, alas, would not have rested content with the "Welfare State": when the "ideal" was set before him of "the capitalist public service. . . brought to perfection", he merely remarked that he "would not walk across the street for the realization of such an 'ideal' ".[3] And even if he had been told of the final overthrow of Marx's theories by several generations of university professors, he would still have excused himself from changing his opinions. "Even supposing I did not understand that there is a definite reason in economics, and that the whole system can be changed", he had told the Northumberland miners in 1887, "I for one would be a rebel against it."

William Morris was the first creative artist of major stature in the world to take his stand, consciously and without shadow of compromise, with the revolutionary working class: to participate in the day-to-day work of building the Socialist movement: to put his brain and his genius at its disposal in the struggle.

It is no small matter for a man of fifty, in the face of the ridicule of society, the indifference of wife and friends, to set aside the work he loves and fashion his life anew. But this was what Morris did:

"To have breasted the Spanish pikes at Leyden, to have drawn sword with Oliver: that may well seem at times amidst the tangles of to-day a happy fate: for a man to be able to say, I have lived like a fool, but now I will cast away fooling for an hour, and die like a man—there is something in that certainly: and yet 'tis clear that few men can be so lucky as to die for a cause, without first of all having lived for it. And

[1] May Morris, II, p. 456.

[2] Morris and Hyndman, *Summary of the Principles of Socialism.* For Morris's opinions of individualism, see May Morris, I, p. 29, and II, p. 121 ("The Dull Level of Life").

[3] *Commonweal,* July 16th, 1887.

as this is the most that can be asked from the greatest man that follows a cause, so it is the least that can be taken from the smallest."[1]

His was the steady enduring courage of the realist, which upheld him in all the drudgery, committee wrangling and trivial duties of the movement.

Morris will always occupy a position of unique importance in the British revolutionary tradition. Some part of his work remains of international significance: *News from Nowhere* has crossed many national boundaries: and the significance of his utopian realism is gaining increasing international recognition.[2] But Morris's strength, no less than the strength of Gramsci, draws deeply upon the strengths of a more local intellectual tradition. The Romantic critique of industrial capitalism, the work of Ruskin and of Carlyle, assumes a new kind of significance in the light of Morris's transformation of the tradition.[3]

Moreover, for all the universality of his interests, Morris's genius was peculiarly English in its most characteristic expressions:

"The land is a little land; too much shut up within the narrow seas as it seems, to have much space for swelling into hugeness: there are no great wastes overwhelming in their dreariness, no great solitudes of forests, no terrible untrodden mountain-walls: all is measured, mingled, varied, gliding easily one thing into another: little rivers, little plains, swelling, speedily-changing uplands, all beset with handsome orderly trees; little hills, little mountains, netted over with the walls of sheep-walks: all is little; yet not foolish and blank, but serious rather, and abundant of meaning for such as choose to seek it: it is neither prison nor palace, but a decent home. . .

"Some people praise this homeliness overmuch, as if the land were

[1] "The Beauty of Life", *Works,* XXII, p. 176.

[2] See especially the work of M. Meier and M. Abensour discussed in the Postscript below.

[3] The first edition of this book was published before Raymond Williams's superb re-evaluation of this tradition, *Culture and Society,* had appeared. I have not revised my own account, which complements that of Williams: see also below, p. 793.

the very axle-tree of the world; so do not I... yet when we think what a small part of the world's history, past, present, and to come, is this land we live in, and how much smaller still in the history of the arts, and yet how our forefathers clung to it, and with what care and pains they adorned it, this unromantic, uneventful-looking land of England, surely by this too our hearts may be touched, and our hope quickened."[1]

"The movement is going on in all civilized countries", he wrote to one correspondent, "some of which are riper for the change than England is. England's adhesion would put the coping stone on the New Society."[2] If there is a trace of chauvinism here (and Wales and Scotland had a movement "going on" at least as vigorous as England's), he extended the same respect to the national traditions of others. The society of the future he saw not as a rupture of all continuities but as a resolution of past contradictions: it must *grow* out of the older positives in human labour, art and sociability.

"Intelligence enough to conceive, courage enough to will, power enough to compel. If our ideas of a new Society are anything more than a dream, these three qualities must animate the due effective majority of the working-people; and then, I say, the thing will be done."[3]

The *power* is the power of the organized working class. The *intelligence* is their revolutionary theory, Marxism. The *courage*—that is a moral quality. And it is here, above all, that we need William Morris to-day. "Think of it a little!" he exclaimed in one of his lectures on Communism:

"What amount of wealth we should produce if we are all working cheerfully at producing the things that we all genuinely want; if all the intelligence, all the inventive power, all the inherited skill of handicraft, all the keen wit and insight, all the healthy bodily strength were

[1] "The Lesser Arts", *Works*, XXII, pp. 17-18.
[2] Brit. Mus. Add. MSS. 45346.
[3] "Communism", *Works*, XXIII, p. 270.

engaged in doing this and nothing else, what a pile of wealth we should have! How would poverty be a word whose meaning we should have forgotten! Believe me, there is nothing but the curse of inequality which forbids this."[1]

So he still paces ahead of us, no longer "lonely" but still in the van—beckoning us forward to the measureless bounty of life. He is one of those men whom history will never overtake.

[1] "Communism", Brit. Mus. Add. MSS. 45331.

APPENDICES

APPENDIX I

THE MANIFESTO OF THE SOCIALIST LEAGUE

WRITTEN BY WILLIAM MORRIS

Adopted at the General Conference, July 5th, 1885 (With selections from the annotations of Morris and Bax to the Second Edition)

FELLOW CITIZENS,—We come before you as a body advocating the principles of Revolutionary International Socialism; that is, we seek a change in the basis of Society—a change which would destroy the distinctions of classes and nationalities.

As the civilised world is at present constituted, there are two classes of Society—the one possessing wealth and the instruments of its production, the other producing wealth by means of those instruments but only by the leave and for the use of the possessing classes.

These two classes are necessarily in antagonism to one another. The possessing class, or non-producers, can only live as a class on the unpaid labour of the producers—the more unpaid labour they can wring out of them, the richer they will be; therefore the producing class—the workers—are driven, to strive to better themselves at the expense of the possessing class, and the conflict between the two is ceaseless. Sometimes it takes the form of open rebellion, sometimes of strikes, sometimes of mere widespread mendicancy and crime; but it is always going on in one form or other, though it may not always be obvious to the thoughtless looker-on (see Note A).

We have spoken of unpaid labour: it is necessary to explain what that means. The sole possession of the producing class is the power of labour inherent in their bodies; but since, as we have already said, the rich classes possess all the instruments of labour, that is, the land, capital, and machinery, the producers or workers are forced to sell their sole possession, the power of labour, on such terms as the possessing classes will grant them.

These terms are, that after they have produced enough to keep them in working order, and enable them to beget children to take their places when they are worn out, the surplus of their product shall belong to the possessors of property, which bargain is based on the fact that every man working in a civilised community can produce more than he needs for his own sustenance (Note B).

This relation of the possessing class to the working class is the essential basis of the system of producing for a profit, on which our modern Society is founded. The way in which it works is as follows. The manufacturer produces to sell at a profit to the broker or factor, who in his turn makes a profit to the retailer, who must make his profit out of the general public, aided by various degrees of fraud and adulteration and the ignorance of the value and quality of goods to which this system has reduced the consumer.

The profit-grinding system is maintained by competition, or veiled war, not only between the conflicting classes, but also within the classes themselves: there is always war among the workers for bare subsistence, and among their masters, the employers and middle-men for the share of the profit wrung out of the workers; lastly, there is competition always, and sometimes open war, among the nations, of the civilised world for their share of the world-market. For now, indeed, all the rivalries of nations have been reduced to this one—a degrading struggle for their share of the spoils of barbarous countries to be used at home for the purpose of increasing the riches of the rich and the poverty of the poor.

For, owing to the fact that goods are made primarily to sell, and only secondarily for use, labour is wasted on all hands; since the pursuit of profit compels the manufacturer competing with his fellows to force his wares on the markets by means of their cheapness, whether there is any real demand for them or not. In the words of the Communist manifesto of 1847:

"Cheap goods are their artillery for battering down Chinese walls and for overcoming the obstinate hatred entertained against foreigners by semi-civilised nations: under penalty of ruin the Bourgeoisie compel by competition the universal adoption of their system of production; they force all nations to accept what is called civilization—to become bourgeois—and thus the middle-class shapes the world after its own image."

Moreover, the whole method of distribution under this system is full of waste; for it employs whole armies of clerks, travellers, shopmen, advertisers, and what not, merely for the sake of shifting money from one person's pocket to another's; and this waste in production and waste in distribution, added to the maintenance of the useless lives of the possessing and non-producing class, must all be paid for out of the products of the workers, and is a ceaseless burden on their lives.

Therefore the necessary results of this so-called civilization are only too obvious in the lives of its slaves, the working-class—in the anxiety and want of leisure amidst which they toil, in the squalor and wretchedness of those parts of our great towns where they dwell; in the degradation of their bodies, their wretched health, and the shortness of their lives; in the terrible brutality so common among them, and which is indeed but the reflection of the cynical selfishness found among the well-to-do classes, a brutality as hideous as the other; and lastly, in the crowd of criminals who are as much manufactures of our commercial system as the cheap and nasty wares which are made at once for the consumption and the enslavement of the poor.

What remedy, then, do we propose for this failure of our civilization, which is now admitted by almost all thoughtful people?

We have already shown that the workers, although they produce all the wealth of society, have no control over its production or distribution: the *people,* who are the only really organic part of society, are treated as a mere appendage to capital—as a part of its machinery. This must be altered from the foundation: the land, the capital, the machinery, factories, workshops, stores, means of transit, mines, banking, all means of production and distribution of wealth, must be declared and treated as the common property of all. Every man will then receive the full value of his labour, without deduction for the profit of a master, and as all will have to work, and the waste now incurred by the pursuit of profit will be at an end, the amount of labour necessary for every individual to perform in order to carry on the essential work of the world will be reduced to something like two or three hours daily; so that every one will have abundant leisure for following intellectual and other pursuits congenial to his nature (Note C).

This change in the method of production and distribution would enable every one to live decently, and free from the sordid anxieties for daily livelihood which at present weigh so heavily on the greatest part of mankind (Note D).

But, moreover, men's social and moral relations would be seriously modified by this gain of economical freedom, and by the collapse of the superstitions, moral and other, which necessarily accompany a state of economical slavery: the test of duty would now rest on the fulfilment of clear and well-defined obligations to the community rather than on the moulding of the individual character and actions to some preconceived standard outside social responsibilities (Note E).

Our modern bourgeois property-marriage, maintained as it is by its necessary complement, universal venal prostitution, would give place to kindly and human relations between the sexes (Note F).

Education freed from the trammels of commercialism on the one hand and superstition on the other, would become a reasonable drawing out of men's varied faculties in order to fit them for a life of social intercourse and happiness; for mere work would no longer be proposed as the end of life, but happiness for each and all.

Only by such fundamental changes in the life of man, only by the transformation of Civilisation into Socialism, can those miseries of the world before-mentioned be amended (Note G).

As to mere politics, Absolutism, Constitutionalism, Republicanism, have all been tried in our day and under our present social system, and all have alike failed in dealing with the real evils of life.

Nor, on the other hand, will certain incomplete schemes of social reform now before the public solve the question.

Co-operation so-called—that is, competitive co-operation for profit—would merely increase the number of small joint-stock capitalists, under the mask of creating an aristocracy of labour, while it would intensify the severity of labour by its temptations to overwork (Note H).

Nationalisation of the land alone, which many earnest and sincere persons are now preaching, would be useless so long as labour was subject to the fleecing of surplus value inevitable under the Capitalist system (Note I).

No better solution would be that State Socialism, by whatever name it may be called, whose aim it would be to make concessions to the working class while leaving the present system of capital and wages still in operation: no number of merely administrative changes, until the workers are in possession of all political power, would make any real approach to Socialism (Note J).

The Socialist League therefore aims at the realisation of complete Revolutionary Socialism, and well knows that this can never happen in any one country without the help of the workers of all civilization. For us neither geographical boundaries, political history, race, nor creed makes rivals or enemies; for us there are no nations, but only varied masses of workers and friends, whose mutual sympathies are checked or perverted by groups of masters and fleecers whose interest it is to stir up rivalries and hatreds between the dwellers in different lands.

It is clear that for all these oppressed and cheated masses of workers and their masters a great change is preparing: the dominant classes are uneasy, anxious, touched in conscience even, as to the condition of those they govern; the markets of the world are being competed for with an eagerness never before known; everything points to the fact that the great commercial system is becoming unmanageable, and is slipping from the grasp of its present rulers.

The one change possible out of all this is Socialism. As chattel-slavery passed into serfdom, and serfdom into the so-called free-labour system, so most surely will this latter pass into social order.

To the realization of this change the Socialist League addresses itself with all earnestness. As a means thereto it will do all in its power towards the education of the people in the principles of this great cause, and will strive to organise those who will accept this education, so that when the crisis comes, which the march of events is preparing there may be a body of men ready to step into their due places and deal with and direct the irresistable movement.

Close fellowship with each other, and steady purpose for the advancement of the Cause, will naturally bring about the organisation and discipline amongst ourselves absolutely necessary to success; but we shall look to it that there shall be no distinctions of rank or dignity amongst us to give opportunities for the selfish ambition of leadership which has so often injured the cause of the workers. We are working *for* equality and brotherhood for all the world, and it is only *through* equality and brotherhood that we can make our work effective.

Let us all strive, then, towards this end of realising the change towards social order, the only cause worthy the attention of the workers of all that are proffered to them: let us work in that cause patiently, yet hopefully, and not shrink from making sacrifices to it. Industry in learning its principles, industry in teaching them, are most necessary to our progress; but to these we must add, if we wish to avoid speedy failure, frankness and fraternal trust in each other, and single-hearted devotion to the religion of Socialism, the only religion which the Socialist League professes.

Notes on the Manifesto

A. Refers to the *necessary* distributors who "belong really to the class of the producers": also to professional workers, like doctors: "Such men have nothing to lose and everything to gain from a social revolution. . ."

B. "The standard of livelihood varies at different times and in different countries: it has always been the subject of bitter contention between employers and employed. . . but the whole result of this higgling has always been to leave at least a *lowest* class of labour existing only a little above actual starvation. . ."

C. "The end which true Socialism sets before us is the realization of absolute equality of condition, helped by the development of variety of capacity, according to the motto, *from* each one according to his capacity, *to* each one according to his needs; but it may be necessary, and probably will be, to go through a transitional period, during which currency will still be used as a medium of exchange, though of course it will not bear with it the impress of surplus value. Various suggestions have been made as to the payment of labour during this period. The community must compel a certain amount of labour from every person not in nonage, or physically or mentally incapable, such compulsion being in fact but the compulsion of nature, who gives us nothing for nothing. 1st. This labour may be arranged on the understanding that each person does an amount of work calculated on the average that an ordinary healthy person can turn out in a given time, the standard being the time necessary for the production of a definite quantity of bread-stuff. It is clear that under this system, owing to the difference of capacity one man may have to work a longer and another a shorter time than the estimated average, and thus the result would fall short of the Communistic ideal of absolute equality; but it is probable that these differences would not have much practical effect on social life; because the advantages gained by the better workers could not be transmuted into the power of compelling unpaid labour from others, since rent, profit, and interest would have ceased to exist. Those who obtained the extra goods would have to consume them themselves, otherwise they would be of no use to them. It should also be remembered that the tendency of modern production is to equalise the capacities of labour by means of machinery. . .

"But 2ndly, labour might be so arranged that an estimated necessary average of time should be its basis, so that no one would have to work longer than another, and the community would have to put up with the differences between various capacities. . . The bourgeois will of course cry out that this would be offering a premium to idleness and stupidity; but once more we must not forget that the use of machinery would much reduce the difficulty; and further, that as each would be encouraged to develop his special capacity; a position of usefulness could be found for everyone. . . Whatever residuum of disadvantages was left would be met by the revolutionized ethics of a Socialist epoch, which would make all feel their first duty to be the energetic performance of social functions: shirking work would be felt to be as much of a disgrace then to an ordinary man as cowardice in the face of an enemy is now to an officer in the army, and would be avoided accordingly.

"Finally, we look forward to the time when any definite exchange will have entirely ceased to exist; just as it never existed in that primitive Communism which preceded Civilization.

"The enemy will say, 'This is retrogression not progress'; to which we answer, All progress, every distinctive stage of progress, involves a backward as well as a forward movement; the new development returns to a point which represents the older principle elevated to a higher plane; the old principle reappears transformed, purified, made stronger, and ready to advance on the fuller life it has gained through its seeming death. . . The progress of all life must be not on the straight line, but on the spiral."

D. "The freedom from these sordid anxieties offers the only chance to escape from the insipidity or the bitterness, into one of which the lives of most men fall at present. Then would real variety and healthy excitement be introduced into human life. Then would come to an end that *'dull level of mediocrity'* which is a necessary characteristic of an epoch of Capitalist production, which forces all but a very small minority to become mere machines. Individuality of character is the real child of communal production; it is the reckless scramble for individual gain which reduces all character to a level by giving it one object in life, an object sordid in itself, and to which all other objects and aspirations, however noble, must bend and be subsidiary."

E. "A new system of industrial production must necessarily bear with it its own morality. Morality, which in a due state of Society, should mean nothing more than the responsibility of the individual man to the social whole of which he forms a part, has come to mean his responsibility to a supernatural being who arbitrarily creates and directs his conscience and the laws which are to govern it; although the attributes of this being are but the reflex of some passing phase of man's existence, and change more or less with that phase. A purely theological morality, therefore, means simply a survival from a past condition of Society; it may be added that, however sacred it may be deemed conventionally, it is set aside with little scruple when it clashes with the necessities (unforeseen at its birth) which belong to the then existing state of things.

"The economical change which we advocate, therefore, would not be stable unless accompanied by a corresponding revolution in ethics, which, however, is certain to accompany it, since the two things are inseparable elements of one whole, to wit social evolution."

F. "Under a Socialistic system contracts between individuals would be voluntary and unenforced by the community. This would apply to the marriage contract as well as others, and it would become a matter of simple inclination. Women also would share in the certainty of livelihood which would be the lot of all; and children would be treated from their birth as members of the community entitled to share in all its advantages; so that economical compulsion could be no more brought to bear on the contract than legal compulsion could be. Nor would a truly enlightened public opinion, freed from mere theological views as to chastity, insist on its permanently binding nature in the face of any discomfort or suffering that might come of it."

G. A Baxian note on historical progress, concluding: " 'Happy', says the proverb, 'is the people which has no history.' Socialism closes [the] era of antagonisms, and, whatever may be the case as time goes on, and though we cannot accept finality, at present we can see nothing beyond it."

H. A critical note on "so-called co-operative bodies."

I. A note stressing that land, under the capitalist system, "is *but one* of the forms of capital."

J. "By political power we do not mean the exercise of the franchise, or even the fullest development of the representative system, but the direct control by the people of the whole administration of the community, whatever the ultimate destiny of that administration is to be." Suggests that the enactment of a law of minimum wage and maximum price might be a first step in the transition to Communism.

E. BELFORT BAX.
WILLIAM MORRIS.

APPENDIX II

WILLIAM MORRIS, BRUCE GLASIER AND MARXISM

I. John Bruce Glasier

"MORRIS", Shaw once wrote, "when he had to define himself politically, called himself a Communist. . . It was the only word he was comfortable with. . . He was on the side of Karl Marx *contra mundum*."[1] Since there is a general impression among biographers of Morris and political journalists that Morris "repudiated" Marxism, it is necessary to examine the source of this confusion.

Those writers who have sought to divorce the name of Morris from that of Marx have based their interpretation almost entirely upon two sources. These are, first, one or two good-humoured references in Morris's own writings to his failings in the comprehension of economic theory; and, second, the reminiscences of two or three acquaintances of Morris who were themselves hostile to Marxism, the only one of whom who is in the least specific in his accounts is John Bruce Glasier.

In the first category, the main source is to be found in Morris's article (*Justice,* June 1894), "How I Became a Socialist":

> "I put some conscience into trying to learn the economic side of Socialism, and even tackled Marx, though *I must confess that, whereas I thoroughly enjoyed the historical part of Capital,* I suffered agonies of confusion of the brain over reading the *pure* economics of that *great* work."

Morris's first biographer, Dr. J.W. Mackail, was the first to employ this quotation outside of its context. Mackail, accord-

[1] May Morris, II, p. ix.

ing to Shaw, regarded Morris's Socialism "as a deplorable aberration, and even in my presence was unable to quite conceal his opinion of me as Morris's most undesirable associate. From his point of view Morris took to Socialism as Poe took to drink."[1] Mackail, indeed, goes so far as to describe Socialism as "a disturbing influence" upon Morris—

> "the patient revenge of the modern or scientific spirit, so long fought against, first by his aristocratic, and then by his artistic instincts, when it took hold of him against his will and made him a dogmatic Socialist."[2]

When referring to Morris's reading of Marx, Mackail omitted (without the customary dots to indicate a hiatus) every word italicized in the above quotation.[3] The passage, when doctored in this way, appears as a confession that Morris was completely unable to comprehend Marx's writings, rather than (as Morris intended it) as a mild rebuff to the more dogmatic of Hyndman's party, and as an encouraging note to those who, like himself, had found parts of *Capital* hard going. The ordinary reader may be excused for being misled by Mackail: but there is less excuse for successive commentators who have borrowed the quotation from Mackail without verifying it. So much for the first "source".

In the second category, by far the most important source is Glasier's book, *William Morris and the Early Days of the Socialist Movement.* This book contains many vivid pictures of the early propaganda, and there can be no doubt that Glasier had a profound admiration for Morris. There is also little doubt that, even if the two men were not on quite such intimate terms as Glasier suggests, Morris looked upon Glasier as one of the best of the Scottish Leaguers, and worked closely with him during the "parliamentary" struggle within the League. Nevertheless, it is necessary to look into Glasier's claims to be Morris's Boswell somewhat closely.

[1] *Observer,* November 6th, 1949. [2] Mackail, I, p. 80.
[3] *Ibid.,* II, p. 80.

James Leatham, of Aberdeen, who knew Glasier in the days of the League, has left a vivid picture of him. "When I first knew him he was a 'barricades man' ":

> "His ideas were ardently revolutionary, and when in one of his frequent rhapsodies he threw back his high head, with its shock of fair hair, and his blue eyes lighted up with their splendid visions, you felt that he was the constructive communist incarnate."[1]

Glasier, in the 'Eighties, shared many of the characteristics, both weak and strong, of some other Socialist Leaguers. The Glasgow Branch (Morris noted in his diary in 1887) included "some very nice fellows. . . a good deal made up of clerks, designers and the like and rather under the thumbs of their employers." Glasier himself was only sporadically employed in these years, as an architectural designer and draughtsman. Enthusiastic in the propaganda, an aspiring poet, interested in questions of art and morality, he carried idealism to the point of romanticism, and made a virtue of his own weakness in serious political theory. His insistence that Morris should fit into the same romantic myth grated sometimes on Morris's nerves. "As to your chaff about a poet, &c.", he wrote on one occasion to Glasier, when he was sweating over accounts in the Faringdon Road office, trying to get the Glasgow Branch to pay their long-standing debt for *Commonweals*, "Chaff away! only please remember that the said poet is *dunned* and has to pass it on. . . as other people have."[2] If there was a tendency among some members of the S.D.F. to harden into dogmatism, there was a counter-tendency with Glasier and several other Leaguers and members of the early I.L.P. to adopt a pose of unpractical "idealism", a self-consciously elevated and priggish "moral tone". The real fervour which had filled Glasier's youth began to degenerate, as it was bound to do, when he

[1] James Leatham, *Glasgow in the Limelight*, p. 35.

[2] Morris to Glasier, August 16th, 1886, Glasier MSS. See also Laurence Thompson, *The Enthusiasts*, (1971), p. 48.

conceived his "idealism", not as complementary to a serious study of political theory, but as opposed to it.

We now have, in Laurence Thompson's *The Enthusiasts,* a sympathetic biography of Glasier and of his wife, Katharine St. John Conway. This does something to redress the sour portrait which I offered of Glasier in the first edition of this Appendix. Undoubtedly the Glasiers were, and remained, "enthusiasts" in the councils of the I.L.P.; and their confused political record retains moments of honour, notably in their opposition to the First World War. But Laurence Thompson's account does not seek to hide Glasier's political amateurishness and his increasingly nebulous ethical religiosity.[1] In 1893 he published a paper on *The Religion of Socialism* as "the highest faith and purpose of life", and set himself forward as a lay preacher of that Ethical Socialism which, in Stanley Pierson's view, constituted a dilution (and adulteration) of William Morris's writings. "Having subordinated strategy and doctrine to quality of faith, Glasier felt free to identify himself with almost any expression of Socialism he judged to be sincere."[2] Soon after the I.L.P. was founded, Glasier became active as one of its itinerant propagandists:

> "Free and unconventional in dress and manner, a disreputable hat crowning his shaggy locks, a picturesque flowing cloak for wet weather, and a Gaberlunzie's wallet slung over his shoulder, he bravely trudged from village to town, carrying song and sunshine wherever he went",

according to one romanticized account.[3] The dress, the shaggy locks, the cloak, the wallet—all were imitative of Morris, and (with Morris's death) Glasier became the prophet of a "moral" Socialism, more "idealistic" than the Socialism of class struggle. In his Chairman's address to the 1901 I.L.P.

[1] For an excellent assessment of Glasier's politics, see Fred Reid's review of *The Enthusiasts* in *Bulletin of the Society for the Study of Labour History.* no. 24, Spring 1972, pp. 69-73.

[2] Stanley Pierson, *Marxism and the Origins of British Socialism* (Ithaca, 1973), p. 144 and chapter six *passim.*

[3] *J. Bruce Glasier: a Memorial* (1920), p. 9.

Conference he declared that "Socialism sought the ending of the selfish individual and class struggle that was going on for wealth, and the gratification of brutal instincts." At the Amsterdam Conference of the International, in 1904, he shocked not only most of the foreign delegates but also most of the British delegation by the vigour of his attack on the "reactionary and Whiggish" dogma of the class war. In the same years he was noting in his diary that Marx "had quite diverted Socialist teaching from its true line–i.e. the *rightness* of Socialism and the theory of Commonweal" (1903), and so-called scientific Socialism was "totally unscientific and of little real value" (1905). In the view of his biographer, "Glasier's most distinctive contribution to Socialist propaganda lay in his passionate anti-Marxism", and the continuing vehemence of his dislike for Hyndman and the S.D.F. coloured all his reminiscences of Morris and of the days of the League.[1]

A sad but significant episode took place two years after Morris's death which illustrates the distance which had already opened up between the master and the self-proclaimed disciple. Morris by no means gave up his efforts to promote a united socialist party with the failure of the S.D.F.-Fabian-Hammersmith joint committee of 1893 (pp. 605-10). In January 1894 he wrote in the *Labour Prophet:*

> "The tendency of the English to neglect organization till it is forced upon them by immediate necessity, their ineradicable personal conceit, which holds them aloof from one another, is obvious in the movement. The materials for a great Socialist party are all around us, but no such party exists. We have only the scattered limbs of it. . ."

Throughout 1894 and 1895 Morris supported *Clarion's* campaign for the unification of S.D.F. and I.L.P., proposing the means of affiliation or federation.[2] From 1895 opinion in favour of unification built up in the membership of both

[1] Laurence Thompson, *op. cit.*, pp. 90-1, 190, 41.

[2] See Laurence Thompson, *Robert Blatchford: Portrait of an Englishman* (1951), p. 97; *Report of the Fourth Annual Conference of the I.L.P.* (1896), p. 16; first edition, pp. 700-1.

bodies, expressed (in 1897) in affirmative ballots: such a merger might have had a profound effect upon the character of the subsequent Labour Party. But at its annual conference in 1898 the I.L.P. rejected unity, and a significant influence in bringing the delegates to this decision was a long "paper" read by a member of the Executive, John Bruce Glasier:

"Socialism is a very great and a very marvellously pervading and encompassing power. It is the most human spirit that has grown up in the world, and it is the divinest of all things we have ever had vision of with our eyes. We who call ourselves Socialists cannot ourselves comprehend its might or magnitude. We are as reeds shaken in the wind of its coming. We can only receive knowledge of it so far as the space and peculiarities of our minds will allow, and of the knowledge which we receive we can only give out according to the little measure of our powers. Is it not, therefore, somewhat perilous that we should do anything that might tend to narrow or lessen the inlet of Socialist ideas upon ourselves, or confine and constrain the message of Socialism, which is to be given forth to the whole nation, into one single channel. . .? Is it not, think you, better for a land that there be many pleasant rivers and brooks—yea, and mountain torrents—of Socialism than that there be one straight, flat, unfertilizing central canal?"[1]

Such rhetoric swung the delegates against unity, despite an 85% majority of the I.L.P. membership voting in its favour. One may see in this passage, only too clearly, the wind that was blowing up the "Morris tradition" into a sentimental afflatus. Glasier catches one or two of Morris's tricks of rhetoric well enough, although with the additive of a local preacher's humbug ("Is it not, think you, better for a land that there be many pleasant rivers and brooks—yea, and mountain torrents. . .?"). But the extra-mundane Spirit of Socialism of which he served as Prophet was only too close to the spirit which inspired his close friend, James Ramsay MacDonald. To old comrades a change in his whole outlook and character was apparent. James Leatham wrote:

[1] *Report of the Sixth Annual Conference of the I.L.P.* (1898), pp. 25-8; S. Pierson, *op. cit.*, pp. 258-9.

"The old gaiety seemed to have left him when in 1908 we met after a long interval. From being a revolutionary, impatient of pedestrian politics, he had swung round so far that he preferred the title 'Labour' to the more explicit word 'Socialist'."[1]

His book of reminiscences was written on his own deathbed, in 1919 and 1920, and it is clear that there were powerful subjective forces at work making for the distortion of his recollections.[2] Glasier recalled the spirit of his pioneering days with genuine excitement and nostalgia: but at the same time he 'read back' into those days the reformist views he held at the end of his life. The passages which refer to Morris's attitude to Marxism, to religion, and his relations with Glasier himself, cannot be accepted as trustworthy evidence.

There is no independent evidence that Morris expressed the views of Marxism which Glasier attributes to him, although the impression which Glasier's book is calculated to leave is that the inadequacy of Marxism was a frequent topic of discussion between the two men. In all Morris's letters to Glasier (published and unpublished) there is no reference to Marx's name. Glasier gives only two specific examples of Morris's supposed statements. The first is the famous "labour theory of value" incident (see pp. 356-7 above). The second is even more doubtful, and lays Glasier open to the charge of deliberate falsification. He was aware that Morris had given (in 1890) an interview to *Cassell's Saturday Journal* which undermined his whole case. Morris had been asked how he had come to Socialism, and had given the following reply:

"Oh, I had for a long time given a good deal of attention to social problems, and I got hold of a copy of Carl Marx's work in French; unfortunately I don't read German. It was Carl Marx, you know, who originated the present Socialist movement; at least, it is pretty certain that that movement would not have gathered the force it has done if there had been no Carl Marx to start it on scientific lines. . .

[1] *The Gateway,* Mid-January, 1941.

[2] For the circumstances in which the book was written, see Laurence Thompson, *The Enthusiasts,* pp. 244-5.

"The general purpose of his great work is to show that Socialism is the natural outcome of the past. From the entire history of the past, he shows that it is a mere matter of evolution, and that, whether you like it or whether you don't, you will have to have it; that just as chattel slavery gave way to mediaeval feudalism and feudalism to free competition, so the age of competition must inevitably give place to organism. It is the natural order of development."[1]

Glasier, attempting to explain this interview away, relates that he quizzed Morris about it on his next visit to London:

"I don't think the *Cassell's Magazine* chap quite put it as I gave it to him", Morris replied [according to Glasier]; "but it is quite true that I put some emphasis on Marx—more than I ought to have done, perhaps. The fact is that I have often tried to read the old German Israelite, but have never been able to make head or tail of his algebraics. He is stiffer reading than some of Browning's poetry. But you see most people think I am a Socialist because I am a crazy sort of artist and poet chap, and I mentioned Marx because I wanted to be upsides with them and make them believe that I am really a tremendous Political Economist—which, thank God, I am not! I don't think I ever read a book on Political Economy in my life—barring, if you choose to call it such, Ruskin's "Unto This Last"—and I'll take precious good care I never will!"[2]

Glasier, in presenting this story, did not quote the interview to which (he alleges) Morris's remarks refer: indeed, he cannot have had the published interview before him, since he stated both its date and the title of the paper incorrectly.[3] We have here two pieces of evidence. The first, a published interview during Morris's lifetime. The second, a "verbatim" account of an unwitnessed conversation, recorded thirty years afterwards by a sick man with an obvious bias. By all normal laws of evidence, the first must be accepted as the most accurate source. But despite this, successive writers have credited Glasier's account without question. Under examination, the story falls to pieces. *Cassell's* may have misquoted Morris in detail, but is exceedingly unlikely to have invented

[1] *Cassell's Saturday Journal,* October 18th, 1890. [2] Glasier, p. 142.

[3] *Ibid.* Glasier gives *Cassell's Saturday Magazine* "a year or two" after December, 1884.

a whole paragraph containing a brief exposition of historical materialism. If it *had* done so (and if, as Glasier suggests, Morris wished to be dissociated from Marxism) Morris could have sent a correction to the paper. But Glasier's account has other signs of being specious. At the time of the interview, the two men were in correspondence on the issues which provoked the Hammersmith Branch to leave the League: but this topic is not mentioned. Moreover, the whole story is overdone. Morris, as we know from a number of sources, certainly *had* read *Capital* in 1883: he had *re*-read much of it in 1887, together with the *Communist Manifesto* and Engels's *Socialism: Utopian and Scientific* when preparing his articles, "Socialism From the Root Up" (see p. 423). By 1890, he had read many other works of political economy. Why should he lie to Glasier in this way? Why should he call Marx a "German Israelite"? Why—but the questions are unnecessary. It is easier to answer why Glasier would have *liked* Morris to have said these things.

Further, there is a kind of bluff whimsy in Glasier's renderings of Morris's words which has also become part of the "Morris myth". Morris certainly was blunt in his speech and manners: but he was also a profoundly serious and responsible man, capable of very great patience and self-restraint. This latter Morris rarely appears in Glasier's book: only too often his vivid pictures of Morris's comradeship in the movement are hazed over by the picture of the great romantic poet acting the clown. His picture of Morris is so close to the truth, and heightens so many lovable characteristics, that one reads it with pleasure; only afterwards does one realize one has been presented, not with Morris himself, but with a sort of jolly comic. "Head or tail", "crazy sort of artist", "poet chap", "upsides"—all these phrases are in character, but *not* all in the same breath and strung together with a looseness of thought which suggests a man with a mouthful of cotton-wool. This picture, in its turn, has served a hundred later commentators, and made it easy for them to adopt Morris with condescension and to call him a great "visionary", while paying no attention whatsoever to his real actions and his political writings.

If the second of Glasier's stories is a fraud built round a doubtful mustard seed, what of the first, concerning the labour theory of value (see p. 356)? Despite the fact that the whole thing is over-written in the same way—"everyone will live and work jollily together"—the story, in view of the circumstances of the meeting, has a more authentic flavour. Morris might very well have said that it was not *necessary* to know either Marx's work or to understand the theory of value to be a Socialist. Since Hyndman was at the time attempting to blacken Scheu by suggesting that he deviated from Marxism and was an "anarchist", Morris may well have burst out in fury against this dogmatism. But that he used the form of words attributed to him—and related, out of its context, on every possible occasion, ever since Glasier's book was published—is very dubious. "I do not know what Marx's theory of value is; and I'm damned if I want to know"—if Morris *did* actually say this, then, on the evidence of his own writings at the time, he was lying on both counts. He *might* have lied, of course, in order to make his point against dogmatism more effectively, or merely in the heat of the discussion. But at least it is worth placing on record that a similar story was going the rounds in the early movement, and was attributed not to Morris but to another member of the Glasgow S.D.F., Robert Hutchinson, a shoemaker, who—according to Leatham—used to declare: "Do I need to read Marx or anyone else in order to learn that I am robbed and how the robbery is done?"[1] Hutchinson may have got the phrase from Morris. Leatham may have been mistaken in his memory. Glasier may have got the idea from Hutchinson. In itself the incident is of little importance, and the facts can never be established. So much for the second source upon which both the learned commentators and the hasty journalists have leant.

[1] James Leatham, *Glasgow in the Limelight*, p. 35. Hutchinson was brother-in-law to the inquisitorial W.J. Nairne who supposedly occasioned Morris's explosion: see above p. 356 and L. Thompson, *The Enthusiasts*, p. 40.

II. William Morris and Marxism

It is typical of critics of Marxism that they should rest their case upon subjective secondary sources, and should pass over the obvious primary source—Morris's own political writings. The evidence here that Morris associated himself with the Marxist tradition is of three kinds—negative, specific, and corroborative.

Negative. With the exception of the case discussed below—the Carruthers "heresy"—Morris neither states nor implies at any time that he was opposed on any major theoretical principle to either Marx or Scientific Socialism.

Specific. The evidence that Morris had a profound admiration for the work of Marx and Engels, and explicitly identified himself with Scientific Socialism, or Communism, is to be found in every phase of his Socialist activities. It includes:

(a) Notes made by Morris upon *Capital.*[1]

(b) References in the *Summary of the Principles of Socialism,* written in 1884, with Hyndman.

(c) Interviews in the Press both after the "Split" and shortly before leaving the League, at both of which critical periods Morris was at pains to identify his views with Marx and with Scientific Socialism (see p. 333 and the Cassell's interview).

(d) Many passing references, all complimentary, in lectures and articles to *Capital* ("that great book"), Marx ("great man"), "the great Socialist economist, F. Engels", and to German, or Scientific Socialism. Morris was sparing of such epithets (unless in such a context as "great scoundrel"), and the adjective was not thrown in for rhetoric's sake.

(e) The central position given to both Marx and Engels in the *Commonweal* articles, "Socialism from the Root Up", which Morris wrote with Belfort Bax in 1886 and 1887. The historical exposition of the class struggle in these articles

[1] Among Walthamstow MSS. Mr. R. Page Arnot refers in *William Morris, A Vindication,* p. 7, to a MS. among the papers of J.L. Mahon "in the handwriting of Morris, being a short precis of one of the 'economic portions' of *Capital*".

closely follows Marx. The Utopian Socialists are discussed, with frequent quotations from the French edition of Engels's *Socialism: Utopian and Scientific.*[1] In 1887, no less than seven articles were devoted to the economic theory of Volume One of *Capital,* which is described as "the full development of the complete Socialist theory".[2]

This evidence must appear conclusive, but Bruce Glasier (once again) attempted to discount it. The articles he described as "most unsatisfactory", and (he implied) Bax, not Morris, was their real author:

> "No one who knew him personally, or was familiar with the general body of his writings, could fail to perceive that these Marxist ideas did not really belong to his own sphere of Socialist thought, but were adopted by him because of their almost universal acceptance by his fellow Socialists, and because he did not feel disposed to bother about doctrines which, whether true or false, hardly interested him."[3]

A wave of the wand–and Morris's lectures, articles, and *Commonweal* notes, all are spirited away! It must seem astonishing that successive commentators should have preferred this passage of Glasier to the weight of evidence in Morris's writings themselves. But, since this is so, it is necessary to examine Glasier's suggestion.

There are several entries in Morris's *Socialist Diary* which relate to the composition of the articles. These do not support the suggestion that Bax wrote the articles and Morris only "said ditto" to them. In the first entry: "Tuesday to Bax at Croydon where we did our first article on Marx: or rather he

[1] *Commonweal,* October 30th, 1886, February 5th, 1887. Morris and Bax translated from the French edition of Engels's book, not yet published in English.

[2] *Ibid.,* February 26th, March 12th, March 26th, April 30th, June 18th, July 23rd and August 6th, 1887.

[3] Glasier, p. 143. I have restored a clause here (as to "almost universal acceptance") which was cut in the first edition, since a Professor Le Bourgeois *(sic)* has been buzzing around this Appendix like an angry wasp, and accusing me of "suppression". The restored clause of course makes Glasier look even sillier: see J.Y. Le Bourgeois, "William Morris and the Marxist Myth", *Durham University Journal,* December 1976: and my forthcoming reply, "A Wasp in September."

did it: I don't think I should ever make an economist even of the most elementary kind: but I am glad of the opportunity this gives me of hammering some Marx into myself".[1] Bax was clearly taking priority in drafting the articles on Marx's economic theory, as one would expect: but this is not the same as Morris saying "ditto". The next entry reads: "Yesterday all day long with Bax trying to get our second article on Marx together; a very difficult job: I hope it may be worth the trouble."[2] The article which caused Morris such difficulty concerned the theory of Money. In the result, Morris and Bax succeeded in presenting Marx's essential theory clearly, and with telling historical illustrations, some drawn from *Capital,* some from their own knowledge. Moreover, anyone familiar with the style of both men can detect at a glance that—in this article as in the others—it is *Morris's* direct manner and tricks of thought which predominate rather than Bax's intelligent but pompous prose.[3] The humourless Bax was hardly likely to have borrowed a phrase from Mr. Boffin to illustrate the Labour Theory of Value: while in the very choice of quotations from *Capital* ("says Marx with a grin") one can trace Morris's warm response to the play of passion and humour with which parts of *Capital* are written.

The evidence, indeed, is so overwhelming that Glasier's suggestion recoils upon his own head, revealing nothing about Morris's interest in "doctrines", but throwing further doubt upon Glasier's own integrity. Confirmation that Morris *did* find the articles "worth the trouble" is to be found in the fact that he and Bax later revised them thoroughly for publication

[1] Brit. Mus. Add. MSS. 45335, entry for February 15th, 1887. I have included this entry once again to satisfy the buzzing of Le Bourgeois.

[2] Brit. Mus. Add. MSS. 45335, entry for February 23rd.

[3] See, for example, a characteristic passage from the article on Money: "In the first stage, illustrated by the proceedings of the Craftsmen of the time of Homer, which were pretty much those of the Mediaeval Craftsman also, the village potter sold his pots and with the money he got from them, which, possible trickery apart, represented just the *value* or embodied labour of the pots, he bought meal, oil, wine, flesh, etc., for his own livelihood and consumed them."

in *Socialism: Its Growth and Outcome* (1893) (see p. 615), referring to *Capital,* at the end of the long chapter on Marx as an "epoch-making work."[1] Finally—as if in anticipation of Glasier's suggestion—they made a point of stating in the Preface that the book "has been in the true sense of the word a *collaboration,* each sentence having been carefully considered by both the authors in common, although now one, now the other, has had more to do with initial suggestions in different portions of the work."[2]

Corroborative. Evidence that the body of Morris's political writings draws upon and is consonant with the Marxist tradition has been frequently presented in this book. It has now been re-examined with immense thoroughness by M. Paul Meier in *La Pensée Utopique de William Morris* (Paris, 1972). M. Meier's examination is conclusive—even if (as I argue in my Postscript) at times excessively literal and theoretically restrictive.

Once these primary facts have been established, certain secondary factors which, to some degree, complicated Morris's attitude to political theory, must be borne in mind. Morris came to Socialism in his fiftieth year, with almost no previous acquaintance with serious economic theory, and he always found difficulty in mastering what he often termed the "economic side", as opposed to the historical side, of Marxism. It is necessary to glance for a moment at those among his colleagues who might have helped to guide him through these problems, in order to understand his difficulty. Scheu, Hyndman, and Bax, each of whom was closely associated with Morris in 1883 and 1884, were all partial advocates who influenced his understanding. Scheu undoubtedly encouraged Morris's "Leftist" leanings, and helped to implant the "anti-parliamentary" bias in his mind. Hyndman was a determined exponent of the "Iron Law of Wages" theory which encouraged opposition to all "palliatives". Moreover, after the "Split" Hyndman's claim to be the only true

[1] *Socialism: Its Growth and Outcome* (1893), p. 267. [2] *Ibid.,* p. vi.

disciple of Marx, and his doctrinaire use of Marx's name, prompted Morris to be especially careful to avoid this kind of dogmatism. As for Bax, there were occasions when the Marxist dialectic was reduced, in his hands, to a Hegelian mystique. He was the author of the first pamphlet to be published by the Socialist League which was addressed directly to trades unionists, and he wrote in its final paragraph:

> "Current antagonisms are thus reduced by their own exhaustion to the shadows of their former selves, only to receive a new significance, in which their opposition vanishes. They are destroyed in their preservation, and preserved in their destruction. They are superseded. . ."[1]

No wonder that Engels exclaimed later in a moment of irritation that Bax was "a hunter of philosophical paradoxes!"[2]

Two other colleagues who might, in the 1880s, have helped in guiding Morris through his difficulties with economic theory were Edward Aveling and John Carruthers. But neither was capable of giving this guidance. Aveling commenced in 1885 a series of "Lessons in Socialism" in the *Commonweal* which he claimed were "the first attempt to put the ideas of Marx. . . simply and clearly before the English people, in their own language."[3] The first Lesson was good, but, by the fourth Lesson, Aveling himself noted that "some bewailing has reached my ears on the subject of the formulae used."[4] There is little wonder. As the Lessons proceeded, Aveling tended to discard all concrete illustrations and historical exposition, and to abstract from *Capital* only the "pure economics", expressed in algebraic formulae, and, only too often, in a mechanical and schematic form. "Aveling on Marx is a matter for general astonishment", Mahon wrote from Leeds. "Workingmen are utterly perplexed as to the meaning of it all. Only one

[1] *Address to Trades Unions,* The Socialist Platform, No. 1 (1885).
[2] Engels to Sorge, April 29th, 1886, *Labour Monthly,* November, 1933.
[3] *Commonweal,* April, 1885.
[4] *Ibid.,* July, 1885.

member... reads them."[1] But despite Morris's rooted objection to Socialist propaganda which was "all figures",[2] he appears to have been a staunch supporter of Aveling in this series. When advising a correspondent on Socialist theory, in February 1885, he strongly recommended Aveling's lectures "which are very good: they are on Marx really... They would make *reading* Marx comparatively easy to you."[3] When the lectures came under criticism at the Annual Conference in the summer, Morris came to Aveling's defence.[4]

After 1885 Morris was also influenced to some degree by John Carruthers, a member of the Hammersmith Branch, who took little active part in the propaganda of the League. Two years younger than Morris, Carruthers was a constructional engineer who had built railways, bridges, canals, and port installations in Canada, the United States, Northern Europe, Mauritius, Egypt, India, and South America, and had served as consultant engineer to the New Zealand and Western Australian Governments.[5] In 1883—before reading Marx—he had published a remarkable book, *Communal and Commercial Economy,* which deserves to be remembered in the tradition of English Socialist thought. Largely concerned with an acute, passionate, but at times disorganized, critique of the economic theory of Ricardo and Mill, Carruthers concluded with a warm advocacy of Communism, which he envisaged (as did Morris in *News from Nowhere*) as a loose association of

[1] J.L. Mahon to Soc. League Council, January 23rd, 1886, S.L. Correspondence, Int. Inst. Soc. Hist. On the other hand, Lyons, a London clothing worker, declared at the First Annual Conference that "the workers, he knew by personal experience, to a large extent bought the paper just on account of the scientific articles on Socialism": *Commonweal,* August, 1885.

[2] Walthamstow MSS. Recollections of H.A. Barker referring not to Aveling, but to the articles of John Sketchley, which, for the general reader, were overloaded with statistics. Since Sketchley was a regular contributor to *Commonweal* until 1890, Morris did not allow his own prejudice against "figures" to influence his editorial policy.

[3] See p. 761, note 1 below.

[4] *Commonweal,* August Supplement, 1885.

[5] See *Economic Studies* (Selections from the writings of John Carruthers) (1915), for biographical foreword.

small communes. He revealed clearly that "the whole class of labourers. . . have common interests antagonistic to those of the capitalists",[1] but through a failure in historical understanding he tended to present the exploitation of the working class in a mechanical and rigid manner—not as an active relationship of struggle with the capitalist class. To the capitalist (he wrote)—

> "it is a matter of indifference what natural agents are instrumental in the production of his wealth, and the labour of men does not, in his estimation, differ generically from that of birds or horses, and is more important only because the men are the phenomena over which he has most control."[2]

"The workman, in commercial economy, is simply an implement that costs nothing".[3] Something in the emotional tone, rather than in the economic reasoning of this argument appealed to Morris, for he noted in his *Socialist Diary:*

> "Tuesday I spent with Bax doing the next Marx article, which went easier: as a contrast I had a long spell with Carruthers. . . and he read me the 2nd (and important) chapter of his Political Economy, which is by the standard of Marx quite heretical. It seemed to me clear & reasonable; and at any rate has this advantage, that it sets forth the antagonism of classes in the nakedest manner: the workman is nothing but part of the capitalist machinery; and if he is rebellious is to be treated like a rebellious spade would be, or say a troublesome piece of land."[4]

It is clear that the "heresy" which was attracting Morris was parallel to his political "Leftism" at this time, and was more a confusion of terms than a serious disagreement with the Marxist position.

What is, however, somewhat less clear is what this Marxist position was, in any public sense, in the 1880s. Marxist, as well as anti-Marxist and agnostic, historians have made anachronis-

[1] Carruthers, *Communal and Commercial Economy* (1883), p. 5.
[2] *Ibid.*, p. 10. [3] *Ibid.*, p. 39.
[4] Brit. Mus. Add. MSS. 45335.

tic judgements which contemporary scholarship is only now beginning to detect. As the late Henry Collins has pointed out, Marx's repudiation of the "Iron Law of Wages" was scarcely a public matter, was not published in any extended form until 1898, and, while it was no doubt a point of discussion in Engels's circle, Bax (Engels's closest English disciple) was still re-stating the "Iron Law" in 1901.[1] From such Marxist texts as were available, as *Wage-Labour and Capital* (1885), readers could well derive support for down-grading trade-union struggles in favour of legislative struggles to limit the working-day.[2] And the confusion becomes even greater when we consider the complex positions through which one other colleague who was close to Morris in 1884-7 was moving—George Bernard Shaw.

Shaw, when Morris first came to know him, was one of the few English intellectuals who had studied *Capital* with care. He was thought to be an expounder and interpreter of Marx, and perhaps thought himself to be so, although early in 1884 he inserted in *Justice* a criticism of the theory of surplus value, expressed characteristically in the form of jest (signed, "G.B.S. Larking").[3] Through 1885 and into 1886 Shaw was a member of the Hampstead Marx Circle, which met fortnightly to study *Capital,* and which wrestled with critiques of Marx from the Jevonian position of marginal utility.[4] In the same period Shaw was working very closely with the Socialist

[1] Henry Collins, "The Marxism of the Social Democratic Federation", in *Essays in Labour History, 1886-1923,* eds. Asa Briggs and John Saville (1971), pp. 52-3. Bax and Quelch re-affirmed the "Iron Law" which "stands as firmly today as when stated by Lassalle" in *A New Catechism of Socialism* (1901).

[2] Henry Collins, *op. cit.,* pp. 59-61.

[3] *Justice,* March 15th, 1884; and G.B. Shaw to M.E. McNulty, April 15th, 1884, *Bernard Shaw: Collected Letters, 1874-97,* ed. Dan H. Laurence (New York, 1965), pp. 81-7.

[4] For the early evolution of Shaw and the Fabians, see especially A.M. McBriar, *Fabian Socialism and English Politics, 1884-1918* (Cambridge, 1962); S. Pierson, *op. cit.,* pp. 119-29; Willard Wolfe, *From Radicalism to Socialism: Men and Ideas in the Formation of Fabian and Socialist Doctrines* (New Haven, 1975); D.M. Ricci, "Fabian Socialism: A Theory of Rent as Exploitation", *Journal of British Studies,* IX (1969), pp. 105-21.

League and lecturing frequently for its branches. Throughout 1886 League members, including Morris, took part in a series of joint conferences with Fabians and others on Socialist strategy: these broke down, not on any issue of "Marxism" but on the vexed question of political action.[1] As late as February 1887, when the League challenged Bradlaugh to public debate, Shaw was invited (and agreed, subject to conditions) to act as the League's champion.[2] In May 1886 Morris clearly supposed Shaw still to be, in general, on the side of the Marxist theory of surplus value against the Jevonian theory of marginal utility, and he wrote to him soliciting an "economical" article for *Commonweal,* "tackling Jevons".[3] But it is fairly clear that by that time it was Jevons who had tackled Shaw, although Shaw's full critique of Marx's economic theory did not appear until he reviewed *Capital* in the *National Reformer* in October 1887.[4] Even so, we should be cautious of a doctrinaire hindsight in which the theory of surplus value is seen as some litmus-paper testing adhesion to "Marxism". Shaw remained a deeply-divided man: in one part of himself he was (and was to remain) strongly influenced by Morris.[5] Perhaps this split found expression in a divided attitude to Marx. On the one hand, "Marx was wrong about value", as Newton was wrong about light and Goethe was wrong about colours; on the other hand, Marx's economic fallacies did no essential damage to the "super-structure" of his theories, to his historical and contemporary analysis of the class struggle. "Read Jevons and

[1] Brief reports of Fabian Society activities in 1886 appeared in *Our Corner* and the *Practical Socialist:* see also S. Pierson, *op. cit.,* p. 126.

[2] *Bernard Shaw: Collected Letters,* pp. 164-6.

[3] James W. Hulse, *Revolutionists in London* (Oxford, 1970), p. 123.

[4] Shaw's first explicit critique of the theory of value was in correspondence in the *Pall Mall Gazette,* May 7th and 12th 1887: there followed articles reviewing *Capital* in the *National Reformer,* October 7th, 14th, 21st, 1887.

[5] I find James Hulse's treatment of the Shaw-Morris relationship in *Revolutionists in London,* pp. 122-30 very much more satisfactory than his treatment of Morris's thought, for which see Postscript below. See also E.E. Stokes, "Morris and Bernard Shaw", *Journal of William Morris Society,* I, Winter 1961.

the rest for your economics", he advised, and "read Marx for the history of their working in the past, and the conditions of their application in the present. And never mind the metaphysics."[1]

The bearing upon Morris of Shaw's idiosyncratic intellectual pilgrimage from something akin to Marxism ("I have done more up and down fighting for Marx than any other Socialist in the country"[2]) to something akin to Fabianism remains unclear. Eventually, the rejection of the Marxist theory of value and its replacement by the Fabian theory of rents (rent of land, of capital, and of ability) smoothed the way for the rejection of a theory of class struggle and for the adoption of the strategies of gradualism in the *Fabian Essays* of 1889. But this need not have seemed inevitable at any time before 1888 and, with Hyndman presenting himself as an orthodox Marxist, one is chiefly struck by the confusion and intricacy of the issues.

One is also struck by the steadfastness of Morris to the Marxist side of these arguments, even when he felt himself to be a novice in economics and even when he was at odds both with Hyndman and with the "Marxists" of the Bloomsbury Branch. He always emphasised that the study of *Capital* was difficult:

> "The more learned socialist literature, like Marx's celebrated book, requires such hard, and close study that those who have not approached the subject by a more easy road are not likely to begin on that side, or if they did, would find that something like a guide was necessary to them before they could follow the arguments steadily."[3]

But for those who could undertake it, the best entry into Socialist theory was through *Capital.* In February 1885 he replied to a correspondent enquiring as to Socialist reading: "If you read German or French, you should tackle Karl Marx

[1] Shaw to Aveling (draft), May 17th, 1887, *Collected Letters,* pp. 168-9; *National Reformer,* October 21st, 1887.

[2] *Collected Letters,* p. 121.

[3] William Morris, Preface to Frank Fairman, *The Principles of Socialism Made Plain* (1887): the Preface is dated December 5th, 1887.

Das Capital at once." In the second place he recommended Gronlund's *Co-operative Commonwealth* ("of some use"), then Carruthers's *Commercial and Communal Economy* ("well argued and worth reading"), then three pamphlets with "useful information" by Lassalle, Joynes and Sorge, then Hyndman's *Historical Basis of Socialism* which "states in some of its chapters the Marxian theory", although Gronlund "carries it further" and Hyndman's book "is ill put together, & not always accurate":

"On the whole tough as the job is you ought to read Marx if you can: up to date he is the only completely scientific Economist on our side."[1]

A final confirmation of this steadfast respect—and a confirmation rather more conclusive than Glasier's thirty-year-old memories—may be found in an episode involving Annie Besant. The courageous champion of Secularism and contraception had been converted, rather suddenly, to Socialism late in 1885. She argued her new convictions in a series of articles in *Our Corner,* February to May 1886. The second article commenced (March 1886): "In Karl Marx's somewhat prolix and often pedantic work, 'Das Capital', may be found a carefully elaborated exposition of 'surplus value' . . ." The reader was directed to a footnote:

"The well-read student of economics will find little that is new in Marx, but he will find some lucid expositions of well-known truths. Marx is, on many points, a very useful intellectual middleman, and a condensation of his book—edited by a capable scientific Socialist, who would expunge the prolixities and the pseudo-scientific formulas—would be of real service to those whose time for study is limited."[2]

[1] Morris to an Unknown Correspondent, February 28th [1885]. I am indebted to Mr. Stuart B. Schimmel of New York, the owner of this letter, for permission to quote extracts: the full letter will appear in Professor Norman Kelvin's *Collected Letters.* In this same letter Morris recommends his correspondent to attend Aveling's lectures.

[2] *Our Corner,* Vol. 7, March 1886, p. 133.

The ink was scarcely dry upon the articles when Annie Besant prepared to put them together in a pamphlet, *Modern Socialism,* and in course of doing so she sent them to Morris for an opinion. Morris's reply does not seem to have been preserved, but we may deduce its tenor from Besant's acknowledgement: "I have cancelled the footnote about Marx, and the 'prolix and pedantic', for the reprint of the articles on Socialism. I am glad you think they will be useful."[1] What makes this small episode the more piquant is that there is strong reason to suppose that (unknown to Morris) the "intellectual middleman" who was the real author of that banal philistinism in the footnote was none other than George Bernard Shaw, who was at this time conducting a secret *amour* with Annie Besant, who had sent to him all articles for advice in advance of their first publication.[2]

In conclusion, it can be said that it is a cause for surprise, not that Morris found difficulty in advanced economic theory, nor that he fell into certain errors in political tactics, but that—despite all the confusion of issues in his period, and the discord of voices surrounding him (not least in importance being the voice of Shaw)—he should have stood from 1883 until the end of his life "on the side of Karl Marx *contra mundum*".

[1] Annie Besant to William Morris, March 9th, 1886, Brit. Mus. Add. MSS. 45346. The articles were published with almost no revision as *Modern Socialism* (1886: reprinted 1890), with the footnote and "prolix and pedantic" deleted. The resultant treatment of Marx is level and respectful.

[2] Arthur H. Nethercot, *The First Five Lives of Annie Besant* (Chicago, 1960), p. 226 and *passim.* The suggestion that, while the footnote may have come from Besant's pen, the true author was Shaw rests not only upon the circumstances of Shaw and Besant's relations at the time, Shaw's consultation in the writing, and the fact that Besant was not a particularly "well-read student of economics". We must add to this: 1) The proposal that a "capable scientific Socialist" should edit and condense *Capital* recalls a similar "condensation" which Shaw had recently performed on Gronlund's *Co-operative Commonwealth* (see Shaw: *Collected Letters,* pp. 101, 112); 2) There is reason to suppose that Shaw, rather than Annie Besant, was the real author of a letter over her name criticising Marx's theory of value in the *Pall Mall Gazette,* May 24th, 1887 (after a letter from Shaw had been refused); 3) Besant's articles and pamphlet continued to distinguish between Marx's economic exposition and his irrelevant "metaphysics", a distinction which Shaw was also making at this time; compare Besant, *Modern Socialism* (1886), p. 17 and Shaw, cited in Pierson, *op. cit.,* p. 121.

POSTSCRIPT: 1976

In twenty-one years (the interval between this book's first publication and this revised edition) the terrain of scholarship changes, and so also do the preoccupations of scholars. I have no intention of offering here a comprehensive bibliography of recent writing which bears on Morris studies. But some books must be mentioned and others must be discussed more carefully.

First mention may go to the William Morris Society which, over the past twenty years, has organised a valuable series of events, lectures, and publications. The Society's *Journal* carries an up-to-date bibliography, and in 1961 the Society's Honorary Secretary, Mr. R.C.H. Briggs, published a *Handlist* of Morris's addresses. A more complete list of lectures and speeches, and their dates of delivery, is to be found in Eugene D. LeMire's *Unpublished Lectures of William Morris:*[1] this presents in full for the first time ten lectures which had before been drawn upon only in my text or in May Morris's two volumes. Another interesting lecture (of 1889), and notes for a further one, have been published by Paul Meier.[2] Few important new letters have been published, apart from Morris's letters to J.L. Mahon.[3] A valuable collection of critical notices of Morris's work has been brought together by Peter Faulkner,[4] and at least two new selections of political writings have been made available.[5]

Much has been written on Morris's practice of the arts. I've done little to revise my own chapter on these, although I am aware that it is inadequate to its several themes. When so much of expert authority has been published, the wisest course for one without such expertise is reticence. An important revision to received views of Morris's influence was made by the late Peter Floud, who contested the view that the revolution in mid-Victorian taste was the consequence of "the Morris movement", and who emphasised his—sometimes idiosyncratic, sometimes conservative—part within a wider tradition of innovation.[6] Since Floud was kind enough to write to me approving of my chapter, I've let it stand, even though it follows at points the older convention. More recently there have been important new contributions from Paul Thompson, Ray Watkinson and others.[7] Philip Henderson, in his biography of Morris, has also enlarged our knowledge of the Firm, drawing upon the correspondence of Warington Taylor and of Morris to Sir Thomas Wardle.[8] From these materials, and from others in California, a definitive history of the Firm could now be written.[9]

By contrast, twenty-one years harvest of critical writing on Morris's poetry and prose is disappointing. Apart from one lecture by Jack Lindsay[10] and John Goode's important study (discussed at the end of this Postscript) I find little that I can recommend. This may indicate a continuing adverse judgment upon Morris's poetry, although I had expected that my own treatment of *The Defence of Guenevere* and *The Earthly Paradise* might have provoked a little comment, or at least disagreement, among scholars of English literature.[11] These chapters constitute an important part of my argument about the crisis of Romanticism in early Victorian England, and I remain as ready to defend them today as when they were first written. In one area one may detect the first signs of a "thaw" in the icy resistance to Morris: a generation nourished upon Tolkien and C.S. Lewis (himself a sympathetic critic of Morris),[12] is now willing to read with more complaisance the late prose romances. This increasing tolerance has enabled critics, whose prior interest is in Morris's political thought, to show a renewed respect for *The House of the Wolfings* and *The Roots of the Mountains.*[13] When this book first appeared, the only notice (so far as I am aware) that it received from the literary establishment was in a comminatory review in the *Times Literary Supplement,* which reported that many pages—

"are dedicated to defending the language of the saga translations and of the prose romances such as *The Earthly Paradise [sic!]* and *The Well at the World's End.* Mr. Thompson, in fact, concentrates upon just those aspects of Morris's work and thought which seem least relevant today."[14]

Criteria of relevance have now changed, and I suspect that I may today be criticised, more properly, for giving inadequate attention to the prose romances than for "defending" them to excess.

Paul Thompson's study of Morris is not limited to his work as a designer but offers a more comprehensive biography, structured around his work. Philip Henderson's new biography is strongest in its recovery of Morris's personal life and conflicts. Henderson repairs the obligatory silence of Mackail as to relations between William and Janey Morris and Dante Gabriel Rossetti, and he draws upon surviving correspondence between Janey and Rossetti which, at the time of my first writing, was not open to inspection. These letters illuminate the predicament of the three friends, but do not lead me to revise my earlier treatment. Philip Henderson is always perceptive[15] upon all matters other than Morris's political thought and action, and he often catches the nuances of personal relations better than I do: but where his interpretation rests upon Morris's poems I prefer to stand by my own account. Perhaps the most significant new evidence to come to light relates not to the Morrises but to Edward and Georgie Burne-Jones: for it now appears that during the height of Janey's and Rossetti's mutual obsession, Ned Burne-Jones was also preoccupied in a love-affair, with Mary Zambaco. Undoubtedly this will have thrown Georgie and Morris more upon each other's sympathy.[16] As for the relations between Morris and Rossetti in later years, the new evidence can lead only to mournful conclusions. Janey was beset with unexplained illnesses, perhaps of neurotic origin. Rossetti mocked at Morris in his private letters to Janey, calling him, during the Eastern Question agitation, "the Odger of the Future",[17] while Morris commented, on Rossetti's death:

"It makes a hole in the world, though I have seen so little of him lately, and might very likely never have seen him again: he was very kind to me when I was a youngster. He had some of the very greatest qualities of genius, most of them indeed; what a great man he would have been but for the arrogant misanthropy that marred his work, and killed him before his time: the grain of humility which makes a great man one of the people and no lord over them, he lacked, and with it lost the enjoyment of life which would have kept him alive, and sweetened all his work for him and us."[18]

Some part of Janey Morris's correspondence remains in private hands in the United States. It was made available to Henderson and (previously) to Rosalie Glynn Grylls (Lady Mander) for her *Portrait of Rossetti* (1964). Mrs. Grylls, as may be proper in a biographer, is always ready to extend sympathy to her subject, and, as may also be proper, she extends it also to the woman whom he loved. It needn't follow that she should feel obliged to write ungenerously about William Morris. But she loses few opportunities of doing so. She implies, in a knowing way, that Morris was a failure as a lover: his early love poems were thrown together in a few minutes snatched from tapestry or wall-paper (but Morris was at work in neither medium when *The Defence of Guenevere* poems were written). Morris was drawn to the North, Janey and Rossetti to the South, and Grylls, who is one for the South also, commiserates with Janey. If Janey was often silent (Grylls notes with mature self-congratulation) this was only because she "saw through" Morris's Socialist friends, notably Shaw. And more of all this.

I don't wish to be misunderstood. It's no part of my intention to offer a moralistic judgment on Janey's and Rossetti's behaviour. William and Janey Morris were not happy together, and in another time it might have been better if they could have separated and found other partners. But what gives offence is Gryll's implication that if Morris accepted the role of *mari complaisant* (even of a wounded and miserable one) this allows her to portray him as unmanly and as a subject for ridicule. This is one of the most ancient and most disabling of male-dominative stereotypes of sexual relations, and one which, in my own view, derives its damaging potency more from the universal dictatorship of the stereotype itself than from any inherent sexual determinations. Moreover, it is one which has been transmitted with peculiar force within feminine conventions. For generations women advised each other to condone or overlook the infidelities of their husbands, but to despise the husband who extended a similar courtesy to his wife. In short, while wishing in no way to pass judgment on Janey and Rossetti, I suggest that it was a matter of honour in Morris that he did not, in that difficult situation, act the conventional Victorian part of the "wronged" husband. For the rest, I haven't myself attempted to consult any still-published letters from Janey in Mrs. Troxell's collection. I think the matter has been pried into enough.[19]

Much new work has appeared on the Socialists of the 1880s and 1890s, although little bears directly on the Socialist League. My own account inevitably concentrated on Morris's relations with Hyndman and gave inadequate attention to the S.D.F. at branch or district level. Chushichi Tsuzuki's study of Hyndman gives a fair account of his end of the story.[20] I have serious disagreements with Tsuzuki's judgements here,[21] but fewer with his capable study of Eleanor Marx.[22] At the time of writing only the first volume of Yvonne Kapp's definitive life of Eleanor Marx has appeared.[23] The next volume, due to appear very shortly, should give us the first complete study of the Avelings' work for the League and in the Bloomsbury Socialist Society: to judge by its predecessor, the book is likely to be both illuminating and persuasively partisan. And we now have fuller accounts of the activity of other colleagues of Morris in the Socialist propaganda.[24] Dona Torr's study of Tom Mann is indispensable for understanding the choppy period of new unionist upsurge and of the fragmentation of Socialist organization in the late 1880s.[25] My own study of Tom Maguire enlarges upon the history of the League in the West Riding in the same years.[26] The Fabian Society has also attracted a lot of scholarly attention.[27] And more is now known about the ideas and the indefatigable Socialist propaganda in the 1880s of George Bernard Shaw: from his diary it appears that he was delivering up to 100 lectures and talks, under various auspices, each year. And it also appears from these sources that the theoretical confrontation between Fabianism and "Morrisism" was even more conscious and prolonged than I had supposed.[28] This by no means exhausts the relevant new studies; no doubt I have overlooked work of importance; but this survey must suffice.

There remain some more substantive questions (and books) to be discussed. Several of the most recent studies of Morris or of British Socialism draw heavily upon my work, sometimes with generous acknowledgement and sometimes without. In short, my book came to be recognised as a "quarry" of information, although in one or two instances it appears that it was a suspect quarry, to be worked surreptitiously for doctoral advancement. One ought not to object to this: a quarry should release materials into the general fabric of scholarship. But what if my book was not a quarry but a construction meriting attention in its own right? And what if the stones lifted from it end up by adding only to the featureless sprawl of academic suburbia?

At least the question may be put. But one must be careful as to *how* the question is put. Several of my successors, in volumes appearing from the most reputable academic presses, are in agreement that the question can be put in only one way: my scholarship is vitiated by Marxist dogmatism. A work "of intelligent and exhaustive scholarship", in one generous account, "but it is marred by the author's intense Marxian bias." Morris's activities "are examined through the prism of the class struggle and the result is a somewhat distorted view of Morris's ideas."[29] Another finds my book "flawed by its misguided attempt to present its object as an orthodox Marxist."[30] A less generous critic notes that my book devoted "some 900 pages to demonstrate that Morris was really a Marxist."[31]

I had thought that the book was something rather different. It is, in a central respect, an argument about the Romantic tradition and its transformation by Morris. (It is of interest that I and Raymond Williams, whose important *Culture and Society* appeared three years after this book, should have been, unknown to each other, working upon different aspects of the Romantic critique of Utilitarianism). But, leaving this aside, one has to ask whether it may not be the political commitment of Morris, and not of Marx, which has given offence to these authors? In which case my own offence has been chiefly that of showing an intense *Morrisian* bias? The question is difficult: it is true that in 1955 I allowed some hectoring political moralisms, as well as a few Stalinist pieties, to intrude upon the text. I had then a somewhat reverent notion of Marxism as a received orthodoxy, and my pages included some passages of polemic whose vulgarity no doubt makes contemporary scholars wince. The book was published at the height of the Cold War. Intellectual McCarthyism was not confined to the United States, although few in the subsequent generations understand its discreet British modes of operation. Marxist sympathies were so disreputable that they could find little expression outside of Communist publications; and the vulgarity of my own polemic[32] can only be understood against the all-pervasive and well-furnished vulgarities of the anti-Marxist orthodoxies of that time.

The climate can be illustrated by the welcome afforded my book in the non-Socialist press.[33] This welcome was mainly a silence, broken by the review in the *Times Literary Supplement,* headed "Morris and Marxism". The reviewer reported that my book was "heavily biased by Marxism" and "splenetic in tone"; the "remarkable feat" of its author is that "he manages to sustain a mood of ill-temper through a volume of 900 pages". My citations from Morris's political writings "show how fluffy were Morris's socialist views", and the book as a whole "merely serves to emphasize aspects of

Morris which are better left forgotten."[34] It is clear that it was Morris, and not Thompson, nor even Marx, who must be pushed back into the silence of disrepute.

All this was (in those days) predictable. So far from dismaying one it was a tonic to one's fighting-blood: in a sense, even one's self-righteous sectarian errors were confirmed within the circular field of antagonism to such official lampoons and silences. Despite this (and perhaps because of the post-1956 "thaw") the book found its way into university and public libraries. Some years afterwards it began to find its way out again, being rather widely stolen; for several years (I am told) it has been "missing" from both the British Museum and the Bodleian, although whether through the agency of the Congress for Cultural Freedom or of readers converted by Morris to an over-literal repudiation of bourgeois property-rights (but what is bourgeois about the common use-rights of a library?) must be left undetermined. In all this, the book became typed, by enemies and even by some friends, as offering only one finding: the Morris=Marx equation. And yet the book, while perhaps offering too tidy an account of that relation, by no means contented itself with showing Morris ending his life in an orthodox Marxist terminus. The point was, rather, that Morris was an original Socialist thinker whose work was complementary to Marxism. And in repeated emphases, and in particular in the stress upon Morris's genius as a moralist, it should not have been difficult for a sensitive reader to have detected a submerged argument within the orthodoxy to which I then belonged.

But this line of argument is an uneasy one, since it focusses attention on my own intellectual evolution (and apologetics) and distracts attention from our proper concern: William Morris and his political thought. And we should return to the question already proposed: have some recent writers used the criticism of my book to mask their ulterior dislike of Morris, so that for Thompson's "intense Marxian bias" we ought really to read "Morris's uncompromising commitment to revolutionary Socialism?" For if I had really falsified my account of Morris's positions, one would suppose that these critics would go on to correct my account, in informed and accurate ways. But I don't find that this has been done. Thus Willard Wolfe, who affirms that my attempt to present Morris as a Marxist is "misguided", offers no close examination of Morris's Socialist writings, and presents, in succession, the following judgments on Morris's Socialism: a) his lectures of the 1880s "advocated a form of Radical-individualist utopianism that was very similar to Shaw's" (p. 132 n.48);* b) his Socialism was "ethical-aesthetic" (p. 162); and c) Morris "must be classed among the Christian Socialist recruits" to the S.D.F. since his Socialism was "essentially religious in character" and was "grounded on an essentially Christian ideal of brotherhood" (p. 174, 301). This may be good enough for Yale University Press, but it would have been rejected by the Editor of *Commonweal:* what it seems to argue is that Morris's Socialism was really very nice, and never rude, although it leaves unresolved the question as to how "Radical-individualist Utopianism" was reconciled with the "Christian ideal of brotherhood".

J.W. Hulse, in *Revolutionists in London,*[35] does a little better: but not much. He has had a good idea for a book and has executed that idea unevenly. His intention was to treat the inter-relations between the ideas of five remarkable men, co-habitants of London in the 1880s and 1890s—Stepniak, Kropotkin, Morris, Shaw and Bernstein. Despite the fact that the ideas under discussion float around in a state of political weightlessness, some parts of the study are executed well. It may be because I know the subject best that I find the study of Morris to be the worst. Hulse, who knows that my book is marred by "intense Marxian bias",[36] knows a great many more things about Morris's Socialism, although his knowledge is supported more often by assertion than by argument:

* In this Postscript I distinguish references back to the revised text of this book by placing these in italics thus (*162*), from references to the works of other authors under discussion, which are thus (p. 162).

thus (of the Manifesto of the Socialist League (*Appendix I*)), "it incorporates several of the Marxian arguments, but the basic tone was moderate" (p. 85); of the Split:

> "Morris found it necessary to make the break because Hyndman's faction was too authoritarian, too wildly militant, and too opportunistic—in short, too Marxist." (p. 85).

We are also reassured that "the doctrine of the class struggle was one of the Marxian ideas that was only gradually and partially assimilated by Morris." (p. 81). In short, once again Morris's Socialism is shown to have been nice; and if Marxism is defined as "authoritarian", "wild", and "opportunistic" (i.e. *not* nice) then Morris can scarcely have been associated with it unless by accident. But it is not clear that Hulse has helped us towards any precisions. Since he has evidently made no study of *Commonweal* or of the actual political movement[37] his assertions cannot be shown to be supported by anything more than academic self-esteem.

This is a pity, since Hulse does have a correction of substance to offer to my account. He argues that Morris may have been more influenced by Kropotkin and by the Communist-Anarchists than has been generally allowed: in particular in his notion of federated communes, as envisaged in "The Society of the Future" and in *News from Nowhere.* It is a fair point: the "withering away of the State" was not a major preoccupation of Engels or of the Marxist circles of the 1880s, whereas it was a preoccupation shared by Morris and Kropotkin. (Morris noted in 1887 that he had "an Englishman's wholesome horror of government interference & centralization which some of our friends who are built on the German pattern are not quite enough afraid of" (*451*)). Morris's imagination may well have been stimulated more by Kropotkin and by arguments with his followers in the League than I have suggested. But Hulse damages his own argument by special pleading and thin scholarship, thickened up with anti-Marxist rancour. His conclusion offers an eclectic's bazaar which might stand in for a dozen other contemporary academic accounts: "Morris's Socialism might best be described as catholic, borrowing from the Middle Ages and from Russian nihilism, as well as from Mill and from Marx" (p. 110). It might "best be described" in this way if the object of the exercise is polite conversation, but not if it is accurate definition: *what,* one wonders, was borrowed, and how were these unlikely elements combined? "It serves little purpose", Hulse concludes, "to insist that Morris belonged more to one branch of Socialism, or Communism, or anarchism, than to another" (p. 109). That may be so: the "claiming" of Morris for this or that tendency has less purpose than I once supposed myself. But what, surely, may serve a purpose, if we wish to attend to Morris, is to define what Morris's Socialism *was,* what were its controlling ideas, values and strategies? And this can scarcely be done if we disregard his polemic against Fabianism on the one hand, and Anarchism on the other. By neglecting both, and by straining the case for Kropotkin's influence, Hulse ends up as only one more (muddled) claimant.

I would not have laboured my disagreements with Hulse if they didn't illustrate a very general problem of the interpretation of Morris. What is being done, again and again, is that a stereotype of Marxism in its subsequent evolution is being brought back to Morris, and the attempt is then made either to dissociate Morris from it or to assimilate him altogether to it (discarding anything unassimilable as "immaturities" or Romantic hang-overs). But the important question might be not whether Morris was or was not a Marxist, but whether he was a Morrisist; and, if he was, whether this was a serious and coherent position in its own right? The problem is illustrated, from different directions, by two studies, both more serious than any noticed up to this point: Stanley Pierson's *Marxism and the Origins of British Socialism*[38] and Paul Meier's *La Pensée Utopique de William Morris.*

Stanley Pierson does not offer a stereotype of Marxism, and his study is in most respects well-founded. He is interested in the intellectual tendencies within British Socialism between 1880 and 1900, and he takes us steadily through intellectual precursors, and thence to Hyndman, Morris, Bax, Carpenter, the Fabians, Glasier, Blatchford, Mahon, Hardie, the Anarchists, the Labour Churches. They are all put together between the same covers, informatively and often shrewdly, and they are held in place, not only by the binding, but also by a controlling argument which, summarised, is this: when Marxist ideas became a presence in British life, they operated upon a ground of native intellectual traditions: those of Utilitarianism, of Christian nonconformity, and of the Romantic tradition as mediated by Carlyle and Ruskin. No sooner had the new ideas appeared than they became subject to a process of assimilation within the older traditions: they became "attached to deeply ingrained attitudes and feelings". "Marxist theory, in any strict sense, disintegrated rapidly in the Britain of the eighties", but only through "a complex process of mediation" which diverted the native traditions into new channels. Pierson argues that in different ways both Fabianism and the Marxism of Hyndman reverted to the control of the utilitarian tradition; Morris, of course, signals the junction of the Marxist and Romantic traditions, but it was an incomplete junction ("The new system of thought was superimposed on his earlier ideas rather than integrated with them" (p. 80)), and in the result those activists most influenced by Morris "fell back on the moral sentiments released by a disintegrating [Nonconformist] religious tradition" (p. 275). "Marxist ideas entered creatively into the working-class movement only through the breakup of the distinctive synthesis which Marx had constructed" (pp. 276-7). In this breakup any inheritance from Morris came largely by way of *Merrie England,* or through the ethical and sometimes religious Socialism of I.L.P. evangelists like the Glasiers—a Socialism which had lost both "the cutting edge of serious theoretical analysis" and the "reach" for creative alternatives (p. 276).

This account is fair and persuasive. At one level it is an

acceptable account of what took place; and Pierson only strengthens his argument when he points out that, so far from British development being unique, "later European Marxism has followed much the same pattern of breakdown and re-assimilation" to national traditions (p. 278), even when the resulting mixture was sometimes acclaimed as orthodox "Marxism". But at another level, which must most concern the student of Morris, the account is less acceptable. To begin with, this intellectual history is seen in terms of the polite culture: but when we consider the problem of the relation of Socialist theory to the working-class movement in 1880-1900, the "inherited pattern of thought and feeling" which demands attention is not that of Utilitarianism, nor of Romanticism, nor even (except for certain regions) Non-conformity, but that of Labourism—that is, a class culture, already with a long history of struggle, with its own organisational forms and strategies, as well as a certain class morale, although these strategies and forms were in important ways influenced by, and sometimes subordinated to, the ideas which Pierson describes. This need not contradict Pierson's argument; for this class culture was able to assimilate the "ethical Socialism" of *Merrie England* and of some part of Morris, in ways which were not negligible but which still fell short of challenging the controlling strategies of the movement; leaving, nevertheless, a residue in terms of motivation, goal, rhetoric, "Clause Four" obstinacy and even—more than some Marxist historians are willing to allow—Socialist priorities expressed at local levels, which have contributed much to the ambiguities of the modern Labour movement and to the difficulties of its more abject parliamentary leaders.

What this raises, acutely, is the problem of ideology, and this is not a problem which Pierson addresses.[39] For the record is something more than one of intellectual "mediations" or "assimilations". Very sharp theoretical confrontations were taking place, in which emergent Socialist thought contested with the "common-sense" of Victorian liberal-capitalist society and its dominant ideological illusions. And the reminder leads us to two attendant considerations. First, in what sense did the new Socialist theory (and its strategies) constitute a critical break, or rupture, not with this or that point of liberal Victorian thought, but with the organising ideas of bourgeois Liberalism? If we argue that it did constitute such a rupture, it need not follow that the new Socialist theory was in all respects mature, coherent and without self-contradiction;[40] it follows only that at critical points, and in certain controlling ideas, this theory was antagonistic to bourgeois ideology, and, specifically, proposed not the amelioration of the liberal capitalist state but its revolutionary transformation. It will follow that, when we attend to Pierson's arguments about "assimilation", we will be alert to see how far such assimilation went, and whether it went so far as to dissolve the revolutionary pretentions of the new theory and drag it back, across the "rupture", into an accommodation with the old: or whether it served only to confuse and constrict (perhaps in serious ways) the new. Thus Pierson may be right (I think he is) to argue that the Fabians and the Marxists of the S.D.F. (and of other European sections) shared an abbreviated notion of economic man which had a good deal in common with the utilitarian tradition. But the Fabians matched this with theories of rent and of value, of the State, and of history, and with a strategy of permeation, which clearly dragged them back across the ideological divide; whereas the S.D.F., despite all the difficulties which Hyndman presents, continued to offer, until the eve of the World War, a confused and sectarian theory of revolutionary Socialism.[41]

I'm not suggesting that there are some talismanic concepts (Marx's theory of value, the theory of the State) which allow us instantly to identify whether the controlling theory of any person or group is "bourgeois" or "revolutionary". Analysis will never be as easy as that. Still less am I suggesting that there is one single, "correct", immanent Socialist orthodoxy. I'm arguing, as I argued twenty-one years ago, that there *is* a "river of fire". One has to resist a tendency in historians of ideas to see concepts only in their lineage of inheritance and in their mutations: this was mediated by that, and that was assimilated into the other, and all this went on in a world of discourse as congenial as the reading-rooms in which we consult the old periodicals. But—and this is our second consideration—these ideas inhabited actual people in actual contexts (often contexts of serious class confrontation—Bloody Sunday, the miners' strikes, the Sudan War, the new unionism), and the ideas had work to do in the present before they were passed on down the line. It might even be asked (although this is at odds with certain notions of the academic discipline) whether certain ideas were *right*?

In the face of these considerations, doubts as to Pierson's analysis multiply. It lacks not only any argument about critical breaks between opposing intellectual systems, but also any sense of *politics*. We can follow the argument only as it bears upon Morris. The entry might best be through the problem of imperialism, which Pierson never faces, since imperialism is not, in his sense of the term, an intellectual tradition. But if we set ourselves in 1890, and employ hindsight, the major disaster which was bearing down upon the European Socialist and working-class movements was the World War and the ignominious collapse of the Second International. Insofar as this disaster was the consequence of those complex processes which we group together as "imperialism", then surely the responses to these processes, and to national-chauvinist complicity within the working-class movement, will dwarf in importance Pierson's more intellectual criteria of classification? Applying this test, we find that the response of the S.D.F. to imperialism was contradictory; the response of the I.L.P. was evasive and ambiguous. The Fabian response was wholly unambiguous; indeed, at one time the Fabians were unabashed advocates of imperial "rationalisation".[42] The response of William Morris was also, as I show in detail, unambiguous and indeed prophetic.

This might suggest two things: either that Pierson's conventional description of the "Romantic" derivation of Morris's ideas (with Marxist concepts "superimposed" upon Romanticism but not "integrated" with it) is an inadequate account: or that the Romantic tradition had possibilities of antagonism to capitalist common-sense a good deal tougher than it is usual to attribute to it. I believe that *both* suggestions are correct. For Pierson's account of Morris's political theory manages, in some way, to leave out Morris's politics: his *Commonweal* notes, his active organization, his anti-imperialist and internationalist actions, his struggle to defeat chauvinism within the movement. Pierson's inattention is such that he is able to write that Morris "virtually dissolved moral claims in aesthetic feelings", (p. 275)[43] and that "Morris carried much further the tendency (evident in Carlyle and Ruskin) toward eliminating clear acknowledgement of those impulses in men which did not harmonize with their desire for fellowship and beauty."[44] These are odd comments to make upon a thinker who argued that "the death of all art" was preferable to its survival among an élite which owed its condition to class supremacy (*664*); and who, more than any other of this time, cast his eye forward to the disasters of our century, identified the "Manichean hatred of the world" loose in the polite culture (*240*), envisaged the possibility of imperialism leading on to "a regular epoch of war" (*428*), and of the transition to Socialism proving to be "more terrible, far more confused and full of suffering than the period of the fall of Rome" (*723*), and who, finally, argued that the "tremendous organization under which we live", rather than "lose anything which really is its essence. . . will pull the roof of the world down upon its head" (*542*).[45] It's not easy to see how Pierson can derive such startingly prophetic foresight from a consciousness which refused to acknowledge impulses in men other than their desire for fellowship and beauty. "From the Marxist standpoint", Pierson assures us, "the Socialism of Morris was regressive—a relapse into the subjectivism and idealism from which Marx has attempted to rescue earlier Socialist reformers"; in short, Morris reverted to "Utopianism" (pp. 274, 84).[46]

So there are two disagreements, and each of them is large.

First, I hold, against Pierson, that certain critical and controlling Socialist concepts were not "superimposed" upon Morris's Romantic critique, but were indeed integrated with it, and in such a way as to constitute a rupture in the older tradition, and to signal its transformation.[47] Insofar as these concepts were consonant with those of Marx, and were in some cases derived directly from Marxist sources, we ought to call them Marxist. Second, I hold, against Pierson, that the Romantic tradition is not to be defined only in terms of its traditional, conservative, "regressive", "escapist", and "utopian" characteristics—and hence to be seen as a continual undertow threatening to draw Morris back to "subjectivism" and "idealism"—but contained within it resources of a quite different nature, capable of undergoing this transformation independently of the precipitate of Marx and Engels's writing. This is to say, the moral critique of capitalist process was pressing forward to conclusions consonant with Marx's critique, and it was Morris's particular genius to think through this transformation, effect this juncture, and seal it with action. Nor should Pierson have been unaware that the typing of this Romantic critique as "regressive", "utopian", and "idealist" is a facile way of getting out of the problem, for an alternative way of reading that tradition had been proposed, not only in this book, in 1955, but, very cogently, by Raymond Williams in *Culture and Society* in 1958. If Pierson is right that "from the Marxist standpoint the Socialism of Morris was regressive"—and we can't know how Marx himself would have seen it—this may only be a comment on the imaginative lethargy and theoretical constriction which orthodox Marxism was undergoing from the 1880s. It need not prove (if it is true) that the juncture was impossible or that Morris was an intellectual incompetent. It might even mean that orthodox Marxism turned its back upon a juncture which it neglected to its own peril and subsequent disgrace.

I prefer to press the issue in this way, since I can now see, very much more clearly than when I first wrote this book, the danger of the other stereotype. This argues that William

Morris "became *a* Marxist", was "converted *to* Marxism", &c. The danger is to be found throughout M. Paul Meier's weighty and often helpful study.[48] I'm sorry that I must take issue with him, for this major attention paid to Morris's political thought by a scrupulous French scholar is yet one more indication that this thought is alive and is not confined to a national idiom. Meier has carefully considered classical, utopian and other influences upon Morris; he has examined with the greatest care every evidence of Marxist influence upon him, either through texts or by way of conversations with Engels and with Bax;[49] and he has then assembled all the elements of Morris's writings about Communist society (and the transitional stage of Socialism) and has presented these with greater system than I (or, it must be said, Morris) attempted. All this is done lucidly and with generous respect for his subject. One can be assured that the book will put a final end to much rubbish.

But major difficulties remain. Meier offers Morris to us as an orthodox Marxist, and his notion of this orthodoxy is heavily influenced by its subsequent Marxist-Leninist definition. When Morris fails to match these requirements, Meier is able to apologise for him, with sympathetic allusion to his weaknesses in economic analysis, the lack of available Marxist texts, or to his Leftist immaturities or vestigial idealist survivals. The notion of Marxism as a correct truth is assumed throughout, and Morris is judged approvingly in terms of his approximation to this. Meier by no means intends to diminish his subject's stature or to disallow his original influence upon Socialist thought; but, in the result, he does both.

A small part of this lies in the treatment of Morris-Engels relations, already discussed in my text. The Engels-Lafargue correspondence[50] became available subsequent to my first edition: at some places, where Meier derives from it illumination, I derive only irritation. It is impossible, in my view, to study this and other evidence without concluding that on occasion Engels and the extended political family of Marx (operating largely through the German party) had a mischievous and élitist influence upon the European movement. This is perhaps only a small defect to set against the immense and positive influence of Engels's central work, and the perspicacity of many of his judgments. But this small defect rubbed rather sharply, on occasion, against Morris's shins, and (after reading the Lafargue letters) I sharpened my own judgments at one point in the revision (*470-1*). By 1887-8 Morris had reason to feel that his shins were raw. The actions of the "Marxists" of the League had been damaging and uncomradely; although their strategy was an improvement upon Morris's purism, it was folly in them to force matters to an issue on the least significant issue (that of parliamentary candidatures);[51] the attempt to manipulate a doctrinal unity of the European movement on the basis of the German party's programme justified Morris's irritation at Bax being "steeped in the Marxite pickle" (*471*); and (a point I had overlooked) on top of all this Morris's continued solidarity with the German party resulted, early in 1888, in his being dunned for the very heavy sum of £1,000 in a libel action.[52] Indeed, in Morris's personal encounters with the Marxist family circle, one is chiefly impressed by his forbearance.

But, questions of tactics and of personality apart, other questions remain. Meier presses the claim that Engels's subterranean influence can be sensed throughout Morris's writings; indeed, he presses this very far, and further than I can possibly follow him. Again and again, when Meier notes a congruity between Morris and Marxist text, he assumes that Morris could not have reached such a position independently, and he speculates upon a derivation—a sight of an unpublished manuscript, a mediation through Bax. Sometimes the case is well-sustained.[53] At other times it is sustained by little more than the assumption that Morris was incapable of arriving at any original "Marxist" conclusion by his own route:[54] "Malgré notre sincère admiration pour son génie," Meier writes, "et notre refus de ne voir en lui qu'un rêveur, il nous est difficile de croire qu'il ait pu s'élever tout seul à ce niveau théorique" (p. 409).[55] At other times, again we are faced with exactly that juncture between Morris and Marxism which has been my theme. We needn't waste time on the trivial question of ascribing priority of thought to Morris or to Engels. What Meier is doing, when he insists that Morris's Socialist concepts must always be derivative from "Marxism", is, first, narrowing the notion of Marxism to a kind of family tradition—a sort of Royal Legitimacy from which alone descent may be derived—and, second, gravely underestimating the vigour of the tradition which Morris had transformed, and which still stood quite as much at his back as Hegel stood at the back of Marx.

A striking example arises in Meier's treatment of dialectical historical consciousness. He cites the famous passage from the conclusion to *A Dream of John Ball* ("I pondered how men fight and lose the battle. . .") and notes, as I had noted, its congruity with a passage of Engels's *Ludwig Feuerbach* (*722*). But for Meier such a coincidence can't be accidental, and he goes on to speculate upon Morris's knowledge of unpublished sources of Marxist dialectics. This speculation has a little point to it. As Meier notes, the conclusion to Note C in the League's *Manifesto* (*739*) expresses a dialectical sense of historical process, written in Morris's style, although we know that the metaphor of "the spiral" is one that he owed to Bax (pp. 689-92, 693). And, as Meier also notes, there was then no available instruction-kit of Marxist dialectics. *Ergo,* Morris had received tuition in this, either directly from the author of *The Dialectics of Nature* (unpublished until 1925) or by way of Bax.

There are two objections to this. The first (too complex to press here) is that it is a matter of argument whether anything was gained by formalising "the dialectic" in this way. If we are thinking of contradiction, and of the "double-edged, double-tongued" process of social change, Morris had already grasped this, and was confirmed in it by his reading of *Capital.* The second is that, once Morris had reached Socialist conclusions and effected a definitive rupture with Whiggish notions of progress, he must—and did—arrive at a dialectical understanding of process, not just because he had arrived at "Marxism", but because of the whole force of the Romantic tradition that pressed behind him. Indeed, few passages of his writings have a greater sense of inevitability than the final meditations in *John Ball.* The Romantic critique is easily described as "regressive" or "nostalgic" because it is grounded upon an appeal to pre-capitalist values: and this is most specifically so in Morris, with his imaginative location of value in medieval, Old Icelandic and Germanic contexts. As Williams has noted, Morris carries directly through into his Socialist thought some of the terms of the Romantic critique of Utilitarianism, as in the opposition of the notion of community (or "true society") to "mechanical civilization".[56] So that it is difficult to see how Morris could have transformed that tradition if he had *not* attained to a dialectical notion (Bax's "spiral") of the reassertion at a new level and in new forms of pre-capitalist values of community and of "barbarism".[57]

Meier, in presenting Morris's thought as system, clarifies much: but he loses the understanding of its own authentic dynamic—how and where it broke through on its own. And I must insist upon the importance of my chapter, "The 'Anti-Scrape' ", a chapter which I dare say impatient Socialist readers generally skip. For this, as much as "The River of Fire", analyses Morris at the point of transforming a tradition, when he is confronted by problems which demand a solution both in practice and in theory. "The essence of what Ruskin taught us", Morris said, "was really nothing more recondite than this, that the art of any epoch must of necessity be the expression of its social life."[58] This was, please note, what Ruskin taught, and not Marx, and in 1880, when he had never so much as heard of Marx's name, Morris was writing:

> "So the life, habits, and aspirations of all groups and classes of the community are founded on the economical conditions under which the mass of the people live, and it is impossible to exclude socio-political questions from the consideration of aesthetics."[59]

It was to "Anti-Scrape" that he spoke, in 1884, of the new

understanding of history:

"Inchoate order in the remotest times... moving forward ever towards something that seems the very opposite of that which it started from and yet the earlier order never dead but living in the new, and slowly moulding it to a recreation of its former self." (*236*).

The thought prefigures *A Dream of John Ball,* and entails the same dialectical sense of process. Bax (or Engels) may have found a name for this (the "spiral") but Morris was already immersed in the problems which it named: why was it impossible to reproduce Gothic architecture? How were the handicrafts of an earlier social order (unless by some spiral of change) to be revived? And in the same Address Morris paused to acknowledge *both* Ruskin and the Marx of *Capital.* But what he acknowledged as a debt to Marx was not some total and new revelation as to historical process but a specific understanding of the effects of the capitalist mode of production, for profit rather than use, upon the workshops of the "manufacturing system". (*238*) This can't be seen just as a conversion *by* Marx *to* "Marxism". It is a juncture of *two* strong traditions, and the second didn't attain to its supremacy only after assassinating the first.

So that I can accept neither Pierson's notion that certain Marxist concepts were "superimposed" upon Morris's Romanticism, without integration; nor Meier's implicit judgment that Romanticism is co-terminous with "idealism" (in its orthodox Marxist connotation), and hence to be sloughed off when Morris became "a Marxist".[60] And if we have to choose between errors, it may be the second which is the more disabling. I may seem to be dancing on the point of a pin, but others have danced there before me. Raymond Williams, when offering in 1958 a cogent criticism of the self-contradictions of English Marxist critics (including myself) noted:

"It certainly seems relevant to ask English Marxists who have interested themselves in the arts whether this is not Romanticism absorbing Marx, rather than Marx transforming Romanticism. It is a matter of opinion which one would prefer to happen." (p. 274)

But, if we let Morris stand in for "Romanticism", these are not the only alternatives. It is possible also to envisage the Romantic tradition, transformed as it was by Morris (in part through his encounter with Marx), entering into a common Communist tradition to which it could contribute its particular emphases, vocabulary and concerns. It was a distinctive contribution of *Culture and Society* to show how tough this long Romantic critique of industrial capitalism had been; and I would add that Williams's own writing, over two decades, has exemplified how tough a mutation of that tradition can still be, and how congruent to the thought of Marx.

At least we have to ask what could lie inside the phrase, "Marx transforming Romanticism?" This might stand for what was actually effected in Morris's own thought. Or it might only mean that Marxism could gobble Romanticism up, both beak and quill, assimilating its good faith as useful nutriment, and discarding its "sentimentalism", its moral realism, and its utopian courage as so much idealist excrement. And it is this second response which only too often appears to characterise Engels's reactions to Morris. There was a brief moment of mutual warmth at the time of the "Split", when Morris was delighted to find the Old Norse Edda on Engels's table and responded by reading him some passages from *Sigurd:* "It went off very well."[61] Thereafter the disdainful and dismissive references multiply: Engels could not be bothered to "manage" this "rich artist-enthusiast" and "sentimental socialist". (*471*) There is no evidence that he read *Hopes and Fears for Art* (1882) nor *Signs of Change* (1888), and there is evidence that he left *News from Nowhere* unread. He did read *Socialism, Its Growth and Outcome,* and signalled a tepid approval, but this was a text of the movement which he was scanning for its utility: there is not the least suggestion that he might have had anything to learn from Morris in his turn. As I noted in 1959, "while Morris strained hard and successfully to understand and absorb much of Engels's tradition, Engels made no comparable effort in Morris's direction."[62]

Marx, whose early revolt was germane to the Romantic tradition, might have met Morris more warmly. But this can't be passed off as a matter of temperament. Engels's disdain for Morris exemplifies the narrowing orthodoxy of those years, a narrowing noted not only in his own writings but in the Marxist tradition more generally. As tendencies towards determinism and positivism grew, so the tradition suffered a general theoretical closure, and the possibility of a juncture between traditions which Morris offered was denied. The Romantic critique of capitalism, however transformed, became suspect as "moralism" and "utopianism". I should not need, in 1976, to labour the point that the ensuing lack of moral self-consciousness (and even vocabulary) led the major Marxist tradition into something worse than confusion.[63] But this helps us to identify two important points about Morris's contemporary significance. First, it is more important to understand him as a (transformed) Romantic than as a (conforming) Marxist. Second, his importance within the Marxist tradition may be seen, today, less in the fact of his adhesion to it than in the Marxist "absences" or failures to meet that adhesion half-way. Morris's "conversion" to Marxism offered a juncture which Marxism failed to reciprocate, and this failure—which is in some sense a *continuing* failure, and not only within the majority Communist tradition—has more to teach us than have homilies as to Morris's great-hearted commitment.[64]

One would expect that the most significant new studies of Morris would be directed to these problems. And it is heartening to find two writers, Miguel Abensour and John Goode, whose work carries my points a great deal further. Abensour has presented a new study of the Utopian tradition, which, after a chain of subtle analysis, places exceptional emphasis upon Morris's critical (and unexhausted) significance.[65] Since

M. Abensour's work will not be easily available to English-speaking readers for some time, I must report his conclusions with care. He writes from a critical position (a position of the "Left") within French Marxist culture; and he attends with especial care to what other Socialist writers have written about Morris: Guyot, Page Arnot, A.L. Morton, John Middleton Murry,[66] Williams, Meier and myself: and none of us escapes criticism. Abensour recognises the importance of Page Arnot's *Vindication* of Morris (1934) in confronting the anti-Marxist myths of the time. But he argues that this also established the countervailing myth within the Marxist tradition, in which all that was "valuable" in Morris's thought had first to be passed through the sieve of an orthodoxy, and any bits of Utopianism too large to be pushed through the holes could be forgiven by invoking the licence afforded to a poet (p. 252). The new myth was not wrong to show that Morris was a practical and theoretical adherent to the Marxist tradition: it was wrong in passing over or apologising for significant differences of emphasis within that tradition (where Morris stood, with Domela Nieuwenhuis, on the "Left"), and in neglecting aspects of his thought which could not be assimilated. I am found less guilty of such assimilation and neglect than some others, but Abensour finds that I run aground, alongside A.L. Morton, on the problem of Utopianism; and he chides me for evasion in accepting the formula, "Scientific Utopia"; for *News from Nowhere* (p. 263).[67] Behind this formula he detects a rejection of the validity of the utopian mode in any form: a "Scientific Utopia" may be condoned only because it is not *really* utopian.

Abensour argues that the critique of Utopian Socialism in the *Communist Manifesto* and, even more, in Engels's *Socialism, Utopian and Scientific,* gave rise in the subsequent Marxist tradition to a doctrinal antinomy: Science (good), Utopianism (bad). At any point after 1850 Scientific Socialism had no more need for Utopias (and doctrinal authority for suspecting them). Speculation as to the society of the future was repressed, and displaced by attention to strategy. Beyond "the Revolution" little more could be known than certain skeletal theoretical propositions, such as the "two stages" foreseen in *The Critique of the Gotha Programme.* It must follow that orthodox Marxists must approach William Morris with great uneasiness. What was this throwback to Utopianism doing within the Marxist tradition at all? Perhaps his was a case of misrecognition? The usual solution was to propose a respect for Morris (for his good intentions and his more explicit political texts) beneath which was hidden a yawning condescension: Morris, who became "a Marxist" at fifty, couldn't be expected to shed all his old Romantic habits, most of which were charming or amusing; but while the form of his writings remains "utopian", the content became, in good part, "scientific"; and what can not be shown to conform to Marxist text may be passed over. The solution, in short, has been to propose that Morris was not really a Utopian at all.

These are not Abensour's words but a gloss upon his argument. And I will gloss also certain of his counter-proposals: (i) While one may assent (as he does) to the criticisms by Marx and Engels of the pre-1850 Utopian Socialists, these are local political judgments which need not condemn, once and for all, any generic utopian mode; (ii) Morris is, inescapably, a utopian Communist, not only in *News from Nowhere,* but also on the evidence of a large part of his more directly political writing, and any judgment which fails to confront this squarely is guilty of evasion; (iii) The question of Morris's relations to Marxism raises acutely the question, not as to whether Marxists should criticise Morris, but whether Marxism should criticise itself?

Let us now see, in more detail, how Abensour pursues these arguments. The conventional Marxist approach to Morris (he argues) combines an exercise of "domestication" and "repression", in which the utopian components in his thought are reduced to an expression of Scientific Socialism (p. 270). It is Meier who draws upon himself Abensour's sharpest critique. In admitting *News from Nowhere* to the Marxist canon, Meier must first pass it through a double scrutiny: first, he must extract from it certain propositions, which are then compared with propositions in Morris's more explicit political writings: then these propositions are compared, in their turn, with the texts of Marx and Engels, as "a kind of Supreme Court, alone qualified to pronounce a final verdict". The theoretical texts are thus used as a master-key to de-code the utopian work (p. 345). As a result, Meier at last "gives a name to the 'Nowhere' from which we've had news: the name of the continent is Marxism" (p. 346). But we are permitted to respond to the work only insofar as it has been found correct, by way of this double textual verification. Where it is correct, the Utopia may be said to be "scientific". Primacy is given, in Meier's analysis, to the "theory of the two stages", as found in *The Critique of the Gotha Programme,* a text which we might well be advised to hold in our right hand and study carefully, while we scan *News from Nowhere* in our left. The function of this "Scientific Utopia" is then reduced to the "illustration" of truths already disclosed elsewhere (p. 347). What Meier offers as a sympathetic appreciation of Utopianism is in effect an *exercise of closure,* confining the utopian imagination within textually-approved limits. Meier has been guilty of an exercise of theoretical repression (p. 350).

A summary would not do justice to Abensour's alternative analysis of *News from Nowhere.* But we should report certain of his general propositions. First, the scientific/utopian antinomy of Engels must be rejected. Second, a new kind of utopian writing may be found among European Socialists after 1850, prefigured by Déjacque and Coeurderoy, and of which Morris is the most notable exemplar. This new Utopianism turned away from the forms of classical Utopianism—those of juridico-political model-building (p. 296)—and turned towards a more open heuristic discourse. Third, and we are now specifically taking the case of Morris, it is possible to show how, around the body of general expectations ("prévision generique") of Marxist thought, further hypotheses as to the future might be advanced by the utopian imagination—hypotheses which are neither Marxist nor anti-Marxist but simply "*a*-Marxist". Morris could (and did) take certain Marxist propositions as his point of departure, but used these as a springboard from which his imagination made a utopian leap (p. 277). If the major Marxist tradition has sought to reduce his insights back to their point of departure, that is because that tradition was becoming enclosed within a self-confirming doctrinal circularity.

What, then, is the function of the new Utopianism of Morris, if it brings back neither propositions which can be validated in relation to text, nor offers, in the classical way, a strict societal model? Communism (as Morris saw it) involved the subversion of bourgeois society and a reversal of the whole order of social life: "the attainment of that immediate end will bring about such a prodigious and overwhelming change in society, that those of us with a grain of imagination in them cannot help speculating as to how we shall live then."[68] It was not Morris's intention, in any of his utopian writings, to offer either doctrine or systematic description of the future society (pp. 295-6). He was often deliberately evasive as to "arrangements". Exactly for this reason he drew upon his Romantic inheritance of dream and of fantasy, accentuated further by the distancing of an archaic vocabulary, instead of adopting the spurious naturalism of Bellamy. His intention was to embody in the forms of fantasy alternative values sketched in an alternative way of life (p. 298). And what distinguishes this enterprise is, exactly, its *open,* speculative, quality, and its *detachment* of the imagination from the demands of conceptual precision.[69] Neither in *News from Nowhere* nor in such lectures as "A Factory as it might be" or "The Society of the Future" is Morris offering precise "solutions". Nor does it even matter (as a first criterion) whether the reader approves of his approximations. Assent may be better than dissent, but more important than either is the challenge to the imagination to become immersed in the same open exploration. And in such an adventure two things happen: our habitual values (the "commonsense" of bourgeois society) are thrown into disarray. And we enter into Utopia's proper and new-found space: *the education of desire.* This is not the same as "a moral education" towards a given end: it is, rather, to open a way to aspiration, to "teach desire to desire, to desire better, to desire more, and above all to desire in a different way" (p. 330). Morris's Utopianism, when it succeeds, liberates desire to an uninterrupted interrogation of our values and also to its own self-interrogation:[70]

"In fact, in William Morris's case, the recourse to utopian writing signifies exactly the desire to make a breakthrough, to risk an adventure, or an experience, in the fullest sense of the word, which allows one to glimpse, to see or even to think what a theoretical text could never, by its very nature, allow us to think, enclosed as it is within the limits of a clear and observable meaning." (p. 347)

Nor is Abensour even willing to allow us to see this as a form of political criticism, since it is, at the deepest level, a criticism of all that we understand by "politics" (p. 341).

This remarkable study despatches the old questions into the past, and proposes new problems. Where the argument had been, "was Morris a Marxist or a not-Marxist?", it turns out that, in a major part of his Communist propaganda, he was neither. He was somewhere else, doing something else, and the question is not so much wrong as inappropriate. This explains the difficulty which all critics, except the "repressive" M. Meier, have in reducing his Socialist writings to system; and why these unsystematic writings should still challenge in such profound ways. We may say, and should say, that Morris was a Marxist *and* a Utopian, but we must not allow either a hyphen or a sense of contradiction to enter between the two terms. Above all, the second term may not be reduced to the first. Nor can we allow a condescension which assumes that the "education of desire" is a subordinate part.

I welcome Abensour's insight the more since it is the insight which, at a submerged level, structured this book when it was first written, but which I finally failed to articulate. In my emphasis upon "aspiration" within the Romantic tradition, upon "moral realism", upon Morris's repeated play on the word "hope", and in the very title of Part Four ("Necessity and Desire"), I was reaching towards a conclusion which, in the end, I turned away from out of piety towards politics-as-text and timidity before the term, "utopian". But it stares one in the face: Morris was a Communist Utopian,[71] with the full force of the transformed Romantic tradition behind him.

The pin-point upon which we have been dancing has imperceptibly enlarged, until it stretches as far as eye can see on every side. To define Morris's position as a Socialist it has proved necessary to submit Marxism itself to self-criticism: and in particular to call in question the scientific/utopian antinomy. But this self-criticism involves very much larger consequences than the local judgment as to William Morris's relation to that tradition. Indeed, "the case of Morris" may be a critical one in diagnosing the case of post-1880 Marxism. A Marxism which could not reciprocate or live without disdain alongside Morris, or which, even while "claiming" him, sought to close what he had opened and to repress his insights, was likely to find equal difficulty in co-habiting with any other Romantic or utopian mode. And "desire", uneducated except in the bitter praxis of class struggle, was likely—as Morris often warned—to go its own way, sometimes for well, and sometimes for ill, but falling back again and again into the "common-sense" or habitual values of the host society. So that what may be involved, in "the case of Morris", is the whole problem of the subordination of the imaginative utopian faculties within the later Marxist tradition: its lack of a moral self-consciousness or even a vocabulary of desire, its inability to project any images of the future, or even its tendency to fall back in lieu of these upon the Utilitarian's earthly paradise—the maximisation of economic growth. But this is to extend the argument further than is proper in this place. Let it suffice to say that this pin has a big enough point; and that to vindicate Morris's Utopianism may at the same time be to vindicate Utopianism itself, and set it free to walk the world once more without shame and without accusations of bad faith.

To vindicate Utopianism (in the sense that Abensour has proposed) does not, of course, mean that *any* (non-classical, non-juridico-political) utopian work is as good as any other. The "education of desire" is not beyond the criticism of sense and of feeling, although the procedures of criticism must be closer to those of creative literature than those of political theory. There are disciplined and undisciplined ways of "dreaming", but the discipline is of the imagination and not of science. It remains to be shown that Morris's utopian thought survives this criticism, as well as the criticism of ninety rather sombre years. I have not changed my view that it does. Raymond Williams reached a more nuanced judgment, which has been challenged by both Abensour and John Goode. Williams wrote:

> "For my own part, I would willingly lose *A Dream of John Ball* and the romantic socialist songs and even *News from Nowhere*—in all of which the weaknesses of Morris's general poetry are active and disabling, if to do so were the price of retaining and getting people to read such smaller things as *How we Live, and How we might Live, The Aims of Art, Useful Work versus Useless Toil,* and *A Factory as it might be.* The change of emphasis would involve a change in Morris's status as a writer, but such a change is critically inevitable. There is more life in the lectures, where one feels that the whole man is engaged in the writing, than in any of the prose and verse romances. . . Morris is a fine political writer, in the broadest sense, and it is on that, finally, that his reputation will rest."[72]

This is not very far from my own judgment (*717*). Nor need the question of utopian vision necessarily be at issue here, in the examples which Williams gives, and taking in "the broadest sense" of political writing. But Abensour fears that Williams is leaving a way open to evasion, much as I did with "Scientific Utopia". For the judgment might easily reduce the utopian to the political, in its customary notation ("a fine political writer"), which may then be judged by normal political canons.[73]

Abensour's objection rests in part upon his own fine and

close reading of *News from Nowhere*—of its structure and its openness—and in part upon a criticism of Williams's neglect of the prior utopian tradition. But the questions may be reduced to one: why should the utopian and the "political" works be set off against each other, when so obviously they must be taken together? Why should we be invited to pay this price at all? Williams gives up *Nowhere* and *John Ball* too easily, as perhaps *Pilgrim's Progress* or *Gulliver's Travels* may once have been given up by readers to whom they had become over-familiar furniture of the mind. And John Goode asks much the same question. It is fascinating to observe how Abensour and Goode, working on different materials and drawing upon the respective strengths—analytic and critical—of their respective disciplines and idioms, approach to similar conclusions.

Goode's work is readily available and I needn't report it at length.[74] He notes of Williams's judgment that it "suggests the right order in which to read Morris", but that as a critical judgment it "needs to be challenged", for such drastic de-valuing of Morris's creative writing would bring a change in his status, and Williams "does not seem to realize how great that change would be." A similar criticism is extended to me: I also offer a "split between aesthetic and moral judgments" which "again reduces Morris's creative work to a marginal role".[75] Goode then returns to Morris's creative writing, from *Sigurd* onwards, but he doesn't attempt to rehabilitate this within the conventional terms of literary criticism. What he does is to enquire into the problems which Morris had to surmount in the creative writing of his Socialist years. This writing should be seen as "a formal response to problems which are theoretically insoluble, except in terms of metaphors which are unsatisfactory and intractable in the actual historical situation" (p. 222). In this view Goode is close to the view of Pierson that "the fusion Morris effected between the romantic vision and Marxism", as one consequence, "sharpened the divorce between consciousness and objective social reality which had characterized the thought of Carlyle and Ruskin."[76] The deeper Morris's understanding became of the determinations of capitalist process, the more intransigeant became the protest against these of aspiration or "desire", the more impossible it became to clothe these aspirations within contemporary forms, and the more urgent it became for "desire" to master "necessity". Goode shares my view that despair, rather than vision, moved Morris in the first place towards revolutionary Socialism (p. 235); and while Marxism "gives his vision an historical basis, the central concept of his socialist ideology is one which has been with him from the beginning, alienation" (p. 236).[77] Not only are we entitled to use "alienation" in an analytic rather than merely descriptive way, but Goode shows that Morris was very conscious of this diagnosis, as when he wrote that "civilization has bred desires which she forbids us to satisfy, and so is not merely a niggard but a torturer also", or that "all civilization has cultivated our sensibility only to disappoint it" (p. 236).[78] Thus Morris faced this contradiction, in a tension brought about by a vision of a Socialist future which "is in some way beyond immediate consciousness although in theoretical terms it is conceivable" (p. 238),—a tension expressed also in his own work (which Goode suggests is the true subject of the later creative writing) between "the vision of the historical potential" and the humdrum or depressing actualities of the movement. Faced with contradictions between Socialist aspiration and the overwhelming presence of capitalist actuality (with its "common-sense" signalling at every turn the "impossibility" of Socialist realisation) a general reaction within the Marxist tradition was (as Gramsci saw) a relapse into mechanical predestinarian determinism—a stamina fortified by a faith in the inevitability of the victory of "the Cause".[79] It is not only that Morris, perhaps increasingly, doubted such determinism or evolutionism;[80] it is also, as Goode very well notes, a pseudo-resolution of the problem of alienation: a resolution (or "Revolution") "achieved by forces outside himself: man's alienation will be brought to an end by alien forces" (p. 270). It is in the face of these contradictions that we should see how Morris's works "attempt, with much success, to find a mode in which the creative mind can be portrayed in its determined and determining relationship to historical actuality" (p. 222), and also how people themselves may be seen "as a determining as well as determined force" (p. 271).

This can't be done, however, within the received forms of realism. It is therefore inevitable and right that Morris should turn to new account his old Romantic inheritance of dream. "The affirmation of the responsibility of dream in a world in which consciousness has become ineradicably dislocated from the field of its existence is an assumed feature of all of Morris's socialist writings" (p. 239).

The test of Goode's defence of Morris's practice must depend not on this argument (although this argument puts us into the right critical relation to the works) but upon Goode's own very close criticism of particular works. This includes a remarkable revaluation of *Sigurd the Volsung,* which reveals hitherto unperceived levels of complexity of mythic organization in the work, but which leaves me not wholly convinced;[81] a very rich, subtle, and convincing analysis of *A Dream of John Ball;* and a significant reappraisal of *The House of the Wolfings.* In my view, although differences of local judgment of course remain, Goode emphatically sustains his challenge to Williams and myself. Henceforward these works and the "political writings" must be taken together.

But what are they to be taken as? It's here that Goode approaches to the same solution as that of Abensour, but (as it seems to me) finally takes alarm and backs away. Goode also challenges the term "Scientific Utopia"; but, as it turns out, he does so because he finds that *News from Nowhere* may neither be described adequately as "Scientific" nor as "Utopia". The work is primarily "not so much a picture of enacted values as a reversal of the rejected values of modern life" (p. 277), and it expresses the exhaustion and even pessimism in the mind of its author: "Nowhere is nowhere except as a conceptual antithesis in the mind of an exhausted activist." But why, in these clauses, does Goode insist upon such an opposition? Is it possible, in this kind of work, to reject present values without enacting alternatives? How can one be done without the other? Perhaps the weight falls on "antithesis": Nowhere's values are those of the not-present, or anti-present, they are not boldly imagined *ex nihilo?* But it has to be shown, first, that this is so (as Goode does not); and second, that a utopian writer can proceed in any other way than by re-ordering the values of present or past, or by proposing antitheses to these. What Goode seems to be doing is, like so many before him, and like myself in 1955, running away from the acceptance of Utopianism as a valid imaginative form, because of a fright given to us by Engels in 1880.[82] Goode therefore concentrates upon one component only of *News from Nowhere* (the "never-ending contrast" between future, past and present, which, as I noted (*695*), is essential to the work's structure) at the expense of all others:

> "It seems to me that we have, in this novel, much less a Utopia than an account of the agony of holding the mind together, committed as it is to the conscious determinants of history and the impersonal forces of change—united only in conceptual terms." (p. 278)

So that, in conclusion, Goode can say that he has identified the achievement in the last creative works in that Morris "discovers forms which dramatize the tensions of the revolutionary mind". This is a part of the truth, especially of *John Ball,* and Goode is the first to have identified this part so well. But is *News from Nowhere* really to be read, responsively, only as an "agony"? And is this not a somewhat cerebral account of a work which does, indeed, enact alternative values? At least it seems a somewhat introverted judgment ("the tensions of the revolutionary mind") upon a work which succeeded rather well in communicating something very different to an audience not given to the intellectual's narcissistic obsession with his own mental agonies.[83]

I may well be wrong: but it seems to me that Goode has come to a conclusion at odds with his own evidence, and that he has done so because he leaves the problem of Utopianism unexamined. For earlier in his study he moves very close to the positions of Abensour. He warns that there is nothing "facile" in Morris's use of dream "as a convention within which to realize concretely socialist insight". Morris's use of dream is "not polemical but exploratory" (p. 246), and, again, he uses it:

> ". . . not in order to escape the exigencies of the depressing actuality but in order to insist on a whole structure of values and perspectives which must emerge in the conscious mind in order to assert the inner truth of that actuality, and give man the knowledge of his own participation in the historical process which dissolves that actuality." (p. 270)

This is, almost, to rehabilitate Utopianism. But not quite. For there is a little fuzz of evasion. Utopia is accepted as "convention" to realize "insight", and dream allows perspectives to emerge "in the conscious mind" which afford "knowledge". (We recall Goode's judgment that "Nowhere" is a "conceptual antithesis" and the work enacts an agony of the "mind".) What one notes is a certain tendency to intellectualise art, and to insist that it can be validated only when translated into terms of knowledge, consciousness and concept: art seen, not as an enactment of values, but as a re-enactment in different terms of theory. What is lost is Abensour's insistence upon "the education of desire". "The role of Morris's art", Goode writes, "seems increasingly to be one which combats the tendency to collapse into a determinist act of faith by presenting the potentialities of human growth in a situation in which it is enabled and compelled to take the initiative" (p. 261). This is fine, and what this expresses is, precisely, the utopian "leap". If Goode has lingered over "initiative" he might have concluded, with Abensour, that one part of Morris's achievement lies in the open, exploratory character of Utopianism: its leap out of the kingdom of necessity into an imagined kingdom of freedom in which desire may actually indicate choices or impose itself as need; and in its innocence of system and its refusal to be cashed in the same medium of exchange as "concept", "mind", "knowledge" or political text.

Whether Utopianism succeeds in what it offers must in each work be submitted to the test of local criticism. And Goode's criticism of *A Dream of John Ball* is by far the best appreciation (and vindication) of any of Morris's Socialist works of art. His work, taken together with Abensour's, carries Morris studies into different territory. These bring, at last, news from somewhere new. That is what is important.

In this review, both of my own work and of Morris studies over the past twenty-one years, I've concentrated perhaps overmuch on one problem: the Morris/Marxism relation. I think that this is where the significant questions lie. The older attempts to assimilate Morris to Labourism, or even to Fabianism, were given a check long ago. Very clearly, the course which British Labourism has pursued in this century has not only departed from the perspectives advocated by Morris, but has led into exactly that general deadlock which he foresaw. The people must "take over for the good of the community *all the means of production:* i.e. *credit,* railways, mines, factories, shipping, land, machinery," he wrote to a correspondent in 1884: "Any partial scheme *elaborated as a scheme* which implies the existence with it side by side of the ordinary commercial competition is doomed to fail. . . it will be sucked into the tremendous stream of commercial production and vanish into it, after having played its part as a red-herring to spoil the scent of revolution."[84] In "The Policy of Abstention" in 1887 he envisaged, with some precision, the course of a parliamentary Labourism which fell into the errors of "*depending* on parliamentary agitation", which did not support "a great organization outside parliament actively engaged in reconstructing society" and which would move "earth & sea to fill the ballot boxes with Socialist votes which will not represent Socialist *men*" (*460*). At about the same time he wrote:

> "They are already beginning. . . to stumble about with attempts at State Socialism. Let them make their experiments and blunders, and prepare the way for us by so doing. . . We—sect or party, or group of self-seekers, madmen, and poets, which you will—are at least the only set of people who have been able to see that there is and has been a great class-struggle going on. Further, we can see that this class-struggle cannot come to an end till the classes themselves do: one class must absorb the other."[85]

Morris already at that time envisaged "experiments" leading on to a "transitional condition" which reads uncomfortably like some passages in the history of this century:

> "Attempts at bettering the condition of the workers will be made, which will result in raising one group of them at the expense of another, will create a new middle-class and a new proletariat; but many will think the change the beginning of the millenium. . . This transitional condition will be chiefly brought about by the middle-class, the owners of capital themselves, partly in ignorant good-will towards the proletariat (as long as they do not understand its claims), partly with the design both conscious and unconscious, of making our civilization hold out a little longer against the incoming flood of corruption on the one hand, and revolution on the other."[86]

In his last years Morris became reconciled to the inevitability of the course upon which Labourism was set. But, in his final lectures, he asked repeatedly "how far the betterment of the working people might go and yet stop short at last without having made any progress on the *direct* road to Communism?"

> "Whether, in short, the tremendous organization of civilized commercial society is not playing the cat and mouse game with us socialists. Whether the Society of Inequality might not accept the quasi-socialist machinery. . . and work it for the purpose of upholding that society in a somewhat shorn condition, maybe, but a safe one. . . The workers better treated, better organized, helping to govern themselves, but with no more pretence to equality with the rich, nor any more hope of it than they have now."[87]

What are being counterposed here are the alternative notions of Equality of Opportunity, within a competitive society: and of a Society of Equals, a Socialist community. Utopianism suddenly reveals itself as more realistic than "science", the exploratory historical imagination overleaps its own circumstances and searches the dilemmas of our own time with a moral insight so searching that it can be mistaken as callous. "I must tell you that my *special* leading motive as a Socialist is hatred of civilization; my ideal of the new Society would not be satisfied unless that Society destroyed civilization" (*718*).

We have to make up our minds about William Morris. Either he was an eccentric, isolated figure, personally-admirable, but whose major thought was wrong or irrelevant and long left behind by events. This could be so, although it needn't mean that we must dismiss his subsidiary interests and emphases. He will always remain of major importance in the history of the decorative arts and in the narrative history of British Socialism. And certain other themes can be taken out of his writings, which will swim up now and then into re-vitalised discourse: thus it has recently been noted (remarkable discovery!) that he is a pioneer of responsible "ecological" consciousness, and it has never been forgotten that he had definite and uncomfortable views on the question of work.[88] On the other hand, it may be that Morris was a major intellectual figure. As such he may be seen as our greatest diagnostician of alienation, in terms of the concrete perception of the moralist and within the context of a particular English cultural tradition. And if he was that, then he remains a contemporary figure. And it then must be important to establish the relation in which he stands to contemporary thought. And if the British Labour movement has now reached, rather exactly, the deadlock which, some ninety years ago, he foresaw, then we can expect an intense renewal of interest in his work and a number of claimants to his inheritance to come forward.

The most plausible, and most vocal, claimant is "Marxism",

and that is why my discussion has turned on this point. I must confess that, when I first read M. Meier, I was thrown into depression. It seemed that one had extricated Morris, twenty-one years ago, from an anti-Marxist myth, only to see him assimilated curtly within a myth of Marxist orthodoxy. The result was not only repressive, it was also distancing and boring—Morris's portrait might now be hung safely on the wall, with *The Critique of the Gotha Programme* on his lap. But since Meier was only writing out at large certain pieties and evasions in my own original treatment, I hardly had the heart to enter the argument again. Thanks to M. Abensour and Mr. Goode I've got back my morale. We can now see that Morris may be assimilated to Marxism only in the course of a process of self-criticism and re-ordering within Marxism itself.

The question turns upon Morris's independent derivation of Communism out of the logic of the Romantic tradition; upon the character of his Utopianism; and upon the relations in which the moral sensibility stands to political consciousness. "My Socialism began", he wrote, "where that of some others ended, with an intense desire for complete equality of condition for all men". And "I became a Communist before I knew anything about the history of Socialism or its immediate aims". It was at this point that he turned to Marx and became "a practical Socialist"—"in short I was born again".[89] But to be born again did not mean renouncing his own parentage. "Ideal" and "science" continued to co-exist and to argue with each other.

"Equality is in fact our ideal", he said, and "I can only explain the fact that some socialists do not put this before them steadily by supposing that their eager pursuit of the means have somewhat blinded them to the end." This was aimed at the Fabians, whom he was then addressing.[90] In one sense this ideal could be defined simply as a negation of class society: Socialism aims at "the full development of human life set free from artificial regulations in favour of a class".[91] The implicit underlying metaphor, drawing upon the old

Romantic critique of Utilitarianism, is the "organic" one: the natural growth of "life" will be set free from the artificial (or "mechanical") constraints of "civilization". Fulfilled Communist society will not depend upon a new race arising of morally-admirable people but upon the growth of a communal value-system made habitual by the absence of private property in the means of production and the attendant competition for the means of life. In "Nowhere" a "habit of life", "a habit of acting on the whole for the best" has "been growing on us"—"it is easy for us to live without robbing each other." (*697*) In this sense, the alternative value-systems of capitalism and socialism are seen, in ways which some contemporary anthropologists might approve, as being both supportive to and supported by the organization of economic and social life.

But this is not quite all that Morris is saying. For in another sense, his use of moral criteria and his assertions of "ideal" ends and of prior values, is *indicative* also: it indicates a direction towards which historical development may move, suggests choices between alternative directions, asserts a preference between these choices, and seeks to educate others in his preferences. These indications are never absolute and "utopian" in that sense: Morris never proposes that men may live in any way they may suppose that they might choose, according to any value-system imaginable. The indications are placed within a firm controlling historical and political argument. But they are certainly there and they are important. They are perhaps an occasion for Engels's dismissal of him as a "sentimental Socialist"—an accusation which left Morris pugnaciously unrepentant ("I *am* a sentimentalist. . . and I am proud of the title" (*718*)). They indicate where a crack lies between Morris's avowed and conscious positions and a moral determinism (from these relations of production, these values and this consonant morality) which has occupied much Marxist thought. In Morris's critique of capitalist society, there is no sense in which morality is seen as secondary, power and productive relations as primary. The ugliness of

Victorian social relations and "the vulgarities of civilization" were "but the outward expression of the innate moral baseness into which we are forced by our present form of society. . ."[92] This moral baseness was "innate", within the societal form: "economics" and "morality" were enmeshed in the same nexus of systematised social relationships, and from this nexus an economic *and* a moral logic must ensue.

It must follow that the revolt against this logic must equally be "economic" and "moral" in character. But a moral revolt, no less than an economic one, must have somewhere to go, somewhere to point towards. And pointing must involve choosing, not between any direction one likes, but between inflexions of direction. When Morris looked forward to the society of the future, he proposed that a quarrel between desire and utilitarian determinations would continue, and that desire must and could assert its own priorities. For to suppose that our desires must be determined by our material needs may be to assume a notion of "need" itself already determined by the expectations of existing society.[93] But desire also can impose itself as "need": in class society it may be felt in the form of alienation, desire unsatisfied: in the society of the future in the form of more open choices between needs:

"We may have in appearance to give up a great deal of what we have been used to call material progress, in order that we may be freer, happier and more completely equal."[94]

And he went on, in the same lecture, to warn that differential rewards and "different standards of livelihood" accorded to different kinds of work would "create fresh classes, enslave the ordinary man, and give rise to parasitical groups", ensuing in "the creation of a new parasitical and servile class". With a quizzical glance at the determinism of evolutionary theory, he concluded:

"My hope is, that now we know, or have been told that we have been evolved from unintelligent germs (or whatever the word is) we shall consciously resist the reversal of the process, which to some seems inevitable, and do our best to remain men, even if in the struggle we become barbarians."[95]

"Civilization" and "barbarism" were terms which he always employed with ironic inversion, drawing in part upon the inheritance from Carlyle and Ruskin, in part upon the very deep commitment he had learned for certain pre-capitalist values and modes. To "become barbarians" alarmed him not at all. " 'Civilization' " (he wrote to Georgie Burne-Jones in May 1885) "I *know* now is doomed to destruction". This "knowledge" is what he had gained as "a practical Socialist", thus being saved from "a fine pessimistic end of life" (*175*). But the assent of desire had preceded this knowledge. "What a joy it is to think of it!", his letter to Georgie continued:

"And how often it consoles me to think of barbarism once more flooding the world, and real feelings and passions, however rudimentary, taking the place of our wretched hypocrisies. With this thought in my mind all the history of the past is lighted up and lives again to me. I used really to despair once because I thought what the idiots of our day call progress would go on perfecting itself. . ."[96]

It is not a comfortable passage, after the barbarism of blood and race into which twentieth-century "civilization" in fact debouched. True, Morris would have seen this outcome, which indeed he almost predicted ("the doom of Blood and Iron in our own day" (*720*)), as being no barbarism in his sense, but an authentic outcome of the logic of capitalist "civilization". But that is a little too easy as a way out from the accusation that Morris, like other alienated intellectuals, was allowing his outraged aesthetic feelings to commit him to a dangerous course of emotional arson. And we have to put his private comment to Georgie together with other private and public evidence to take a full measure. For if Morris was emphatically a revolutionary Socialist, he didn't suppose that "the Revolution" would, at one throw, "liberate" some mass of healthy "barbarism", some underground reserves of repressed desire. And if he toyed with such notions on his first commitment to "the Cause" between 1883 and 1885,[97] he was rescued from any revolutionary Romanticism (of the Swinburne variety) exactly by the sobering experience of very hard and applied mundane political agitation. Neither his audiences nor his comrades in the quarrelling Socialist sects were "barbarians" of that kind; nor, as he knew *far* better than most Victorian intellectuals, out of his immense practical experience in the decorative arts, was the "ordinary man in the street" an unspoiled vessel of true barbaric art ("Let us once for all get rid of the idea of the mass of the people having an intuitive idea of Art" (*666*)).. The false consciousness of "civilization" was not seen by him as masking some healthy proletarian Unconscious. Necessity itself would impell the workers into struggle, but this struggle could attain no goal unless the goal was located by desire and a strategy for its attainment prescribed by Socialist theory. First we must have "courage enough to will"; "*conscious* hope" must match the response to "commercial ruin" (*428*). Moreover, if Socialists failed to educate desire, and to enlarge this conscious hope, "to sustain steadily their due claim to that fullness and completeness of life which no class system can give them", then they would the more easily fall victim of the "humbug" of "a kind of utilitarian sham Socialism" (*429*). Or, if the existing society failed to provide even that, and "if we give it all up into the hands of necessity", the result will be a volcanic disaster (*724*).[98] The end itself was unobtainable without the prior education of desire or "need". And science cannot tell us what to desire or how to desire. Morris saw it as a task of Socialists (his own first task) to help people to find out their wants, to encourage them to want more, to challenge them to want differently, and to envisage a society of the future in which people, freed at last of necessity, might choose between different wants. "It is to stir you up not to be contented with a little that I am here tonight" (*361*).

When I say that Morris may be assimilated to Marxism only in the course of a re-ordering of Marxism itself, I don't of course imply that Marxist thinkers have not noticed these problems or proposed solutions. But it is in this area that (I think) the problem still lies. And "the case of Morris", and Marxism's bewilderment before it, emphasises that the problem is unresolved. Moreover, it should now be clear that there is a sense in which Morris, as a Utopian and moralist, can never be assimilated to Marxism, not because of any contradiction of purposes but because one may not assimilate desire to knowledge, and because the attempt to do so is to confuse two different operative principles of culture. So that I've phrased the problem wrongly, and Marxism requires less a re-ordering of its parts than a sense of humility before those parts of culture which it can never order. The motions of desire may be legible in the text of necessity, and may then become subject to rational explanation and criticism. But such criticism can scarcely touch these motions at their source. "Marxism", on its own, we now know, has never made anyone "good" or "bad", although a faith, arising from other sources but acclaimed as Marxism, has sustained epic courage, and a bad faith, arising from other sources but acclaimed as Marxism, has defiled the first premises of Marx. So that what Marxism might do, for a change, is sit on its own head a little in the interests of Socialism's heart. It might close down one counter in its universal pharmacy, and cease dispensing potions of analysis to cure the maladies of desire. This might do good politically as well, since it would allow a little space, not only for literary Utopians, but also for the unprescribed initiatives of everyday men and women who, in some part of themselves, are also alienated and utopian by turns.

This won't be how all other readers see it. So it is time for me to get out of Morris's way, and put this book to bed. I shan't revise it again. It must now stand like this, for people to use as they will. If they want to use it as a quarry, that's all right. The bits of Morris are what matter. But I would hope that one part of its structure—the part least noted by its critics—might receive a little attention before it is pulled down: that is, the analysis of Romanticism and of its trajectory in Morris's life. I don't mean only the way in which Morris rejected the reactionary "Feudal Socialism" of Carlyle and turned to new account the Ruskin of "The Nature of Gothic". I mean, even more, the trajectory from the profoundly-subjective Romanticism of Keats (in which aspiration, denied of realisation, circulated between the integrity of the artist and the ideal artefact of Beauty), through the sublimated rebellion of *The Defence of Guenevere,* to the crisis of despair of *The Earthly Paradise,* in which all the values of subjective individualism were poisoned by the taint of mortality; and thence, through the recuperative societal myths of Icelandic saga, to the Socialist resolution.

This trajectory may be viewed from two aspects. In Morris's own poetry it appears as fragmentary and suggestive, but as unfulfilled. His aesthetic premises were modified least of all, and his devotion to pre-capitalist achievements in the visual and architectural arts re-inforced his stubborn attachment to Keatsian and Pre-Raphaelite notions of "Beauty". This led him to his rash attempt to invent (or re-invent) a language which would put at a distance Victorian society. From this aspect we can see how Morris intended the arch of his creative writing to go. But, as I've argued sufficiently, his premises were wrong, and to attempt to "make a new tongue" in that way was to disengage from, rather than to challenge, the sensibility of his time. The attempt succeeded only when it was matched by the form of dream, when disengagement was itself a means by which criticism of the age's common-sense could be brought to bear.

From another aspect the arch is that of aspiration fulfilled. Morris's youthful Romantic rebellion was not a rebellion of individual sensibility against "society", but a rebellion of value, or aspiration, against actuality. When he stood, with young Burne-Jones, entranced by his first sight of medieval Rouen, what seized him like a passion was the sense of a whole alternative way of life: "no words can tell you how its mingled beauty, history, and romance took hold on me" (*4*). This mingled sense was the accent which he gave to Romanticism, and in later years he specifically identified this sense with the historical consciousness:

> "As for romance, what does romance mean? I have heard people miscalled for being romantic, but what romance means is the capacity for a true conception of history, a power of making the past part of the present."[99]

Nor was this sense confined to reverie; Morris's close practical knowledge of the medieval craftsman's mode of work gave to it an unusual substance. But it also threw into deeper shadow the actuality of his own society, in which both the values and the artefacts of the past were doomed to decay. This nourished the pessimism—the impulse to use art as a means of escape—of his early middle years. And I remain convinced that these *were* years of despair, and that the acute sense of mortality within a purposeless social universe was sapping the very sources of Morris's psychic life. When his arduous quest ended in Socialist conclusions, he was able, in one motion, to re-appropriate that "power of making the past part of the present" and extend it into an imagined future. The aspirations of the past were themselves infused with new meaning: "the past is lighted up and lives again to me." For the present, "I did not measure my hope, nor the joy it brought me" (*126*). The old fear of death relaxed, as aspiration was extended, vicariously, into the future: when he imagined that society, he asked, not "How Will They Live?", but "How Shall We Live Then?" The trajectory was completed. And what was transformed was, not only his tradition, but his own personality and sensibility. So that we may see in William Morris, not a late Victorian, nor even a "contemporary", but a new kind of sensibility. If he sometimes appears as an isolated and ill-understood figure, that is because few men or women of his kind were then about—or have happened since.

If I write about Morris again it will be in my character, not as historian, but as Socialist. For I must set one misunderstanding at rest. It might seem that, in the revaluation proposed in this Postscript, I've been setting myself up as yet one more "claimant" of Morris, in the attempt to attach him to an idiosyncratic Thompsonian position. But the case is the reverse. Morris, by 1955, had claimed me. My book was then, I suppose, already a work of muffled "revisionism". The Morris/Marx argument has worked inside me ever since. When, in 1956, my disagreements with orthodox Marxism became fully articulate, I fell back on modes of perception which I'd learned in those years of close company with Morris, and I found, perhaps, the will to go on arguing from the pressure of Morris behind me. To say that Morris claimed me, and that I've tried to acknowledge that claim, gives me no right to claim him. I have no license to act as his interpreter. But at least I can now say that this is what I've been trying, for twenty years, to do.

August, 1976.

NOTES

1 Detroit, 1969.

2 Paul Meier, "An Unpublished Lecture of William Morris: 'How Shall We Live Then?' ", *International Review of Social History,* XVI, 1971, Part 2: "Justice and Socialism", extended notes for a lecture in 1885, in Appendix I to Paul Meier, *La Pensée Utopique de William Morris* (Paris, 1972).

3 In R. Page Arnot, *William Morris, the Man and the Myth* (1964). Professor Norman Kelvin of the Department of English, City College, City University of New York, N.Y. 10031, has for some ten years been assembling materials for a full collection of letters. Anyone with knowledge of unpublished letters is invited to get in touch with him.

4 Peter Faulkner (ed.), *William Morris: The Critical Heritage* (1973).

5 Asa Briggs (ed.), *William Morris: Selected Writings and Designs* (1962); A.L. Morton (ed.), *Political Writings of William Morris* (1973).

6 Unfortunately Floud's early death robbed us of his full conclusions: but see his articles in the *Listener,* October 7th & 14th, 1954; "Dating Morris Patterns", *Architectural Review,* July 1959; "English Chintz: the Influence of William Morris", *CIBA Review,* 1961.

7 Paul Thompson, *The Work of William Morris* (1967); Ray Watkinson, *William Morris as Designer* (1967). Also Graeme Shankland in (ed.) Asa Briggs, *op. cit.,;* R. Furneaux Jordan, *The Medieval Vision of William Morris* (1960); A.C. Sewter, *The Stained Glass of William Morris and his Circle* (New Haven, 1975); E. Goldzamt, *William Morris et La Genèse Sociale de L'Architecture Moderne* (Warsaw, 1967).

8 Warington Taylor, Victoria & Albert Museum, Reserve Case JJ35; Sir Thomas Wardle, V. & A. Box II 86. zz. See especially Philip Henderson, *William Morris: His Life, Work and Friends* (1967: Penguin edition 1973), pp. 105-12 (Taylor) and pp. 193-5 (letters to Wardle on dyeing).

9 Some minute-books of Morris & Co. are in the Hammersmith Public Library. Account-books, pattern-books and other materials of the Firm are now in the private collection of Sanford and Helen Berger at their home in Carmel near San Francisco. It is unfortunate that the Firm's records should be divided by the Atlantic and between public and private hands. But scholars who can get to California will find (as I have done) that the present owners of these records are generous in providing access to them.

10 *William Morris, Writer* (William Morris Society, 1961). A brief essay in general interpretation by George Levine in (eds.) H.J. Dyos and M. Wolff, *The Victorian City* (1973), II, pp. 495-517, is also fresh and perceptive.

11 Disagreement has been expressed by Jessie Kocmanova, "Some Remarks on E.P. Thompson's Opinions of the Poetry of William Morris", *Philologica Pragensia*, III, 3, 1960, and in *The Poetic Maturing of William Morris* (Prague, 1964). But I have not been convinced by her critical re-appraisals.

12 C.S. Lewis, *Rehabilitations and Other Essays* (Oxford, 1939).

13 Notably John Goode's work, discussed below. Also Lionel Munby, "William Morris's Romances and the Society of the Future", *Zeitschrift fur Anglistik u. Amerikanistik*, X, 1, 1962. I find Jessie Kocmanova's studies on *A Dream of John Ball* and on the late prose romances more helpful than her studies of Morris's poetry: see *Brno Studies in English*, II, no. 68, 1960 and VI, no. 109, 1966.

14 July 15th, 1955.

15 Jack Lindsay, who had the benefit of Henderson's work, as well as Meier's, also offers some perceptive suggestions in his helter-skelter biography: *William Morris: His Life and Work* (1975).

16 See Henderson, *op. cit.*, pp. 124-5; C. Doughty and Robert Wahl (eds.), *Letters of Dante Gabriel Rossetti* (Oxford, 1965), II, p. 685; Penelope Fitzgerald, *Edward Burne-Jones* (1975), esp. chapter 10.

17 "Has Top perhaps thrown trade after poetry, & now executes none but wholesale orders in philanthropy,—the retail trade being beneath a true humanitarian? But no—without a shop he could not be the Odger of the Future!": D.G. Rossetti to Janey Morris, April 1st, 1878, cited in Jack Lindsay, *William Morris*, pp. 224-5. George Odger, the shoemakers leader, had repeatedly fought parliamentary elections, with strong support, against both Liberal and Conservative candidates, on a Radical working-men's platform: he had died in 1877.

18 Morris to W. Bell Scott, April 9th, 1882, cited in Philip Henderson, *op. cit.*, p. 260.

19 This judgment of mine is perhaps smug in the light of the full surviving correspondence between Rossetti and Janey Morris which has become available while these pages were in proof: *Dante Gabriel Rossetti and Jane Morris: Their Correspondence*, ed. John Bryson (Oxford, 1976). Unrevealing in some ways, these letters (the bulk of them from Rossetti) do appear to disclose the general shape of the relationship. There are several letters of 1868-70, when the mutual passion of Janey and Rossetti appears to be first fully disclosed. In 1869 Janey had her first breakdown and Morris took her to recuperate at Ems: the three friends appear to have been attempting to live through the triangular situation with mutual affection and confessional frankness: "All that concerns you" (Rossetti wrote to Janey at Ems, July 1869) "is the all absorbing question with me, as dear Top will not mind my telling you at this anxious moment. The more he loves you, the more he knows that you are too lovely and noble not to be loved. . ." In whatever way the three friends attempted to "handle" the situation, it seems clear that the attempt broke down. No letters survive for the years of

crisis, 1870-75. These are the years of Morris's two Icelandic journeys—years when Janey and Rossetti were often together at Kelmscott. By the time the correspondence resumes in 1877, a sad change has come over the situation. Gabriel is preparing to move out of Kelmscott and there are no more friendly messages (and a few sneers) for "Top". Janey appears to have entered a settled melancholia and hypochondria (the symptoms mentioned include lumbago, sciatica, neuralgia, migraine, sore throats, fevers) which matches the melancholia of Rossetti. "I hope", Gabriel writes on Christmas Eve 1879, "you will have a Xmas not too unlike a merry one." In her reply Janey says nothing about her Christmas, but writes of her daughter May: "she is excessively delicate this winter, and I think will not drag through a long life. So much the better for her!". (May was in fact to live well into her seventies). It is altogether a sad correspondence, of two self-preoccupied people conjoined by a melancholy retrospective obsession, redeemed by reciprocal concern and respect. Much of the nature of the relationship remains unclear; one does not know how far to credit the statement of Hall Caine (which Meier has brought to light) that Rossetti told him that he had been made impotent by a serious accident (at some time during these years?); moreover, the letters reveal little of the paradoxes of Rossetti's own feeling and behaviour (his mistress, Fanny Cornforth, is never mentioned). It is clear only that the relationship falls easily into no stereotype, and that an emotional distance had opened up between Morris on one hand and Janey and Rossetti on the other.

20 *H.M. Hyndman and British Socialism* (Oxford, 1961). For London, see also Paul Thompson, *Socialists, Liberals and Labour: The Struggle for London, 1885-1914* (1967), and (for class relations generally) Gareth Stedman Jones, *Outcast London* (Oxford, 1971).

21 See my review in the *Bulletin of the Society for the Study of Labour History*, no. 3, Autumn 1961, pp. 66-71.

22 C. Tsuzuki, *The Life of Eleanor Marx, 1855-1898* (Oxford, 1967).

23 *Eleanor Marx: Family Life, 1855-83* (1972). This volume introduces Eleanor fully and also introduces Aveling.

24 S. Pierson, "Ernest Belfort Bax: the Encounter of Marxism and Late Victorian Culture", *Journal of British Studies*, 1972; Laurence Thompson, *The Enthusiasts* (1971)—on Bruce and Katherine Glasier; W.J. Fishman, *East End Jewish Radicals, 1875-1914*. New information on the Labour Emancipation League, Frank Kitz and other London pioneers is in Stan Shipley, *Club Life and Socialism in Mid-Victorian London* (History Workshop, 1972), and on London anarchism in Rudolf Rocker, *The London Years* (1956).

25 *Tom Mann and his Times* (1965).

26 "Homage to Tom Maguire", in Asa Briggs and John Saville (eds.), *Essays in Labour History* (1960).

27 Especially A.M. McBriar, *Fabian Socialism and English Politics, 1884-1918* (Cambridge, 1962); Margaret Cole, *The Story of Fabian Socialism* (1961); E.J. Hobsbawm, "The Fabians Reconsidered" in *Labouring Men* (1964). Also Wolfe and Pierson (discussed below).

28 The new sources on Shaw and the relations between Fabians and Socialist League in 1886, are discussed in Appendix II.

29 James W. Hulse, *Revolutionists in London* (Oxford, 1970), p. 27.

30 Willard Wolfe, *From Radicalism to Socialism: Men and Ideas in the Formation of Fabian and Socialist Doctrines* (New Haven, 1975), p. 320.

31 J.Y. Le Bourgeois, "William Morris and the Marxist Myth", *Durham University Journal*, December 1976.

32 I have taken out certain passages (e.g. first edition, pp. 735-46) not because I apologise for them in 1955 but because they are not relevant to 1976.

33 In fact my book was better received than most books from Lawrence &

Wishart (a Communist publishing-house), getting a generous notice from G.D.H. Cole in the *Listener* and a knockabout, but not unfair, criticism from A.J.P. Taylor in the *Manchester Guardian*.

34 July 15th, 1955.

35 Oxford, 1970.

36 By contrast Hulse offers Lloyd Wendell Eshleman (alias Lloyd Eric Grey), *A Victorian Rebel: The Life of William Morris* (New York, 1940: and, under a different title and different author, London, 1949) as "the most readily available general biography for the past quarter century... based on competent research and a sympathetic understanding of Morris". For Mackail's opinion, in 1940, as to Eshleman's "lack of sincerity", see Meier, *op. cit.*, p. 303. I dissected Eshleman/Grey's nauseous and thoroughly dishonest book in "The Murder of William Morris", *Arena*, April-May 1951; and abused it further in first edition, pp. 741-3.

37 Hulse notes (p. 17) that the S.D.F., League and Fabians "filled the columns of their respective periodicals with criticisms of the other organizations": this is rubbish, most of all for *Commonweal*. Of Bloody Sunday he notes, "it... needed only a few officers to disperse the crowd" (p. 93). And so on.

38 Ithaca and London, 1973.

39 This point is made forcefully in Keith Nield's review of Pierson in the *Bulletin of the Society for the Study of Labour History*, no. 27, Autumn 1973.

40 Nor need it follow that we must endorse all of Althusser's notions of "rupture". I do not.

41 We have been reminded that Hyndman's ideas were not co-terminous with those of the whole S.D.F.: see E.J. Hobsbawm, *Labouring Men*.

42 See Bernard Semmel, *Imperialism and Social Reform*, (Cambridge, U.S.A., 1960).

43 *Cf.* Morris: "I am not pleading for the production of a little more beauty in the world, much as I love it, and much as I would sacrifice for its sake; it is the lives of human beings I am pleading for...", "Art and its Producers" (1888); "Once again I warn you against supposing, you who may specially love art, that you will do any good by attempting to revivify art by dealing with its dead exterior. I say it is the *aims of art* that you must seek rather than the *art itself;* and in that search we may find ourselves in a world blank and bare, as a result of our caring at least this much for art, that we will not endure the shams of it", "The Aims of Art" (1886). See also the letter on the miners' strike of 1893, "The Deeper Meaning of the Struggle", in *Letters*, pp. 355-7 and above, *665*.

44 See pp. 274-5. Also p. 84, where Morris is held to have tended to refuse to acknowledge "those forces in life, formerly categorized as the sinful or the tragic".

45 When I say "more than any other of his time", I am thinking of British Socialists. But it isn't easy to suggest European comparisons, unless we move to cosmic (non-Socialist) pessimists. If Engels in his last years allowed himself to confront a similar pessimistic realism, he kept it to himself.

46 Pierson is fond of this term "regressive". In another place (*The Victorian City*, eds. H.J. Dyos and M. Wolff, 1972, II., p. 879) he has Morris trying to rescue "the rural vision" by "attaching it to Marxism". "Ideological impulses within Marxism encouraged the project, but it was incompatible with the social and economic realism of that system of thought and it soon collapsed. In Morris's Socialism the Romantic regression ended virtually in anarchism..." The "collapse" here is not of Morris's thought but of Pierson's more nuanced appraisal in the book under discussion.

47 I prefer the term "transformation" to the term "extension", employed by Raymond Williams in *Culture and Society* (1958), p. 158, since it insists upon "rupture" as well as continuity. I argued the point rather loudly in a review of *The Long Revolution* in *New Left Review*, 9 & 10, May/June & July/August 1961, to be reprinted shortly in my political essays (Merlin Press, 1977). Any differences

between myself and Williams have (I think) diminished over the years, and neither of us would argue in exactly the same way today. The choice of terms is unimportant, but the point remains of interest.

48 An English edition of *La Pensée Utopique de William Morris* (Paris, 1972) is announced as forthcoming from the Harvester Press.

49 See also Meier, "Friedrich Engels et William Morris", *La Pensée,* no. 156, Avril, 1971, pp. 68-80.

50 F. Engels and Paul & Laura Lafargue, *Correspondence* (Moscow, 1959), 2 vols.

51 As early as July 24th, 1884 Morris wrote to Robert Thompson: "I believe (and have always done so)... that the most important thing to press... at present is the legal reduction of the working day: every working man can see the immediate advantage to him of this: the Trades Unions *may* be got to take it up..." This would become "an international affair" *Letters,* p. 205. When the Marxists of the Bloomsbury Branch split from the League they put their best efforts exactly into the Eight Hour agitation, and not into parliamentary candidatures. Had they made this their main plank while still within the League, no break would have been necessary.

52 In brief, *Commonweal* (January 7th, 1888) publicised the exposure in the *Sozial-Demokrat* of 13 German police-spies, one of whom, Reuss, lived in England. Reuss commenced an action; Engels noted that Morris was "funky" but tried to collect evidence to support a defence. When the case was lost, Morris appears to have been allowed to carry the damages and costs out of his own purse.

53 I find helpful the suggestion that *The House of the Wolfings,* and Morris's articles on "The Development of Modern Society" in *Commonweal* (1890) may have drawn upon ideas in *The Origin of the Family,* derived from conversations with Engels or with Bax. But it still has to be shown that Morris was drawing upon Engels rather than (as John Goode has suggested) turning Morgan's *Ancient Society* to a similar account: see Meier, *La Pensée Utopique,* pp. 308, 359-65; Goode (cited below), pp. 261-5.

54 I find especially strained Meier's attribution of an influence from Marx's theses on Feuerbach (p. 347); and the notion that Morris's wholly characteristic insistence that a Communist morality must rest upon the habits induced by the general conditions of life in Communist society must depend upon knowledge of the manuscript of *The German Ideology* (unpublished until 1932): Meier, pp. 706-8.

55 The case being argued at this point is difficult. Meier ascribes a very general influence to ideas (as yet unpublished) in *The Critique of the Gotha Programme.* Possibly some of these derive from conversations with Engels, Bax, the Avelings and others, while some were of Morris's own definition.

56 *Op. cit.,* p. 149. See also George Levine, *op. cit.,* on the continuity of the underlying "organic metaphor".

57 In making these criticisms I should add that Meier treats well the questions of "barbarism" and "civilization" in Morris's thought: see esp. his discussion of Richard Jefferies, *After London,* and its influence (pp. 107-13) and Part III, chapter 1. But, as Goode points out, Morgan also envisaged that "civilization" contained within itself "the elements of self-destruction", since private property had become an "unmanageable power"; the "next higher plane of society" will be "a revival, in a higher form, of the liberty, equality and fraternity of the ancient *gentes*"—a view as influential upon Morris as upon Engels, who cited it at the conclusion to *The Origin of the Family.*

58 "The Revival of Architecture" (1888).

59 "The Revival of Handicraft" (1880).

60 See Meier (p. 646) where he refers to "un passage progressif des positions idéalistes du début au materialisme marxiste de sa maturité."

61 Engels to Laura Lafargue, November 23rd, 1884, *Correspondence,* I, p. 245.

62 *The Communism of William Morris* (William Morris Society, 1965)—a lecture

delivered in May 1959.

63 Since I did not myself take the point when I first wrote this book, it would be pharisaical to labour it now.

64 *Cf.* Asa Briggs' comment that Morris's writings "provide the material for a critique of twentieth-century Socialism (and Communism) as much as for a critique of nineteenth-century capitalism": *William Morris: Selected Writings,* p. 17.

65 M. M-H. Abensour, "Les Formes de L'Utopie Socialiste-Communiste", thèse pour le Doctorat d'Etat en Science politique, Paris 1, 1973, esp. chapter 4. Forthcoming as *Utopies et dialectique du socialisme*, Payot, Paris (1977?).

66 Abensour re-directs attention to Murry's neglected articles, "The Return to Fundamentals: Marx and Morris", *Adelphi,* V, nos. 1 & 2 (October-November, 1932); "Bolshevism and Bradford", *Adelphi,* IV, no. 5 (August 1932).

67 See above *693.* I accept Abensour's criticism, but have let my passage stand, as a text in this argument.

68 "How Shall We Live Then?", *op. cit.,* p. 6.

69 "L'utopie se détache du concept pour devenir image, image médiatrice et ouverture à la vérite du désir" (p. 329).

70 "Sa fonction est de donner libre cours au désir d'interroger, de voir, de savoir, au desire même" (p. 349).

71 I write "Communist Utopian" when I refuse the term "Marxist Utopian" (just as Abensour refuses "Scientific Utopia") since the term "Communist" may appertain to value-systems as well as to theoretical system in a way in which "Marxist" has ceased to do. By "Communist" I mean especially those values which Morris himself attributed to the society of the future.

72 *Culture and Society,* 1958, pp. 155-6.

73 "Privilégiant une lecture politique, l'interprète s'expose à minimiser ou à même passer sous silence la critique de la politique dans l'oeuvre de William Morris, si fondamentale qu'elle vise une fin de la politique at que son auteur ne peut être dit un penseur politique au sens classique du terme" (Abensour, p. 341).

74 John Goode, "William Morris and the Dream of Revolution" in John Lucas (ed.), *Literature and Politics in the Nineteenth Century* (1971).

75 Goode, pp. 222-3 and first edition of this work, *779.* In this case the judgment properly criticised by Goode as "complacent" was too pious to be allowed to stand in this revision.

76 Pierson, *op. cit.,* p. 274. This is the only place where Pierson allows the term "fusion".

77 I strongly support Goode's judgment here, as to the unitary theme of alienation in Morris's work from youth to maturity. But I wish that Goode, in common with many English Marxists, would not use "ideology" in such a sloppy way. Morris did not have "a socialist ideology".

78 I'm aware that "alienation" is used in several senses in Marxist writing. But this sense of alienated sensibility seems permissible and consonant with some passages of Marx.

79 Goode, p. 260, citing *The Modern Prince,* 1967, p. 69.

80 Until the mid-1880s, and occasionally thereafter (e.g. *748*), Morris refers to the "new understanding of history" in terms of "evolution" of a necessary kind. It's my impression that he came to doubt this evolutionism after 1887 (see e.g. *427-30*). Engels, Bax, Aveling, Hyndman &c were all also in the habit of using evolutionary metaphors (sometimes with explicit parallels with Darwinism); and Goode notes with justice (p. 270) that some of Engels's comments on the English scene show a "merely reflexive" defeatism fortified by determinist stamina.

81 Undoubtedly no-one can approach *Sigurd* after this analysis without a new kind of respect. The problem is that Goode can show this mythic elaboration only by extricating it from the poem's "linguistic fog" and then offering it as an analytic

precis; also, how much was already given to Morris in his materials?
82 1880 is the date of the first French edition of *Socialism, Utopian and Scientific.*
83 In the post-1929 depression Harold Laski reported that he found copies of *A Dream of John Ball* and *News from Nowhere* in the Tyneside area (which Morris had visited in 1887) "in house after house of the miners", even when most of the furniture had been sold off: see Paul Thompson, *William Morris,* p. 219.
84 Morris to Robert Thomson, July 24th [1884], Houghton Library, Harvard University, MS. Eng. 798; *Letters,* p. 205.
85 "Feudal England", *Signs of Change,* (1888), pp. 82-3.
86 *Commonweal,* Mayday issue, 1886.
87 "Communism" (1893).
88 These views are discussed lucidly by Alasdair Clayre, *Work and Play* (1974), esp. chapter 6.
89 Morris carefully emphasised this sequence in "How Shall We Live Then?", *op. cit.,* p. 10. *Cf.* Raymond Williams, *op. cit.,* p. 265: "The economic reasoning, and the political promise, came to him from Marxism; the general rebellion was in older terms."
90 "How Shall We Live Then?", p. 20.
91 William Morris, Preface to Frank Fairman, *Socialism Made Plain* (1888), p. iv. *Cf.* another definition by negation: "the great central power of modern times, the world-market... with all the ingenious and intricate system which profit hunting commerce has built up about it" must develop into "its contradiction, which is the conscious mutual exchange of services between equals": "How Shall We Live Then?", p. 16.
92 Preface to *Signs of Change* (1888). I am here revising a very confused discussion of moral consciousness and the Marxist tradition, in my first edition, pp. 83-5 (cut from this edition), and am replacing it with points first argued in "The Communism of William Morris", *op. cit.,* p. 17.
93 See Morris's criticism of some "practical" Socialists: "he is thinking entirely of the conservative side of human nature... and ignores that which exists just as surely, its revolutionary side": *Commonweal,* February 18, 1888.
94 "How Shall We Live Then?", p. 23. Another unequivocal preference which, of course, Morris never ceased to nourish as a want, was the need for artistic expression: "For without art Socialism would remain as sterile as the other forms of social organization: it would not meet the real and perpetual wants of mankind". Preface to Ruskin's "On the Nature of Gothic" (Kelmscott Press, 1892). And ("How I Became a Socialist"): "It is the province of art to set the true ideal of a full and reasonable life before him, a life to which the perception and creation of beauty... shall be felt to be as necessary to man as his daily bread."
95 "How Shall We Live Then?", pp. 23-4. The last comment was perhaps a crack at Bax's notion that evolutionary changes "in the human organism" would eradicate "the coarser side of the sexual passion" (*705*), but Morris is hanging on this peg a more general irony.
96 *Letters,* p. 236.
97 See "Art and Socialism" (1884): "the change in store for us hidden in the breast of the Barbarism of civilization—the Proletariat".
98 When writing in this sense, Morris offered the alternatives of Socialism or social disaster in a way which anticipates Rosa Luxembourg's "Socialism or Barbarism".
99 May Morris, I, p. 148.

AUTHOR'S NOTE TO THE REVISED EDITION

When this book was first published in 1955 I described it as a study of William Morris rather than a biography. It was a very long study (running to 900 pages), but even so the treatment was selective and interpretive. It made no attempt to replace the standard biography of Morris by J.W. Mackail, first published in 1899. But Mackail's undisguised dislike of Morris's revolutionary convictions resulted in a wholly inadequate treatment of the political activities and writings which absorbed Morris's energy in the years of his maturity. Hence my study was written against the background of Mackail: where his *Life of William Morris* is most sympathetic and thorough (in the years up to 1880) my methods are interpretive and critical: and where his sympathies lapsed (after 1880) I introduce a great deal of new biographical material and, in effect, write out at length the history of the Socialist League (1885–90) from many hitherto unexamined sources.

The first edition of this book had a mixed history. I wrote it in an embattled mood, from a position of strong political commitment, addressing an audience in the adult education movement and in the political movements of the Left rather than a more academic public. It is not surprising that it dropped into an academic silence. As a consequence some part of what has been written about William Morris in the past twenty years continues to nourish misconceptions which ought not to have survived the evidence of Morris's own writings and actions as presented fully in these pages. But for reasons too complicated to enter into here the book did not engage with the interests of the new intellectual Left. For over the same period a new generation of Marxist intellectuals has matured in Britain, one of whose tenets is that there has been no significant Marxist influence within our intellectual life until the last decade. And yet William Morris was an outstanding member of the first generation of European Communist intellectuals, the friend of Engels, and the comrade and peer of Bebel, Liebknecht, Eleanor Marx and Bernstein. In the tangled context of his time he associated himself generally with the Marxist tradition, and his original contributions to this tradition seem to me to be quite as significant as those of (let us say) Plekhanov or Labriola. I would myself argue that they are of considerably more relevance to us today, for, while Morris remained always an avowed amateur in economic theory, in his historical and utopian thought he filled in certain silences of Marx and proposed certain qualifications to the already-hardening doctrines of the Marxists of the 1880s, all of which assume—or ought to assume—greater importance in the present time. It is extraordinary that in a time of manifest capitalist crisis the ideas of this very remarkable British Socialist should continue to be ignored or should be condescended to.

The first edition of this book should have made these ideas more generally available. It did reach some attentive and sympathetic readers. That it failed to reach more was in some part the book's fault. It was too long and the length showed self-indulgence in the author. I allowed myself too many digressions, in pursuit of the minor episodes of the early Socialist movement, and, worse than this, I intruded far too often upon the text with moralistic comments and pat political sentiments. William Morris spoke so clearly in his own voice that he did not need my commentary. Hence the work of this revision has been made more easy. I have simply cut out the fat, most of which was my own callow fat. The result is not only a shorter but a better book.

I have taken out almost nothing of Morris's own writings. What have gone, in the main, are my own intrusions. I have been forced, here and there, to cut out details (for example, as to peripheral activities of the Socialist League) which will still be of interest to specialist scholars: these must still consult the first edition. I have also for reasons of space cut out two of the original appendices: the correspondence between Engels and J.L. Mahon and five letters of William Morris to Fred Henderson. These letters are sufficiently cited in the revised text. For the rest, it is not possible after the passage of twenty years to rewrite a book of this kind, not because the subject has changed but because the author has. I have made corrections or inserted footnotes where new information has come to light which modified my original account, and I have rewritten several other sections to take in evidence from the Engels-Lafargue Correspondence and from the William Morris to J.L. Mahon Correspondence published by Mr. R. Page Arnot in *William Morris, the Man and the Myth* (1964).

There have of course been other significant contributions to William Morris studies in the past twenty years: I discuss several of these in the Postscript. But none of these have trenched centrally upon the themes of this study nor have they led me to revise my central interpretation.

My full thanks and acknowledgements to the many people and institutions who gave me assistance in the original research are given in the Foreword to the first edition. These need not now be repeated. But I cannot let this revised edition go out without repeating the thanks which I expressed in the first edition to the late Dona Torr: "She has repeatedly laid aside her own work in order to answer my enquiries or to read drafts of my material, until I have felt that parts of the book were less my own than a collaboration in which her guiding ideas have the main part. It has been a privilege to be associated so closely with a Communist scholar so versatile, so distinguished, and so generous with her gifts."

SEPTEMBER, 1976

INDEX

Abensour, Miguel, 786-91, 793-4, 796, 798-9, 802
Adams, W. Bridges, 366
Allingham, William, 43, 194, 207
Allman, James, 484-5
"Anti-Scrape". *See* Society for the Protection of Ancient Buildings
Arnold, Matthew, 139-40, 144, 243-5
Arnot, R. Page, 787
Art Workers' Guild, 557, 636
Arts and Crafts Exhibition Society, 504, 540, 557
Austin, Alfred, 149
Aveling, Edward, 337; and Engels, 342 n 2, n 3, 422, 467; and "Split", 345-8, 348 n 2, 349, 357, 359-60; character and influence, 345-6, 346 n 1, 366-72, 449, 468-71; and League, 366, 380-1, 383, 387, 391-2, 395-6, 398, 412, 427, 453, 504; and Bloomsbury Socialist Society, 520, 564-5, 585; and I.L.P., 610, 610 n 1; and Mahon, 449 n 1, 468-70, 755-6; and Marxism, 332, 755-6, 761 n 1.
Aveling, Eleanor Marx–. *See* Marx, Eleanor

Banner, Robert, 269, 298, 307, 332, 350, 357, 359, 398, 416, 520, 586
Barclay, Tom, 298-300, 391, 517-8, 566
Barker, Ambrose G., 359
Barker, H.A., 485
Barry, Maltman, 281
Bax, Ernest Belfort, 301, 586, 629, 682, 710-11; and Engels, 342 n 2, n 3, 370, 422, 615-6, 755; and Marx, 288, 332, 335, 755, 758; and "Split", 343, 346, 348 n 2, 349, 357, 359-60, 364-5; character, 315, 372-5, 705; and League, 383, 391-2, 404, 445; 448-9, 452-3, 471 n 2, 520; and "Bloody Sunday", 497-8; and imperialism, 514-5, 780-2, 784
–(with Morris), *Socialism: its Growth and Outcome*, 372, 391, 676-7, 751-3
Bebel, A., 383, 534
Beesly, Professor E.S., 247, 386
Bell, Sir Lowthian, 249-50
Bellamy, Edward *(Looking Backward)*, 542, 551, 575, 577, 688, 692-3
Bernstein, Edouard, 367, 369, 623, 534, 586, 771
Besant, Annie, 387, 395, 488, 493-4, 497, 524 n 2, 528, 535, 538, 548, 577, 761-2, 762 n 2
Binning, Thomas, 375, 416, 446, 448, 453, 504, 520, 563
Blackwell, James, 549-51
Bland, Hubert, 548, 553
Blatchford, Robert, 603, 611, 618, 622, 638
–*Clarion*, 586, 600, 603-4, 618, 638
–*Merrie England*, 622, 774-5
Bloomsbury Socialist Society, 509, 564-5
Blunt, Wilfred Scawen, 167, 625, 638, 713
Bradlaugh, Charles, 301, 345, 346 n 1, 386-7, 399, 492, 499 n 4, 667, 759
Bright, John, 136, 328-9
Broadhurst, Henry, 211-3, 218-9, 221, 261-3, 265, 473, 532
Brooke, Rev. Stopford, 207, 716
Brown, Ford Madox, 42, 45, 58, 60, 62, 92-3, 99 n 1, 160, 163, 194
Browning, Robert, 45, 55, 77, 80, 83-4, 207, 748
Bryce, James, 228
Bullock, Sam, 523, 598, 618, 623
Burden, Jane. *See* Morris, Jane
Burne-Jones, Sir Edward, 64-5, 76-9, 146, 151, 165, 194, 207, 221, 228, 233, 261 n 2, 394, 627, 633, 636, 765, 809; at Oxford, 3, 23-5, 29, 33; and Pre-Raphaelites, 41-9, 52-62, 64; and Firm, 92-4, 97, 99 n 1; shocked by Morris's socialism, 274, 322; and Kelmscott Press, 627-8, 633-4
Burne-Jones, Georgiana ("Georgie"), 94, 101, 153, 159, 164-5, 167, 219, 239-40, 250, 256-8, 267, 319-20, 322,

325-7, 394, 424-6, 628, 631, 633, 635
Burns, John, 298-9, 312, 315, 328-30, 358, 364 n 3, 387-8, 398, 404, 406-7, 409, 412, 427, 435, 473, 478, 483, 490, 492, 496-7, 524-5, 528-30, 532, 542, 599, 636, 638
Burrows, Herbert, 296, 315, 358, 364 n 3, 494, 586
Burt, Thomas, 212-4, 259, 386

Cailes, Victor, 591-2
Caine, Hall, 59, 160, 163 n 3
Cantwell, T., 508, 594-5, 596 n 1
Capital. *See* Marx, Karl
Carlyle, Thomas, 29-33, 40, 58, 198, 207, 228, 643-4, 647, 687, 728, 774, 778, 808
Carpenter, Edward, 106, 109, 289-90, 295, 313, 347-8, 361, 520, 528, 562, 589, 637-8, 701 n 2, 705, 711, 714
Carruthers, John, 399-400, 586, 621, 634, 756-7, 761
Catterson-Smith, R., 556
Chamberlain, Joseph, 404, 543
Champion, Henry Hyde, 270, 298-9, 301, 313, 315, 328, 337, 349, 358, 364 n 3, 388, 406-7, 412, 427, 471-2, 476-7, 483, 524-6, 535, 561, 609
Charles, Fred. *See* F.C. Slaughter
Charles, Henry, 416
Chesson, F.W., 219, 221, 223
Chicago Anarchists, 484, 487, 506-7, 518, 549
Clarion. *See* Blatchford, Robert
Clark, Dr. G.B., 352
Clark, W.J., 349, 357-9, 364, 366
Clough, Arthur Hugh, 25-6, 71-2
Cobbett, William, 269, 306
Cobden-Sanderson, T.J., 318, 556-7, 635, 711
Cockerell, Sir Sydney, 247, 556, 702
Commonweal, 372-3, 375, 413, 667, 670, 671, 684; first numbers, 382-5; character and circulation, 391-2, 414, 420-1, 432, 453, 460-1, 504, 508, 523, 561, 569; Morris as Editor, 416-7, 432, 467 n 2, 513, 561, 587, 604, 743; decline, 461, 463-4, 516-21; Morris removed as Editor, 566, 587; edited by Kitz and Nicoll, 566-70; last numbers, 586-95
Commons Preservation Society, 257
Commune, The Paris, 196-7, 200-1, 213, 277-8, 282, 284, 288, 314, 335-6, 377, 412, 518, 672
Conway, Katharine St. John (Mrs. Bruce Glasier), 744
Cooper, J., 359, 366
Coronio, Aglaia, 159, 162-6, 174, 181
Coulon, Auguste, 590-3
Cowen, Joseph, 208
Craig, E.T., 366, 383, 387, 520
Crane, Walter, 94-7, 101-2, 495, 555, 557, 598, 636
Creaghe, Dr., 588, 591
Curner, W.B., 491 n 1, 493 n 1

Dave, Victor, 278, 282
Davis, H., 508, 523
Davitt, Michael, 291, 496
Democratic Federation. *See* Social-Democratic Federation
De Morgan, William, 207, 261 n 2, 322
Derby, Lord, 204, 214, 224
Dickens, Charles, 8-9, 30, 40-1, 54, 137-9
Dilke, Sir Charles, 261 n 2, 283
Disraeli, Benjamin, 203-4, 208-9, 211, 214-9, 223-5, 229, 259-60, 264, 479
Dixon, Canon R.W., 5-6, 23, 33, 46, 76, 78-9, 142-3
Donald, Alexander Karley, 418, 441-2, 445, 449, 451, 453-4, 466-7, 504, 508, 522, 526, 563, 570, 609

Eastern Question Association, 193, 203, 211, 214, 216-7, 220-1, 224, 259, 265-6
Ellis, F.S., 207, 318 n 3
Engels, Frederick, 298, 721-2; and the English movement, 276-7, 288, 345, 370-2, 379-84, 448-9, 452-3, 465-71, 531, 564-5, 577-9, 585, 601-2, 610-11; and the "Split", 341-2, 344, 346, 359-60; and Morris, 342, 371, 422, 453, 471, 564, 751-2, 780-2, 784-6, 803; and Socialist League, 405, 414,

422, 448 n 1, 453-4, 470, 564-5, 601; and North of England Socialist Federation, 454, 464-7; and Second International, 534-5; and Utopianism, 787-91, 797

Fabian Essays, 541, 546-8, 598, 760
Fabian Society, Fabianism, 332 n 2, 333, 395, 412, 421 n 3, 446, 459, 461, 499, 501, 537-42, 575, 577, 598, 605-8, 610, 618, 682-3, 726, 759-60, 773-4, 776-7, 802
Faulkner, Charles, 6, 46, 179, 194, 207, 209, 220, 227, 274, 519; part in socialist movement, 322, 366, 390, 420, 452
Fawcett, Professor Henry, 207, 328
Fielden, Samuel, 137
Fitzgerald, C.L., 364 n 3, 412
Floud, Peter, 763-4
Freedom, 505, 589, 638

George, Henry, 269, 290-1, 351
Gissing, George, 287, 316-7, 397, 420-2, 712
Gladstone, W.E., 204-7, 210-11, 214, 217, 221-3, 225, 229, 260-4, 285, 335-6, 343, 486, 603, 603 n 1, 700
Glasier, John Bruce, 230, 351-7, 430, 451, 462, 508-9, 518, 518 n 2, 520-2, 552, 560-1, 570-1, 624, 635, 638, 713, 742-7; and Marxism, 741-2, 745, 747-50, 752-4, 761
Glasse, Rev. John, 354, 409, 450, 555
Goode, John, 786, 793-9, 802
Graham, Cunninghame, 488, 490, 492-4, 496-7, 535, 585, 636-7
Guile, Daniel, 213

Hales, John, 213, 263
Hall, Leonard, 517, 563, 563 n 2, 598, 609
Hammersmith Socialist Record, 586-7, 593-4, 598
Hammersmith Socialist Society, 571, 580-1, 586-8, 594, 598, 600-2, 609-10, 613, 621-2, 625-6, 628-9, 633, 636-7, 745
Hardie, J. Keir, 464, 475, 478 n 4, 509-10, 510 n 1, 524, 535-6, 561, 586, 599, 609, 611, 618, 624, 634, 715
Harrison, Frederick, 142-4, 196, 208, 259 n 2
Hartington, Lord, 205-6
Headlam, Rev. Stewart, 488, 494, 586
Henderson, Fred, 14, 418, 517-8, 598, 672
Herbert, Aubderon, 221
Hoare, Dr. Dorothy, 187, 190
Hopkins, Gerard Manley, 142-3
Houghton, Lord, 228
Howard, George (earl of Carlisle), 266
Howard, Hon. Mrs. George, 172, 195
Howell, George, 211-3, 261-2, 265
Hudson, W., 366
Hughes, Thomas, 213, 407
Hulse, J.W., 771-2
Hunt, William Holman, 41-2, 49-51, 53, 59, 61, 63, 228
Hyndman, Henry Mayers, 6, 208, 224 n 3, 268, 287, 301, 395, 398, 404, 440-1, 478, 523-4, 534-5, 715, 754-5, 774, 776; character and entry into socialist movement, 292-6, 301, 303-4, 312-4, 328, 332-3, 335-7; and "Split", 331, 338, 340-50, 352-5, 357-65, 379-80; and unemployed riots, 406-10; and "Bloody Sunday", 496-7; refuses reconciliation with League, 412-3, 415, 441; reconciliation with Morris, 570, 586; and negotiations for unity, 605-6, 508-10
—*The Coming Revolution in England,* 295-6
—*England for All,* 288, 293, 313, 631
—*The Historical Basis for Socialism in England,* 295, 333, 335-7, 711, 761
—*Socialism Made Plain,* 296, 301, 330, 333
—(with Morris), *Summary of the Principles of Socialism,* 333, 751

Independent Labour Party, 598-9, 608-11, 621, 624, 633, 744-7, 774, 776

James, Henry, 75, 89, 188, 660
Jones, Ernest, 136
Jowett, F.W., 560, 609, 667-8

Joynes, J.L., 290-1, 296, 299, 301, 313-5, 332, 336, 348-9, 520, 761
Jung, Hermann, 277
Justice, 301, 304, 312-3, 328, 347-50, 358, 383, 413, 523, 570, 638, 667; Morris's contributions to, 310 n 4, 324-5, 340, 597, 604, 616-9, 623, 631-2

Keats, John, 10-21, 27-8, 44, 50-4, 60, 65, 67, 77, 85, 118, 121, 129, 131-2, 147, 694
Kelmscott Press, 106, 375, 556, 559, 581, 583-5, 624-5, 627-8, 630, 633-4, 679
Kitz, Frank, 281-5, 375-7, 383, 387, 395, 399-400, 415-6, 420, 453, 463, 479, 481, 507-8, 520, 522-3, 535-6, 552, 560, 566-7, 569, 587, 594-5, 595 n 3, 712-3
Kropotkin, Prince, 307, 377 n 1, 432, 441, 505-6, 549, 567, 589, 636, 771-3
Kyrle Society, 257

Labour Emancipation League, 282, 285-7, 328-30, 344-5, 359, 375-8, 412, 414, 453-4; Hoxton branch, 381 n 1, 414-5, 422, 433, 453, 509
Labour Representation League, 206, 209, 211-3, 216-7, 223-4, 261
Lafargue, Laura, 346, 780-1
Lafargue, Paul, 383, 534, 780-1
Land and Labour League, 282 n 1, 286 n 1
Lane, Joseph, 282-7, 328, 337, 344-6, 350, 357, 359, 375-7, 383, 404, 412, 415, 446, 453, 507-8, 520, 523
–*Anti-Statist, Communist Manifesto,* 447-9, 705
Lansbury, George, 619-20, 629
Lassalle, Ferdinand, 758 n 1, 761
Law and Liberty League, 488, 493, 495-6
Leatham, James, 474-5, 618-20, 638, 743, 746-7, 750
Lenin, V.I., 578
Leno, John Bedford, 281, 713
Lessner, Frederick, 277, 299, 307, 372, 520
Lethaby, W.R., 99, 107-8, 227
Liebknecht, W., 213, 383, 534, 632-3
Linnell, Alfred, 491 n 1, 492-6, 667
Looking Backward. See Bellamy, Edward
Lowson, Malcolm, 495
Lyons, Lewis, 395-6, 398, 756 n 1

MacDonald, James, 277, 285, 301, 313-4
MacDonald, J. Ramsay, 746
McMillan, Margaret, 715
Mackail, J.W., 88, 153, 741-2
Magnússon, Eiríkr, 177-9, 186, 625-6
Maguire, Tom, 298-9, 366, 378, 417, 427, 435, 520, 528-9, 533, 560-3, 598, 600, 608-9
Mahon, John Lincoln, 369, 755, 763; entry into socialist movement, 298, 332, 350-1; and "Split", 352, 357, 359; and League, 375, 381, 386, 390, 395, 412, 415-17, 427, 435, 438-42, 445-6, 448, 449 n 1, 451-3, 509-10, and North of England Socialist Federation, 439-40, 451-2, 454, 464-7, 447-8; theory of Labourism, 472-3, 478, 525; and Labour Union, 518, 522, 525-6, 563; Scottish propaganda, 473-7, 516, 525; and I.L.P., 609; correspondence with Engels, 454 n 2, 464-70, 472, 476
Mainwaring, Sam, 330, 357, 359, 375, 399-402, 413, 463, 507-9, 520, 523, 587, 589, 594-5, 595 n 3
Malatesta, E., 567, 569
Manifesto of English Socialists, 606-8, 610
Mann, Tom, 298-9, 312-3, 375, 392, 427, 435, 464, 473, 476 n 2, 478, 523-7, 529-30, 535, 586, 634, 716
Marx, Eleanor (Marx-Aveling), 331, 347; and "Split", 345, 348, 348 n 2, 357, 359; character and influence, 367 n 1, 368-72; and League, 372, 380-1, 383, 380-1, 383, 387, 392, 396, 427, 453, 504, 520; and new unionism, 527, 535, 564-5; and Mahon, 467, 469-70
Marx, Karl, 29, 31, 269, 271-3, 287-8,

291, 313-14, 332, 370 469-70, 757-62, 786; and Eastern Question, 208, 212-3, 224 n 3. *See* also Morris, William (and Marxism)
–*Capital*, 38-9, 238, 270-1, 288, 292, 294, 306-7, 318, 367, 641, 690, 721, 741-2, 747-9, 751-5, 758-62, 782, 784
Mattison, Alfred, 421, 528, 560, 598, 600, 609, 637, 713
Mavor, James, 355-6, 366
Maxwell, J. Shaw, 351-2, 586, 609
Meier, Paul, 690 n 2, 754, 763, 773, 780-4, 788-9, 791, 802
Merrie England. See Blatchford, Robert
Merlino, Dr., 535-6
Michel, Louise, 590
Mill, John Stuart, 243, 291, 756
Millais, J.E., 41-2, 50-1, 57-8, 60-1, 63
Morley, John, 144-5
Morley, Samuel, 211-2, 221
Morris, Jane (Mrs. William Morris), 48, 64-8, 74-6, 153-70, 173-4, 179, 217-8, 319, 556, 584, 624, 635, 637, 712, 765-7, 811-2, n 19
Morris, Jenny, 157, 171, 268, 319, 581-2, 584
Morris, May, 157, 171, 373, 500, 581, 598, 618, 713
Morris, William; early life, 1-9, 22; and romanticism, 10-21; at Oxford, 5-7, 23-5, 29, 76-7; and architecture, 27-8, 43-4; and medievalism, 27-9; and Carlyle, 29-33; and Ruskin, 32-8, 40; and Pre-Raphaelites, 41-60, 657-8, 658 n 1, 672; marriage, 64-8, 74-6; and Red House, 76, 88, 91-4, 96, 111; and the Firm, 88, 91-109, 171, 247-50; and Victorianism, 128-30, 134-42, and Janey, 64, 153-70, 766-7; and Kelmscott Manor, 161-2, 169-75, 267, 513; northern influence, 175-9, 182-6; visits to Iceland, 162-4, 166-7, 179-82, 184; and Ruskin's political writings, 196-201; and Eastern Question, 192-3, 202-25; and "Anti-Scrape", 226-42; first lectures, 245-8, 252-8; and National Liberal League, 261-5; conversion to socialism, 267-74, 299; and Democratic Federation, 268-71, 273, 297, 301-3; first socialist lectures, 304-5, 308-12, 423; middle-class reactions, 308-10, 316-27; opposition to "palliatives", 337-40, 381-2; and "Split", 341-65; and Engels, 371, 383, 780-1, 784-5; and League policy, 378-82; and imperialism, 259-60, 264-6, 272, 384-9, 514-5, 629-32, 718-9; and Irish independence, 388-9; and *Commonweal*, 382-3, 391-2, 416-7, 423-4, 467 n 2, 518-9, 561, 569-70; and fight for free speech, 393-403; as a propagandist, 419, 423-6, 430-5, 511; and Northumberland miners, 439-45; anti-parliamentary theory, 455-60; on the monarchy, 480-2; and "Bloody Sunday", 488-503, 683; and new unionism, 530-3, 575, 615-6; and Second International, 534-7; on Fabianism, 459-60, 501-3, 537-42, 546-8, 575, 577, 618, 682-3, 687, 726; on anarchism, 549-52; "The Class Struggle", 542-5; artistic colleagues, 552-9; leaves League, 567-72; and Hammersmith Socialist Society, 580-1, 586-7; and Kelmscott Press, 583-5; revises anti-parliamentary views, 597-602; breaks with anarchists, 587-8, 593-4, 596-7; and poet laureatship, 603-4, 673; appeals for socialist unity, 605-10, 745; mature theory, 610-6, 620-4; reconciliation with S.D.F., 601-2, 616-20, 623; last year, 624-35
Theory of the arts, 253-6, 641-8, 655-67; views on machinery, 649-54; socialist poems, 667-73; prose romances, 673-82; and women's equality, 681-2, 707-10, 713, 740; political theory, 682-5; on the society of the future, 685-91; personality and influence, 698-717; views on sexual morality, 161-2, 705-10; on religion, 699-700, 710-1; his moral realism, 717-27; Morris and Marxism, 38-9, 270-2, 333, 355-7, 534, 547, 570, 577-8, 619, 643, 682-3, 690,

721, 727, 741-62, and Postscript, *passim;* and Utopianism, 692-7, and Postscript, *passim*
–*Chants for Socialists,* 304, 315, 667, 669
–*The Defence of Guenevere,* 1, 10, 66-71, 74, 76, 111, 118-19, 123, 157, 173, 694, 764, 808
–*A Dream of John Ball,* 391, 423, 425, 512, 637, 667, 675, 694, 717, 722-3, 782-4, 793-4, 796-7, 799
–*The Earthly Paradise,* 27, 88, 110, 112, 114-34, 151-5, 159, 190, 396, 400, 658, 675, 680-1, 694, 764, 808; reviews of, 134-5, 143-50
–Homer (Morris's *Odyssey*), 423, 432, 700
–*Hopes and Fears for Art,* 785
–*The House of the Wolfings,* 504, 511, 513, 667, 673, 675-9, 687, 694, 764, 796
–"How I Became a Socialist", 125, 175-6, 269, 619, 714
–*Icelandic Journals,* 179-81
–*Killian of the Close,* 630
–*Life and Death of Jason,* 110-11, 679
–*Love is Enough,* 151-5, 158, 658
–*News from Nowhere,* 150, 157, 161, 169-70, 502-3, 512, 514, 542, 551, 559, 567-70, 602, 633, 649, 654, 667, 677, 682, 684 n 3, 685-6, 690, 692-8, 704-5, 717, 728, 756, 772, 785, 787-90, 793-4, 796-7, 803
–*The Pilgrims of Hope,* 161, 196, 277, 312, 383-4, 391, 423, 512, 667, 669-72, 674
–*Poems By The Way,* 559
–*The Roots of the Mountains,* 559, 673, 675, 678-9, 764
–*The Saga of Gunnlaug Worm-tongue,* 177
–*Scenes from the Fall of Troy,* 111-4
–*Signs of Change,* 539-41, 602, 785
–*Sigurd the Volsung,* 88, 188-92, 658, 785, 794, 796
–*Socialist Diary,* 430-4, 440-2, 445-6, 752-3, 757
–*The Story of the Glittering Plain,* 559, 679-80
–*The Story of Grettir the Strong,* 177
–*The Sundering Flood,* 625, 630, 634, 667, 674, 679
–*The Tables Turned: or Nupkins Awakened,* 683, 698-9
–*The Water of the Wondrous Isles,* 625, 674, 679, 680 n 1, 681
–*The Well at the World's End,* 625, 674, 679
–*The Wood beyond the World,* 625, 674, 679
–(with Bax) *Socialism, it's Growth and Outcome* ("Socialism from the root up"), 372, 391, 423, 615-6, 676-7, 749, 751-4, 785
–(with Hyndman) *Summary of the Principles of Socialism,* 333, 751
Morton, A.L., 697, 787
Most, Johann, 268-9, 278, 282, 285 n 2, 354, 377, 592
Mottershead, Thomas, 213
Mowbray, Charles, 375, 387-8, 395, 417, 507, 517-8, 520, 569, 588-9, 591, 593
Muirhead, R.F., 555
Mundella, A.J., 206-7, 210-2, 218, 222-3, 225, 228, 265, 543
Murray, Charles, 280-1, 283, 285, 296
Murray, James, 280-3, 285, 296, 358

Nairne, W.J., 352, 455-6, 750 n 1
National Liberal League, 106, 261-3, 265, 285
Nicoll, David, 454, 507-8, 522, 529-30, 566-71, 586, 589, 591-3, 595
North of England Socialist Federation, 381 n 1, 439-40, 451-2, 454, 464-6, 477-8

O'Brien, J. Bronterre, 280-1, 376
O'Brien, William, 488, 496-7
Olivier, Sidney, 586, 606, 608
Owen, Robert, 269-70, 276, 306

Parsons, Lucy, 507
Pater, Walter, 147
Paylor, Tom, 528-9, 560, 562
Pease, E.R., 608
Pickles, Fred, 390-1, 609

Pierson, Stanley, 744, 773-9, 784, 794-5
Plint, Thomas, 52, 58-9
Pre-Raphaelite Brotherhood, 20, 41-61, 63
Price, Cormell, 26, 40, 46, 76
Prinsep, Val, 48-9, 58, 77

Quelch, Harry, 295, 298, 315, 332, 358, 364 n 3, 495, 585, 638

Rogers, John, 281
Rogers, Thorold, 207, 386-7
Rossetti, Christina, 42
Rossetti, Dante Gabriel, 3, 40-9, 51-65, 74, 77, 92-3, 109, 172-3, 207, 243-4; and Morris, 61-4, 765-7, 778; and Janey Morris, 160-3, 173-4, 765-7, 778, 811-2
Rossetti, Mrs. D.G. *See* Siddal, Lizzie
Rossetti, William Michael, 41, 49, 51, 57, 59, 62, 162, 192, 289
Ruskin, John, 32-8, 40, 99-100, 207, 245, 728, 774, 808; and Pre-Raphaelites, 42, 51-2; and Victorianism, 140-2; on architectural restoration, 228, 234-5, 237-8; and Morris's socialism, 270, 274; artistic theories, 641-3, 655-67, 783-4
–*The Stones of Venice* ("The Nature of Gothic"), 33-8, 198, 237
–*Unto This Last,* and *Fors Clavigera,* 196-201, 664, 748
Rutherford, Mark (W. Hale White), 142-3

Salt, Henry, 276, 290, 368
Samuels, H.B., 518, 523, 562, 568, 576
Scheu, Andreas, 2, 98, 168, 182, 184, 251, 269, 278-9, 296, 299, 301, 306-7, 315, 319, 332, 337, 339, 342-5, 347, 350-4, 358, 365-6, 378, 392, 404, 418, 520, 572, 586, 750, 754
Scott, Sir Gilbert, 99, 226-8
Scott, W. Bell, 194, 207
Scottish Land and Labour League, 350-7, 378, 414, 454, 466, 472-7, 516, 524-5, 560
Sharp, William, 701
Shaw, George Bernard, 168, 191, 299, 332, 336, 367, 553, 585-6, 624, 629, 709-10; on the "Split", 347; and League, 383, 388, 393-4, 398; and Fabian Society, 332 n 2, 459, 537-8, 546-8, 598, 618, 760; and "Bloody Sunday", 483-4, 490, 498-502; rejects socialist unity, 606-9; and Marxism, 758-60, 762, 762 n 2; on Morris, 252, 302-3, 654, 659-61, 698, 702, 716-7, 726, 741-2, 768, 771
–*An Unsocial Socialist,* 291-2
Shelley, Percy Bysshe, 669
Siddal, Lizzie (Mrs. D.G. Rossetti), 62, 74, 162
Sketchley, John, 279-80, 350, 392, 756 n 2
Slaughter, Fred ("Fred Charles"), 417, 454, 507-8, 598, 598 n 2, 591-3, 637
Smith, Frank, 494, 599
Social-Democratic Federation (and Democratic Federation), 110, 268-9, 276, 415, 464; formation, 287, 295-7, 301, 338, 344-5; the "Split", 342-65; and unemployed, 378, 406-9, 483-2, 483 n 1; and free speech, 394-403, 412-3; and new unionism, 523-4, 530; criticism by Engels, 564-5; unity discussions, 605-6, 608-9; Morris reconciled with, 570, 616, 620, 629 n 3, 634; and Marxist theory, 776-7. *See* also *Justice*
Socialist League; formation, 360-2, 366; and imperialism, 384-9; 1885-1886, 393, 412-22; Third Annual Conference, 448-54, 462-3; and Jubilee, 479-81; Fourth Annual Conference, 462, 504-8; last years, 516-23, 560-3, 565-72, 576, 587-95; Morris breaks with, 567-79; membership, 390-1; 413-4, 414 n 3, 415-22, 460, 460 n 3, 461-3, 571-2. *See* also *Commonweal;* Engels, F., (on League)
–Branches: Aberdeen, 474-6, 560, 563, 580 n 1; Acton, 461; Bingley, 415, 528; Birmingham, 414-5; Bloomsbury, 414-5, 467, 504-5, 508-9, 570; Blyth, 478; Bradford, 390, 414, 461-2, 528, 533, 560; Bristol,

463; Clerkenwell, 412, 414, 522 n 4; Croydon, 412, 414-5, 449, 452; Dublin, 414-5; East Holywell, 478; East London, 522 n 4, 571; Edinburgh, 414, 418, 437, 462, 473-4, 507, 522 n 4, 560; Fulham, 415, 461; Glasgow, 399 n 3, 413-4, 418, 430, 436-7, 440-1, 451-2, 461-2, 472-4, 477, 485 n 1, 506-7, 516, 522, 552, 558, 560, 571, 588, 743; Hackney, 412, 414-5, 434; Hamilton, 415, 438, 462, 474; Hammersmith, 277, 339 n 4, 340, 362, 394, 414-5, 421-4, 431-2, 449-50, 452, 461-2, 508, 516, 518-9, 522, 552-3, 571-2, 590; Hoxton—*see* Labour Emancipation League; Hull, 412, 415, 438, 462, 588; Ipswich, 415, 462, 507; Lancaster, 415, 462; Leeds, 378, 381, 414, 417, 438, 461-2, 518, 527-9, 533, 560-3, 588; Leicester, 414, 418-9, 462-3, 517, 522 n 4, 560, 571, 588; Manchester, 414-5, 517, 522 n 4, 533, 560, 563, 571; Marylebone, 400, 403, 414-5; Merton Abbey, 318, 414, 430; Mile End, 414-5; Mitcham, 415, 432-4; North Kensington, 461, 571, 590; North London, 414-5, 552 n 4, 571; Norwich, 415, 462, 477-8; North Shields, 414, 417-8, 461-2, 507, 513, 517-8, 522 n 4, 588; Nottingham Socialist Society, 419, 463, 517, 560; Notting Hill, 461; Oldham, 414-5; Oxford, 322, 378, 390, 414, 462, 522 n 4, 571; St George's-in-the-East, 522 n 4; Sheffield Socialist Society, 517, 533, 588; Southampton, 463; South London, 414-5; Stratford, 414-5; Streatham, 571; Walsall, 415, 462, 560, 588, 591-2; Wednesbury, 463; Yarmouth, 463, 522 n 4, 560, 571. *See* also Bloomsbury Socialist Society; Labour Emancipation League; North of England Socialist Federation; Scottish Land and Labour League
Society for the Protection of Ancient Buildings ("Anti-Scrape"), 88, 106, 228-41, 249, 252-3, 504, 585, 626, 628, 641-2, 783-4
Sparling, H. Halliday, 292, 438, 500, 508, 523, 566, 581-3, 598, 624, 700
Stead, W.T., 207, 488, 493-4, 497, 500
Stephen, Leslie, 228
Stepniak, Sergius, 306-7, 383, 586, 629, 661 n 2, 771
Street, G.E., 3, 43, 229 n 1
Sturt, George, 413 n 4
Swinburne, Algernon, 48, 194, 274, 633-4, 667

Tarleton, H.B., 500, 523, 535
Taylor, Mrs., 490, 500
Taylor, Warington, 99 n 1, 177, 249
Tennyson, Alfred Lord, 45, 55, 71, 77-81, 128, 145-6, 603, 698-9
Thomson, James, 126, 127 n 1, 128, 131
Thorne, Will, 527, 564
Tillett, Ben, 529, 599
Tochatti, James, 393, 508, 587, 589, 594-7, 623
Today, 332, 348 n 2, 369, 539
Townshend, W., 281, 285
Travis, Dr. Henry, 281
Trollope, Anthony, 211
Tupper, Martin, 72-3
Turner, Ben, 561
Turner, John, 523, 589, 595, 595 n 3

Unwin, Raymond, 555
Utley, W.H., 453

Victoria Queen ("Mrs. Brown"), 203, 209, 215-9, 223, 479-82

Walker, Emery, 339 n 4, 519-20, 556-7, 571, 582
Wallace, Henry, 269
Wallas, Graham, 548, 553, 586
Wallis, Henry, 207, 229 n 1
Wardle, George, 247
Wardle, Thomas, 321
Warr, Professor, 246-7
Warren, Sir Charles, 488, 492, 503
Watson, Edward, 366
Watts, J. Hunter, 439, 523
Watts-Dunton, Theodore, 63 n 3, 172-

3, 274, 699-700
Webb, Philip, 43, 91, 93, 97, 100, 172, 207, 274, 582, 584; and "Anti-Scrape", 227-8, 230-1, 249; and socialist movement, 322, 423, 508, 520, 523, 555, 566, 630-1, 633
Webb, Sidney, 546-7, 682-3
Wells, H.G., 552-3, 555
Westminster, duke of, 211
Whitman, Walt, 194, 289
Wicksteed, P.H., 332, 538
Wilde, Oscar, 148
Williams, John E. ("Jack"), 284 n 3, 295-6, 312-4, 328-9, 358, 364 n 3, 394, 400, 402, 404, 407, 409, 412-3, 439, 636
Williams, Raymond, 769, 779, 783-5, 793-4
Woolner, Thomas, 45, 61-2, 192
Wyatt, A.J., 625

Yeats, W.B., 85, 554-5, 681, 691, 716

Zambaco, Marie, 165 n 2, 765